W9-BLB-603

THE LASTword

10th

CANADIAN EDITION

Microeconomics

Campbell R. McConnell

Professor of Economics, Emeritus
University of Nebraska, Lincoln

Stanley L. Brue

Professor of Economics
Pacific Lutheran University

Thomas P. Barbiero

Professor of Economics
Ryerson University

McGraw-Hill Ryerson

Toronto Montréal Boston Burr Ridge, IL Dubuque, IA Madison, WI New York San Francisco
St. Louis Bangkok Bogotá Caracas Kuala Lumpur Lisbon London Madrid
Mexico City Milan New Delhi Santiago Seoul Singapore Sydney Taipei

**McGraw-Hill
Ryerson Limited**

A Subsidiary of The McGraw·Hill Companies

Microeconomics
10th Canadian Edition

Statistics Canada information is used with the permission of the Minister of Industry, as Minister responsible for Statistics Canada. Information on the availability of the wide range of data from Statistics Canada can be obtained from Statistics Canada's Regional Offices, its World Wide Web site at http://www.statcan.ca, and its toll-free access number 1-800-263-1136.

ISBN: 0-07-091657-8

1 2 3 4 5 6 7 8 9 10 TRI 0 9 8 7 6 5

Printed and bound in Canada

Care has been taken to trace ownership of copyright material contained in this text; however, the publisher will welcome any information that enables them to rectify any reference or credit for subsequent editions.

Vice President, Editorial and Media Technology: Patrick Ferrier
Executive Sponsoring Editor: Lynn Fisher
Economics Editor: Ron Doleman
Developmental Editor: Daphne Scriabin
Marketing Manager: Kelly Smyth
Supervising Editor: Joanne Murray
Copy Editor: Nick Gamble
Production Coordinator: Andrée Davis
Formatter: Michelle Losier, Finelines
Interior Design: Dianna Little
Cover Design: Dianna Little
Cover Image Credit: Background trees © Miles Ertman/Masterfile; Evergreen seedling © Corbis Corporation/Roy Morsch
Printer: Tri-Graphic Printing Limited

National Library of Canada Cataloguing in Publication

McConnell, Campbell R.
   Microeconomics / Campbell R. McConnell, Stanley L. Brue, Thomas P. Barbiero. — 10th Canadian ed.

Includes bibliographical references and index.
ISBN 0-07-091657-8

1. Microeconomics—Textbooks. I. Brue, Stanley L., 1945- II. Barbiero, Thomas Paul, 1952- III. Title.

HB172.M115 2003   338.5   C2003-905306-7

Dedication

This book is dedicated to Elsa, Marta, Emilia, and Robert.

About the Authors

Campbell R. McConnell earned his Ph.D. from the University of Iowa after receiving degrees from Cornell College and the University of Illinois. He taught at the University of Nebraska-Lincoln from 1953 until his retirement in 1990. He is also coauthor of *Contemporary Labor Economics*, 5th ed. (McGraw-Hill) and has edited readers for the principles and labour economics courses. He is a recipient of both the University of Nebraska Distinguished Teaching Award and the James A. Lake Academic Freedom Award, and is past-president of the Midwest Economics Association. Professor McConnell was awarded an honorary Doctor of Laws degree from Cornell College in 1973 and received its Distinguished Achievement Award in 1994. His primary areas of interest are labour economics and economic education. He has an extensive collection of jazz recordings and enjoys reading jazz history.

Stanley L. Brue did his undergraduate work at Augustana College (SD) and received his Ph.D. from the University of Nebraska-Lincoln. He teaches at Pacific Lutheran University, where he has been honoured as a recipient of the Burlington Northern Faculty Achievement Award. He has also received the national Leavey Award for excellence in economic education. Professor Brue is past president and a current member of the International Executive Board of Omicron Delta Epsilon International Economics Honorary. He is coauthor of *Economic Scenes*, 5th ed. (Prentice-Hall) and *Contemporary Labor Economics*, 5th ed. (McGraw-Hill) and author of *The Evolution of Economic Thought*, 5th ed. (HB/Dryden). For relaxation, he enjoys boating on Puget Sound and skiing trips with his family.

Thomas P. Barbiero received his Ph.D. from the University of Toronto after completing undergraduate studies at the same university. He has published papers on the role of the agricultural sector in the industrial development of northern Italy in the period 1861–1914. His research interest in the last few years has turned to economic methodology and the application of economic theory to explain social phenomena. Professor Barbiero spends part of his summer on the Amalfi Coast in Italy.

Brief Contents

Web Site Bonus Chapters (found at www.mcgrawhill.ca/college/mcconnell)

Contents

Web Site Bonus Chapters (found at www.mcgrawhill.ca/college/mcconnell)

CHAPTER 3W:
Applications and Extensions of Supply and Demand Analysis

CHAPTER 19W:
Canadian Agriculture: Economics and Policy

Preface

Welcome to the Tenth Canadian Edition of *Microeconomics*, the world's best-selling economics textbook. An estimated 13 million students worldwide have now used this book. *Microeconomics* is available in American and Australian editions, and has been translated into Italian, Russian, Chinese, French, Spanish, Portuguese, and other languages.

Fundamental Objectives

We have three main goals for *Microeconomics*, to:

- Help the beginning student master the principles essential for understanding economic problems, specific Canadian economic issues, and the policy alternatives.
- Help the student understand and apply the economic perspective and to reason accurately and objectively about economic matters.
- Promote a lasting student interest in economics and the economy.

What's New and Improved?

One of the benefits of writing a text that has met the market test is the opportunity to revise—to delete the outdated and install the new, to rewrite misleading or ambiguous statements, to introduce more relevant Canadian illustrations, to improve the organizational structure, and to enhance the learning aids. The more significant changes to the Tenth Canadian Edition include the following:

Consider This Boxes

New to the book are 18 analogies, examples, and stories that help drive home central economic ideas in a student-oriented, real-world manner. For instance, the income of street entertainers is shown to suffer from the fact that they provide a type of public good (Chapter 4, page 89). These brief vignettes drive home key points in a lively, colourful, and easy-to-remember way.

Consumer and Producer Surplus

There is expanded coverage of consumer surplus and producer surplus. For example, Chapter 9 on monopoly now includes a discussion of deadweight loss.

Game Theory

There is improved coverage of game theory. Chapter 10, on monopolistic competition and oligopoly, now includes a section that discusses the prisoner's dilemma and the Nash equilibrium.

Contemporary Discussions and Examples

The Tenth Canadian Edition contains discussions of many new or extended topics, some of special relevance to Canadian students. Here are a few:

- Canadian health care issues
- The Kyoto Accord and the Canadian economy
- Corporate financial and accounting misconduct
- The explosion of demand for DVDs, DVD players, and digital cameras
- Minimum efficient scale applications
- Effects of rising insurance costs on the cost curves of individual firms

- Strategic behaviour as an entry barrier
- Global warming issues
- Alternative anti-combines philosophies
- The Microsoft anti-combines case
- The Gini ratio as a measure of income inequality
- High executive compensation

Revised Chapters on Demand and Supply and on Elasticity

We have moved the discussion of price floors and price ceilings in Chapter 6 of the previous edition to Chapter 3 on demand and supply. Chapter 5 (" Supply and Demand: Elasticities and Applications") now has new sections on the economics of agricultural price supports and the economics of health care, and also has room for new elasticity of supply applications that relate to antiques versus reproductions and to the volatile price of gold.

Two Bonus Web Chapters, Including a Second Supply and Demand Chapter

Two chapters are available for use at our Web site (www.mcgrawhill.ca/college/mcconnell). The first of these, "Chapter 3W: Applications and Extensions of Supply and Demand Analysis," is entirely new and provides real-world examples of changes in supply and demand, shortages and surpluses arising from pre-set prices, and overconsumption of non-priced goods (or factors of production). For instructors who want to extend the supply and demand analysis of Chapter 3, this chapter also has an extensive coverage of consumer surplus, producer surplus, and efficiency losses. The other Web chapter, "Chapter 19W: Canadian Agriculture: Economics and Policy," is also available for instructors and students who have a special interest in that topic. The two Web chapters have the same design and features of regular book chapters. They are in Adobe Acrobat (PDF) format and can be printed if desired.

New Last Word Topics and Global Perspective Boxes

New Last Word topics are efficiency gains from generic drugs (Chapter 3W); efficiency and the Canadian health care system (Chapter 8); the controversy over CEO pay (Chapter 14); and a brief biography of James M. Buchanan, one of the founders of public choice theory (Chapter 18). In addition, a few Last Word topics have been relocated to match reorganized content. New Global Perspective boxes include lists of the top 12 globalized nations (Chapter 4) and the world's 10 largest corporations (Chapter 7).

Streamlined Presentations

A major revision goal was to streamline presentations, where possible, without compromising the thoroughness of our explanations. Our efforts resulted in a more efficient organization and greater clarity. As an example, Chapter 4, "The Market System and International Trade," amalgamates the contents of two chapters from the previous edition. You will find similar improvements throughout the Tenth Canadian Edition. Where needed, of course, the "extra sentence of explanation" remains a distinguishing characteristic of *Microeconomics*. Brevity at the expense of clarity is a false economy.

Other New Topics and Revised Discussions

Along with the improvements just discussed, there are many other revisions. The following are some of the many changes made:

- ***Part 1.***   *Chapter 1*: Introduced the term "utility" very early on. *Chapter 2*: Changed examples to reflect introduction of new products, such as MP3 players; substituted "factors of production" for "resources" where appropriate. *Chapter 3*: New applications section on price ceilings and price floors. *Chapter 4*: New chapter title and introduction; rewritten section on public goods to reflect the more recent nomenclature and treatment by economists; a new brief section entitled "Limitation of the Market System."

- **Part 2.** *Chapter 5*: A completely revised presentation of the price elasticity of demand equation that introduces the arch elasticity upfront; and new sections entitled "Applications of Price Elasticity of Supply," "The Economics of Agricultural Price Supports," and "The Economics of Health Care."*Chapter 6*: A new section entitled "Consumer Surplus" has been added. *Chapter 7*: The Last Word now includes the Canadian story of Nortel Networks and how a rapidly changing industry led to some of the company's previous investments becoming virtually worthless. Chapter 8: A new section that evaluates the efficiency of pure competition with the concepts of consumer surplus and producer surplus. *Chapter 9*: A new section entitled "Monopoly and Deadweight Loss." *Chapter 10*: A new section on game theory, introducing the prisoner's dilemma, Nash equilibrium, and dominant strategy. *Chapter 11*: A new section entitled "Health Care, Technological Advance, and Efficiency." *Chapter 12*: Discussion of a new case involving the decision brought down by the Competition Bureau on price fixing.

- **Part 3.** New title for this part to reflect the use of the term "factor markets." *Chapter 13*: New chapter title to reflect the use of the term "factor markets." *Chapter 14*: A new section entitled "The Principal–Agent Problem and Health Care Suppliers," which discusses the possibility of demand creation by health care suppliers and the possible repercussions for the Canadian health care system. *Chapter 16*: The introduction of the Gini ratio into the discussion of the Lorenz curve.

- **Part 4.** *Chapter 17*: The addition of a new section entitled "The Moral Hazard Problem and Canada's National Health Care System." *Chapter 18*: Expanded definition of public choice theory; a new section entitled "Benefits Received versus Ability to Pay."

Distinguishing Features

- **Comprehensive Explanations at an Appropriate Level.** *Microeconomics* is comprehensive, analytical, and challenging yet fully accessible to a wide range of students. Its thoroughness and accessibility enable instructors to select topics for special classroom emphasis with confidence that students can independently read and comprehend other assigned material in the book.

- **Fundamentals of the Market System.** Many economies throughout the world are making difficult transitions from planning to markets. Our detailed description of the institutions and operation of the market system in Chapter 4 is even more relevant than before. We pay particular attention to property rights, entrepreneurship, freedom of enterprise and choice, competition, and the role of profits, because these concepts are often misunderstood by beginning students.

- **Early Integration of International Economics.** We give the principles and institutions of the global economy early treatment. Chapter 4 examines specialization and comparative advantage (without the more difficult graphs). This strong introduction to international economics facilitates the study of globalization issues throughout the textbook.

- **Early and Extensive Treatment of Government.** Government is an integral component of modern capitalism. We introduce the economic functions of government early on, and give them systematic treatment in Chapter 4. Chapter 17 examines government and market failure in further detail, and Chapter 18 looks at salient facets of public choice theory and taxation. The text includes several issues- and policy-oriented chapters.

- **Stress on the Theory of the Firm and Technological Advances.** We have given much attention to microeconomics in general and to the theory of the firm in particular, for two reasons: First, because the concepts of microeconomics are difficult for most beginning students, and abbreviated expositions usually compound these difficulties by raising more questions than they answer; and second, because we have coupled analysis of the various market structures with a discussion of the impact of each market arrangement on price, output levels, resource allocation, and the rate of technological advance. Chapter 11, on the microeconomics of technology, is unique to principles books.

- **Focus on Economic Issues.**   For many students, Canadian issues related to health care, the environment, agriculture, income inequality, and labour are where the action is. We guide their interest along logical lines through the application of appropriate analytical tools.

- **Integrated Text and Web site.**   *Microeconomics* and its Web site are highly integrated through in-text Web buttons, Web-based end-of-chapter questions, bonus Web chapters, multiple-choice self-tests at the Web site, Web math notes, and other features. Our Web site is part and parcel of our student learning package, and is customized to the book.

Organizational Alternatives

Although instructors generally agree as to the content of the principles of microeconomics course, they often differ in how they arrange the material. *Microeconomics* includes four parts, which provides considerable organizational flexibility. The Web chapter on agriculture may follow Chapter 8 on pure competition; Chapter 12 on anti-combines and regulation may follow Chapters 9 and 10 on imperfect competition models and technological advance. Chapter 16 on income inequality may follow Chapters 14 and 15 on distributive shares of national income.

Pedagogical Aids for Students

Microeconomics has always been student oriented. Economics is concerned with efficiency—accomplishing goals using the best methods. Therefore, we offer the student some brief introductory comments on how to improve efficiency and hence grades.

- **In This Chapter You Will Learn**   We set out the learning objectives at the start of each chapter so the chapter's main concepts can be easily recognized. We have also tied the learning objectives to each of the numbered headings in each chapter. In addition, the chapter summaries are now organized by numbered headings.

IN THIS CHAPTER YOU WILL LEARN:

3.1 What markets are.

3.2 What demand is and what affects it.

3.3 What supply is and what affects it.

3.4 How demand and supply together determine market equilibrium.

3.5 What government-set prices are and how ~~they affect mark...~~

According to an old joke, if you teach a parrot to say "demand and supply," you have an economist. There is much truth in this quip. The tools of demand and supply can take us far in understanding both specific economic issues and how the entire economy works.

With our circular flow model in Chapter 2, we identified the participants in the product market and factor market. We asserted that prices were determined by the "interaction" between buyers and sellers in those markets. In this chapter we examine that interaction in detail and explain how prices and output quantities are determined.

- **Terminology**   A significant portion of any introductory course is terminology. In this edition key terms are highlighted in bold type the first time they appear in the text. Key terms are defined in the margin and a comprehensive list appears at the end of each chapter. A glossary of definitions can also be found at the end of the book and on the Web site.

- **Ten Key Concepts**   Ten Key Concepts have been identified to help students organize the main principles. The Ten Key Concepts are introduced in Chapter 1 and each one is reinforced throughout the textbook by its individual icon.

CONCEPT 3 ("Choosing a Little More or Less"): Choices are usually made at the **margin**; we choose a "little" more or a "little" less of something.

CONCEPT 4 ("The Influence of Incentives"): The choices you make are influenced by **incentives**.

- **Data Updates**   Data updates for selected graphs and tables can be found on the McConnell-Brue-Barbiero Web site (www.mcgrawhill.ca/college/mcconnell).

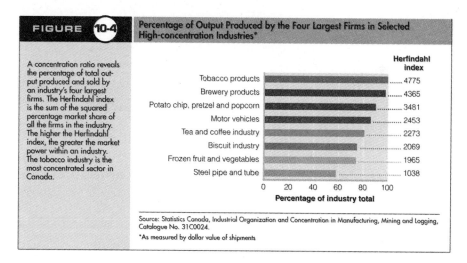

FIGURE 10-4   Percentage of Output Produced by the Four Largest Firms in Selected High-concentration Industries*

A concentration ratio reveals the percentage of total output produced and sold by an industry's four largest firms. The Herfindahl index is the sum of the squared percentage market share of all the firms in the industry. The higher the Herfindahl index, the greater the market power within an industry. The tobacco industry is the most concentrated sector in Canada.

	Herfindahl index
Tobacco products	4775
Brewery products	4365
Potato chip, pretzel and popcorn	3481
Motor vehicles	2453
Tea and coffee industry	2273
Biscuit industry	2069
Frozen fruit and vegetables	1965
Steel pipe and tube	1038

Source: Statistics Canada, Industrial Organization and Concentration in Manufacturing, Mining and Logging, Catalogue No. 31C0024.
*As measured by dollar value of shipments

- **Graphics with Supporting Data**   Where possible we have provided data to support our graphs. In such cases a data table now appears in the same figure with the graph.

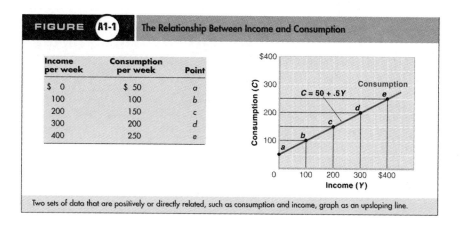

FIGURE A1-1   The Relationship Between Income and Consumption

Income per week	Consumption per week	Point
$ 0	$ 50	a
100	100	b
200	150	c
300	200	d
400	250	e

$C = 50 + .5Y$

Two sets of data that are positively or directly related, such as consumption and income, graph as an upsloping line.

- **Key Graphs** We have labelled graphs that have special relevance as Key Graphs. Each Key Graph includes a quick quiz of four questions, with answers provided below.

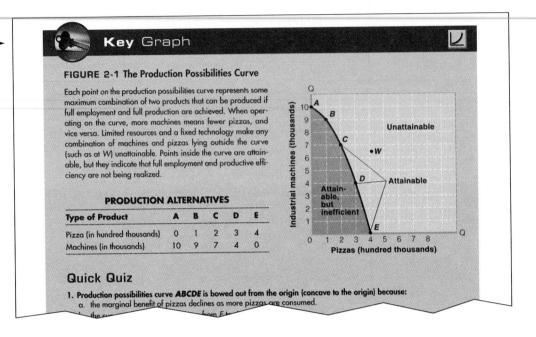

Key Graph

FIGURE 2-1 The Production Possibilities Curve

Each point on the production possibilities curve represents some maximum combination of two products that can be produced if full employment and full production are achieved. When operating on the curve, more machines means fewer pizzas, and vice versa. Limited resources and a fixed technology make any combination of machines and pizzas lying outside the curve (such as at *W*) unattainable. Points inside the curve are attainable, but they indicate that full employment and productive efficiency are not being realized.

PRODUCTION ALTERNATIVES

Type of Product	A	B	C	D	E
Pizza (in hundred thousands)	0	1	2	3	4
Machines (in thousands)	10	9	7	4	0

Quick Quiz

1. Production possibilities curve **ABCDE** is bowed out from the origin (concave to the origin) because:
    a. the marginal benefit of pizzas declines as more pizzas are consumed.

- **Interactive Graphs** For selected Key Graphs, interactive graphs are available on the McConnell-Brue-Barbiero Web site (www.mcgrawhill.ca/college/mcconnell). Developed under the supervision of Norris Peterson of Pacific Lutheran University, this interactive feature depicts major graphs and instructs students to shift the curves, observe the outcomes, and derive relevant generalizations. New interactive graphs have been added in this edition.

- **Reviewing the Chapter** Important things should be said more than once. You will find a Chapter Summary at the conclusion of every chapter, as well as two or three Quick Reviews within each chapter. The end-of-chapter summary is presented by numbered chapter section. These review statements will help students to focus on the essential ideas of each chapter and to study for exams.

QUICK REVIEW

- The monopolist maximizes profit (or minimizes loss) at the output where MR = MC and charges the price that corresponds to that output on its demand curve.

- The monopolist has no supply curve, since any of several prices can be associated with a specific quantity of output supplied.

- Assuming identical costs, a monopolist will be less efficient than a purely competitive industry because the monopolist produces less output and charges a higher price.

- The inefficiencies of monopoly may be offset or lessened by economies of scale and, less likely, by technological progress, but may be intensified by the presence of X-inefficiency and rent-seeking expenditures.

- ***Global Perspective Boxes***   Each nation functions increasingly in a global economy. To help the student gain appreciation of this wider economic environment, we provide Global Perspectives features, which compare Canada to other nations.

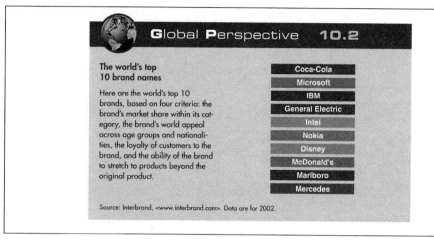

- ***Consider This***   This new feature highlights and emphasizes an important theoretical issue in each chapter, and makes it interesting to students through examples and analogies.

- **The Last Word**   *The Last Word* features, which reinforce chapter material with topics of interest, have been revised and updated.

THE LASTword | Efficiency and the Canadian Health Care System

The Canadian national health care system has been under strain in the last decade as patients have had to endure longer and longer line-ups for the medical services they need. Although the Canadian health care sector does not function in a competitive market structure, solutions have been put forward to improve the efficiency and delivery time of health-care services.

Productive efficiency implies getting the most output for the least cost. Another way of expressing productive efficiency is getting the most output from available resources. Although it is very difficult to accurately measure the efficiency of a country's national health care system, there are some measures that can be used as a rough proxy. One such proxy is the infant mortality rate per

nomic Cooperation and Development (OECD) data shown here presents some interesting contrasts. The Czech Republic spends under $1000 per citizen and has 4.6 deaths per 1000 live births. (All spending is in U.S. dollars.) The United States spends over $4000 per citizen, but has a relatively high infant mortality rate of 7.2. This suggests the Czech health care system is more efficient than the American

per capita spending on health care is the highest in the world.

Canada's health care system does not fare much better when we use the infant mortality rate as a measure. It ranks only 17th in the world, though Canada has the world's 4th highest per capita expenditure on health care. Contrast this with Spain, which ranks 13th in the world in infant mortality despite being only the 22nd

---

- **Appendix on Graphs**   Being comfortable with graphical analysis and a few related quantitative concepts will be a big advantage to students in understanding the principles of economics. The appendix to Chapter 1, which reviews graphing, slopes of lines, and linear equations, should not be skipped.

- **Study Questions**   A comprehensive list of questions is located at the end of each chapter. The old cliché that we learn by doing is very relevant to economics. Use of these questions will enhance students' understanding. For each chapter, we designate several as Key Questions and answer them in the Study Guide.

- **Internet Application Questions**   Students are presented with questions, relevant to the topic discussed in the chapter, to explore on the Internet. On the McConnell-Brue Barbiero Web site (www.mcgrawhill.ca/college/mcconnell), students will find direct links to the Web sites included in these questions.

INTERNET APPLICATION QUESTIONS

1. **More Labour Resources—What is the Evidence for Canada and France?** Use the link in the McConnell-Brue-Barbiero Web site (Chapter 2) to find Canadian civilian employment data for the last 10 years. How many more workers were there at the end of the 10-year period than at the beginning? Next, find total employment growth in France over the last 10 years. In which of the two countries did "more labour resources" have the greatest impact in shifting the nation's production possibilities curve outward over the 10-year period?

2. **Relative Size of the Military—Who's Incurring the Largest Opportunity Cost?** To obtain military goods, a nation must sacrifice civilian goods. Of course, that sacrifice may be worthwhile in terms of national defence and protection of national interests. Use the link in the McConnell-Brue-Barbiero Web site (Chapter 2) to determine the amount of military expenditures, and military expenditures as a percentage of GDP, for each of the following five nations: Canada, Japan, North Korea, Russia, and the United States. Who is bearing the greatest opportunity costs?

- **Origin of the Idea** These brief histories, which can be found on the Web site, examine the origins of major ideas identified in the book. Students will find it interesting to learn about the person who first developed such ideas as opportunity cost, equilibrium price, the multiplier, comparative advantage, and elasticity.

- **∑-STAT** ∑-STAT is Statistics Canada's education resource that allows socioeconomic and demographic data to be viewed in charts, graphs, and maps. Access to ∑-STAT and the CANSIM II database is made available to purchasers of the book, via the McConnell-Brue-Barbiero Web site, by special agreement between McGraw-Hill Ryerson and Statistics Canada. The Online Learning Centre provides additional information.

Supplements for the Instructor

- **i-Learning Sales Specialist** Your Integrated Learning Sales Specialist is a McGraw-Hill Ryerson representative who has the experience, product knowledge, training, and support to help you assess and integrate any of the below-noted products, technology, and services into your course for optimum teaching and learning performance. Whether it's using our test bank software, helping your students improve their grades, or putting your entire course online, your *i*-Learning Sales Specialist is there to help you do it. Contact your local *i*-Learning Sales Specialist today to learn how to maximize all of McGraw-Hill Ryerson's resources.

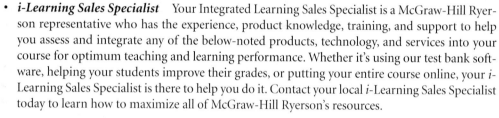

- **The Instructor Online Learning Centre** The Instructor Online Learning Centre (www. mcgrawhill.ca/college/mcconnell) includes a password-protected Web site for instructors. The site offers downloadable supplements and PageOut, the McGraw-Hill Ryerson course Web site development centre. New to the Tenth Canadian Edition is the **Integrator**. This pioneering instructional resource from McGraw-Hill Ryerson is your road map to all the other elements of your text's support package. Keyed to the chapters and topics of the textbook, the **Integrator** ties together all the elements in your resource package, guiding you to corresponding coverage in each component of the support package.

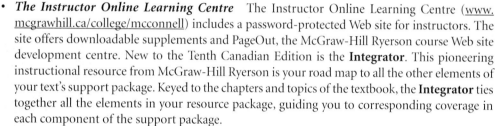

- **Instructor's CD-ROM** This CD-ROM contains all the necessary Instructor Supplements including:

  - **Instructor's Manual.** Thomas Barbiero, Ryerson University, has revised and updated the Instructor's Manual. It includes chapter summaries, listings of "what's new" in each chapter, teaching tips and suggestions, learning objectives, chapter outlines, and data and visual aid sources with suggestions for classroom use. It also provides answers to all end-of-chapter questions as well as an extra set of parallel end-of-chapter problems and solutions.

  - **Microsoft® PowerPoint® Slide Powernotes.** Prepared by Judith Skuce, Georgian College, this presentation system is found on the Instructor's CD-ROM and on the Instructor's Site of the Online Learning Centre. It offers visual presentations that may be edited and manipulated to fit a particular course format. They have been significantly revised for this edition and contain many animated graphs and figures that have been imported from Excel.

  - **Computerized Test Bank I.** Prepared by Nargess Kayhani, Mount St. Vincent University, the test bank includes more than 5400 mixed multiple-choice and true/false questions that are categorized by topic and learning objective. Each question has been checked for accuracy and content.

  - **Test Bank II.** Prepared by Tom Fulton, Langara College. This test bank, available in Microsoft Word, contains for each chapter over 30 short-answer questions, with suggested answers.

- Also available, from the U.S. supplement list, is *U.S. Test Bank II*. This test bank contains more than 5200 multiple-choice and true/false questions. All *Test Bank II* questions are categorized according to level of difficulty.

- **CBC Videos and Video Cases**   These videos have been chosen to visually help students relate real-world economics issues to the text, and to illuminate key ideas and concepts presented in the text. A set of instructor notes accompanies the segments and is available at the Instructor Online Learning Centre. The video segments are available in VHS format for use in class and through video-streaming on the Online Learning Centre (where they are accessible by both instructors and students).

- **PageOut**   Visit www.mhhe.com/pageout to create a Web page for your course using our resources. PageOut is the McGraw-Hill Ryerson Web site development centre. This Web page generation software is free to adopters and is designed to help faculty create an online course, complete with assignments, quizzes, links to relevant Web sites, lecture notes, and more—all in a matter of minutes.

- In addition, content cartridges are available for course management systems such as WebCT and Blackboard. These platforms provide instructors with user-friendly, flexible teaching tools. Please contact your local McGraw-Hill Ryerson *i*-Learning Sales Specialist for additional information.

- **iLearning Services Program**   McGraw-Hill Ryerson offers a unique services package designed for Canadian faculty. It includes technical support, access to our educational technology conferences, and custom e-courses, to name just a few. Please speak to your *i*-Learning Sales Specialist for details.

Supplements for Students

- **Online Learning Centre**   The student Online Learning Centre is prepared by Beverly and Norman Cameron, University of Manitoba. This electronic learning aid, located at www.mcgrawhill.ca/college/mcconnell, offers a wealth of materials, including multiple-choice quizzes, interactive graphing exercises, Internet exercises, annotated Weblinks, CBC video cases, Econ GraphKit, access to $\sum$-STAT and the CANSIM II database, Want to See the Math and much more!

- **Study Guide**   Torben Andersen, Chairperson of Humanities and Social Sciences at Red Deer College, has prepared the Tenth Edition of the Study Guide (ISBN 007-092239X), which many students find indispensable. Each chapter contains an overview of the major topics, a review of each numbered A-level head with a discussion of the learning objectives that apply to that section, a list of important terms, fill-in questions, true/false questions, multiple-choice tests, problems and projects identified by topic, discussion questions, and an answer section.

- **GradeSummit**   GradeSummit (www.gradesummit.com) is an Internet-based self-assessment service that offers a variety of ways for students to analyze what they know and don't know. By revealing subject strengths and weaknesses and by providing detailed feedback and direction, GradeSummit enables students to focus their study time on those areas where they are most in need of improvement. GradeSummit provides data about how much students know while they study for an exam—not after they have taken it. It helps the professor measure an individual student's progress and assess his or her progress relative to others in the class.

Acknowledgements

The Tenth Canadian Edition has benefited from a number of perceptive reviews, which were a rich source of suggestions for this revision. Reviewers include:

Morris Altman, University of Saskatchewan
Sal AmirKhalkhali, Saint Mary's University
Torben Andersen, Red Deer College
Michael Benarroch, University of Winnipeg
Beverly Cameron, University of Manitoba
Douglas Curtis, Trent University
Santo Dodaro, St. Francis Xavier University
Bruno Fullone, George Brown College
Ibrahim Hayani, Seneca College
Geraldine Joosse, Lethbridge Community College
Nargess Kayhani, Mount St. Vincent University
Allan Matadeen, Simon Fraser University
Fiona MacPhail, University of Northern British Columbia
John Pirrie, St. Lawrence College
Paul Pieper, Humber College
Judith Skuce, Georgian College
Steve Rakoczy, Humber College
Richard Schwindt, Simon Fraser University
Andrew Wong, Grant MacEwan College

Special thanks must be given to Morris Altman and to Torben Andersen, both of whom reviewed all stages of the manuscript in development and provided many suggestions for improvement. And special praise should go to Audrey Laporte, University of Toronto, for her vigilant efforts as the technical reviewer for the text. Her keen eye and attention to detail has contributed greatly to the quality of the final product.

We are greatly indebted to the many professionals at McGraw-Hill Ryerson—in particular Lynn Fisher, Executive Sponsoring Editor; Ron Doleman, Economics Editor; Daphne Scriabin, Developmental Editor; Kelly Dickson, Manager, Editorial Services; Joanne Murray, Supervising Editor; and Kelly Smyth, Marketing Manager—for their publishing and marketing expertise. We thank Nick Gamble for his thorough and sensitive editing and Jacques Cournoyer for his vivid Last Word illustrations. Dianna Little developed the interior design and the colourful cover.

We also strongly acknowledge the McGraw-Hill Ryerson sales staff, who greeted this new Canadian edition with wholehearted enthusiasm.

Campbell R. McConnell
Stanley L. Brue
Thomas Barbiero

Learning Centre

www.mcgrawhill.ca/college/mcconnell

FOR THE STUDENT

- Want to get higher grades?

- Want instant feedback on your comprehension *and* retention of the course material?

- Want to know how ready you *really* are to take your next exam?

- Want the extra help at *your* convenience?

Of course you do!

Then check out your Online Learning Centre!

- Online Quizzes
- Interactive Graphing Exercises
- CBC Videos and Cases
- Econ Graph Kit

Microeconomics

10th CANADIAN EDITION

FOR THE INSTRUCTOR

- Want an easy way to test your students prior to an exam that *doesn't* create more work for you?

- Want to access your supplements *without* having to bring them all to class?

- Want to integrate current happenings into your lectures *without* all the searching and extra work?

- Want an *easy* way to get your course on-line?

- Want to *free up more time* in your day to get more done?

Of course you do!

Then check out your
Online Learning Centre!

- Downloadable Supplements
- PageOut
- Online Resources
- The Integrator!

Part 1

An Introduction to Economics and the Economy

The Nature and Method of Economics

> Want is a growing giant whom the coat of Have was never large enough to cover.
>
> Ralph Waldo Emerson
> *The Conduct of Life,* 1860

People's wants are many and diverse. Biologically, humans need only air, water, food, clothing, and shelter. But in contemporary Canada, as in many other nations, we also want the many goods and services associated with a comfortable standard of living. Fortunately, Canada is blessed with productive resources—labour and managerial talent, tools and machinery, land and mineral deposits—that are used to produce goods and services. This production satisfies many of our wants and takes place through the organizational mechanism called the *economic system* or, more simply, the *economy.*

economics
The social science concerned with the efficient use of scarce resources to obtain the maximum satisfaction of society's unlimited wants.

The blunt reality, however, is that our wants far exceed the productive capacity of our limited resources. So the complete satisfaction of society's wants is impossible. This fact provides our definition of **economics**: *it is the social science concerned with the efficient use of scarce resources to obtain the maximum satisfaction of society's unlimited wants.*

Numerous problems and issues arise from the challenge of using limited resources efficiently. Although it is tempting to plunge into them, that sort of analysis must wait. In this chapter, we need to discuss some important preliminaries.

1.1   Ten Key Concepts to Retain for a Lifetime

Economics is concerned with the efficient use of scarce resources to obtain the maximum satisfaction of society's unlimited wants.

Suppose you unexpectedly meet your introductory economics professor on the street five or ten years after you complete this course. What will you be able to tell her you retained from the course she taught? More than likely you will not be able to remember very much. To help you retain the main ideas that economics has to offer, we have come up with **Ten Key Concepts** we believe are essential to understand the world around you and help you in your chosen career. These key concepts will be reinforced throughout the textbook. When a key concept is about to be discussed you will be alerted with an icon and the concept description.

The 10 key concepts will simply be listed here; elaboration on each of the key concepts will be found as we progress through the textbook. At the end of the course you should review these 10 key concepts. They will help you organize and better understand the materials you have studied. We have divided the 10 key concepts into three categories: (a) those pertaining to the individual; (b) concepts that explain the interaction among individuals; and (c) concepts that deal with the economy as a whole and the standard of living.

The Individual

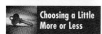

CONCEPT 1 ("Facing Tradeoffs"): Scarcity in relation to wants means you face **tradeoffs**; therefore you have to make choices.

CONCEPT 2 ("Opportunity Costs"): The cost of the choice you make is what you give up for it, or the **opportunity cost**.

CONCEPT 3 ("Choosing a Little More or Less"): Choices are usually made at the **margin**; we choose a "little" more or a "little" less of something.

CONCEPT 4 ("The Influence of Incentives"): The choices you make are influenced by **incentives**.

Interaction Among Individuals

CONCEPT 5 ("Specialization and Trade"): **Specialization** and **trade** will improve the well-being of all participants.

CONCEPT 6 ("The Effectiveness of Markets"): **Markets** usually do a good job of coordinating trade among individuals, groups, and nations.

CONCEPT 7 ("The Role of Governments"): **Governments** can occasionally improve the coordinating function of markets.

The Economy as a Whole and the Standard of Living

CONCEPT 8 ("Production and the Standard of Living"): The **standard of living** of the average person in a particular country is dependent on its production of goods and services. A rise in the standard of living requires a rise in the output of goods and services.

CONCEPT 9 ("Money and Inflation"): If the monetary authorities of a country annually print money in excess of the growth of output of goods and services it will eventually lead to **inflation**.

CONCEPT 10 ("Inflation–Unemployment Tradeoff"): In the short run, society faces a short-run **tradeoff** between **inflation** and its level of **unemployment**.

These concepts will be elaborated on throughout this textbook. Be sure to be on the lookout for the icon that alerts you that one of these concepts is being discussed. We now turn to our first topic, the economic way of thinking.

1.2   The Economic Perspective

Close your eyes for a minute and pretend you are in paradise, a place where you can have anything you want whenever you desire it. On a particular day you may decide you want a new pair of jeans, a new notebook computer, a cellular phone, tickets to see Avril Lavigne, and a new yellow Lamborghini sports car to cruise around in. Your friends may have a completely different list of wants, but all of their desires will also be satisfied. Indeed, everyone's desires are satisfied. The following day you can start all over and make any request you have, and they will all be fulfilled. And so it will continue forever. Your body will never get old or sick, you will have all the friends and love you want, etc., etc.

economic perspective
A viewpoint that envisions individuals and institutions making rational decisions by comparing the marginal benefits and marginal costs associated with their actions.

Of course, paradise may be waiting for us in the afterlife, but in this world our wants greatly outstrip our ability to satisfy them. Anytime there is a situation in which wants are greater than the resources to meet those desires, we have an economic problem. It is this reality that gives economists their unique perspective. This **economic perspective** or *economic way of thinking* has several critical and closely interrelated features.

Scarcity and Choice

From our definition of economics, it is easy to see why economists view the world through the lens of scarcity. Since resources are scarce (limited), it follows that the goods and services we produce must also be limited. Scarcity limits our options and means that we must make choices. Because we "can't have it all," we must decide what we will have, and what we must forgo.

Limited resources have given economics its core: the idea that "there is no free lunch." You may get treated to lunch, making it "free" to you, but there is a cost to someone or a group of people (see the Consider This box). Scarce inputs of land, equipment, farm labour, the labour of cooks and waiters, and managerial talent are required. Because these resources could be used in other production activities, they and the other goods and services they could have produced are sacrificed in making the lunch available. Economists call these sacrifices *opportunity costs*. To get more of one thing, you forgo the opportunity of getting something else. So, the cost of that which you get is the value of that which is sacrificed to obtain it. We will say much more about opportunity costs in Chapter 2.

Rational Behaviour

The economic approach assumes that human behaviour reflects "rational self-interest." Individuals look for and pursue opportunities to increase their **utility**—that is, pleasure or satisfaction. They allocate their time, energy, and money to maximize their well-being. Because they weigh costs and benefits, their decisions are purposeful, not random.

utility
The satisfaction a person gets from consuming a good or service.

Rational behaviour means that the same person may make different choices under different circumstances. For example, Gagnon may decide to buy Coca-Cola cans in bulk at a warehouse store rather than at a convenience store where they are much more expensive. That will leave him with extra money to buy something else that provides satisfaction. Yet, while on a Saturday drive, he may stop at a Mac's store to buy a single can of Coca-Cola. Both actions are rational.

Consider This

The Idea of a "Free Lunch"

If you have never been offered a free product, you must be living on a deserted island. Sellers from time to time offer free software (Corel Corp. of Ottawa), free cellphones (Telus and Rogers), and no-fee chequing accounts (all the major Canadian chartered banks). Dentists give out free toothbrushes. Advertisers tout that if you buy three tires, you get one free. At provincial visitors' centres, there are free brochures and maps. Publishers provide free CD-ROMs along with some of their textbooks.

You might think that the presence of so many free products contradicts the economist's assertion that "there is no free lunch." You would be wrong! Scarce resources are used to produce each of these products, and because those resources have alternative uses, society incurs an opportunity cost. Where there are opportunity costs, there are no free lunches.

So why are these goods offered for free? In a word: marketing. Firms sometimes offer free products to entice people to try them, hoping they will then purchase them (or upgraded versions of them) later. That free version of WordPerfect software from Corel may eventually entice you to buy the next upgraded version. In other instances, the product contains advertising. Those free brochures contain advertising for shops and restaurants and free access to the Internet is filled with ads. In still other cases, the product is only "free" in conjunction with a purchase. To get the soft drink you must buy the large pizza. To get the free cellphone from Rogers or Telus you need to sign up for a year (or more) of cellphone service.

QUESTION: Is health care "free" in Canada?

Rational behaviour also means that choices will vary greatly among individuals. High school graduate Andrée, living in Montreal, may decide to attend college or university to major in business. Baker, in Saskatoon, may opt to take a job at a warehouse and buy a new car. Chin, from Kelowna, may accept a signing bonus and join the Armed Forces. All three choices reflect the pursuit of self-interest and are rational, but they are based on different preferences and circumstances.

Of course, rational decisions may change as costs and benefits change. Gagnon may switch to Pepsi when it is on sale. And, after taking a few business courses, Andrée may decide to change her major to social work.

Rational self-interest is not the same as selfishness. Many individuals make personal sacrifices to help family members or friends, and they contribute to charities because they derive pleasure from doing so. Parents help pay for their children's education for the same reason. These self-interested, but unselfish, acts help maximize the givers' satisfaction as much as any personal purchase of goods or services. Self-interested behaviour is simply behaviour that enables a person to achieve personal satisfaction, whatever the source of that satisfaction.

Marginal Analysis: Benefits and Costs

marginal analysis
The comparison of marginal ("extra" or "additional") benefits and marginal costs, usually for decision making.

The economic perspective focuses on **marginal analysis**—comparisons of *marginal benefits* and *marginal costs*. (Used this way, "marginal" means "extra," "additional," or "a change in.") Most choices or decisions involve changes in the status quo (the existing state of affairs). Should you attend school for another year or not? Should you study an extra hour for an exam? Should you add fries to your fast-food order? Similarly, should a business expand or reduce its output? Should government increase or decrease health care funding?

Choosing a Little More or Less

Each option will have marginal benefits and marginal costs. In making choices, the decision maker will compare those two amounts. Example: You and your fiancé are shopping for an engagement ring. Should you buy a ¼-carat diamond, a ½-carat diamond, a ¾-carat diamond, or a larger one? The marginal cost of the larger diamond is the added expense beyond the smaller diamond. The marginal benefit is the greater lifetime pleasure (utility) from the larger stone. If the marginal benefit of the larger diamond exceeds its marginal cost, you buy the larger stone. But if the marginal cost is more than the marginal benefit, you purchase the smaller diamond instead.

In a world of scarcity, the marginal benefit associated with some specific option always includes the marginal cost of forgoing something else. For example, the money spent on the larger diamond may mean forgoing a honeymoon to an exotic location.

One surprising implication of decisions based on marginal analysis is that there can be too much of a good thing. Although certain goods and services such as education, health care, and a pristine environment are desirable, we can in fact produce too much of them. "Too much" occurs when we keep obtaining them beyond the point where their marginal cost (the value of the forgone options) equals their marginal benefit. Then we are sacrificing alternative products that are more valuable *at the margin*. Thus, society can have too much health care and you can buy too large a diamond. *(Key Question 4)*

This chapter's Last Word, on page 14, provides an everyday application of the economic perspective.

QUICK REVIEW

- Economics is concerned with obtaining maximum satisfaction through the efficient use of scarce resources.

- The economic perspective stresses (a) resource scarcity and the necessity of making choices, (b) the assumption of rational behaviour, and (c) comparisons of marginal benefit and marginal cost.

1.3   Economic Methodology

scientific method
The systematic pursuit of knowledge through the formulation of a problem, collection of data, and the formulation and testing of hypotheses.

Like the physical and life sciences, as well as other social sciences, economics relies on the **scientific method**. It consists of a number of elements:

- The observation of facts (real world data).

- Based on those facts, the formulation of possible explanations of cause and effect (hypotheses).

- The testing of these explanations by comparing the outcomes of specific events to the outcomes predicted by the hypotheses.

- The acceptance, rejection, or modification of the hypotheses, based on these comparisons.

- The continued testing of the hypotheses against the facts. As favourable results accumulate, the hypotheses evolve into a *theory*, sometimes referred to as a *model*. A very well-tested and widely accepted theory is referred to as a *law* or *principle*.

Laws, principles, and models enable the economist, like the natural scientist, to understand and explain economic phenomena and to predict the various outcomes of particular actions. But as we will soon see, economic laws and principles are usually less certain than the laws of physics or chemistry.

Deriving Theories

Economists develop models of the behaviour of individuals (consumers, workers) and institutions (business, government) engaged in the production, exchange, and consumption of goods and services. They start by gathering facts about economic activity and economic outcomes. Because the world is cluttered with innumerable interrelated facts, economists, like all scientists, must select what they consider useful information. They must determine which facts are relevant to the problem under consideration. But even when this sorting process is complete, the relevant information may at first seem random and unrelated.

The economist draws on the facts to establish cause–effect hypotheses about economic behaviour. Then the hypotheses are tested against real world observation and data. Through this process,

FIGURE 1-1

The Relationship Between Facts, Theories, and Policies in Economics

Theoretical economics involves establishing economic theories by gathering, systematically arranging, and generalizing from facts. Economic theories are tested for validity against facts. Economists use these theories—the most reliable of which are called *laws* or *principles*—to explain and analyze the economy. *Policy economics* entails using the economic laws and principles to formulate economic policies.

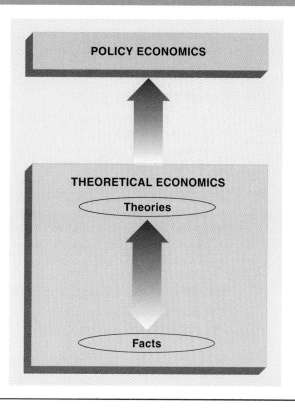

POLICY ECONOMICS

THEORETICAL ECONOMICS

Theories

Facts

---

theoretical economics
The process of deriving and applying economic theories and principles.

the economist tries to discover hypotheses that can eventually rise to the level of theories and principles (or laws)—well-tested and widely accepted generalizations about how individuals and institutions behave. The process of deriving theories and principles is called **theoretical economics** (see the lower box in Figure 1-1). *The role of economic theorizing is to systematically arrange facts, interpret them, and generalize from them.* Theories and principles bring order and meaning to facts by arranging them in cause-and-effect order.

Observe that the arrow between "theories" and "facts" in Figure 1-1 moves in both directions. Some understanding of factual, real-world evidence is required to formulate meaningful hypotheses. And hypotheses are tested through gathering and organizing factual data to see if the hypotheses can be verified.

principles
Statements about economic behaviour that enable prediction of the probable effects of certain actions.

Economic theories and **principles** *are statements about economic behaviour that enable prediction of the probable effects of certain actions.* Good theories are those that explain and predict well. They are supported by facts of how individuals and institutions behave in producing, exchanging, and consuming goods and services. But these facts may change over time, so economists must continually check theories against the shifting economic environment.

Several other points relating to economic principles are important to know.

TERMINOLOGY

Economists speak of "hypotheses," "theories," "models," "laws," and "principles." These terms overlap but usually reflect the degree of confidence in the generalizations. A hypothesis needs initial testing; a theory has been tested but needs more testing; a law or principle is a theory that has proved highly reliable, over and over. The terms *economic laws* and *principles* are useful, even though they imply a degree of exactness and universal application that is rare in any social science. The word *theory* is often used in economics even though many people incorrectly believe theories have nothing to do with real-world applications.

In this book, custom and convenience will govern the use of "theory," "law," "principle," and "model." Thus, we will use the term *law of demand* to describe the relationship between the price of a product and the amount of it purchased, rather than the theory or principle of demand, simply because this is the custom. We will refer to the *circular flow model*, not the circular flow law, because it combines several ideas into a single representation.

GENERALIZATIONS

generalization
Statement of the nature of the relation between two or more sets of facts.

As we have already mentioned, economic theories, principles, and laws are **generalizations** relating to economic behaviour or to the economy itself. They are imprecise because economic facts are usually diverse; no two individuals or institutions act in exactly the same way. *Economic principles are expressed as the tendencies of typical or average consumers, workers, or business firms.* For example, when economists say that Canadian consumer spending rises when personal income increases, they are well aware that some Canadian households may save *all* of an increase in their incomes. But, on average, and for the entire economy, spending goes up when income increases. Similarly, economists claim that consumers buy more of a particular product when its price falls. Some consumers may increase their purchases by a large amount, others by a small amount, and a few not at all. This "price–quantity" principle, however, holds for the typical consumer and for consumers as a group.

OTHER-THINGS-EQUAL ASSUMPTION

other-things-equal assumption
The assumption that factors other than those being considered are held constant.

Like other scientists, economists use the *ceteris paribus* or **other-things-equal assumption** to arrive at their generalizations. They assume that all other variables except those under immediate consideration are held constant for a particular analysis. For example, consider the relationship between the price of Pepsi and the amount of it purchased. It helps to assume that, of all the factors that might influence the amount of Pepsi purchased (for example, the price of Pepsi, the price of Coca-Cola, and consumer incomes and preferences), only the price of Pepsi varies. We can then focus on the "price of Pepsi–purchases of Pepsi" relationship without being confused by changes in other variables.

Natural scientists such as chemists or physicists can usually conduct controlled experiments where "all other things" are in fact held constant (or virtually so). They can test with great precision the assumed relationship between two variables. For example, they might examine the height from which an object is dropped and the length of time it takes to hit the ground. But economics is not a laboratory science. Economists test their theories using real-world data, which are generated by the actual operation of the economy. In this complex environment, "other things" *do* change. Despite the development of sophisticated statistical techniques designed to hold other things equal, control is less than perfect. As a result, economic theories are less certain and less precise than those of laboratory sciences. That also means they generate more debate than many scientific theories (for example, the law of gravity.)

ABSTRACTIONS

Economic theories are *abstractions*—simplifications that omit irrelevant facts and circumstances. Economic models do *not* mirror the full complexity of the real world. The very process of sorting out and analyzing facts involves simplification and removal of clutter. Unfortunately, this "abstraction" leads some people to consider economic theory impractical and unrealistic. That is simply nonsense! Economic theories are practical precisely because they are abstractions. The full scope of economic reality itself is too complex to be understood as a whole. Economists abstract—that is, develop theories and build models—to give meaning to an otherwise overwhelming and confusing maze of facts. Theorizing for this purpose is highly practical.

GRAPHICAL EXPRESSION

Many of the economic models in this book are expressed graphically; the most important are labelled *Key Graphs*. Be sure to read the appendix to this chapter as a review of graphs.

Policy Economics

Applied economics, or **policy economics**, is the application of theories and data to formulate *policies* that aim to resolve a specific economic problem or bring about a desired economic outcome. Economic theories are the foundation of economic policy, as shown in the upper part of Figure 1-1. Economic policy normally is applied to problems after they arise. However, if economic analysis can predict some undesirable event, such as unemployment, inflation, or an increase in poverty, then it may be possible to avoid or moderate that event through economic policy. For example, you may read in the newspaper that the Bank of Canada has reduced interest rates to increase spending and prevent a recession.

FORMULATING ECONOMIC POLICY

Here are the basic steps in policy-making:

- *State the goal.* The first step is to make a clear statement of the economic goal. If we say that we want "full employment," do we mean that everyone between, say, 16 and 65 years of age should have a job? Or do we mean that everyone who *wants* to work should have a job? Should we allow for some unemployment caused by inevitable changes in the structure of industry and workers voluntarily changing jobs? The goal must be specific.

- *Determine the policy options.* The next step is to formulate alternative policies designed to achieve the goal, and determine the possible effects of each policy. This requires a detailed assessment of the economic impact, benefits, costs, and political feasibility of the alternative policies. For example, to achieve full employment in Canada, should the federal and provincial governments use fiscal policy (which involves changing government spending and taxes), monetary policy (which entails altering the supply of money), an education and training policy that enhances worker employability, or a policy of wage subsidies to firms that hire disadvantaged workers?

- *Implement and evaluate the policy that was selected.* After implementing the policy, we need to evaluate how well it worked. Only through unbiased evaluation can we improve on economic policy. Did a specific change in taxes or the money supply alter the level of employment to the extent predicted? Did deregulation of a particular industry (for example, banking) yield the predicted beneficial results? If not, why not? What were the harmful side effects, if any? How might the policy be altered to make it work better? *(Key Question 8)*

ECONOMIC GOALS

If economic policies are designed to achieve specific economic goals, then we need to recognize a number of goals that are widely accepted in Canada and many other countries. They include:

- *Economic growth*   Produce more and better goods and services, or, more simply, achieve a higher standard of living.

- *Full employment*   Provide suitable jobs for all citizens who are willing and able to work.

- *Economic efficiency*   Achieve the maximum output and satisfaction using the available productive resources.

- *Price-level stability*   Avoid large upswings and downswings in the general price level; that is, avoid inflation and deflation.

policy economics
The formulation of courses of action to bring about desired economic outcomes or to prevent undesired occurrences.

www.bankofcanada.ca
Bank of Canada

- *Economic freedom*   Guarantee that businesses, workers, and consumers have a high degree of freedom of choice in their economic activities.

- *Equitable distribution of income*   Ensure that no group of citizens faces poverty while most others enjoy abundance.

- *Economic security*   Provide for those who are chronically ill, disabled, laid off, aged, or otherwise unable to earn minimal levels of income.

- *Balance of trade*   Seek a reasonable overall balance with the rest of the world in international trade and financial transactions.

Although most of us might accept these goals as generally stated, we might also disagree substantially on their specific meanings. What are "large" changes in the price level? What is a "high degree" of economic freedom? What is an "equitable" distribution of income? How can we measure precisely such abstract goals as "economic freedom"? These objectives are often the subject of spirited public debate.

Also, some of these goals are complementary; when one is achieved, some other one will also be realized. For example, achieving full employment means eliminating unemployment, which is a basic cause of inequitable income distribution. But other goals may conflict or even be mutually exclusive. They may entail **tradeoffs**, meaning that to achieve one we must sacrifice another. For example, efforts to equalize the distribution of income may weaken incentives to work, invest, innovate, and take business risks, all of which promote economic growth. Taxing high-income people heavily and transferring the tax revenues to low-income people is one way to equalize the distribution of income. But then the incentives to high-income individuals may diminish because higher taxes reduce their rewards for working. Similarly, low-income individuals may be less motivated to work when government stands ready to subsidize them.

When goals conflict, society must develop a system to prioritize the objectives it seeks. If more economic freedom is accompanied by less economic security and more economic security allows less economic freedom, society must assess the tradeoffs and decide on the optimal (best) balance between them.

tradeoffs
The sacrifice of some or all of one economic goal, good, or service to achieve some other goal, good, or service.

QUICK REVIEW

- Economists use the scientific method to establish theories, laws, and principles. Economic theories (laws, principles, or models) are generalizations relating to the economic behaviour of individuals and institutions; good theories are grounded in facts.

- Theoretical economics involves formulating theories (or laws and principles) and using them to understand and explain economic behaviour and the economy;

- policy economics involves using the theories to fix economic problems or promote economic goals.

- Policy-making requires a clear statement of goals, a thorough assessment of options, and an unbiased evaluation of results.

- Some of society's economic goals are complementary, while others conflict; where conflicts exist, tradeoffs arise.

1.4   Macroeconomics and Microeconomics

Economists derive and apply principles about economic behaviour at two levels.

macroeconomics
The part of economics concerned with the economy as a whole.

Macroeconomics

aggregate
A collection of specific economic units treated as if they were one unit.

Macroeconomics examines either the economy as a whole or its basic subdivisions or aggregates such as the government, household, and business sectors. An **aggregate** is a collection of specific economic units treated as if they were one unit. Therefore, we might lump together the millions of consumers in the Canadian economy and treat them as if they were one huge unit called "consumers."

In using aggregates, macroeconomics seeks to obtain an overview, or general outline, of the structure of the economy and the relationships of its major aggregates. Macroeconomics is concerned with such economic measures as *total* output, *total* employment, *total* income, *aggregate* expenditures, and the *general* level of prices in analyzing various economic problems. Very little attention is given to specific units making up the various aggregates. Macroeconomics examines the beach, not the sand, rocks, and shells.

Microeconomics

microeconomics
The part of economics concerned with such individual units as industries, firms, and households.

Microeconomics looks at specific economic units. At this level of analysis, we observe the details of an economic unit, or very small segment of the economy, under the microscope. In microeconomics we investigate an individual industry, firm, or household. We measure the price of a *specific* product, the number of workers employed by a *single* firm, the revenue or income of a *particular* firm or household, or the expenditures of a *specific* firm, government entity, or family. In microeconomics, we examine the sand, rocks, and shells, not the beach.

The macro–micro distinction does not mean that every topic can be readily labelled as either macro or micro; many topics and subdivisions of economics are rooted in both. Example: While the problem of unemployment is usually treated as a macroeconomic topic (because unemployment relates to *aggregate* spending), the decisions made by *individual* workers in searching for jobs and the way *specific* product and labour markets operate are also critical in determining the unemployment rate. *(Key Question 10)*

Positive and Normative Economics

positive economics
The analysis of facts or data to establish scientific generalizations about economic behaviour.

normative economics
The part of economics involving value judgments about what the economy should be like.

Both macroeconomics and microeconomics use facts, theories, and policies. Each contains elements of *positive* economics and *normative* economics. **Positive economics** focuses on facts and cause-and-effect relationships. Positive economics avoids value judgments, tries to establish scientific statements about economic behaviour, and deals with what the economy is actually like. Such factually based analysis is critical to good policy analysis.

In contrast **normative economics** incorporates a person's (or group of people's) value judgments about what the economy should be like. Normative economics looks at the subjective desirability of certain aspects of the economy, or the expressions of support for particular economic policies.

Positive economics concerns *what is,* while normative economics embodies subjective feelings about *what ought to be.* Here are some examples. Positive statement: "The unemployment rate in several European nations is higher than that in Canada." Normative statement: "European nations ought to undertake policies to reduce their unemployment rates." A second positive statement: "Other things equal, if tuition is substantially increased, college and university enrolment will fall." Normative statement: "College and university tuition should be lowered so that more students can obtain an education." Whenever words such as "ought" or "should" appear in a sentence, there is a strong chance you are encountering a normative statement.

Most of the disagreement among economists involves normative, value-based policy questions. Of course, there is often some disagreement about which theories or models best represent the economy and its parts. But economists agree on a full range of economic principles. Most economic controversy thus reflects differing opinions or value judgments about what society should be like. *(Key Question 11)*

There is one more thing to add to the normative–positive dichotomy, and that is to distinguish them from *prediction* about future factual issues. If I believe that Mary Smith will be elected the next prime minister of Canada, such a prediction of a future event should be distinguished from a value-based opinion, such as "Mary Smith should be elected the next prime minister of Canada."

1.5   Pitfalls to Objective Thinking

Because they often affect us so personally, we often have difficulty thinking objectively about economic issues. Here are some common pitfalls to avoid in successfully applying the economic perspective.

Biases

Most people bring a bundle of biases and preconceptions when thinking about economic issues. For example, you might think that corporate profits are excessive or that borrowing money is never a good idea. Perhaps you believe that government is necessarily less efficient than businesses or that more government regulation is always better than less. Biases cloud thinking and interfere with objective analysis. The novice economics student must be willing to shed biases and preconceptions that are not supported by facts.

Loaded Terminology

The economic terminology used in newspapers and popular magazines is sometimes emotionally biased, or loaded. The writer or the interest group he or she represents may have a cause to promote or an axe to grind and may slant an article accordingly. High profits may be labelled "obscene," low wages may be called "exploitive," or self-interested behaviour may be "greed." Government workers may be referred to as "mindless bureaucrats," and those favouring stronger government regulations may be called "socialists." To objectively analyze economic issues, you must be prepared to reject or discount such terminology.

Definitions

Some of the terms used in economics have precise technical definitions that are quite different from those implied by their common usage. This is generally not a problem if everyone understands these definitions and uses them consistently. For example, *investment* to the average citizen means the purchase of stocks and bonds in security markets, as when someone "invests" in Royal Bank stock or government bonds. But to the economist, *investment* means the purchase of newly created real (physical) capital assets such as machinery and equipment or the construction of a new factory building.

Fallacy of Composition

fallacy of composition
Incorrectly reasoning that what is true for the individual (or part) is necessarily true for the group (or whole).

Another pitfall in economic thinking is the assumption that what is true for one individual is necessarily true for a group of individuals. This is a logical fallacy called the **fallacy of composition**; the assumption is *not* correct. A statement that is valid for an individual or part is *not* necessarily valid for the larger group.

Consider the following example from outside of economics. You are at a football game in Winnipeg and the home team makes an outstanding play. In the excitement, you leap to your feet to get a better view. A valid statement: "If you, *an individual*, stand, your view of the game is improved." But is this also true for the group—for everyone watching the play? Not necessarily. If *everyone* stands to watch the play, it is likely that nobody—including you—will have a better view than when all remain seated.

A second example comes from economics: An *individual* farmer who reaps a particularly large crop is likely to realize a sharp gain in income. But this statement cannot be generalized to farmers as a *group*. The individual farmer's large or "bumper" crop will not noticeably influence (reduce) crop prices because each farmer produces a negligible fraction of the total farm output. But for *all* farmers as a group, prices decline when total output increases. Thus, if all farmers reap bumper crops, the total output of farm products will rise, depressing crop prices. If the price declines are relatively large, total farm income might actually *fall*.

Recall our earlier distinction between macroeconomics and microeconomics: *The fallacy of composition reminds us that generalizations valid at one of these levels of analysis may or may not be valid at the other.*

Causation Fallacies

Causation is sometimes difficult to identify in economics. Two important fallacies often interfere with economic thinking.

POST HOC FALLACY

post hoc, ergo propter hoc fallacy
Incorrectly reasoning that when one event precedes another the first event must have caused the second event.

You must think very carefully before concluding that because event A precedes event B, A is the cause of B. This kind of faulty reasoning is known as the ***post hoc, ergo propter hoc*** or **"after this, therefore because of this" fallacy**.

Example: Suppose that early each spring the medicine man of a tribe performs a special dance. A week or so later the trees and grass turn green. Can we safely conclude that event A, the medicine man's dance, has caused event B, the landscape's turning green? Obviously not. The rooster crows before dawn, but that does not mean the rooster is responsible for the sunrise!

The Toronto Maple Leafs hire a new coach and the team's record improves. Is the new coach the cause? Maybe. But perhaps the presence of more experienced and talented players or an easier schedule is the true cause.

CORRELATION VERSUS CAUSATION

Do not confuse correlation, or connection, with causation. Correlation between two events indicates only that they are associated in some systematic and dependable way. For example, we may find that when variable X increases, Y also increases. But this correlation does not necessarily mean that there is causation—that an increase in X is the cause of an increase in Y. The relationship could be purely coincidental or dependent on some other factor, Z, not included in the analysis.

Here is an example: Economists have found a positive correlation between education and income. In general, people with more education earn higher incomes than those with less education. Common sense suggests education is the cause and higher incomes are the effect; more education implies a more knowledgeable and productive worker, and such workers receive larger salaries.

But causation could also partly run the other way. People with higher incomes could buy more education, just as they buy more furniture and organic foods. Or is part of the relationship explainable in still other ways? Are education and income correlated because the characteristics required to succeed in education—ability and motivation—are the same ones required to be a productive and highly paid worker? If so, then people with those traits will probably obtain more education *and* earn higher incomes. But greater education will not be the sole cause of the higher income. ***(Key Question 12)***

A Look Ahead

The ideas in this chapter will come into much sharper focus as you advance through Part 1, where we develop specific economic principles and models. Specifically, in Chapter 2 we will build a model of the production choices facing an economy. In Chapter 3 we develop laws of demand and supply that will help you understand how prices and quantities of goods and services are established in markets. In Chapter 4 we combine all markets in the economy to see how the *market system* works and then proceed to look at international markets and the structure of the Canadian economy.

THE LASTword — Fast-Food Lines: An Economic Perspective

How can the economic perspective help us understand the behaviour of fast-food consumers?

You enter a fast-food restaurant on the outskirts of Halifax. Do you immediately look to see which line is the shortest? What do you do when you are in the middle of a long line and a new serving station opens? Have you ever gone to a fast-food restaurant, seen very long lines, and then left? Have you ever become annoyed when someone in front of you in line placed an order that took a long time to fill?

The economic perspective is useful in analyzing the behaviour of fast-food customers. These consumers are at the restaurant because they expect the marginal benefit from the food they buy to match or exceed its marginal cost. When customers enter the restaurant, they go to the shortest line, believing that it will minimize the time cost of obtaining their food. They are acting purposefully; time is limited and people prefer using it in some way other than standing in line.

If one fast-food line is temporarily shorter than other lines, some people will move toward that line. These movers apparently view the time saving associated with the shorter line to exceed the cost of moving from their present line. The line switching tends to equalize line lengths. No further movement of customers between lines occurs once all lines are about equal.

Fast-food customers face another cost–benefit decision when a clerk opens a new station at the counter.

Should they move to the new station or stay put? Those who shift to the new line decide that the time saving from the move exceeds the extra cost of physically moving. In so deciding, customers must also consider just how quickly they can get to the new station compared with others who may be contemplating the same move. (Those who hesitate in this situation are lost!)

Customers at the fast-food establishment do not have perfect information when they select lines. For example, they do not first survey those in the lines to determine what they are ordering before deciding which line to enter. There are two reasons for this. First, most customers would tell them "It's none of your business," and therefore no information would be forthcoming. Second, even if they could obtain the information, the amount of time necessary to get it (a cost) would most certainly exceed any time saving associated with finding the best line (the benefit). Because information is costly to obtain, fast-food patrons select lines without perfect information. Thus, not all decisions turn

out as expected. For example, you might enter a short line and find someone in front of you is ordering hamburgers and fries for 40 people in the Greyhound bus that just arrived from Moncton and is parked out back (and the employee is a trainee)! Nevertheless, at the time you made your decision, you thought it was optimal.

Imperfect information also explains why some people who arrive at a fast-food restaurant and observe long lines decide to leave. These people conclude that the marginal cost (monetary plus time costs) of obtaining the fast food is too large relative to the marginal benefit. They would not have come to the restaurant in the first place had they known the lines would be so long. But getting that information by, say, employing an advance scout with a cellphone would cost more than the perceived benefit.

Finally, customers must decide what food to order when they arrive at the counter. In making their choices they again compare marginal costs and marginal benefits in attempting to obtain the greatest personal satisfaction or well-being for their expenditure.

Economists believe that what is true for the behaviour of customers at fast-food restaurants is true for economic behaviour in general. Faced with an array of choices, consumers, workers, and businesses rationally compare marginal costs and marginal benefits in making decisions.

CHAPTER SUMMARY

1-1 TEN KEY CONCEPTS TO RETAIN FOR A LIFETIME

- There are ten key concepts to remember: four deal with the individual, three with interaction among individuals, and three with the economy as a whole.

1-2 THE ECONOMIC PERSPECTIVE

- Economics is the study of the efficient use of scarce resources in the production of goods and services to obtain the maximum satisfaction of society's unlimited wants.

- The economic perspective includes three elements: scarcity and choice, rational behaviour, and marginalism. It sees individuals and institutions making rational decisions based on comparisons of marginal costs and marginal benefits.

1-3 ECONOMIC METHODOLOGY

- Economists employ the scientific method to form and test hypotheses of cause-and-effect relationships, in order to generate theories, laws, and principles.

- Generalizations are called principles, theories, laws, or models. Good theories explain real-world relationships and predict real-world outcomes.

- Economic policy is designed to identify and solve problems to the greatest extent possible and at the least pos-

sible cost. This application of economics is called policy economics.

- Our society accepts certain shared economic goals, including economic growth, full employment, economic efficiency, price-level stability, economic freedom, equity in the distribution of income, economic security, and a reasonable balance in international trade and finance. Some of these goals are complementary; others entail tradeoffs.

1-4 MACROECONOMICS AND MICROECONOMICS

- Macroeconomics looks at the economy as a whole or its major aggregates; microeconomics examines specific economic units or institutions.

- Positive statements state facts ("what is"); normative statements express value judgments ("what ought to be").

1-5 PITFALLS TO OBJECTIVE THINKING

- In studying economics we encounter pitfalls to straight thinking such as biases and preconceptions, unfamiliar or confusing terminology, the fallacy of composition, and the difficulty of establishing clear cause–effect relationships.

TERMS AND CONCEPTS

economics, p. 3
economic perspective, p. 4
utility, p. 4
marginal analysis, p. 5
scientific method, p. 6
theoretical economics, p. 7
principles, p. 7

generalization, p. 8
"other-things-equal"
   assumption, p. 8
policy economics, p. 9
tradeoffs, p. 10
macroeconomics, p. 10
aggregate, p. 10

microeconomics, p. 11
positive economics, p. 11
normative economics, p. 11
fallacy of composition, p. 12
post hoc, ergo propter hoc
   fallacy, p. 13

STUDY QUESTIONS

1. "Buy two, get one free." Explain why the "one free" is free to the buyer, but not to society.

2. What is meant by the term "utility" and how does it relate to the economic perspective?

3. Cite three examples of recent decisions that you made in which, at least implicitly, you weighed marginal costs and marginal benefits.

4. **KEY QUESTION**   Use the economic perspective to explain why someone who is normally a light eater at a standard restaurant may become a bit of a glutton at

a buffet-style restaurant that charges a single price for all you can eat.

5. What is the scientific method and how does it relate to theoretical economics? What is the difference between a hypothesis and an economic law or principle?

6. Why is it significant that economics is not a laboratory science? What problems may be involved in deriving and applying economic principles?

7. Explain the following statements:

   a. Good economic policy requires good economic theory.

b. Generalization and abstraction are nearly synonymous.

c. Facts serve to sort out good and bad hypotheses.

d. The *other things equal assumption* helps isolate key economic relationships.

8. **KEY QUESTION**   Explain in detail the interrelationships between economic facts, theory, and policy. Critically evaluate this statement: "The trouble with economic theory is that it is not practical. It is detached from the real world."

9. To what extent do you accept the eight economic goals stated and described in this chapter? What priorities do you assign to them?

10. **KEY QUESTION**   Indicate whether each of the following statements applies to microeconomics or macroeconomics:

a. The unemployment rate in Canada was 7.4 percent in January 2003.

b. The fish processing plant in Torbay, Newfoundland, laid off 15 workers last month.

c. An unexpected freeze in central Florida reduced the citrus crop and caused the price of oranges to rise.

d. Canadian output, adjusted for inflation, grew by 13.4 percent in 2002.

e. Last week the Royal Bank lowered its interest rate on business loans by one-half of 1 percentage point.

f. The consumer price index rose by 2.7 percent in 2002.

11. **KEY QUESTION**   Identify each of the following as either a positive or a normative statement:

a. The high temperature today was 30 degrees.

b. It was too hot today in Edmonton.

c. Other things equal, higher interest rates reduce the total amount of borrowing.

d. Interest rates are too high.

12. **KEY QUESTION**   Explain and give an example of (a) the fallacy of composition, and (b) the "after this, therefore because of this" fallacy. Why are cause-and-effect relationships difficult to isolate in economics?

13. Suppose studies show that students who study more hours receive higher grades. Does this relationship guarantee that any particular student who studies longer will get higher grades?

14. Studies indicate that married men on average earn more income than unmarried men of the same age. Why must we be cautious in concluding that marriage is the *cause* and higher income is the *effect*?

15. **(Last Word)** Use the economic perspective to explain the behaviour of the *workers* (rather than the customers) observed at a fast-food restaurant. Why are these workers there, rather than, say, cruising around in their cars? Why do they work so diligently? Why do so many of them quit these jobs once they have graduated high school?

INTERNET APPLICATION QUESTIONS

1. **Three Economic Goals—Are They Being Achieved?** Three primary economic goals are economic growth (an increase in real GDP), full employment (less than 7 percent unemployment), and price-level stability (less than 2 percent as measured by the Consumer Price Index—CPI). Use the links to Canadian economic data on the McConnell-Brue-Barbiero Web site (Chapter 1) to assess whether these three goals are being met in Canada.

Σ-STAT

2. **Normative Economics—Canadian Politics.** Many economic policy statements made by the Liberal Party, the Reform Party, the Progressive Conservative Party, and the NDP can be considered normative rather than positive economic statements. Use the links on the McConnell-Brue-Barbiero Web site (Chapter 1) and compare and contrast their views on how to achieve economic goals. How much of the disagreement is based on positive statements and how much on normative statements? Give an example of loaded terminology from each site.

Appendix to Chapter 1

A1.1   Graphs and Their Meaning

If you glance quickly through this text, you will find many graphs. Some seem simple, others more complicated. All are important. They are used to help you visualize and understand economic relationships. Physicists and chemists sometimes illustrate their theories by building arrangements of multicoloured wooden balls, representing protons, neutrons, and electrons, which are held in proper relation to one another by wires or sticks. Economists use graphs to illustrate their models. By understanding these "pictures," you can more readily make sense of economic relationships. Most of our principles or models explain relationships between just two sets of economic facts, which can be conveniently represented with two-dimensional graphs.

Construction of a Graph

A graph is a visual representation of the relationship between two variables. Figure A1-1 is a hypothetical illustration showing the relationship between income and consumption for the economy as a whole. Without having studied economics, we would intuitively expect that people would buy more goods and services when their incomes go up. Thus it is not surprising to find in Figure A1-1 that total consumption in the economy increases as total income increases.

The information in Figure A1-1 is expressed both graphically and in table form. Here is how it is done: We want to show visually or graphically how consumption changes as income changes. Since income is the determining factor, we represent it on the **horizontal axis** of the graph, as is customary. And because consumption depends on income, we represent it on the **vertical axis** of the graph, as is also customary. Actually, what we are doing is representing the *independent variable* on the horizontal axis and the *dependent variable* on the vertical axis.

Now we arrange the vertical and horizontal scales of the graph to reflect the ranges of values of consumption and income, and we mark the scales in convenient increments. As you can see in Figure A1-1, the values marked on the scales cover all the values in the table. The increments on both scales are $100 for approximately each 1.25 centimetres.

Because this type of *graph* has two dimensions, each point within it represents an income value and its associated consumption value. To find a point that represents one of the five income-consumption combinations in the table, we draw perpendiculars from the appropriate values on the vertical and horizontal axes. For example, to plot point *c* (the $200 income–$150 consumption point), perpendiculars are drawn up from the horizontal (income) axis at $200 and across from the vertical (consumption) axis at $150. These perpendiculars intersect at point *c*, which represents this particular income–consumption combination. You should verify that the other income–consumption combinations shown in the table are properly located in the graph. Finally, by assuming that the same general relationship between income and consumption prevails for all other incomes, we draw a line or smooth curve to connect these points. That line or curve represents the income–consumption relationship.

horizontal axis
The "left-right" or "west-east" axis on a graph or grid.

vertical axis
The "up-down" or "north-south" axis on a graph or grid.

FIGURE A1-1 The Relationship Between Income and Consumption

Income per week	Consumption per week	Point
$ 0	$ 50	a
100	100	b
200	150	c
300	200	d
400	250	e

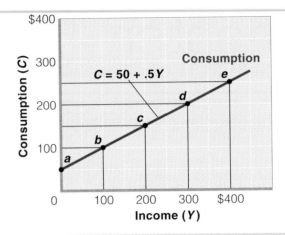

Two sets of data that are positively or directly related, such as consumption and income, graph as an upsloping line.

If the graph is a straight line, as in Figure A1-1, we say the relationship is *linear*.

Direct and Inverse Relationships

direct relationship
The (positive) relationship between two variables that change in the same direction, for example, product price and quantity supplied.

The line in Figure A1-1 slopes upward to the right, depicting a direct relationship between income and consumption. By a **direct relationship** (or positive relationship) we mean that two variables—in this case, consumption and income—change in the *same* direction. An increase in consumption is associated with an increase in income; a decrease in consumption accompanies a decrease in income. When two sets of data are positively or directly related, they always graph as an *upsloping* line, as in Figure A1-1.

In contrast, two sets of data may be inversely related. Consider Figure A1-2, which shows the relationship between the price of basketball tickets and game attendance at Informed University (IU). Here we have an **inverse relationship** (or negative relationship) because the two variables change in *opposite* directions. When ticket prices decrease, attendance increases. When ticket prices increase, attendance decreases. The six data points in the table are plotted in the graph. Observe that an inverse relationship always graphs as a *downsloping* line.

inverse relationship
The (negative) relationship between two variables that change in opposite directions, for example, product price and quantity demanded.

Dependent and Independent Variables

independent variable
The variable causing a change in some other (dependent) variable.

dependent variable
A variable that changes as a consequence of a change in some other (independent) variable; the "effect" or outcome.

Although it is not always easy, economists seek to determine which variable is the "cause" and which is the "effect." Or, more formally, they seek the independent variable and the dependent variable. The **independent variable** is the cause or source; it is the variable that changes first. The **dependent variable** is the effect or outcome; it is the variable that changes because of the change in the independent variable. As noted in our income–consumption example, income generally is the independent variable and consumption the dependent variable. Income causes consumption to be what it is rather than the other way around. Similarly, ticket prices (set in advance of the season) determine attendance at IU basketball games; attendance at games does not determine the ticket prices for those games. Ticket price is the independent variable, and the quantity of tickets purchased is the dependent variable.

You may recall from your high school courses that mathematicians always put the independent variable (cause) on the horizontal axis and the dependent variable (effect) on the vertical axis.

Economists are less tidy; their graphing of independent and dependent variables is more arbitrary. Their conventional graphing of the income–consumption relationship is consistent with mathematical presentation, but economists put price and cost data on the vertical axis.

Other Things Equal

Our simple two-variable graphs purposely ignore many other factors that might affect the amount of consumption occurring at each income level or the number of people who attend IU basketball games at each possible ticket price. When economists plot the relationship between any two variables, they employ the *ceteris paribus* (other things equal) assumption. Thus, in Figure A1-1 all factors other than income that might affect the amount of consumption are held constant. Similarly, in Figure A1-2 all factors other than ticket price that might influence attendance at IU basketball games are held constant. In reality, "other things" are not equal; they often change, and when they do, the relationship represented in our two tables and graphs will change. Specifically, the lines we have plotted will shift to new locations.

Consider a stock market "crash." The dramatic drop in the value of stocks might cause people to feel less wealthy and therefore less willing to consume at each level of income. The result might be a downward shift of the consumption line. To see this, you should plot a new consumption line in Figure A1-1, assuming that consumption is, say, $20 less at each income level. Note that the relationship remains direct; the line merely shifts downward to reflect less consumption spending at each income level.

Similarly, factors other than ticket prices might affect IU game attendance. If IU loses most of its games, attendance at IU games might fall at each ticket price. To see this, redraw the graph in Figure A1-2, assuming that 2000 fewer fans attend IU games at each ticket price. (***Key Appendix Question 2***)

FIGURE A1-2   The Relationship Between Ticket Prices and Attendance

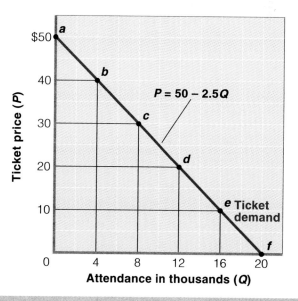

Ticket price	Attendance, thousands	Point
$50	0	a
40	4	b
30	8	c
20	12	d
10	16	e
0	20	f

Two sets of data that are negatively or inversely related, such as ticket price and the attendance at basketball games, graph as a downsloping line.

Slope of a Line

slope of a line
The ratio of the vertical change (the rise or fall) to the horizontal change (the run) between any two points on a line. The slope of an upward sloping line is positive, reflecting a direct relationship between two variables; the slope of a downward sloping line is negative, reflecting an inverse relationship between two variables.

Lines can be described in terms of their slopes and their intercepts. The **slope of a straight line** is the ratio of the vertical change (the rise or drop) to the horizontal change (the run) between any two points of the line, or "rise" over "run."

POSITIVE SLOPE

Between point b and point c in Figure A1-1 the rise or vertical change (the change in consumption) is +$50 and the run or horizontal change (the change in income) is +$100. Therefore:

$$\text{Slope} = \frac{\text{vertical change}}{\text{horizontal change}} = \frac{+50}{+100} = \frac{1}{2} = .5$$

Note that our slope of ½ or .5 is positive because consumption and income change in the same direction; that is, consumption and income are directly or positively related.

The slope of .5 tells us there will be a $1 increase in consumption for every $2 increase in income. Similarly, it indicates that for every $2 decrease in income there will be a $1 decrease in consumption.

NEGATIVE SLOPE

Between any two of the identified points in Figure A1-2, say, point c and point d, the vertical change is –10 (the drop) and the horizontal change is +4 (the run). Therefore:

$$\text{Slope} = \frac{\text{vertical change}}{\text{horizontal change}} = \frac{-10}{+4} = -2\frac{1}{2} = -2.5$$

This slope is negative because ticket price and attendance have an inverse or negative relationship.

Note that on the horizontal axis attendance is stated in thousands of people. So the slope of –10/+4 or –2.5 means that lowering the price by $10 will increase attendance by 4000 people. This is the same as saying that a $2.50 price reduction will increase attendance by 1000 people.

SLOPES AND MEASUREMENT UNITS

The slope of a line will be affected by the choice of units for either variable. If, in our ticket price illustration, we had chosen to measure attendance in individual people, our horizontal change would have been 4000 and the slope would have been

$$\text{Slope} = \frac{-10}{+4000} = \frac{-1}{+400} = -.0025$$

The slope depends on the units by which variables are measured.

SLOPES AND MARGINAL ANALYSIS

Recall that economics largely deals with changes from the status quo. The concept of slope is important in economics because it reflects marginal changes—those involving one more (or one less) unit. For example, in Figure A1-1 the .5 slope shows that $.50 of extra or marginal consumption is associated with each $1 change in income. In this example, people collectively will consume $.50 of any $1 increase in their incomes and reduce their consumption by $.50 for each $1 decline in income.

INFINITE AND ZERO SLOPES

Many variables are unrelated or independent of one another. For example, the quantity of digital cameras purchased is not related to the price of bananas. In Figure A1-3(a) we represent the price of bananas on the vertical axis and the quantity of digital cameras demanded on the

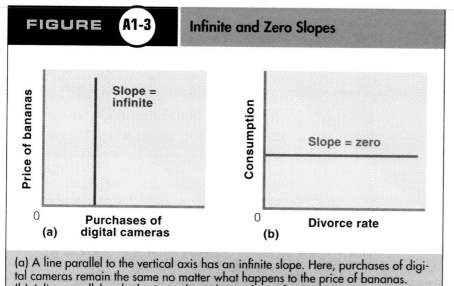

FIGURE A1-3   Infinite and Zero Slopes

(a) A line parallel to the vertical axis has an infinite slope. Here, purchases of digital cameras remain the same no matter what happens to the price of bananas. (b) A line parallel to the horizontal axis has a slope of zero. Here, consumption remains the same no matter what happens to the divorce rate. In both (a) and (b), the two variables are totally unrelated to one another.

horizontal axis. The graph of their relationship is the line parallel to the vertical axis, indicating that the same quantity of cameras is purchased no matter what the price of bananas. The slope of such a line is *infinite*.

Similarly, aggregate consumption is completely unrelated to the nation's divorce rate. In Figure A1-3(b) we put consumption on the vertical axis and the divorce rate on the horizontal axis. The line parallel to the horizontal axis represents this lack of relatedness. This line has a slope of *zero*.

Vertical Intercept

A line can be located on a graph (without plotting points) if we know its slope and its vertical intercept. The **vertical intercept** of a line is the point where the line meets the vertical axis.

vertical intercept
The point at which a line meets the vertical axis of a graph.

In Figure A1-1 the intercept is $50. This intercept means that if current income were zero, consumers would still spend $50. They might do this through borrowing or by selling some of their assets. Similarly, the $50 vertical intercept in Figure A1-2 shows that at a $50 ticket price, IU's basketball team would be playing in an empty arena.

Equation of a Linear Relationship

If we know the vertical intercept and slope, we can describe a line succinctly in equation form. In its general form, the equation of a straight line is

$$y = a + bx$$

where y = dependent variable

a = vertical intercept

b = slope of line

x = independent variable

For our income–consumption example, if C represents consumption (the dependent variable) and Y represents income (the independent variable), we can write $C = a + bY$. By substituting the known values of the intercept and the slope, we get

$$C = 50 + .5Y$$

This equation also allows us to determine the amount of consumption C at any specific level of income. You should use it to confirm that at the $250 income level, consumption is $175.

When economists reverse mathematical convention by putting the independent variable on the vertical axis and the dependent variable on the horizontal axis, then y stands for the independent variable, rather than the dependent variable in the general form. We noted previously that this case is relevant for our IU ticket price–attendance data. If P represents the ticket price (independent variable) and Q represents attendance (dependent variable), their relationship is given by

$$P = 50 - 2.5Q$$

FIGURE **A1-4** **Determining the Slopes of Curves**

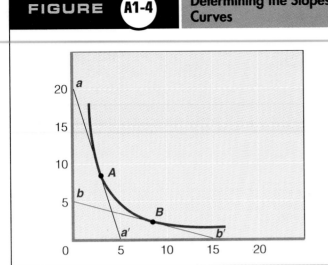

The slope of a non-linear curve changes from point to point on the curve. The slope at any point (say, *B*) can be determined by drawing a straight line that is tangent to that point (line *bb*) and calculating the slope of that line.

where the vertical intercept is 50 and the negative slope is –2½ or –2.5. Knowing the value of *P* lets us solve for *Q*, our dependent variable. You should use this equation to predict IU ticket sales when the ticket price is $15. *(Key Appendix Question 3)*

Slope of a Non-Linear Curve

We now move from the simple world of linear relationships (straight lines) to the more complex world of non-linear relationships. The slope of a straight line is the same at all its points. The slope of a line representing a non-linear relationship changes from one point to another. Such lines are referred to as *curves*. (It is also permissible to refer to a straight line as a "curve.")

Consider the downsloping curve in Figure A1-4. Its slope is negative throughout, but the curve flattens as we move down along it. Thus, its slope constantly changes; the curve has a different slope at each point.

To measure the slope at a specific point, we draw a straight line tangent to the curve at that point. A line is *tangent* at a point if it touches, but does not intersect, the curve at that point. Thus line *aa'* is tangent to the curve in Figure A1-4 at point *A*. The slope of the curve at that point is equal to the slope of the tangent line. Specifically, the total vertical change (drop) in the tangent line *aa'* is –20 and the total horizontal change (run) is +5. Because the slope of the tangent line *aa'* is –20/+5, or –4, the slope of the curve at point *A* is also –4.

Line *bb'* in Figure A1-4 is tangent to the curve at point *B*. Following the same procedure, we find the slope at *B* to be –5/+15, or –⅓. Thus, in this flatter part of the curve, the slope is less negative. *(Key Appendix Question 7)*

APPENDIX SUMMARY

A1.1 GRAPHS AND THEIR MEANING

- Graphs are a convenient and revealing way to represent economic relationships.

- Two variables are positively or directly related when their values change in the same direction. The line (curve) representing two directly related variables slopes upward.

- Two variables are negatively or inversely related when their values change in opposite directions. The curve representing two inversely related variables slopes downward.

- The value of the dependent variable (the "effect") is determined by the value of the independent variable (the "cause").

- When the "other factors" that might affect a two-variable relationship are allowed to change, the graph of the relationship will likely shift to a new location.

- The slope of a straight line is the ratio of the vertical change to the horizontal change between any two points. The slope of an upsloping line is positive; the slope of a downsloping line is negative.

- The slope of a line or curve depends on the units used in measuring the variables. It is especially relevant for economics because it measures marginal changes.

- The slope of a horizontal line is zero; the slope of a vertical line is infinite.

- The vertical intercept and slope of a line determine its location; they are used in expressing the line—and the relationship between the two variables—as an equation.

- The slope of a curve at any point is determined by calculating the slope of a straight-line tangent to the curve at that point.

APPENDIX TERMS AND CONCEPTS

horizontal axis, p. 17
vertical axis, p. 17
direct relationship, p. 18

inverse relationship, p. 18
independent variable, p. 18
dependent variable, p. 18

slope of a line, p. 20
vertical intercept, p. 21

APPENDIX STUDY QUESTIONS

1. Briefly explain the use of graphs as a way to represent economic relationships. What is an inverse relationship? How does it graph? What is a direct relationship? How does it graph? Graph and explain the relationships you would expect to find between (a) the number of centimetres of rainfall per month and the sale of umbrellas, (b) the amount of tuition and the level of enrolment at a college or university, and (c) the popularity of a music artist and the price of her concert tickets.

   In each case cite and explain how variables other than those specifically mentioned might upset the expected relationship. Is your graph in part (b), above, consistent with the fact that, historically, enrolments and tuition have both increased? If not, explain any difference.

2. **KEY APPENDIX QUESTION** Indicate how each of the following might affect the data shown in Figure A1-2 of this appendix:

   a. IU's athletic director schedules higher-quality opponents.

   b. A National Basketball Association (NBA) team locates in the city where IU also plays.

   c. IU contracts to have all its home games televised.

3. **KEY APPENDIX QUESTION** The following table contains data on the relationship between saving and income. Rearrange these data into a meaningful order and graph them on the accompanying grid. What is the slope of the line? The vertical intercept? Interpret the meaning of both the slope and the intercept. Write the equation that represents this line. What would you predict saving to be at the $12,500 level of income?

Income (per year)	Saving (per year)
$15,000	$1,000
0	−500
10,000	500
5,000	0
20,000	1,500

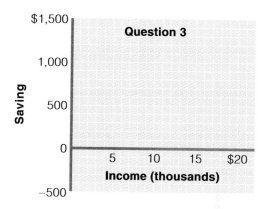

4. Construct a table from the data shown on the graph below. Which is the dependent variable and which the independent variable? Summarize the data in equation form.

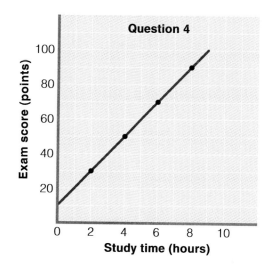

5. Suppose that when the interest rate on loans is 16 percent, businesses find it unprofitable to invest in machinery and equipment. However, when the interest rate is 14 percent, $5 billion worth of investment is profitable. At 12 percent interest, a total of $10 billion of investment is profitable. Similarly, total investment increases by $5 billion for each successive 2-percentage-point decline in the interest rate. Describe the relevant relationship between the interest rate and investment in

words, in a table, graphically, and as an equation. Put the interest rate on the vertical axis and investment on the horizontal axis. In your equation use the form $i = a - bI$, where i is the interest rate, a is the vertical intercept, $-b$ is the slope of the line (which is negative), and I is the level of investment. Comment on the advantages and disadvantages of the verbal, tabular, graphical, and equation forms of description.

6. Suppose that $C = a + bY$, where C = consumption, a = consumption at zero income, b = slope, and Y = income.

   a. Are C and Y positively related or are they negatively related?

   b. If graphed, would the curve for this equation slope upward or slope downward?

   c. Are the variables C and Y inversely related or directly related?

   d. What is the value of C if $a = 10$, $b = .50$, and $Y = 200$?

   e. What is the value of Y if $C = 100$, $a = 10$, and $b = .25$?

7. **KEY APPENDIX QUESTION** The accompanying graph shows curve XX' and tangents at points A, B, and C. Calculate the slope of the curve at these three points.

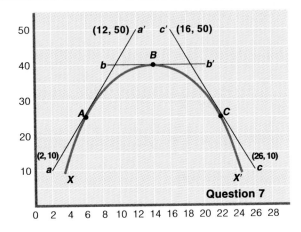

Question 7

8. In the accompanying graph, is the slope of curve AA' positive or negative? Does the slope increase or decrease as we move along the curve from A to A'? Answer the same two questions for curve BB'.

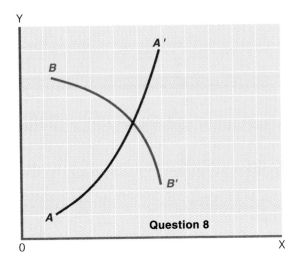

Question 8

2

Chapter

The Economic Problem
Scarcity, Wants, and Choices

You make decisions every day that capture the essence of economics. Suppose you have $40 and are deciding how to spend it. Should you buy a new pair of jeans? Two or three compact discs? A ticket for a concert?

Should you forgo work while you are attending college or university and concentrate solely on your coursework and grades? Is that an option for you, given the rising cost of post-secondary education? If you decide to work, should it be full-time or part-time? Should you work on campus at lower pay or off campus at higher pay? What are the implications for your course grades if you decide to take a job?

Money and time are both scarce, and making decisions in the context of scarcity always means there are costs. If you choose the jeans, the cost is the forgone CDs or concert. If you work full-time, the cost might be greater stress, poorer performance in your classes, or an extra year or two in school.

This chapter examines the fundamentals of economics—scarcity, wants and choices. We first examine the *economic problem*, focusing closely on *wants* and *resources*. Next, we develop two economic models: (1) a *production possibilities model* that incorporates and illustrates several key ideas, and (2) a simple *circular flow model* that identifies the major decision makers and markets in the economy.

2.1   The Foundation of Economics

economic problem
Choices are necessary because society's material wants for goods and services are unlimited but the resources available to satisfy these wants are limited (scarce).

Two fundamental facts together create the **economic problem** and provide a foundation for economics:

- Society's wants are virtually unlimited.
- The resources for producing the goods and services to satisfy society's wants are limited (or scarce).

All that follows depends directly on these two facts.

Unlimited Wants

By "wants" we mean the desires of consumers to obtain and use various goods and services that provide utility—that is, pleasure or satisfaction. These wants extend over a wide range of products, from *necessities* (food, shelter, and clothing) to *luxuries* (perfumes, yachts, race cars). Some wants—basic food, clothing, and shelter—have biological roots. Other wants—for example, the specific kinds of food, clothing, and shelter we seek—are rooted in the conventions and customs of society.

Over time, wants change and tend to multiply, fuelled by new products. Not long ago, we did not want personal computers, Internet service, digital cameras, or cellphones because they simply did not exist. Also, the satisfaction of certain wants tends to trigger others: The acquisition of a Focus or Civic has been known to whet the appetite for a Ferrari or a BMW.

Services, as well as products, satisfy our wants. Car repair work, the removal of an inflamed appendix, legal and accounting advice, and haircuts all satisfy human wants. Actually, we buy many goods, such as automobiles and washing machines, for the services they render. The differences between goods and services are often smaller than they appear to be.

Businesses and units of government add to the wants of consumers. Businesses want factories, machinery, trucks, warehouses, and phone systems to help them achieve their production goals. Government, reflecting the collective wants of its citizens or goals of its own, seeks highways, schools, and hospitals.

All these wants are *insatiable*, or *unlimited*, meaning that our desires for goods and services cannot be completely satisfied. Our desires for a *particular* good or service can be satisfied; over a short period of time we can surely get enough toothpaste or pasta. And one appendectomy is plenty. But goods and services *in general* are another story. We do not, and presumably cannot, get enough. Suppose all members of society were asked to list the goods and services they would buy if they had unlimited income. That list would probably never end.

In short, individuals and institutions have innumerable unfilled wants. *The objective of all economic activity is to fulfill wants.*

Scarce Resources

economic resources
The land, labour, capital, and entrepreneurial ability that are used in the production of goods and services.

The second fundamental fact is that *resources needed to produce the goods and services people want are limited or scarce.* By **economic resources** we mean all natural, human, and manufactured resources that go into the production of goods and services. That includes all the factory and farm buildings and all the equipment, tools, and machinery used to produce manufactured goods and agricultural products; all transportation and communication facilities; all types of labour; and land and mineral resources. Economists classify all these resources as either *property* resources—land and raw materials and capital—or *human* resources—labour and entrepreneurial ability.

RESOURCE CATEGORIES

Resources used in the production of goods and services can be divided into four categories.

land
Natural resources ("free gifts of nature") used to produce goods and services.

Land   **Land** means much more to the economist than it does to most people. Land includes all natural resources—all "gifts of nature"—used in the production process, such as arable land, forests, mineral and oil deposits, and water resources.

capital
Human-made resources (buildings, machinery, and equipment) used to produce goods and services.

investment
Spending for the production and accumulation of capital and additions to inventories.

Capital   **Capital** (or *capital goods* or *investment goods*) includes all manufactured aids used in producing consumer goods and services—that is, all tools, machinery, equipment, factory, storage, transportation, and distribution facilities. The process of producing and purchasing capital goods is known as **investment**.

   Capital goods differ from consumer goods in that *consumer goods* satisfy wants directly, while capital goods do so indirectly by aiding the production of consumer goods. Note that the term "capital" as used by economists does *not* refer to money, but to *real capital*—tools, machinery, and other productive equipment. Money produces nothing; it is *not* an economic resource. So-called "money capital" or "financial capital" is simply a means for purchasing real capital.

labour
The physical and mental talents and efforts of people used to produce goods and services.

Labour   **Labour** is a broad term for all the physical and mental talents of individuals usable in producing goods and services that individuals want. The services of a logger, retail clerk, machinist, professor, professional football player, and nuclear physicist all fall under the general heading "labour."

entrepreneurial ability
The human talents that combine the other resources to produce a product, make non-routine decisions, innovate, and bear risks.

Entrepreneurial Ability   Finally, there is the special human resource, distinct from labour, that we label **entrepreneurial ability**. The entrepreneur performs several functions:

- The entrepreneur *takes the initiative* in combining the resources of land, capital, and labour to produce a good or a service in what is hoped will be a successful business venture.

- The entrepreneur *makes the non-routine policy decisions* that set the course of a business enterprise.

- The entrepreneur is an *innovator*—the one who commercializes new products or new production techniques, or creates new forms of business organization.

- The entrepreneur is a *risk bearer*. The entrepreneur in a market system has no guarantee of profit. The reward for the entrepreneur's time, efforts, and abilities may be profits *or* losses.

factors of production
Economic resources: land, capital, labour, and entrepreneurial ability.

Because these four productive resources—land, labour, capital, and entrepreneurial ability—are combined to *produce* goods and services, they are called the **factors of production**. *(Key Question 4)*

RESOURCE PAYMENTS

The income received from supplying raw materials and capital equipment (the property resources) is called *rental income* and *interest income,* respectively. The income accruing to those who supply labour is called *wages,* which includes salaries and all wage and salary supplements such as bonuses, commissions, and royalties. Entrepreneurial income is called *profits,* which may be negative—that is, losses.

RELATIVE SCARCITY

The four factors of production, or *inputs*, have one significant characteristic in common: *They are limited in supply.* Our planet contains only finite amounts of arable land, mineral deposits, capital equipment, and labour. Their limited supply, or scarcity, puts a limit on the quantity of goods and services that a society can produce.

2.2   Efficiency: Getting the Most from Available Resources

The economic problem is at the heart of the definition of economics stated in Chapter 1: *Economics is the social science concerned with the efficient use of scarce resources to attain the maximum fulfillment of society's unlimited wants.* Economics is concerned with "doing the best with what we have." Society wants to use its limited resources efficiently; it desires to produce as many goods and services as possible from its available resources, thereby maximizing total satisfaction.

Full Employment: Using Available Resources

full employment
Use of all available resources to produce want-satisfying goods and services.

To get the most from its limited resources, a society must achieve both full employment and full production. By **full employment** we mean the use of all available resources. No workers should be out of work if they are willing and able to work. Nor should capital equipment or arable land sit idle. But note that we say all *available* resources should be employed. Each society has certain customs and practices that determine what resources are available for employment and what resources are not. For example, in most countries legislation and custom provide that children and the very aged should not be employed. And we should conserve some resources—the fishing stocks off the east and west coasts, and Canada's immense forests, for instance—for use by future generations.

Full Production: Using Resources Efficiently

full production
Employment of available resources so that the maximum amount of goods and services is produced.

productive efficiency
The production of a good in the least costly way.

allocative efficiency
The apportionment of resources among firms and industries to obtain the production of the products most wanted by society (consumers).

The employment of all available resources is not enough to achieve efficiency. We also need to achieve full production. **Full production** occurs when all employed resources are used so that they provide the maximum possible output so as to satisfy as many of our material wants as possible. If we fail to realize full production, our resources are *underemployed.*

Full production implies two kinds of efficiency—productive and allocative efficiency. **Productive efficiency** is the production of *goods and services in the least costly way.* When we produce, say, compact discs at the lowest achievable unit cost, we are using the smallest amount of resources to produce CDs, meaning more resources are available to produce other desired products. Suppose society has only $100 worth of resources available. If we can produce a CD for only $5 of those resources, then $95 will be available to produce other goods. This is preferable to producing the CD for $10 and having only $90 of resources available for alternative uses.

In contrast, **allocative efficiency** is the production of *goods and services most wanted by society.* For example, society wants resources allocated to compact discs and MP3 players, not to 45 rpm records. We want personal computers (PCs), not manual typewriters. Furthermore, we do not want to devote *all* our resources to producing CDs and PCs; we want to assign some of them to producing other goods that individuals and businesses desire, such as automobiles and office buildings. Allocative efficiency is achieved when an economy produces the "right" mix of goods and services, meaning the combination of goods and services it wants the most. (*Key Question 5*)

Production Possibilities Table

Because resources are scarce, a full-employment, full-production economy cannot have an unlimited output of goods and services. Consequently, society must choose which goods and services to produce and which to forgo. The necessity and consequences of those choices can best be understood through a *production possibilities model*. We examine the model first as a table, then as a graph.

ASSUMPTIONS

We begin our discussion of the production possibilities model with simplifying assumptions:

- *Full employment and productive efficiency*   The economy is employing all its available resources (full employment) and is producing goods and services at least cost (productive efficiency).

- *Fixed resources*   The available supplies of the factors of production are fixed in both quantity and quality, although they can be reallocated, within limits, among different uses; for example, land can be used either for factory sites or for food production.

- *Fixed technology*   The state of technology does not change during our analysis. We are looking at an economy at a particular point in time or over a very short period of time.

- *Two goods*   The economy produces only two goods: pizzas and industrial machines. Pizzas symbolize **consumer goods**, products that satisfy our wants *directly*; industrial machines symbolize **capital goods**, products that satisfy our wants *indirectly* by making possible more efficient production of consumer goods.

THE NEED FOR CHOICE

Given our assumptions, we see that society must choose among alternatives. Fixed resources mean limited outputs of pizza and machines. And since all available factors of production are fully employed, to increase the production of machines we must shift resources away from the production of pizzas. The reverse is also true: To increase the production of pizzas, we must shift resources away from the production of machines. There is no such thing as a free pizza. This, recall, is the essence of the economic problem.

A **production possibilities table** lists the different combinations of two products that can be produced with a specific set of resources (and with full employment *and* productive efficiency). Table 2-1 is such a table for a pizza–machine economy; the data are, of course, hypothetical. At alternative A, this economy devotes all its available resources to the production of machines (capital goods); at alternative E, all resources are used in pizza production (consumer goods). More typically, an economy produces both capital goods and consumer goods, as in B, C, and D. As we move from alternative A to E, we increase the production of pizza at the expense of machine production.

In producing more pizzas, society increases the current satisfaction of its wants. But there is a cost: more pizzas mean fewer machines. This shift of resources to consumer goods catches up with

consumer goods
Products and services that satisfy human wants directly.

capital goods
Goods that do not directly satisfy human wants.

production possibilities table
A table showing the different combinations of two products that can be produced with a specific set of resources in a full-employment, full-production economy.

society over time as the stock of capital goods dwindles, reducing the potential for greater future production. By moving toward alternative E, society chooses "more now" at the expense of "much more later."

By moving toward A, society chooses to forgo current consumption, freeing up resources that can be used to increase the production of capital goods. By building up its stock of capital, society will have greater future production and, therefore, greater future consumption. By moving toward A, society is choosing "more later" at the cost of "less now."

Generalization: *At any point in time, an economy achieving full employment and productive efficiency must sacrifice some of one good to obtain more of another good.*

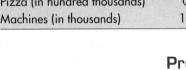

| TABLE 2-1 | Production Possibilities of Pizzas and Machines with Full Employment and Productive Efficiency |

	PRODUCTION ALTERNATIVES				
Type of Product	A	B	C	D	E
Pizza (in hundred thousands)	0	1	2	3	4
Machines (in thousands)	10	9	7	4	0

Production Possibilities Curve

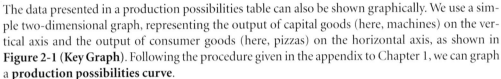

production possibilities curve
A curve showing the different combinations of goods and services that can be produced in a full-employment, full-production economy where the available supplies of resources and technology are fixed.

The data presented in a production possibilities table can also be shown graphically. We use a simple two-dimensional graph, representing the output of capital goods (here, machines) on the vertical axis and the output of consumer goods (here, pizzas) on the horizontal axis, as shown in **Figure 2-1 (Key Graph)**. Following the procedure given in the appendix to Chapter 1, we can graph a **production possibilities curve**.

Each point on the production possibilities curve represents some maximum output of the two products. The curve is a production *frontier* because it shows the limit of attainable outputs. To obtain the various combinations of pizza and machines *on* the production possibilities curve, society must achieve both full employment and productive efficiency. Points lying *inside* the curve are also attainable, but they are inefficient and therefore are not as desirable as points on the curve. Points inside the curve imply that the economy could have more of both machines and pizzas if it achieved full employment and productive efficiency. Points lying *outside* the production possibilities curve, like point *W*, represent a greater output than the output at any point on the curve. Points outside the production possibility curve, however, are unattainable with current supplies of resources and technology.

Law of Increasing Opportunity Cost

opportunity cost
The amount of other products that must be forgone or sacrificed to produce a unit of a product.

Because resources are scarce relative to the virtually unlimited wants they can be used to satisfy, people must choose among alternatives. More pizzas mean fewer machines. The amount of other products that must be sacrificed to obtain one unit of a specific good is called the **opportunity cost** of that good (see the Consider This box on page 32). In our case, the number of machines that must be given up to get another unit of pizza is the *opportunity cost*, or simply the *cost*, of that unit of pizza.

In moving from alternative A to alternative B in Table 2-1, the cost of 1 additional unit of pizzas is 1 less unit of machines. But as we pursue the concept of cost through the additional production possibilities—B to C, C to D, and D to E—an important economic principle is revealed: The opportunity cost of each additional unit of pizza increases. When we move from A to B, just 1 unit of machines is sacrificed for 1 more unit of pizza; but in going from B to C we sacrifice 2 additional units of machines for 1 more unit of pizza; then 3 more of machines for 1 more of pizza; and finally 4 for 1. Conversely, confirm that as we move from E to A, the cost of an additional machine is ¼, ⅓, ½, and 1 unit of pizza, respectively, for the four successive moves.

Note two points about these opportunity costs:

- Here opportunity costs are being measured in *real* terms, that is, in actual goods rather than in money terms.

Key Graph

FIGURE 2-1 The Production Possibilities Curve

Each point *on* the production possibilities curve represents some maximum combination of two products that can be produced if full employment and full production are achieved. When operating on the curve, more machines means fewer pizzas, and vice versa. Limited resources and a fixed technology make any combination of machines and pizzas lying outside the curve (such as at *W*) unattainable. Points inside the curve are attainable, but they indicate that full employment and productive efficiency are not being realized.

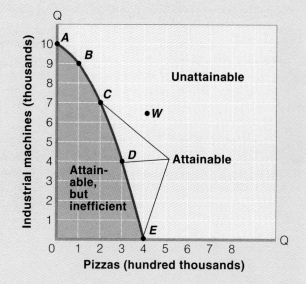

PRODUCTION ALTERNATIVES

Type of Product	A	B	C	D	E
Pizza (in hundred thousands)	0	1	2	3	4
Machines (in thousands)	10	9	7	4	0

Quick Quiz

1. **Production possibilities curve *ABCDE* is bowed out from the origin (concave to the origin) because:**
   a. the marginal benefit of pizzas declines as more pizzas are consumed.
   b. the curve gets steeper as we move from *E* to *A*.
   c. it reflects the law of increasing opportunity costs.
   d. resources are scarce.

2. **The marginal opportunity cost of the second unit of pizza is:**
   a. 2 units of machines.
   b. 3 units of machines.
   c. 7 units of machines.
   d. 9 units of machines.

3. **The total opportunity cost of 7 units of machines is:**
   a. 1 unit of pizza.
   b. 2 units of pizza.
   c. 3 units of pizza.
   d. 4 units of pizza.

4. **All points on this production possibilities curve necessarily represent:**
   a. allocative efficiency.
   b. less than full use of resources.
   c. unattainable levels of output.
   d. productive efficiency.

ANSWERS: 1. c; 2. a; 3. b; 4. d

Consider This

Opportunity Cost

The concept of opportunity cost can be illustrated through the eyes of a small child. Suppose that a young girl named Amber receives a $30 gift certificate from her grandparents to be used at the Hudson's Bay Company. The grandparents take the girl to the store, where she spots several toys she would like—all priced above $30. After gaining a sense of what is affordable, Amber narrows her focus to small stuffed animals ($10 each) and picture books ($5 each).

The grandparents tell Amber that she can buy three stuffed animals, six books, or some limited combinations of the two items. She initially settles on one stuffed animal at $10 and four picture books at $5 each. The grandparents assure her that this selection works; it will exactly use up the $30 certificate. Amber takes the goods to the checkout counter.

But while waiting to pay, she changes her mind. She decides she wants another stuffed animal because they are so cute. What should she do? The grandparents tell her to go pick out a second stuffed animal and then return two of her four books to the shelf. She makes the exchange, ending up with two stuffed animals at $10 each and two picture books at $5 each.

From an adult's perspective, the second stuffed animal cost $10. But in the eyes of the child, *it cost two picture books*. To get the second stuffed animal, Amber had to give up two books. That sacrifice was the *opportunity cost* of her last-minute decision. Amber's way of looking at cost is one of the fundamental ideas in economics.

Question: List some of the opportunity costs of going to a party on a Friday night.

- We are discussing *marginal* (meaning "extra") opportunity costs, rather than cumulative or total opportunity costs. For example, the marginal opportunity cost of the third unit of pizza in Table 2-1 is 3 units of machines (= 7 − 4). But the *total* opportunity cost of 3 units of pizza is 6 units of machines (= 1 unit of machines for the first unit of pizza *plus* 2 units of machines for the second unit of pizza *plus* 3 units of machines for the third unit of pizza).

law of increasing opportunity costs
As the production of a good increases, the opportunity cost of producing an additional unit rises.

Our example illustrates the **law of increasing opportunity costs**: The more of a product that is produced, the greater is its opportunity cost.

SHAPE OF THE CURVE

The law of increasing opportunity costs is reflected in the shape of the production possibilities curve: The curve is bowed out from the origin of the graph. Figure 2-1 shows that when the economy moves from *A* to *E*, successively larger numbers of machines (1, 2, 3, and 4) are given up to acquire equal increments of pizza (1, 1, 1, and 1). This is shown in the slope of the production possibilities curve, which becomes steeper as we move from *A* to *E*. A curve that gets steeper as we move down it is "concave to the origin."

ECONOMIC RATIONALE

The economic rationale for the law of increasing opportunity costs is that *resources are not completely adaptable to alternative uses*. Many resources are better at producing one good than at producing others. Fertile farmland is highly suited to producing the ingredients needed to make pizzas, while land rich in mineral deposits is highly suited to producing the materials needed to make machines. As we step up pizza production, resources that are less and less adaptable to making pizzas must be "pushed" into pizza production. Thus, it will take more and more of such resources, and thus greater sacrifices of machines, to achieve each increase of 1 unit in the production of pizzas. This lack of perfect flexibility, or interchangeability, on the part of resources is the cause of increasing opportunity costs. (*Key Question 6*)

Allocative Efficiency Revisited

So far, we have assumed full employment and productive efficiency, both of which are necessary to realize *any point* on an economy's production possibilities curve. We now turn to allocative efficiency, which requires that the economy produce at the most valued, or *optimal*, point on the production possibilities curve. What specific quantities of resources should be allocated to pizzas and what specific quantities to machines in order to maximize satisfaction?

Our discussion of the *economic perspective* in Chapter 1 helps us answer this question. Recall that economic decisions compare marginal benefits and marginal costs. Any economic activity—for example, production or consumption—should be expanded as long as marginal benefit exceeds marginal cost and should be reduced if marginal cost exceeds marginal benefit. The optimal amount of the activity occurs where MB = MC.

Consider pizzas. We already know from the law of increasing opportunity costs that the marginal cost (MC) of additional units of pizzas will rise as more units are produced. This can be shown by an upsloping MC curve, as in Figure 2-2. We also know that we get marginal benefits (MB) from additional units of pizzas. However, although material wants in the aggregate are insatiable, studies reveal that the consumption of the second unit of a particular product or service yields less additional benefit to a person than the first. And a third provides even less MB than the second. So it is for society as a whole. We therefore can portray the marginal benefits from pizzas with a downsloping MB curve, as in Figure 2-2. Although total benefits rise when society consumes more pizzas, marginal benefits decline.

The optimal quantity of pizza production is indicated by the intersection of the MB and MC curves: 200,000 units in Figure 2-2. Why is this the optimal quantity? If only 100,000 pizzas were produced, the marginal benefit of pizzas would exceed its marginal cost. In money terms, MB might be $15, while MC is only $5. This means that society is *underallocating* resources to pizza production and that more of it should be produced.

FIGURE 2-2

Allocative Efficiency: MB = MC

Allocative efficiency requires the expansion of a good's output until its marginal benefit (MB) and marginal cost (MC) are equal. No resources beyond that point should get allocated to the product. Here, allocative efficiency occurs when 200,000 pizzas are produced.

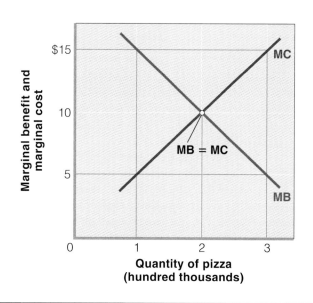

How do we know? Because society values an additional pizza as being worth $15, while the alternative products that those resources could produce are worth only $5. Society benefits whenever it can gain something valued $15 by forgoing something valued only $5. Each additional pizza up to 200,000 would provide such a gain, indicating that allocative efficiency would be improved by that production. Allocative efficiency is achieved where MB = MC.

The production of 300,000 pizzas would represent an *overallocation* of resources to pizza production. Here the MC of pizzas is $15 and its MB is only $5. This means that 1 unit of pizza is worth only $5 to society, while the alternative products that those resources could otherwise produce are valued at $15. By producing 1 less unit, society loses a pizza worth $5. But by reallocating the freed resources, it gains other products worth $15. In Figure 2-2, net gains can be realized until pizza production has been reduced to 200,000.

Generalization: *Resources are being efficiently allocated to any product when the marginal benefit and marginal cost of its output are equal (MB = MC).* Suppose that by applying the above analysis to machines, we find their optimal (MB = MC) output is 7000. This would mean that alternative C on our production possibilities curve—200,000 pizzas and 7000 machines—would result in allocative efficiency for our hypothetical economy. **(Key Question 9)**

QUICK REVIEW

- The production possibilities curve illustrates four concepts: (a) *scarcity* of resources is implied by the area of unattainable combinations of output lying outside the production possibilities curve; (b) *choice* among outputs is reflected in the variety of attainable combinations of goods lying along the curve; (c) *opportunity cost* is illustrated by the downward slope of the curve; (d) the law of *increasing opportunity costs* is implied by the concavity of the curve.

- Full employment and productive efficiency must be realized in order for the economy to operate on its production possibilities curve.

- A comparison of marginal benefits and marginal costs is needed to determine allocative efficiency—the best or optimal output mix on the curve.

2.3   Unemployment, Growth, and The Future

Let's now discard the first three assumptions underlying the production possibilities curve and see what happens.

Unemployment and Productive Inefficiency

The first assumption was that our economy was achieving full employment and productive efficiency. Our analysis and conclusions change if some resources are idle (unemployment) or if least-cost production is not realized.

Graphically, we represent situations of unemployment or productive inefficiency by points *inside* the original production possibilities curve (reproduced in Figure 2-3). Point *U* is one such point. Here the economy is falling short of the various maximum combinations of pizzas and machines that could be produced. The arrows in Figure 2-3 indicate three possible paths back to full employment and least-cost production. A move toward full employment and productive efficiency would yield a greater output of one or both products.

A Growing Economy

Production and the Standard of Living

When we drop the assumptions that the quantity and quality of resources and technology are fixed, the production possibilities curve shifts positions—that is, the potential maximum output of the economy changes.

FIGURE 2-3

Unemployment, Productive Inefficiency, and the Production Possibilities Curve

Any point inside the production possibilities curve, such as *U*, represents unemployment or a failure to achieve productive efficiency. The arrows indicate that, by realizing full employment and productive efficiency, the economy could operate on the curve. This means it could produce more of one or both products than it is producing at point *U*.

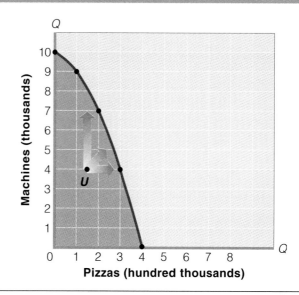

INCREASES IN FACTOR SUPPLIES

Although factor supplies are fixed at any specific moment, they can and do change over time. For example, a nation's growing population will increase the supplies of labour and entrepreneurial ability. Also, labour quality usually improves over time through education and training. Historically, the economy's stock of capital has increased at a significant, though unsteady, rate. And although we are depleting some of our energy and mineral resources, new sources are being discovered. The development of irrigation programs, for example, adds to the supply of arable land.

The net result of these increased supplies of the factors of production is the potential to produce more of both pizzas and machines. Thus, 20 years from now, the production possibilities curve in Figure 2-4 may supersede the one shown in Figure 2-3. The greater abundance of factors of production will result in a greater potential output of one or both products at each alternative. Society will have achieved economic growth in the form of an expanded potential output.

ADVANCES IN TECHNOLOGY

Our second assumption is that we have constant, unchanging technology. In reality, technology has progressed dramatically over time. An advancing technology brings both new and better goods *and* improved ways of producing them. For now, let's think of technological advance as being only improvements in the methods of production, for example, the introduction of computerized systems to manage inventories and schedule production. These advances alter our previous discussion of the economic problem by improving productive efficiency, thereby allowing society to produce more goods with fixed resources. As with increases in resource supplies, technological advances make possible the production of more machines *and* more pizzas.

Thus, when either supplies of factors of production increase or an improvement in technology occurs, the production possibilities curve in Figure 2-3 shifts outward and to the right, as illustrated by curve A′, B′, C′, D′, E′ in Figure 2-4. Such an outward shift of the production possibilities curve represents **economic growth**: *the ability to produce a larger total output.* This growth is the result of (1) increases in supplies of factors of production, (2) improvements in factor quality, and (3) technological advances.

Advancing technology brings both new and better goods and improved ways of producing them.

economic growth
An outward shift in the production possibilities curve that results from an increase in factor supplies or quality or an improvement in technology.

FIGURE 2-4

| FIGURE 2-4 | Economic Growth and the Production Possibilities Curve |

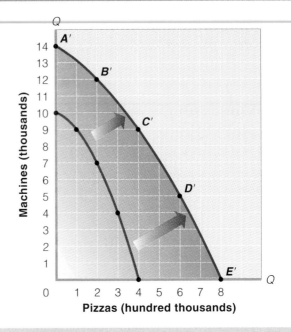

PRODUCTION ALTERNATIVES					
Type of product	A′	B′	C′	D′	E′
Pizzas (in hundred thousands)	0	2	4	6	8
Machines (in thousands)	14	12	9	5	0

The increase in supplies of resources, the improvements in resource quality, and the technological advances that occur in a dynamic economy move the production possibilities curve outward and to the right, allowing the economy to have larger quantities of both types of goods.

The consequence of growth is that our full-employment economy can enjoy a greater output of both machines and pizzas. *While a static, no-growth economy must sacrifice some of one product in order to get more of another, a dynamic, growing economy can have larger quantities of both products.*

Economic growth does not ordinarily mean proportionate increases in a nation's capacity to produce all its products. Note in Figure 2-4 that, at the maximums, the economy can produce twice as many pizzas as before but only 40 percent more machines. To reinforce your understanding of this concept, sketch in two new production possibilities curves: one showing the situation where a better technique for producing machines has been developed while the technology for producing pizzas is unchanged, and the other illustrating an improved technology for pizzas while the technology for producing machines remains constant.

PRESENT CHOICES AND FUTURE POSSIBILITIES

An economy's current position on its production possibilities curve is a basic determinant of the future location of that curve. Let's designate the two axes of the production possibilities curve as *goods for the future* and *goods for the present*, as in Figure 2-5. Goods for the future are such things as capital goods, research and education, and preventive medicine. (Global Perspective 2.1 shows expenditure on research and development in selected countries.) Goods for the future increase the quantity and quality of property resources, enlarge the stock of technological information, and improve the quality of human resources. As we have already seen, goods for the future, like industrial machines, are the ingredients of economic growth. Goods for the present are pure consumer goods, such as pizza, clothing, and soft drinks.

Now suppose there are two economies, Alta and Zorn, which are initially identical in every respect except one: Alta's current choice of positions on its production possibilities curve strongly favours

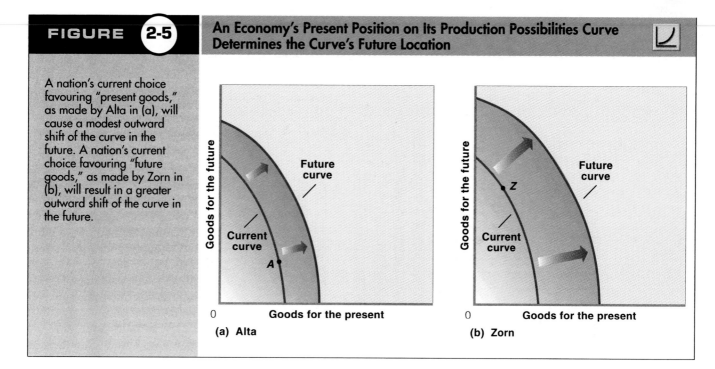

FIGURE 2-5

An Economy's Present Position on Its Production Possibilities Curve Determines the Curve's Future Location

A nation's current choice favouring "present goods," as made by Alta in (a), will cause a modest outward shift of the curve in the future. A nation's current choice favouring "future goods," as made by Zorn in (b), will result in a greater outward shift of the curve in the future.

present goods over future goods. Point *A* in Figure 2-5(a) indicates that choice. It is located quite far down the curve to the right, indicating a high priority for goods for the present, at the expense of fewer goods for the future. Zorn, in contrast, makes a current choice that stresses larger amounts of future goods and smaller amounts of present goods, as shown by point *Z* in Figure 2-5(b).

Other things equal, we can expect the future production possibilities curve of Zorn to be farther to the right than Alta's curve. By currently choosing an output more favourable to technological advances and to increases in the quantity and quality of resources, Zorn will achieve greater economic growth than Alta. In terms of capital goods, Zorn is choosing to make larger current additions to its "national factory"—to invest more of its current output—than Alta. The payoff from this choice for Zorn is more rapid growth—greater future production capacity. The opportunity cost is fewer consumer goods in the present for Zorn to enjoy.

Is Zorn's choice thus "better" than Alta's? It is impossible to say. The different outcomes reflect different preferences and priorities in the two countries. *(Key Questions 10 and 11)*

A Qualification: International Trade

Production possibilities analysis implies that a nation is limited to the combinations of output indicated by its production possibilities curve. *But we must modify this principle when international specialization and trade exist.*

You will see in later chapters that an economy can avoid, through international specialization and trade, the output limits imposed by its domestic production possibilities curve. *International specialization* means directing domestic resources to output that a nation is highly efficient at producing. *International trade* involves the exchange of these goods for goods produced abroad. Specialization and trade enable a nation to get more of a desired good at less sacrifice of some other good. For example, rather than sacrifice three machines to get a third unit of pizza, as in Table 2-1, a nation might be able to obtain the third unit of pizza by trading only two units of machines for it. Specialization and trade have the same effect as having more and better resources or discovering improved production techniques; both increase the quantities of capital and consumer goods available to society.

Global Perspective   2.1

**Research and
Development Spending,
Selected Countries**

Sweden leads the world on
R&D expenditure. Canada
spent just under 2 percent of
GDP on R&D.

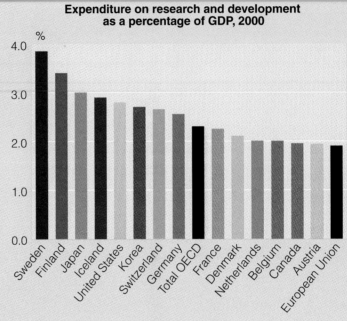

**Expenditure on research and development
as a percentage of GDP, 2000**

Source: Organization for Economic Co-operation and Development (OECD)

QUICK REVIEW

- Unemployment and the failure to achieve productive efficiency cause an economy to operate at a point inside its production possibilities curve.

- Increases in resource supplies, improvements in resource quality, and technological advance cause economic growth, which is depicted as an outward shift of the production possibilities curve.

- Society's present choice of capital and consumer goods helps determine the future location of its production possibilities curve.

- International specialization and trade enable a nation to obtain more goods than its production possibilities curve indicates.

Examples and Applications

There are many possible applications and examples relating to the production possibilities model. We will discuss just a few of them.

UNEMPLOYMENT AND PRODUCTIVE INEFFICIENCY

In the depths of the Great Depression of the 1930s, Canada's economy operated well inside its production possibilities curve. At one point, 20 percent of Canadian workers were unemployed and almost one-third of Canadian production capacity was idle. Canada has suffered a number of much milder downturns since then, the latest occurring in 2001. In that year, unemployment increased, and the economy operated inside its production possibility curve.

Almost all nations have experienced widespread unemployment and unused production capacity at one time or another. Since 1995, for example, several nations including Argentina, Japan, Mexico, Germany, and South Korea have had economic downturns that placed them inside their production possibilities curves, at least temporarily.

Economies that experience substantial discrimination based on race, ethnicity, and gender do not achieve productive efficiency and thus operate inside their production possibilities curves. Because discrimination prevents those discriminated against from obtaining jobs that best use their skills, society has less output than otherwise. Eliminating discrimination would move such an economy from a point inside its production possibilities curve toward a point on its curve. Similarly, economies in which labour usage and production methods are based on custom, heredity, and caste, rather than on efficiency, operate well inside their production possibilities curves.

TRADEOFFS AND OPPORTUNITY COSTS

Many current controversies illustrate the tradeoffs and opportunity costs indicated in movements along a particular production possibilities curve. (Any two categories of "output" can be placed on the axes of production possibilities curves.) Should old-growth forests in British Columbia be used for logging or preserved as wilderness? If the land is used for logging, the opportunity cost is the forgone benefits of wilderness. If the land is used for wilderness, the opportunity cost is the lost value of the lumber that Canadian society forgoes.

Should Canadian society devote more resources to the health care system (doctors, medical equipment, and hospitals) or to education (teachers, books, and schools)? If Canada decides to devote more resources to the health care system, other things equal, the opportunity cost is forgone improvements in education. If more resources are allocated to education, the opportunity cost is the forgone benefits from an improved health care system.

SHIFTS IN PRODUCTION POSSIBILITIES CURVES

Canada has recently experienced a spurt of new technologies relating to computers, communications, and biotechnology. Technological advances have dropped the prices of computers and greatly enhanced their speed. Cellular phones and the Internet have increased communications capacity, enhancing production and improving the efficiency of markets. Advances in biotechnology, specifically genetic engineering, have resulted in important agricultural and medical discoveries. Many economists believe that these new technologies are so significant that they are contributing to faster-than-normal economic growth (faster rightward shifts of the production possibilities curve).

In some circumstances a nation's production possibilities curve can collapse inward. For example, in the late 1990s Yugoslavian forces began to "ethnically cleanse" Kosovo by driving out its Muslim residents. A decisive military response participated in by Canada and its allies eventually pushed the Yugoslavians out of Kosovo. The military action also devastated Yugoslavia's economy. Allied bombing inflicted great physical damage on Yugoslavia's production facilities and its system of roads, bridges, and communication. Consequently, Yugoslavia's production possibilities curve shifted inward.

2.4   Economic Systems

economic system
A particular set of institutional arrangements and a coordinating mechanism for producing goods and services.

Every society needs to develop an **economic system**—*a particular set of institutional arrangements and a coordinating mechanism*—to produce the goods and services its members desire. Economic systems differ as to (1) who owns the factors of production and (2) the method used to coordinate and direct economic activity. There are two general types of economic systems: the market system and the command system.

The Market System

market system
An economic system in which
property resources are privately
owned and markets and prices
are used to direct and coordinate economic activities.

The private ownership of resources and the use of markets and prices to coordinate and direct economic activity characterize the **market system**, or *capitalism*. In that system each participant acts in his or her own self-interest; each individual or business seeks to maximize its satisfaction or profit through its own decisions regarding consumption or production. The system allows for the private ownership of capital, communicates through prices, and coordinates economic activity through *markets*—places where buyers and sellers come together. Goods and services are produced and resources are supplied by whoever is willing and able to do so. The result is competition among independently acting buyers and sellers of each product and resource. Thus, economic decision making is widely dispersed.

In *pure* capitalism—or *laissez-faire* capitalism—government's role is limited to protecting private property and establishing an environment appropriate to the operation of the market system. The term *laissez-faire* means "let it be," that is, keep government from interfering with the economy. The idea is that such interference will disturb the efficient working of the market system.

But in the capitalism practised in Canada and most other countries, government plays a substantial role in the economy. It not only provides the rules for economic activity but also promotes economic stability and growth, provides certain goods and services that would otherwise be underproduced or not produced at all, and modifies the distribution of income. The government, however, is not the dominant player in deciding what to produce, how to produce it, and who will get it. These decisions are determined by market forces.

The Command System

command system
An economic system in which
most property resources are
owned by the government and
economic decisions are made
by a central government body.

The alternative to the market system is the **command system**, also known as *socialism* or *communism*. In that system, government owns most property resources and economic decision making occurs through a central economic plan. A government central planning board determines nearly all the major decisions concerning the use of resources, the composition and distribution of output, and the organization of production. The government owns most of the business firms, which produce according to government directives. A central planning board determines production goals for each enterprise and specifies the amount of resources to be allocated to each enterprise so that it can reach its production goals. The division of output among the population is centrally decided, and capital goods are allocated among industries on the basis of the central planning board's long-term priorities.

A pure command economy would rely exclusively on a central plan to allocate the government-owned property resources. But, in reality, even the pre-eminent command economy—the Soviet Union—tolerated some private ownership and incorporated some markets before its demise in 1991. Recent reforms in Russia and most of the eastern European nations have to one degree or another transformed their command economies to market-oriented systems. China's reforms have not gone as far, but have reduced the reliance on central planning. Although there is still extensive government ownership of resources and capital in China, it has increasingly relied on free markets to organize and coordinate its economy. North Korea and Cuba are the last remaining examples of largely centrally planned economies.

2.5   The Circular Flow Model

Because nearly all of the major nations now use the market system, we need to gain a good understanding of how this system operates. Our goal in the remainder of this chapter is to identify the market economy's decision makers and major markets. In Chapter 3 we will explain how prices are established in individual markets. Then in Chapter 4 we will detail the characteristics of the market system and explain how it addresses the economic problem.

As shown in **Figure 2-6 (Key Graph)**, the market economy has two groups of decision makers: *households* and *businesses*. It also has two broad markets: the *factor market* and the *product market*.

Key Graph

FIGURE 2-6
The Circular Flow Diagram

Factors of production flow from households to businesses through the factor market and products flow from businesses to households through the product market. Opposite these real flows are monetary flows. Households receive income from businesses (their costs) through the factor market and businesses receive revenue from households (their expenditures) through the product market.

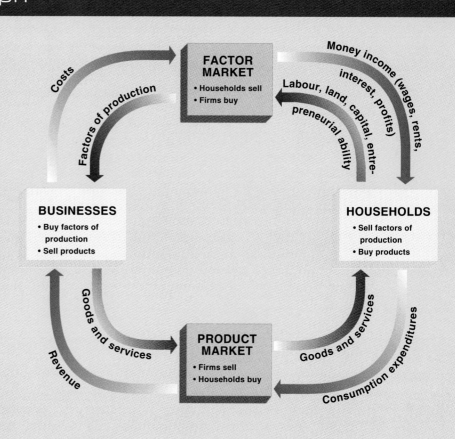

Quick Quiz

1. The factor market is where:
a. households sell products and businesses buy products.
b. businesses sell factors of production and households sell products.
c. households sell factors of production and businesses buy factors of production (or the services of factors).
d. businesses sell factors of production and households buy factors of production (or the services of factors).

2. Which of the following would be determined in the product market?
a. a manager's salary
b. the price of equipment used in a bottling plant
c. the price of 80 hectares of farmland
d. the price of a new pair of athletic shoes

3. In this circular flow diagram:
a. money flows counterclockwise.
b. resources flow counterclockwise.
c. goods and services flow clockwise.
d. households are on the selling side of the product market.

4. In this circular flow diagram:
a. households spend income in the product market.
b. firms sell resources to households.
c. households receive income through the product market.
d. households produce goods.

ANSWERS: 1. c; 2. d; 3. b; 4. a

factor market
A market in which households sell and firms buy factors of production.

The upper half of the diagram represents the **factor market**: *the place where factors of production are bought and sold*. In the factor market, households sell factors of production and businesses purchase them. Households (that is, people) own all factors of production, either directly as workers or entrepreneurs or indirectly through their ownership (through stocks) of business corporations. They sell their resources to businesses, which buy them because they are necessary for producing goods and services. The money that businesses pay for factors of production are costs to businesses but are flows of wage, rent, interest, and profit income to the households. Resources therefore flow from households to businesses, and money flows from businesses to households.

product market
A market in which products are sold by firms and bought by households.

Next consider the lower part of the diagram that represents the **product market**: *the place where goods and services produced by businesses are bought and sold*. In the product market, businesses combine the resources they have obtained to produce and sell goods and services. Households use the income they have received from the sale of resources to buy goods and services. The monetary flow of consumer spending on goods and services yields sales revenues for businesses.

circular flow model
The flow of resources from households to firms and of products from firms to households.

The **circular flow model** shows the interrelated web of decision making and economic activity involving businesses and households. Businesses and households are both buyers and sellers. Businesses buy resources and sell products. Households buy products and sell resources. As shown in Figure 2-6, there is a counterclockwise *real flow* of factors of production and finished goods and services, and a clockwise *money flow* of income and consumption expenditures.

THE LASTword — Women and Expanded Production Possibilities

A large increase in the number of employed women has shifted the Canadian production possibilities curve outward.

One of the more remarkable trends of the past half-century in Canada has been the substantial rise in the number of women working in the paid workforce. Today, nearly 70 percent of women in Canada work full-time or part-time in paid jobs, compared to only 31 percent in 1965. There are many reasons for this increase.

Women's Rising Wage Rates
Over recent years, women have greatly increased their productivity in the workplace, mostly by becoming better educated and professionally trained. As a result, they can earn higher wages. Because those higher wages have increased the opportunity costs—the forgone wage earnings—of staying at home, women have substituted employment in the labour market for more "expensive" traditional home activities. This substitution has been particularly pronounced among married women.

Women's higher wages and longer hours away from home have produced creative reallocations of

time and purchasing patterns. Day-care services have partly replaced personal child care. Restaurants, take-home meals, and pizza delivery often substitute for traditional home cooking. Convenience stores and catalogue and Internet sales have proliferated, as have lawn-care and in-home cleaning services. Microwave ovens, dishwashers, automatic washers and dryers, and other household "capital goods" enhance domestic productivity.

Expanded Job Access Greater access to jobs is a second factor increasing the employment of women. Service industries—teaching, nursing, and clerical work, for instance—that traditionally have employed mainly women have expanded in the past several decades. Also, population in general has shifted from farms and rural regions to urban areas, where jobs for women are more abundant and more geographically accessible. The decline in the average length of the workweek and the increased availability of part-time jobs have also made it easier for women to combine labour market employment with child-rearing and household activities.

Changing Preferences and Attitudes Women collectively have changed their preferences from household activities to employment in the labour market. Many find personal fulfillment in jobs, careers, and earnings, as evidenced by the huge influx of women into law, medicine, business, and other professions. More broadly, most industrial societies now widely accept and encourage labour force participation by women, including those with very young children. Today about 60 percent of Canadian mothers with preschool children participate in the labour force, compared to only 30 percent in 1970. More than half return to work before their youngest child has reached the age of two.

Declining Birthrates There were 3.8 lifetime births per woman in 1957 at the peak of the baby boom. Today the number is less than 2. This marked decline in the size of the typical family, the result of changing lifestyles and the widespread availability of birth control, has freed up time for greater labour-force participation by women. Not only do women now have fewer children, their children are spaced closer together in age. Thus women who leave their jobs during their children's early years can return to the labour force sooner. Higher wage rates have also been a factor. On average, women with relatively high wage earnings have fewer children than women with lower earnings. The opportunity cost of children—the income sacrificed by not being employed—rises as wage earnings rise. In the language of economics, the higher "price" associated with children has reduced the "quantity" of children demanded.

Rising Divorce Rates Marital instability, as evidenced by high divorce rates, may have motivated many women to enter and remain in the labour market. Because alimony and child support payments are often erratic or non-existent, the economic impact of divorce on non-working women may be disastrous. Most non-working women enter the labour force for the first time following divorce. And many married women—perhaps even women contemplating marriage—may have joined the labour force to protect themselves against the financial difficulties of potential divorce.

Slower Growth of Male Wages The earnings of many low-wage and middle-wage male workers grew slowly or even fell in Canada over the past three decades. Many wives may have entered the labour force to ensure the rise of household living standards. The median income of couples with children grew 28 percent between 1969 and 2002. Without the mothers' income, that growth would have been only 2 percent. Couples of all income levels may be concerned about their family income compared to other families. So, the entry of some women into the labour force may have encouraged still other women to enter in order to maintain their families' *relative* standard of living.

Taken together, these factors have produced a rapid rise in the presence of women workers in Canada. This increase in the *quantity of resources* has helped push the Canadian production possibilities curve outward. In other words, it has contributed greatly to Canada's economic growth, and thus per capita income.

CHAPTER SUMMARY

2.1 THE FOUNDATION OF ECONOMICS

- Economics is grounded on two basic facts: (a) wants are virtually unlimited; (b) resources are scarce.

- Resources may be classified as property resources—raw materials and capital—or as human resources—labour and entrepreneurial ability. These resources constitute the factors of production.

- Economics is concerned with the problem of using scarce resources to produce the goods and services that satisfy the material wants of society. Both full employment and the efficient use of available resources are essential to maximize want satisfaction.

2.2 EFFICIENCY: GETTING THE MOST FROM AVAILABLE RESOURCES

- Efficient use of resources consists of productive efficiency (producing all output combinations in the least costly way) and allocative efficiency (producing the specific output mix most desired by society).

- An economy that is achieving full employment and productive efficiency—that is operating on its production possibilities curve—must sacrifice the output of some types of goods and services in order to increase the production of others. Because resources are not equally productive in all possible uses, shifting resources from one use to another brings the law of increasing opportunity costs into play. The production of additional units of one product requires the sacrifice of *increasing* amounts of the other product.

- Allocative efficiency means operating at the optimal point on the production possibilities curve. That point represents the highest-valued mix of goods and is determined by expanding the production of each good until its marginal benefit (MB) equals its marginal cost (MC).

2.3 UNEMPLOYMENT, GROWTH, AND THE FUTURE

- Over time, technological advances and increases in the quantity and quality of resources enable the economy to produce more of all goods and services—that is, to experience economic growth. Society's choice as to the mix of consumer goods and capital goods in current output is a major determinant of the future location of the production possibilities curve and thus of economic growth.

2.4 ECONOMIC SYSTEMS

- The market system and the command system are the two broad types of economic systems used to address the economic problem. In the market system (or capitalism) private individuals own most resources and markets coordinate most economic activity. In the command system (or socialism or communism), government owns most resources and central planners coordinate most economic activity.

2.5 THE CIRCULAR FLOW MODEL

- The circular flow model locates the product and factor markets and shows the major real and money flows between businesses and households. Businesses are on the buying side of the factor market and the selling side of the product market. Households are on the selling side of the factor market and the buying side of the product market.

TERMS AND CONCEPTS

economic problem, p. 26
economic resources, p. 27
land, p. 27
capital, p. 27
investment, p. 27
labour, p. 27
entrepreneurial ability, p. 27
factors of production, p. 27
full employment, p. 28

full production, p. 28
productive efficiency, p. 28
allocative efficiency, p. 28
consumer goods, p. 29
capital goods, p. 29
production possibilities table, p. 29
production possibilities curve, p. 30
opportunity cost, p. 30

law of increasing opportunity costs, p. 32
economic growth, p. 35
economic system, p. 39
market system, p. 40
command system, p. 40
factor market, p. 42
product market, p. 42
circular flow model, p. 42

STUDY QUESTIONS

1. Critically analyze: "Wants aren't unlimited. I can prove it. I get all the coffee I want to drink every morning at breakfast." Explain: "Wants change as we move from childhood to adulthood, but do not diminish."

2. What are economic resources? What categories do economists use to classify them? Why are resources also called "factors of production?" Explain: "If resources were unlimited and freely available, there would be no subject called *economics*."

3. Why isn't money considered to be a capital resource in economics? Why is entrepreneurial ability considered to be a category of economic resource, distinct from "labour?" What are the major functions of the entrepreneur?

4. **KEY QUESTION**   Classify the following Microsoft factors of production as labour, land, capital, or entrepreneurial ability: code writers for software; Bill Gates; production facility for Windows CD-ROMs; "campus" on which Microsoft buildings sit; grounds crew at Microsoft campus; Microsoft corporate jet.

5. **KEY QUESTION**   Distinguish between "full employment" and "full production" as it relates to production possibilities analysis. Distinguish between "productive efficiency" and "allocative efficiency." Give an illustration of achieving productive efficiency but not achieving allocative efficiency.

6. **KEY QUESTION**   Here is a production possibilities table for war goods and civilian goods:

PRODUCTION ALTERNATIVES

Type of production	A	B	C	D	E
Automobiles	0	2	4	6	8
Missiles	30	27	21	12	0

a. Show these data graphically. Upon what specific assumptions is this production possibilities curve based?

b. If the economy is at point C, what is the cost of one more automobile? One more rocket? Explain how the production possibilities curve reflects the law of increasing opportunity costs.

c. What must the economy do to operate at some point on the production possibilities curve?

7. What is the opportunity cost of attending college or university? In 2001 nearly 80 percent of Canadians with post-secondary education held jobs, whereas only about 40 percent of those who did not finish high school held jobs. How might this difference relate to opportunity costs?

8. Suppose you arrive at a store expecting to pay $100 for an item but learn that a store 2 kilometres away is charging $50 for it. Would you drive there and buy it? How does your decision benefit you? What is the opportunity cost of your decision? Now suppose you arrive at a store expecting to pay $6000 for an item but discover that it costs $5950 at the other store. Do you make the same decision as before? Perhaps surprisingly, you should! Explain why.

9. **KEY QUESTION**   Specify and explain the shapes of the marginal-benefit and marginal-cost curves. How are these curves used to determine the optimal allocation of resources to a particular product? If current output is such that marginal cost exceeds marginal benefit, should more or fewer resources be allocated to this product? Explain.

10. **KEY QUESTION**   Label point G *inside* the production possibilities curve you drew in question 6. What does it indicate? Label point H *outside* the curve. What does that point indicate? What must occur before the economy can attain the level of production shown by point H?

11. **KEY QUESTION**   Referring again to question 6, suppose improvement occurs in the technology of producing missiles but not in the technology of producing automobiles. Draw the new production possibilities curve. Now assume that a technological advance occurs in producing automobiles but not in producing missiles. Draw the new production possibilities curve. Now draw a production possibilities curve that reflects technological improvement in the production of both products.

12. Explain how, if at all, each of the following events affects the location of the production possibilities curve:

a. Standardized examination scores of high school, university, and college students decline.

b. The unemployment rate falls from 9 to 6 percent of the labour force.

c. Defence spending is reduced to allow government to spend more on health care.

d. A new technique improves the efficiency of extracting copper from ore.

13. Explain: "Affluence tomorrow requires sacrifice today."

14. Suppose that, based on a nation's production possibilities curve, an economy must sacrifice 10,000 pizzas domestically to get the one additional industrial machine it desires, but that it can get the machine from another country in exchange for 9000 pizzas. Relate this information to the following statement: "Through international specialization and trade, a nation can reduce its opportunity cost of obtaining goods and thus 'move outside its production possibilities curve.' "

15. Contrast how a market system and a command economy respond to the economic problem.

16. Distinguish between the factor market and product market in the circular flow model. In what way are businesses and households both *sellers and buyers* in this model? What are the flows in the circular flow model?

17. **(Last Word)** Which two of the six reasons listed in the Last Word do you think are the *most important* in explaining the rise in participation of women in the workplace? Explain your reasoning.

INTERNET APPLICATION QUESTIONS

1. **More Labour Resources—What is the Evidence for Canada and France?** Use the link in the McConnell-Brue-Barbiero Web site (Chapter 2) to find Canadian civilian employment data for the last 10 years. How many more workers were there at the end of the 10-year period than at the beginning? Next, find total employment growth in France over the last 10 years. In which of the two countries did "more labour resources" have the greatest impact in shifting the nation's production possibilities curve outward over the 10-year period?

2. **Relative Size of the Military—Who's Incurring the Largest Opportunity Cost?** To obtain military goods, a nation must sacrifice civilian goods. Of course, that sacrifice may be worthwhile in terms of national defence and protection of national interests. Use the link in the McConnell-Brue-Barbiero Web site (Chapter 2) to determine the amount of military expenditures, and military expenditures as a percentage of GDP, for each of the following five nations: Canada, Japan, North Korea, Russia, and the United States. Who is bearing the greatest opportunity costs?

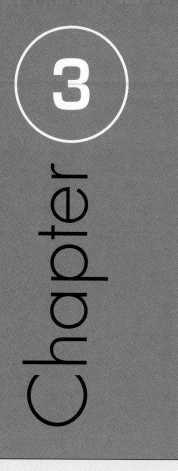

3

Chapter

Individual Markets
Demand and Supply

According to an old joke, if you teach a parrot to say "demand and supply," you have an economist. There is much truth in this quip. The tools of demand and supply can take us far in understanding both specific economic issues and how the entire economy works.

With our circular flow model in Chapter 2, we identified the participants in the product market and factor market. We asserted that prices were determined by the "interaction" between buyers and sellers in those markets. In this chapter we examine that interaction in detail and explain how prices and output quantities are determined.

3.1   Markets

market
Any institution or mechanism that brings together buyers and sellers of particular goods, services, or resources for the purpose of exchange.

www.tse.com
Toronto Stock Exchange

Recall from Chapter 2 that a **market** is *an institution or mechanism that brings together buyers ("demanders") and sellers ("suppliers") of particular goods, services, or factors for the purpose of exchange.* Markets exist in many forms. The corner gas station, e-commerce sites, the local music store, a farmer's roadside stand—all are familiar markets. The Toronto Stock Exchange and the Chicago Board of Trade are markets where buyers and sellers of stocks and bonds and farm commodities from all over the world communicate with one another to buy and sell. Auctioneers bring together potential buyers and sellers of art, livestock, used farm equipment, and, sometimes, real estate. In labour markets, the professional hockey player and his agent bargain with the owner of an NHL team. A graduating finance major interviews with the Royal Bank or the Bank of Montreal at the university placement office.

All situations that link potential buyers with potential sellers are markets. Some markets are local, while others are national or international. Some are highly personal, involving face-to-face contact between demander and supplier; others are impersonal, with buyer and seller never seeing or knowing each other.

To keep things simple, we will focus in this chapter on markets consisting of large numbers of buyers and sellers of standardized products. These are the highly competitive markets such as a central grain exchange, a stock market, or a market for foreign currencies in which the price is "discovered" through the interacting decisions of buyers and sellers. They are *not* the markets in which one or a handful of producers "set" prices, such as the markets for commercial airplanes or operating software for personal computers.

3.2   Demand

demand
A schedule or curve that shows the various amounts of a product that consumers are willing and able to purchase at each of a series of possible prices during a specified period of time.

Recall from Chapter 2 that the economic problem consists of unlimited wants and limited resources to produce the goods and services to satisfy those wants. We begin now to take a closer look at the nature of wants, or demand. Later in the chapter we will investigate the nature of supply.

Demand is *a schedule or a curve that shows the various amounts of a product that consumers are willing and able to purchase at each of a series of possible prices during a specified period of time.*[1] Demand shows the quantities of a product that will be purchased at various possible prices, *other things equal.* Demand can easily be shown in table form. Figure 3-1 shows a hypothetical demand schedule for a *single consumer* purchasing bushels of corn.

Figure 3-1 reveals the relationship between the various prices of corn and the quantity of corn a particular consumer would be willing *and able* to purchase at each of these prices. We say willing *and able* because willingness alone is not effective in the market. You may be willing to buy a Porsche, but if that willingness is not backed by the necessary dollars, it will not be effective and, therefore, will not be reflected in the market. If the price of corn was $5 per bushel, our consumer would be willing and able to buy 10 bushels per week; if it was $4, the consumer would be willing and able to buy 20 bushels per week; and so forth.

Figure 3-1 does not tell us which of the five possible prices will actually exist in the corn market. That depends on demand and supply. Demand is simply a statement of a buyer's plans, or intentions, with respect to the purchase of a product.

To be meaningful, the quantities demanded at each price must relate to a specific period—a day, a week, a month. Saying "A consumer will buy 10 bushels of corn at $5 per bushel" is meaningless. Unless a specific time period is stated, we do not know whether the demand for a product is large or small.

---

[1]This definition obviously is worded to apply to product markets. To adjust it to apply to factor markets, substitute the word "factor" for "product" and the word "businesses" for "consumers."

FIGURE 3-1	An Individual Buyer's Demand for Corn

Price per bushel	Quantity demanded (bushels per week)
$5	10
4	20
3	35
2	55
1	80

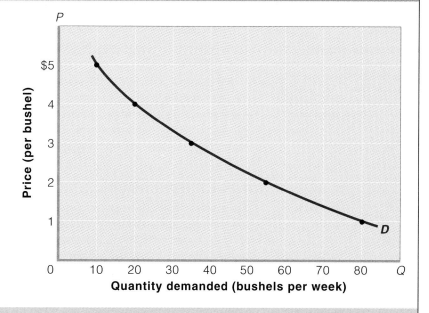

Because price and quantity demanded are inversely related, an individual's demand schedule graphs as a downsloping curve such as D. Specifically, the law of demand says that, other things equal, consumers will buy more of a product as its price declines. Here and in later figures, P stands for price, and Q stands for quantity (either demanded or supplied).

As price falls, the quantity demanded rises, and as price rises, the quantity demanded falls.

law of demand
All else equal, as price falls, the quantity demanded rises, and vice versa.

marginal utility
The extra utility a consumer obtains from the consumption of one additional unit of a good or service.

Law of Demand

A fundamental characteristic of demand is this: *All else equal, as price falls, the quantity demanded rises, and as price rises, the quantity demanded falls.* There is a negative or *inverse* relationship between price and quantity demanded. This inverse relationship is called the **law of demand**.

The "other things equal" assumption is critical here. Many factors other than the price of the product being considered affect the amount purchased. The quantity of Nikes purchased will depend not only on the price of Nikes but also on the prices of such substitutes as Reeboks, Adidas, and Filas. The law of demand in this case says that fewer Nikes will be purchased if the price of Nikes rises *and if the prices of Reeboks, Adidas, and Filas all remain constant.* Another way of stating it is that if the *relative price* of Nikes rises, fewer Nikes will be bought. However, if the price of Nikes and all other competing shoes increase by some amount—say, $5—consumers might buy more, fewer, or the same amount of Nikes.

Why the inverse relationship between price and quantity demanded? Let's look at two explanations:

• In any specific time period, each buyer of a product will derive less satisfaction (or benefit, or utility) from each successive unit of the product consumed. The second Big Mac will yield less satisfaction to the consumer than the first, and the third still less than the second. That is, consumption is subject to diminishing **marginal utility**. And because successive units of a particular product yield less and less marginal utility, consumers will buy additional units only if the price of those units is progressively reduced.

income effect
A change in the price of a product changes a consumer's real income (purchasing power) and thus the quantity of the product purchased.

substitution effect
A change in the price of a consumer good changes the relative expensiveness of that good and hence changes the willingness to buy it rather than other goods.

• We can also explain the law of demand in terms of income and substitution effects. The **income effect** indicates that a lower price increases the purchasing power of a buyer's money income, enabling the buyer to purchase more of the product than she or he could buy before. A higher price has the opposite effect. The **substitution effect** suggests that at a lower price, buyers have the incentive to substitute what is now a less expensive product for similar products that are now *relatively* more expensive. The product whose price has fallen is now "a better deal" relative to the other products.

For example, a decline in the price of chicken will increase the purchasing power of consumer incomes, enabling them to buy more chicken (the income effect). At a lower price, chicken is relatively more attractive and consumers tend to substitute it for pork, beef, and fish (the substitution effect). The income and substitution effects combine to make consumers able and willing to buy more of a product at a low price than at a high price.

The Demand Curve

The inverse relationship between price and quantity demanded for any product can be represented on a simple graph, in which, by convention, we measure *quantity demanded* on the horizontal axis and *price* on the vertical axis. In Figure 3-1 we have plotted the five price–quantity data points listed in the table and connected the points with a smooth curve, labelled *D*. Such a curve is called a **demand curve**. Its downward slope reflects the law of demand—more people buy more of a product or service as its price falls. The relationship between price and quantity demanded is inverse.

demand curve
A curve illustrating the inverse (negative) relationship between the quantity demanded of a good or service and its price, other things equal.

The table and graph in Figure 3-1 contain exactly the same data and reflect the same relationship between price and quantity demanded. But the graph shows that relationship more simply and clearly than a table or a description in words.

Market Demand

So far, we have concentrated on just one consumer. By adding the quantities demanded by all consumers at each of the various possible prices, we can get from *individual* demand to *market* demand. If there are just three buyers in the market, as represented in Figure 3-2, it is relatively easy to determine the total quantity demanded at each price. Figure 3-2 shows the graphical summing procedure: At each price we add the individual quantities demanded to obtain the total quantity demanded at that price; we then plot the price and the total quantity demanded as one point of the market demand curve.

Of course, there are usually many more than three buyers of a product. To avoid hundreds or thousands or millions of additions, we suppose that all the buyers in a market are willing and able to buy the same amounts at each of the possible prices. Then we just multiply those amounts by the number of buyers to obtain the market demand. This is the way we arrived at curve D_1, in Figure 3-3 on page 52, for a market with 200 corn buyers. The table in Figure 3-3 shows the calculations for 200 corn buyers.

In constructing a demand curve such as D_1 in Figure 3-3, we assume that price is the most important influence on the amount of any product purchased, even though other factors can and do affect purchases. These factors, called **determinants of demand**, are assumed to be constant when a demand curve like D_1 is drawn. They are the "other things equal" in the relationship between price and quantity demanded. When any of these determinants changes, the demand curve will shift to the right or left.

determinants of demand
Factors other than its price that determine the quantities demanded of a good or service.

The basic determinants of demand are (1) consumers' tastes (preferences), (2) the number of consumers in the market, (3) consumers' incomes, (4) the prices of related goods, and (5) consumer expectations about future prices and incomes.

FIGURE 3-2	Market Demand for Corn, Three Buyers

| Price per bushel | Quantity demanded | | | Total quantity demanded per week |
	First buyer	Second buyer	Third buyer	
$5	10 +	12 +	8 =	30
4	20 +	23 +	17 =	60
3	35 +	39 +	26 =	100
2	55 +	60 +	39 =	154
1	80 +	87 +	54 =	221

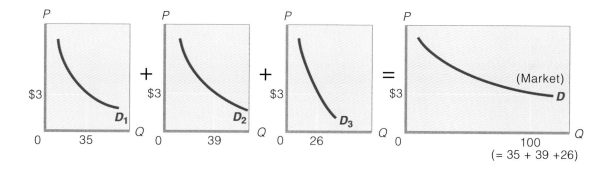

We establish the market demand curve D by adding horizontally the individual demand curves (D_1, D_2, and D_3) of all the consumers in the market. At the price of $3, for example, the three individual curves yield a total quantity demanded of 100 bushels.

Change in Demand

A change in one or more of the determinants of demand will change the demand data (the demand schedule) and therefore the location of the demand curve in Figure 3-3. A change in the demand schedule or, graphically, a shift in the demand curve, is called a *change in demand*.

If consumers desire to buy more corn at each possible price than is reflected in column 4 of the table in Figure 3-3, that *increase in demand* is shown as a shift of the demand curve to the right, say, from D_1 to D_2. Conversely, a *decrease in demand* occurs when consumers buy less corn at each possible price than is indicated in column 4 of the table in Figure 3-3. The leftward shift of the demand curve from D_1 to D_3 in Figure 3-3 shows that situation.

Now let's see how changes in each determinant affect demand.

TASTES

A favourable change in consumer tastes (preferences) for a product—a change that makes the product more desirable—means that more of it will be demanded at each price. Demand will increase; the demand curve will shift rightward. An unfavourable change in consumer preferences will decrease demand, shifting the demand curve to the left.

FIGURE 3-3   Changes in the Demand for Corn

A change in one or more of the determinants of demand causes a change in demand. An increase in demand is shown as a shift of the demand curve to the right, as from D_1 to D_2. A decrease in demand is shown as a shift of the demand curve to the left, as from D_1 to D_3. These changes in demand are to be distinguished from a change in quantity demanded, which is caused by a change in the price of the product, as shown by a movement from, say, point a to point b on fixed demand curve D_1.

MARKET DEMAND FOR CORN, 200 BUYERS

(1) Price per bushel	(2) Quantity demanded per week, single buyer		(3) Number of buyers in the market		(4) Total quantity demanded per week
$5	10	×	200	=	2,000
4	20	×	200	=	4,000
3	35	×	200	=	7,000
2	55	×	200	=	11,000
1	80	×	200	=	16,000

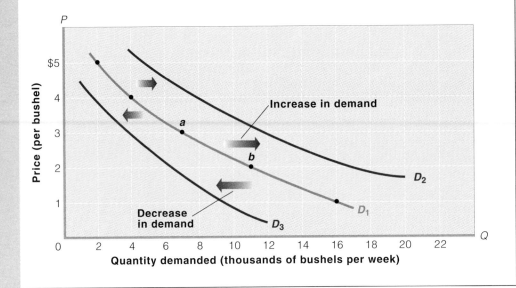

New products may affect consumer tastes; for example, the introduction of compact discs greatly decreased the demand for cassette tapes. Consumers' concern over the health hazards of cholesterol and obesity have increased the demand for broccoli, low-calorie sweeteners, and fresh fruit, while decreasing the demand for beef, veal, eggs, and whole milk.

NUMBER OF BUYERS

An increase in the number of buyers in a market increases demand. A decrease in the number of buyers in a market decreases demand. For example, the baby boom after World War II increased demand for diapers, baby lotion, and the services of obstetricians. When the baby boomers reached their 20s in the 1970s, the demand for housing increased. Also, an increase in life expectancy has increased the demand for medical care, retirement communities, and nursing homes.

INCOME

How changes in income affect demand is more complex. For most products, a rise in income causes an increase in demand. Consumers typically buy more steaks, furniture, and computers as their incomes increase. Conversely, the demand for such products declines as income falls. Products for which demand *varies* directly with money income are called **normal goods**.

normal good
A good or service whose consumption rises when income increases and falls when income decreases, price remaining constant.

Although most products are normal goods, there are some exceptions. As incomes increase beyond some point, the demand for used clothing, retread tires, and third-hand automobiles may decrease, because the higher incomes enable consumers to buy new versions of those products. Similarly, rising incomes may cause the demand for charcoal grills to decline as wealthier consumers switch to gas grills. Goods for which demand varies *inversely* with money income are called **inferior goods**.

inferior good
A good or service whose consumption declines as income rises (and conversely), price remaining constant.

PRICES OF RELATED GOODS

A change in the price of a related good may either increase or decrease the demand for a product, depending on whether the related good is a substitute or a complement.

substitute goods
Products or services that can be used in place of each other.

- A **substitute good** is one that can be used in place of another good.
- A **complementary good** is one that is used together with another good.

complementary goods
Products and services that are used together.

Substitutes   Beef and chicken are examples of substitute goods, or simply *substitutes*. When the price of beef rises, consumers buy less beef, increasing the demand for chicken. Conversely, as the price of beef falls, consumers buy more beef, decreasing the demand for chicken. *When two products are substitutes, the price of one and the demand for the other move in the same direction.* So it is with pairs such as Nikes and Reeboks, Colgate and Crest, Toyotas and Hondas, and Coke and Pepsi. So-called *substitution in consumption* occurs when the price of one good rises relative to the price of a similar good. One can also buy services that are close substitutes. Examples include obstetricians and midwives, and, increasingly, physicians and nurse practitioners. Although in Canada government insurance pays for these services, if waiting times to see an obstetrician or a physician increase, consumers may turn to their close substitutes, for example, nurse practitioners.

Complements   Complementary goods (or simply *complements*) are goods that are used together and are usually demanded together. If the price of gasoline falls and, as a result, you drive your car more often, the extra driving increases your demand for motor oil. Thus, gas and motor oil are jointly demanded; they are complements. So it is with ham and eggs, tuition and textbooks, movies and popcorn, cameras and film. *When two products are complements, the price of one good and the demand for the other good move in opposite directions.*

Unrelated Goods   The vast majority of goods that are not related to one another are called *independent goods*. Examples are butter and golf balls, potatoes and automobiles, and bananas and wristwatches. A change in the price of one does not affect the demand for the other.

Expectations   Changes in consumer expectations may shift demand. A newly formed expectation of higher future prices may cause consumers to buy now in order to "beat" the anticipated price rises, thus increasing current demand. For example, when freezing weather destroys much of Florida's citrus crop, consumers may reason that the price of orange juice will rise. They may stock up on orange juice by purchasing large quantities now. In contrast, a newly formed expectation of falling prices or falling income may decrease current demand for products.

Finally, a change in expectations concerning future income may prompt consumers to change their current spending. For example, first-round NHL draft choices may splurge on new luxury cars in anticipation of a lucrative professional hockey contract. Or workers who become fearful of losing their jobs may reduce their demand for, say, vacation travel.

In summary, an *increase* in demand—the decision by consumers to buy larger quantities of a product at each possible price—may be caused by:

- A favourable change in consumer tastes

- An increase in the number of buyers

- Rising incomes if the product is a normal good

- Falling incomes if the product is an inferior good

- An increase in the price of a substitute good

- A decrease in the price of a complementary good

- A new consumer expectation that prices and income will be higher in the future

You should "reverse" these generalizations to explain a *decrease* in demand. Table 3-1 provides additional illustrations of the determinants of demand. *(Key Question 2)*

Changes in Quantity Demanded

change in demand
A change in the quantity demanded of a good or service at every price.

A *change in demand* must not be confused with a *change in quantity demanded*. A **change in demand** is a shift of the entire demand curve to the right (an increase in demand) or to the left (a decrease in demand). It occurs because the consumer's state of mind about purchasing the product has been altered in response to a change in one or more of the determinants of demand. Recall that *demand* is a schedule or a curve; therefore, a *change in demand* means a change in the entire schedule and a shift of the entire curve.

change in quantity demanded
A movement from one point to another on a demand curve.

In contrast, a **change in quantity demanded** is a movement from one point to another point—from one price–quantity combination to another—on a fixed demand schedule or demand curve. The cause of such a change is an increase or decrease in the price of the product under consideration. In Figure 3-3, for example, a decline in the price of corn from $5 to $4 will increase the quantity of corn demanded from 2000 to 4000 bushels.

TABLE 3-1	Determinants of Demand Curve Shifts
Determinant	**Examples**
Change in buyer tastes	Physical fitness rises in popularity, increasing the demand for jogging shoes and bicycles; Latin American music becomes more popular, increasing the demand for Latin CDs.
Change in number of buyers	A decline in the birthrate reduces the demand for children's toys.
Change in income	A rise in incomes increases the demand for such normal goods as butter, lobster, and filet mignon while reducing the demand for such inferior goods as cabbage, turnips, and cheap wine.
Change in the prices of related goods	A reduction in airfares reduces the demand for bus transportation (substitute goods); a decline in the price of compact disc players increases the demand for compact discs (complementary goods).
Change in expectations	Inclement weather in South America creates an expectation of higher future prices of coffee beans, thereby increasing today's demand for coffee beans.

In Figure 3-3 the shift of the demand curve D_1 to either D_2 or D_3 is a change in demand. But the movement from point *a* to point *b* on curve D_1 represents a change in quantity demanded: *demand has not changed; it is the entire curve, and it remains fixed in place.*

QUICK REVIEW

- A market is any arrangement that facilitates the purchase and sale of goods, services, or resources.

- Demand is a schedule or a curve showing the amount of a product that buyers are willing and able to purchase at each possible price in a series of prices, in a particular time period.

- The law of demand states that, other things equal, the quantity of a good purchased varies inversely with its price.

- The demand curve shifts because of changes in (a) consumer tastes, (b) the number of buyers in the market, (c) consumer income, (d) the prices of substitute or complementary goods, and (e) consumer expectations.

- A change in demand is a shift of the entire demand curve; a change in quantity demanded is a movement from one point to another on a demand curve.

3.3 Supply

supply
A schedule or curve that shows the amounts of a product that producers are willing and able to make available for sale at each of a series of possible prices during a specific period.

Up to this point we have concentrated our attention on the nature of wants. In order for wants to be satisfied someone must produce the goods and services desired. We now turn to investigate the nature of supply.

Supply is *a schedule or curve that shows the amounts of a product that producers are willing and able to make available for sale at each of a series of possible prices during a specific period.*[2] Figure 3-4 is a hypothetical supply schedule for a single producer of corn. It shows the quantities of corn that will be supplied at various prices, other things equal.

Law of Supply

law of supply
The principle that, other things equal, an increase in the price of a product will increase the quantity of it supplied; and conversely for a price decrease.

The table of Figure 3-4 shows a direct relationship between price and quantity supplied. *As price rises, the quantity supplied rises; as price falls, the quantity supplied falls.* This relationship is called the **law of supply**. A supply schedule tells us that firms will produce and offer for sale more of their product at a high price than at a low price. To a supplier, price represents *revenue*, which serves as an incentive to produce and sell a product. The higher the price, the greater the incentive and the greater the quantity supplied.

Consider a farmer in Manitoba who can shift resources among alternative farm products. As price moves up, as shown in Figure 3-4, the farmer finds it profitable to take land out of wheat, oats, and soybean production and put it into corn. And the higher corn prices enable the Manitoba farmer to cover the increased costs associated with more intensive cultivation and the use of more seed, fertilizer, and pesticides. The overall result is more corn.

Now consider a manufacturer. Beyond some quantity of production, manufacturers usually encounter increasing costs per added unit of output. The firm will not produce those more costly units unless it receives a higher price for them. Again, price and quantity supplied are directly related.

---

[2]This definition is worded to apply to product markets. To adjust it to apply to factor markets, substitute *factor* for *product* and *owner* for the word *producer.*

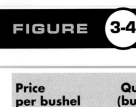

FIGURE 3-4   **An Individual Producer's Supply of Corn**

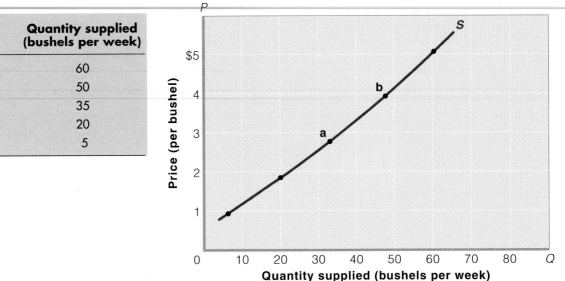

Price per bushel	Quantity supplied (bushels per week)
$5	60
4	50
3	35
2	20
1	5

Because price and quantity supplied are positively related, a firm's supply schedule is an upward-sloping curve such as S. Specifically, the law of supply says that, other things equal, firms will supply more of a product as its price rises.

The Market Supply Curve

In Figure 3-5, curve S_1 is a graph of the market supply data given in the table. Those data assume there are 200 suppliers in the market, each willing and able to supply corn according to the data in the table of Figure 3-4. The market **supply curve** is derived by horizontally adding the supply curves of the individual producers.

supply curve
A curve illustrating the positive (direct) relationship between the quantity supplied of a good or service and its price, other things equal.

Determinants of Supply

In constructing a supply curve, we assume that price is the most significant influence on the quantity supplied of any product. But other factors (the "other things equal") can and do affect supply. The supply curve is drawn on the assumption that these other things are fixed and do not change. If one of them does change, a *change in supply* will occur, meaning that the entire supply curve will shift.

determinants of supply
Causes other than its price that determine the quantities supplied of a good or service.

The basic **determinants of supply** are (1) factor prices, (2) technology, (3) taxes and subsidies, (4) prices of other goods, (5) price expectations, and (6) the number of sellers in the market. A change in any one or more of these determinants of supply will move the supply curve for a product either to the right or to the left. A shift to the *right*, as from S_1 to S_2 in Figure 3-5, signifies an *increase* in supply: Producers supply larger quantities of the product at each possible price. A shift to the *left*, as from S_1 to S_3, indicates a *decrease* in supply.

Changes in Supply

Let's consider how changes in each of the determinants affect supply. The key idea is that costs are a major factor underlying supply curves; anything that affects costs (other than changes in output itself) usually shifts the supply curve.

FIGURE 3-5   Changes in the Supply of Corn

A change in one or more of the determinants of supply causes a shift in supply. An increase in supply is shown as a rightward shift of the supply curve, as from S_1 to S_2. A decrease in supply is depicted as a leftward shift of the curve, as from S_1 to S_3. In contrast, a change in the *quantity supplied* is caused by a change in the product's price and is shown by a movement from one point to another, as from *a* to *b*, on a fixed supply curve.

MARKET SUPPLY OF CORN, 200 PRODUCERS

(1) Price per bushel	(2) Quantity supplied per week, single producer		(3) Number of sellers in the market		(4) Total quantity supplied per week
$5	60	×	200	=	12,000
4	50	×	200	=	10,000
3	35	×	200	=	7,000
2	20	×	200	=	4,000
1	5	×	200	=	1,000

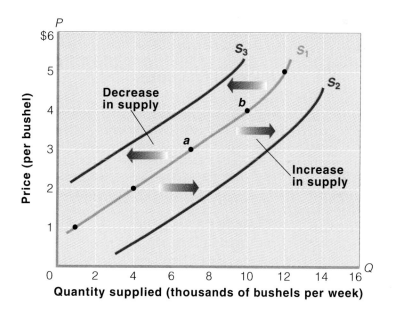

FACTOR PRICES

The prices of the factors used as inputs in the production process determine the costs of production. Higher *factor* prices raise production costs and, assuming a particular *product* price, squeeze profits. That reduction in profits reduces the incentive for firms to supply output at each product price. For example, an increase in the prices of iron ore and coke will increase the cost of producing steel for Dofasco and reduce its supply.

In contrast, lower *factor* prices reduce production costs and increase profits. So, when input prices fall, firms supply greater output at each product price. For example, a decrease in the prices of seed and fertilizer will increase the supply of corn.

TECHNOLOGY

Improvements in technology (techniques of production) enable firms to produce units of output with fewer inputs. Because inputs are costly, using fewer of them lowers production costs and increases supply. Example: Recent improvements in the fuel efficiency of aircraft engines have reduced the cost of providing passenger air service. Thus, Air Canada and other airlines now offer more flights than previously at each ticket price; the supply of air service has increased. Similarly, technological improvement of medical diagnostic equipment can increase the number of patients that can have tests.

TAXES AND SUBSIDIES

Businesses treat most taxes as costs. An increase in sales or property taxes will increase production costs and reduce supply. In contrast, subsidies are "taxes in reverse." If the government subsidizes the production of a good, it in effect lowers the producers' costs and increases supply. Government subsidies will, for example, help increase the number of rural medical practitioners.

PRICES OF OTHER GOODS

Firms that produce a particular product, say, soccer balls, can sometimes use their plant and equipment to produce alternative goods, say, basketballs and volleyballs. The higher prices of these "other goods" may entice soccer ball producers to switch production to those other goods in order to increase profits. This *substitution in production* results in a decline in the supply of soccer balls. Alternatively, when the prices of basketballs and volleyballs decline relative to the price of soccer balls, producers of those goods may decide to produce more soccer balls instead, increasing their supply.

PRICE EXPECTATIONS

Changes in expectations about the future price of a product may affect the producer's current willingness to supply that product. It is difficult, however, to generalize about how a new expectation of higher prices affects the present supply of a product. Ontario farmers anticipating a higher corn price in the future might withhold some of their current corn harvest from the market, thereby causing a decrease in the current supply of corn. In contrast, in many types of manufacturing industries, newly formed expectations that price will increase may induce firms to add another shift of workers or to expand their production facilities, causing current supply to increase.

NUMBER OF SELLERS

Other things equal, the larger the number of suppliers, the greater the market supply. As more firms enter an industry, the supply curve shifts to the right. Conversely, the smaller the number of firms in the industry, the less the market supply. This means that as firms leave an industry, the supply curve shifts to the left. Example: Canada and the United States have imposed restrictions on haddock fishing to replenish dwindling stocks. As part of that policy, the federal government has bought the boats of some of the haddock fishermen as a way of putting them out of business and decreasing the catch. The result has been a decline in the market supply of haddock.

Table 3-2 is a checklist of the determinants of supply, along with further illustrations. (*Key Question 5*)

CHANGES IN QUANTITY SUPPLIED

change in supply
A change in the quantity supplied of a good or service at every price; a shift of the supply curve to the left or right.

The distinction between a *change in supply* and a *change in quantity supplied* parallels the distinction between a change in demand and a change in quantity demanded. Because supply is a schedule or curve, a **change in supply** means a change in the entire schedule and a shift of the entire curve. An increase in supply shifts the curve to the right; a decrease in supply shifts it to the left. The cause of a change in supply is a change in one or more of the determinants of supply.

TABLE 3-2 Determinants of Supply Curve Shifts

Determinant	Examples
Change in factor prices	A decrease in the price of microchips increases the supply of computers; an increase in the price of crude oil reduces the supply of gasoline.
Change in technology	The development of more effective wireless technology increases the supply of cell phones.
Changes in taxes and subsidies	An increase in the excise tax on cigarettes reduces the supply of cigarettes; a decline in subsidies to universities reduces the supply of higher education.
Change in prices of other goods	An increase in the price of cucumbers decreases the supply of watermelons.
Change in expectations	An expectation of a substantial rise in future log prices decreases the supply of logs today.
Change in number of suppliers	An increase in the number of Internet service providers increases the supply of such services; the formation of women's professional basketball leagues increases the supply of women's professional basketball games.

change in quantity supplied
A movement from one point to another on a fixed supply curve.

In contrast, a **change in quantity supplied** is a movement from one point to another on a fixed supply curve. The cause of such a movement is a change in the price of the specific product being considered. In Figure 3-5, a decline in the price of corn from $5 to $4 decreases the quantity of corn supplied per week from 12,000 to 10,000 bushels. This is a change in quantity supplied, not a change in supply. *Supply is the full schedule of prices and quantities shown, and this schedule does not change when price changes.*

QUICK REVIEW

- A supply schedule or curve shows that, other things equal, the quantity of a good supplied varies directly with its price.

- The supply curve shifts because of changes in (a) factor prices, (b) technology, (c) taxes or subsidies, (d) prices of other goods, (e) expectations of future prices, and (f) the number of suppliers.

- A change in supply is a shift of the supply curve; a change in quantity supplied is a movement from one point to another on a fixed supply curve.

3.4 Supply and Demand: Market Equilibrium

We can now bring together supply and demand to see how the buying decisions of households and the selling decisions of businesses interact to determine the price of a product and the quantity actually bought and sold. In the table of **Figure 3-6 (Key Graph)**, columns 1 and 2 repeat the market supply of corn (from Figure 3-5), and columns 2 and 3 repeat the market demand for corn (from Figure 3-3). We assume that this is a competitive market—neither buyers nor sellers can set the price (see the Consider This box).

Key Graph

FIGURE 3-6 Equilibrium Price and Quantity

The intersection of the downsloping demand curve *D* and the upsloping supply curve *S* indicates the equilibrium price and quantity, here $3 and 7000 bushels of corn. The shortages of corn at below-equilibrium prices (for example, 7000 bushels at $2), drive up price. These higher prices increase the quantity supplied and reduce the quantity demanded until equilibrium is achieved. The surpluses caused by above-equilibrium prices (for example, 6000 bushels at $4), push price down. As price drops, the quantity demanded rises and the quantity supplied falls until equilibrium is established. At the equilibrium price and quantity, there are neither shortages nor surpluses of corn.

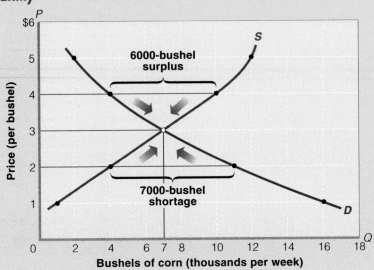

(1) Total quantity supplied per week	(2) Price per bushel	(3) Total quantity demanded per week	(4) Surplus (+) or shortage (−)
12,000	$5	2,000	+10,000↓
10,000	4	4,000	+ 6,000↓
7,000	3	7,000	0
4,000	2	11,000	− 7,000↑
1,000	1	16,000	−15,000↑

The arrows indicate the effect on price.

Quick Quiz

1. **Demand curve *D* in Figure 3-6 is downsloping because:**
   a. producers offer less product for sale as the price of the product falls.
   b. lower prices of a product create income and substitution effects, which lead consumers to purchase more of it.
   c. the larger the number of buyers in a market, the lower the product price.
   d. price and quantity demanded are directly (positively) related.

2. **Supply curve *S*:**
   a. reflects an inverse (negative) relationship between price and quantity supplied.
   b. reflects a direct (positive) relationship between price and quantity supplied.
   c. depicts the collective behaviour of buyers in this market.
   d. shows that producers will offer more of a product for sale at a low product price than at a high product price.

3. **At the $3 price:**
   a. quantity supplied exceeds quantity demanded.
   b. quantity demanded exceeds quantity supplied.
   c. the product is abundant and a surplus exists.
   d. there is no pressure on price to rise or fall.

4. **At price $5 in this market:**
   a. there will be a shortage of 10,000 units.
   b. there will be a surplus of 10,000 units.
   c. quantity demanded will be 12,000 units.
   d. quantity demanded will equal quantity supplied.

ANSWERS: 1. b; 2. b; 3. d; 4. b

Consider This

Supply and Demand

In viewing demand and supply curves such as those shown in Figure 3-6, students taking introductory economics often wonder if demand is more important than supply in determining equilibrium price and quantity or if supply is more important than demand. The answer is that demand and supply are equally important.

Economist Alfred Marshall (1842–1924) used a vivid analogy to make this point. He likened demand and supply to the two blades of a pair of scissors. Which blade of the scissors cuts the paper? To be sure, if the lower blade is held in place and the upper blade is closed down upon it, one could argue that the upper blade has cut the paper. But would the paper have been cut without the lower blade? And if the upper blade is held in place and the lower blade is closed up against it, would the paper have been cut without the upper blade?

The answer to these questions is that it is the interaction of the two blades of the scissors that cuts the paper. Both are necessary and both are important. So it is with demand and supply in competitive markets. Demand (which reflects utility) and supply (which reflects costs) jointly determine equilibrium price and quantity. Without a demand curve, there is no equilibrium price and quantity. But the same is true for supply. Without it, no equilibrium price and quantity exist. Equilibrium price and quantity result from the *interaction* of demand and supply, and each is *equally* important.

Question: With the aid of demand and supply analysis, explain why prostitution exists.

Surpluses

surplus
The amount by which the quantity supplied of a product exceeds the quantity demanded at a specific (above-equilibrium) price.

We have limited our example to only five possible prices. Of these, which will actually prevail as the market price for corn? We can find an answer through trial and error. For no particular reason, let's start with $5. We see immediately that this cannot be the prevailing market price. At the $5 price, producers are willing to produce and offer for sale 12,000 bushels of corn, but buyers are willing to buy only 2000 bushels. The $5 price encourages farmers to produce lots of corn but discourages most consumers from buying it. The result is a 10,000-bushel **surplus** or *excess supply* of corn. This surplus, shown in column 4 of the table in Figure 3-6, is the excess of quantity supplied over quantity demanded at $5. Corn farmers would find themselves with 10,000 unsold bushels of output.

A price of $5, even if it existed temporarily in the corn market, could not persist over a period of time. The very large surplus of corn would drive competing sellers to lower the price to encourage buyers to take the surplus off their hands.

Shortages

shortage
The amount by which the quantity demanded of a product exceeds the quantity supplied at a particular (below-equilibrium) price.

Let's jump now to $1 as the possible market price of corn. Observe in column 4 of the table that at this price, quantity demanded exceeds quantity supplied by 15,000 units. The $1 price discourages farmers from devoting resources to corn production and encourages consumers to buy more than is available. The result is a 15,000-bushel **shortage** of, or *excess demand* for, corn. The $1 price cannot persist as the market price. Many consumers who want to buy at this price will not get corn. They will express a willingness to pay more than $1 to get some of the available output. Competition among these buyers will drive up the price to something greater than $1.

Equilibrium Price and Quantity

At $3, *and only at this price*, the quantity of corn that farmers are willing to produce and supply is identical with the quantity consumers are willing and able to buy. There is neither a shortage nor a surplus of corn at that price.

equilibrium price
The price in a competitive market at which the quantity demanded and the quantity supplied are equal.

equilibrium quantity
The quantity demanded and supplied at the equilibrium price in a competitive market.

With no shortage or surplus at $3, there is no reason for the price of corn to change. Economists call this price the *market-clearing* or **equilibrium price**, equilibrium meaning "in balance" or "at rest." At $3, quantity supplied and quantity demanded are in balance at the **equilibrium quantity** of 7000 bushels. So $3 is the only stable price of corn under the supply and demand conditions shown in Figure 3-6.

The price of corn, or of any other product bought and sold in competitive markets, will be established where the supply decisions of producers and the demand decisions of buyers are mutually consistent. Such decisions are consistent only at the equilibrium price (here, $3) and equilibrium quantity (here, 7000 bushels). At any higher price, suppliers want to sell more than consumers want to buy and a surplus results; at any lower price, consumers want to buy more than producers make available for sale and a shortage results. Such discrepancies between the supply and demand intentions of sellers and buyers then prompt price changes that bring the two sets of intentions into accord.

A graphical analysis of supply and demand yields these same conclusions. Figure 3-6 shows the market supply and demand curves for corn on the same graph. (The horizontal axis now measures both quantity demanded and quantity supplied.)

 Graphically, the intersection of the supply curve and the demand curve for a product indicates the market equilibrium. Here, equilibrium price and quantity are $3 per bushel and 7000 bushels. At any above-equilibrium price, quantity supplied exceeds quantity demanded. This surplus of corn causes price reductions by sellers who are eager to rid themselves of their surplus. The falling price causes less corn to be offered and simultaneously encourages consumers to buy more. The market moves to its equilibrium.

Any price below the equilibrium price creates a shortage; quantity demanded then exceeds quantity supplied. Buyers try to obtain the product by offering to pay more for it; this drives the price upward toward its equilibrium level. The rising price simultaneously causes producers to increase the quantity supplied and prompts many buyers to leave the market, thus eliminating the shortage. Again the market moves to its equilibrium.

Rationing Function of Prices

rationing function of prices
The ability of market forces in a competitive market to equalize quantity demanded and quantity supplied and to eliminate shortages via changes in prices.

The ability of the competitive forces of supply and demand to establish a price at which selling and buying decisions are consistent is called the **rationing function of prices**. In our case, the equilibrium price of $3 clears the market, leaving no burdensome surplus for sellers and no inconvenient shortage for potential buyers. And it is the combination of freely made individual decisions that sets this market-clearing price. In effect, the market outcome says that all buyers who are willing and able to pay $3 for a bushel of corn will obtain it; all buyers who cannot or will not pay $3 will go without corn. Similarly, all producers who are willing and able to offer corn for sale at $3 a bushel will sell it; all producers who cannot or will not sell for $3 per bushel will not sell their product. (**Key Question 7**)

Changes in Supply, Demand, and Equilibrium

We know that demand might change because of fluctuations in consumer tastes or incomes, changes in consumer expectations, or variations in the prices of related goods. Supply might change in response to changes in resource prices, technology, or taxes. What effects will such changes in supply and demand have on equilibrium price and quantity?

CHANGES IN DEMAND

Suppose that supply is constant and demand increases, as shown in Figure 3-7(a). As a result, the new intersection of the supply and demand curves is at higher values on both the price and quantity axes. An increase in demand raises both equilibrium price and equilibrium quantity. Conversely, a decrease in demand, such as that shown in Figure 3-7(b), reduces both equilibrium price and equilibrium quantity. (The value of graphical analysis is now apparent: We need not fumble with columns of figures to determine the outcomes; we need only compare the new and the old points of intersection on the graph.)

CHANGES IN SUPPLY

Now suppose that demand is constant but supply increases, as in Figure 3-7(c). The new intersection of supply and demand is located at a lower equilibrium price but at a higher equilibrium quantity. An increase in supply reduces equilibrium price but increases equilibrium quantity. In contrast, if supply decreases, as in Figure 3-7(d), the equilibrium price rises while the equilibrium quantity declines.

FIGURE 3-7 Changes in Demand and Supply and the Effects on Price and Quantity

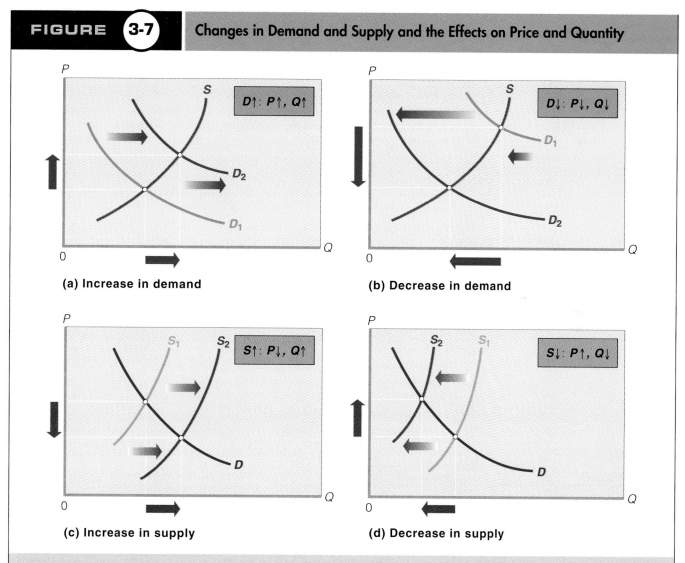

(a) Increase in demand

(b) Decrease in demand

(c) Increase in supply

(d) Decrease in supply

The increase in demand from D_1 to D_2 in (a) increases both equilibrium price and quantity. The decrease in demand from D_1 to D_2 in (b) decreases both equilibrium price and quantity. The increase in supply from S_1 to S_2 in (c) decreases equilibrium price and increases equilibrium quantity. The decline in supply from S_1 to S_2 in (d) increases equilibrium price and decreases equilibrium quantity. The boxes in the top right corners summarize the respective changes and outcomes. The upward arrows in those boxes signify increases in demand (D), supply (S), equilibrium price (P), and equilibrium quantity (Q); the downward arrows signify decreases in these items.

COMPLEX CASES

When both supply and demand change, the effect is a combination of the individual effects. As you study the following cases, keep in mind that each effect on the demand and supply curves has to be considered independently.

1. **Supply Increase; Demand Decrease**   What effect will a supply increase and a demand decrease have on equilibrium price? Both changes decrease price, so the net result is a price drop greater than that resulting from either change alone.

   What about equilibrium quantity? Here the effects of the changes in supply and demand are opposed: The increase in supply increases equilibrium quantity, but the decrease in demand reduces it. The direction of the change in quantity depends on the relative sizes of the changes in supply and demand. If the increase in supply is larger than the decrease in demand, the equilibrium quantity will increase. But if the decrease in demand is greater than the increase in supply, the equilibrium quantity will decrease.

2. **Supply Decrease; Demand Increase**   A decrease in supply and an increase in demand both increase price. Their combined effect is an increase in equilibrium price greater than that caused by either change separately. But their effect on equilibrium quantity is again indeterminate, depending on the relative sizes of the changes in supply and demand. If the decrease in supply is larger than the increase in demand, the equilibrium quantity will decrease. In contrast, if the increase in demand is greater than the decrease in supply, the equilibrium quantity will increase.

3. **Supply Increase; Demand Increase**   What if supply and demand both increase? A supply increase drops equilibrium price, while a demand increase boosts it. If the increase in supply is greater than the increase in demand, the equilibrium price will fall. If the opposite holds, the equilibrium price will rise.

   The effect on equilibrium quantity is certain: The increases in supply and in demand each raise equilibrium quantity. Therefore, the equilibrium quantity will increase by an amount greater than that caused by either change alone.

4. **Supply Decrease; Demand Decrease**   What about decreases in both supply and demand? If the decrease in supply is greater than the decrease in demand, equilibrium price will rise. If the reverse is true, equilibrium price will fall. Because decreases in supply and in demand each reduce equilibrium quantity, we can be sure that equilibrium quantity will fall.

Table 3-3 summarizes these four cases. To understand them fully you should draw supply and demand diagrams for each case to confirm the effects listed in Table 3-3.

Special cases arise when a decrease in demand and a decrease in supply, or an increase in demand and an increase in supply, exactly cancel out. In both cases, the net effect on equilibrium price will be zero; price will not change. **(Key Question 8)**

TABLE 3-3	Effects of Changes in Both Supply and Demand		
Change in supply	**Change in demand**	**Effect on equilibrium price**	**Effect on equilibrium quantity**
1 Increase	Decrease	Decrease	Indeterminate
2 Decrease	Increase	Increase	Indeterminate
3 Increase	Increase	Indeterminate	Increase
4 Decrease	Decrease	Indeterminate	Decrease

A Reminder: "Other Things Equal"

We must stress once again that specific demand and supply curves (such as those in Figure 3-7) show relationships between prices and quantities demanded and supplied, *other things equal*.

If you forget the other-things-equal assumption, you can encounter situations that *seem* to be in conflict with these basic principles. For example, suppose salsa manufacturers sell one million bottles of salsa at $4 a bottle in one year, two million bottles at $5 in the next year; and three million at $6 in the year thereafter. Price and quantity purchased vary directly, and these data seem to be at odds with the law of demand. But there is no conflict here; these data do not refute the law of demand. The catch is that the law of demand's other-things-equal assumption has been violated over the three years in the example. Specifically, because of changing tastes and rising incomes, the demand for salsa has increased sharply, as in Figure 3-7(a). The result is higher prices *and* larger quantities purchased.

Another example: The price of coffee occasionally has shot upward at the same time that the quantity of coffee produced has declined. These events seemingly contradict the direct relationship between price and quantity denoted by supply. The catch again is that the other-things-equal assumption underlying the upsloping supply curve was violated. Poor coffee harvests decreased supply, as in Figure 3-7(d), increasing the equilibrium price of coffee and reducing the equilibrium quantity.

These examples emphasize the importance of our earlier distinction between a change in quantity demanded (or supplied) and a change in demand (supply). In Figure 3-7(a) a change in demand causes a change in the quantity supplied. In Figure 3-7(d) a change in supply causes a change in quantity demanded.

3.5　Application: Government-set Prices

Prices in most markets are free to rise or fall to their equilibrium levels, no matter how high or low that might be. However, government sometimes concludes that supply and demand will produce prices that are unfairly high for buyers or unfairly low for sellers. So government may place legal limits on how high or low a price or prices may go. Is that a good idea?

Price Ceilings and Shortages

price ceiling
A legally established maximum price for a good or service.

A **price ceiling** is the maximum legal price a seller may charge for a product or service. A price at or below the ceiling is legal; a price above it is not. The rationale for establishing price ceilings (or ceiling prices) on specific products is that they purportedly enable consumers to obtain some essential good or service that they could not afford at the equilibrium price. Examples are rent controls and usury laws, which specify maximum prices in the forms of rent and interest that can be charged to borrowers. Also, the government has at times imposed price ceilings either on all products or on a very wide range of products—so-called price controls—to try to restrain inflation. Price controls were invoked in Canada during World War II and in the 1970s.

GRAPHICAL ANALYSIS

To be effective, a price ceiling on gasoline must be below the equilibrium price.

We can easily demonstrate the effects of price ceilings graphically. Let's suppose that rapidly rising world income boosts the purchase of automobiles and shifts the demand for gasoline to the right so that the equilibrium or market price reaches $1.25 per litre, shown as P_0 in Figure 3-8. The rapidly rising price of gasoline greatly burdens low-income and moderate-income households who pressure the federal government to "do something." To keep gasoline affordable for these households, the government imposes a ceiling price, P_c, of $.75 per litre. To be effective, a price ceiling must be below the equilibrium price. A ceiling price of $1.50, for example, would have no immediate effect on the gasoline market.

What are the effects of this $.75 ceiling price? The rationing ability of the free market is rendered ineffective. Because the ceiling price, P_c, is below the market-clearing price, P_0, there is a shortage of gasoline. The quantity of gasoline demanded at P_c is Q_d and the quantity supplied is only Q_s; an excess demand or shortage of amount $Q_d - Q_s$ occurs.

The important point is that the price ceiling, P_c, prevents the usual market adjustment in which competition among buyers bids up price, inducing more production and rationing some buyers out of the market. That process would continue until the shortage disappeared at the equilibrium price and quantity, P_0 and Q_0.

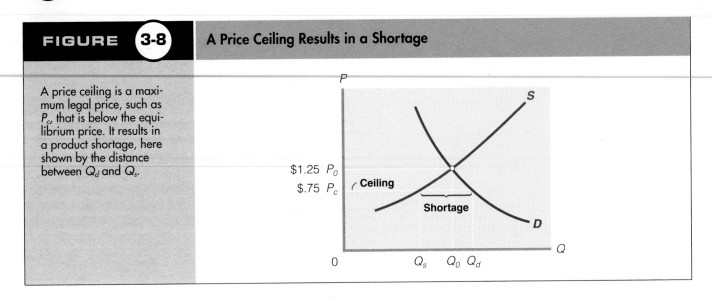

FIGURE 3-8

A Price Ceiling Results in a Shortage

A price ceiling is a maximum legal price, such as P_c, that is below the equilibrium price. It results in a product shortage, here shown by the distance between Q_d and Q_s.

RATIONING PROBLEM

How will the government apportion the available supply, Q_s, among buyers who want the greater amount Q_d? Should gasoline be distributed on a first-come, first-served basis, that is, to those willing and able to get in line the soonest and to stay in line? Or should gas stations distribute it on the basis of favouritism? Since an unregulated shortage does not lead to an equitable distribution of gasoline, the federal government must establish some formal system for rationing it to consumers. One option is to issue ration coupons, which allow coupon-holders to purchase a fixed amount of gasoline per month. The rationing system would require the printing of coupons for Q_s litres of gasoline and then the equitable distribution of the coupons among consumers so that the wealthy family of four and the poor family of four both receive the same number of coupons.

BLACK MARKETS

Ration coupons would not prevent a second problem from arising. The demand curve in Figure 3-8 tells us that many buyers are willing to pay more than the ceiling price P_c, and, of course, it is more profitable for gasoline stations to sell at prices above the ceiling. Thus, despite the sizable enforcement bureaucracy that will accompany the price controls, *black markets* in which gasoline is illegally bought and sold at prices above the legal limits will flourish. Counterfeiting of ration coupons will also be a problem, and since the price of gasoline is now set by the federal government, there would be political pressure to set the price even lower.

CREDIT CARD INTEREST CEILINGS

Over the years there have been many calls in Canada for interest-rate ceilings on credit card accounts. The usual rationale for interest-rate ceilings is that the chartered banks and retail stores issuing such cards are presumably taking unfair advantage of users and, in particular, lower-income users by charging interest rates that average about 18 percent per year.

What might be the responses if the Canadian government imposed a below-equilibrium interest rate on credit cards? The lower interest income associated with a legal interest ceiling would require the issuers of cards to reduce their costs or enhance their revenues:

- Card issuers might tighten credit standards to reduce losses due to non-payment and collection costs. Then, low-income and young Canadians who have not yet established their creditworthiness would find it more difficult to obtain credit cards.

- The annual fee charged to cardholders might be increased, as might the fee charged to merchants for processing credit card sales. Similarly, card users might be charged a fee for every transaction.

- Card users now have a post-purchase grace period during which the credit provided is interest-free. That period might be shortened or eliminated.

- Certain "enhancements" that accompany some credit cards (for example, extended warranties on products bought with a card) might be eliminated.

- Retail stores, such as Hudson's Bay Company, that issue their own cards might increase their prices to help offset the decline of interest income; customers who pay cash would in effect be subsidizing customers who use credit cards.

Price Floors and Surpluses

price floors
Legally determined prices above equilibrium prices.

Supported prices for some agricultural products are an example of price floors.

Price floors are minimum prices fixed by the government. A price at or above the price floor is legal; a price below it is not. Price floors above equilibrium prices are usually invoked when society believes that the free functioning of the market system has not provided a sufficient income for certain groups of resource suppliers or producers. Supported prices for some agricultural products and current minimum wages are two examples of price (or wage) floors. Let's look at the former.

Suppose the equilibrium price for wheat is $3 per bushel and, because of that low price, many Prairie farmers have extremely low incomes. The federal government decides to help by establishing a legal price floor or price support of $4 per bushel.

What will be the effects? At any price above the equilibrium price, quantity supplied will exceed quantity demanded—that is, there will be an excess supply or surplus of the product. Prairie farmers will be willing to produce and offer for sale more than private buyers are willing to purchase at the price floor. As we saw with a price ceiling, an imposed legal price disrupts the rationing ability of the free market.

Figure 3-9 illustrates the effect of a price floor. Suppose that S and D are the supply and demand curves for wheat. Equilibrium price and quantity are P_0 and Q_0, respectively. If the federal government imposes a price floor of P_f, farmers will produce Q_s, but private buyers will purchase only Q_d. The surplus is the excess of Q_s over Q_d.

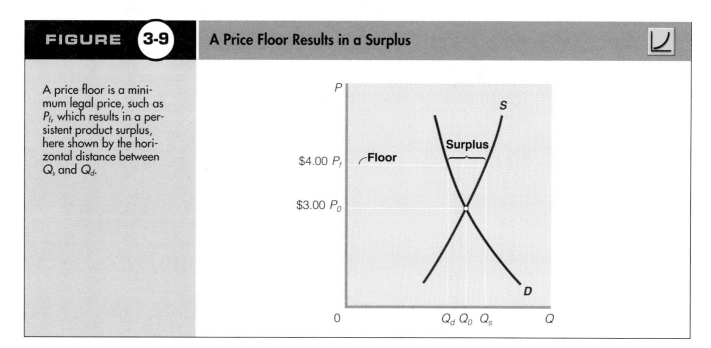

FIGURE 3-9	**A Price Floor Results in a Surplus**

A price floor is a minimum legal price, such as P_f, which results in a persistent product surplus, here shown by the horizontal distance between Q_s and Q_d.

The government can cope with the surplus resulting from a price floor in only two ways:

1. It can restrict supply (for example, by asking farmers in Alberta, Saskatchewan, and Manitoba to agree to take a certain amount of land out of production) or increase demand (for example, by researching new uses for the product involved). These actions may reduce the difference between the equilibrium price and the price floor and thereby reduce the size of the resulting surplus.

2. The federal government can purchase the surplus output at the $4 price (thereby subsidizing Prairie farmers) and store or otherwise dispose of it.

Controversial Tradeoffs

In a free market, the competitive forces match the supply decisions of producers and the demand decisions of buyers, but price ceilings and floors interfere with such an outcome. The government must provide a rationing system to handle product shortages stemming from price ceilings and devise ways to eliminate product surpluses arising from price floors. Legal maximum and minimum prices thus lead to controversial tradeoffs. The alleged benefits of price ceilings to consumers and price floors to producers must be balanced against the costs associated with shortages and surpluses.

Our discussion of price controls and interest-rate ceilings on credit cards shows that government interference with the market can have unintended, undesirable side effects. Price controls, for example, create illegal black markets. Rent controls may discourage housing construction and repair. Instead of protecting low-income families from higher interest charges, interest-rate ceilings may simply deny credit to those families. For all these reasons, economists generally oppose government-imposed prices.

ADDITIONAL CONSEQUENCES

Price floors such as P_f in Figure 3.9 not only disrupt the rationing ability of prices but also distort resource allocation. Without the price floor, the $3 equilibrium price of wheat would cause financial losses and force high-cost wheat producers to plant other crops or abandon farming altogether. But the $4 price floor allows them to continue to grow wheat and remain farmers. So society devotes too many of its scarce resources to wheat production and too little to producing other, more valuable, goods and services. It fails to achieve allocative efficiency.

That's not all. Consumers of wheat-based products pay higher prices because of the price floor. Taxpayers pay higher taxes to finance the government's purchase of the surplus. Also, the price floor causes potential environmental damage by encouraging wheat farmers to bring "marginal land" into production. The higher price also prompts imports of wheat. But, since such imports would increase the quantity of wheat supplied and thus undermine the price floor, the government needs to erect tariffs (taxes on imports) to keep the foreign wheat out. Such tariffs usually prompt other countries to retaliate with their own tariffs against Canadian agricultural or manufacturing exports.

 It is easy to see why economists "raise the caution flag" when politicians advocate imposing price ceilings or price floors. In both cases, good intentions typically lead to bad economic outcomes. *(Key Question 12)*

QUICK REVIEW

- In competitive markets, prices adjust to the equilibrium level at which quantity demanded equals quantity supplied.

- The equilibrium price and quantity are those indicated by the intersection of the supply and demand curves for any product or resource.

- An increase in demand increases equilibrium price and quantity; a decrease in demand decreases equilibrium price and quantity.

- An increase in supply reduces equilibrium price but increases equilibrium quantity; a decrease in supply increases equilibrium price but reduces equilibrium quantity.

- Over time, equilibrium price and quantity may change in directions that seem at odds with the laws of demand and supply because the other-things-equal assumption is violated.

THE LASTword   Ticket Scalping: A Bum Rap?

Some market transactions get a bad name that is not warranted.

The Effectiveness of Markets

Tickets to athletic and artistic events are sometimes resold at higher-than-original prices—a market transaction known by the term "scalping." For example, the original buyer may resell a $50 ticket to an NHL game for $200, $250, or more. The media often denounce scalpers for "ripping off" buyers by charging "exorbitant" prices. Scalping and extortion are synonymous in some people's minds.

But is scalping really sinful? We must first recognize that such ticket resales are voluntary transactions. Both buyer and seller expect to gain from the exchange. Otherwise it would not occur! The seller must value the $200 more than seeing the event, and the buyer must value seeing the event more than the $200. So there are no losers or victims here: Both buyer and seller benefit from the transaction. The

"scalping" market simply redistributes assets (game or concert tickets) from those who value them less to those who value them more.

Does scalping impose losses or injury on other parties, in particular the sponsors of the event? If the sponsors are injured, it is because they initially priced tickets below the equilibrium level. In so doing they suffer an economic loss in the form of less revenue and profit than they might have otherwise received. But the loss is self-inflicted because of their pricing error.

That mistake is quite separate and distinct from the fact that some tickets were later sold at a higher price.

What about spectators? Does scalping deteriorate the enthusiasm of the audience? No! People who have the greatest interest in the event will pay the scalper's high prices. Ticket scalping also benefits the teams and performing artists, because they will appear before more dedicated audiences—ones that are more likely to buy souvenir items or CDs.

So, is ticket scalping undesirable? Not on economic grounds. Both seller and buyer of a "scalped" ticket benefit, and a more interested audience results. Event sponsors may sacrifice revenue and profits, but that stems from their own misjudgment of the equilibrium price.

CHAPTER SUMMARY

3.1 MARKETS

- A market is an institution or arrangement that brings together buyers and sellers of a product, service, or resource for the purpose of exchange.

3.2 DEMAND

- Demand is a schedule or curve representing the willingness of buyers in a specific period to purchase a particular product at each of various prices. The law of demand implies that consumers will buy more of a product at a low price than at a high price. Therefore, other things equal, the relationship between price and quantity demanded is negative or inverse and is graphed as a downsloping curve. Market demand curves are found by adding horizontally the demand curves of the many individual consumers in the market.

- Changes in one or more of the determinants of demand (consumer tastes, the number of buyers in the market, the money incomes of consumers, the prices of related goods, and price expectations) shift the market demand curve. A shift to the right is an increase in demand; a shift to the left is a decrease in demand. A change in demand is different from a change in the quantity demanded, the latter being a movement from one point to another point on a fixed demand curve because of a change in the product's price.

3.3 SUPPLY

- Supply is a schedule or curve showing the amounts of a product that producers are willing to offer in the market at each possible price during a specific period. The law of supply states that, other things equal, producers will offer more of a product at a high price than at a low price. Thus, the relationship between price and quantity supplied is positive or direct, and supply is graphed as an upsloping curve. The market supply curve is the horizontal summation of the supply curves of the individual producers of the product.

- Changes in one or more of the determinants of supply (resource prices, production techniques, taxes or subsidies, the prices of other goods, price expectations, or the number of sellers in the market) shift the supply curve of a product. A shift to the right is an increase in supply; a shift to the left is a decrease in supply. In contrast, a change in the price of the product being considered causes a change in the quantity supplied, which is shown as a movement from one point to another point on a fixed supply curve.

3.4 SUPPLY AND DEMAND: MARKET EQUILIBRIUM

- The equilibrium price and quantity are established at the intersection of the supply and demand curves. The interaction of market demand and market supply adjusts the price to the point at which the quantity demanded and supplied are equal. This is the equilibrium price. The corresponding quantity is the equilibrium quantity.

- The ability of market forces to synchronize selling and buying decisions to eliminate potential surpluses and shortages is known as the rationing function of prices.

- A change in either demand or supply changes the equilibrium price and quantity. Increases in demand raise both equilibrium price and equilibrium quantity; decreases in demand lower both equilibrium price and equilibrium quantity. Increases in supply lower equilibrium price and raise equilibrium quantity; decreases in supply raise equilibrium price and lower equilibrium quantity.

- Simultaneous changes in demand and supply affect equilibrium price and quantity in various ways, depending on their direction and relative magnitudes.

3.5 APPLICATION: GOVERNMENT-SET PRICES

- A price ceiling is a maximum price set by government and is designed to help consumers. A price floor is a minimum price set by government and is designed to aid producers.

- Legally fixed prices stifle the rationing function of prices and distort the allocation of resources. Effective price ceilings produce persistent product shortages, and if an equitable distribution of the product is sought, government must ration the product to consumers. Price floors lead to product surpluses; the government must either purchase the product or eliminate the surplus by imposing restrictions on production or increasing private demand.

TERMS AND CONCEPTS

market, p. 48
demand, p. 48
law of demand, p. 49
marginal utility, p. 49
income effect, p. 50

substitution effect, p. 50
demand curve, p. 50
determinants of demand, p. 50
normal good, p. 53
inferior good, p. 53

substitute goods, p. 53
complementary goods, p. 53
change in demand, p. 54
change in quantity demanded, p. 54
supply, p. 55

STUDY QUESTIONS

1. Explain the law of demand. Why does a demand curve slope downward? What are the determinants of demand? What happens to the demand curve when each of these determinants changes? Distinguish between a change in demand and a change in the quantity demanded, noting the cause(s) of each.

2. **KEY QUESTION**   What effect will each of the following have on the demand for product B?

   a. Product B becomes more fashionable.

   b. The price of substitute product C falls.

   c. Income declines and product B is an inferior good.

   d. Consumers anticipate the price of product B will be lower in the near future.

   e. The price of complementary product D falls.

3. Explain the following news dispatch from Hull, England: "The fish market here slumped today to what local commentators called 'a disastrous level'—all because of a shortage of potatoes. The potatoes are one of the main ingredients in a dish that figures on almost every café menu—fish and chips."

4. Explain the law of supply. Why does the supply curve slope upward? What are the determinants of supply? What happens to the supply curve when each of these determinants changes? Distinguish between a change in supply and a change in the quantity supplied, noting the cause(s) of each.

5. **KEY QUESTION**   What effect will each of the following have on the supply of product B?

   a. A technological advance in the methods of producing product B.

   b. A decline in the number of firms in industry B.

   c. An increase in the prices of resources required in the production of B.

   d. The expectation that the equilibrium price of B will be lower in the future than it is currently.

   e. A decline in the price of product A, a good whose production requires substantially the same techniques and resources as does the production of B.

   f. The levying of a specific sales tax on B.

   g. The granting of a 50-cent per-unit subsidy for each unit of B produced.

6. "In the corn market, demand often exceeds supply and supply sometimes exceeds demand." "The price of corn rises and falls in response to changes in supply and demand." In which of these two statements are the terms *supply* and *demand* used correctly? Explain.

7. **KEY QUESTION**   Suppose the total demand for wheat and the total supply of wheat per month in the Winnipeg grain market are as follows:

Thousands of bushels demanded	Price per bushel	Thousands of bushels supplied	Surplus (+) or shortage (−)
85	$3.40	72	_____
80	$3.70	73	_____
75	$4.00	75	_____
70	$4.30	77	_____
65	$4.60	79	_____
60	$4.90	81	_____

   a. What is the equilibrium price? What is the equilibrium quantity? Fill in the surplus–shortage column and use it to explain why your answers are correct.

   b. Graph the demand for wheat and the supply of wheat. Be sure to label the axes of your graph correctly. Label equilibrium price *P* and equilibrium quantity *Q*.

   c. Why will $3.40 not be the equilibrium price in this market? Why not $4.90? "Surpluses drive prices up; shortages drive them down." Do you agree?

8. **KEY QUESTION**   How will each of the following changes in demand and/or supply affect equilibrium price and equilibrium quantity in a competitive market; that is, do price and quantity rise, fall, or remain unchanged, or are the answers indeterminate because they depend on the magnitudes of the shifts? Use supply and demand diagrams to verify your answers.

   a. Supply decreases and demand is constant.

   b. Demand decreases and supply is constant.

   c. Supply increases and demand is constant.

   d. Demand increases and supply increases.

   e. Demand increases and supply is constant.

   f. Supply increases and demand decreases.

g. Demand increases and supply decreases.

h. Demand decreases and supply decreases.

9. In 2001, an outbreak of foot-and-mouth disease in Europe led to the burning of millions of cattle carcasses. What impact do you think this had on the supply of cattle hides, hide prices, the supply of leather goods, and the price of leather goods?

10. Explain: "Even though parking meters may yield little or no revenue, they should nevertheless be retained because of the rationing function they perform."

11. Refer to the table in Question 7. Suppose that the government establishes a price ceiling of $3.70 for wheat. What might prompt the government to establish this price ceiling? Explain carefully the main effects. Demonstrate your answer graphically. Next, suppose that the government establishes a price floor of $4.60 for wheat. What will be the main effects of this price floor? Demonstrate your answer graphically.

12. **KEY QUESTION**   What do economists mean when they say that "price floors and ceilings stifle the rationing function of prices and distort resource allocation?"

13. Critically evaluate: "In comparing the two equilibrium positions in Figure 13-7(a), I note that a larger amount is actually purchased at a higher price. This refutes the law of demand."

14. **Advanced analysis:** Assume that demand for a commodity is represented by the equation $P = 10 - .2Q_d$ and supply by the equation $P = 2 + .2Q_s$, where Q_d and Q_s are quantity demanded and quantity supplied, respectively, and P is price. Using the equilibrium condition $Q_s = Q_d$, solve the equations to determine equilibrium price. Now determine equilibrium quantity. Graph the two equations to substantiate your answers.

15. **(Last Word)** Discuss the economic aspects of ticket scalping, specifying gainers and losers.

INTERNET APPLICATION QUESTION

1. **Changes in Demand—Baby Diapers and Retirement Villages** Other things equal, an increase in the number of buyers for a product or service will increase demand. Baby diapers and retirement villages are two products designed for different population groups. The McConnell-Brue-Barbiero Web site (Chapter 3) provides links to population pyramids (graphs that show the distribution of population by age and sex) for countries for the current year, 2025, and 2050. View the population pyramids for Mexico, Japan, and Canada. Which country would you expect to have the greatest percentage increase in demand for baby diapers in the year 2050? For retirement villages? Which country would you expect to have the greatest absolute increase in demand for baby diapers? For retirement villages?

Math Appendix to Chapter 3

A3.1   The Mathematics of Market Equilibrium

A market equilibrium is the price and the quantity, denoted as the pair (Q^*, P^*), of a commodity bought or sold at price P^*. The following mathematical note provides an introduction of how a market equilibrium (Q^*, P^*) is derived.

The market equilibrium is found by using the market demand (buyers' behaviour), the market supply (sellers' behaviour), and the negotiating process (to find the agreed upon price and quantity, namely P^* and Q^*, on which to transact). The market equilibrium is identified by the condition reached at the end of the negotiating process that at the price they negotiated, P^*, the quantity of the commodity that buyers are willing to buy, denoted as Q_d, and the quantity sellers are willing to sell, denoted as Q_s, matches exactly.

The Demand Curve

The equation describing the downward sloping demand when the demand curve is a straight line, in which Q_d represents the quantity demanded by buyers and P the price, is

$$P = a - bQ_d$$

The demand equation and curve below tell us that if the price is higher than a then the buyers will not buy; thus, for a transaction to occur the price must be lower. The demand equation and curve also tell us that at a price lower than a the quantity demanded by the buyers increases. Buyers' behaviour, as described by the demand equation, is that at lower prices buyers buy more quantity.

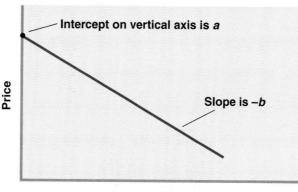

Intercept on vertical axis is *a*

Slope is *−b*

Price

Quantity demanded

The Supply Curve

The equation describing the upward sloping market supply function when the supply curve is a straight line, in which Q_s represents the quantity supplied by sellers and P the price, is

$$P = c + dQ_s$$

If the price is lower than c then the sellers will sell nothing, as the figure below shows. If the price is c or higher, then the supply equation states that sellers facing higher prices sell more quantity. Sellers' behaviour, as described by the supply curve and equation, is that at higher prices sellers make more quantity available.

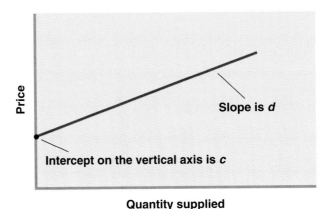

Quantity supplied

The Market Equilibrium

The negotiating process (in which price and quantity or both adjust) provides the mechanism by which, eventually, buyers and sellers agree upon a price, P^*, and a quantity, Q^*, at which they can buy and sell and thus complete the transaction. At the end of the negotiating process, the quantity demanded by the buyers, Q_d, is equal to the quantity supplied by the sellers, Q_s (at the agreed-upon price), and thus the market is in equilibrium. The mathematical representation of such a negotiating process is described as follows.

At the agreed price, P^*, the equilibrium condition of the negotiating process, the equality in the quantity demanded and supplied, is

$$Q_d = Q_s$$

Having denoted Q^* as the equilibrium quantity, then it must be that $Q^* = Q_d = Q_s$. To solve for the equilibrium quantity Q^* and the equilibrium price P^* the demand and supply functions are used. With Q^* the equilibrium quantity, for the buyers

$$P^* = a - bQ^*,$$

and for the sellers

$$P^* = c + dQ^*.$$

Now, since P^* is the same agreed-upon price by both buyer and seller, then

$$a - bQ^* = c + dQ^*,$$

giving the equilibrium quantity, Q^*, as

$$Q^* = \frac{(a - c)}{(b + d)}.$$

To find P^* substitute $\dfrac{(a-c)}{(b+d)}$ in the supply (or demand) function.

$$P^* = c + d\,\frac{(a-c)}{(b+d)},\ \text{thus}$$

$$P^* = \frac{(ad+bc)}{(b+d)}.$$

The equilibrium is $(Q^*, P^*) = \left[\dfrac{(a-c)}{(b+d)}, \dfrac{(ad+bc)}{(b+d)}\right]$.

The market equilibrium may also be represented diagrammatically, as shown below.

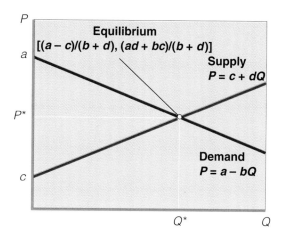

Example

Assume the demand for a pair of jeans is represented by the equation:

$$P = 100 - .2Q_d$$

Assume the supply of a pair of jeans is represented by the equation:

$$P = 20 + .2Q_s$$

Assume quantities are expressed in jeans per day, and the price in dollars.

To find the equilibrium price P^*, and equilibrium quantity Q^*, substitute Q^* for Q_d and Q_s and P^* for P in the demand and supply equations. To solve for Q^*:

$$100 - .2Q^* = 20 + .2Q^*$$

$$.4Q^* = 80$$

$$Q^* = 200$$

To solve for P^*:

$$P^* = 100 - .2(200)$$

$$= 60$$

The equilibrium quantity of jeans is 200 per day, and the equilibrium price is $60 per pair of jeans.

4

Chapter

The Market System and International Trade

Suppose that you were assigned to compile a list of all the individual goods and services available at a large shopping mall, including the different brands and variations of each type of product. We think you would agree that this task would be daunting and the list would be long! And, although a single shopping mall contains a remarkable quantity and variety of goods, it is only a minuscule part of the Canadian economy.

Who decided that the particular goods and services available at the mall and in the broader economy should be produced? How did the producers determine which technology and types of resources to use in producing these particular goods? Who will obtain these products? What accounts for the new and improved products among these goods?

In Chapter 3 we saw how equilibrium prices and quantities are established in *individual* product and factor markets. We now widen our focus to take in *all* product markets and factor markets, variously referred to as *capitalism, the private enterprise system,* or simply the *market system*. In this chapter we examine the characteristics of the market system and how it addresses the economic problem. We then look at international markets and Canada's trade with the rest of the world.

4.1   Characteristics of the Market System

A market brings together buyers and sellers for the purpose of exchange. It can be a local market in which relatively few people participate, or it can be on an international scale where hundreds of millions of buyers and sellers from all over the globe participate. In order for the market system to function, several characteristics must be present: private property, freedom of enterprise and choice, self-interest as the dominant motive, competition, and a limited role for government.

Private Property

private property
The right of private persons and firms to obtain, own, control, employ, dispose of, and bequeath land, capital, and other property.

In a market system, individuals and firms, not the government, own most of the property resources (land and capital). In fact, it is the private ownership of capital that gives capitalism its name. This right of **private property**, coupled with the freedom to negotiate binding legal contracts, enables individuals and businesses to obtain, use, and dispose of property resources as they see fit. Also, with private property rights owners can designate who will receive their property when they die.

Property rights encourage investment, innovation, exchange, maintenance of property, and the expansion of the production of goods and services. Individuals stock stores, build factories, or clear land for farming because they can reap the rewards. Why would they do so if the government, or anyone else, could take that property from them?

Property rights also extend to intellectual property through patents, copyrights, and trademarks. Long-term protection encourages people to write books, music, and computer programs and to invent new products and production processes without fear that others will steal them and the rewards they may bring.

Property rights also facilitate exchange. The title to an automobile or the deed to a cattle ranch assures the buyer that the seller is the legitimate owner. Moreover, property rights encourage owners to maintain or improve their property so as to preserve or increase its value. Finally, property rights enable people to use their time and resources to produce more goods and services, rather than using them to protect and retain the property they have already produced or acquired.

If property rights did not exist, or were not enforced, it would make market exchange much more costly; it would also increase the price of goods and services exchanged on markets. Buyers would have to ascertain the origins of what they bought, and property would need to be protected from burglars.

Freedom of Enterprise and Choice

freedom of enterprise
The freedom of firms to obtain economic resources, to use these resources to produce products of the firm's own choosing, and to sell their products in markets of their choice.

Closely related to private ownership of property is freedom of enterprise and choice. The market system requires that various economic units make choices, which are expressed and implemented in the economy's markets.

- **Freedom of enterprise** ensures that entrepreneurs and private businesses are free to obtain and use resources to produce their choice of goods and services, and to sell them in the markets of their choice.

freedom of choice
The freedom of owners of property resources to employ or dispose of them as they see fit, and of consumers to spend their incomes in a manner that they think is appropriate.

- **Freedom of choice** allows owners to employ or dispose of their property and money as they see fit. It also allows workers to enter any line of work for which they are qualified. Finally, it ensures that consumers are free to buy the goods and services that best satisfy their wants.

These choices are free only within broad legal limitations, of course. Illegal choices such as selling human organs or buying illicit drugs are punished through fines and imprisonment. (Global Perspective 4.1 reveals that the degree of economic freedom varies greatly from nation to nation.)

Self-interest

self-interest
That which each firm, property owner, worker, and consumer believes is best for itself.

In the market system, **self-interest** is the motivating force of all the various economic units as they express their free choices. Self-interest means that each economic unit tries to do what is best for itself. Entrepreneurs try to maximize profit or minimize loss. Property owners try to get the highest price for the sale or rent of their resources. Workers try to maximize their utility (satisfaction) by finding jobs that offer the best combination of wages, hours, fringe benefits, and working conditions. Consumers try to obtain the products they want at the lowest possible price and apportion their expenditures to maximize their utility.

The pursuit of self-interest is not the same as selfishness. Self-interest simply means maximizing some benefit, and can include helping others. A stockholder in Halifax may invest to receive the best available corporate dividends and then donate a portion of them to the local United Way or give them to grandchildren. A worker in Winnipeg may take a second job to help pay college or university tuition for her or his children. An entrepreneur in Toronto may make a fortune and donate much of it to a charitable foundation.

Competition

competition
The presence in a market of a large number of independent buyers and sellers competing with one another and the freedom of buyers and sellers to enter and leave the market.

The market system fosters **competition** among economic units. The basis of this competition is freedom of choice exercised in pursuit of the best return. Very broadly defined, *competition* requires:

- Independently acting sellers and buyers operating in a particular product or factor market

- Freedom of sellers and buyers to enter or leave markets, based on their self-interest

Competition diffuses economic power within the businesses and households that make up the economy. When there are independently acting sellers and buyers in a market, no one buyer or seller is able to dictate the price of the product.

Consider the supply side of the product market. When a product becomes scarce, its price rises. An unseasonable frost in Southern Ontario may seriously reduce the supply of apple crops and sharply increase the price of apples. Similarly, if a single producer can restrict the total output of a product, the product's price will rise. By controlling market supply, a firm can "rig the market" to its own advantage. But that is not possible in markets in which suppliers compete. A firm that raises its price will lose part or all of its business to competitors.

The same reasoning applies to the demand side of the market. With multiple buyers, single buyers cannot manipulate the market to their own advantage by refusing to pay the market price.

Competition also implies that producers can enter or leave an industry; there are no insurmountable barriers to an industry expanding or contracting. This freedom of an industry to expand or contract provides the economy with the flexibility needed to remain efficient over time. Freedom of entry and exit enables the economy to adjust to changes in consumer tastes, technology, and resource availability.

The diffusion of economic power inherent in competition limits the potential abuse of that power. A producer who charges more than the competitive market price will lose sales to other producers. An employer who pays less than the competitive market wage will lose workers to other employers. A firm that fails to exploit new technology will lose profits to firms that do. Competition is the basic regulatory force in the market system.

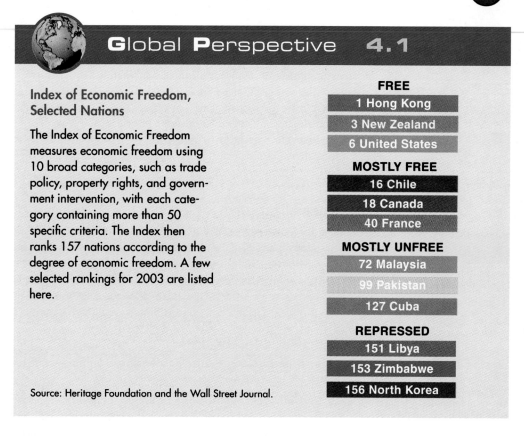

Global Perspective 4.1

Index of Economic Freedom, Selected Nations

The Index of Economic Freedom measures economic freedom using 10 broad categories, such as trade policy, property rights, and government intervention, with each category containing more than 50 specific criteria. The Index then ranks 157 nations according to the degree of economic freedom. A few selected rankings for 2003 are listed here.

Source: Heritage Foundation and the Wall Street Journal.

FREE
1 Hong Kong
3 New Zealand
6 United States

MOSTLY FREE
16 Chile
18 Canada
40 France

MOSTLY UNFREE
72 Malaysia
99 Pakistan
127 Cuba

REPRESSED
151 Libya
153 Zimbabwe
156 North Korea

Markets and Prices

Markets and prices are key characteristics of the market system. They give the market system its ability to coordinate millions of daily economic decisions. A market system is necessary to convey the decisions made by buyers and sellers of products and resources. The decisions made on each side of the market determine a set of product and resource prices that guide resource owners, entrepreneurs, and consumers as they make and revise their choices and pursue what is best for themselves.

The market system is an organizing mechanism. It serves as an elaborate communication network through which innumerable individual free choices are recorded, summarized, and balanced. Those who respond to market signals and obey market dictates are rewarded with greater profit and income; those who do not respond to these signals and choose to ignore market dictates are penalized. Through this mechanism millions of independent decisions by producers and consumers determine what the economy should produce, how production can be organized efficiently, and how the fruits of production are to be distributed among the various units that make up the economy.

Active but Limited Government

Another characteristic of the market system, as evidenced in modern economies, is an active but limited government. Although a market system promotes a high degree of efficiency in the use of its resources, it has certain shortcomings. We will discover later in this chapter that government can increase the overall effectiveness of the economic system in several ways.

Technology and Capital Goods

The market system facilitates the extensive use of capital goods. In the market system, competition, freedom of choice, self-interest, and personal reward provide the opportunity and motivation for technological advance. The monetary rewards for new products or production techniques accrue directly to the innovator. The market system therefore encourages extensive use and rapid development of complex capital goods: tools, machinery, large-scale factories, and facilities for storage, communication, transportation, and marketing.

roundabout production
The construction and use of capital to aid in the production of consumer goods.

Advanced technology and capital goods are important because the most direct methods of production are the least efficient. The only way to avoid that inefficiency is to rely on **roundabout production**. It would be ridiculous for a Prairie farmer to go at production with bare hands. There are huge benefits—in the form of more efficient production and, therefore, a more abundant output— to be derived from creating and using such tools of production (capital equipment) as plows, tractors, storage bins, and so on.

Specialization

specialization
The use of the resources of an individual, a firm, a region, or a nation to produce one or a few goods and services.

The extent to which market economies rely on **specialization** is extraordinary. The majority of consumers produce virtually none of the goods and services they consume, and they consume little or nothing of what they produce. The worker who devotes eight hours a day to installing windows in Fords may own a Honda. Many farmers sell their milk to the local dairy and then buy margarine at the local grocery store. Society learned long ago that self-sufficiency breeds inefficiency. The jack-of-all-trades may be a very colourful individual but is certainly not an efficient producer.

DIVISION OF LABOUR

division of labour
Dividing the work required to produce a product into a number of different tasks that are performed by different workers.

Human specialization—called the **division of labour**—contributes to a society's output in several ways.

- *Specialization makes use of differences in ability.*   Specialization enables individuals to take advantage of existing differences in their abilities and skills. If caveman A is strong and swift, and good at tracking animals, and caveman B is weak and slow but patient, their distribution of talents can be most efficiently used if A hunts and B fishes.

- *Specialization fosters learning by doing.*   Even if the abilities of A and B are identical, specialization may still be advantageous. By devoting all your time to a single task, you are more likely to develop the skills it requires and to devise improved techniques than you would by working at a number of different tasks. You learn to be a good hunter by going hunting every day.

- *Specialization saves time.*   By devoting all your time to a single task you avoid the loss of time incurred in shifting from one job to another.

For all these reasons, specialization increases the total output society can get from limited resources.

GEOGRAPHIC SPECIALIZATION

Specialization also works on a regional and international basis. It is conceivable that apples could be grown in Saskatchewan, but because of the unsuitability of the land, rainfall, and temperature, the costs would be very high. And it is conceivable that wheat could be grown in British Columbia. But for similar reasons such production would be costly. So, Saskatchewan farmers produce products—wheat in particular—for which their resources are best suited, and British Columbians (in the Okanagan Valley) do the same, producing apples and other fruits. By specializing, both provinces' economies produce more than is needed locally. Then, very sensibly, they exchange some of their surpluses—wheat for apples, apples for wheat.

Similarly, on an international scale, Canada specializes in producing such items as telecommunication equipment (Nortel Networks) and small commercial aircraft (Bombardier), which it sells abroad in exchange for video recorders from Japan, bananas from Honduras, and woven baskets from Thailand. Both human specialization and geographical specialization are needed to achieve efficiency in the use of limited resources.

Use of Money

Specialization and trade require the use of money. Money performs several functions, but first and foremost it is a **medium of exchange**. It makes trade easier.

A convenient means of exchanging goods is required for specialization. Exchange can, and sometimes does, occur through **barter**—swapping goods for goods, say, wheat for apples. But barter poses serious problems for the economy because it requires a *coincidence of wants* between the buyer and seller. In our example, we assumed that Saskatchewan had excess wheat to trade and wanted apples. And we assumed that British Columbia had excess apples to trade and wanted wheat. So an exchange occurred. But if such a coincidence of wants is missing, trade cannot occur.

Suppose Saskatchewan has no interest in British Columbia's apples but wants potatoes from Prince Edward Island. And suppose that Prince Edward Island wants British Columbia's apples but not Saskatchewan's wheat. And, to complicate matters, suppose that British Columbia wants some of Saskatchewan's wheat but none of PEI's potatoes. We summarize the situation in Figure 4-1.

In none of these cases shown in the figure is there a coincidence of wants, thus trade by barter clearly would be difficult. Instead, people in each province use **money**, which is simply a convenient social invention to facilitate exchanges of goods and services. Historically, people have used cattle, cigarettes, shells, stones, pieces of metal, and many other commodities, with varying degrees of success, as a medium of exchange. But to serve as money, an item needs to pass only one test: *It must be generally acceptable to sellers in exchange for their goods and services.* Money is socially defined; whatever society accepts as a medium of exchange *is* money.

Most economies use pieces of paper as money. The use of paper dollars (currency) as a medium of exchange is what enables Saskatchewan, B.C., and P.E.I. to overcome their non-coincidence of wants.

On a global basis the fact that different nations have different currencies complicates specialization and exchange. However, markets in which currencies are bought and sold make it possible for residents of Canada, Japan, Germany, Britain, and Mexico, through the swapping of dollars, yen, euros, pounds, and pesos, one for another, to exchange goods and services.

medium of exchange
Items sellers generally accept and buyers generally use to pay for a good or service.

barter
The exchange of one good or service for another good or service.

www.swp.com
Saskatchewan Wheat Pool

money
Any item that is generally acceptable to sellers in exchange for goods and services.

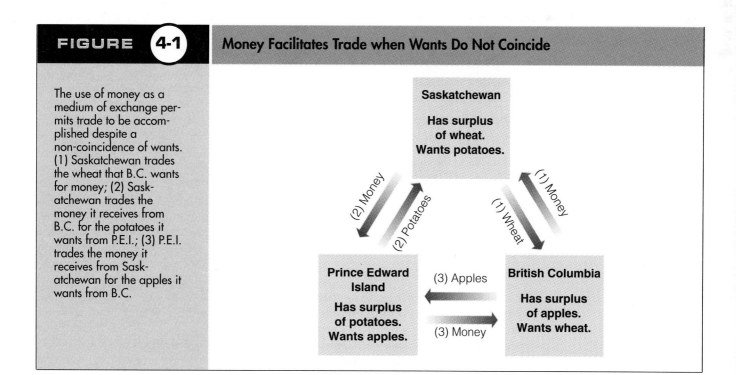

FIGURE 4-1

Money Facilitates Trade when Wants Do Not Coincide

The use of money as a medium of exchange permits trade to be accomplished despite a non-coincidence of wants. (1) Saskatchewan trades the wheat that B.C. wants for money; (2) Saskatchewan trades the money it receives from B.C. for the potatoes it wants from P.E.I.; (3) P.E.I. trades the money it receives from Saskatchewan for the apples it wants from B.C.

QUICK REVIEW

- The market system requires private ownership of property, freedom of enterprise, and freedom of choice.

- The market system permits economic entities—business, resource suppliers, and consumers—to pursue and further their self-interest. It prevents any single economic entity from dictating the prices of products or resources.

- The coordinating mechanism of the market system is a system of markets and prices.

- The market systems of modern industrial economies are characterized by extensive use of technologically advanced capital goods. Such goods help these economies achieve greater efficiency in production.

- Specialization is extensive in market systems; it enhances efficiency and output by enabling individuals, regions, and nations to produce those goods and services for which their resources are best suited.

- The use of money in market systems facilitates specialization and the exchange of goods and services.

4.2   The Market System at Work

household
An economic unit (of one or more persons) that provides the economy with resources and uses the income received to purchase goods and services that satisfy material wants.

firm
An organization that employs resources to produce a good or service for profit.

Four Fundamental Questions
The four questions that every economy must answer.

There are two primary *decision makers* in a market economy: **households** (consumers) and **firms** (businesses). Households are the ultimate suppliers of economic resources (factors of production) and simultaneously the major spending group in the economy. Firms provide goods and services to the economy.

We have noted that a market system is characterized by competition, freedom of enterprise, and choice. Consumers are free to buy what they choose; entrepreneurs and firms are free to produce and sell what they choose; and resource suppliers are free to make their property and human resources available in whatever use or occupation they choose. We may wonder why such an economy does not collapse in chaos. If Canadian consumers want breakfast cereal but businesses choose to produce athletic shoes and resource suppliers decide to manufacture computer software, production would seem to be deadlocked by the apparent inconsistency of these free choices.

In reality, the millions of decisions made by Canadian households and businesses are highly consistent with one another. Firms *do* produce the goods and services that consumers want, and households *do* provide the kinds of labour that businesses want.

To understand the operation of the market system, you must first recognize that every economy must address **Four Fundamental Questions**:

- What goods and services will be produced?

- How will the goods and services be produced?

- Who will get the goods and services?

- How will the system accommodate change?

The Four Fundamental Questions highlight the economic choices underlying the production possibilities curve discussed in Chapter 2. Let's examine how the market system answers each of these questions and thus addresses the economic problem.

What Will Be Produced?

With product and resource prices in place, established through competition in both the product and factor markets, what will determine the specific types and quantities of goods that will be produced in the market system? *Because businesses seek profits and avoid losses, those goods and services produced at a continuing profit* will *be produced and those produced at a continuing loss will not.* Profits and losses depend on the difference between the total revenue a firm receives from selling its product and the total cost of producing the product.

Consumers register their preferences on the demand side of the product market; producers and suppliers of factors of production respond appropriately in seeking to further their own welfare. The market system communicates the wants of consumers to businesses and suppliers of factors of production and elicits appropriate responses.

CONSUMER SOVEREIGNTY AND "DOLLAR VOTES"

consumer sovereignty
Determination by consumers of the types and quantities of goods and services that will be produced with the scarce resources of the economy.

dollar votes
The "votes" that consumers and entrepreneurs cast for the production of consumer and capital goods, respectively, when they purchase them in product and factor markets.

In the market system, consumers are sovereign (in command). **Consumer sovereignty** works through consumer demand, and consumer demand is crucial in determining the types and quantities of goods produced. Consumers spend the income they earn from the sale of their resources on those goods they are most willing and able to buy. Through these **dollar votes** consumers register their wants via the demand side of the product market. If the dollar votes for a certain product are great enough to provide a normal profit, businesses will produce that product. If there is an increase in consumer demand, so that enough dollar votes are cast to provide above normal profit, the industry will expand, as will the output of the product.

Conversely, a decrease in consumer demand—meaning fewer dollar votes cast for the product—will result in losses, and, in time, the industry will contract. As firms leave the industry, the output of the product will decline. Indeed, the industry may even cease to exist. Again, the consumers are sovereign; they collectively direct resources away from industries that are not meeting consumer wants and toward those industries that do.

The dollar votes of consumers determine not only which industries will continue to exist but also which products will survive or fail. Example: In 1991, responding to doctors and nutritionists, McDonald's introduced its low-fat McLean burger. Good idea? Not really. Most consumers found the new product "too dry" and "not tasty," so sales were meagre. In 1996 McDonald's quietly dropped the McLean burger from its menu at the same time that it introduced its higher-fat Arch Deluxe burger. In effect, consumers had collectively "voted out" the McLean burger.

MARKET RESTRAINTS ON FREEDOM

Firms are not really free to produce whatever they wish. Consumers' buying decisions make the production of some products profitable and the production of other products unprofitable, thus restricting the choice of firms in deciding what to produce. Firms must match their production choices with consumer choices or else face losses and eventual bankruptcy.

derived demand
The demand for a factor of production that depends on the demand for the products it can be used to produce.

The same holds true for suppliers of factors of production. The demand for factors is a **derived demand**—derived, that is, from the demand for the goods and services that the factors help produce. There is a demand for autoworkers in Canada because there is a demand for automobiles. There is no demand for buggy-whip braiders because there is no demand for buggy whips. Suppliers of factors of production are not free to allocate their resources to the production of goods that consumers do not value highly. Consumers register their preferences on the demand side of the product market; producers and factor suppliers, prompted by their own self-interest, respond appropriately.

How Will the Goods and Services Be Produced?

The market system steers resources (factors of production) to those industries that have products consumers want—simply because those industries survive, are profitable, and pay for resources. Within each industry, the firms that survive are the ones that are profitable. Because competition weeds out high-cost producers, continued profitability requires that firms produce their output at minimum cost. Achieving least-cost production necessitates, among other things, that firms locate their production facilities optimally, taking into consideration such variables as factor prices, factor productivity, and transportation costs. Least-cost production also means that firms must employ the most economically efficient technique of production in producing their output.

Who Will Get the Goods and Services?

The market system enters the picture in two ways when solving the problem of distributing total output. Generally, any product will be distributed to consumers based on their ability and willingness to pay its existing market price. If the price of some product, say, a pocket calculator, is $15, then those buyers who are able and willing to pay that price will get a pocket calculator. This is the rationing function of equilibrium prices.

The ability to pay the equilibrium prices for pocket calculators and other products depends on the amount of income that consumers earn. If they earn sufficient income and want to spend their money on a particular good, they can have it. The amount of income they earn depends on (1) the quantities of the factors of production they supply and (2) the prices those factors of production command in the factor market. This in turn is dependent on the demand for the items produced with those factors. The prices of factors of production (wages and salaries in particular) are key in determining the size of each household's income and therefore each household's ability to buy part of the economy's output.

How Will the System Accommodate Change?

Consumer preferences, technology, and supplies of factors constantly change. A particular allocation of resources that is now the most efficient for a *specific* pattern of consumer tastes, range of technological alternatives, and supplies of resources may become obsolete and inefficient as consumer preferences change, new techniques of production are discovered, and factor supplies change over time. Can the market economy adjust to such changes and still use resources efficiently?

GUIDING FUNCTION OF PRICES

Suppose consumer tastes change. For instance, assume that consumers in Alberta decide they want more apple juice and less milk than the economy currently provides. Those changes in consumer tastes will be communicated to producers through an increase in demand for apples and a decline in demand for milk. Apple prices will rise and milk prices will fall.

Now, assuming that firms in both industries were enjoying profits before these changes in consumer demand set in, the higher apple prices will mean higher profit for the apple growing industry, and the lower milk prices will mean losses for the milk industry. Self-interest will induce new competitors to enter the prosperous apple growing industry and will in time force firms to leave the depressed milk industry.

The higher profit that initially follows the increase in demand for apples will not only induce that industry to expand but will also give it the revenue needed to obtain the resources essential to its growth. Higher apple prices will permit apple growers to pay higher prices for resources, thereby increasing resource demand and drawing resources from less urgent alternative employment. The reverse occurs in the milk industry, where resource demand declines and fewer workers and other factors of production are employed. These adjustments in the economy are appropriate responses to the changes in consumer tastes. This is consumer sovereignty at work.

The market system is a gigantic communications system. Through changes in prices it communicates changes in such basic matters as consumer tastes and elicits appropriate responses from businesses and the suppliers of factors of production. By affecting product prices and profits, changes in consumer tastes direct the expansion of some industries and the contraction of others. Those adjustments are conveyed to the factor market as expanding industries demand more resources and contracting industries demand fewer; the resulting changes in factor prices guide resources from the contracting industries to the expanding industries.

guiding function of prices
The ability of price changes to bring about changes in the quantities of products and factors of production demanded and supplied.

This *directing* or **guiding function of prices** is a core element of the market system. Without such a system, some administrative agency, such as a government planning board, would have to direct businesses and resources into the appropriate industries. A similar analysis shows that the system can and does adjust to other fundamental changes—for example, to changes in technology and in the availability of various resources.

ROLE IN PROMOTING PROGRESS

Adjusting to changes is one thing; initiating desirable changes is another. How does the market system promote technological improvements and capital accumulation—two changes that lead to greater productivity and a higher level of material well-being for society?

Technological Advance   The market system provides a strong incentive for technological advance and over time enables better products and processes to brush aside inferior ones. An entrepreneur or firm that introduces a popular new product will gain profit. Technological advance also includes new and improved methods that reduce production or distribution costs. By passing part of its cost reduction on to the consumer through a lower product price, the firm can increase sales and obtain above-normal profit at the expense of rival firms. Moreover, the market system is conducive to the *rapid spread* of technological advance throughout an industry. Rival firms must follow the lead of the most innovative firm or else suffer immediate losses and eventual failure. In some cases, the result is **creative destruction**: The creation of new products and production methods completely destroys the market positions of firms that are wedded to existing products and older ways of doing business. Example: The advent of personal computers and word processing software (for example, WordPerfect, produced by Corel Corp. of Ottawa) demolished the market for electric typewriters.

creative destruction
The hypothesis that the creation of new products and production methods simultaneously destroys the market power of existing monopolies.

Capital Accumulation   Most technological advances require additional capital goods. The market system provides the resources necessary to produce those goods by adjusting the product market and the factor market through increased dollar votes for capital goods.

But who will register votes for capital goods? Entrepreneurs and owners of businesses often use part of their profit income to purchase capital goods. Doing so yields even greater profit income in the future if the technological innovation is successful. Also, by paying interest or selling ownership shares, the entrepreneur and firm can attract some of the income of households to cast dollar votes for the production of more capital goods. *(Key Question 9)*

Competition and the "Invisible Hand"

In his 1776 book *The Wealth of Nations,* Adam Smith first noted that the operation of a market system creates a curious unity between private interests and public interests. Firms and suppliers of factors of production, seeking to further their own self-interest and operating within the framework of a highly competitive market system, will simultaneously, as though guided by an **"invisible hand,"** promote the public or social interest. In a competitive environment, businesses use the least-costly combination of resources to produce a specific output because it is in their self-interest to do so. To act otherwise would be to forgo profit or even to risk business failure. But, at the same time, to use scarce resources in the least-costly (most efficient) way is also in the public interest.

invisible hand
The tendency of firms and resource suppliers seeking to further their own self-interests in competitive markets to also promote the interests of society as a whole.

The Effectiveness of Markets

In our more-apple-juice-less-milk illustration, it is self-interest that induces responses appropriate to the change in society's wants. Canadian businesses seeking to make higher profits and to avoid losses, and suppliers of factors of production pursuing greater monetary rewards, negotiate changes in the allocation of resources and end up with the output that Canadians demand. Competition controls or guides self-interest in such a way that it automatically, and quite unintentionally, furthers the best interests of society. The "invisible hand" ensures us that when firms maximize their profits, they also maximize society's output and income.

Of the many virtues of the market system, three merit special emphasis:

- *Efficiency*   The basic economic argument for the market system is that it promotes the efficient use of resources, by guiding them into the production of those goods and services most wanted by society. It forces the use of the most efficient techniques in organizing resources for production, and it encourages the development and adoption of new and more efficient production techniques.

QUICK REVIEW

- The output mix of the market system is determined by profits, which in turn depend heavily on consumer preferences. Profits cause efficient industries to expand; losses cause inefficient industries to contract.

- Competition forces industries to use the least-costly (most efficient) production methods.

- In a market economy, consumer income and product prices determine how output will be distributed.

- Competitive markets reallocate resources in response to changes in consumer tastes, technological advances, and changes in supplies of factors of production.

- The "invisible hand" of the market system channels the pursuit of self-interest to the good of society.

- *Incentives*   The market system encourages skill acquisition, hard work, and innovation. Greater work skills and effort mean greater production and higher incomes, which translate into a higher standard of living. Similarly, the assuming of risks by entrepreneurs can result in substantial profit incomes. Successful innovations generate economic rewards.

- *Freedom*   The major non-economic argument for the market system is its emphasis on personal freedom. In contrast to central planning, the market system coordinates economic activity without coercion. The market system permits—indeed, it thrives on—freedom of enterprise and choice. Entrepreneurs and workers are free to further their own self-interest, subject to the rewards and penalties imposed by the market system itself.

4.3   Market Failure

market failure
The inability of markets to bring about the allocation of resources that best satisfies the wants of society.

The market system has many positive aspects in its favour. Unfortunately, there are instances when it doesn't work. **Market failure** occurs when the competitive market system (1) produces the "wrong" amounts of certain goods and services or (2) fails to allocate any resources whatsoever to the production of certain goods and services that are economically justified. The first type of failure results from what economists call *spillovers,* and the second type involves *public goods.* Both kinds of market failure can be corrected by government action.

Spillovers or Externalities

When we say that competitive markets automatically bring about the efficient use of resources, we assume that all the benefits and costs for each product are fully reflected in the market demand and supply curves. That is not always the case. In some markets certain benefits or costs may escape the buyer or seller.

A spillover occurs when some of the costs or the benefits of a good are passed on to or "spill over to" someone other than the immediate buyer or seller. Spillovers are also called *externalities* because they are benefits or costs that accrue to some third party that is external to the market transaction.

SPILLOVER COSTS

spillover costs
A cost imposed without compensation on third parties by the production or consumption of sellers or buyers.

Production or consumption costs inflicted on a third party without compensation are called **spillover costs**. Environmental pollution is an example. When a chemical manufacturer in southern Ontario or a meatpacking plant in Alberta dumps its wastes into a lake or river, swimmers, fishers, and boaters—and perhaps those who drink the water—suffer spillover costs. When a petroleum refinery in Sarnia, Ontario, pollutes the air with smoke or a paper mill in St-Félicien, Quebec, creates obnoxious odours, the local community experiences spillover costs for which it is not compensated. Cigarette smokers impose costs on those in close proximity by releasing second-hand smoke; in Canada, smokers also impose costs on others through increased use of the taxpayer-funded health care system.

What are the economic effects? Recall that costs determine the position of the firm's supply curve. When a firm avoids some costs by polluting, its supply curve lies farther to the right than it does when the firm bears the full costs of production. As a result, the price of the product is too low and the output of the product is too large to achieve allocative efficiency. A market failure occurs in the form of an overallocation of resources to the production of the good.

CORRECTING FOR SPILLOVER COSTS

Government can do two things to correct the overallocation of resources. Both solutions internalize external costs—that is, they make the offending firm pay the costs rather than shift them to others:

- *Legislation*   In cases of air and water pollution, the most direct action is legislation prohibiting or limiting the pollution. Such legislation forces potential polluters to pay for the proper disposal of industrial wastes—here, by installing smoke-abatement equipment or water-purification facilities. The idea is to force potential offenders, under the threat of legal action, to bear *all* the costs associated with production. For example, both Quebec and British Columbia have passed legislation to prevent pulp and paper mills from damaging the environment.

- *Specific taxes*   A less direct action is for government to levy a *specific tax*—that is, a tax confined to a particular product—on each unit of the polluting firm's output. The amount of this tax would roughly equal the estimated amount of the spillover cost arising from the production of each unit of output. Through this tax, government would pass back to the offending firm a cost equivalent to the spillover cost the firm is avoiding. This would shift the firm's supply curve to the left, reducing equilibrium output and eliminating the overallocation of resources. Governments in Canada levy high taxes on cigarettes to induce smokers to internalize the costs they impose on the rest of Canadians.

SPILLOVER BENEFITS

Sometimes spillovers appear as benefits. The production or consumption of certain goods and services may confer spillover or external benefits on third parties or on the community at large without compensating payment. Immunization against measles and polio results in direct benefits to the immediate consumer of those vaccines. But it also results in widespread substantial spillover benefits to the entire community.

spillover benefits
Benefit obtained without compensation by third parties from the production or consumption of sellers or buyers.

Education is another example of **spillover benefits**. Education benefits individual consumers: "Better-educated" people generally achieve higher incomes than "less-well-educated" people. But education also provides benefits to society, in the form of a more versatile and more productive labour force, on the one hand, and smaller outlays for crime prevention, law enforcement, and welfare programs, on the other.

Spillover benefits mean that the market demand curve, which reflects only private benefits, understates total benefits. The demand curve for the product lies farther to the left than it would if the market took all benefits into account. As a result, a smaller amount of the product will be produced or, alternatively, there will be an *underallocation* of resources to the product—again a market failure.

CORRECTING FOR SPILLOVER BENEFITS

How can the underallocation of resources associated with spillover benefits be corrected? The answer is either to subsidize consumers (to increase demand), to subsidize producers (to increase supply), or, in the extreme, to have government produce the product.

- *Subsidize consumers*   To correct the underallocation of resources to higher education, the federal and provincial governments provide low-interest loans to students so that they can afford more education. Those loans help increase the demand for higher education.

- *Subsidize suppliers*   In some cases governments find it more convenient and administratively simpler to correct an underallocation by subsidizing suppliers. For example, in Canada, provincial governments provide substantial portions of the budgets of public elementary and high schools, and colleges and universities. Such subsidies lower the costs of producing education and increase its supply. Publicly subsidized immunization programs, hospitals, and medical research are other examples.

- *Provide goods via government*   A third policy option may be appropriate where spillover benefits are extremely large: Government may finance or, in the extreme, own and operate the industry that is involved. In Canada, most hospitals are publicly owned and operated through provincial governments.

Public Goods and Services

Certain goods called *private goods* are produced through the competitive market system. Examples are the many items sold in stores. Private goods have two characteristics—*rivalry* and *excludability*. *Rivalry* means that when one person buys and consumes a product or service, it is not available for purchase and consumption by another person. What Joan purchases, Jane cannot have. *Excludability* means that buyers who are willing and able to pay the market price for the product obtain its benefits, but those unable or unwilling to pay that price do not. This characteristic makes it possible for private firms to profitably produce goods and services.

Certain other goods and services called **public goods** have the opposite characteristics—*non-rivalry* and *non-excludability*. Everyone can simultaneously obtain the benefit from a public good such as a global positioning system satellite, national defence, street lighting, and environmental protection. One person's benefit does not reduce the benefit available to others. More important, there is no effective way of excluding individuals from the benefit of the good once it comes into existence (see the Consider This box). The inability to exclude individuals from consumption of a good creates the **free-rider problem**, in which people can receive benefits from a public good without paying for it. The free-rider problem makes it unprofitable for a private firm to provide the product or service.

An example of a public good is the war on global terrorism. This expenditure on heightened security, for example at airports, is economically justified because the benefits to Canadians are thought to exceed the costs. Once these efforts are undertaken, however, the benefits accrue to all Canadians (non-rivalry). And, there is no practical way to exclude any Canadian from benefiting from these efforts (non-excludability).

No private firm will undertake the war on terrorism because the benefits cannot be profitably sold (due to the free-rider problem). So here we have a service that yields substantial benefits but to which the market system would not allocate resources. The war on terrorism is a public good. Society signals its desire for such goods by voting for particular political candidates who support their provision. Because of the free-rider problem, the public sector must provide these goods and finance them through compulsory charges in the form of taxes.

Quasi-public Goods

Government provides many goods that fit the economist's definition of a public good. However, it also provides other goods and services that could be produced and delivered in such a way that the exclusion principle would apply. Such goods, called **quasi-public goods**, include health care, education, streets and highways, police and fire protection, libraries and museums, preventive medicine, and sewage disposal. They could all be priced and provided by private firms through the

A public good can be simultaneously consumed by everyone. One person's benefit does not reduce the benefit available to others.

public good
A good or service that can be simultaneously consumed by everyone, and from which no one can be excluded, even if they don't pay for it.

free-rider problem
The inability of potential providers of an economically desirable but indivisible good or service to obtain payment from those who benefit.

quasi-public good
A good or service to which the exclusion principle could apply, but that has such a large spillover benefit that government sponsors its production to prevent an underallocation of resources.

Consider This

Public Goods

Street entertainers are often found in tourist areas of major cities, such as Vancouver and Quebec City. They can also be found in the subway stations of Toronto and Montreal. Some play violins, tubas, harmonicas, accordions, or other instruments, while others team up to sing songs or juggle various objects. Some street entertainers are highly creative and talented; others "need more practice." But, regardless of talent level, these entertainers illuminate the concepts of free riders and public goods.

Most street entertainers have a hard time earning a living from their activities (unless event organizers pay them). Their problem is that they have no way of excluding non-payers from the benefits of their entertainment. They essentially are providing public, not private, goods and must rely on voluntary payments.

The result is a significant free-rider problem. Only a few in the audience put money in the container or instrument case, and many who do contribute put in only token amounts. The rest are free riders. Because they did not ask the entertainers to perform, they rightfully feel no obligation to pay for the performances. Free riders obtain the benefits of the street entertainment and keep their money for purchases that *they* initiate.

Street entertainers are acutely aware of the free-rider problem and some have found creative ways to lessen it. For example, some entertainers involve the audience directly in the act. This usually creates a greater sense of audience willingness (or obligation) to contribute money at the end of the performance.

"Pay for performance" is another creative approach to lessening the free-rider problem. A good example is the street entertainer painted up to look like a statue. When people drop coins into the container, the "statue" makes a slight movement. The greater the contributions, the greater the movement. But these human "statues" still face the free-rider problem: Non-payers also get to enjoy the acts.

Some street entertainers supplement their earnings by selling CDs of their music to appreciative audience members. Unlike their public performances, the CDs are private goods. Only consumers who pay for the CDs obtain the benefits.

Finally, because talented street entertainers create a festive street environment, cities or retailers sometimes hire them to perform. The "free entertainment" attracts crowds of shoppers who buy goods from nearby retailers. In these instances the cities or retailers use tax revenue or commercial funds to pay the entertainers, in the former case validating them as public goods.

Question: If government is not providing street entertainment, why is it considered a public good?

market system. But, as we noted earlier, because they all have substantial spillover benefits, they would be underproduced by the market system. Therefore, government often provides them to avoid the underallocation of resources that would otherwise occur.

The Reallocation Process

How are resources reallocated from the production of private goods to the production of public and quasi-public goods? If the resources of the economy are fully employed, government must free up resources from the production of private goods and make them available for the production of public and quasi-public goods. It does so by reducing private demand for them. And it does that by levying taxes on households and businesses, taking some of their income out of the circular flow. With lower incomes, households and businesses are obliged to curtail their consumption and investment spending. As a result, the private demand for goods and services declines, as does the private demand for resources. So by diverting purchasing power from private spenders to government, taxes remove resources from private use. (Global Perspective 4.2 shows the extent to which various countries divert labour from the private sector to the public sector.)

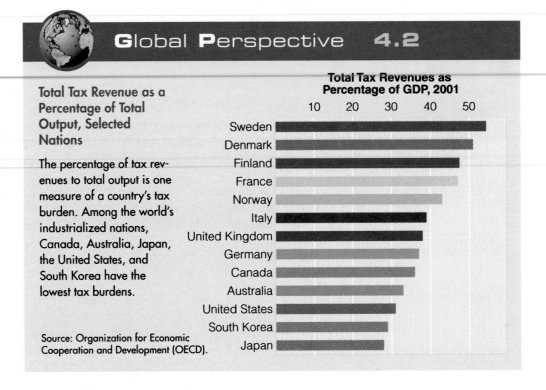

Global Perspective 4.2

Total Tax Revenue as a Percentage of Total Output, Selected Nations

The percentage of tax revenues to total output is one measure of a country's tax burden. Among the world's industrialized nations, Canada, Australia, Japan, the United States, and South Korea have the lowest tax burdens.

Source: Organization for Economic Cooperation and Development (OECD).

Total Tax Revenues as Percentage of GDP, 2001

Sweden
Denmark
Finland
France
Norway
Italy
United Kingdom
Germany
Canada
Australia
United States
South Korea
Japan

Government then spends the tax proceeds to provide public and quasi-public goods and services. Taxation releases resources from the production of private consumer goods (food, clothing, television sets) and private investment goods (printing presses, boxcars, warehouses). Government shifts those resources to the production of public and quasi-public goods (post offices, health care, parks), changing the composition of the economy's total output. (Global Perspective 4.2 shows total tax revenues as a percentage of national output in several nations.) *(Key Questions 12 and 13)*

Limitations of the Market System

We end our discussion of the market system by re-emphasizing an important caution. Although the market system has remarkable virtues, its operation is not as smooth as some of its proponents imply. Both in its purest form and as practised in reality, the market system has well-known limitations. It fails to provide public goods. Unscrupulous people occasionally abuse it. Resource allocation does not always accurately reflect all costs and benefits, including those that spill over to society at large. It may generate more income inequality than many individuals feel is justified. It does not always produce full employment and price-level stability. And so on. In subsequent chapters, we discuss these limitations and how to address them.

The Circular Flow Revisited

Figure 4-2 integrates government into the circular flow model first shown in Figure 2-6. Here flows (1) through (4) are the same as the corresponding flows in that figure. Flows (1) and (2) show business expenditures for the factors of production provided by households. These expenditures are costs to businesses but represent wage, rent, interest, and profit income to households. Flows (3) and (4) show household expenditures for the goods and services produced by businesses.

Now consider what happens when we add government. Flows (5) through (8) illustrate that government makes purchases in both product and factor markets. Flows (5) and (6) represent government purchases of such products as paper, computers, and military hardware from private businesses. Flows (7) and (8) represent government purchases of resources. The federal government employs and pays salaries to members of Parliament, the armed forces, lawyers, meat inspectors, and so on. Provincial and municipal governments hire and pay teachers, bus drivers, police, and firefighters. The federal government might also lease or purchase land to expand an airport and a city might buy land on which to build a new elementary school.

Government then provides public goods and services to both households and businesses as shown by flows (9) and (10). To finance those public goods and services, businesses and households are required to pay taxes, as shown by flows (11) and (12). These flows are labelled as *net* taxes to indicate that they also include "taxes in reverse" in the form of transfer payments to households and subsidies to businesses. Thus, flow (11) includes various subsidies to farmers, shipbuilders, and airlines as well as income, sales, and excise taxes paid by businesses to government. Most subsidies to business are "concealed" in the form of low-interest loans, loan guarantees, tax concessions, or public facilities provided at prices below their cost. Similarly, flow (12) includes both taxes collected by government directly from households and transfer payments such as child-care benefits paid by the government.

We can use Figure 4-2 to review how government alters the distribution of income, reallocates resources, and changes the level of economic activity. The structure of taxes and transfer payments significantly affects income distribution. In flow (12), a tax structure that draws tax revenues primarily from well-to-do households, combined with a system of transfer payments to low-income households, reduces income inequality.

Flows (5) through (8) show that government diverts goods and resources away from private sector consumption and directs them to the public sector. This resource reallocation is required to provide public goods and services.

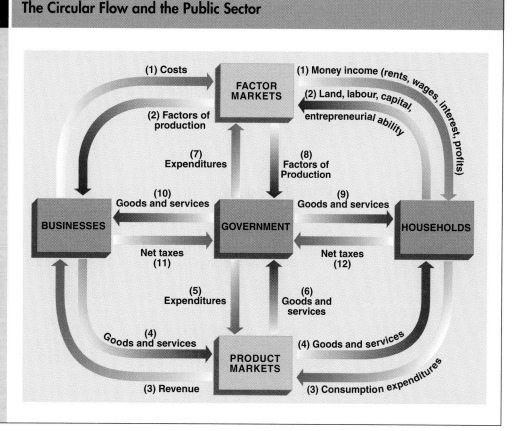

FIGURE 4-2

The Circular Flow and the Public Sector

Government buys products from the product market and employs factors of production from the factor market to provide public goods and services to households and businesses. Government finances its expenditures through the net tax revenues (taxes minus transfer payments) it receives from households and businesses.

4.4   Canada and International Trade

Canadians consume many goods that are produced abroad.

As we noted earlier in the chapter, markets are made up of buyers and sellers that want to exchange goods. Up to this point we have implicitly assumed that markets are national in scope: Canadians buying and selling from each other. But a visit to any retail outlet will reveal that Canadians consume many goods produced abroad. And if you were to go abroad—say, to Europe—you would probably not have great difficulty finding beer, telecommunication equipment, or software produced in Canada.

Canadian backpackers in the wilderness of Banff National Park may like to think they are "leaving the world behind" but, like Atlas, they carry the world on their shoulders. Much of their equipment is likely imported—knives from Switzerland, rain gear from South Korea, cameras from Japan, aluminum pots from England, miniature stoves from Sweden, sleeping bags from China, and compasses from Finland. Moreover, they may have driven to the trailheads in Japanese-made Toyotas or Swedish-made Volvos, sipping coffee from Brazil or snacking on bananas from Honduras. Equally, Swiss backpackers may be carrying tents, prepackaged dehydrated meals, and hiking boots made in Canada.

Canada, with a limited domestic market, cannot efficiently produce the variety of goods its citizens want. Therefore, we must import goods from other nations. That, in turn, means that we must export, or sell abroad, some of our own products. For Canada, exports make up about 40 percent of our gross domestic product (GDP)—the market value of all goods and services produced in an economy. Other countries, such as the United States, have a large internal market. Although the total volume of trade in the United States is huge, it constitutes a much smaller percentage of GDP than in a number of other nations.

Global Trade and Competition

Globalization—the integration of industry, commerce, communication, travel, and culture among the world's nations—is one of the major trends of our time. (See Global Perspective 4.3 for a list of the top 12 globalized nations, according to one set of criteria.). There is a lively debate internationally as to whether globalization is a positive or negative force. Those who support globalization focus on the improvements to general standards of living that it brings. Those who oppose it express concerns about its impacts on the environment, unskilled and semi-skilled workers, and the poor.

One thing about globalization is certain and relevant to our present discussion: It has brought intense competition both within Canada and across the globe. In Canada, imports have gained major shares of many markets, including those for cars, tires, steel, clothing, sporting goods, electronics, and toys. Nevertheless, hundreds of Canadian firms have prospered in the global marketplace. Such firms as Bombardier, Nortel, Alcan, JDS Uniphase, ATI Technologies, and Cognos have continued to hold high market shares at home while greatly expanding their sales abroad. Of course, not all firms have been successful. Some have not been able to compete, because their

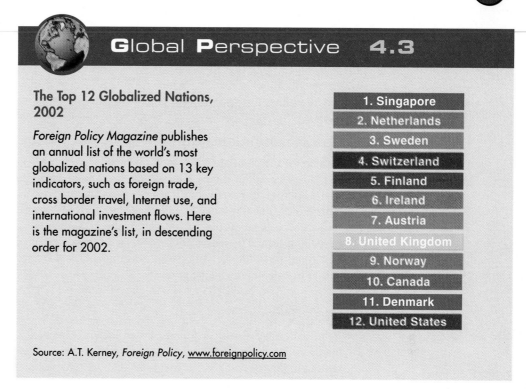

Global Perspective 4.3

The Top 12 Globalized Nations, 2002

Foreign Policy Magazine publishes an annual list of the world's most globalized nations based on 13 key indicators, such as foreign trade, cross border travel, Internet use, and international investment flows. Here is the magazine's list, in descending order for 2002.

1. Singapore
2. Netherlands
3. Sweden
4. Switzerland
5. Finland
6. Ireland
7. Austria
8. United Kingdom
9. Norway
10. Canada
11. Denmark
12. United States

Source: A.T. Kerney, *Foreign Policy*, www.foreignpolicy.com

international competitors either make higher-quality products, have lower production costs, or both.

International trade and the global economy affect all Canadians daily, whether we are hiking in the wilderness, driving our cars, listening to music, or working at our jobs. We cannot "leave the world behind." We are enmeshed in a global web of economic relationships—trading of goods and services, multinational corporations, cooperative ventures among the world's firms, and ties among the world's financial markets. That web is so complex that sometimes it is difficult to determine just what is a Canadian product. A Finnish company owns Wilson sporting goods; a Swiss company owns Gerber baby food; and a British corporation owns Burger King. The Toyota Corolla sedan is manufactured in Canada. Some Volvo models are assembled in Nova Scotia. Many "Canadian" products are made with components from abroad, and, conversely, many "foreign" products contain numerous Canadian-produced parts.

International Linkages

Several economic flows link the Canadian economy and the economies of other nations:

- *Goods and services flows*   Canada exports goods and services to other nations and imports goods and services from them.

- *Capital and labour flows*   Canadian firms establish production facilities in foreign countries and foreign firms establish production facilities in Canada. Labour also moves between nations. Each year between 200,000 and 400,000 people immigrate to Canada and some Canadians move to other nations.

- *Information and technology flows*   Canada transmits information to other nations about Canadian products, prices, interest rates, and investment opportunities and receives such information from abroad. Firms in other countries use technology created in Canada and Canadian businesses incorporate technology developed abroad.

- *Financial flows*   Money is transferred between Canada and other countries for several purposes, for example, paying for imports, buying foreign assets, paying interest on debt, and providing foreign aid.

We will soon see that international trade provides significant benefits to each participating nation. We now turn to investigating how the gains from international trade come about.

Specialization and Comparative Advantage

Recall from Chapter 2 that the economic problem consists of limited resources, unlimited wants, and thus the need for choice. If a nation can get more output from its limited resources, the constraint it faces is less severe. In Chapter 2 we also pointed out that specialization and international trade provide one way to get more output from limited resources. *Specialization and international trade increase the productivity of a nation's resources and allow for greater total output than would otherwise be possible.* This idea is not new. Adam Smith pointed it out over 200 years ago. Nations specialize and trade for the same reasons as individuals do: Specialization and exchange result in greater overall output and income.

Basic Principle

In the early 1800s British economist David Ricardo expanded Smith's idea, observing that it pays for a person or a country to specialize and exchange even if that person or nation is more productive than a potential trading partner in *all* economic activities.

Consider an example of a chartered accountant (CA) who is also a skilled house painter. Suppose the CA can paint her house in less time than the professional painter she is thinking of hiring. Also suppose the CA can earn $50 per hour doing her accounting and must pay the painter $15 per hour. Let's say that it will take the accountant 30 hours to paint her house; the painter, 40 hours.

Should the CA take time from her accounting to paint her own house or should she hire the painter? The CA's opportunity cost of painting her house is $1500 (= 30 hours × $50 per hour of sacrificed income). The cost of hiring the painter is only $600 (40 hours × $15 per hour paid to the painter). The CA is better at both accounting and painting—she has an **absolute advantage** in both accounting and painting. But her relative advantage (about which more below) is in accounting. She *will get her house painted at a lower cost by specializing in accounting and using some of the earnings from accounting to hire a house painter.*

Similarly, the house painter can reduce his cost of obtaining accounting services by specializing in painting and using some of his income to hire the CA to prepare his income tax forms. Suppose that it would take the painter ten hours to prepare his tax return, while the CA could handle this task in two hours. The house painter would sacrifice $150 of income (= 10 hours × $15 per hour of sacrificed time) to accomplish a task that he could hire the CA to do for $100 (= 2 hours × $50 per hour of the CA's time). By using the CA to prepare his tax return, the painter lowers *his cost of getting the tax return prepared.*

What is true for our CA and house painter is also true for nations. Specializing enables nations to reduce the cost of obtaining the goods and services they desire.

Comparative Costs

Our simple example shows that specialization is economically desirable because it results in more efficient production. Let's now put specialization in the context of trading nations, using the familiar concept of the production possibilities table for our analysis. Suppose production possibilities for two products in Mexico and Canada are as shown in Tables 4-1 and 4-2. In these tables we assume constant costs. Each country must give up a constant amount of one product to secure a particular increment of the other product. (This assumption simplifies our discussion without impairing the validity of our conclusions.)

absolute advantage
When a region or nation can produce more of good Z and good Y with less resources compared to other regions or nations.

TABLE 4-1	Mexico's Production Possibilities Table (in Tonnes)				
PRODUCTION ALTERNATIVES					
Product	**A**	**B**	**C**	**D**	**E**
Corn	0	20	24	40	60
Soybeans	15	10	9	5	0

TABLE 4-2	Canada's Production Possibilities Table (in Tonnes)				
PRODUCTION ALTERNATIVES					
Product	**R**	**S**	**T**	**U**	**V**
Corn	0	30	33	60	90
Soybeans	30	20	19	10	0

comparative advantage
When a region or nation can produce a good at a lower domestic opportunity cost compared to a potential trading partner.

Specialization and trade are mutually beneficial or "profitable" to the two nations if the comparative costs of the two products within the two nations differ. What are the comparative costs of corn and soybeans in Mexico? By comparing production alternatives A and B in Table 4-1, we see that 5 tonnes of soybeans (= 15 − 10) must be sacrificed to produce 20 tonnes of corn (= 20 − 0). Or more simply, in Mexico it costs one tonne of soybeans (S) to produce four tonnes of corn (C); that is, $1S \equiv 4C$. Because we assumed constant costs, this domestic *comparative-cost ratio* will not change as Mexico expands the output of either product. This is evident from looking at production possibilities B and C, where we see that four more tonnes of corn (= 24 − 20) cost one tonne of soybeans (= 10 − 9).

Similarly, in Table 4-2, comparing Canadian production alternatives R and S reveals that in Canada it costs 10 tonnes of soybeans (= 30 − 20) to obtain 30 tonnes of corn (= 30 − 0). That is, the domestic comparative-cost ratio for the two products in Canada is $1S \equiv 3C$. Comparing production alternatives S and T reinforces this; an extra three tonnes of corn (= 33 − 30) comes at the direct sacrifice of one tonne of soybeans (= 20 − 19).

The comparative costs, or internal terms of trade, of the two products within the two nations are clearly different. Economists say that Canada has a **comparative advantage** over Mexico in soybeans. Canada must forgo only three tonnes of corn to get one tonne of soybeans, but Mexico must forgo four tonnes of corn to get one tonne of soybeans. In terms of domestic opportunity costs, soybeans are relatively cheaper in Canada. *A nation has a comparative advantage in some product when it can produce that product at a lower domestic opportunity cost than can a potential trading partner.* Mexico, in contrast, has a comparative advantage in corn. While one tonne of corn costs one-third tonne of soybeans in Canada, it costs only one-quarter tonne of soybeans in Mexico. Comparatively speaking, corn is cheaper in Mexico. We summarize the situation in Table 4-3.

Because of these differences in domestic comparative costs, if both nations specialize, each according to its comparative advantage, each can achieve a larger total output with the same total input of resources. Together they will be using their scarce resources more efficiently.

terms of trade
The amount of one good or service that must be given up to obtain one unit of another good or service.

Terms of Trade

Canada can shift production between soybeans and corn at the rate of 1S for 3C. Thus, Canadians would specialize in soybeans only if they could obtain *more than* three tonnes of corn for one tonne of soybeans by trading with Mexico. Similarly, Mexico can shift production at the rate of 4C for 1S. So it would be advantageous to Mexico to specialize in corn if it could get one tonne of soybeans for *less than* four tonnes of corn.

Suppose that through negotiation the two nations agree on an exchange rate of one tonne of soybeans for three-and-a-half tonnes of corn. These **terms of trade** are mutually beneficial to both countries since each can "do better" through such trade than via domestic production alone. Canadians can get three-and-a-half tonnes of corn by sending one tonne of soybeans to Mexico, while they can get only three tonnes of corn by shifting resources domestically from soybeans to corn. Mexicans can obtain one tonne of soybeans at a lower cost of three-and-a-half tonnes of corn through trade with Canada, compared to the cost of four tonnes if Mexicans produce one tonne of corn themselves.

TABLE 4-3	Comparative Advantage Example: A Summary	
Soybeans		**Corn**
Mexico: Must give up 4 tonnes of corn to get 1 tonne of soybeans		*Mexico:* Must give up ¼ tonne of soybeans to get 1 tonne of corn
Canada: Must give up 3 tonnes of corn to get 1 tonne of soybeans		*Canada:* Must give up ⅓ tonne of soybeans to get 1 tonne of corn
Comparative advantage: Canada		Comparative advantage: Mexico

Gains from Specialization and Trade

Let's pinpoint the size of the gains in total output from specialization and trade. Suppose that before specialization and trade, production alternative C in Table 4-1 and alternative T in Table 4-2 are the optimal product mixes for the two countries. These outputs are shown in column 1 of Table 4-4. That is, Mexicans prefer 24 tonnes of corn and 9 tonnes of soybeans (Table 4-1) and Canadians prefer 33 tonnes of corn and 19 tonnes of soybeans (Table 4-2) to all other alternatives.

Now assume both nations specialize according to comparative advantage, Mexico producing 60 tonnes of corn and no soybeans (alternative E) and Canada producing no corn and 30 tonnes of soybeans (alternative R). These outputs are reflected in column 2 of Table 4-4. Using our 1S = 3½C terms of trade, assume Mexico exchanges 35 tonnes of corn for 10 tonnes of Canadian soybeans. Column 3 of Table 4-4 shows the quantities exchanged in this trade. As indicated in Column 4, after trade Mexicans have 25 tonnes of corn and 10 tonnes of soybeans, while Canadians have 35 tonnes of corn and 20 tonnes of soybeans. Compared with their optimum product mixes before specialization and trade (column 1), *both* nations now enjoy more corn and more soybeans! Specifically, Mexico has gained one tonne of corn and one tonne of soybeans. Canada has gained two tonnes of corn and one tonne of soybeans. These gains are shown in column 5.

Specialization based on comparative advantage improves resource allocation. The same total inputs of world resources result in a larger global output. If Mexico and Canada allocate all their resources to corn and soybeans respectively, the same total inputs of resources can produce more output between them, indicating that resources are being used or allocated more efficiently.

We noted in Chapter 2 that through specialization and international trade a nation can overcome the production constraints imposed by its domestic production possibilities table and curve. Table 4-4 and its discussion show just how this is done. The domestic production possibilities data of the two countries have not changed, meaning that neither nation's production possibilities curve has shifted. But specialization and trade mean that citizens of both countries enjoy increased consumption. Thus, specialization and trade have the same effect as an increase in resources or technological progress: they make more goods available to an economy. *(Key Question 16)*

Back to the Circular Flow Model

We can easily add "the rest of the world" to the circular flow model. We do so in Figure 4-3 via two adjustments.

1. Our previous "Factor Markets" and "Product Markets" now become "Canadian Factor Markets" and "Canadian Product Markets." Similarly, we add the modifier "Canadian" to the "Businesses," "Government," and "Households" sectors.

TABLE 4-4	Specialization According to Comparative Advantage and the Gains from Trade (in Tonnes)				
Country	(1) Outputs before specialization	(2) Outputs after specialization	(3) Amounts traded	(4) Outputs available after trade	(5) Gains from specialization and trade (4) − (1)
Mexico	24 corn	60 corn	−35 corn	25 corn	1 corn
	9 soybeans	0 soybeans	+10 soybeans	10 soybeans	1 soybeans
Canada	33 corn	0 corn	+35 corn	35 corn	2 corn
	19 soybeans	30 soybeans	−10 soybeans	20 soybeans	1 soybeans

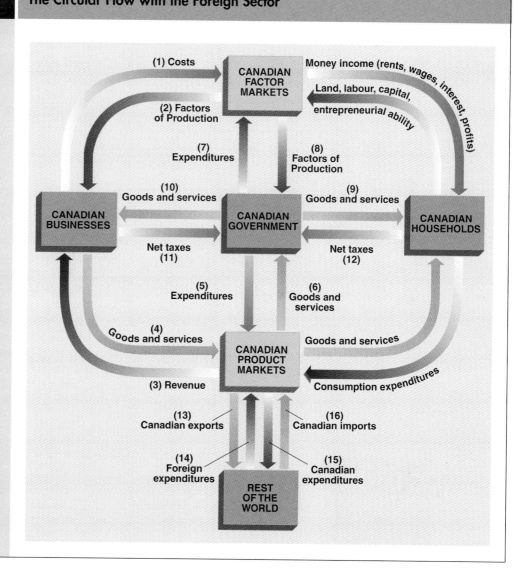

FIGURE 4-3

The Circular Flow with the Foreign Sector

Flows 13–16 in the lower portion of the diagram show how the Canadian economy interacts with the "Rest of the World." People abroad buy Canadian exports, contributing to our business revenue and money income. Canadians, in turn, spend part of their incomes to buy imports from abroad. Income from a nation's exports helps pay for its imports.

2. We place the foreign sector—the "Rest of the World"—so that it interacts with Canadian Product Markets. This sector designates all foreign nations that we deal with and the individuals, businesses, and governments that make them up.

Flow (13) in Figure 4-3 shows that people, businesses, and governments abroad buy Canadian products—our exports—from our product market. This goods and services flow of Canadian exports to foreign nations is accompanied by an opposite monetary revenue flow (14) from the rest of the world to us. In response to these revenues from abroad, Canadian businesses demand more domestic factors of production (flow 2) to produce the goods for export; they pay for these inputs with revenues from abroad. Thus, the domestic flow (1) of money income (rents, wages, interest, and profits) to Canadian households rises.

But our exports are only half the picture. Flow (15) shows that Canadian households, businesses, and government spend some of their income on foreign products. These products, of course, are our imports (flow 16). Purchases of imports, say, autos from Japan and electronic equipment from South Korea, contribute to foreign output and income, which in turn provides the means for foreign households to buy Canadian exports.

Canada imports and exports not only products, but also factors of production. For example, we import some crude oil and export raw logs. Moreover, some Canadian firms choose to engage in production abroad, which diverts spending on capital from our domestic market to markets in other nations. For instance, Nortel has an assembly plant in the U.S. Or flowing the other direction, Sony might construct a plant for manufacturing CD players in Canada.

There are also international flows of labour. Hundreds of thousands of immigrants enter Canada each year. These immigrants expand the availability of labour resources in Canada, raising our total output and income.

The expanded circular flow model also demonstrates that a nation engaged in world trade faces potential sources of economic fluctuations that would not affect a "closed" nation. Recessions and inflation can be highly contagious among nations. Suppose the United States experiences a severe recession. As its income declines, its purchases of Canadian exports fall. As a result, flows (13) and (14) in Figure 4-3 decline and inventories of unsold Canadian goods rise. Canadian firms would respond by limiting their production and employment, reducing the flow of money income to Canadian households (flow 1). Recession in the United States in this case contributes to a recession in Canada.

Figure 4-3 also helps us to see that the foreign sector alters resource allocation and incomes in the Canadian economy. With a foreign sector, we produce more of some goods (our exports) and fewer of others (our imports) than we would otherwise. Thus, Canadian labour and other factors are shifted toward export industries and away from import industries. We use more of our own factors of production to manufacture autos and telecommunication equipment. So we ask: "Do these shifts of resources make economic sense? Do they enhance our total output and thus our standard of living?" We look at some answers next.

QUICK REVIEW

- There are four main categories of economic flows linking nations: goods and services flows, capital and labour flows, information and technology flows, and financial flows.

- A country has a comparative advantage when it can produce a product at a lower domestic opportunity cost than can a potential trading partner.

- Specialization based on comparative advantage increases the total output available for nations that trade with one another.

- The circular flow model with foreign trade includes flows of exports from our domestic product market, imports to our domestic product market, and the corresponding flows of spending.

THE LASTword | Market Failure and the Need for Government

Private markets fulfill individual desires very well, but where there is a need for collective action, they often fail.

Suppose a municipality, say, Brandon, Manitoba, requires a new road. In the absence of a government request that a private firm build it, it is unlikely that a private firm will build the required road on its own initiative. Or, to express it in another way, private markets will not make available public goods. The citizens of Brandon have to elect a government to either direct a private firm to build the road, or hire the people and buy the capital equipment needed to construct the road on its own.

Why would a private firm not undertake to build a road on its own? The obstacle is common property rights. The land on which the road is to be built must be owned by the firm before it would consider building the road. Lands used by all citizens are most often held publicly. The firm would thus need to get the consent of all the citizens affected. Such unanimity would be difficult to achieve. Indeed, it is the difficulty of making collective decisions that makes government action essential in the creation of an infrastructure—such as roads and airports—necessary to facilitate the functioning of markets. Not only must

a decision be made to build the road, but then the decision must be made as to who should bear the cost. The free-rider problem arises here. Every individual hopes someone will pay for the needed road. This way he or she can have the benefits without contributing to its cost. The free-rider problem can potentially arise in all situations where collective action must be taken. Unless we have a central authority—government—with the monopoly power to impose costs on all members of a society, many socially useful projects will not be undertaken.

In a pathbreaking book, *The Logic of Collective Action*,[1] Mancur Olson pointed out almost 40 years ago that contrary to popular belief, groups of individuals with common interest do not necessarily attempt to further those common interests. In many instances group members attempt to further their own personal interests. A few years later, the political scientist Garrett Hardin popularized the term "the tragedy of the commons"[2] to describe the problems that arise when there are common property rights. For example, where there are common property rights to a natural resource, it is typi-

cally overexploited. The cod stocks on Canada's east coast have suffered just that fate.

Where collective action is required, or where there are common property rights, governments are needed because markets fail to bring together the interests of the individual and those of society. The federal government has had to impose mandatory fishing restrictions to save the cod stocks from dwindling further. Similarly, governments must make decisions to construct a road, otherwise the road might never get built. Clearly, markets work best where there are private property rights.

But we do not want to leave the impression that all government interventions to rectify market failure succeed. Some individuals point to the failure of the Canadian federal government to properly manage the cod stocks off the eastern seaboard as a case in point.

[1]Mancur Olson, *The Logic of Collective Action* (Cambridge: Cambridge University Press, 1965).

[2]Garrett Hardin, "The Tragedy of the Commons," *Science* 162 (1968): 1243–48.

CHAPTER SUMMARY

4.1 CHARACTERISTICS OF THE MARKET SYSTEM

- The market system—known also as the private-enterprise system or capitalism—is characterized by the private ownership of resources, including capital, and the freedom of individuals to engage in economic activities of their choice to advance their material well-being. Self interest is the driving force of such an economy, and competition functions as a regulatory or control mechanism.

- In the market system, markets and prices organize and make effective the many millions of individual decisions that determine what is produced, the methods of production, and the sharing of output.

- Specialization, use of advanced technology, and the extensive use of capital goods are facilitated by the market system.

- Functioning as a medium of exchange, money eliminates the problems of bartering and permits easy trade and greater specialization, both domestically and internationally.

4.2 THE MARKET SYSTEM AT WORK

- Every economy faces Four Fundamental Questions: (a) What goods and services will be produced? (b) How will the goods and services be produced? (c) Who will get the goods and services? (d) How will the system accommodate changes in consumer tastes, factor supplies, and technology?

- The market system produces those products of which production and sale yield total revenue sufficient to cover all costs, including a profit (a cost). It does not produce those products that do not yield a profit.

- Profit indicates that an industry is prosperous and promotes its expansion. Losses signify that an industry is not prosperous and hasten its contraction.

- Consumer sovereignty means that both businesses and suppliers of factors of production are subject to the wants of consumers. Through their dollar votes, consumers decide on the composition of output.

- Competition forces firms to use the lowest-cost and therefore the most economically efficient production techniques.

- The prices that a household receives for the resources it supplies to the economy determine that household's income. This income determines the household's claim on the economy's output. Those who have income to spend get the products produced in the market system.

- By communicating changes in consumer tastes to suppliers of factors of production and entrepreneurs, the market system prompts appropriate adjustments in the allocation of the economy's resources. The market system also encourages technological advance and capital accumulation.

- Competition, the primary mechanism of control in the market economy, promotes a unity of self-interest and public interests; as though directed by an "invisible hand," competition harnesses the self-interest motives of businesses and suppliers of factors of production to further the public interest.

4.3 MARKET FAILURE

- Spillovers, or externalities, cause the equilibrium output of certain goods to vary from the socially efficient output. Spillover costs result in an overallocation of resources, which can be corrected by legislation or by specific taxes. Spillover benefits are accompanied by an underallocation of resources, which can be corrected by government subsidies to consumers or producers.

- Only government can provide public goods, which are indivisible and entail benefits from which non-paying consumers (free riders) cannot be excluded. Private firms will not produce public goods. Quasi-public goods have some of the characteristics of public goods and some of the characteristics of private goods; government provides them because the private sector would underallocate resources to their production.

4.4 CANADA AND INTERNATIONAL TRADE

- Specialization based on comparative advantage enables nations to achieve higher standards of living through trade with other countries. A trading partner should specialize in products and services for which its domestic opportunity costs are lowest. The terms of trade must be such that both nations can obtain more of some products via trade than they could obtain by producing them at home.

TERMS AND CONCEPTS

STUDY QUESTIONS

1. Explain each of the following statements:

   a. The market system not only accepts self-interest as a fact of human existence, it relies on self-interest to achieve society's material goals.

   b. The market system provides such a variety of desired goods and services precisely because no single individual or small group is deciding what the economy will produce.

   c. Entrepreneurs and business are at the helm of the economy, but their commanders are consumers.

2. Why is private property, and the protection of property rights, so critical to the success of the market system?

3. What are the advantages of "roundabout" production? What is meant by the term "division of labour"? What are the advantages of specialization in the use of human and material resources? Explain: "Exchange is the necessary consequence of specialization."

4. What problem does barter entail? Indicate the economic significance of money as a medium of exchange. What is meant by the statement "We want money only to part with it"?

5. Evaluate and explain the following statements:

   a. The market system is a profit-and-loss system.

   b. Competition is the indispensable disciplinarian of the market economy.

   c. Production methods that are inferior in the engineering sense may be the most efficient methods in the economic sense, once resource prices are considered.

6. In the 1990s, thousands of "dot-com" companies emerged with great fanfare to take advantage of the Internet and new information technologies. A few, like Yahoo, eBay, and Amazon, thrived and prospered but many others struggled and eventually failed. Relate these outcomes to how the market system answers the question, "What goods and services will be produced?"

7. Explain the meaning and implications of the following quotation.

   > The beautiful consequence of the market is that it is its own guardian. If output or prices or certain kinds of remuneration stray away from their socially ordained levels, forces are set into motion to bring them back to the fold. A curious paradox thus ensues: the market, which is the acme of individual economic freedom, is the strictest taskmaster of all. One may appeal the ruling of a planning board or win the dispensation of a [government] minister; but there is no appeal, no dispensation, from the anonymous pressures of the market mechanism. Economic freedom is thus more illusory than at first appears. One can do as one pleases in the market. But if one pleases to do what the market disapproves, the price of individual freedom is economic ruination.[1]

8. Suppose the demand for bagels rises dramatically while the demand for breakfast cereal falls. Briefly explain how the competitive market economy will make the needed adjustments to re-establish an efficient allocation of society's scarce resources.

9. **KEY QUESTION**   Some large hardware stores, such as Canadian Tire, boast of carrying as many as 20,000 different products in each store. What motivated the producers of those products—everything from screwdrivers to ladders to water heaters—to make them and offer them for sale? How did the producers decide on the best combinations of factors of production to use? Who made those factors available, and why? Who decides whether these particular hardware products should continue to get produced and offered for sale?

10. In a single sentence, describe the meaning of the phrase "invisible hand."

11. What divergences arise between equilibrium output and efficient output when (a) spillover costs and (b) spillover benefits are present? How might government correct for these divergences? "The presence of spillover costs suggests the underallocation of resources to a particular product and the need for governmental subsidies." Do you agree? Why or why not? Explain how zoning and seat-belt laws might be used to deal with a problem of spillover costs.

12. **KEY QUESTION**   What are the two characteristics of public goods? Explain the significance of each for public provision as opposed to private provision. What is the free-rider problem, as it relates to public goods? Is Canada's border patrol a public good or a private good? Why or why not? How about satellite TV? Explain.

13. **KEY QUESTION**   Draw a production possibilities curve with public goods on the vertical axis and private goods on the horizontal axis. Assuming the economy is initially operating *on the curve,* indicate how the production of public goods might be increased. How might the output of public goods be increased if the economy is initially operating at a point *inside the curve*?

14. Use your understanding of the characteristics of private and public goods to determine whether the following should be produced through the market system or provided by government: (a) French fries; (b) airport screening; (c) court systems; (d) mail delivery; and (e) medical care. State why you answered as you did in each case.

15. Use the circular flow diagram to show how each of the following government actions simultaneously affect the allocation of resources and the distribution of income:

   a. The construction of a new high school.

   b. A 2 percentage-point reduction of the corporate income tax.

   c. An expansion of preschool programs for disadvantaged children.

   d. The levying of an excise tax on polluters.

---

[1] Robert L. Heilbroner, *The Worldly Philosophers,* 7th ed. (New York: Simon & Schuster, 1999), pp. 57–58.

16. **KEY QUESTION** The following are production possibilities tables for South Korea and Canada. Assume that before specialization and trade the optimal product mix for South Korea is alternative B and for Canada alternative D.

PRODUCT	SOUTH KOREA'S PRODUCTION ALTERNATIVES					
	A	B	C	D	E	F
Radios (in thousands)	30	24	18	12	6	0
Chemicals (in tonnes)	0	6	12	18	24	30

PRODUCT	CANADA'S PRODUCTION ALTERNATIVES					
	A	B	C	D	E	F
Radios (in thousands)	10	8	6	4	2	0
Chemicals (in tonnes)	0	4	8	12	16	20

a. Are comparative-cost conditions such that the two areas should specialize? If so, what product should each produce?

b. What is the total gain in radio and chemical output that results from this specialization?

c. What are the limits of the terms of trade? Suppose actual terms of trade are 1 unit of radios for 1½ units of chemicals and that 4 units of radios are exchanged for 6 units of chemicals. What are the gains from specialization and trade for each area?

d. Can you conclude from this illustration that specialization according to comparative advantage results in more efficient use of world resources? Explain.

17. Suppose that the comparative-cost ratios of two products—baby formula and tuna fish—are as follows in the hypothetical nations of Canswicki and Tunata.

Canswicki: 1 can baby formula ≡ 2 cans tuna fish

Tunata: 1 can baby formula ≡ 4 cans tuna fish

   In what product should each nation specialize? Explain why terms of trade of 1 can baby formula = 2½ cans tuna fish would be acceptable to both nations.

18. **(The Last Word)** Why do private markets fail? In your answer, refer to the dwindling cod stocks on Canada's east coast.

INTERNET APPLICATION QUESTIONS

1. **Sparkly Things—Interested in Buying One?** Use the link in the McConnell-Brue-Barbiero Web site (Chapter 4) to connect to the eBay auction site. How many diamonds are for sale at the moment? How many rubies, sapphires, and opals? Note the wide array of sizes and prices of the gemstones. In what sense is there competition among the sellers in these markets? How does that competition influence prices? In what sense is there competition among buyers? How does that competition influence prices? See something interesting, there or elsewhere on eBay? Go ahead and buy it!

2. **Barter and the Canada Customs and Revenue Agency** Bartering occurs when goods or services are exchanged without the exchange of money. For some, barter's popularity is that it enables them to avoid paying taxes to the government. How might such avoidance occur? Use the link in the McConnell-Brue-Barbiero Web site (Chapter 4) to access the Canada Customs and Revenue Agency's interpretation of barter transactions. Does CCRA treat barter as taxable or non-taxable income? How is the value of a barter transaction determined?

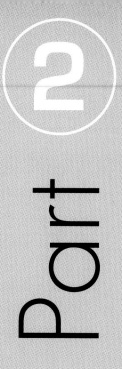

2

Part

Microeconomics of Product Markets

5

Chapter

Supply and Demand
Elasticities and Applications

Modern market economies rely mainly on the activities of consumers, businesses, and resource suppliers to allocate resources efficiently. Those activities and their outcomes are the subject of *microeconomics*, to which we now turn. We begin Part 2 by investigating the behaviours and decisions of consumers and businesses.

In this chapter we extend our previous discussion of demand and supply. First, we introduce three ideas: *price elasticity,* the buying and selling responses of consumers and producers to price changes; *cross elasticity,* the buying response of consumers of one product when the price of another product changes; and *income elasticity,* the buying response of consumers when their incomes change. Second, we discuss a number of real-world applications of the elasticity concept.

5.1   Price Elasticity of Demand

price elasticity of demand
A measure of the responsiveness of buyers to a change in the price of a product or resource.

The law of demand tells us that consumers will buy more of a product when its price declines and less when its price increases. But how much more or less will they buy?

The responsiveness (or sensitivity) of consumers to a price change is measured by a product's **price elasticity of demand**. For some products—for example, restaurant meals—consumers are highly responsive to price changes. Modest price changes cause very large changes in the quantity purchased. Economists say that the demand for such products is *relatively elastic* or simply *elastic.*

For other products—for example, salt—consumers pay much less attention to price changes. Substantial price changes cause only small changes in the amount purchased. The demand for such products is *relatively inelastic* or simply *inelastic.*

The Price Elasticity Coefficient and Formula

We measure the degree of price elasticity of demand with the coefficient E_d, defined as

$$E_d = \frac{\text{percentage change in quantity demanded of product X}}{\text{percentage change in price of product X}}$$

Let's look at a specific example from Table 5-1, rows 1 to 3, to see how the price elasticity of demand is calculated. This table shows the number of movie tickets demanded (in thousands) per week at each specified price. Let's calculate E_d for, say, the $5 to $4 price range. But before we do so, let's look at how we calculate a percentage.

TABLE 5-1	Price Elasticity of Demand for Movie Tickets as Measured by the Elasticity Coefficient and the Total-revenue Test			
(1) Total quantity demanded per week (thousands)	**(2)** Price per unit	**(3)** Elasticity coefficient, E_d	**(4)** Total revenue (1) × (2)	**(5)** Total-revenue test
1	$8		$ 8,000	
		5.00		Elastic
2	7		14,000	
		2.60		Elastic
3	6		18,000	
		1.57		Elastic
4	5		20,000	
		1.00		Unit elastic
5	4		20,000	
		0.64		Inelastic
6	3		18,000	
		0.38		Inelastic
7	2		14,000	
		0.20		Inelastic
8	1		8,000	

CALCULATING A PERCENTAGE

To calculate the percentage change in quantity demanded between two points, we divide the change in quantity demanded ($\triangle Q_d$)* by the original quantity demanded (Q_0) that we are considering:

$$\%\triangle Q_d = \frac{\text{change in quantity demanded of product X}}{\text{original quantity demanded of product X}} \times 100$$

For example, if the quantity demanded increased from 4 to 5 units, the percentage change in quantity demanded would be calculated as follows:

$$\%\triangle Q_d = \frac{\triangle Q_d}{Q_0} = \frac{1}{4} \times 100 = 25\%$$

To calculate the percentage change in price between two points, we would divide the change in price ($\triangle P$) by the original price (P_0):

$$\%\triangle P = \frac{\text{change in price of product X}}{\text{original price of product X}} \times 100$$

For example, if the price dropped from \$5 to \$4, the percentage change in price would be:

$$\%\triangle P = \frac{\triangle P}{P_0} = \frac{1}{5} \times 100 = 20\%$$

AVERAGE PRICE AND QUANTITY

But we can run into confusion as to which original price or quantity to use when calculating the price elasticity of demand. To avoid such confusion we generally use the *average price* and *average quantity*. Thus, we can restate the price elasticity formula as:

$$E_d = \frac{\text{change in quantity}}{\text{sum of quantities/2}} \div \frac{\text{change in price}}{\text{sum of prices/2}} \times 100$$

In symbol, the formula becomes:

$$E_d = \frac{\triangle Q}{(Q_0 + Q_1)/2} \div \frac{\triangle P}{(P_0 + P_1)/2} \times 100$$

Thus, price elasticity of demand for a price change from \$4 to \$5 and a quantity change from 4 to 5, becomes:

$$E_d = \frac{1}{(4 + 5)/2} \div \frac{1}{(4 + 5)/2} \times 100$$

$$= \frac{1}{4.5} \div \frac{1}{4.5} \times 100$$

$$= \frac{22\%}{22\%} = 1$$

Interpretation of E_d

We can interpret the coefficient of price elasticity of demand as follows.

ELASTIC DEMAND

elastic demand
Product demand whose price elasticity is greater than one.

Demand is **elastic** if a specific percentage change in price results in a larger percentage change in quantity demanded. Then E_d will be greater than one. For example, suppose that a 2 percent decline in the price of cut flowers results in a 4 percent increase in quantity demanded. Because $E_d = .04/.02 = 2$, demand for cut flowers is elastic.

---

*The Greek letter delta ($\triangle$) signifies "change in."

INELASTIC DEMAND

inelastic demand
Product or resource demand for which the price elasticity coefficient is less than one.

If a specific percentage change in price produces a smaller percentage change in quantity demanded, demand is **inelastic**. E_d will be less than one. For example, suppose that a 2 percent decline in the price of coffee leads to only a 1 percent increase in quantity demanded. Because E_d = .01/.02 = .5 demand is inelastic.

UNIT ELASTICITY

unit elasticity
Demand or supply for which the elasticity coefficient is equal to one.

The case separating elastic and inelastic demands occurs when a percentage change in price and the resulting percentage change in quantity demanded are the same. For example, suppose that a 2 percent drop in the price of chocolate causes a 2 percent increase in quantity demanded. This special case is termed **unit elasticity** because E_d is exactly one, or unity. In this example, E_d = .02/.02 = 1.

USE OF PERCENTAGES

Note that we use percentages rather than absolute amounts in measuring consumer responsiveness. If we use absolute changes, the choice of units will arbitrarily affect our impression of buyer responsiveness. To illustrate, if the price of a bag of popcorn at the local softball game is reduced from $3 to $2, and consumers increase their purchases from 60 to 100 bags, it appears that consumers are quite sensitive to price changes and, therefore, that demand is elastic. After all, a price change of one unit has caused a change of 40 units in the amount demanded. But by changing the monetary unit from dollars to pennies (why not?), we find that a price change of 100 units (pennies) causes a quantity change of 40 units. This result may falsely lead us to believe that demand is inelastic. We avoid this problem by using percentage changes. This particular price decline is 33 percent whether we measure in dollars ($1/$3) or pennies (100¢/300¢).

Also, by using percentages, we can correctly compare consumer responsiveness to changes in the prices of different products. It makes little sense to compare the effects on quantity demanded of a $1 increase in the price of a $10,000 used car with a $1 increase in the price of a $1 soft drink. Here the price of the used car increased by .01 percent while the price of the soft drink increased by 100 percent.

ELIMINATION OF THE MINUS SIGN

We know from the downsloping demand curve shown in Chapter 3 that price and quantity demanded are inversely related. Thus, the price elasticity coefficient of demand E_d will always be a negative number. We usually ignore the minus sign and simply present the absolute value of the elasticity coefficient to avoid an ambiguity that might otherwise arise. It can be confusing to say that an E_d of −4 is greater than one of −2. This possible confusion is avoided when we say an E_d of 4 reveals greater elasticity than one of 2.

EXTREME CASES

perfectly inelastic demand
Quantity demanded does not respond to a change in price.

When we say demand is *inelastic,* we do not mean that consumers are completely unresponsive to a price change. In that extreme situation, when a price change results in no change whatsoever in the quantity demanded, economists say that demand is **perfectly inelastic**. The price elasticity coefficient is zero because there is no response to a change in price. Approximate examples include a diabetic's demand for insulin or an addict's demand for heroin. A line parallel to the vertical axis, such as D_1 in Figure 5-1(a), shows perfectly inelastic demand graphically.

perfectly elastic demand
Quantity demanded can be of any amount at a particular product price.

Conversely, when demand is *elastic,* we do not mean that consumers are completely responsive to a price change. In that extreme situation, when a small price reduction causes buyers to increase their purchases from zero to all they can obtain, the elasticity coefficient is infinite ($= \infty$), and economists say demand is **perfectly elastic**. A line parallel to the horizontal axis, such as D_2 in Figure 5-1(b), shows perfectly elastic demand.

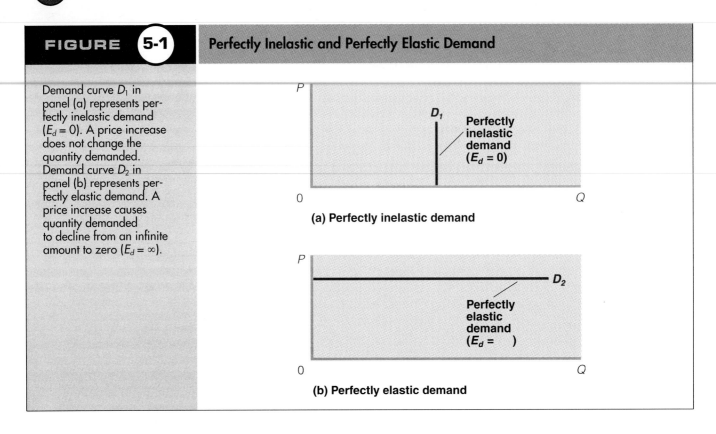

FIGURE 5-1 — Perfectly Inelastic and Perfectly Elastic Demand

Demand curve D_1 in panel (a) represents perfectly inelastic demand ($E_d = 0$). A price increase does not change the quantity demanded. Demand curve D_2 in panel (b) represents perfectly elastic demand. A price increase causes quantity demanded to decline from an infinite amount to zero ($E_d = \infty$).

(a) Perfectly inelastic demand

Perfectly inelastic demand ($E_d = 0$)

(b) Perfectly elastic demand

Perfectly elastic demand ($E_d = \ $)

As an exercise, verify the elasticity coefficients for the $1 to $2 and $7 to $8 ticket price ranges in Table 5-1. The interpretation of E_d for the $1 to $2 range is that a 1 percent change in price will change quantity demanded by 0.20 percent. For the $7 to $8 range, a 1 percent change in price will change quantity demanded by 5 percent.

Graphical Analysis

We used the hypothetical data for movie tickets in columns 1 and 2 of Table 5-1 to plot the demand curve D in Figure 5-2(a). The curve illustrates that elasticity typically varies over the different price ranges of the same demand schedule or curve. For all straight-line and most other demand curves, demand is more elastic toward the upper left (the $5 to $8 price range of D) than toward the lower right (the $4 to $1 price range of D).

This difference is the consequence of arithmetic properties of the elasticity measure. Specifically, in the upper left segment of the demand curve, the percentage change in quantity is large because the original reference quantity is small. Similarly, the percentage change in price is small in that segment because the original reference price is large. The relatively large percentage change in quantity divided by the relatively small change in price yields a large E_d—an elastic demand.

The reverse holds true for the lower right segment of the demand curve. Here the percentage change in quantity is small because the original reference quantity is large; similarly, the percentage change in price is large because the original reference price is small. The relatively small percentage change in quantity divided by the relatively large percentage change in price results in a small E_d—an inelastic demand.

The demand curve in Figure 5-2(a) also illustrates that the slope of a demand curve—its flatness or steepness—is not a sound basis for judging elasticity. The catch is that the slope of the curve is computed from *absolute* changes in price and quantity, while elasticity involves *relative* or

| FIGURE 5-2 | The Relation Between Price Elasticity of Demand for Movie Tickets and Total Revenue |

Demand curve D in panel (a) is based on Table 5-1 and is marked to show that the hypothetical weekly demand for movie tickets is elastic at higher price ranges and inelastic at lower price ranges. The total-revenue curve TR in panel (b) is derived from demand curve D. When price falls and TR increases, demand is elastic; when price falls and TR is unchanged, demand is unit elastic; when price falls and TR declines, demand is inelastic.

(a) Demand curve

(b) Total-revenue curve

percentage changes in price and quantity. The demand curve in Figure 5-2(a) is linear, which by definition means that the slope is constant throughout, but we have demonstrated that such a curve is elastic in its high-price ($8 to $5) range and inelastic in its low-price ($4 to $1) range. *(Key Question 2)*

5.2   The Total-revenue Test

total revenue (TR)
The total number of dollars received by a firm from the sale of a product in a particular period.

total-revenue test
A test to determine elasticity of demand between any two prices.

The importance of elasticity for firms relates to the effect of price changes on total revenue and thus on profits (total revenue minus total costs).

Total revenue (TR) is the total amount the seller receives from the sale of a product in a particular period; it is calculated by multiplying the product price (P) by the quantity demanded and sold (Q). In equation form, TR = $P \times Q$. Total revenue and the price elasticity of demand are related. Indeed, perhaps the easiest way to infer whether demand is elastic or inelastic is to employ the **total-revenue test**, which looks at what happens to total revenue when product price changes.

Elastic Demand

If demand is elastic, a decrease in price will increase total revenue. Even though a lesser price is received per unit, enough additional units are sold to more than compensate for the lower price. For an example, look at demand curve D in Figure 5-2(a), specifically the elastic-demand region at the upper left. (Disregard Figure 5-2(b) for the moment.) At point a on the curve, price is $8 and quantity demanded is 1 unit, or 1000 tickets. So total revenue, or price times quantity, is $8000 (= $8 × 1000 tickets).

If the price of movie tickets declines to $7 (point b), the quantity demanded becomes 2 units, and total revenue is $14,000 (= $2 × 7000 units). As a result of the price decline from $8 to $7, total revenue has increased from $8000 to $14,000. This increase has occurred because the loss in revenue from the lower price per unit is less than the gain in revenue from the larger quantity demanded at the lower price.

The reasoning is reversible: If demand is elastic, a price increase will reduce total revenue. If we shift from b to a on the demand curve, the gain in total revenue caused by the higher ticket price is less than the loss in revenue from the drop in sales. Combining these results tells us that demand is elastic if a price change causes total revenue to change in the opposite direction.

Inelastic Demand

If demand is inelastic, a price decrease will reduce total revenue. The modest increase in ticket sales will not offset the decline in revenue per unit, and the net result is that total revenue will decline. To see this, look toward the lower right of demand curve D in Figure 5-2(a), specifically the inelastic-demand region. At point f on the curve, price is $2 and quantity demanded is 7000 tickets. So total revenue is $14,000. If the price drops to $1 (point h), quantity demanded increases to 8000 tickets. Total revenue becomes $8000, which is clearly less than $14,000.

Again, our analysis is reversible: If demand is inelastic, a price increase will increase total revenue. Together, these results tell us that demand is inelastic if a price change causes total revenue to change in the same direction.

Unit Elasticity

In the special case of unit elasticity, an increase or a decrease in price leaves total revenue unchanged. In Figure 5-2(a) we find that at the $5 price, 4000 tickets will be sold, yielding total revenue of $20,000. At $4, 5000 tickets will be sold, again resulting in $20,000 of total revenue. The $1 price reduction causes the loss of $4000 in revenue on the 4000 tickets that could have been sold for $5 each. This loss is exactly offset by a $4000 revenue gain resulting from the sale of 1000 more tickets at the lower $4 price.

Price Elasticity and the Total-revenue Curve

In Figure 5-2(b) we graphed the total revenue per week to the theatre owner that corresponds to each price–quantity combination indicated along demand curve D in Figure 5-2(a). Comparison of curves D and TR sharply focuses the relationship between elasticity and total revenue. Lowering the ticket price in the elastic range of demand—for example, from $8 to $5—increases total revenue. Conversely, increasing the ticket price in that range reduces total revenue. In both cases, price and total revenue change in opposite directions, confirming that demand is elastic.

The $5 to $4 price range of demand curve D reflects unit elasticity. When price either decreases from $5 to $4 or increases from $4 to $5, total revenue remains $20,000. In both cases, price has changed and total revenue has remained constant, confirming that demand is unit elastic when we consider these particular price changes.

In the inelastic range of demand curve D, lowering the price—for example, from $4 to $1—decreases total revenue, as shown in Figure 5-2(b). Raising the price boosts total revenue. In both cases, price and total revenue move in the same direction, confirming that demand is inelastic.

Table 5-2 summarizes the characteristics of price elasticity of demand. You should review it carefully. *(Key Questions 4 and 5)*

Determinants of Price Elasticity of Demand

What determines the price elasticity of demand? Four main factors stand out.

TABLE 5-2	Price Elasticity of Demand: A Summary			
			Impact on total revenue of a	
Absolute value of elasticity coefficient	**Demand is**	**Description**	**Price increase**	**Price decrease**
Greater than 1 ($E_d > 1$)	Elastic or relatively elastic	Quantity demanded changes by a larger percentage than does price	Total revenue decreases	Total revenue increases
Equal to 1 ($E_d = 1$)	Unit or unitary elastic	Quantity demanded changes by the same percentage as does price	Total revenue is unchanged	Total revenue is unchanged
Less than 1 ($E_d < 1$)	Inelastic or relatively inelastic	Quantity demanded changes by a smaller percentage than does price	Total revenue increases	Total revenue decreases

SUBSTITUTABILITY

Generally, *the larger the number of substitute goods that are available, the greater the price elasticity of demand.* We will see later that in a purely competitive market, where by definition many perfect substitutes exist for the product of any specific seller, the demand curve for the single seller is perfectly elastic. If one competitive seller of carrots or potatoes raises its price, buyers will turn to the readily available perfect substitutes provided by its many rivals. Similarly, we would expect the lowering of world trade barriers to increase the elasticity of demand for most products by making more substitutes available. With unimpeded foreign trade, Mercedes and BMWs become effective substitutes for domestic Cadillacs and Lincolns. At the other extreme, we saw earlier that the diabetic's demand for insulin is highly inelastic because no close substitutes exist.

The elasticity of demand for a product depends on how narrowly the product is defined. Demand for Reebok sneakers is more elastic than is the overall demand for shoes. Many other brands are readily substitutable for Reebok sneakers, but there are few, if any, good substitutes for shoes.

PROPORTION OF INCOME

Other things equal, *the greater the proportion of income spent on a good, the greater the price elasticity of demand for it.* A 10 percent increase in the price of relatively low-priced pencils or chewing gum amounts to a very small proportion of most people's incomes, and quantity demanded will probably decline only slightly. Thus, price elasticity for such items tends to be low. But a 10 percent increase in the price of relatively high-priced automobiles or houses means additional expenditures of perhaps $6000 or $70,000, respectively. These price increases are significant fractions of the annual incomes and budgets of most families, and quantities demanded will likely diminish significantly. Price elasticity for such items tends to be high.

LUXURIES VERSUS NECESSITIES

In general, *the more that a good is considered a luxury rather than a necessity, the greater is the price elasticity of demand.* Bread and electricity are generally regarded as necessities; a price increase will not significantly reduce the amount of bread consumed or the amount of lighting and power used in a household. (Note the very low price elasticity coefficient of these goods in Table 5-3.) In an extreme example, a person does not decline an operation for acute appendicitis because the surgeon has found a way to extra-bill.

However, travel vacations and jewellery are luxuries, which, by definition, can easily be forgone. If the prices of travel vacations or jewellery rise, a consumer need not buy them and will suffer no greater hardship without them.

In general, the more a good is considered a luxury rather than a necessity, the greater is the price elasticity of demand.

TIME

Generally, *product demand is more elastic the longer the period under consideration.* Consumers often need time to adjust to changes in prices. When the price of a product rises, it takes time to find and experiment with other products to see whether they are acceptable. Consumers may not immediately reduce their purchases very much when the price of beef rises by 10 percent, but in time they may switch to chicken or fish.

Studies show that short-run demand for gasoline is more inelastic ($E_d = .2$) than is long-run demand ($E_d = .7$). In the short run, people are stuck with their present cars and trucks, but with rising gasoline prices, they will eventually replace them with smaller, more fuel-efficient vehicles.

Table 5-3 shows estimated price elasticity coefficients for several products. Each coefficient reflects some combination of the elasticity determinants just discussed. As an exercise, select two or three of them and explain how they relate to the determinants. **(Key Question 6)**

TABLE 5-3	Selected Price Elasticities of Demand		
Product or service	**Coefficient of price elasticity of demand, E_d**	**Product or service**	**Coefficient of price elasticity of demand, E_d**
Newspapers	.10	Milk	.63
Electricity (household)	.13	Household appliances	.63
Bread	.15	Movies	.87
Major league baseball tickets	.23	Beer	.90
Telephone service	.26	Shoes	.91
Sugar	.30	Motor vehicles	1.14
Eggs	.32	Beef	1.27
Legal services	.37	China, glassware, tableware	1.54
Automobile repair	.40	Restaurant meals	2.27
Clothing	.49	Lamb and mutton	2.65
Gasoline	.60		

Compiled from numerous studies and sources reporting price elasticity of demand.

QUICK REVIEW

- When the price of a good changes, total revenue will change in the opposite direction if demand for the good is price elastic, in the same direction if demand is price inelastic, and not at all if demand is unit elastic.

- Price elasticity of demand is greater (1) the larger the number of substitutes available, (2) the higher the price of a product relative to one's budget, (3) the greater the extent to which the product is a luxury, and (4) the longer the period involved.

Applications of Price Elasticity of Demand

The concept of price elasticity of demand has great practical significance, as the following examples suggest.

LARGE CROP YIELDS

The demand for most farm products is highly inelastic; E_d is perhaps .20 or .25. As a result, increases in the output of farm products arising from a good growing season or from increased productivity tend to depress both the prices of farm products and the total revenues (incomes) of farmers. For farmers as a group, the inelastic demand for their product means that a large crop may be undesirable. For policymakers it means that achieving the goal of higher total farm income requires that farm output be restricted.

SALES TAXES

Both federal and provincial governments pay attention to elasticity of demand when selecting goods and services on which to levy sales taxes. If a $1 tax is levied on a product and 10,000 units are sold, tax revenue will be $10,000 (= $1 × 10,000 units sold). If the government raises the tax to

$1.50 but the higher price reduces sales to 5000 because of elastic demand, tax revenue will decline to $7500 (= $1.50 × 5000 units sold). Because a higher tax on a product with elastic demand will bring in less tax revenue, legislatures tend to seek out products that have inelastic demand—such as liquor, gasoline, and cigarettes—when levying sales tax.

DECRIMINALIZATION OF ILLEGAL DRUGS

<www.drugwarfacts.org/
economi.htm>
The drug war and economics

In recent years proposals to legalize drugs have been widely debated. Proponents contend that drugs should be treated like alcohol; they should be made legal for adults and regulated for purity and potency. The war on drugs, it is argued, has been unsuccessful and the associated costs—including enlarged police forces, the construction of more prisons, an overburdened court system, and untold human costs—have increased markedly. Some contend that legalization would reduce drug trafficking significantly by taking the profit out of it. Crack cocaine and heroin, for example, are cheap to produce and could be sold at low prices in legal markets. Because the demand of addicts is highly inelastic, the amounts consumed at the lower prices would increase only modestly. Addicts' total expenditures for cocaine and heroin would decline and so would the street crime that finances those expenditures.

Opponents of legalization say that the overall demand for cocaine and heroin is far more elastic than proponents think. In addition to the inelastic demand of addicts, another market segment's demand is relatively elastic. This segment consists of occasional users, who use hard drugs when the prices are low but who abstain or substitute, say, alcohol when the prices of hard drugs are high. Thus, the lower prices associated with the legalization of hard drugs would increase consumption by occasional users. Also, removal of the legal prohibitions against using drugs might make drug use more socially acceptable, increasing the demand for cocaine and heroin.

Many economists predict that the legalization of cocaine and heroin would reduce street prices by up to 60 percent, depending on whether and how much it was taxed. According to a recent study, price declines of that size would increase the number of occasional users of heroin by 54 percent and the number of occasional users of cocaine by 33 percent. The total quantity of heroin demanded would rise by an estimated 100 percent and the quantity of cocaine demanded would rise by 50 percent.[1] Assuming street prices for both heroin and cocaine rose by 60 percent, such changes in quantity demanded imply price elasticity of demand of 1.66 for heroin and 0.83 for cocaine. Many existing and first-time users might eventually become addicts. The overall result, say the opponents of legalization, would be higher social costs, possibly including an increase in street crime.

MINIMUM WAGE

The minimum wage prohibits employers from paying workers less than a specified hourly wage. The minimum wage in Canada ranges from a low of $5.80 in Nova Scotia to $8.00 in British Columbia. Critics say that such a minimum wage, if it is above the equilibrium market wage, moves employers upward along their downsloping labour demand curves toward lower quantities of labour demanded, which causes unemployment, particularly among teenage workers. However, workers who remain employed at the minimum wage receive higher incomes than they otherwise would. The amount of income lost by the newly unemployed and the amount of income gained by those who keep their jobs depend on the elasticity of demand for teenage labour. Research suggests that the demand for teenage labour is relatively inelastic. If correct, this means that income gains associated with the minimum wage would exceed income losses. The "unemployment argument" made by critics of the minimum wage would be stronger if the demand for teenage workers were elastic.

---

[1]Henry Saffer and Frank Chaloupka, "The Demand for Illegal Drugs," *Economic Inquiry*, July 1999, pp. 401–411.

5.3   Price Elasticity of Supply

The concept of price elasticity also applies to supply. If producers are relatively responsive to price changes, supply is elastic. If they are relatively insensitive to price changes, supply is inelastic.

We measure the degree of price elasticity of supply with the coefficient E_s, defined almost like E_d except that we substitute "percentage change in quantity supplied" for "percentage change in quantity demanded":

$$E_s = \frac{\text{percentage change in quantity supplied of product X}}{\text{percentage change in price of product X}}$$

For reasons explained earlier, the averages, or midpoints, of the before and after quantities supplied and the before and after prices are used as reference points for the percentage changes. Suppose an increase in the price of a good from \$4 to \$6 increases the quantity supplied from 10 units to 14 units. The percentage change in price would be 2/5, or 40 percent, and the percentage change in quantity would be 4/12, or 33 percent: $E_s = .33/.40 = .83$. In this case, supply is inelastic, since the price elasticity coefficient is less than one. If E_s is greater than one, supply is elastic. If it is equal to one, supply is unit elastic. Also, E_s is never negative, since price and quantity supplied are directly related. Thus, there are no minus signs to drop, as was necessary with elasticity of demand.

price elasticity of supply
The ratio of the percentage change in quantity supplied of a product or resource to the percentage change in its price.

The main determinant of **price elasticity of supply** is the amount of time producers have to respond to a change in product price. A firm's response to, say, an increase in the price of Christmas trees depends on its ability to shift inputs from the production of other products (whose prices we assume remain constant) to the production of trees. Shifting inputs takes time: the longer the time available, the greater the ability to shift inputs. So, we can expect a greater response, and therefore greater elasticity of supply, the longer a firm has to adjust to a price change.

In analyzing the impact of time on elasticity, we distinguish among the immediate market period, the short run, and the long run.

Price Elasticity of Supply: The Market Period

market period
A period in which producers of a product are unable to change the quantity produced in response to a change in its price.

The **market period** is the period that occurs when the time immediately after a change in market price is too short for producers to respond with a change in quantity supplied. Suppose the owner of a small farm in southwestern Ontario brings to market one truckload of tomatoes, which is the entire season's output. The supply curve for the tomatoes is perfectly inelastic (vertical); the farmer will sell the truckload whether the price is high or low. Why? Because the farmer can offer only one truckload of tomatoes even if the price of tomatoes is much higher than anticipated. The farmer might like to offer more tomatoes, but tomatoes cannot be produced overnight. Another full growing season is needed to respond to a higher-than-expected price by producing more than one truckload. Similarly, because the product is perishable, the farmer cannot withhold it from the market. If the price is lower than anticipated, the farmer will still sell the entire truckload.

The farmer's costs of production, incidentally, will not enter into this decision to sell. Though the price of tomatoes may fall far short of production costs, the farmer will nevertheless sell out to avoid a total loss through spoilage. During the market period, our farmer's supply of tomatoes is fixed: only one truckload is offered no matter how high or low the price.

Figure 5-3(a) shows the farmer's vertical supply curve during the market period. Supply is perfectly inelastic because the farmer does not have time to respond to a change in demand, say from D_1 to D_2. The resulting price increase from P_0 to P_m simply determines which buyers get the fixed quantity supplied; it elicits no increase in output.

However, not all supply curves need be perfectly inelastic immediately after a price change. If the product is not perishable and the price rises, producers may choose to increase quantity supplied by drawing down their inventories of unsold, stored goods, causing the market supply curve to attain some positive slope. For our tomato farmer, the market period may be a full growing season; for producers of goods that can be inexpensively stored, there may be no market period at all.

FIGURE **5-3**   **Time and the Elasticity of Supply**

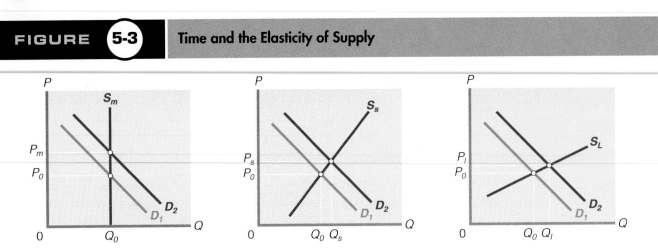

(a) Immediate market period   **(b) Short run**   **(c) Long run**

The greater the amount of time producers have to adjust to a change in demand, here from D_1 to D_2, the greater will be their output response. In the immediate market period in panel (a), producers have insufficient time to change output, and so supply is perfectly inelastic. In the short run in panel (b), plant capacity is fixed, but changing the intensity of its use can alter output; supply is therefore more elastic. In the long run in panel (c), all desired adjustments, including changes in plant capacity, can be made, and supply becomes still more elastic.

Price Elasticity of Supply: The Short Run

short run
A period of time in which producers are able to change the quantities of some but not all of the resources they employ.

In the **short run**, the plant capacity of individual producers and of the entire industry is fixed. Even so, firms do have time to use their fixed plants more or less intensively. In the short run, our farmer's plant (land and farm machinery) is fixed, but time is available in the short run to cultivate tomatoes more intensively by applying more labour and more fertilizer and pesticides to the crop. The result is a somewhat greater output in response to a presumed increase in demand; this greater output is reflected in a more elastic supply of tomatoes, as shown by figure S_s in Figure 5-3(b). Note now that the increase in demand from D_1 to D_2 is met by an increase in quantity (from Q_0 to Q_s), so there is a smaller price adjustment (from P_0 to P_s) than in the market period. The equilibrium price is, therefore, lower in the short run than in the market period.

Price Elasticity of Supply: The Long Run

long run
A period of time long enough to enable producers of a product to change the quantities of all the resources they employ.

The **long run** is a period long enough for firms to adjust their plant sizes and for new firms to enter (or existing firms to leave) the industry. In the tomato industry, for example, our farmer has time to acquire additional land and buy more machinery and equipment. Furthermore, other farmers may, over time, be attracted to tomato farming by the increased demand and higher price. Such adjustments create a larger supply response, as represented by the more elastic supply curve S_L in Figure 5-3(c). The outcome is a smaller price rise (P_0 to P_1) and a larger output increase (Q_0 to Q_1) in response to the increase in demand from D_1 to D_2. *(Key Question 10)*

There is no total-revenue test for elasticity of supply. Supply shows a positive or direct relationship between price and amount supplied; the supply curve is upsloping. Regardless of the degree of elasticity or inelasticity, price and total revenue always move together.

5.4   Cross Elasticity and Income Elasticity of Demand

Price elasticities measure the responsiveness of the quantity of a product demanded or supplied when its price changes. The consumption of a good also is affected by a change in the price of a related product or by a change in income.

Cross Elasticity of Demand

cross elasticity of demand
The ratio of the percentage change in quantity demanded of one good to the percentage change in the price of some other good.

The **cross elasticity of demand** measures how sensitive consumer purchases of one product (say, X) are to a change in the price of some other product (say, Y). We calculate the coefficient of cross elasticity of demand E_{xy} just as we do the coefficient of simple price elasticity, except that we relate the percentage change in the consumption of X to the percentage change in the price of Y:

$$E_{xy} = \frac{\text{percentage change in quantity demanded of product X}}{\text{percentage change in price of product Y}}$$

This cross elasticity (or cross price elasticity) concept allows us to quantify and more fully understand substitute and complementary goods, introduced in Chapter 3.

SUBSTITUTE GOODS

If cross elasticity of demand is positive, meaning that sales of X move in the same direction as a change in the price of Y, then X and Y are substitute goods. An example is Kodak film (X) and Fuji film (Y). An increase in the price of Kodak film causes consumers to buy more Fuji film, resulting in a positive cross elasticity. The larger the positive cross elasticity coefficient, the greater the substitutability between the two products.

COMPLEMENTARY GOODS

When cross elasticity is negative, we know that X and Y move together; an increase in the price of one decreases the demand for the other. They are complementary goods. For example, an increase in the price of cameras will decrease the amount of film purchased. The larger the negative cross elasticity coefficient, the greater is the complementarity between the two goods.

INDEPENDENT GOODS

A zero or near-zero cross elasticity tells us that the two products being considered are unrelated or independent goods. An example is walnuts and film; we would not expect a change in the price of walnuts to have any effect on purchases of film, and vice versa.

APPLICATIONS

The degree of substitutability of products, measured by the cross elasticity coefficient, is important to businesses and government. For example, suppose that Coca-Cola is considering whether to lower the price of its Sprite brand. Not only will it want to know something about the price elasticity of demand for Sprite (will the price cut increase or decrease total revenue?), it will also be interested in knowing whether the increased sale of Sprite will come at the expense of its Coke brand. How sensitive are the sales of one of its products (Coke) to a change in the price of another of its products (Sprite)? By how much will the increased sales of Sprite reduce the sales of Coke? A low cross elasticity would indicate that Coke and Sprite are weak substitutes for each other and that a lower price for Sprite would have little effect on Coke sales.

Government also implicitly uses the idea of cross elasticity of demand in assessing whether a proposed merger between two large firms will substantially reduce competition and violate the anti-combines laws. For example, the cross elasticity between Coke and Pepsi is high, making them strong substitutes for each other. Consequently, the government would likely block a merger between the two companies because it would lessen competition. In contrast, the cross elasticity between film and gasoline is low or zero. A merger between Kodak and Petro-Canada would have a minimal effect on competition, so government would be more likely to allow it.

Income Elasticity of Demand

Income elasticity of demand measures the degree to which consumers respond to a change in their income by buying more or less of a particular good. The coefficient of income elasticity of demand, E_i, is determined with the formula

$$E_i = \frac{\text{percentage change in quantity demanded}}{\text{percentage change in income}}$$

NORMAL GOODS

For most goods, the income elasticity coefficient E_i is positive, meaning that more of them are demanded as incomes rise. Such goods are called normal goods, which we first described in Chapter 3. The value of E_i varies greatly among normal goods. For example, income elasticity of demand for automobiles is about +3.00, while income elasticity for most farm products is only about +0.20.

INFERIOR GOODS

A negative income elasticity coefficient designates an inferior good. Retread tires, cabbage, long-distance bus tickets, used clothing, and muscatel wine are likely candidates. Consumers decrease their purchases of inferior goods as incomes rise.

INSIGHTS

Coefficients of income elasticity of demand provide insights into the economy. For example, income elasticity helps to explain the expansion and contraction of industries in the Canadian economy. On average, total income in the economy has grown by 2 to 3 percent annually. As income has expanded, industries producing products for which demand is quite income elastic have expanded their outputs. Thus, automobiles ($E_i = +3.0$), housing ($E_i = +1.5$), books ($E_i = +1.4$), and restaurant meals ($E_i = +1.4$) have all experienced strong growth of output. Also, studies show that the demand for health services is income elastic. The implication of this is that the demand on the Canadian health care system will continue to outpace income growth. Meanwhile, industries producing products for which income elasticity is low or negative have tended to grow slowly or to decline. For example, agriculture ($E_i = +0.20$) has grown far more slowly than has the economy's total output. We do not eat twice as much when our incomes double.

As another example, when recessions occur and people's incomes decline, grocery stores fare relatively better than stores selling electronic equipment. People do not substantially cut back on their purchases of food when their incomes fall; income elasticity of demand for food is relatively low. But they do substantially cut back on their purchases of electronic equipment; income elasticity on such equipment is relatively high. *(Key Questions 12 and 13)*

In Table 5-4 we provide a synopsis of the cross elasticity and income elasticity concepts.

5.5   Elasticity and Real-world Applications

Supply and demand analysis and the elasticity concept are applied repeatedly in the remainder of this book. Let's strengthen our understanding of these analytical tools and their significance by examining elasticity and tax incidence.

TABLE 5-4	Cross and Income Elasticities of Demand	
Value of coefficient	**Description**	**Type of good(s)**
Cross elasticity:		
Positive ($E_{wz} > 0$)	Quantity demanded of W changes in same direction as change in price of Z	Substitutes
Negative ($E_{xy} < 0$)	Quantity demanded of X changes in opposite direction from change in price of Y	Complements
Income elasticity:		
Positive ($E_i > 0$)	Quantity demanded of the product changes in same direction as change in income	Normal
Negative ($E_i < 0$)	Quantity demanded of the product changes in opposite direction from change in income	Inferior

Elasticity and Tax Incidence

In Figure 5-4, *S* and *D* represent the pre-tax market for a certain domestic wine from the Niagara Peninsula. The no-tax equilibrium price and quantity are $4 per bottle and 15 million bottles. If the Ontario government levies a tax of $1 per bottle directly on the winery for every bottle sold, who actually pays it?

FIGURE 5-4	The Incidence of a Tax

A tax of a specified amount per unit levied on producers, here $2 per unit, shifts the supply curve upward by the amount of the tax per unit: the vertical distance between *S* and *S*ₜ. This shift results in a higher price (here $9.00) to the consumer and a lower after-tax price (here $7.00) to the producer. Thus, consumers and producers share the burden of the tax in some proportion (here equally at $1.00 per unit).

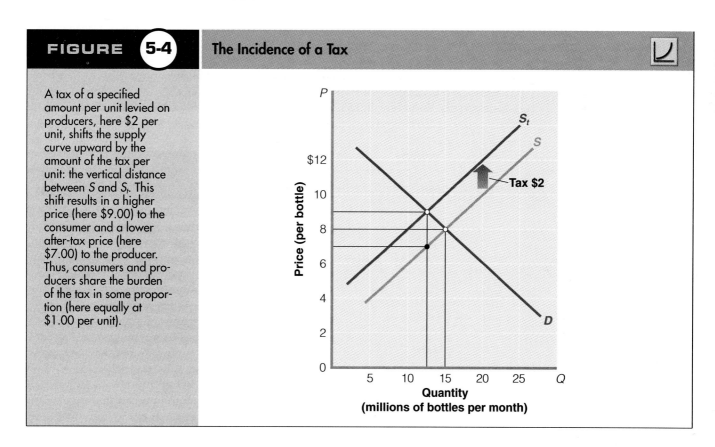

DIVISION OF BURDEN

Since provincial government places the tax on the sellers (suppliers), the tax can be viewed as an addition to the marginal cost of the product. Now sellers must get $2 more for each bottle to receive the same per-unit profit they were getting before the tax. While sellers are willing to offer, for example, five million bottles of untaxed wine at $4 per bottle, they must now receive $6 per bottle—$4 plus the $2 tax—to offer the same five million bottles. The tax shifts the supply curve upward (leftward) as shown in Figure 5-4, where S_t is the after-tax supply curve.

The after-tax equilibrium price is $9.00 per bottle, whereas the before-tax price was $8.00. So, in this case, half the $2 tax is paid by consumers as a higher price; the other half must be paid by producers in a lower after-tax per-unit revenue. That is, after paying the $2.00 tax per unit to the provincial government, producers receive $7.00, or $1.00 less than the $8.00 before-tax price. In this instance, consumers and producers share the burden of this tax equally; producers shift half the tax to consumers in a higher price and bear the other half themselves.

Note also that the equilibrium quantity decreases as a result of the tax levy and the higher price it imposes on consumers. In Figure 5-4, that decline in quantity is from 15 million bottles per month to 12.5 million bottles per month.

ELASTICITIES

If the elasticities of demand and supply were different from those shown in Figure 5-4, the incidence of tax would also be different. Two generalizations are relevant.

First, *with a specific supply, the more inelastic the demand for the product, the larger the portion of the tax shifted to consumers.* To verify this, sketch graphically the extreme cases where demand is perfectly elastic or perfectly inelastic. In the first case, the incidence of the tax is entirely on sellers; in the second, the tax is shifted entirely to consumers.

Figure 5-5 contrasts the more usual cases where demand is either relatively elastic or relatively inelastic in the relevant price range. With elastic demand, shown in Figure 5-5(a), a small portion of the tax $(P_e - P_1)$ is shifted to consumers and most of the tax $(P_1 - P_a)$ is borne by the producers. With inelastic demand, shown in Figure 5-5(b), most of the tax $(P_i - P_1)$ is shifted to consumers and only a small amount $(P_1 - P_b)$ is paid by producers. In both graphs the per-unit tax is represented by the vertical distance between S_t and S.

Note also that the decline in equilibrium quantity $(Q_1 - Q_2)$ is smaller when demand is more inelastic, which is the basis of our previous applications of the elasticity concept: Revenue-seeking

---

FIGURE **5-5**	Demand Elasticity and the Incidence of a Tax

Panel (a): If demand is elastic in the relevant price range, price rises modestly (P_1 to P_e) when a tax is levied. Hence, the producer bears most of the tax burden. Panel (b): If demand is inelastic, the price to the buyer will increase substantially (P_1 to P_i) and most of the tax will be shifted to consumers.

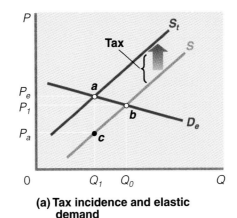

(a) Tax incidence and elastic demand

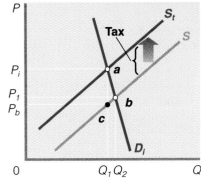

(b) Tax incidence and inelastic demand

legislatures place heavy sales taxes on liquor, cigarettes, and other products whose demands are thought to be inelastic. Since demand for these products is relatively inelastic, the tax does not reduce sales much, so the tax revenue stays high.

Second, *with a specific demand, the more inelastic the supply, the larger the portion of the tax borne by producers.* When supply is elastic, as in Figure 5-6(a), most of the tax ($P_e – P_1$) is shifted to consumers, and only a small portion ($P_1 – P_a$) is borne by sellers. But when supply is inelastic, as in Figure 5-6(b), the reverse is true; the major portion of the tax ($P_1 – P_b$) falls on sellers, and a relatively small amount ($P_i – P_1$) is shifted to buyers. The equilibrium quantity also declines less with an inelastic supply than it does with an elastic supply.

Gold is an example of a product with an inelastic supply, one where the burden of a tax would mainly fall on producers. Conversely, because the supply of baseballs is elastic, producers would pass on to consumers much of a tax on baseballs.

You may want to reverse the analysis and assume that the government levies a (sales) tax on consumers. *(Key Question 15)*

Rent Controls

Rent controls are maximum rents established by law (and recently, rent controls have set maximum rent increases for existing tenants). Such laws are well intended; their goals are to protect low-income families from escalating rents caused by perceived housing shortages and to make housing more affordable to the poor.

When controls are first imposed, they usually restrict increases in rents above current levels. The short-run supply curve for rental accommodation is inelastic because it takes landlords some time to react to price changes and bring new units on the market. Most tenants benefit, since the quantity of rental accommodation currently on the market or under construction is not significantly affected. Thus, the program appears to be successful even if shortages begin to appear. Figure 5-7(a) portrays a market for rental accommodation with rents fixed at R_c and a short-run supply curve, S_s. A shortage $Q_1 – Q_2$ exists in the short run.

In the long run the shortage of rental accommodation will worsen since the supply of rental accommodation becomes more elastic. Construction of new units decreases and landlords try to convert existing units to other uses or allow them to deteriorate. The supply curve becomes more elastic in the long run, shown by S_L in Figure 5-7(b), making the shortage worse, and increasing it to $Q_1 – Q_3$.

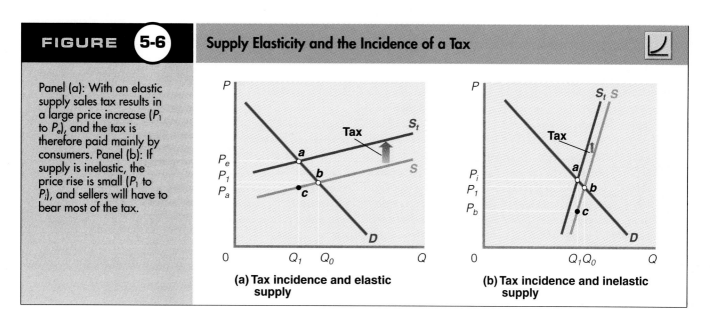

FIGURE 5-6 Supply Elasticity and the Incidence of a Tax

Panel (a): With an elastic supply sales tax results in a large price increase (P_1 to P_e), and the tax is therefore paid mainly by consumers. Panel (b): If supply is inelastic, the price rise is small (P_1 to P_i), and sellers will have to bear most of the tax.

(a) Tax incidence and elastic supply

(b) Tax incidence and inelastic supply

FIGURE 5-7 **Rent Controls**

In the short run (panel a) the supply for rental accommodation is inelastic. If rent controls are set at R_c, a shortage of $Q_1 - Q_2$ will occur in the short run. In the long run (panel b), supply becomes more elastic as landlords are able to add or withdraw rental units from the market. In the long run the shortage will worsen to $Q_1 - Q_3$. On the black market, rents of as much as R_2 will be charged.

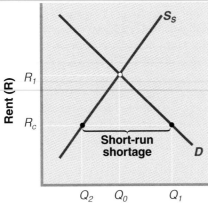

(a) Short run

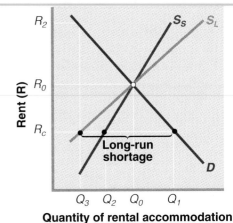

(b) Long run

The gradually worsening shortage in the long run leads to several related problems. As in the case of controls on food prices, a black market will emerge. The black market in rental accommodation is often characterized by the charging of "key money." Prospective tenants are often forced to bribe a landlord or a subletting tenant to acquire a particular rental unit. The acceptance of key money is illegal in most jurisdictions with rent controls, but the practice is difficult to stamp out because it is to the advantage of both parties. Those desperate for rental accommodation will have to pay the black market rate of as much as R_2, shown in Figure 5-7(b).

Consider This

Below-equilibrium Prices

Below-equilibrium pricing should not be associated solely with government policies. Rock superstars, such as Canada's Avril Lavigne, sometimes price their concert tickets below the market-clearing price. The tickets are usually rationed on a first-come, first-served basis, and ticket scalping is common. Why should these stars want to subsidize their fans—at least those fortunate enough to obtain tickets—with below-equilibrium prices? Why not set ticket prices at a higher, market-clearing level and realize more income from a tour?

The answer is that long lines of fans waiting hours or days for bargain-priced tickets catch the attention of the press. (Some of the people in the lines, however, are there to buy tickets for resale!) The millions of dollars' worth of free publicity that results undoubtedly stimulates CD sales, from which much of any musician's income is derived. Thus the gift of

below-equilibrium ticket prices from a rock star to fans also benefits the star. And the gift imposes a cost on fans—the opportunity cost of time spent waiting in line to buy tickets.

Incidentally, many people regard the ticket scalping often associated with musical or athletic events as a form of extortion, where the extortionist's (the seller's) gain is the victim's (the buyer's) loss. But the fact that scalping is a voluntary transaction suggests that both seller and buyer gain; otherwise, the exchange would not occur. Such exchanges redistribute assets (tickets) from those who value them less to those who value them more.

Question: Explain what would occur if a rock star such as Avril Lavigne priced concert tickets at above the market-clearing price.

Another problem that results from controls is the emergence of a dual rental market if new buildings are exempt from controls. Apartment units whose rents are below market levels are almost always rented informally or with some form of key money attached. The units that have recently come on the market will be offered at rents above the levels that would exist without controls as landlords attempt to compensate for future restrictions on rent increases. Because of discrimination by landlords and the ability to pay key money, middle-class tenants will find it easier to secure units in the controlled market, while the poor will be forced to seek units in the uncontrolled market. Perversely, tenants with higher incomes can be the major beneficiaries of the program.

Rent controls distort market signals and misallocate resources. Too few resources are allocated to rental housing, too many to alternative uses. Ironically, although rent controls are often legislated to lessen the effects of perceived housing shortages, controls are a primary cause of such shortages.

Refer to the Consider This box for other examples of below-equilibrium prices.

Applications of Price Elasticity of Supply

The idea of price elasticity of supply has widespread applicability, as suggested by the following examples.

ANTIQUES AND REPRODUCTIONS

There are several places across Canada in which people bring antiques to a central location for appraisal by experts. Some people are pleased to learn that their old piece of furniture or funky folk art is worth a large amount, say, $30,000 or more.

The high price of an antique results from strong demand and limited, highly inelastic supply. Because a genuine antique can no longer be reproduced, the quantity supplied either does not rise or rises only slightly as its price goes up. The higher price might prompt the discovery of a few more of the remaining originals and thus add to the quantity available for sale, but this quantity response is usually quite small. So the supply of antiques and other collectibles tends to be inelastic. For one-of-a-kind antiques, the supply is perfectly inelastic.

Factors such as increased population, higher income, and greater enthusiasm for collecting antiques have increased the demand for antiques over time. Because the supply of antiques is limited and inelastic, those increases in demand have greatly boosted the prices of antiques.

Contrast the inelastic supply of original antiques with the elastic supply of modern "made-to-look-old" reproductions. Such faux antiques are quite popular and widely available. When the demand for reproductions increases, the firms making them simply boost production. Because the supply of reproductions is highly elastic, increased demand raises their price only slightly.

VOLATILE GOLD PRICES

The price of gold is quite volatile, sometimes shooting upward one period and plummeting downward the next. The main sources of these fluctuations are shifts in demand and highly inelastic supply. Gold production is a costly and time-consuming process of exploration, mining, and refining. Moreover, the physical availability of gold is highly limited. For both reasons, increases in gold prices do not elicit substantial increases in quantity supplied. Conversely, gold mining is costly to shut down and existing gold bars are expensive to store. Price decreases therefore do not produce large drops in the quantity of gold supplied. In short, the supply of gold is inelastic.

The demand for gold is partly derived from the demand for its uses such as for jewellery, dental fillings, and coins. But people also demand gold as a speculative financial investment. They increase their demand for gold when they fear general inflation or domestic or international turmoil that might undermine the value of currency and more traditional investments. They reduce their demand when events settle down. Because of the inelastic supply of gold, even relatively small changes in demand produce relatively large changes in price.

5.6 The Economics of Agricultural Price Supports

Canadian federal and provincial agricultural policy aims to protect farmers from fluctuations in farm income. The main tools used are a national income safety net system, and supply programs through marketing boards and **price supports**, which are government-supported minimum prices.

price supports
Government-supported minimum prices for agricultural products.

Net Income Stabilization

An income safety net for all Canadian farmers is provided by the Net Income Stabilization Account (NISA). It is designed to protect farmers from fluctuations in farm income and to provide long-term farm income stability. NISA is essentially a risk management tool. Individual farmers and the federal and provincial governments contribute money annually into a fund. Farmers may withdraw funds when farm income falls below specified trigger levels. There is also crop insurance to protect farmers against crop failure due to the weather or other natural hazards. As with NISA, the individual farmer and the federal and provincial governments contribute to a crop insurance fund.

Canadian federal and provincial agricultural policy aims to protect farmers from fluctuations in farm income.

<www.cwb.ca>
Canadian Wheat Board

Supply Management Programs

Both federal and provincial governments are involved in supply management programs, whose aim is to regulate supply so as to ensure a stable, minimum level of income for Canadian farmers. Supply management is carried out through provincial marketing boards and federal agencies. The three main commodity groups for which marketing boards regulate supply are dairy and poultry products and eggs.

The Canadian Wheat Marketing Board, created in 1935, also manages supply, but also acts as the sole marketing agency for Canadian wheat producers, who are not allowed to sell any of the wheat they produce. In a high-profile case in 2002, a small number of Prairie wheat farmers were jailed for marketing their own wheat (they had actually donated the wheat to a U.S. charity group). These farmers were protesting the monopoly power of the Wheat Marketing Board.

As of 2003, the Wheat Board still had complete control over the price and marketing of western wheat. When farmers deliver their wheat to the Wheat Board, they receive an initial payment per bushel that is 75 percent of the expected average selling price. This is in effect a floor price and is set low enough that the Wheat Board is reasonably certain to be able to sell the wheat at least at that price. The producers subsequently get the full average selling price the Wheat Board is able to get on the domestic and international markets, less transportation costs, storage costs, and administrative expenses. Farmers get the average price the Wheat Board is able to realize over the course of the year.

Supply management policies ensure higher incomes to farmers can be accomplished through price supports. There are three basic methods of supporting prices above their market equilibrium values: (1) offers to purchase, (2) deficiency payments, and (3) supply restrictions.

OFFERS TO PURCHASE

A marketing board can increase farm income by ensuring that the price farmers get for their produce does not fall below a specified minimum. In Figure 5-8(a) let's assume that the *floor price*—or, as it is commonly called, the support price—is P_s. The major effects are as follows:

- **Surplus output** The most obvious result is product surplus. Consumers are willing to purchase only Q_o units at the supported price, while farmers will supply Q_s units. The government must buy the surplus ($Q_s - Q_o$) to make the above-equilibrium support price effective. The surpluses are undesirable on two counts. First, their very existence indicates a misallocation of the economy's resources. Government-held surpluses mean that the economy is devoting too many resources to the production of commodities that, at existing supported prices, are not wanted by consumers. Second, since surplus products have to be stored, they will add to the cost of the farm program and, ultimately, to the consumer's tax bill. For example, in the late 1950s the federal government accumulated more than 45 million kilograms of butter as it tried to maintain

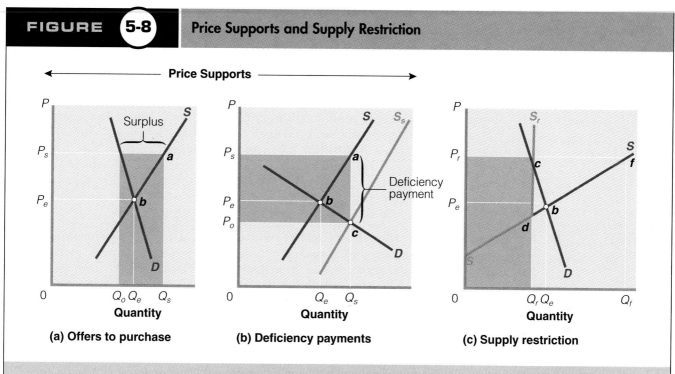

FIGURE 5-8 Price Supports and Supply Restriction

Panel (a): Offers to purchase result in surpluses. Panel (b): Deficiency payments or subsidies do not result in surpluses. Panel (c): Supply restriction results in neither surpluses nor government payments. All costs (the higher price) are borne by consumers.

an above-equilibrium price. The solution was to convert the butter into butter oil, which the government then sold abroad at half the butter price.

- **Loss to consumers** Consumers lose because they pay a higher price (P_s rather than P_e) and consume less (Q_o rather than Q_e) of the product. They also pay higher taxes to finance the government's purchase of the surplus. In Figure 5-8(a), this added tax burden will amount to the surplus output $Q_o - Q_s$ multiplied by its price, P_s. Storage costs add to this tax burden. Unfortunately, the higher food prices fall disproportionately on the poor because they spend a larger portion of their incomes on food.

- **Gain to farmers** Farmers gain from price supports. In Figure 5-8(a), gross receipts rise from the free market level of $0P_ebQ_e$ to the larger supported level of area $0P_saQ_s$.

DEFICIENCY PAYMENTS

deficiency payments
Subsidies that make up the difference between market prices and government-supported prices.

Deficiency payments, another method of price supports, are subsidies that make up the difference between the market price and the government-supported price. In Figure 5-8(b) suppose that the support price is P_s. Also, at price P_s farmers expand production from Q_e to Q_s. However, with demand as shown by D, consumers will only buy Q_s if the price is P_o. The government arranges for this to be the market price by simply subsidizing production by the amount $P_o - P_s$. The government makes a deficiency payment to each producer equal to $P_o - P_s$ times the quantity sold.

The total consumer expenditure is $0P_ocQ_s$, and total government expenditure is $0P_sac$ = deficiency payment times Q_s. The producers are still on the original supply curve S. However, S_s is the supply curve as seen by the consumer and is created by the deficiency payment. When we analyze the economic effect of these payments, two considerations arise: elasticity of supply and demand, and resource overallocation.

Elasticity of Supply and Demand   The incidence of the subsidy, like the sales tax, depends on the elasticity of the supply and demand curves. In Figure 5-8(b), the combined effects of the elastic demand curve in the price range P_oP_s and the inelastic supply curve result in the subsidy going mostly to the producer: the producer gets P_eP_s of the deficiency payment, the consumer only P_eP_o. The effect of elasticity on the incidence of a subsidy is precisely the same as that of a sales tax.

Comparing Offers to Purchase and Deficiency Payments   Assuming, as we have done, that P_s is the same in both Figures 5-8(a) and (b), farmers will benefit equally from the two programs: their total income will increase in each case. Consumers prefer deficiency payments since they receive a large amount of output (Q_s) at a low price (P_o). This compares with a high price (P_s) and small quantity (Q_o) under a program of offers to purchase. But when the subsidies of taxpayers to farmers (the green areas) are taken into account, total payments by the public (consumption expenditures plus tax-financed subsidies) to farmers are identical under both programs.

Resource Overallocation   A more subtle cost exists in both offers to purchase and deficiency payments. Society loses because price supports contribute to economic inefficiency by encouraging an overallocation of resources to agriculture. A price floor (P_s) attracts more resources to the agricultural sector than would the free market price (P_e). The market supply curve in Figures 5-8(a) and (b) represents the marginal costs of all farmers producing this product at various outputs Q_o. An efficient allocation of resources occurs at point b, where the market price P_e is equal to marginal costs. The output Q_e reflects an efficient allocation of resources.

In contrast, the output Q_s associated with the price support P_s represents an overallocation of resources; the marginal cost of the extra production exceeds its marginal benefit to society. Society incurs an *efficiency loss* from the price-support system.

SUPPLY RESTRICTIONS

Another method of increasing the prices farmers get for their output is to restrict supply. In the case of crops, the government would set the total number of hectares to be planted, and then divide these among existing farmers. This form of supply management is know as **crop restriction**. For farmers producing dairy and poultry products and eggs, the government, through the marketing boards, sets a **quota**, or a maximum amount each farm is allowed to produce.

Suppose in Figure 5-8(c) that government wants to guarantee farmers price P_r. In this case neither offers to purchase nor deficiency payments would work because of the price-elastic supply. An offer to purchase at price P_r results in a surplus of $Q_r - Q_f$, a greater amount than presently demanded. A deficiency payment program would also not work for the same reason.

In this situation the government-desired price P_r can only be ensured by restricting supply through a quota system. *(Key Question 16)*

crop restriction
In return for guaranteed prices for their crops, farmers agree to limit the number of hectares they plant in that crop.

quota
A restriction on the amount of a product that a farm is allowed to produce in a given period.

5.7   The Economics of Health Care

There is a major controversy over the funding, delivery, and cost of health care in Canada. The heated debate has arisen because some Canadians are concerned about declining standards and increasing waiting time to see specialists and have surgery. The Canadian health care system provides universal access for covered services. There are no user fees across Canada for basic health services, including hospital and physician services. The Canadian health care system is in essence an insurance program funded by both provincial and federal governments, with zero deductibility. To the individual consumer, health services are "free," even if in reality these services are paid by Canadian taxpayers.

We noted in Chapter 3 that competitive markets will eliminate surpluses or shortages of a particular product or service. If markets clear, why are there "shortages" in the current Canadian health care system as manifested through longer waiting times for needed health service?

Peculiarities of the Health Care Market

Competitive markets bring about both allocative and productive efficiency, two concepts you came across in Chapter 2. But the health care sector in Canada is not a competitive market industry. Indeed, a competitive market system in health care may not be desirable or attainable because of the unique properties of health care. What follows are some of the unique properties of the health care market.

ETHICAL AND EQUITY CONSIDERATIONS

Ethical questions inevitably intervene in markets when decisions involve the quality of life, or literally life or death. Although we might not consider it immoral if a person cannot buy a Mercedes or a personal computer, Canadians regard the denial of basic health care as unjust. Generally, Canadians look upon health care as an "entitlement" or a "right" and are reluctant to ration it on the basis of price and income.

ASYMMETRIC INFORMATION

asymmetric information
Unequal knowledge by the parties to a market transaction.

Competitive markets may not be fully appropriate in health care delivery because of **asymmetric information**—unequal knowledge possessed by the parties to a market transaction. Health care buyers typically have little or no understanding of the complex diagnostic and treatment procedures, while the physicians who are the health care sellers of those procedures possess detailed information. This creates the unusual situation in which the doctor (supplier) as the agent of the patient (consumer) tells the patient what health care services he or she should consume. For example, if a physician tells a patient she needs a follow-up visit in a few weeks, few health care consumers would be informed enough to know whether such a visit was actually needed.

THE MORAL HAZARD PROBLEM

moral hazard problem
The possibility that individuals or institutions will change their behaviour as a result of a contract or agreement.

The **moral hazard problem** is the tendency of one party to an agreement to alter her or his behaviour in a way which is costly to the other party. Health care insurance can change behaviour in two ways. First, some insured people might be less careful about their health, taking fewer steps to prevent accident or illness. Second, insured individuals have greater incentives to use health care more intensively than they would if they did not have insurance.

ADVERSE SELECTION

adverse selection problem
The problem that arises when information known to the first party to a contract is not known by the second, who then incurs costs.

Another information problem arising from inadequate information is the **adverse selection problem**. This problem arises when information known to the first party to a contract is not known by the second, and, as a result, the second party incurs major costs. In health insurance, the adverse selection problem is that people who are most likely to need insurance payouts are those who buy insurance. Those with the poorest health will seek to buy the most generous health insurance policies. Private insurers, knowing this, will try to attract those clients least likely to get sick. Thus, in a competitive health care industry, people either already sick or at a high risk of serious illness will find it difficult to get health insurance except at very high premiums. Those who cannot afford the high premiums will not be covered if they get sick. In the present Canadian system, government insurance covers every citizen, no matter what their state of health.

SPILLOVER BENEFITS

The medical care market generates positive externalities (spillover benefits), a concept you learned in Chapter 4. For example, an immunization against polio, smallpox, or measles benefits the immediate purchaser, but it also benefits society because it reduces the risk that other members of society will be infected with highly contagious diseases. Similarly, a healthy labour force is more productive, contributing to the general prosperity and well-being of society. In Chapter 4 we noted that freely functioning markets underallocate resources to products and services that generate spillover benefits. Thus, a competitive health care sector may not deliver as much output as society deems desirable.

In Canada, most essential health care expenses are paid primarily through public insurance.

THIRD PARTY PAYMENTS: INSURANCE

In Canada most essential health care expenses are paid primarily through public insurance. Health care consumers do not pay out-of-pocket "prices" they would otherwise. The zero prices are distortions that result in "excess" consumption of health care services.

GRAPHICAL PORTRAYAL

A simple demand and supply model illustrates the effect of health insurance on the health care market. Figure 5-9(a) depicts a competitive market for health care services; curve D shows the demand for health care services if all consumers are uninsured, and S represents the supply of health care services. At market price P_u the equilibrium quantity of health care is Q_u. The market clears, and there is no excess demand or supply.

What happens when we introduce private or government health insurance that covers, say, one half of all health care costs? In Figure 5-9(b), with health insurance paying half the price, the consumer is confronted with price P_i $(=\frac{1}{2}P_u)$. The health care consumer reacts by purchasing Q_i units rather than Q_u. An excess demand for health care services has been created. If the health care consumer does not pay any portion of health care costs, as is the case in Canada, the shortage would become more acute.

Possible Solutions to Excess Demand

Solutions to the existing excess demand for health care services in Canada come down to either increasing the supply by diverting more tax revenues to health care, or instituting user fees to reduce quantity demanded of health care services. An infusion of more resources is depicted by a rightward shift the supply curve to S_1 in Figure 5.9(b). Although increased resources for health care services will resolve the excess demand, there is as yet no consensus as to whether this is the way Canadians want to move.

In Chapter 2 we discussed the necessary tradeoffs that face any society with limited resources. The federal and provincial governments must either divert tax revenues from other government programs or increase taxes to properly fund the health care needs of Canadians. Neither option is pleasant, but more importantly, it is not clear which option the majority of Canadians prefer. Critics argue that even if more resources are made available to the Canadian health care system, it will not solve the current shortage problem. They point out that the demand for health care rises with

FIGURE 5-9 | **Insurance and the Overallocation of Resources to Health Care**

Panel (a) Without health insurance, the optimal amount of health care consumed is Q_u, where the marginal benefit and marginal cost of health care are equal. Panel (b) The availability of private and public insurance reduces the direct price of health care from P_u to P_i, resulting in its overconsumption (Q_i rather than Q_u) and an overallocation of resources to the health care industry. The area abc represents the efficiency loss from that overallocation.

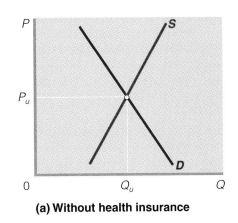
(a) Without health insurance

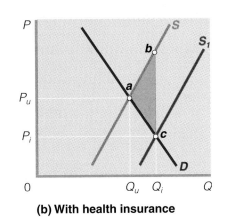
(b) With health insurance

income and the age of its citizens. Both will rise in the future, particularly the number of older Canadians, who generally require more health care services. Critics also point out that there is little competition for the delivery of health care services in Canada, which has created what they see as "inefficiencies" that waste scarce resources.

Proponents of the national health care system in Canada emphasize that compared to the system in the U.S., our system is efficient. Administrative costs of health care delivery are lower in Canada, and the Canadian system costs less than the American system. Canada spends just under 10 percent of Gross Domestic Product (GDP) on health care, while the U.S. health care system consumes almost 14 percent of GDP. The advocates of the existing national health care system in Canada say that even if we have to divert more resources to health care, knowing every Canadian will have the health care he or she needs is a comfort well worth paying for. *(Key Question 17)*

QUICK REVIEW

- Price elasticity of supply measures the sensitivity of suppliers to changes in the price of a product. The price elasticity of supply coefficient E_s is the ratio of the percentage change in quantity supplied to the percentage change in price. The elasticity of supply varies directly with the amount of time producers have to respond to the price change.

- The cross elasticity of demand coefficient E_{xy} is computed as the percentage change in the quantity demanded of product X divided by the percentage change in the price of product Y. If the cross elasticity coefficient is positive, the two products are substitutes; if it is negative, they are complements.

- The income elasticity coefficient E_i is computed as the percentage change in quantity demanded divided by the percentage change in income. A positive coefficient indicates a normal good. The coefficient is negative for an inferior good.

- Government-controlled prices in the form of ceilings and floors stifle the rationing function of prices and cause unintended side effects.

- Insurance generally leads to excess consumption of the insured product or service. But many believe that there is a place for public health insurance in Canada because of the peculiarities of the health care market.

THE LASTword — A Market for Human Organs?

A market might eliminate the present shortage of human organs for transplant. But many serious objections exist to turning human body parts into commodities for purchase and sale.

Advances in medical technology make it possible for surgeons to replace some human body parts with donated used parts, much like a mechanic might replace a worn-out alternator in an automobile with one from a junked vehicle. It has become increasingly commonplace in medicine to transplant kidneys, lungs, livers, eye corneas, pancreases, and hearts from deceased individuals to those whose organs have failed or are failing. But surgeons and many of their patients face a growing problem: too few donated organs are available for transplant. Not everyone who needs a transplant can get one. Indeed, an inadequate supply of donated organs causes an estimated 400 Canadian deaths per year.

Why Shortages? Seldom, if ever, do we hear of shortages of used auto parts such as alternators, batteries, transmissions, or water pumps. What is different about organs for transplant? One difference is that a market exists for used auto parts but not for human organs. To understand this situation, observe the demand curve D_1 and supply curve S_1 in the accompanying figure. The downward slope of the demand curve tells us that if there were a market for human organs, the quantity of organs demanded would be greater at lower prices than at higher prices. Perfectly inelastic supply curve S_1 represents the fixed quantity of human organs now donated via consent before death. Because the price of these donated organs is in effect zero, quantity demanded, Q_3, exceeds quantity supplied, Q_1. The shortage of $Q_3 - Q_1$ is rationed through a waiting list of those in medical need of transplants. Many people die while still on the waiting list.

Use of a Market A market for human organs would increase the incentive to donate organs. Such a market might work like this: An individual might specify in a legal document a willingness to sell one or more usable human organs on death or brain death. The person could specify where the money from the sale would go, for example, to family, a church, an educational institution, or a charity. Firms would then emerge to purchase organs and resell them where needed for profit. Under such a system, the supply curve of usable organs would take on the normal upward slope of typical supply curves. The higher the expected price of an organ, the greater the number of people willing to have their organs sold at death. Suppose that the supply curve is S_2 in the figure. At the equilibrium price P_1, the number of organs made available for transplant (Q_2) would equal the number purchased for transplant (also Q_2). In this generalized case, the shortage of organs would be eliminated and, of particular importance, the number of organs available for transplanting would rise from Q_1 to Q_2. More lives would be saved and enhanced than is the case under the present donor system.

Objections In view of this positive outcome, why is there no such market for human organs? Critics of market-based solutions have two main objections. The first is a moral objection: Critics feel that turning human organs into commodities commercializes human beings and diminishes the special nature of human life. They say there is something unseemly about selling and buying body organs as if they were bushels of wheat or ounces of gold. Moreover, critics note that the market would ration the available organs (as represented by Q_2 in the figure) to people who either can afford them (at P_1) or have health insurance for transplants.

Second, a health cost objection suggests that a market for body organs would greatly increase the cost of health care. Rather than obtaining freely donated (although too few) body organs, patients would have to pay market prices for them, increasing the cost of medical care. As transplant procedures are further perfected, the demand for transplants is expected to increase significantly. Rapid increases in demand relative to supply would boost the prices of human organs and thus further contribute to the problem of escalating health care costs.

Supporters of market-based solutions to organ shortages point out that the market is simply being driven underground. Worldwide, an estimated $1 billion annual illegal market in human organs has emerged. As in other illegal markets, the unscrupulous tend to thrive. Those who support legalization say that it would be greatly preferable to legalize and regulate the market for the laws against selling transplantable human organs.

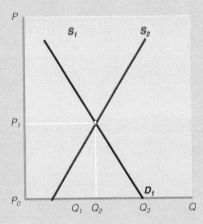

CHAPTER SUMMARY

5.1 PRICE ELASTICITY OF DEMAND

- Price elasticity of demand measures consumer response to price changes. If consumers are relatively sensitive to price changes, demand is elastic. If they are relatively unresponsive to price changes, demand is inelastic.

- The price elasticity coefficient E_d measures the degree of elasticity or inelasticity of demand. The coefficient is found by the formula

$$E_d = \frac{\text{percentage change in quantity demanded of X}}{\text{percentage change in price of X}}$$

The averages of prices and quantities under consideration are used as reference points in determining percentage changes in price and quantity. If E_d is greater than one, demand is elastic. If E_d is less than one, demand is inelastic. Unit elasticity is the special case in which E_d equals one.

- Perfectly inelastic demand is graphed as a line parallel to the vertical axis; perfectly elastic demand is shown by a line above and parallel to the horizontal axis.

- Elasticity varies at different price ranges on a demand curve, tending to be elastic in the upper left segment and inelastic in the lower right segment. Elasticity cannot be judged by the steepness or flatness of a demand curve.

5.2 THE TOTAL-REVENUE TEST

- If total revenue changes in the opposite direction from prices, demand is elastic. If price and total revenue change in the same direction, demand is inelastic. Where demand is of unit elasticity, a change in prices leaves total revenue unchanged.

- The number of available substitutes, the size of an item's price relative to one's budget, whether the product is a luxury or a necessity, and the time given to adjust are all determinants of elasticity of demand.

5.3 PRICE ELASTICITY OF SUPPLY

- The elasticity concept also applies to supply. The coefficient of price elasticity of supply is found by the formula

$$E_d = \frac{\text{percentage change in quantity supplied of X}}{\text{percentage change in price of X}}$$

The averages of the price and quantities under consideration are used as reference points for computing percentage changes. Elasticity of supply depends on the ease of shifting resources between alternative uses, which in turn varies directly with the time producers have to adjust to a particular price change.

5.4 CROSS ELASTICITY AND INCOME ELASTICITY OF DEMAND

- Cross elasticity of demand indicates how sensitive the purchase of one product is to changes in the price of another product. The coefficient of cross elasticity of demand is found by the formula

$$E_{xy} = \frac{\text{percentage change in quantity demanded of X}}{\text{percentage change in price of Y}}$$

Positive cross elasticity of demand identifies substitute goods; negative cross elasticity identifies complementary goods.

- Income elasticity of demand indicates the responsiveness of consumer purchases to a change in income. The coefficient of income elasticity of demand is found by the formula

$$E_i = \frac{\text{percentage change in quantity demanded of X}}{\text{percentage change in income}}$$

The coefficient is positive for normal goods and negative for inferior goods.

5.5 ELASTICITY AND REAL-WORLD APPLICATIONS

- Excise taxes affect supply and, therefore, equilibrium price and quantity. The more inelastic the demand for a product, the greater is the proportion of an excise tax that is shifted to consumers. The greater the inelasticity of supply, the larger the portion of the tax that is borne by the seller.

- Legally fixed prices stifle the rationing function of equilibrium prices. Effective price ceilings result in persistent product shortages, and if an equitable distribution of the product is sought, government must ration the product to consumers. Price floors lead to product surpluses; the government must either purchase these surpluses or eliminate them by imposing restrictions on production or by increasing private demand.

5.6 THE ECONOMICS OF AGRICULTURAL PRICE SUPPORTS

- The use of price floors or price supports has many economic effects: (a) surplus production occurs, (b) the incomes of farmers are increased, (c) consumers pay higher prices for farm products, (d) an overallocation of resources to agriculture occurs, and (e) society pays higher taxes to finance the purchase and storage of surplus output.

5.7 THE ECONOMICS OF HEALTH CARE

- Special characteristics of the health care market include (a) ethical and equity considerations, (b) an imbalance of information between consumers and suppliers, (c) the moral hazard problem, (d) the adverse selection problem, (e) the presence of spillover benefits, and (f) the payment of most health care expenses by public insurance.

TERMS AND CONCEPTS

price elasticity of demand, p. 105	total-revenue test, p. 110	price supports, p. 124
elastic demand, p. 106	price elasticity of supply, p. 115	deficiency payments, p. 125
inelastic demand, p. 107	market period, p. 115	crop restriction, p. 126
unit elasticity, p. 107	short run, p. 116	quota, p. 126
perfectly inelastic demand, p. 107	long run, p. 116	asymmetric information, p. 127
perfectly elastic demand, p. 107	cross elasticity of demand, p. 117	moral hazard problem, p. 127
total revenue (TR), p. 110	income elasticity of demand, p. 118	adverse selection problem, p. 127

STUDY QUESTIONS

1. Explain why the choice between discussing 1, 2, 3, 4, 5, 6, 7, and 8 units or 1000, 2000, 3000, 4000, 5000, 6000, 7000, and 8000 movie tickets makes no difference in determining elasticity in Table 5-1.

2. **KEY QUESTION** Graph the accompanying demand data and then use the midpoint formula for E_d to determine price elasticity of demand for each of the four possible $1 price changes. What can you conclude about the relationship between the slope of a curve and its elasticity? Explain in a non-technical way why demand is elastic in the northwest segment of the demand curve and inelastic in the southeast segment.

Product price	Quantity demanded
$5	1
4	2
3	3
2	4
1	5

3. Draw two linear demand curves parallel to one another. Demonstrate that for any specific price change, demand is more elastic on the curve closer to the origin.

4. **KEY QUESTION** Calculate total-revenue data from the demand schedule in question 2. Graph total revenue below your demand curve. Generalize about the relationship between price elasticity and total revenue.

5. **KEY QUESTION** How would the following changes in price affect total revenue? That is, would total revenue increase, decline, or remain unchanged?

   a. Price falls and demand is inelastic.

   b. Price rises and demand is elastic.

   c. Price rises and supply is elastic.

   d. Price rises and supply is inelastic.

   e. Price rises and demand is inelastic.

   f. Price falls and demand is elastic.

   g. Price falls and demand is unit elastic.

6. **KEY QUESTION** What are the major determinants of price elasticity of demand? Use those determinants and your own reasoning in judging whether demand for each of the following products is probably elastic or inelastic: (a) bottled water, (b) toothpaste, (c) Crest toothpaste, (d) ketchup, (e) diamond bracelets, (f) Microsoft Windows operating system.

7. What effect would a rule stating that university students must live in university or college dormitories have on the price elasticity of demand for dormitory space? What impact might this in turn have on room rates?

8. "If the demand for farm products is highly price inelastic, a large crop yield may reduce farm incomes." Evaluate this statement and illustrate it graphically.

9. You are chairperson of a provincial tax commission responsible for establishing a program to raise new revenue through sales taxes. Would elasticity of demand be important to you in determining on which products the taxes should be levied? Explain.

10. **KEY QUESTION** In November 1998 Vincent van Gogh's self-portrait sold at auction for $71.5 million. Portray this sale in a demand and supply diagram and comment on the elasticity of supply. Comedian George Carlin once mused, "If a painting can be forged well enough to fool some experts, why is the original so valuable?" Provide an answer.

11. Suppose that because of a legal settlement over health care claims, tobacco companies raise the average price of a pack of cigarettes from $1.95 to $2.45. Also suppose the projected decline in cigarette sales was 8 percent. What does this imply about the elasticity of demand for cigarettes? Explain.

12. **KEY QUESTION** Suppose the cross elasticity of demand for products A and B is +3.6 and for products C and D is −5.4. What can you conclude about how products A and B are related? products C and D?

13. **KEY QUESTION** The income elasticities of demand for movies, dental services, and clothing have been estimated to be +3.4, +1.0, and +0.5, respectively. Interpret these coefficients. What does it mean if an income elasticity coefficient is negative?

14. A recent study found that an increase in the price of beer would reduce the amount of marijuana consumed. Is cross elasticity of demand between the two products positive or is it negative? Are these products substitutes, or are they complements? What might be the logic behind this relationship?

15. **KEY QUESTION**   What is the incidence of a tax when demand is highly inelastic? highly elastic? What effect does the elasticity of supply have on the incidence of a tax?

16. **KEY QUESTION**   Why is it desirable for price ceilings to be accompanied by government rationing? Why is it desirable for price floors to be accompanied by programs that purchase surpluses, restrict output, or increase demand? Show graphically why price ceilings produce shortages and price floors cause surpluses.

17. **KEY QUESTION**   Can insurance cause overconsumption? How does insurance relate to the Canadian national health care system.

18. **(The Last Word)** Do you favour the establishment of a market for donated human organs? Why or why not?

INTERNET APPLICATION QUESTIONS

1. Go to the McConnell-Brue-Barbiero Web site (Chapter 5) to find the very latest price of gold. Compare that price to the price at the beginning of the day. What was the highest price during the last 12 months? The lowest price? Assume the price fluctuations observed resulted exclusively from changes in demand. Would the observed price changes have been greater or less if the gold supply had they been elastic rather than inelastic? Explain.

2. On the McConnell-Brue-Barbiero Web site (Chapter 5), select NBER Working Papers. In the search space, type "alcohol." Use the titles and summaries of the papers to answer the following questions relating to elasticity:

   a. Do the mentally ill have perfectly inelastic demands for cigarettes and alcohol?

   b. Does alcohol consumption increase in bad times?

   c. What is the effect of cigarette taxes (and smuggling) on the consumption of alcohol? What does that imply about the cross elasticity of demand between the two?

   d. Is binge drinking among college and university students sensitive to the price of alcohol?

6

Chapter

The Theory of Consumer Choice

If you were to compare the shopping carts of almost any two consumers, you would observe striking differences. Why does Paula have potatoes, peaches, and Pepsi in her cart while Sam has sugar, saltines, and 7-Up in his? Why didn't Paula also buy pasta and plums? Why didn't Sam have soup and spaghetti on his grocery list?

In this chapter, you will see how individual consumers allocate their income among the various goods and services available to them. Given a particular budget, how does a consumer decide what goods and services to buy? Why does the typical consumer buy more of a product when its price falls? As we answer these questions, you will also strengthen your understanding of the law of demand.

6.1   A Closer Look at the Law of Demand

The law of demand is based on common sense. A high price discourages consumers from buying; a low price encourages them to buy. In Chapter 3 we mentioned two explanations of the downward-sloping demand curve (income and substitution effects and the law of diminishing marginal utility) that supported this observation. We now want to say more about these explanations in the context of consumer behaviour, the subject of this chapter. A third explanation, based on indifference curves, is summarized in the appendix to this chapter.

Income and Substitution Effects

Our first explanation of the downward slope of the demand curve involves the income and substitution effects.

THE INCOME EFFECT

income effect
A change in the quantity demanded of a product that results from the change in real income (purchasing power) produced by a change in the product's price.

The **income effect** is the impact that a change in a product's price has on a consumer's real income and, consequently, on the quantity of that good demanded. Let's suppose our product is a coffee drink such as a latte or cappuccino. If the price of such drinks declines, the real income or purchasing power of anyone who buys them increases; that is, they are able to buy more with the same income. The increase in real income will be reflected in increased purchases of many normal goods, including coffee drinks.

For example, with a constant money income of $20 every two weeks, you can buy 10 coffee drinks at $2 each. If the price falls to $1 for each coffee drink and you buy 10 of them, you will have $10 per week left over to buy more coffee drinks and other goods. This relationship is the income effect.

THE SUBSTITUTION EFFECT

substitution effect
A change in the quantity demanded of a consumer good that results from a change in its relative price.

The **substitution effect** is the impact that a change in a product's price has on its relative expensiveness, and, consequently, on the quantity demanded. When the price of a product falls, that product becomes cheaper relative to all other products. Consumers will substitute the cheaper product for other products that are now relatively more expensive. In our example, if the prices of other products remain unchanged and the price of coffee drinks falls, lattes and cappuccinos become more attractive to the buyer. Coffee drinks are a relatively better buy at $1 than at $2. The lower price will induce the consumer to substitute coffee drinks for some of the now relatively less attractive items in the budget—perhaps colas, bottled water, or iced tea. This relationship is the substitution effect.

The income and substitution effects combine to increase a consumer's *ability* and *willingness* to buy more of a specific good when its price falls.

Law of Diminishing Marginal Utility

Choosing a Little More or Less

A second explanation of the downward-sloping demand curve is that, although consumer wants in general may be insatiable, wants for particular commodities can be satisfied. In a specific span of time over which consumers' tastes remain unchanged, consumers can get as much of a particular good or service as they can afford. But, the more of that product they obtain, the less additional product they want.

Consider durable goods, for example. Consumers' desires for an automobile, when they have none, may be very strong, but the desire for a second car is less intense, and for a third or fourth, weaker and weaker. Unless they are collectors, even the wealthiest families rarely have more than a half-dozen cars, although their income would allow them to purchase a whole fleet of vehicles.

TERMINOLOGY

Evidence indicates that consumers can fulfill specific wants with succeeding units of a commodity but that each added unit provides less utility than the previous unit purchased. Recall that a product has utility if it can satisfy a want: utility is want-satisfying power. The utility of a good or service is the satisfaction or pleasure one gets from consuming it. Three characteristics of this concept must be emphasized:

1. "Utility" and "usefulness" are not synonymous. Paintings by Picasso may offer great utility to art connoisseurs but are useless functionally (other than for hiding a crack in a wall!)

2. Implied in the first characteristic is the fact that utility is subjective. The utility of a specific product may vary widely from person to person. A Celine Dion CD has tremendous utility for one of her fans, but no utility to someone who listens only to the Tragically Hip.

3. Because utility is subjective, it is difficult to quantify. But for purposes of illustration, we assume that people can measure satisfaction with units called *utils* (units of utility). For example, a particular consumer may get 100 utils of satisfaction from a smoothie, 10 utils of satisfaction from a candy bar, and 1 util of satisfaction from a stick of gum. These imaginary units of satisfaction are convenient for quantifying consumer behaviour.

TOTAL UTILITY AND MARGINAL UTILITY

total utility
The total amount of satisfaction derived from the consumption of a single product or a combination of products.

marginal utility
The extra utility a consumer obtains from the consumption of one additional unit of a good or service.

We must distinguish carefully between total utility and marginal utility. **Total utility** is the total amount of satisfaction or pleasure a person derives from consuming some specific quantity—for example, 10 units—of a good or service. **Marginal utility** is the *extra* satisfaction a consumer realizes from one additional unit of that product, for example, from the 11th unit. Alternatively, we can say that marginal utility is the change in total utility that results from the consumption of one more unit of a product.

Figure 6-1 (Key Graph) and the accompanying table reveal the relation between total utility and marginal utility. We have drawn the curves from the data in the table. Column 2 shows the total utility at each level of consumption of this particular product, tacos; column 3 shows the marginal utility—the change in total utility—that results from the consumption of each successive taco. Starting at the origin in Figure 6-1(a), we observe that each of the first five units increases total utility (TU) but by a diminishing amount. Total utility reaches a maximum at the sixth unit and then declines.

So, in Figure 6-1(b) we find that marginal utility (MU) remains positive but diminishes through the first five units (because total utility increases at a declining rate). Marginal utility is zero for the sixth unit (because that unit doesn't change total utility). Marginal utility then becomes negative with the seventh unit as the diner becomes ill (because total utility is falling). Figure 6-1(b) and column 3 of the table tell us that each successive taco yields less extra utility, meaning fewer utils, than the preceding one as the consumer's want for tacos comes closer and closer to fulfillment.[1] The principle that marginal utility declines as the consumer acquires additional units of a given product is known as the **law of diminishing marginal utility**. (See the Consider This box for other examples of the law of diminishing marginal utility). **(Key Question 2)**

law of diminishing marginal utility
As a consumer increases the consumption of a good or service, the marginal utility obtained from each additional unit of the good or service decreases.

MARGINAL UTILITY, DEMAND, AND ELASTICITY

How does the law of diminishing marginal utility explain why the demand curve for a given product slopes downward? The answer is that, if successive units of a good yield smaller and smaller amounts of marginal, or extra, utility, then the consumer will buy additional units of a product only if its price falls. The consumer for whom Figure 6-1 is relevant may buy two tacos at a price of $1 each, but because less marginal utility is obtained from additional tacos, the consumer will choose

---

[1]In Figure 6-1(b) we graphed marginal utility at half-units. For example, we graphed the marginal utility of 4 utils at 3½ units because the 4 utils refers neither to the third nor the fourth unit per se but to the *addition* or *subtraction* of the fourth unit.

Consider This

Diminishing Marginal Utility

Newspaper dispensing devices and soft drink vending machines are similar in their basic operations. Both allow consumers to buy a product by inserting coins. But there is an important difference in the two devices. The newspaper dispenser opens to the full stack of papers and seemingly "trusts" the customer to take only a single copy, whereas the vending machine displays no such "trust," requiring the consumer to buy one can at a time. Why the difference?

The idea of diminishing marginal utility is key to solving this puzzle. Most consumers take only single copies from the newspaper box because the marginal utility of a second newspaper is nearly zero. They could grab a few extra papers and try to sell them on the street, but the revenue obtained would be small relative to their time and effort. So, in selling their product newspaper publishers rely on "zero marginal utility of the second unit," not on "consumer honesty." Also, newspapers have little "shelf life"; they are obsolete the next day. In contrast, soft drink sellers do not allow

buyers to make a single payment and then take as many cans as they want. If they did, consumers would clean out the machine because the marginal utility of successive cans of pop diminishes slowly, so buyers could take extra cans and consume them later. As a result, soft drink firms sell their products on a pay-per-can basis.

In summary, newspaper publishers and soft drink firms use alternative vending techniques because of the very different rates of decline in marginal utility for their products. The newspaper seller uses inexpensive dispensers that open to the full stack of papers. The soft drink seller uses expensive vending machines that limit the consumer to a single can at a time. Each vending technique is optimal under the particular economic circumstance.

Question: Some restaurants offer "All you can eat" buffets at a set price. How can they afford to make such offers?

If successive units of a good yield smaller and smaller amounts of marginal utility, then the consumer will buy additional units only if its price falls.

not to buy more at that price. The consumer would rather spend additional dollars on products that provide more (or equal) utility, not less utility. Therefore, additional tacos with less utility are not worth buying unless the price declines. (When marginal utility becomes negative, the restaurant would have to pay you to consume another taco!) Thus, diminishing marginal utility supports the idea that price must decrease for quantity demanded to increase.

The amount by which marginal utility declines as more units of a product are consumed helps us to determine that product's price elasticity of demand. Other things equal, if marginal utility (MU) falls sharply as successive units of a product are consumed, demand is inelastic. A given decline in price will elicit only a relatively small increase in quantity demanded, since the MU of extra units falls so rapidly. Conversely, modest declines in marginal utility as consumption increases imply an elastic demand. A particular decline in price will entice consumers to buy considerably more units of the product, since the MU of additional units declines so slowly.

QUICK REVIEW

- The law of demand can be explained in terms of the income effect (a decline in price raises the consumer's purchasing power) and the substitution effect (a product whose price falls is substituted for other products).

- Utility is the benefit or satisfaction a person receives from consuming a good or a service.

- The law of diminishing marginal utility indicates that gains in satisfaction become smaller as successive units of a specific product are consumed.

- Diminishing marginal utility provides another rationale for the law of demand, as well as one for differing price elasticities.

Key Graph

FIGURE 6-1 Total and Marginal Utility

Curves TU and MU are graphed from the data in the table. Panel (a): As more of a product is consumed, total utility increases at a diminishing rate, reaches a maximum, and then declines. Panel (b): Marginal utility, by definition, reflects the changes in total utility. Thus marginal utility diminishes with increased consumption, becomes zero when total utility is at a maximum, and is negative when total utility declines. As shown by the shaded rectangles in panels (a) and (b), marginal utility is the change in total utility associated with each additional taco. Or, alternatively, each new level of total utility is found by adding marginal utility to the preceding level of total utility.

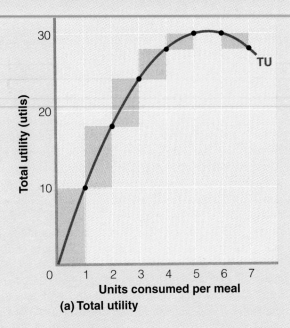

(a) Total utility

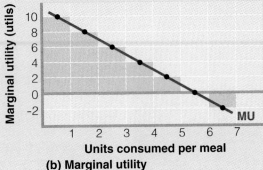

(b) Marginal utility

(1) Tacos consumed per meal	(2) Total utility, utils	(3) Marginal utility, utils
0	0	
		10
1	10	
		8
2	18	
		6
3	24	
		4
4	28	
		2
5	30	
		0
6	30	
		-2
7	28	

Quick Quiz

1. **Marginal utility**
   a. is the extra output a firm obtains when it adds another unit of labour.
   b. explains why product supply curves slope upward.
   c. typically rises as successive units of a good are consumed.
   d. is the extra satisfaction from the consumption of one more unit of some good or service.

2. **Marginal utility in Figure 6-1(b) is positive, but declining, when total utility in Figure 6-1(a) is positive and**
   a. rising at an increasing rate.
   b. falling at an increasing rate.
   c. rising at a decreasing rate.
   d. falling at a decreasing rate.

3. **When marginal utility is zero in panel (b), total utility in panel (a) is**
   a. also zero.

b. neither rising nor falling.

c. negative.

d. rising but at a declining rate.

4. Suppose the person represented by these graphs experienced a diminished taste for tacos. As a result the

a. TU curve would get steeper.

b. MU curve would get flatter.

c. TU and MU curves would shift downward.

d. MU curve, but not the TU curve, would collapse to the horizontal axis.

ANSWERS: 1. d.; 2. c.; 3. b.; 4. c.

6.2   Theory of Consumer Choice

Choosing a Little More or Less

In addition to explaining the law of demand, the idea of diminishing marginal utility explains how consumers allocate their money income among the many goods and services available for purchase.

Consumer Choice and Budget Constraint

The typical consumer's situation has the following dimensions.

- *Rational behaviour*   Consumers are rational in that they try to use their money incomes to get the greatest amount of satisfaction, or utility, from them. Consumers want to get the most for their money or, technically, to maximize their total utility. Maximizing total utility may include giving money to the poor. They engage in **rational behaviour**.

- *Preferences*   Each consumer has clear-cut preferences for certain goods and services of those available in the market. We assume buyers also have a good idea of how much marginal utility they will get from successive units of the various products they purchase.

- *Budget constraint*   Since each consumer supplies a finite amount of factors of production to society, each earns only limited income. Thus, every consumer faces what economists call a **budget constraint** (budget limitation), even those who earn millions of dollars a year. Of course, those budget constraints are more severe for consumers with average incomes than for those with extraordinarily high incomes.

- *Prices*   Goods are scarce relative to the demand for them, so every good carries a price tag. We assume that those price tags are not affected by the amounts of specific goods that each person buys. Since the consumer has a limited number of dollars, each can buy only a limited amount of goods. Consumers cannot buy everything they want. This point drives home the reality of scarcity to each consumer.

So the consumer must compromise and must choose the most satisfying affordable combination of goods and services. Different individuals will choose different mixes. As Global Perspective 6.1 shows, the mix may vary from nation to nation.

Utility-maximizing Rule

To maximize satisfaction, *consumers should allocate their money income so that the last dollar spent on each product yields the same amount of extra (marginal) utility.* We call this the **utility-maximizing rule**. When the consumer has balanced his or her margins using this rule, no incen-

rational behaviour
Human behaviour that seeks to maximize total utility.

budget constraint
The limit that a consumer's income (and the prices that must be paid for goods and services) imposes on the ability of that consumer to obtain goods and services.

utility-maximizing rule
To obtain the greatest utility, the consumer should allocate money income so that the last dollar spent on each good or service yields the same marginal utility.

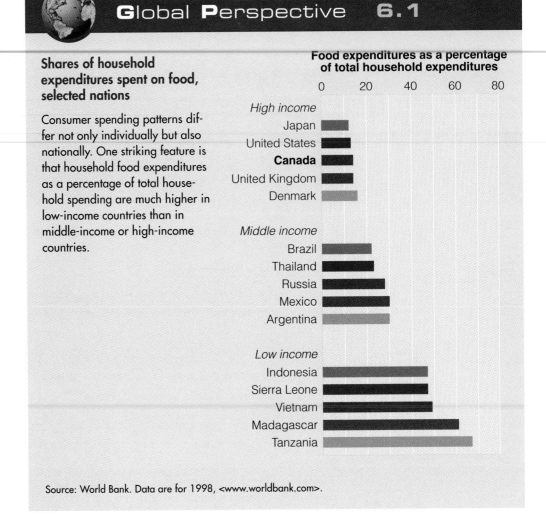

Global Perspective 6.1

Shares of household expenditures spent on food, selected nations

Consumer spending patterns differ not only individually but also nationally. One striking feature is that household food expenditures as a percentage of total household spending are much higher in low-income countries than in middle-income or high-income countries.

Food expenditures as a percentage of total household expenditures

0   20   40   60   80

High income
Japan
United States
Canada
United Kingdom
Denmark

Middle income
Brazil
Thailand
Russia
Mexico
Argentina

Low income
Indonesia
Sierra Leone
Vietnam
Madagascar
Tanzania

Source: World Bank. Data are for 1998, <www.worldbank.com>.

tive exists to alter the expenditure pattern. The consumer is in equilibrium and would be worse off—total utility would decline—if any alteration occurred in the bundle of goods purchased, providing no change occurs in taste, income, products, or prices.

Numerical Example

An illustration will help explain the utility-maximizing rule. For simplicity our example is limited to two products, but the analysis would apply if there were more. Suppose consumer Holly is trying to decide which combination of two products she should purchase with her fixed daily income of $10. These products might be asparagus and breadsticks, apricots and bananas, or apples and broccoli. Let's just call them A and B.

Holly's preferences for products A and B, their prices, and her income are the basic data determining the combination that will maximize her satisfaction. Table 6-1 summarizes those data, with column 2(a) showing the amount of marginal utility Holly will derive from each successive unit of A and column 3(a) showing the same thing for product B. Both columns reflect the law of diminishing marginal utility, which is assumed to begin with the second unit of each product purchased.

<www.econtools.com/jevons/java/choice/Choice.html>
Illustrates utility maximization subject to a budget constraint

TABLE 6-1	The Utility-maximizing Combination of Products A and B Obtainable with an Income of $10				
(1) **Unit of product**	**(2)** **Product A: price = $1**		**(3)** **Product B: price = $2**		
	(a) **Marginal utility, utils**	**(b)** **Marginal utility per dollar (MU/price)**	**(a)** **Marginal utility, utils**	**(b)** **Marginal utility per dollar (MU/price)**	
First	10	10	24	12	
Second	8	_8_	20	10	
Third	7	7	18	9	
Fourth	6	6	16	_8_	
Fifth	5	5	12	6	
Sixth	4	4	6	3	
Seventh	3	3	4	2	

It is assumed in this table that the amount of marginal utility received from additional units of each of the two products is independent of the quantity of the other product. For example, the marginal-utility schedule for product A is independent of the amount of B obtained by the consumer.

MARGINAL UTILITY PER DOLLAR

Before applying the utility-maximizing rule to these data, we must put the marginal utility information in columns 2(a) and 3(a) on a per-dollar-spent basis. Holly's choices are influenced not only by the extra utility that successive units of product A will yield, but also by how many dollars (and therefore how many units of alternative product B) she must give up to obtain those added units of A.

The rational consumer must compare the extra utility from each product with its added cost (that is, its price). Suppose you prefer a pizza whose marginal utility is, say, 36 utils to a movie whose marginal utility is 24 utils. But if the pizza's price is $12 and the movie costs only $6, you would choose the movie rather than the pizza! Why? Because the marginal utility per dollar spent would be 4 utils for the movie (= 24 utils ÷ $6) compared to only 3 utils for the pizza (= 36 utils ÷ $12). You could buy two movies for $12 and, assuming that the marginal utility of the second movie is, say, 16 utils, your total utility would be 40 utils. Clearly, 40 units of satisfaction from two movies are superior to 36 utils from the same $12 expenditure on one pizza.

To make the amounts of extra utility derived from differently priced goods comparable, marginal utilities must be put on a per-dollar-spent basis. We do this in columns 2(b) and 3(b) by dividing the marginal utility data of columns 2(a) and 3(a) by the prices of A and B, $1 and $2, respectively.

DECISION-MAKING PROCESS

In Table 6-1 we have Holly's preferences on a unit basis and a per-dollar basis, as well as the price tags of A and B. With $10 to spend, in what order should Holly allocate her dollars on units of A and B to achieve the highest degree of utility within the $10 limit imposed by her income? What specific combination of A and B will she have obtained at the time she uses up her $10?

Concentrating on columns 2(b) and 3(b) in Table 6-1, we find that Holly should first spend $2 on the first unit of B, because its marginal utility per dollar of 12 utils is higher than A's 10 utils. Now Holly finds herself indifferent about whether she should buy a second unit of B or the first unit of A because the marginal utility per dollar of both is 10 utils. So she buys both of them. Holly now has one unit of A and two units of B. Also, the last dollar she spent on each good yielded the same marginal utility per dollar (10 utils), but this combination of A and B does not represent the maximum amount of utility that Holly can obtain. It cost her only $5 [= (1 × $1) + (2 × $2)], so she has $5 remaining, which she can spend to achieve a still higher level of total utility.

Examining columns 2(b) and 3(b) again, we find that Holly should spend the next $2 on a third unit of B because marginal utility per dollar for the third unit of B is nine compared with eight for the second unit of A. Now, with one unit of A and three units of B, she is again indifferent between a second unit of A and a fourth unit of B because both provide eight utils per dollar. So Holly purchases one more unit of each. Now the last dollar spent on each product provides the same marginal utility per dollar (eight utils), and Holly's money income of $10 is exhausted.

The utility-maximizing combination of goods attainable by Holly is two units of A and four of B. By summing marginal utility information from columns 2(a) and 3(a), we find that Holly is obtaining 18 (= 10 + 8) utils of satisfaction from the two units of A and 78 (= 24 + 20 + 18 + 16) utils of satisfaction from the four units of B. Her $10, optimally spent, yields 96 (= 18 + 78) utils of satisfaction.

Table 6-2, which summarizes our step-by-step process for maximizing Holly's utility, merits careful study. Note that we have implicitly assumed that Holly spends her entire income. She neither borrows nor saves. However, saving can be regarded as a commodity that yields utility and be incorporated into our analysis. In fact, we treat it that way in question 4 at the end of this chapter. (*Key Question 4*)

INFERIOR OPTIONS

Holly can obtain other combinations of A and B with $10, but none will yield as great a total utility as do two units of A and four of B. As an example, she can obtain four units of A and three of B for $10. However, this combination yields only 93 utils, clearly inferior to the 96 utils provided by two units of A and four of B. Furthermore, other combinations of A and B exist (such as four of A and five of B or one of A and two of B) in which the marginal utility of the last dollar spent is the same for both A and B. All such combinations are either unobtainable with Holly's limited money income (as four of A and five of B) or do not exhaust her money income (as one of A and two of B) and, therefore, fail to yield the maximum utility attainable.

As an exercise, suppose Holly's money income is $14 rather than $10. What is the utility-maximizing combination of A and B? Are A and B normal or inferior goods?

Algebraic Restatement

Our allocation rule says that a consumer will maximize satisfaction by allocating money income so that the last dollar spent on product A, the last on product B, and so forth, yield equal amounts of

TABLE 6-2	Sequence of Purchases to Achieve Consumer Equilibrium, Given the Data in Table 6-1			
Choice number	Potential choices	Marginal utility per dollar	Purchase decision	Income remaining
1	First unit of A First unit of B	10 12	First unit of B for $2	$8 = $10 − $2
2	First unit of A Second unit of B	10 10	First unit of A for $1 and second unit of B for $2	$5 = $8 − $3
3	Second unit of A Third unit of B	8 9	Third unit of B for $2	$3 = $5 − $2
4	Second unit of A Fourth unit of B	8 8	Second unit of A for $1 and fourth unit of B for $2	$0 = $3 − $3

marginal utility. The marginal utility per dollar spent on A is indicated by MU of product A divided by the price of A (column 2(b) in Table 6-1), and the marginal utility per dollar spent on B by MU of product B divided by the price of B (column 3(b) in Table 6-1). Our utility-maximizing rule merely requires that these ratios be equal. Algebraically,

$$\frac{\text{MU of Product A}}{\text{Price of A}} = \frac{\text{MU of Product B}}{\text{Price of B}}$$

Of course, the consumer must exhaust her available income. Table 6-1 shows us that the combination of two units of A and four of B fulfills these conditions in that

$$\frac{8 \text{ utils}}{\$1} = \frac{16 \text{ utils}}{\$2}$$

and the consumer's $10 income is spent.

   If the equation is not fulfilled, then some reallocation of the consumer's expenditures between A and B (from the low to the high marginal-utility-per-dollar product) will increase the consumer's total utility. For example, if the consumer spent $10 on four units of A and three of B, we would find that

$$\frac{\text{MU of A: 6 utils}}{\text{Price of A: \$1}} < \frac{\text{MU of B: 18 utils}}{\text{Price of B: \$2}}$$

Here the last dollar spent on A provides only six utils of satisfaction, and the last dollar spent on B provides nine (= 18 ÷ $2). So, the consumer can increase total satisfaction by purchasing more of B and less of A. As dollars are reallocated from A to B, the marginal utility per dollar of A will increase while the marginal utility per dollar of B will decrease. At some new combination of A and B, the two will be equal, and consumer equilibrium will be achieved. Here, that combination is two units of A and four of B.

6.3   Utility Maximization and the Demand Curve

Once you understand the utility-maximizing rule, you can easily see why product price and quantity demanded are inversely related. Recall that the basic determinants of an individual's demand for a specific product are (1) preferences or tastes, (2) money income, and (3) the prices of other goods. The utility data in Table 6-1 reflect our consumer's preferences. We continue to suppose that her money income is $10. Concentrating on the construction of a simple demand curve for product B, we assume that the price of A, representing other goods, is still $1.

Deriving the Demand Schedule and Curve

We can derive a single consumer's demand schedule for product B by considering alternative prices at which B might be sold and then determining the quantity the consumer will purchase. We have already determined one such price–quantity combination in the utility-maximizing example: given tastes, income, and prices of other goods, our rational consumer will purchase four units of B at $2.

   Now let's assume the price of B falls to $1. The marginal-utility-per-dollar data of column 3(b) in Table 6-1 will double because the price of B has been halved; the new data for column 3(b) are identical to those in column 3(a), but the purchase of two units of A and four of B is no longer an equilibrium combination. By applying the same reasoning we used in the initial utility-maximizing example, we now find that Holly's utility-maximizing combination is four units of A and six units of B. As summarized in the table in Figure 6-2, Holly will purchase six units of B when the price of B is $1. Using the data in this table, we can sketch the downward-sloping demand curve D_B shown in Figure 6-2. This exercise, then, clearly links the utility-maximizing behaviour of a consumer and that person's demand curve for a particular product.

144

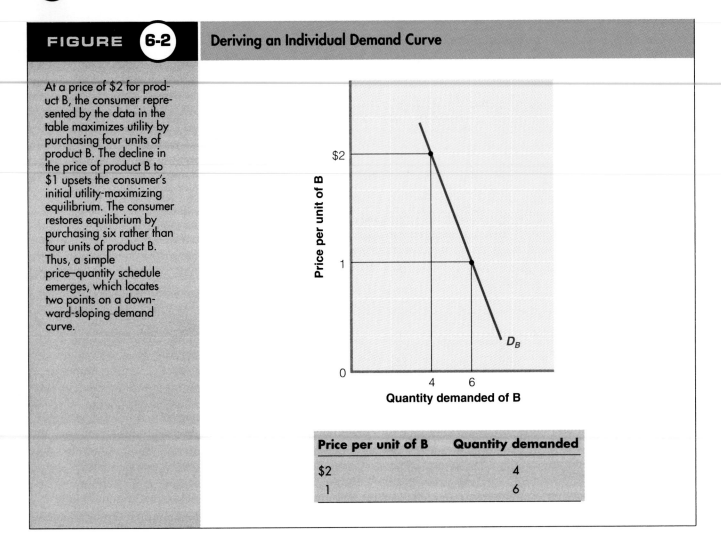

Deriving an Individual Demand Curve

At a price of $2 for product B, the consumer represented by the data in the table maximizes utility by purchasing four units of product B. The decline in the price of product B to $1 upsets the consumer's initial utility-maximizing equilibrium. The consumer restores equilibrium by purchasing six rather than four units of product B. Thus, a simple price–quantity schedule emerges, which locates two points on a downward-sloping demand curve.

Price per unit of B	Quantity demanded
$2	4
1	6

Income and Substitution Effects Revisited

At the beginning of this chapter we mentioned that the law of demand can be understood in terms of the substitution and income effects. Our analysis does not let us sort out these two effects quantitatively. However, we can see through utility maximization how each is involved in the increased purchase of product B when the price of B falls.

To see the substitution effect, recall that before the price of B declined, Holly was in equilibrium when purchasing two units of A and four units of B in that $MU_A(8)/P_A(\$1) = MU_B(16)/P_B(\$2)$. After B's price falls from $2 to $1, we have $MU_A(8)/P_A(\$1) < MU_B(16)/P_B(\$1)$; more simply stated, the last dollar spent on B now yields more utility (16 utils) than does the last dollar spent on A (8 utils). This result indicates that a switching of purchases from A to B is needed to restore equilibrium; that is, a *substitution* of the now cheaper B for A will occur when the price of B drops.

What about the *income effect*? The assumed decline in the price of B from $2 to $1 increases Holly's real income. Before the price decline, Holly was in equilibrium when buying two units of A and four of B. At the lower $1 price for B, Holly would have to spend only $6 rather than $10 on this same combination of goods. She has $4 left over to spend on more of A, more of B, or more of both. The price decline of B has caused Holly's *real* income to increase so that she can now obtain larger amounts of A and B with the same $10 of *money* income. The portion of the increase in her purchases of B due to this increase in real income is the income effect. (***Key Question 5***)

6.4   Applications and Extensions

Many real-world phenomena can be explained by applying the theory of consumer choice.

DVDs and DVD Players

Every now and then a new product captures the consumer's imagination. One such product is the digital video disc (DVD) and the DVD player. DVDs and DVD players made their debut in Canada in 1997, when about 30,000 DVD players were sold. In 2002, Canadian sales of DVD players hit over a million and the cumulative number of players in Canada exceeded four million. Nearly $800 million was spent on DVD movies in 2002.

This swift ascendancy of the DVD and DVD player has resulted from both price and quality considerations. Although the price of DVDs has declined relatively slightly, the price of DVD players has nosedived. Costing $1000 or more when first introduced, most players currently sell for under $250. DVDs and DVD players are *complementary goods.* The lower price for DVD players has expanded their sales and greatly increased the demand for DVD movies.

Moreover, DVDs provide higher quality audio and video than video cassettes (VCs) and are much easier to store. For playing movies, DVDs and VCs are *substitute goods.* The improved audio and video experience of DVDs—the greater consumer satisfaction—has produced a substitution away from VCs and toward DVDs.

In terms of our analysis, many consumers have concluded that DVDs have higher marginal utility-to-price ratios (MU/P) than do VCs. Those consumers have enhanced the total utility by shifting spending toward DVDs.

The Diamond–Water Paradox

Early economists such as Adam Smith were puzzled by the fact that some essential goods had much lower prices than some unimportant goods. Why would water, essential to life, be priced below diamonds, which have much less usefulness? The paradox is resolved when we consider that water is in great supply relative to demand and thus has a very low price per litre. Diamonds, in contrast, are rare and are costly to mine, cut, and polish. Because their supply is small relative to demand, their price is very high per caret.

The marginal utility of the last unit of water consumed is very low. The reason follows from our utility-maximizing rule. Consumers (and producers) respond to the very low price of water by using a great deal of it for generating electricity, irrigating crops, heating buildings, watering lawns, quenching thirst, and so on. Consumption is expanded until marginal utility, which declines as more water is consumed, equals its low price. Conversely, relatively few diamonds are purchased because of their prohibitively high price, meaning that their marginal utility remains high. In equilibrium

<william-king.www.drexel.edu/top/prin/txt/MUch/Eco412.html>
Adam Smith and the diamond–water paradox

$$\frac{\text{MU of water (low)}}{\text{Price of water (low)}} = \frac{\text{MU of diamonds (high)}}{\text{Price of diamonds (high)}}$$

Although the marginal utility of the last unit of water consumed is low and the marginal utility of the last diamond purchased is high, the total utility of water is very high and the total utility of diamonds quite low. The total utility derived from the consumption of water is large because of the enormous amounts of water consumed. Total utility is the sum of the marginal utilities of all the litres of water consumed, including the trillions of litres that have far higher marginal utilities than the last unit consumed. In contrast, the total utility derived from diamonds is low since their high price means that relatively few of them are bought. Thus the diamond–water paradox is solved: water has much more total utility (roughly, usefulness) than diamonds even though the price of diamonds greatly exceeds the price of water. These relative prices relate to marginal utility, not total utility.

The Value of Time

The theory of consumer choice has been generalized to account for the economic value of *time*. Both consumption and production take time. Time is a valuable economic commodity; by using an hour in productive work, a person can earn $6, $10, $50, or more, depending on education and skills. By using that hour for leisure or in consumption activities, the individual incurs the opportunity cost of forgone income and sacrifices the $6, $10, or $50 that could have been earned by working.

Imagine a self-employed consumer in Winnipeg who is considering buying a round of golf on the one hand, and a concert ticket on the other. The market price of the golf game is $30 and that of the ticket is $40, but the golf game takes more time than the concert. Suppose this consumer spends four hours on the golf course but only two hours at the concert. If the consumer's time is worth $10 per hour as evidenced by the $10 wage obtained by working, then the full price of the golf game is $70 (the $30 market price plus $40 worth of time), while the full price of the concert is $60 (the $40 market price plus $20 worth of time). We find that, contrary to what market prices alone indicate, the full price of the concert is really less than the full price of the golf game.

Another example is the consumption of health care services. In Canada, government-sponsored insurance pays the full amount of a doctor's visit. The price the consumer pays is zero. But if we consider the time and cost of travelling to the doctor's office, and the waiting time in the office, the full price is considerably more than zero.

By accounting for time, we can see that it may be rational for the unskilled worker or retiree whose time has little market value to ride a bus from Edmonton to Saskatoon, but the corporate executive, whose time is very valuable, will find it cheaper to fly, even though bus fare is only a fraction of plane fare. It is sensible for the retiree, living on a modest income and having ample time, to spend many hours shopping for bargains at the mall or taking long trips in a motor home. It is equally rational for the highly paid physician, working 55 hours per week, to buy a new personal computer over the Internet and take short vacations at expensive resorts.

People in poor nations often conclude that affluent Canadians are wasteful of food and other material goods but overly economical in their use of time. Canadians who visit developing countries may think that time is used casually or squandered, while material goods are very highly prized and carefully used. These differences are not a paradox or a case of radically different temperaments; the differences are primarily a rational reflection that the high productivity of labour in an industrially advanced society gives time a high market value, whereas the opposite is true in a low-income, developing country.

Cash and Non-cash Gifts

Marginal utility analysis also helps us understand why people generally prefer cash gifts to non-cash gifts costing the same amount. The reason is simply that consumers know their own preferences better than the gift giver does and the cash gift provides more choices.

Look back at Table 6-1. Suppose Holly has zero earned income but is given the choice of a $2 cash gift or a non-cash gift of two units of A. Because two units of A can be bought with $2, these two gifts are of equal monetary value, but by spending the $2 cash gift on the first unit of B, Holly could obtain 24 utils. The non-cash gift of the first two units of A would yield only 18 (= 10 + 8) units of utility; the non-cash gifts yields less utility to the beneficiary than the cash gift.

Since giving of non-cash gifts is common, considerable value of those gifts is potentially lost because they do not match their recipients' tastes. For example, Aunt Flo may have paid $15 for the Celine Dion CD she gave you for your birthday, but you would pay only $7.50 for it. Thus, a $7.50, or 50 percent, value loss is involved. Multiplied by billions spent on gifts each year, the potential loss of value is large.

Some of that loss is avoided by the creative ways individuals handle the problem. For example, newlyweds set up gift registries for their weddings to help match their wants to the non-cash gifts received. Also, people obtain cash refunds or exchanges for gifts, so they can buy goods that provide more utility. And people have even been known to recycle gifts by giving them to someone else at a later time. All three actions support the proposition that individuals take actions to maximize their total utility.

6.5　　Consumer Surplus

consumer surplus
The difference between the maximum price a consumer (or consumers) is willing to pay for an additional unit of a product or service and its actual market price.

The individual demand curve depicted in Figure 6-2 can help us to understand the crucial distinction between total utility and marginal utility. An appreciation of the distinction between total utility and marginal utility is essential to understand how a consumer chooses to purchase an amount of a particular good, or a bundle of goods, given the market price. The concept of *consumer surplus* can help sharpen the distinction.

Suppose you have been invited to a party next weekend. You realize that there is nothing in your wardrobe that you want to wear for this social event, so you decide to finally buy a new pair of jeans. You head out to the local mall in search of jeans, prepared to pay $65 for a pair. After searching for an hour you locate the perfect pair, and the price is only $50. You quickly snap up the jeans, believing you have got a bargain. The difference between the maximum price a consumer (or consumers) is willing to pay for an additional unit of a product or service and its actual market price is called **consumer surplus**. Recall that a consumer compares the marginal utility of a good or service and its price when deciding whether to buy. You were the beneficiary of a consumer surplus of $15 on the jeans you purchased because you actually valued the first pair of jeans at $65, and were willing to pay that price. Would the purchase of a second pair of jeans result in a consumer surplus? It depends on whether a second pair of jeans will give you more than $50 worth of utility. Certainly, your total utility would increase with a second pair of jeans, but perhaps the marginal utility may not be enough to persuade you to shell out another $50 for an additional, identical pair. You may value the second pair of jeans at only $5 because the additional utility you get from it is relatively low.

In almost all markets, consumers collectively obtain more utility (total satisfaction) from their purchases than the amount of their expenditures (product price × quantity). The surplus of utility arises because, as we have just seen, some consumers are willing to pay more than the equilibrium price but need not do so.

Let's go through an example. Consider the market for jeans depicted in Figure 6-3. The demand curve *D* (which is also the marginal benefit curve) tells us that at $70 no consumers are willing to buy jeans, but some consumers of jeans are willing to pay more than the $50 market price. For example, assume Vijay is willing to pay $65; Elise, $60; Dieter, $55; while Andrea, in contrast, is unwilling to pay one penny more than the $50 market price.

There are many other consumers besides Vijay, Elise, and Dieter in this market who are willing to pay prices above $50. Only Andrea pays exactly the price she is willing to pay; the others receive some amount of utility beyond their expenditures. The difference between that utility value (measured by the vertical height of the points on the demand curve) and the $50 price is the consumer surplus. For example, Vijay is willing to pay $65 for his pair of jeans, but he pays only the $50 mar-

In almost all markets, consumers collectively obtain more utility from their purchases than their expenditures.

ket price, for a utility surplus of $15 (= $65 – 50). When we add together each buyer's utility surplus, we obtain the consumer surplus for all the consumers in the market. In Figure 6-3, consumers collectively are willing to pay the sum of the amounts represented by the blue triangle and grey rectangle to get Q* of jeans. However, consumers only have to pay the amount represented by the grey rectangle. The blue triangle thus represents consumer surplus.

A glance at Figure 6-3 shows that the amount of consumer surplus—the size of the blue triangle—would be less if the sellers could charge a price above $50. As just one example, at a price of $65, only a very small triangle of consumer surplus would exist.

Consumer surplus is one of the two key elements that are considered in *cost-benefit analysis*, which you encountered in Chapters 1 and 2. The demand curve is also a marginal benefit curve, and thus is essential in determining the marginal benefits of a particular project. Consumer surplus is also used to measure the efficiency of the market structures you will study in Chapters 8–10.

FIGURE 6-3   **Consumer Demand and Consumer Surplus**

Consumer surplus—shown as the blue triangle—reflects the differences between the maximum prices consumers are willing to pay for a product and the lower equilibrium price, here assumed to be $50. For quantity Q*, consumers are willing to pay the sum of the amounts represented by the blue triangle and the gray rectangle. Because they need pay only the amount shown as the gray rectangle, the blue triangle reflects consumer surplus.

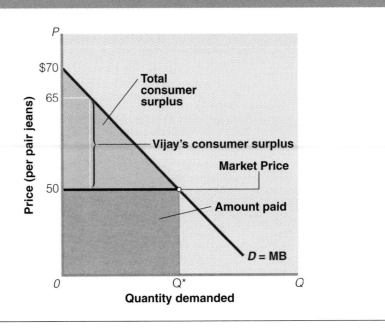

THE LASTword   Criminal Behaviour

Although economic analysis is not particularly relevant in explaining some crimes of violence, it does provide interesting insights into such property crimes as robbery, burglary, and auto theft.

Through extension, the theory of rational consumer behaviour provides some useful insights on criminal behaviour. Both the lawful consumer and the criminal try to maximize their total utility (or net benefit). For example, you can remove a textbook from the campus bookstore either by purchasing it or by stealing it. If you *buy* the book, your action is legal; you have fully compensated the bookstore for the product. (The bookstore would rather have your money than the book.) If you *steal* the book, you have broken the law. Theft is outlawed because it imposes uncompensated costs on others. In this case, your action reduces the bookstore's revenue and profit and also may impose costs on other buyers who now must pay higher prices for their textbooks.

Why might someone engage in criminal activity such as stealing? Just like the consumer who compares the marginal utility of a good with its price, the potential criminal compares the marginal benefit from an action with the price or cost. If the marginal benefit (to the criminal) exceeds the price or marginal cost (also to the criminal), the individual undertakes the criminal activity.

Most people, however, do not engage in theft, burglary, or fraud. Why not? The answer is that they perceive the personal price of engaging in these illegal activities to be too high relative to the marginal benefit. That price or marginal cost to the potential criminal has several facets. First, there are the guilt costs, which for many people are substantial. Such individuals would not steal from others even if there were no penalties for doing so; their moral sense of right and wrong would entail too great a guilt cost relative to the benefit from the stolen good. Other types of costs include the direct costs of the criminal activity (supplies and tools) and the forgone income from legitimate activities (the opportunity cost to the criminal).

Unfortunately, guilt costs, direct costs, and forgone income are not sufficient to deter some people from stealing. So society imposes other costs, mainly fines and imprisonment, on lawbreakers. The potential of being fined increases the marginal cost to the criminal. The potential of being imprisoned boosts marginal cost still further. Most people highly value their personal freedom and lose considerable legitimate earnings while incarcerated.

Given these types of costs, the potential criminal estimates the marginal cost and benefit of committing the crime. As a simple example, suppose that the direct cost and opportunity cost of stealing an $80 textbook are both zero. The probability of getting caught is 10 percent, and, if apprehended, there will be a $500 fine. The potential criminal will estimate the marginal cost of stealing the book as $50 (= $500 fine × .10 chance of apprehension). Someone who has guilt costs of zero will choose to steal the book because the marginal benefit of $80 will exceed the marginal cost of $50. In contrast, someone having a guilt cost of, say, $40, will not steal the book. The marginal benefit of $80 will not be as great as the marginal cost of $90 (= $50 of penalty cost + $40 of guilt cost).

This perspective on illegal behaviour has some interesting implications. For example, other things equal, crime will rise (more of it will be bought) when its price falls. This explains, for instance, why some people who do not steal from stores under normal circumstances participate in looting stores during riots, when the marginal cost of being apprehended declines substantially.

Another implication is that society can reduce unlawful behaviour by increasing the price of crime. It can nourish and increase guilt costs through family, educational, and religious efforts. It can increase the direct costs of crime by using more sophisticated security systems (locks, alarms, video surveillance) so that criminals will have to buy and use more sophisticated tools. It can undertake education and training initiatives to enhance the legitimate earnings of people who might otherwise engage in illegal activity. It can increase policing to raise the probability of being apprehended for crime, and it can impose greater penalties for those who are caught and convicted.

CHAPTER SUMMARY

6.1 A CLOSER LOOK AT THE LAW OF DEMAND

- The income and substitution effects and the law of diminishing marginal utility help explain why consumers buy more of a product when its price drops and less of a product when its price increases.

- The income effect implies that a decline in the price of a product increases the consumer's real income and enables the consumer to buy more of that product with a fixed money income. The substitution effect implies that a lower price makes a product relatively more attractive and, therefore, increases the consumer's willingness to substitute it for other products.

6.2 THEORY OF CONSUMER CHOICE

- The law of diminishing marginal utility states that, beyond a certain quantity, additional units of a specific good will yield declining amounts of extra satisfaction to a consumer.

- We assume that the typical consumer is rational and acts based on well-defined preferences. Because income is limited and goods have prices, consumers cannot purchase all the goods and services they might want. Consumers therefore select the attainable combination of goods that maximizes their utility or satisfaction.

- A consumer's utility is maximized when income is allocated so that the last dollar spent on each product purchased yields the same amount of extra satisfaction.

Algebraically, the utility-maximizing rule is fulfilled when

$$\frac{\text{MU of product A}}{\text{Price of A}} = \frac{\text{MU of product B}}{\text{Price of B}}$$

and the consumer's total income is spent.

6.3 UTILITY MAXIMIZATION AND THE DEMAND CURVE

- The utility-maximizing rule and the demand curve are logically consistent. Because marginal utility declines, a lower price is needed to induce the consumer to buy more of a particular product.

6.4 APPLICATION AND EXTENSIONS

- The theory of consumer choice can be used to explain real-world phenomena. For example, consumers have switched from video cassettes (VCs) to DVDs because as the price of DVD players has fallen, the utility-to-price ratio of DVDs has risen compared to VCs; and the price of diamonds is high compared to the price of water because it is the marginal utility (MU) of diamonds that is high, and it is MU, not total utility, that determines what people are prepared to pay for an item.

6.5 CONSUMER SURPLUS

- Consumer surplus is the difference between what a consumer is willing to pay for an additional unit of a product or service and its market price.

TERMS AND CONCEPTS

income effect, p. 135
substitution effect, p. 135
total utility, p. 136
marginal utility, p. 136

law of diminishing marginal utility, p. 136
rational behaviour, p. 139
budget constraint, p. 139

utility-maximizing rule, p. 139
consumer surplus, p. 147

STUDY QUESTIONS

1. Explain the law of demand through the income and substitution effects, using a price increase as a point of departure. Explain the law of demand in terms of diminishing marginal utility.

2. **KEY QUESTION** Complete the following table and answer the questions that follow.

Units consumed	Total utility	Marginal utility
0	0	
1	10	10
2	—	8
3	25	—
4	30	—
5	—	3
6	34	—

a. At which rate is total utility increasing: a constant rate, a decreasing rate, or an increasing rate? How do you know?

b. "A rational consumer will purchase only one unit of the product represented by these data, since that amount maximizes marginal utility." Do you agree? Explain why or why not.

c. "It is possible that a rational consumer will not purchase any units of the product represented by these data." Do you agree? Explain why or why not.

3. Mrs. Wilson buys loaves of bread and litres of milk each week at prices of $1 and $.80, respectively. At present she is buying these two products in amounts such that the marginal utilities from the last units purchased of the two products are 80 and 70 utils, respectively. Is she buying the utility-maximizing combination of bread and milk? If not, how should she reallocate her expenditures between the two goods?

4. **KEY QUESTION** Columns 1 through 4 in the table below show the marginal utility, measured in utils, that Ricardo would get by purchasing various amounts of products A, B, C, and D. Column 5 shows the marginal utility Ricardo gets from saving. Assume that the prices of A, B, C, and D are $18, $6, $4, and $24, respectively, and that Ricardo has an income of $106.

a. What quantities of A, B, C, and D will Ricardo purchase in maximizing his utility?

b. How many dollars will Ricardo choose to save?

c. Check your answers by substituting them into the algebraic statement of the utility-maximizing rule.

5. **KEY QUESTION** You are choosing between two goods, X and Y, and your marginal utility from each is as shown below. If your income is $9 and the prices of X and Y are $2 and $1, respectively, what quantities of each will you purchase to maximize utility? What

total utility will you realize? Assume that, other things remaining unchanged, the price of X falls to $1. What quantities of X and Y will you now purchase? Using the two prices and quantities for X, derive a demand schedule (price–quantity demanded table) for X.

Units of X	MU_x	Units of Y	MU_y
1	10	1	8
2	8	2	7
3	6	3	6
4	4	4	5
5	3	5	4
6	2	6	3

6. How can time be incorporated into the theory of consumer behaviour? Explain the following comment: "Want to make millions of dollars? Devise a product that saves Canadians lots of time."

7. Explain:

a. "Before economic growth, there were too few goods; after growth, there is too little time."

b. "It is irrational for an individual to take the time to be completely rational in economic decision making."

c. "Telling Santa what you want for Christmas makes sense in terms of utility maximization."

8. In the past decade or so there has been a dramatic expansion of small retail convenience stores (such as Mac's, 7-Elevens, Beckers), although their prices are generally much higher than prices in large supermarkets. What explains the success of the convenience stores?

9. Many apartment-complex owners are installing water meters for each apartment and billing the occupants according to the amount of water they use, in contrast to the former procedure of having a central meter for the

Column 1		Column 2		Column 3		Column 4		Column 5	
Units of A	MU	Units of B	MU	Units of C	MU	Units of D	MU	Number of dollars saved	MU
1	72	1	24	1	15	1	36	1	5
2	54	2	15	2	12	2	30	2	4
3	45	3	12	3	8	3	24	3	3
4	36	4	9	4	7	4	18	4	2
5	27	5	7	5	5	5	13	5	1
6	18	6	5	6	4	6	7	6	½
7	15	7	2	7	3½	7	4	7	¼
8	12	8	1	8	3	8	2	8	⅛

entire complex and dividing up the water expense as part of the rent. Where individual meters have been installed, water usage has declined 10 to 40 percent. Explain that drop, referring to price and marginal utility.

10. How does the term "maximum willingness to pay" relate to consumer surplus?

11. **Advanced analysis**: A mathematically fair bet is one in which a gambler bets, say, $100, for a 10 percent chance to win $1000 dollars ($100 = .10 × 1000). Assuming diminishing marginal utility of dollars, explain why this is *not* a fair bet in terms of utility. Why is it even a less fair bet when the house takes a cut of each dollar bet? So is gambling irrational?

12. **Advanced analysis**: Let $MU_A = z = 10 - x$ and $MU_B = z = 21 - 2y$, where z is marginal utility per dollar measured in utils, x is the amount spent on product A, and y is the amount spent on product B. Assume that the consumer has $10 to spend on A and B—that is, $x + y = 10$. How is the $10 best allocated between A and B? How much utility will the marginal dollar yield?

13. **(The Last Word)** In what way is criminal behaviour similar to consumer behaviour? Why do most people obtain goods via legal behaviour as opposed to illegal behaviour? What are society's main options for reducing illegal behaviour?

INTERNET APPLICATION QUESTIONS

1. Assume that you and several classmates each receive a $300 credit voucher (good for today only) from the Hudson's Bay Company. Go to the McConnell-Brue-Barbiero Web site (Chapter 6) to access the Bay's home page and select $300 worth of merchandise. Use "Add to Basket" to keep a running total. Compare your list with your classmates' lists. What explains the differences? Would you have purchased your items if you had received $300 in cash to be spent whenever and wherever you pleased?

Appendix to Chapter 6

A6.1   Indifference Curve Analysis

A more advanced explanation of consumer behaviour and equilibrium is based on (1) budget lines and (2) so-called indifference curves.

The Budget Line: What Is Attainable

budget line
A line that shows various combinations of two products a consumer can purchase with a specific money income, given the products' prices.

A **budget line** (or, more technically, a *budget constraint*) is a schedule or curve that shows various combinations of two products a consumer can purchase with a specific money income. If the price of product A is $1.50 and the price of product B is $1.00, a consumer could purchase all the combinations of A and B shown in the table of Figure A6-1 with $12 of money income. At one extreme, the consumer might spend all the income on eight units of A and have nothing left to spend on B. Or, by giving up two units of A and thereby freeing $3, the consumer could have six units of A and three of B. At the other extreme, the consumer could buy 12 units of B at $1.00 each, spending his or her entire money income on B with nothing left to spend on A.

FIGURE   A6-1   A Consumer's Budget Line

Units of A (price = $1.50)	Units of B (price = $1.00)	Total expenditure
8	0	$12 (= $12 + $0)
6	3	$12 (= $9 + $3)
4	6	$12 (= $6 + $6)
2	9	$12 (= $3 + $9)
0	12	$12 (= $0 + $12)

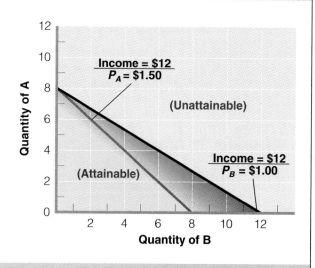

The budget line shows all the combinations of any two products that can be purchased given the prices of the products and the consumer's money income.

Figure A6-1 also shows the same budget line graphically. Note that the graph is not restricted to whole units of A and B as is the table. Every point on the graph represents a possible combination of A and B, including fractional quantities. The slope of the graphed budget line measures the ratio of the price of B to the price of A; more precisely, the absolute value of the slope is $P_B/P_A = \$1.00/\$1.50 = 2/3$. This is the mathematical way of saying that the consumer must forgo two units of A (measured on the vertical axis) to buy three units of B (measured on the horizontal axis). In moving down the budget or price line, two units of A (at \$1.50 each) must be given up to obtain three more units of B (at \$1.00 each). This yields a slope of 2/3.

The budget line has two other significant characteristics:

1. **Income changes**   The location of the budget line varies with money income. An increase in money income shifts the budget line to the right; a decrease in money income shifts it to the left. To verify this, recalculate the table in Figure A6-1, assuming that money income is (a) \$24 and (b) \$6, and plot the new budget lines.

2. **Price changes**   A change in product prices also shifts the budget line. A decline in the prices of both products—the equivalent of an increase in real income—shifts the curve to the right. (You can verify this by recalculating the table in Figure A6-1 and replotting the graph, assuming that $P_A = \$.75$ and $P_B = \$.50$.) Conversely, an increase in the prices of A and B shifts the curve to the left. (Assume $P_A = \$3$ and $P_B = \$2$ and rework the table and the graph to substantiate this statement.)

Note what happens if P_B changes while P_A and money income remain constant. In particular, if P_B drops, say, from \$1.00 to \$.50, the lower end of the budget line fans outward to the right. Conversely, if P_B increases, say, from \$1.00 to \$1.50, the lower end of the line fans inward to the left. In both instances the line remains anchored at eight units on the vertical axis because P_A has not changed.

Indifference Curves: What Is Preferred

Budget lines reflect objective market data, specifically income and prices. They reveal combinations of products A and B that can be purchased given current money income and prices.

indifference curves
Curves showing the different combinations of two products that yield the same satisfaction or utility to a consumer.

Indifference curves, however, reflect subjective information about consumer preferences for A and B. An indifference curve shows all the combinations of two products A and B that will yield the same total satisfaction or total utility to a consumer. Figure A6-2 presents a hypothetical indifference curve for products A and B. The consumer's subjective preferences are such that he or she will realize the same total utility from each combination of A and B shown in the table or on the curve. The consumer will be indifferent (will not care) as to which combination is actually obtained.

Indifference curves have several important characteristics.

INDIFFERENCE CURVES ARE DOWNSLOPING

An indifference curve slopes downward because more of one product means less of the other, if total utility is to remain unchanged. Suppose the consumer moves from one combination of A and B to another, say, from j to k in Figure A6-2. In so doing, the consumer obtains more of product B, increasing total utility. But because total utility is the same everywhere on the curve, the consumer must give up some of the other product, A, to reduce total utility by a precisely offsetting amount. Thus more of B necessitates less of A, and the quantities of A and B are inversely related. A curve that reflects inversely related variables is downward sloping.

FIGURE A6-2 A Consumer's Indifference Curve

Combination	Units of A	Units of B
j	12	2
k	6	4
l	4	6
m	3	8

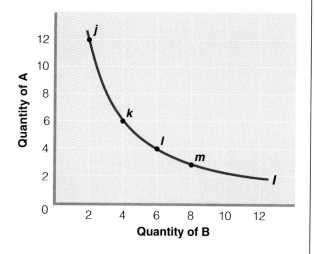

Every point on indifference curve I represents some combination of products A and B, and all those combinations are equally satisfactory to the consumer. That is, each combination of A and B on the curve yields the same total utility.

INDIFFERENCE CURVES ARE CONVEX TO THE ORIGIN

A downward-sloping curve can be concave (bowed outward) or convex (bowed inward) to the origin. A concave curve has an increasing (steeper) slope as one moves down the curve, while a convex curve has a diminishing (flatter) slope as one moves down the curve. Note in Figure A6-2 that the indifference curve is convex to the origin. Its slope diminishes or becomes flatter as we move from *j* to *k* to *l*, and so on down the curve. Technically, the slope of the indifference curve at each point measures the **marginal rate of substitution (MRS)** of the combination represented by that point. The slope or MRS shows the rate at which the consumer who possesses that combination will substitute one good for the other (say, B for A) to remain equally satisfied. The diminishing slope of the indifference curve means the willingness to substitute B for A diminishes as we move down the curve.

The rationale for this convexity—that is, for a diminishing MRS—is that consumers' subjective willingness to substitute B for A (or A for B) will depend on the amounts of B and A they have to begin with. Consider Figure A6-2 again, beginning at point *j*. Here, in relative terms, the consumer has a substantial amount of A and very little of B. Within this combination, a unit of B is very valuable (that is, its marginal utility is high), while a unit of A is less valuable (its marginal utility is low). The consumer will then be willing to give up a substantial amount of A to get, say, two more units of B. In this case, the consumer is willing to forgo six units of A to get two more units of B; the MRS is 6/2 or 3.

But at point *k* the consumer has less A and more B. Here A is somewhat more valuable and B less valuable at the margin. In a move from point *k* to point *l*, the consumer is willing to give up only two units of A to get two more units of B, so the MRS is only

marginal rate of substitution (MRS)
The rate at which a consumer is prepared to substitute one good for another (from a given combination of goods) and remain equally satisfied (have the same total utility).

<ingrimayne.saintjoe.edu/
econ/MaximizingBeha/
Indifference.html>
Another look at indifference curves

2/2 or 1. Having still less of A and more of B at point *l*, the consumer is willing to give up only one unit of A in return for two more units of B and the MRS falls to 1/2.

Generally, as the amount of B *increases,* the marginal utility of additional units of B *decreases.* Similarly, as the quantity of A *decreases,* its marginal utility *increases.* In Figure A6-2 we see that in moving down the curve, the consumer will be willing to give up smaller and smaller amounts of A to offset acquiring each additional unit of B. The result is a curve with a diminishing slope, a curve that is convex to the origin. The MRS declines as one moves southeast along the indifference curve.

The Indifference Map

indifference map
A series of indifference curves, each of which represents a different level of total utility and together show the preferences of the consumer.

equilibrium position
The combination of products that yields the greatest satisfaction or utility.

The single indifference curve of Figure A6-2 reflects some constant (but unspecified) level of total utility or satisfaction. It is possible and useful to sketch a whole series of indifference curves or an **indifference map**, as shown in Figure A6-3. Each curve reflects a different level of total utility. Specifically, each curve to the right of our original curve (labelled I_3 in Figure A6-3) reflects combinations of A and B that yield more utility than I_3. Each curve to the left of I_3 reflects less total utility than I_3. As we move out from the origin, each successive indifference curve represents a higher level of utility. To demonstrate this fact, draw a line in a northeasterly direction from the origin; note that its points of intersection with successive curves entail larger amounts of both A and B and, therefore, higher levels of total utility.

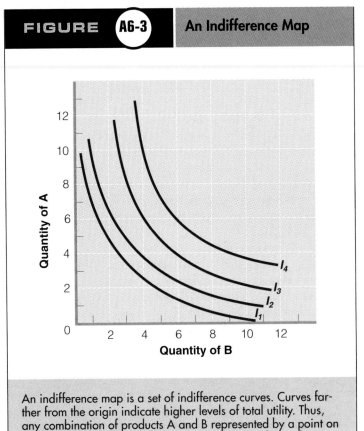

FIGURE A6-3 — An Indifference Map

An indifference map is a set of indifference curves. Curves farther from the origin indicate higher levels of total utility. Thus, any combination of products A and B represented by a point on I_4 has greater total utility than any combination of A and B represented by a point on I_3, I_2, and I_1.

Equilibrium at Tangency

Since the axes in Figures A6-1 and A6-3 are identical, we can superimpose a budget line on the consumer's indifference map, as shown in Figure A6-4. By definition, the budget line indicates all the combinations of A and B that the consumer can attain with his or her money income given the prices of A and B. Of these attainable combinations, the consumer will prefer that combination that yields the greatest satisfaction or utility. Specifically, the utility-maximizing combination will be the combination lying on the highest attainable indifference curve, which is called the consumer's **equilibrium position**.

In Figure A6-4 the consumer's equilibrium position is at point X, where the budget line is *tangent* to I_3. Why not point Y? Because Y is on a lower indifference curve, I_2. By moving down the budget line—by shifting dollars from purchases of A to purchases of B—the consumer can attain an indifference curve farther from the origin and thereby increase the total utility derived from the same income. Why not point Z? For the same reason as for Y: point Z is on a lower indifference curve, I_1. By moving up the budget line—by reallocating dollars from B to A—the consumer can get on the higher indifference curve I_3 and increase total utility.

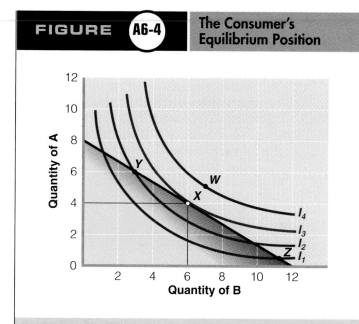

FIGURE A6-4 The Consumer's Equilibrium Position

The consumer's equilibrium position is represented by point *X*, where the black budget line is tangent to indifference curve *I₃*. The consumer buys four units of A at $1.50 per unit and six of B at $1.00 per unit with a $12 money income. Points *Z* and *Y* represent attainable combinations of A and B that yield less total utility, as is evidenced by the fact that they are on lower indifference curves. Point *W* would entail more utility than *X*, but it requires a greater income than the $12 represented by the budget line.

How about point *W* on indifference curve *I₄*? While it is true that *W* would yield a greater total utility than *X*, point *W* is beyond (outside) the budget line and, hence, is *not* attainable by the consumer. Point *X* represents the optimal *attainable* combination of products A and B. Note that, according to the definition of tangency, the slope of the highest attainable indifference curve equals the slope of the budget line. Because the slope of the indifference curve reflects the MRS (marginal rate of substitution) and the slope of the budget line is P_B/P_A, the consumer's optimal or equilibrium position is the point where

$$\text{MRS} = \frac{P_B}{P_A}$$

(You may benefit by trying to answer Appendix *Key Question 3* at this time.)

The Measurement of Utility

There is an important difference between the marginal utility theory of consumer demand and the indifference curve theory. The marginal utility theory assumes that utility is *numerically* measurable, that is, that the consumer can say how much extra utility he or she derives from each extra unit of A or B. The consumer needs that information to realize the utility-maximizing (equilibrium) position, as indicated by

$$\frac{\text{Marginal utility of A}}{\text{Price of A}} = \frac{\text{Marginal utility of B}}{\text{Price of B}}$$

The indifference curve approach imposes a less stringent requirement on the consumer, who need only specify whether a particular combination of A and B will yield more, less, or the same amount of utility than some other combination of A and B. The consumer need only say, for example, that six units of A and seven of B will yield more (or less) satisfaction than four of A and nine of B. Indifference curve theory does not require that the consumer specify *how much* more (or less) satisfaction will be realized.

When we compare the equilibrium situations in the two theories, we find that in the indifference curve analysis, the MRS equals P_B/P_A at equilibrium; however, in the marginal utility approach, the ratio of marginal utilities equals P_B/P_A. We therefore deduce that at equilibrium, the MRS is equivalent in the marginal utility approach to the ratio of the marginal utilities of the last purchased units of the two products.[2]

---

[2]If we begin with the utility-maximizing rule, $MU_A/P_A = MU_B/P_B$, and then multiply through by P_B and divide through by MU_A, we obtain $P_B/P_A = MU_B/MU_A$. In indifference curve analysis we know that at the equilibrium position MRS = P_B/P_A. Hence, at equilibrium, MRS also equals MU_B/MU_A.

158

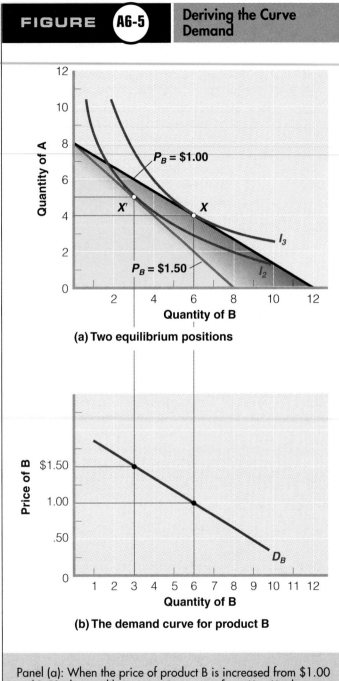

FIGURE A6-5 Deriving the Curve Demand

(a) Two equilibrium positions

(b) The demand curve for product B

Panel (a): When the price of product B is increased from $1.00 to $1.50, the equilibrium position moves from X to X', decreasing the quantity of product B demanded from six to three units. Panel (b): The demand curve for product B is determined by plotting the $1.00–six-unit and $1.50–three-unit price–quantity combinations for product B.

The Derivation of the Demand Curve

We noted earlier that with a fixed price for A, an increase in the price of B will cause the bottom of the budget line to fan inward to the left. We can use that fact to derive a demand curve for product B. In Figure A6-5(a) we reproduce the part of Figure A6-4 that shows our initial consumer equilibrium at point X. The budget line determining this equilibrium position assumes that money income is $12 and that $P_A = \$1.50$ and $P_B = \$1.00$. Let's see what happens to the equilibrium position when we increase P_B to $1.50 and hold both money income and the price of A constant.

The result is shown in Figure A6-5(a). The budget line fans to the left, yielding a new equilibrium point X' where it is tangent to lower indifference curve I_2. At X' the consumer buys three units of B and five of A compared with four of A and six of B at X. Our interest is in B, and we now have sufficient information to locate two points on the demand curve for product B. We know that at equilibrium point X, the price of B is $1.00 and six units are purchased; at equilibrium point X', the price of B is $1.50 and three units are purchased.

These data are shown graphically in Figure A6-5(b) as points on the consumer's demand curve for B. Note that the horizontal axes of Figure A6-5(a) and (b) are identical; both measure the quantity demanded of B. We can therefore drop vertical reference lines from Figure A6-5(a) down to the horizontal axis of Figure A6-5(b). On the vertical axis of Figure A6-5(b) we locate the two chosen prices of B. Knowing that these prices yield the relevant quantities demanded, we locate two points on the demand curve for B. By simple manipulation of the price of B in an indifference curve–budget line context, we have obtained a downward-sloping demand curve for B. We have thus again derived the law of demand assuming other things are equal, since only the price of B was changed (the price of A and the consumer's money income and tastes remained constant). In this case, we have derived the demand curve without resorting to the questionable assumption that consumers can measure utility in units called utils. In this indifference curve approach, consumers simply compare combinations of products A and B and determine which combination they prefer given their incomes and the prices of the two products.

APPENDIX SUMMARY

A6.1 INDIFFERENCE CURVE ANALYSIS

- The indifference curve approach to consumer behaviour is based on the consumer's budget line and indifference curves.

- The budget line shows all combinations of two products that the consumer can purchase given product prices and money income.

- A change in either product prices or money income moves the budget line.

- An indifference curve shows all combinations of two products that will yield the same total utility to a consumer. Indifference curves are downward sloping and convex from the origin.

- An indifference map consists of a number of indifference curves; the farther from the origin, the higher the total utility associated with a curve.

- The consumer is in equilibrium (utility is maximized) at the point on the budget line that lies on the highest attainable indifference curve. At that point the budget line and indifference curve are tangent.

- Changing the price of one product shifts the budget line and determines a new equilibrium point. A downsloping demand curve can be determined by plotting the price–quantity combinations associated with two or more equilibrium points.

APPENDIX TERMS AND CONCEPTS

budget line, p. 153
indifference curves, p. 154

marginal rate of substitution (MRS), p. 155

indifference map, p. 156
equilibrium position, p. 156

APPENDIX STUDY QUESTIONS

1. What information is embodied in a budget line? What shifts occur in the budget line when money income (a) increases and (b) decreases? What shifts occur in the budget line when the price of the product shown on the vertical axis (a) increases and (b) decreases?

2. What information is contained in an indifference curve? Why are such curves (a) downward sloping and (b) convex from the origin? Why does total utility increase as the consumer moves to indifference curves farther from the origin? Why can't indifference curves intersect?

3. **APPENDIX KEY QUESTION**   Using Figure A6-4, explain why the point of tangency of the budget line with an indifference curve is the consumer's equilibrium position. Explain why any point where the budget line intersects an indifference curve is not equilibrium. Explain: "The consumer is in equilibrium where MRS = P_B/P_A."

4. Assume that the data in the accompanying table give an indifference curve for Mr. Chen. Graph this curve, putting A on the vertical axis and B on the horizontal axis. Assuming that the prices of A and B are $1.50 and $1.00, respectively, and that Mr. Chen has $24 to spend, add his budget line to your graph. What combination of A and B will Mr. Chen purchase? Does your answer meet the MRS = P_B/P_A rule for equilibrium?

Units of A	Units of B
16	6
12	8
8	2
4	24

5. Explain graphically how indifference analysis can be used to derive a demand curve.

6. Advanced analysis: Demonstrate mathematically that the equilibrium condition MRS = P_B/P_A is the equivalent of the utility-maximizing rule $MU_A/P_A = MU_B/P_B$.

Chapter 7

The Organization and Costs of Production

Our attention now turns from the behaviour of consumers to the behaviour of producers. In market economies, a wide variety of businesses, from family-owned businesses to large corporations, produce an even wider variety of goods and services. Each business requires inputs to produce its products. To acquire the needed inputs, a firm makes monetary payments to resource owners (for example, workers) and incurs opportunity costs when using resources it already owns (for example, entrepreneurial talent). Those payments and opportunity costs together make up the firm's *costs of production,* which we discuss in this chapter.

Then in the next several chapters, we bring product demand, product prices, and revenue back into the analysis and explain how firms compare revenues and costs in determining how much to produce. Our ultimate purpose is to show how those comparisons relate to economic efficiency.

7.1   The Firm and the Business Sector

A firm can be organized several ways. It will be useful to distinguish among a plant, a firm, and an industry.

- A **plant** is a physical establishment—a factory, farm, mine, store, or warehouse—that performs one or more functions in producing, fabricating, and distributing goods and services.

- A **firm** is a business organization that owns and operates plants. Some firms operate only one plant, but many own and operate several.

- An **industry** is a group of firms that produce the same, or similar, products.

The organizational structures of firms are often complex and varied. *Multiplant firms* may be organized horizontally, with several plants performing much the same function. Examples are the multiple bottling plants of Coca-Cola and the many individual Canadian Tire stores. Firms may be *vertically integrated,* meaning they own plants that perform different functions in the various stages of the production process. For example, oil companies such as Petro-Canada own oil fields, refineries, and retail gasoline stations. Some firms are *conglomerates,* so named because they have plants that produce products in several industries. For example, Power Corp. of Montreal operates in such diverse fields as communications and industrial, financial, and energy services.

Legal Forms of Businesses

The business population is diverse, ranging from giant corporations such as George Weston Ltd., with sales in 2001 of over $24 billion and more than 126,000 employees, to neighbourhood specialty shops and mom-and-pop groceries with one or two employees and sales of only $200 to $300 per day. There are three major legal forms of businesses.

1. A **sole proprietorship** is a business owned and operated by one person. Usually, the proprietor (the owner) personally supervises its operation.

2. The **partnership** form of business organization is a natural outgrowth of the sole proprietorship. In a partnership, two or more individuals (the partners) agree to own and operate a business together. Usually they pool their financial resources and business skills. Consequently, they share the risks and the profits or losses.

3. A **corporation** is a legal creation that can acquire resources, own assets, produce and sell products, incur debts, extend credit, sue and be sued, and perform the functions of any other type of enterprise. A corporation is distinct and separate from the individual stockholders who own it. Hired managers run most corporations.

Advantages and Disadvantages

Each form of business enterprise has advantages and disadvantages.

SOLE PROPRIETORSHIP

Sole proprietorships are very numerous because they are easy to set up and organize; there is virtually no red tape or legal expense. There are an estimated three million businesses classified as sole proprietorships in Canada. The proprietor is the boss and has substantial freedom of action. Because the proprietor's profit income depends on the enterprise's success, strong incentive exists to manage the business efficiently.

---

plant
A physical establishment that performs one or more functions in producing, fabricating, and distributing goods and services.

firm
An organization that employs resources to produce a good or service for profit and owns and operates one or more plants.

industry
A group of firms that produce the same or similar products.

sole proprietorship
An unincorporated firm owned and operated by one person.

partnership
An unincorporated firm owned and operated by two or more people.

corporation
A legal entity chartered by the federal or provincial governments that operates as a distinct and separate body from the individuals who own it.

Sole proprietorships also have several disadvantages. With rare exceptions, the financial resources of a sole proprietorship are insufficient to permit the firm to grow into a large enterprise. Finances are usually limited to what the proprietor has in the bank and can borrow. Since proprietorships often fail, chartered banks are not eager to extend them credit. In some sectors, more than 50 percent of new sole-proprietor businesses have gone out of business within five years of initiating activity.

Also, being totally in charge of an enterprise means that the proprietor carries out all management functions. A proprietor must make decisions on buying and selling, the hiring and training of personnel, and producing, advertising, and distributing the firm's product. Thus, the potential benefits of specialization in business management are not available to the typical small-scale proprietorship.

Finally, and most important, the proprietor is subject to *unlimited liability*. Individuals in business for themselves risk not only the assets of the firm but their personal assets as well. If the assets of an unsuccessful sole proprietorship are insufficient to pay the firm's bills, creditors can file claims against the proprietor's personal property.

PARTNERSHIP

Like the sole proprietorship, a partnership is easy to organize. Although the partners usually sign a written agreement, there is not much legal red tape or legal expense. Also, greater specialization in management is possible, because a partnership has two or more participants, and, because there is more than one owner, the financial resources of a partnership are likely to be greater than the resources of a sole proprietorship. Consequently, chartered banks regard partnerships as somewhat better risks than sole proprietorships.

Partnerships have some of the shortcomings of the proprietorship and also some of their own. Whenever several people participate in management, the divided authority may lead to inconsistent policies or to inaction when action is required. Worse, the partners may disagree on basic policy. Although the finances of partnerships are generally superior to those of sole proprietorships, the finances of partnerships are still severely limited. The combined financial resources of three or four partners may still not be enough to ensure the growth of a successful enterprise.

The continuity of a partnership is precarious. Generally, when one partner dies or withdraws, the partnership must be dissolved and reorganized, with inevitable disruption of its operations. Finally, unlimited liability plagues a partnership, just as it does a proprietorship. Each partner is liable for all business debts incurred, not only as a result of his or her own performance but also as a result of the performance of any other partner. Wealthy partners risk their wealth on the prudence of less affluent partners.

CORPORATION

The advantages of the corporate form of business enterprise have catapulted it into a dominant position in Canada. Although corporations are relatively small in number, many of them are large in size and in scale of operations. The corporation is by far the most effective form of business organization for raising financial capital (money). The corporation employs unique methods of finance—the selling of stocks and bonds—that enable it to pool the financial resources of large numbers of people. **Stocks** are shares of ownership of a corporation, whereas **bonds** are promises to repay a loan, usually at a set rate of interest (see The Last Word at the end of this chapter).

Financing via sales of stocks and bonds also provides advantages to those who purchase these *securities*. Such financing makes it possible for a household to own a part of the business and to share the expected monetary rewards without actively managing the firm. An individual investor can spread risks by buying the securities of several corporations, and it is usually easy for holders of corporate securities to sell their holdings. Organized stock exchanges simplify the transfer of securities from sellers to buyers. This ease of sale increases the willingness of savers to make financial investments in corporate securities. Corporations have easier access to bank credit than other

stocks
Ownership shares in a corporation.

bonds
Financial devices through which a borrower (a firm or government) is obligated to pay the principal and interest on a loan at a specific date in the future.

types of business organizations do, and since corporations are better risks, they are more likely to become profitable clients of banks.

Corporations have the distinct advantage of **limited liability**. The owners (stockholders) of a corporation risk only what they paid for their stock. Their personal assets are not at stake if the corporation defaults on its debts. Creditors can sue the corporation as a legal entity but cannot sue the owners of the corporation as individuals.

Because of their ability to attract financial capital, successful corporations can easily expand the scope of their operations and realize the benefits of expansion. They can take advantage of mass-production technologies and division of labour, and hire specialists in production, accounting, and marketing functions, and thus improve efficiency.

As a legal entity, the corporation has a life independent of its owners and its officers. Legally, at least, corporations are immortal. The transfer of corporate ownership through inheritance or the sale of stock does not disrupt the continuity of the corporation. Corporations have permanence that is conducive to long-range planning and growth.

The corporation's advantages are of tremendous significance and typically override any associated disadvantages, yet the corporate form has certain drawbacks. Some red tape and legal expense are involved in obtaining a corporate charter. From the social point of view, the corporate form of enterprise lends itself to certain abuses; because the corporation is a legal entity, unscrupulous business owners can sometimes avoid personal responsibility for questionable business activities by adopting the corporate form of enterprise.

A disadvantage to the owners of corporations is the **double taxation** of some corporate income. Corporate profit that is shared among stockholders as *dividends* is taxed twice—once as corporate profit and again as stockholders' personal income.

The Principal–Agent Problem

Many Canadian corporations are extremely large and that size creates a potential problem. In sole proprietorships and partnerships, the owners of the real and financial assets of the firm enjoy direct control of those assets, but ownership of large corporations is spread over tens or hundreds of thousands of stockholders. The owners of a corporation usually do not manage it, but instead hire others to do so.

That practice can create a **principal–agent problem**. The *principals* are the stockholders who own the corporation and who hire executives as their agents to run the business on their behalf. The interests of these managers (the agents) and the wishes of the owners (the principals) do not always coincide. The owners typically want maximum company profit and stock price. The agents, however, may want the power, prestige, and pay that usually accompany control over a large enterprise, independent of its profitability and stock price.

So, a conflict of interest may develop. For example, executives may build expensive office buildings, enjoy excessive perks such as corporate jets, and pay too much to acquire other corporations. Consequently, the firm will have bloated costs, and profits and stock prices will not be maximized for the owners.

Many corporations have addressed the principal–agent problem by providing a substantial part of executive pay as shares of the companies' stock. The idea is to align the interest of the executives more closely with those of the broader corporate owners. By pursuing high profits and share prices—which benefit the broader owners—the executives enhance their own income.

But the principal–agent problem is certainly not completely resolved by paying public company executives a significant part of their pay with company stock. In 2002, there were some spectacular bankruptcies of very large corporations in the U.S., Enron and WorldCom among the most prominent. In Canada, 360 Networks, a less well-known telecommunications firm, also filed for bankruptcy protection. Executives fudged financial statements to hide the dismal financial state of their companies from investors, in an effort to keep the stock price high. In the meantime, executives in

limited liability
Restriction of the maximum loss to a predetermined amount for the owners (stockholders) of a corporation.

double taxation
The taxation of both corporate net income (profits) and the dividends paid from this net income when they become the personal income of households.

principal–agent problem
A conflict of interest that occurs when agents (workers or managers) pursue their own objectives to the detriment of the principal's (stockholders) goals.

these very same firms were selling their shares while the stock price was still at lofty heights. Once the true financial state of these companies became known, their stock prices plummeted.

Also in Canada, investors in Nortel Networks stock were burned when the stock fell from over $100 in 2000 to under $1 in October 2002. Many investors in Nortel blamed management for misleading them with overly optimistic sales projections. Many executives in Canada's largest telecommunications company sold their stock when the going was good. Clearly, the principal–agent problems that exist in corporate governance continue to plague many companies. (*Key Question 2*)

QUICK REVIEW

- A plant is a physical establishment that contributes to the production of goods and services; a firm is a business organization that owns and operates plants; plants may be arranged horizontally, be vertically integrated, or take on a conglomerate form.

- The three basic legal forms of business are the sole proprietorship, the partnership, and the corporation.

- The major advantages of corporations are their ability to raise financial capital, the limited liability they bestow on owners, and their continuing life beyond the life of their owners and managers.

- The principal–agent problem is the conflict of interest that can occur when agents (executives) pursue their own objectives to the detriment of the principals' (stockholders') goals.

7.2   Economic Costs

Opportunity Costs

economic (opportunity) cost
Equal to the quantity of other products that cannot be produced when resources are instead used to make a particular product.

Costs exist because resources are scarce and have alternative uses. When society uses a combination of resources to produce a particular product, it forgoes all alternative opportunities to use those resources for any other purpose. The measure of the **economic cost** or **opportunity cost** of any resource used to produce a good is the value or worth it would have in its best alternative use.

We stressed this point in our analysis of production possibilities in Chapter 2, where we found that the opportunity cost of producing more pizzas is the industrial machines that must be forgone. Similarly, the opportunity cost of the steel used in constructing office buildings is the value it would have in manufacturing automobiles or refrigerators. The paper used for printing economics textbooks is not available for printing encyclopedias or romance novels. And if an assembly line worker is capable of assembling either personal computers or washing machines, then the cost to society of employing that worker in a computer plant is the contribution that worker would otherwise have made in producing washing machines.

Explicit and Implicit Costs

Now let's consider costs from the firm's viewpoint. Keeping opportunity costs in mind, we can say that *economic costs are the payments a firm must make, or the incomes it must provide, to attract the the factors of production it needs away from alternative production opportunities.* Those payments to suppliers of factors are explicit (revealed and expressed) or implicit (present but not obvious). So, in producing products firms incur explicit costs and implicit costs:

explicit costs
The monetary payments a firm must make to an outsider to obtain a resource.

- A firm's **explicit costs** are the monetary payments it makes to those who supply labour services, materials, fuel, transportation services, and the like. Such money payments are for the use of resources owned by others.

implicit costs
The monetary income a firm sacrifices when it uses a resource it owns rather than supplying the resource in the market; equal to what the resource could have earned in the best-paying alternative employment (includes a normal profit).

- A firm's **implicit costs** are the opportunity costs of using its self-owned, self-employed resources. To the firm, implicit costs are the money payments that self-employed inputs could have earned in their best alternative use.

For example, suppose you are earning $22,000 a year as a sales representative for a T-shirt manufacturer in Calgary. At some point you decide to open a retail store of your own in the centre of the city to sell T-shirts. You invest $20,000 of savings that has been earning you $1000 per year in interest. You decide that your new firm will occupy a small store that you own and have been renting out for $5000 per year. You hire one clerk to help you in the store, paying her $18,000.

A year after you open the store, you total up your accounts and find the following:

Total sales revenue	$120,000
Cost of T-shirts	$40,000
Clerk's salary	18,000
Utilities	5,000
Total (explicit) costs	63,000
Accounting profit	57,000

Costs of production exist because resources are scarce and have alternative uses.

Looks good. But unfortunately your accounting profit of $57,000 ignores your implicit costs and thus overstates the economic success of your venture. By providing your own financial capital, building, and labour, you incur implicit costs (forgone incomes) of $1000 of interest, $5000 of rent, and $22,000 of wages. And, if your entrepreneurial talent is worth, say, $5000 annually in other business endeavours of similar scope, you have also ignored that implicit cost. So:

Accounting profit	$57,000
Forgone interest	$ 1,000
Forgone rent	5,000
Forgone wages	22,000
Forgone entrepreneurial income	5,000
Total implicit costs	33,000
Economic profit	24,000

Normal Profit as a Cost

normal profit
Payment that must be made by a firm to obtain and retain entrepreneurial ability.

The $5000 implicit cost of your entrepreneurial talent in the above example is a **normal profit**. As is true of the forgone rent and forgone wages, the payment you could otherwise receive for performing entrepreneurial functions is indeed an implicit cost. If you did not realize at least this minimum, or normal, payment for your effort, you could withdraw from this line of business and shift to a more attractive endeavour. So a normal profit is a cost of doing business.

Costs of production include all costs—explicit and implicit, including a normal profit—required to attract and retain factors of production in a specific line of production. A firm's economic costs are the opportunity costs of the inputs used, whether those inputs are owned by others or by the firm. In our example, economic costs are $96,000 (= $63,000 of explicit costs + $33,000 of implicit costs).

Economic Profit

Obviously, then, economists use the term *profit* differently from the way accountants use it. To the accountant, profit is the firm's total revenue less its explicit costs (or accounting costs). To the econ-

economic profit
The total revenue of a firm less its economic costs (which includes both explicit costs and implicit costs), also called pure profit and above-normal profit.

omist, **economic profit** is total revenue less economic costs (explicit and implicit costs, the latter including a normal profit to the entrepreneur). So, when an economist says a certain firm is earning only enough revenue to cover its costs, this means it is meeting all explicit and implicit costs and the entrepreneur is receiving a payment just large enough to retain his or her talents in the present line of production.

If a firm's total revenue exceeds all its economic costs (explicit + implicit), any residual goes to the entrepreneur. That residual is called an economic, or pure, profit. In short:

Economic profit = total revenue – economic cost (the sum of all explicit and implicit costs)

In our example, economic profit is $24,000, found by subtracting the $96,000 of economic cost from the $120,000 of revenue. An *economic* profit is not a cost, because it is a return in excess of the normal profit that is required to retain the entrepreneur in this particular line of production. Even if the economic profit is zero, the entrepreneur is still covering all explicit and implicit costs, including a normal profit. In our example, as long as accounting profit is $33,000 or more (so that economic profit is zero or more), you will be earning a $5000 normal profit and will, therefore, continue to operate your T-shirt store.

Figure 7-1 shows the relationship among the various cost and profit concepts that we have just discussed. To test yourself, you might want to enter cost data from our example in the appropriate blocks. *(Key Question 4)*

Short Run and Long Run

When the demand for a firm's product changes, the firm's profitability may depend on how quickly it can adjust the amounts of the various factors it employs. It can easily and quickly adjust the quantities employed of many resources such as hourly labour, raw materials, fuel, and power. It needs much more time, however, to adjust its *plant capacity*—the size of the factory building, the amount of machinery and equipment, and other capital resources. In some heavy industries such as aircraft manufacturing, a firm such as Bombardier in Quebec may need several years to alter plant capacity. Because of these differences in adjustment time, economists find it useful to distinguish between two conceptual periods: the short run and the long run. We will discover that costs differ in these two periods.

short run
A period of time in which producers are able to change the quantities of some but not all of the resources they employ.

SHORT RUN: FIXED PLANT

The **short run** is a period too brief for a firm to alter its plant capacity yet long enough to permit a change in the degree to which the fixed plant is used. The firm's plant capacity is fixed in the short

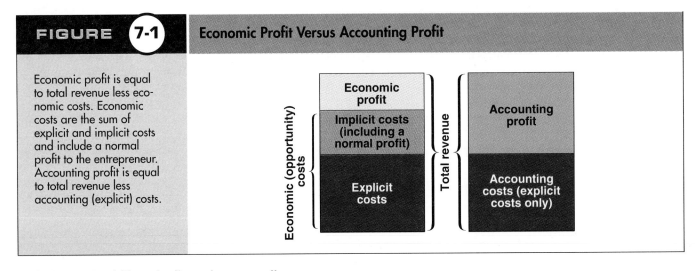

FIGURE 7-1   **Economic Profit Versus Accounting Profit**

Economic profit is equal to total revenue less economic costs. Economic costs are the sum of explicit and implicit costs and include a normal profit to the entrepreneur. Accounting profit is equal to total revenue less accounting (explicit) costs.

run. However, the firm can vary its output by applying larger or smaller amounts of labour, materials, and other inputs to that plant, using its existing plant capacity more or less intensively in the short run.

LONG RUN: VARIABLE PLANT

long run
A period of time long enough to enable producers of a product to change the quantities of all the resources they employ.

For an existing firm, the **long run** is a period long enough for it to adjust the quantities of all the factors that it employs, including plant capacity. For the industry, the long run also includes enough time for existing firms to dissolve and leave the industry or for new firms to be created and enter the industry. While the short run is a "fixed-plant" period, the long run is a "variable-plant" period.

ILLUSTRATIONS

If Bombardier hires 100 extra workers for one of its Ski-doo plants or adds an entire shift of workers, we are speaking of the short run. If it adds a new production facility and installs more equipment, we are referring to the long run. The first situation is a *short-run adjustment;* the second is a *long-run adjustment.*

The short run and the long run are conceptual periods rather than calendar periods. In light-manufacturing industries, changes in plant capacity may be accomplished almost overnight. A small T-shirt manufacturer can increase its plant capacity in a matter of days by ordering and installing two or three new cutting tables and several extra sewing machines. But for heavy industry the long run is a different matter. Petro-Canada may require several years to construct a new oil refinery.

QUICK REVIEW

- Explicit costs are money payments a firm makes to outside suppliers of factors of production; implicit costs are the opportunity costs associated with a firm's use of inputs its owns.

- Normal profit is the implicit cost of entrepreneurship. Economic profit is total revenue less all explicit and implicit costs, including normal profit.

- In the short run, a firm's plant capacity is fixed; in the long run, a firm can vary its plant size and firms can enter or leave the industry.

7.3   Short-run Production Relationships

A firm's costs of producing a specific output depend on the prices of the needed inputs and the quantities of inputs needed to produce that output. Factor supply and demand determine input prices. The technological aspects of production, specifically the relationships between inputs and output, determine the quantities of factors of production needed. Our focus will be on the *labour-output* relationship, given a fixed-plant capacity. But before examining that relationship, we need to define three terms:

total product (TP)
The total output of a particular good or service produced by a firm.

1. **Total product (TP)** is the total quantity, or total output, of a particular good produced.

marginal product (MP)
The extra output or added product associated with adding a unit of a variable factor (labour) to the production process.

2. **Marginal product (MP)** is the extra output associated with adding a unit of variable input, in this case labour, to the production process. Thus,

$$\text{Marginal product} = \frac{\text{change in total product}}{\text{change in labour input}}$$

average product (AP)
The total output divided by the quantity of the factor employed (labour).

3. **Average product (AP)**, also called labour productivity, is output per unit of labour input:

$$\text{Average product} = \frac{\text{total product}}{\text{units of labour}}$$

In the short run, a firm can for a time increase its output by adding units of labour to its fixed plant. But by how much will output rise when a firm adds another unit of labour? Why do we say "for a time"?

Law of Diminishing Returns

law of diminishing returns
As successive increments of a variable factor are added to a fixed factor, the marginal product of the variable factor will eventually decrease.

The answers are provided in general terms by the **law of diminishing returns**, also called the *law of diminishing marginal product*. This law assumes that technology is fixed, so that the techniques of production do not change. It states that as *successive units of a variable factor (say, labour) are added to a fixed factor (say, capital or land), beyond some point the extra, or marginal, product that can be attributed to each additional unit of the variable factor will decline.* If additional workers are hired to work with a constant amount of capital equipment, output will eventually rise by smaller and smaller amounts as more workers are hired. (See the Consider This box for a non-economic example of diminishing returns.)

RATIONALE

Suppose a farmer in Ontario has a fixed supply of 80 hectares planted in corn. If the farmer does not cultivate the cornfields (clear the weeds) at all, the yield will be 40 bushels per hectare. If he cultivates the land once, output may rise to 50 bushels per hectare. A second cultivation may increase output to 57 bushels per hectare, a third to 61, and a fourth to 63. Succeeding cultivations would add less and less to the land's yield. If this were not so, the world's need for corn could be fulfilled by extremely intense cultivation of this single 80-hectare plot of land. Indeed, if diminishing returns did not occur, the world could be fed out of a flowerpot. Why not? Just keep adding more seed, fertilizer, and harvesters!

The law of diminishing returns also holds true in non-agricultural industries. Assume a wood shop is manufacturing chairs. It has a specific amount of equipment such as lathes, planers, saws,

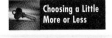

Choosing a Little More or Less

 Consider **T**his

Diminishing Returns

Here is a non-economic example of a hypothetical relationship between "inputs" and "output" that may help you better understand the idea of diminishing returns. Suppose that:

    Total Attractiveness = f (Physical Features; Personality,
    Clothing, and Perfume/Cologne)

where f means "function of" or "depends on." So this hypothetical relationship supposes that total attractiveness depends on physical features, personality, clothing, and the amount of perfume or cologne used. For analytical purposes, let's assume that one's physical features, personality, and clothing are fixed. Now let's add units of perfume or cologne to "produce" greater attractiveness. The first dab of perfume or cologne increases total attractiveness. Will the second dab enhance attractiveness by as much as the first? By how much will the third, fourth, fifth, or thirty-fifth dab contribute to total attractiveness relative to the *immediate previous dab*?

We think you will agree that eventually diminishing returns will set in as successive dabs of perfume or cologne are added. At some point the marginal product of extra dabs of perfume or cologne will decline and, at some further point, it will become zero. Thereafter, an extra dab of perfume will reduce total attractiveness.

So it is with production relationships within firms. As successive units of a variable input (say, labour) are added to a fixed input (say, capital), the marginal product of the variable input will eventually decline. In short, diminishing returns will eventually occur. Total product eventually will rise at a diminishing rate, reach a maximum, and then decline.

Question: Most people agree that the amount of studying you do for a course will largely determine the mark you will achieve. Does this mean that studying is not subject to diminishing returns?

and sanders. If this shop hired just one or two workers, total output and productivity (output per worker) would be low. (Note that we assume all units of labour are of equal quality.) The workers would have to perform many different jobs, and the advantages of specialization would not be realized. Time would be lost switching from one job to another, and machines would stand idle much of the time. In short, the plant would be understaffed, and production would be inefficient because there would be too much capital relative to the amount of labour.

The shop could eliminate those difficulties by hiring more workers. Then the equipment would be more fully used, and workers could specialize in doing a single job. Time would no longer be lost switching from job to job. As more workers were added, production would become more efficient and the marginal product of each succeeding worker would rise.

But the rise could not go on indefinitely. If still more workers were added, beyond a certain point, overcrowding would set in. Since workers would then have to wait in line to use the machinery, it would be underused. Total output would increase at a diminishing rate, because, given the fixed size of the plant, each worker would have less capital equipment to work with as more and more labour was hired. The marginal product of additional workers would decline because there would be more labour in proportion to the fixed amount of capital. Eventually, adding still more workers would cause so much congestion that marginal product would become negative and total product would decline.

TABULAR EXAMPLE

Table 7-1 is a numerical hypothetical illustration of the law of diminishing returns in a wood shop manufacturing chairs. Column 2 shows the total product, or total output, resulting from combining each level of a variable input (labour) in column 1 with a fixed amount of capital.

Column 3 shows the marginal product (MP), the change in total product associated with each additional unit of labour. Note that with no labour input, total product is zero; a plant with no workers will produce no output. The first three units of labour reflect increasing marginal returns, with marginal products of 10, 15, and 20 units, respectively. But beginning with the fourth unit of labour, marginal product diminishes continually, becoming zero with the seventh unit of labour and negative with the eighth.

Average product, or output per labour unit, is shown in column 4. It is calculated by dividing total product (column 2) by the number of labour units needed to produce it (column 1). At five units of labour, for example, AP is 14 (= 70/5).

<www.kanga.nu/
~claw/docs/extess/>
Find out whether free software production in a bazaar obeys the law of diminishing returns

TABLE 7-1	Total, Marginal, and Average Product: The Law of Diminishing Returns		
(1) Units of the variable factor (workers per day)	**(2)** Total product (TP) (chairs per day)	**(3)** Marginal product (MP), change in (2)/change in (1) (chairs per additional worker)	**(4)** Average product (AP), (2)/(1) (chairs per worker)
0	0		—
1	10	10 ⎫ Increasing	10.00
2	25	15 ⎬ marginal returns	12.50
3	45	20	15.00
4	60	15 ⎫ Diminishing	15.00
5	70	10 ⎬ marginal returns	14.00
6	75	5	12.50
7	75	0 ⎫ Negative	10.71
8	70	−5 ⎬ marginal returns	8.75

GRAPHICAL PORTRAYAL

Figure 7-2 (Key Graph) shows the diminishing returns data in Table 7-1 graphically and further clarifies the relationships between total, marginal, and average products. (Marginal product in Figure 7-2(b) is plotted halfway between the units of labour, since it applies to the addition of each labour unit.)

Note first in Figure 7-2(a) that total product, TP, goes through three phases: it rises initially at an increasing rate; then it increases, but at a diminishing rate; finally, after reaching a maximum, it declines.

Geometrically, marginal product—shown by the MP curve in Figure 7-2(b)—is the slope of the total product curve. Marginal product measures the change in total output of chairs associated with each succeeding unit of labour. Thus, the three phases of total product are also reflected in marginal product. Where total product is increasing at an increasing rate, marginal product is rising. Here, extra units of labour are adding larger and larger amounts to total product. Similarly, where total product is increasing but at a decreasing rate, marginal product is positive but falling. Each additional unit of labour adds fewer chairs than did the previous unit. When total product is at a maximum, marginal product is zero. When total product declines, marginal product becomes negative.

Average product, AP in Figure 7-2(b), displays the same tendencies as marginal product. It increases, reaches a maximum, and then decreases as more units of labour are added to the fixed plant. Note the relationship between marginal product and average product: Where marginal product exceeds average product, average product rises, and where marginal product is less than average product, average product declines. It follows that marginal product intersects average product where average product is at a maximum.

This relationship is a mathematical necessity. If you add a larger number to a total than the current average of that total, the average must rise; if you add a smaller number to a total than the current average of that total, the average must fall. You raise your average examination grade only when your score on an additional (marginal) examination is greater than the average of all your past scores.

The law of diminishing returns is reflected in the shapes of all three curves. But, as our definition of the law of diminishing returns indicates, we are most concerned with its effects on marginal product. The regions of increasing, diminishing, and negative marginal product (returns) are shown in Figure 7-2(b). *(Key Question 6)*

7.4   Short-run Production Costs

Production information such as that provided in Table 7-1 and Figure 7-2(a) and (b) must be coupled with prices of factors of production to determine the total and per-unit costs of producing various levels of output. We know that in the short run some factors, those associated with the firm's plant, are fixed. Other factors of production, however, are variable. So short-run costs are either fixed or variable.

Fixed, Variable, and Total Costs

Let's see what distinguishes fixed costs, variable costs, and total costs from one another.

FIXED COSTS

fixed costs
Costs that in total do not change when the firm changes its output.

Fixed costs are *those costs that in total do not vary with changes in output.* Fixed costs are associated with the very existence of a firm's plant and, therefore, must be paid even if its output is zero. Such costs as rental payments, interest on a firm's debts, a portion of depreciation on equipment and buildings, and insurance premiums are generally fixed costs; they do not increase even if a firm produces more. In column 2 in Table 7-2 we assume that the firm's total fixed cost is $100. By definition, this fixed cost is incurred at all levels of output, including zero. The firm cannot avoid paying these costs in the short run.

Key Graph

FIGURE 7-2 The Law of Diminishing Returns

Panel (a): As a variable resource (labour) is added to fixed amounts of other resources (land or capital), the total product that results will eventually increase by diminishing amounts, reach a maximum, and then decline. Panel (b): Marginal product is the change in total product associated with each new unit of labour. Average product is simply output per labour unit. Note that marginal product intersects average product at the maximum average product.

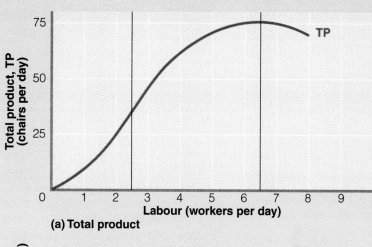

(a) Total product

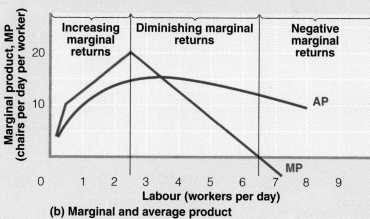

(b) Marginal and average product

Quick Quiz

1. Which of the following is an assumption underlying these figures?
   a. Firms first hire highly skilled workers and then hire less skilled workers.
   b. Capital and labour are both variable, but labour increases more rapidly than capital.
   c. Consumers will buy all the output (total product) produced.
   d. Workers are of equal quality.

2. Marginal product is
   a. the change in total product divided by the change in the quantity of labour.
   b. total product divided by the quantity of labour.
   c. always positive.
   d. unrelated to total product.

3. Marginal product in graph (b) is zero when
   a. average product in graph (b) stops rising.
   b. the slope of the marginal-product curve in graph (b) is zero.

c. total product in graph (a) begins to rise at a diminishing rate.
d. the slope of the total-product curve in graph (a) is zero.

4. Average product in graph (b)
   a. rises when it is less than marginal product.
   b. is the change in total product divided by the change in the quantity of labour.
   c. can never exceed marginal product.
   d. falls whenever total product in graph (a) rises at a diminishing rate.

ANSWERS   1. d; 2. a; 3. d; 4. a

VARIABLE COSTS

variable costs
Costs that increase or decrease with a firm's output.

Variable costs are *those costs that change with the level of output.* They include payments for materials, fuel, power, transportation services, most labour, and similar variable resources. In column 3 of Table 7-2 we find that the total of variable costs changes directly with output, but note that the increases in variable cost associated with succeeding one-unit increases in output are not equal. As production begins, variable cost will for a time increase by a decreasing amount; this is true through the fourth unit of output in Table 7-2. Beyond the fourth unit, however, variable cost rises by increasing amounts for succeeding units of output.

The reason lies in the shape of the marginal product curve. At first, as in Figure 7-2(b), marginal product is increasing, so smaller and smaller increases in the amounts of variable inputs are needed to produce successive units of output. Thus, the variable cost of successive units of output decreases. But when, as diminishing returns are encountered, marginal product begins to decline, larger and larger additional amounts of variable inputs are needed to produce successive units of output. Total variable cost, therefore, increases by increasing amounts.

TOTAL COST

total cost
The sum of fixed cost and variable cost.

Total cost is *the sum of fixed cost and variable cost at each level of output.* It is shown in column 4 in Table 7-2. At zero units of output, total cost is equal to the firm's fixed cost. Then for each unit of the 10 units of production, total cost increases by the same amount as variable cost.

Figure 7-3 shows graphically the fixed-cost, variable-cost, and total-cost data given in Table 7-2. Observe that total variable cost, TVC, is measured vertically from the horizontal axis at each level of output. The amount of fixed cost, shown as TFC, is added vertically to the total variable cost curve to obtain the points on the total-cost curve, TC.

The distinction between fixed and variable costs is significant to the business manager. Variable costs can be controlled or altered in the short run by changing production levels. Fixed costs are beyond the business manager's current control; they are incurred in the short run and must be paid regardless of output level.

Per-unit, or Average, Costs

Producers are certainly interested in their total costs, but they are equally concerned with per-unit, or average, costs. In particular, average-cost data are more meaningful for making comparisons with product price, which is always stated on a per-unit basis. Average fixed cost, average variable cost, and average total cost are shown in columns 5 to 7, Table 7-2.

TABLE 7-2	Total-cost, Average-cost, and Marginal-cost Schedules for an Individual Firm in the Short Run						
TOTAL-COST DATA				**AVERAGE-COST DATA**			**MARGINAL COST**
(1) Total product (Q)	(2) Total fixed cost (TFC)	(3) Total variable cost (TVC)	(4) Total cost (TC)	(5) Average fixed cost (AFC)	(6) Average variable cost (AVC)	(7) Average total cost (ATC)	(8) Marginal cost (MC)
(chairs per day)	(dollars per day)			(dollars per chair)			(dollars per additional chair)
0	$100	$ 0	$ 100				
1	100	90	190	$100.00	$90.00	$190.00	$ 90
2	100	170	270	50.00	85.00	135.00	80
3	100	240	340	33.33	80.00	113.33	70
4	100	300	400	25.00	75.00	100.00	60
5	100	370	470	20.00	74.00	94.00	70
6	100	450	550	16.67	75.00	91.67	80
7	100	540	640	14.29	77.14	91.43	90
8	100	650	750	12.50	81.25	93.75	110
9	100	780	880	11.11	86.67	97.78	130
10	100	930	1,030	10.00	93.00	103.00	150

FIGURE 7-3	Total Cost Is the Sum of Fixed Cost and Variable Cost

Total variable cost (TVC) changes with output. Total fixed cost (TFC) is independent of the level of output. The total cost (TC) at any output is the vertical sum of the fixed cost and variable cost at that output.

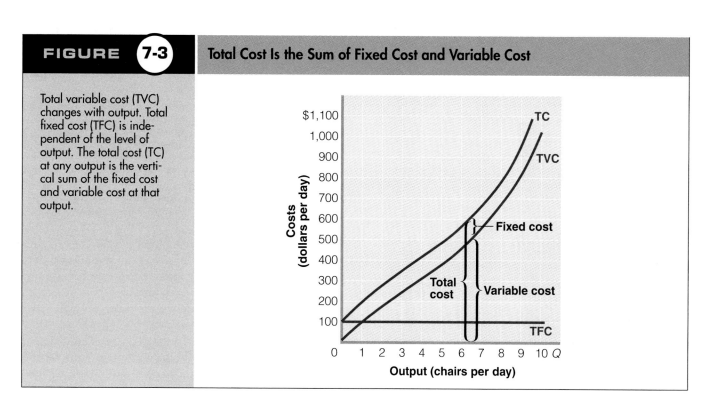

AFC

average fixed cost (AFC)
A firm's total fixed cost divided by output.

Average fixed cost (AFC) for any output level is found by dividing total fixed cost (TFC) by that output (Q). That is,

$$AFC = \frac{TFC}{Q}$$

Because the total fixed cost is, by definition, the same regardless of output, AFC must decline as output increases. As output rises, the total fixed cost is spread over a larger and larger output. When output is just one unit in Table 7-2, TFC and AFC are the same at $100. But at two units of output, the total fixed cost of $100 becomes $50 of AFC or fixed cost per unit; then it becomes $33.33 per unit as $100 is spread over three units, and $25 per unit when spread over four units. This process is sometimes referred to as "spreading the overhead." Figure 7-4 shows that AFC graphs as a continuously declining curve as total output is increased.

AVC

average variable cost (AVC)
A firm's total variable cost divided by output.

Average variable cost (AVC) for any output level is calculated by dividing total variable cost (TVC) by that output (Q):

$$AVC = \frac{TVC}{Q}$$

As added variable inputs increase output, AVC declines initially, reaches a minimum, and then increases again. A graph of AVC is a U-shaped curve, as shown in Figure 7-4.

Because total variable cost reflects the law of diminishing returns, so must AVC, which is derived from total variable cost. Marginal returns increase initially because it takes fewer and fewer additional variable inputs to produce each of the first four units of output. As a result, variable cost per unit declines. AVC hits a minimum with the fifth unit of output, and beyond that point AVC rises as diminishing returns require more variable inputs to produce each additional unit of output.

You can verify the U shape of the AVC curve by returning to Table 7-1. Assume the price of labour is $10 per unit. By dividing average product (output per labour unit) into $10 (price per labour unit), we determine the labour cost per unit of output. Because we have assumed labour to

| FIGURE 7-4 | The Average-cost Curves |

AFC falls as a given amount of fixed costs is apportioned over a larger and larger output. AVC initially falls because of increasing marginal returns but then rises because of diminishing marginal returns. Average total cost (ATC) is the vertical sum of average variable cost (AVC) and average fixed cost (AFC).

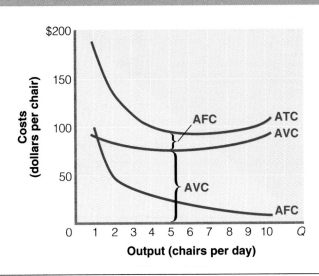

be the only variable input, the labour cost per unit of output is the variable cost per unit of output or AVC. When average product is initially low, AVC is high. As workers are added, average product rises and AVC falls. When average product is at its maximum, AVC is at its minimum. Then, as still more workers are added and average product declines, AVC rises. The hump of the average-product curve is reflected in the U shape of the AVC curve. As you will soon see, the two are mirror images.

ATC

average total cost (ATC)
A firm's total cost divided by output.

Average total cost (ATC) for any output level is found by dividing total cost (TC) by that output (Q) or by adding AFC and AVC at that output:

$$ATC = \frac{TC}{Q} = \frac{TFC}{Q} + \frac{TVC}{Q}$$

$$= AFC + AVC$$

Graphically, ATC can be found by adding vertically the AFC and AVC curves, as in Figure 7-4. Thus, the vertical distance between the ATC and AVC curves measures AFC at any level of output.

Marginal Cost

marginal cost (MC)
The extra or additional cost of producing one more unit of output.

One final and very crucial cost concept remains: **Marginal cost (MC)** is *the extra, or additional, cost of producing one more unit of output.* MC can be determined for each added unit of output by noting the change in total cost that that unit's production entails:

$$MC = \frac{\text{change in TC}}{\text{change in Q}}$$

CALCULATIONS

In column 4, Table 7-2, production of the first unit of output increases total cost from $100 to $190. Therefore, the additional, or marginal, cost of that first unit is $90 (column 8). The marginal cost of the second unit is $80 (= $270 − $190); the MC of the third is $70 (= $340 − $270); and so forth. The MC for each of the 10 units of output is shown in column 8.

MC can also be calculated from the total-variable-cost column, because the only difference between total cost and total variable cost is the constant amount of fixed costs ($100). Thus, the change in total cost and the change in total variable cost associated with each additional unit of output are always the same.

MARGINAL DECISIONS

Choosing a Little More or Less

Marginal costs are costs the firm can control directly and immediately. Specifically, MC designates all the additional cost incurred in producing the last unit of output. Thus, it also designates the cost that can be saved by not producing that last unit.

A firm's decisions as to what output level to produce are typically decisions to produce a few more or a few less units. Marginal cost is the change in costs when one more or one fewer unit of output is produced. When coupled with marginal revenue, marginal cost allows a firm to determine whether it is profitable to expand or contract its production. The analysis in the next three chapters focuses on those marginal calculations.

GRAPHICAL PORTRAYAL

Marginal cost is shown graphically in **Figure 7-5 (Key Graph)**. Marginal cost at first declines sharply, reaches a minimum, and then rises rather abruptly. This pattern reflects the fact that the variable costs, and therefore total cost, increase first by decreasing amounts and then by increasing amounts (see columns 3 and 4, Table 7-2).

Key Graph

FIGURE 7-5 The Relationship of the Marginal-cost Curve to the Average-total-cost and Average-variable-cost Curves

The marginal-cost (MC) curve cuts through the average-total-cost (ATC) curve and the average-variable-cost (AVC) curve at their minimum points. When MC is below average total cost, ATC falls; when MC is above average total cost, ATC rises. Similarly, when MC is below average variable cost, AVC falls; when MC is above average variable cost, AVC rises.

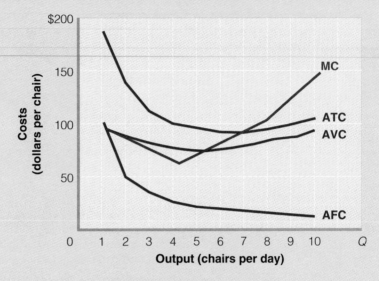

Quick Quiz

1. The marginal-cost curve first declines and then increases because of
  a. increasing, then diminishing, marginal utility.
  b. the decline in the gap between ATC and AVC as output expands.
  c. increasing, then diminishing, marginal returns.
  d. constant marginal revenue.

2. The vertical distance between ATC and AVC measures
  a. marginal cost.
  b. total fixed cost.
  c. average fixed cost.
  d. economic profit per unit.

3. ATC is
  a. AVC − AFC.
  b. MC + AVC.
  c. AFC + AVC.
  d. (AFC + AVC) × Q.

4. When the marginal-cost curve lies
  a. above the ATC curve, ATC rises.
  b. above the AVC curve, ATC rises.
  c. below the AVC curve, total fixed cost increases.
  d. below the ATC curve, total fixed cost falls.

ANSWERS 1. c; 2. c; 3. c; 4. a

MC AND MARGINAL PRODUCT

The shape of the marginal-cost curve is a consequence of the law of diminishing returns. Looking back at Table 7-1, we can see the relationship between marginal product and marginal cost. If all units of a variable factor (here labour) are hired at the same price, the marginal cost of each extra unit of output will fall as long as the marginal product of each additional worker is rising, because marginal cost is the (constant) cost of an extra worker divided by his or her marginal product. Therefore, in Table 7-1, suppose that each worker can be hired for $10. Because the first worker's marginal product is 10 units of output, and hiring this worker increases the firm's costs by $10, the marginal cost of each of these 10 extra units of output is $1 (= $10 ÷ 10 units). The second worker also increases costs by $10, but the marginal product is 15, so the marginal cost of each of these 15 extra units of output is $.67 (= $10 ÷ 15 units). Similarly, the MC of each of the 20 extra units of output contributed by the third worker is $.50 (= $10 ÷ 20 units). To generalize, as long as marginal product is rising, marginal cost will fall.

With the fourth worker, diminishing returns set in and marginal cost begins to rise. For the fourth worker, marginal cost is $.67 (= $10 ÷ 15 units); for the fifth worker, MC is $1.00 ($10 ÷ 10 units); for the sixth, MC is $2.00 (= $10 ÷ 5 units), and so on. If the price (cost) of the variable resource remains constant, diminishing marginal returns will be reflected in a rising marginal cost.

The MC curve is a mirror reflection of the marginal-product curve. As you can see in Figure 7-6, when marginal product is rising, marginal cost is necessarily falling. When marginal product is at its maximum, marginal cost is at its minimum; when marginal product is falling, marginal cost is rising.

FIGURE 7-6   The Relationship Between Productivity Curves and Cost Curves

The marginal-cost (MC) curve and the average-variable-cost (AVC) curve in panel (b) are mirror images of the marginal-product (MP) and average-product (AP) curves in panel (a). Assuming that labour is the only variable input and that its price (the wage rate) is constant, then when MP is rising, MC is falling, and when MP is falling, MC is rising. Under the same assumptions, when AP is rising, AVC is falling, and when AP is falling, AVC is rising.

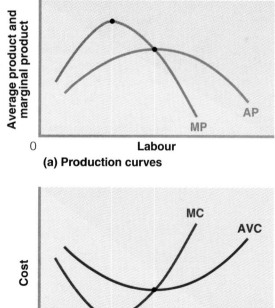

(a) Production curves

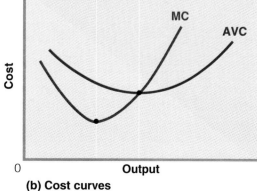

(b) Cost curves

RELATION OF MC TO AVC AND ATC

Figure 7-5 shows that the marginal-cost curve MC intersects both the AVC and ATC curves at their minimum points. As noted earlier, this marginal-average relationship is a mathematical necessity, which a simple illustration will reveal. Suppose a baseball pitcher has allowed his opponents an average of three runs per game in the first three games he has pitched. Now, whether his average falls or rises as a result of pitching a fourth (marginal) game will depend on whether the additional runs he allows in that extra game are fewer or more than his current three-run average. If in the fourth game he allows fewer than three runs, for example one, his total runs will rise from 9 to 10 and his average will fall from 3 to 2.5 (= 10 ÷ 4). Conversely, if in the fourth game he allows more than three runs, say, seven, his total will increase from 9 to 16 and his average will rise from 3 to 4 (= 16 ÷ 4).

So it is with costs. When the amount (the marginal cost) added to total cost is less than the current average total cost, ATC will fall. Conversely, when the marginal cost exceeds ATC, ATC will rise, which means that in Figure 7-5, as long as MC lies below ATC, ATC will fall, and whenever MC lies above ATC, ATC will rise. At the point of intersection, where MC equals ATC, ATC has just stopped falling but has not yet begun rising. This point, by definition, is the minimum point on the ATC curve. The marginal-cost curve intersects the average-total-cost curve at the ATC curve's minimum point.

Marginal cost can be defined as the addition either to total cost or to total variable cost resulting from one more unit of output; thus, this same rationale explains why the MC curve also crosses the AVC curve at the AVC curve's minimum point. No such relationship exists between the MC curve and the average-fixed-cost curve, because the two are not related; marginal cost includes only those costs that change with output, and fixed costs by definition are those that are independent of output. (*Key Question 9*)

Global Perspective 7.1

Relative changes in average labour costs in manufacturing, 1992–1999, selected nations

Average labour costs (labour costs per unit of output) are a significant part of average total costs in most industries. Average labour costs have varied widely among nations at various times in recent years. Other things equal, higher average labour costs at each output level result in higher ATC curves; lower average labour costs result in lower ATC curves.

Source: U.S. Bureau of Labor Statistics, <www.bls.gov/>.

Shifts of Cost Curves

Changes in either factors of production prices or technology will change costs, and therefore the cost curves will shift. If fixed costs were to double from $100 to $200, the AFC curve in Figure 7-5 would shift upward. At each level of output, fixed costs would be higher. The ATC curve would also move upward, because AFC is a component of ATC. The positions of the AVC and MC curves would be unaltered, because their locations are based on the prices of variable rather than fixed factors of production. However, if the price (wage) of labour or some other variable input rose, AVC, ATC, and MC would rise, and those cost curves would all shift upward. The AFC curve would remain in place because fixed costs have not changed.

The discovery of a more efficient technology would increase the productivity of all inputs, and the AVC, ATC and MC cost figures in Table 7-2 would all be lower. To illustrate, if labour is the only variable input, if wages are $10 per hour, and if the average product is 10 units, then AVC would be $1. But if a technological improvement increases the average product of labour to 20 units, then AVC will decline to $.50. More generally, an upward shift in the productivity curves shown in Figure 7-6(a) means a downward shift in the cost curves portrayed in Figure 7-6(b). (Global Perspective 7.1 shows average labour cost in selected countries. Other things equal, higher average labour costs per unit of output will result in higher ATC curves, with negative implications for a nation's competitive position in international trade.)

QUICK REVIEW

- The law of diminishing returns indicates that, beyond some point, output will increase by diminishing amounts as more units of a variable factor (labour) are added to a fixed factor (capital).

- In the short run, the total cost of any level of output is the sum of fixed and variable costs (TC = TFC + TVC).

- Average fixed, average variable, and average total costs are fixed, variable, and total costs per unit of output; mar-

ginal cost is the extra cost of producing one more unit of output.

- Average fixed cost declines continuously as output increases; average-variable-cost and average-total-cost curves are U-shaped, reflecting increasing and then diminishing returns; the marginal-cost curve falls but then rises, intersecting both the average-variable-cost curve and the average-total-cost curve at their minimum points.

7.5   Long-run Production Costs

<hadm.sph.sc.edu/Courses/ Econ/Cost/Cost.html>
A tutorial on total cost, fixed cost, variable cost, and marginal cost

In the long run firms can undertake all desired input adjustments. The firm can alter its plant capacity; it can build a larger plant or revert to a smaller plant than that assumed in Table 7-2. The industry also can change its plant size; the long run allows sufficient time for new firms to enter or for existing firms to leave an industry. We will discuss the impact of the entry and exit of firms to and from an industry in the next chapter; here we are concerned only with changes in plant capacity made by a single firm. Let's couch our analysis in terms of average total cost (ATC), making no distinction between fixed and variable costs because all inputs, and therefore all costs, are variable in the long run.

Firm Size and Costs

Suppose a single-plant manufacturer begins on a small scale and, as the result of successful operations, expands to successively larger plant sizes with larger output capacities. What happens to average total cost as this occurs? For a time, successively larger plants will lower average total cost. However, eventually the building of a still larger plant may cause ATC to rise.

Figure 7-7 illustrates this situation for five possible plant sizes. ATC-1 is the short-run average-total-cost curve for the smallest of the five plants, and ATC-5 the curve for the largest. Constructing larger plants will lower the minimum average total costs through plant size 3, but then larger plants will mean higher minimum average total costs.

The Long-Run Cost Curve

The vertical lines perpendicular to the output axis in Figure 7-7 indicate those outputs at which the firm should change plant size to realize the lowest attainable average total costs of production. These are the outputs at which the per-unit costs for a larger plant drop below those for the current, smaller plant. For all outputs up to 20 units, the lowest average total costs are attainable with plant size 1. However, if the firm's volume of sales expands to between 20 and 30 units, it can achieve lower per-unit costs by constructing larger plant size 2. Although total cost will be higher at the expanded levels of production, the cost per unit of output will be less. For any output between 30 and 50 units, plant size 3 will yield the lowest average total costs. From 50 to 60 units of output, the firm must build plant size 4 to achieve the lowest unit costs. Lowest average total costs for any output over 60 units require construction of the still larger plant size 5.

Tracing these adjustments, we find that the long-run ATC curve for the enterprise is made up of segments of the short-run ATC curves for the various plant sizes that can be constructed. The long-run ATC curve shows the lowest average total cost at which *any output level* can be produced after the firm has had time to make all appropriate adjustments in its plant size. In Figure 7-7 the dark blue, uneven curve is the firm's long-run ATC curve or, as it is often called, the firm's *planning curve*.

In most lines of production, the choice of plant size is much wider than in our illustration. In many industries the number of possible plant sizes is virtually unlimited, and in time quite small changes in the volume of output will lead to changes in plant size. Graphically, this implies an unlimited number of short-run ATC curves, one for each output level, as suggested by **Figure 7-8 (Key Graph)**. Then, rather than consisting of segments of short-run ATC curves as in Figure 7-7, the long-run ATC curve is made up of all the points of tangency of the unlimited number of short-run ATC curves from which the long-run ATC curve is derived. Therefore, the planning curve is

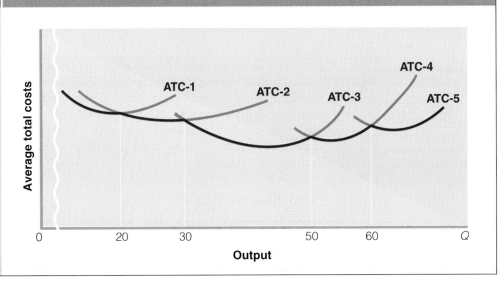

FIGURE 7-7 | **The Long-run Average-total-cost Curve: Five Possible Plant Sizes**

The long-run average-total-cost curve is made up of segments of the short-run cost curves (ATC-1, ATC-2, etc.) of the various-size plants from which the firm might choose. Each point on the planning curve shows the least unit cost attainable for any output when the firm has had time to make all desired changes in its plant size.

Key Graph

FIGURE 7-8 The Long-run Average-total-cost Curve: Unlimited Number of Plant Sizes

If the number of possible plant sizes is very large, the long-run average-total-cost curve approximates a smooth curve. Economies of scale, followed by diseconomies of scale, cause the curve to be U-shaped.

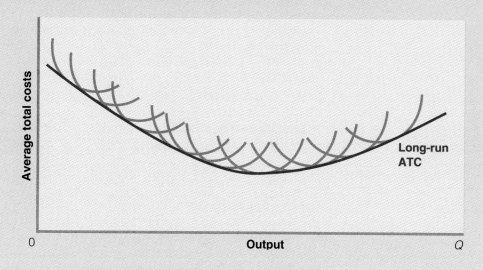

Quick Quiz

1. **The unlabelled light blue curves in this figure illustrate the**
   a. long-run average-total-cost curves of various firms constituting the industry.
   b. short-run average-total-cost curves of various firms constituting the industry.
   c. short-run average-total-cost curves of various plant sizes available to a particular firm.
   d. short-run marginal-cost curves of various plant sizes available to a particular firm.

2. **The unlabelled light blue curves in this figure derive their shapes from**
   a. decreasing, then increasing, short-run returns.
   b. increasing, then decreasing, short-run returns.
   c. economies, then diseconomies, of scale.
   d. diseconomies, then economies, of scale.

3. **The long-run ATC curve in this figure derives its shape from**
   a. decreasing, then increasing, short-run returns.
   b. increasing, then decreasing, short-run returns.
   c. economies, then diseconomies, of scale.
   d. diseconomies, then economies, of scale.

4. **The long-run ATC curve is often called the firm's**
   a. planning curve.
   b. capital-expansion path.
   c. total-product curve.
   d. production possibilities curve.

ANSWERS: 1. c; 2. b; 3. c; 4. a

smooth rather than bumpy. Each point on it tells us the minimum ATC of producing the corresponding level of output.

Economies and Diseconomies of Scale

We have assumed that for a time increasing plant sizes will lead to lower unit costs but that beyond some point successively larger plants will mean higher average total costs. That is, we have assumed that the long-run ATC curve is U-shaped. But why should this be? Note, first, that the law of diminishing returns does not apply in the long run because diminishing returns presumes one factor of production is fixed in supply, while the long run means all factors of production are variable. Also, our discussion assumes factor prices are constant. We can explain the U-shaped long-run average-total-cost curve in terms of economies and diseconomies of large-scale production.

ECONOMIES OF SCALE

economies of scale
Reductions in the average total cost of producing a product as the firm expands the size of plant (its output) in the long run.

Economies of scale, or economies of mass production, explain the downsloping part of the long-run ATC curve. As plant size increases, a number of factors will for a time lead to lower average costs of production.

Labour Specialization   Increased specialization in the use of labour becomes more achievable as a plant increases in size. Hiring more workers means jobs can be divided and subdivided. Each worker may now have just one task to perform instead of five or six. Workers can work full time on those tasks for which they have special skills. In a small plant, skilled machinists may spend half their time performing unskilled tasks, leading to higher production costs.

Further, by working at fewer tasks, workers become proficient at those tasks. The jack-of-all-trades doing five or six jobs is not likely to be efficient in any of them. By concentrating on one task, the same worker may become highly efficient.

Finally, greater labour specialization eliminates the loss of time that accompanies each shift of a worker from one task to another.

Managerial Specialization   Large-scale production also means better use of, and greater specialization in, management. A supervisor who can handle 20 workers is underused in a small plant that employs only 10 people. The production staff could be doubled with no increase in supervisory costs.

Small firms cannot use management specialists to best advantage. In a small plant sales specialists may have to divide their time between several executive functions, for example, marketing, personnel, and finance. A larger scale of operations means that the marketing expert can supervise marketing full time, while specialists perform other managerial functions. Greater efficiency and lower unit costs are the net result.

Efficient Capital   Small firms often cannot afford the most efficient equipment. In many lines of production such machinery is available only in very large and extremely expensive units. Effective use of such equipment demands a high volume of production, and that again requires large-scale producers.

In the automobile industry the most efficient fabrication method in North America employs robotics and elaborate assembly line equipment. Effective use of this equipment demands an annual output of perhaps 200,000 to 400,000 automobiles. Only very large-scale producers can afford to purchase and use this equipment efficiently.

Other Factors   Many products have design and development costs, as well as other start-up costs, that must be incurred irrespective of projected sales. These costs decline per unit as output is increased. Similarly, advertising costs decline per auto, per computer, per stereo system, and per box of detergent as more units are produced and sold. The firm's production and marketing expertise usually rises as it produces and sells more output. This *learning by doing* is a further source of economies of scale.

Where economies of scale are possible, an increase in all inputs of, say, 10 percent will cause a more-than-proportionate increase in output of, say, 20 percent. The result will be a decline in ATC.

In many Canadian manufacturing industries, from automobile to aircraft production, economies of scale have been of great significance. Firms that have expanded their scale of operations to obtain economies of mass production have survived and flourished. Those unable to expand have become relatively high-cost producers, doomed to struggle to survive.

DISECONOMIES OF SCALE

In time the expansion of a firm may lead to diseconomies and, therefore, higher average total costs.

diseconomies of scale
Increases in the average total cost of producing a product as the firm expands the size of its plant (its output) in the long run.

The main factor causing **diseconomies of scale** is the difficulty of efficiently controlling and coordinating a firm's operations as it becomes larger and larger. As a firm grows, many management levels now come between the executive suite and the assembly line; top management is far removed from the actual production operations of the plant. Authority must be delegated to many vice-presidents, second vice-presidents, and so forth. This expansion of the management hierarchy leads to problems of communication and cooperation, bureaucratic red tape, and the possibility that decisions will not be coordinated. Decision making may be slowed down to the point that decisions fail to reflect changes in consumer tastes or technology quickly enough. The result is impaired efficiency and rising average total costs.

Also, in massive production facilities workers may feel alienated from their employers and care little about working efficiently. Opportunities to shirk responsibilities, by avoiding work in favour of on-the-job leisure, may be greater in large plants than in small ones. Countering worker alienation and shirking may require additional worker supervision, which increases costs.

If a firm encounters diseconomies of scale, an increase in all inputs of, say, 10 percent will cause a less-than-proportionate increase in output of, say, 5 percent. As a consequence, ATC will increase. The rising portion of the long-run cost curves in Figure 7-9(a) illustrates diseconomies of scale.

CONSTANT RETURNS TO SCALE

constant returns to scale
The range of output between the output at which economies of scale end and diseconomies of scale begin.

In some industries a rather wide range of output may exist between the output at which economies of scale end and the output at which diseconomies of scale begin. That is, a range of **constant returns to scale** may exist over which long-run average cost does not change. The q_1q_2 output range of Figure 7-9(a), on page 185, is an example. Here a given percentage increase in all inputs of, say, 10 percent will cause a proportionate 10 percent increase in output. Thus, in this range ATC is constant.

Applications and Illustrations

The business world offers many examples of economies and diseconomies of scale. Here are just a few.

SUCCESSFUL STARTUP FIRMS

<www.theshortrun.com/
classroom/glossary/micro/
costprofit.html>
Cost and profit summarized, including constant returns to scale

The Canadian economy has greatly benefited over the past few decades by explosive growth of new startup firms. Where economies of scale are significant, such firms can enjoy years or even decades of growth accompanied by lower average total costs. That has been the case for such firms as Second Cup (coffee), Ballard Power Systems (fuel cells), Celestica (computer components), and JDS Uniphase (fibre optics).

A major source of these economies of scale is the ability to spread huge product development and advertising costs over an increasing number of units of output. These firms also benefit from the greater specialization of labour, management, and capital equipment permitted by larger firm size.

THE DAILY NEWSPAPER

The daily newspaper is undoubtedly one of the economy's great bargains. In every major city, you can buy a high-quality newspaper for just cents. The main reason for such low prices is the low average total costs that result from the spreading of fixed costs and the achievement of economies of scale. If only 100 or 200 people bought the paper each day, the average cost of each paper would be exceedingly high because the overhead costs would be spread over so few buyers. But when publishers sell tens or hundreds of thousands of newspapers each day, they spread the overhead costs very widely. The large volume of sales also enables them to use specialized labour and large, highly efficient printing presses. Given sufficient scale and volume, the average total cost of a paper sinks to a few dimes. Moreover, the greater the number of readers, the greater the amount of money that advertisers are willing to pay for advertising space. That added revenue helps keep the price of the newspaper low.

GENERAL MOTORS

Executives of General Motors, the world's largest auto producer, are well aware of the realities of diseconomies of scale. Auto industry experts say GM's large size may be a liability; it is substantially larger than Ford and Daimler Chrysler and is larger than Toyota and Honda combined. Compared with these competitors, GM has a cost disadvantage that may help explain its substantial decline in long-term market share. Despite billions of dollars of investment in modern equipment, GM still had, up to the recent past, the lowest productivity and the highest cost per car in the industry.

To try to reduce scale diseconomies, GM has taken several actions. It has established joint ventures (combined projects) with smaller foreign rivals such as Toyota to reduce its production costs. It has created Saturn, a separate, stand-alone auto manufacturing company. It has given each of its five automotive divisions (Chevrolet, Buick, Pontiac, Oldsmobile, and Cadillac) greater autonomy with respect to styling, engineering, and marketing decisions to reduce the layers of managerial approval required in decision making. Finally, GM has reorganized into a small-car group and a midsize and luxury group to try to cut costs and bring new cars to the market faster.

The changes at GM seem to have paid off. In the 2001-model year, GM actually earned an average accounting profit of $522 per car produced, while its North American–based competitors DaimlerChrysler and Ford lost $2602 and $2965 per vehicle respectively. Still, GM's performance is not so impressive compared with Honda, which earned $2574 for each car it built in North America. Helping GM was its Oshawa, Ontario plant, where it makes the Impala and Monte Carlo models. In 2002 the GM Oshawa plant was rated the most efficient plant in North America.

Economies and diseconomies of scale are important determinants of an industry's market structure.

Minimum Efficient Scale and Industry Structure

Economies and diseconomies of scale are an important determinant of an industry's structure. We now introduce the concept of **minimum efficient scale (MES)**, which is the lowest level of output at which a firm can minimize long-run average costs. In Figure 7-9(a) that level occurs at q_1 units of output. Because of the extended range of constant returns to scale, firms within the q_1 to q_2 range would be equally efficient, so we would not be surprised to find an industry with such cost conditions to be populated by firms of quite different sizes. The apparel, food processing, furniture, wood products, snowboard, and small-appliance industries are examples. With an extended range of constant returns to scale, relatively large and relatively small firms can coexist in an industry and be equally successful.

minimum efficient scale (MES)
The lowest level of output at which a firm can minimize long-run average costs.

Compare this with Figure 7-9(b), where economies of scale prevail over a wide range of output and diseconomies of scale appear only at very high levels of output. This pattern of declining long-run average total cost may occur over an extended range of output, as in the automobile, aluminum, steel, and other heavy industries. The same pattern holds in several of the new industries related to information technology, for example, computer microchips, operating system software, and Internet service provision.

Given consumer demand, efficient production will be achieved with a few large-scale producers. Small firms cannot realize the minimum efficient scale and will not be able to compete. In the extreme, economies of scale might extend beyond the market's size, resulting in what is termed

FIGURE 7-9 Various Possible Long-run Average-total-cost Curves

In panel (a), economies of scale are rather rapidly obtained as plant size rises, and diseconomies of scale are not encountered until a considerably large scale of output has been achieved. Thus, long-run average total cost is constant over a wide range of output. In panel (b), economies of scale are extensive, and diseconomies of scale occur only at very large outputs. Average total cost, therefore, declines over a broad range of output. In panel (c), economies of scale are exhausted quickly, followed immediately by diseconomies of scale. Minimum ATC thus occurs at a relatively low output.

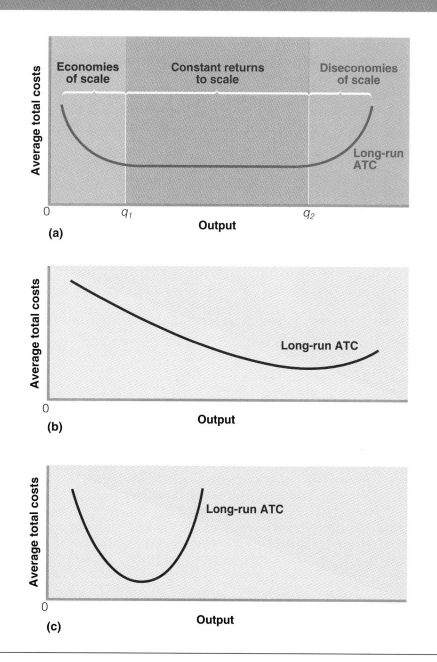

natural monopoly
An industry in which economies of scale are so great that a single firm can produce the product at a lower average total cost than if more than one firm produced the product.

natural monopoly, a relatively rare market situation in which average total cost is minimized when only one firm produces the particular good or service.

Where economies of scale are few and diseconomies come into play quickly, the minimum efficient size occurs at a low level of output, as shown in Figure 7-9(c). In such industries a particular level of consumer demand will support a large number of relatively small producers. Many retail trades and some types of farming fall into this category. So do certain kinds of light manufacturing, such as the baking, clothing, and shoe industries. Fairly small firms are as efficient as, or more efficient than, large-scale producers in such industries.

Our point here is that the shape of the long-run average-total-cost curve is determined by technology and the economies and diseconomies of scale that result. The shape of the long-run ATC curve, in turn, can be significant in determining whether an industry has a relatively large number of small firms or is dominated by a few large producers, or lies somewhere in between.

We must be cautious in our assessment, because industry structure does not depend on cost conditions alone. Government policies, the geographic size of markets, managerial strategy and skill, and other factors must be considered in explaining the structure of a particular industry. *(Key Question 12)*

QUICK REVIEW

- Most firms have U-shaped long-run average-total-cost curves, reflecting economies and then diseconomies of scale.

- Economies of scale are the consequence of greater specialization of labour and management, more efficient capital equipment, and the spreading of startup costs among more units of output.

- Diseconomies of scale are caused by the problems of coordination and communication that arise in large firms.

- Minimum efficient scale is the lowest level of output at which a firm's long-run average total cost is at a minimum.

THE LASTword | Irrelevancy of Sunk Costs

Sunk costs should be disregarded in decision making.

There is an old saying: Don't cry over spilt milk. The message is that once you have spilled a glass of milk, there is nothing you can do to recover it, so you should forget about it and move on from there. This saying has great relevance to what economists call *sunk costs*. Such costs are like sunken ships on the ocean floor: once these costs are incurred, they cannot be recovered.

Let's gain an understanding of this idea by applying it first to consumers and then to businesses. Suppose you buy an expensive ticket to an upcoming Grey Cup football game between the Calgary Stampeders and the Hamilton Tiger Cats. But the morning of the game you wake up with a bad case of the flu. Feeling miserable, you step outside to find that the wind chill is about –20 degrees. You absolutely do not want to go to the game, but you remind yourself that you paid a steep price for the ticket. You call several people to try to sell the ticket, but you soon discover that no one is interested in it, even at a discounted

price. You conclude that everyone who wants a ticket has one.

Should you go to the game? Economic analysis says that you should not take actions for which marginal cost exceeds marginal benefit. In this situation, the price you paid for the ticket is irrelevant to the decision; both marginal or additional costs and marginal or additional benefit are forward-looking. If the marginal cost of going to the game is greater than the marginal benefit, the best decision is to go back to bed. This decision should be the same whether you paid $2, $20, or $200 for the game ticket, because the price that you pay for something does not affect its marginal benefit. Once the ticket has been purchased and cannot be resold, its cost is irrelevant to the decision to attend the game. Since you absolutely do not want to go, clearly the marginal cost exceeds the marginal benefit of the game.

Here is a second consumer example. Suppose a family is on vacation in B.C.'s Okanagan Valley and stops at a roadside stand to buy some apples. The kids get back into the car and bite into their apples, immediately pronouncing them "totally mushy" and unworthy of another bite. Both parents agree that the apples are "terrible," but the father continues to eat his, because, as he says, "We paid a premium price for them." One of the older children replies, "Dad, that's irrelevant." Although not stated very diplomatically, the child is exactly right. In making a new decision, you should ignore all costs that are not affected by the decision. The prior bad decision (in retrospect) to buy the apples should not dictate a second decision for which marginal benefit is less than marginal cost.

Now let's apply the idea of sunk costs to firms. Some of a firm's costs are not only fixed (recurring, but unrelated to the level of output) but are sunk (unrecoverable). For example, a non-refundable annual lease payment for the use of a store cannot be recouped once it has been paid. A firm's decision about whether to move from the store to a more profitable location does not depend on the amount of time remaining on the lease. If moving means greater profit, it makes sense to move whether there are 300 days, 30 days, or 3 days left on the lease.

Or, as another example, suppose a firm spends $1 million on R&D to bring out a new product, only to discover that the product sells very poorly. Should the firm continue to produce the product at a loss even when there is no realistic hope for future success? Obviously, it should not. In making this decision, the firm realizes that the amount it has spent in developing the product is irrelevant; it should stop production of the product and cut its losses. In fact, many firms have dropped products after spending millions of dollars on their development. Examples are the quick decision by Coca-Cola to drop its New Coke and the eventual decision by McDonald's to drop its McLean Burger.

Consider a final real-world example. Nortel Networks is one of the best-known Canadian telecommunications companies. It started business in 1895, when it began making equipment for traditional phone companies. It was originally part of Bell Telephone, before it became known as Northern Telecom, later shortened to Nortel. In the 1990s, especially under the leadership of John Roth beginning in 1997, Nortel experienced explosive growth as it transformed itself from a telephone equipment manufacturer to providing network gear and optical transmission lines for the Internet. By the late 1990s it was also heavily into wireless transmission gear. As the Internet quickly grew, Nortel could not keep up with the large number of orders flowing in. At its peak in early 2000, Nortel employed over 90,000 employees worldwide and the company's stock rose to over $100.

The frenzied expansion came to an abrupt end as over-extended telephone companies sharply reduced capital expenditures, especially on fibre optics equipment. By the end of 2002, Nortel had only 35,000 employees and was shedding part of its unprofitable lines. In October 2002, Nortel sold its optical transmitter and receiver business and its pump laser and amplifiers business, which it had acquired during the heady days of rapid expansion, to a British company for a small fraction of the original purchase price. But at that point, the original acquisition cost was irrelevant because the telecommunication business had changed.

CHAPTER SUMMARY

7.1 THE FIRM AND THE BUSINESS SECTOR

- The firm is the most efficient form of organizing production and distribution. The main goal of a firm is to maximize profit.

- Sole proprietorships, partnerships, and corporations are the major legal forms that business enterprises may assume. Though proprietorships dominate numerically, the bulk of total output is produced by corporations. Corporations have grown to their position of dominance in the business sector primarily because they are characterized by limited liability and can acquire money capital for expansion more easily than other firms can.

7.2 ECONOMIC COSTS

- Economic costs include all payments that must be received by resource owners of factors of production to ensure a continued supply of needed inputs to a particular line of production. Economic costs include explicit costs, which flow to factors of production owned and supplied by others, and implicit costs, which are payments for the use of self-owned and self-employed factors of production. One implicit cost is a normal profit to the entrepreneur. Economic profit occurs when total revenue exceeds total cost (= explicit costs + implicit costs, including a normal profit).

7.3 SHORT-RUN PRODUCTION RELATION-SHIPS

- In the short run a firm's plant capacity is fixed. The firm can use its plant more or less intensively by adding or subtracting units of various factors of production, but it does not have sufficient time in the short run to alter plant size.

- The law of diminishing returns describes what happens to output as a fixed plant is used more intensively. As successive units of a variable factor such as labour are added to a fixed plant, beyond some point the marginal product associated with each additional worker declines.

7.4 SHORT-RUN PRODUCTION COSTS

- Because some factors of production are variable and others are fixed, costs can be classified as variable or fixed in the short run. Fixed costs are independent of the level of output; variable costs vary with output. The total cost of any output is the sum of fixed and variable costs at that output.

- Average fixed costs, average variable costs, and average total costs are fixed, variable, and total costs per unit of output. Average fixed cost declines continuously as output increases because a fixed sum is being spread over an increasing number of units of produc-

tion. A graph of average variable cost is U-shaped, reflecting the law of diminishing returns. Average total cost is the sum of average fixed and average variable costs; its graph is also U-shaped.

- Marginal cost is the extra cost of producing one more unit of output. It is the amount by which total cost and total variable cost change when one more or one fewer unit of output is produced. Graphically, the marginal-cost curve intersects the ATC and AVC curves at their minimum points.

- Lower input prices shift cost curves downward, as does technological progress. Higher input prices shift cost curves upward.

7.5 LONG-RUN PRODUCTION COSTS

- The long run is a period of time sufficiently long for a firm to vary the amounts of all inputs used, including plant size. In the long run all costs are variable. The long-run ATC, or planning, curve is composed of segments of the short-run ATC curves, and it represents the various plant sizes a firm can construct in the long run.

- The long-run ATC curve is generally U-shaped. Economies of scale are first encountered as a small firm expands. Greater specialization in the use of labour and management, the ability to use the most efficient equipment, and the spreading of startup costs among more units of output all contribute to economies of scale. As the firm continues to grow, it will encounter diseconomies of scale stemming from the managerial complexities that accompany large-scale production. The output ranges over which economies and diseconomies of scale occur in an industry are often an important determinant of the structure of that industry.

TERMS AND CONCEPTS

plant, p. 161
firm, p. 161
industry, p. 161
sole proprietorship, p. 161
partnership, p. 161
corporation, p. 161
stocks, p. 162
bonds, p. 162
limited liability, p. 163
double taxation, p. 163
principal–agent problem, p. 163
economic (opportunity) cost, p. 164

explicit costs, p. 164
implicit costs, p. 165
normal profit, p. 165
economic profit, p. 166
short run, p. 166
long run, p. 167
total product (TP), p. 167
marginal product (MP), p. 167
average product (AP), p. 167
law of diminishing returns, p. 168
fixed costs, p. 170
variable costs, p. 172

total cost, p. 172
average fixed cost (AFC), p. 174
average variable cost (AVC), p. 174
average total cost (ATC), p. 175
marginal cost (MC), p. 175
economies of scale, p. 182
diseconomies of scale, p. 183
constant returns to scale, p. 183
minimum efficient scale (MES), p. 184
natural monopoly, p. 185

STUDY QUESTIONS

1. Distinguish between a plant, a firm, and an industry. Why is an industry often difficult to define?

2. **KEY QUESTION** What are the major legal forms of business organization? Briefly state the advantages

and disadvantages of each. How do you account for the dominant role of corporations in the Canadian economy?

3. "The legal form an enterprise takes is dictated primarily by the financial requirements of its particular line of production." Do you agree? Why or why not?

4. **KEY QUESTION**   Gomez runs a small pottery firm. He hires one helper at $12,000 per year, pays annual rent of $5000 for his shop, and spends $20,000 per year on materials. He has $40,000 of his own funds invested in equipment (pottery wheels, kilns, and so forth) that could earn him $4000 per year if alternatively invested. He has been offered $15,000 per year to work as a potter for a competitor. He estimates his entrepreneurial talents are worth $3000 per year. Total annual revenue from pottery sales is $72,000. Calculate the accounting profit and the economic profit for Gomez's pottery firm.

5. Which of the following are short-run and which are long-run adjustments? (a) Wendy's builds a new restaurant. (b) Acme Steel Corporation hires 200 more workers. (c) A farmer increases the amount of fertilizer used on his corn crop. (d) An Alcan aluminum plant adds a third shift of workers.

6. **KEY QUESTION**   Complete the following table by calculating marginal product and average product from the data given.

Inputs of labour	Total product	Marginal product	Average product
0	0		
1	15	_____	_____
2	34	_____	_____
3	51	_____	_____
4	65	_____	_____
5	74	_____	_____
6	80	_____	_____
7	83	_____	_____
8	82	_____	_____

Plot the total, marginal, and average products and explain in detail the relationship between each pair of curves. Explain why marginal product first rises, then declines, and ultimately becomes negative. What bearing does the law of diminishing returns have on short-run costs? Be specific. "When marginal product is rising, marginal cost is falling. When marginal product is diminishing, marginal cost is rising." Illustrate and explain graphically.

7. Why can the distinction between fixed costs and variable costs be made in the short run? Classify the following as fixed or variable costs: advertising expenditures, fuel, interest on company-issued bonds, shipping charges, payments for raw materials, real estate taxes, executive salaries, insurance premiums, wage payments, depreciation and obsolescence charges, sales taxes, and rental payments on leased office machinery. "There are no fixed costs in the long run; all costs are variable." Explain.

8. List several fixed and variable costs associated with owning and operating an automobile. Suppose you are considering whether to drive your car or fly 2000 kilometres for spring break. Which costs—fixed, variable, or both—would you take into account in making your decision? Would any implicit costs be relevant? Explain.

9. **KEY QUESTION**   A firm has $60 in fixed costs and variable costs as indicated in the table below. Complete the table; check your calculations by referring to question 4 at the end of Chapter 8.

Total product	Total fixed cost	Total variable cost	Total cost	Average fixed cost	Average variable cost	Average total cost	Marginal cost
0	$_____	$ 0	$_____	$_____	$_____	$_____	$_____
1	_____	45	_____	_____	_____	_____	_____
2	_____	85	_____	_____	_____	_____	_____
3	_____	120	_____	_____	_____	_____	_____
4	_____	150	_____	_____	_____	_____	_____
5	_____	185	_____	_____	_____	_____	_____
6	_____	225	_____	_____	_____	_____	_____
7	_____	270	_____	_____	_____	_____	_____
8	_____	325	_____	_____	_____	_____	_____
9	_____	390	_____	_____	_____	_____	_____
10	_____	465	_____	_____	_____	_____	_____

a. Graph total fixed cost, total variable cost, and total cost. Explain how the law of diminishing returns influences the shapes of the variable-cost and total-cost curves.

b. Graph AFC, AVC, ATC, and MC. Explain the derivation and shape of each of these four curves and their relationships to one another. Specifically, explain in non-technical terms why the MC curve intersects both the AVC and ATC curves at their minimum points.

c. Explain how the location of each curve graphed in question 9b would be altered if (1) total fixed cost had been $100 rather than $60, and (2) total variable cost had been $10 less at each level of output.

10. Indicate how each of the following would shift the (1) marginal-cost curve, (2) average-variable-cost curve, (3) average-fixed-cost curve, and (4) average-total-cost curve of a manufacturing firm. In each case specify the direction of the shift.

   a. A reduction in business property taxes

   b. An increase in the nominal wages of production workers

   c. A decrease in the price of electricity

   d. An increase in insurance rates on plant and equipment

   e. An increase in transportation costs

11. Suppose a firm has only three possible plant-size options, represented by the ATC curves shown in the accompanying figure. What plant size will the firm choose in producing (a) 50, (b) 130, (c) 160 and (d) 250 units of output? Draw the firm's long-run average-cost curve on the diagram and describe this curve.

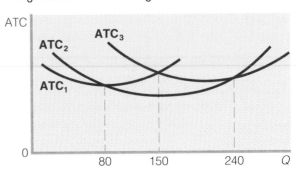

12. **KEY QUESTION**   Use the concepts of economies and diseconomies of scale to explain the shape of a firm's long-run ATC curve. What is the concept of minimum efficient scale? What bearing can the shape of the long-run ATC curve have on the structure of an industry?

13. **(The Last Word)** What is a sunk cost? Provide an example of a sunk cost other than one from the text. Why are such costs irrelevant in making decisions about future actions?

INTERNET APPLICATION QUESTIONS

1. Check out the list of the largest Canadian firms on the McConnell-Brue-Barbiero Web site (Chapter 7). From the top ten profit list, select three firms from three different industries and discuss the likely sources of economies of scale that underlie their large size.

2. Use the McConnell-Brue-Barbiero Web site (Chapter 7) to locate the Web site of a company of your choice. Find and review the company's income statement in its annual report and classify the non-revenue items as either fixed or variable costs. Are all costs clearly identifiable as either fixed or variable? What item would be considered as accounting profit? Would economic profit be higher or lower than this accounting profit?

8 Chapter

Pure Competition

In Chapter 6 we examined the relationship between product demand and total revenue, and in Chapter 7 we discussed costs of production. Now we will put revenues and costs together to see how a business decides what price to charge and how much output to produce. A firm's decisions concerning price and production depend greatly on the market structure of the industry in which it is operating; there is no average or typical industry. At one extreme is a single producer that dominates the market; at the other extreme are industries in which thousands of firms each produce a minute fraction of market supply. Between these extremes are many other market structures.

Since we cannot examine each industry individually, we will focus on four basic models of market structure to help you understand how price and output are determined in the many product markets in the economy. The models will also help you to assess the efficiency or inefficiency of those markets.

8.1   Four Market Structures

Economists group industries into four distinct market structures: pure competition, pure monopoly, monopolistic competition, and oligopoly. These four market models differ in several respects: the number of firms in the industry, whether those firms produce a standardized product or try to differentiate their products from those of other firms, and how easy or how difficult it is for firms to enter the industry.

Very briefly the four models are as follows:

pure competition
A market structure in which a very large number of firms produce a standardized product.

pure monopoly
A market structure in which one firm is the sole seller of a product or service.

monopolistic competition
A market structure in which a relatively large number of sellers produce differentiated products.

oligopoly
A market structure in which a few large firms produce homogeneous or differentiated products.

imperfect competition
The market models of pure monopoly, monopolistic competition, and oligopoly considered as a group.

- **Pure competition** is a market structure characterized by a very large number of firms producing a standardized product (that is, a product identical to that of other producers, such as corn or cucumbers). New firms can enter the industry very easily.

- **Pure monopoly** is a market structure in which one firm is the sole seller of a product or service (for example, a local cable company). Since the entry of additional firms is blocked, one firm constitutes the entire industry. The monopolist produces a unique product, and thus makes no effort to differentiate its product.

- **Monopolistic competition** is characterized by a relatively large number of sellers producing differentiated products (clothing, furniture, books). There is widespread *non-price competition*, a selling strategy in which one firm tries to distinguish its product or service from all competing products based on attributes like design and quality (an approach called *product differentiation*). Entry to monopolistically competitive industries is quite easy.

- **Oligopoly** involves only a few sellers of a homogeneous or differentiated product; consequently each firm is affected by the decisions of its rivals and must take those decisions into account when determining its own price and output.

Table 8-1 summarizes the characteristics of the four models for easy comparison. In discussing these four market models, we will occasionally distinguish the characteristics of a *pure competition* from those of the three other basic market structures, which together we will designate as **imperfect competition**.

8.2   Characteristics of Pure Competition and the Firm's Demand Curve

Purely competitive firms produce a standardized product.

Let's take a fuller look at pure competition, the focus of the remainder of this chapter.

- **Very large numbers**   A basic feature of a purely competitive market is the presence of a large number of sellers acting independently, often offering their products in large national or international markets. Examples include markets for farm commodities, the stock market, and the foreign exchange market.

- **Standardized product**   Purely competitive firms produce a standardized (or homogeneous) product. As long as the price is the same, consumers will be indifferent about which seller to buy the product from. Buyers view the products of firms B, C, D, and E as perfect substitutes for the product of firm A. Because purely competitive firms sell standardized products, they make no attempt to differentiate their products and do not engage in other forms of nonprice competition.

- **Price-takers**   In purely competitive markets individual firms exert no significant control over product price. Each firm produces such a small fraction of total output that increasing or

TABLE 8-1	Characteristics of the Four Basic Market Models

	MARKET MODEL			
Characteristic	**Pure competition**	**Monopolistic competition**	**Oligopoly**	**Pure monopoly**
Number of firms	A very large number	Many	Few	One
Type of product	Standardized	Differentiated	Standardized or differentiated	Unique; no close substitutes
Control over price	None	Some, but within rather narrow limits	Limited by mutual interdependence; considerable with collusion	Considerable
Conditions of entry	Very easy, no obstacles	Relatively easy	Significant obstacles	Blocked
Non-price competition	None	Considerable emphasis on advertising, brand names, trademarks	Typically a great deal, particularly with product differentiation	Mostly public relations advertising
Examples	Agriculture	Retail trade, dresses, shoes	Steel, automobiles, farm implements, many household appliances	Local utilities

price-taker
A firm in a purely competitive market that cannot change market price, only adjust to it.

decreasing its output will not noticeably influence total supply or, therefore, product price. In short, the competitive firm is a **price-taker**: it cannot change market price, it can only adjust to it. Asking a price higher than the market price would be futile; consumers will not buy from firm A at $2.05 when its 9999 competitors are selling an identical product at $2 per unit. Conversely, because firm A can sell as much as it chooses at $2 per unit, it has no reason to charge a lower price, say, $1.95, for to do so would lower its profit.

- *Easy entry and exit* New firms can easily enter, and existing firms can easily leave, purely competitive industries in the long run. No legal, technological, financial, or other obstacles prohibit new firms from selling their output in any competitive market. Exit barriers may include an entrepreneur's emotional ties to an industry or previous financial commitments.

Relevance of Pure Competition

Although pure competition is relatively rare in the real world, this market model is highly relevant. A few industries more closely approximate pure competition than any other market structure. In particular, we can learn much about markets for agricultural goods, fish products, foreign exchange, basic metals, and stock shares by studying the pure competition model. Also, pure competition is a meaningful starting point for any discussion of price and output determination. The operation of a competitive economy provides a standard, or norm, for evaluating the efficiency of the real-world economy.

Demand for a Purely Competitive Firm

To develop a tabular and graphical model of pure competition, we first examine demand from a competitive seller's viewpoint and see how it affects revenue. This seller might be a wheat farmer,

Although pure competition is rare in the real world, by studying it we can learn much about markets such as the market for agricultural products.

a strawberry grower, or a sheep rancher. Each purely competitive firm offers only a negligible fraction of total market supply, so it must accept the price determined by the market; it is a price-taker, not a price-maker.

PERFECTLY ELASTIC DEMAND

The demand curve of the purely competitive firm, as represented by columns 1 and 2 in the table of Figure 8-1, is perfectly elastic. As shown in the table, the market price is $131. The firm represented cannot obtain a higher price by restricting its output, nor does it need to lower its price to increase its sales volume.

We are *not* saying that *market* demand is perfectly elastic in a competitive market. Market demand graphs are the usual downsloping curve, as a glance ahead at Figure 8-7(b) on page 206 will reveal. In fact, the total-demand curves for most agricultural products are quite inelastic, even though agriculture is the most competitive industry in the Canadian economy. An entire industry (all firms producing a particular product) can affect price by changing industry output. For example, all firms, acting independently but simultaneously, can increase price by reducing output, but the individual firm cannot do that. So the demand schedule faced by the *individual firm* in a purely competitive industry is perfectly elastic at the market price, as shown in Figure 8-1.

FIGURE 8-1 — Demand, Marginal Revenue, and Total Revenue of a Purely Competitive Firm

FIRM'S DEMAND SCHEDULE		FIRM'S REVENUE DATA	
(1) Product price, *P* (average revenue)	(2) Quantity demanded, *Q*	(3) Total revenue, TR (1) × (2)	(4) Marginal revenue, MR
$131	0	$ 0	
			$131
131	1	131	
			131
131	2	262	
			131
131	3	393	
			131
131	4	524	
			131
131	5	655	
			131
131	6	786	
			131
131	7	917	
			131
131	8	1,048	
			131
131	9	1,179	
			131
131	10	1,310	

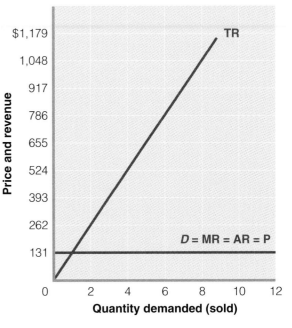

A purely competitive firm can sell additional units of output at the market price, and thus its marginal-revenue curve (MR) coincides with its perfectly elastic demand curve (D). The firm's total-revenue curve (TR) is a straight upward-sloping line.

Average, Total, and Marginal Revenue

The firm's demand schedule is also its revenue schedule. The price per unit to the purchaser is also revenue per unit, or average revenue, to the seller. To say that all buyers must pay $131 per unit is to say that the revenue per unit, or **average revenue**, received by the seller is $131.

The **total revenue** for each sales level is found by multiplying price by the corresponding quantity the firm can sell. (In the table of Figure 8-1, column 1 multiplied by column 2 yields column 3.) In this case, total revenue increases by a constant amount, $131, for each additional unit of sales. Each unit sold adds exactly its constant price to total revenue.

When a firm is pondering a change in its output, it will consider how its total revenue will change as a result. What will be the additional revenue from selling another unit of output? **Marginal revenue** is the change in total revenue that results from selling one more unit of output. In column 3 of the table in Figure 8-1, total revenue is zero when zero units are sold. The first unit of output sold increases total revenue from zero to $131; marginal revenue for that unit is $131. The second unit sold increases total revenue from $131 to $262, and marginal revenue is again $131. Note in column 4 that, as is price, marginal revenue is a constant $131. In pure competition, marginal revenue, average revenue, and price are equal. *(Key Question 3)*

GRAPHICAL PORTRAYAL

Figure 8-1 shows the purely competitive firm's demand curve and total-revenue and marginal-revenue curves. The demand curve (*D*) is horizontal, indicating perfect price elasticity. The marginal-revenue curve (MR) coincides with the demand curve, because the product price (and hence MR) is constant. Total revenue (TR) is a straight line that slopes upward to the right. Its slope is constant because each extra unit of sales increases TR by $131.

average revenue
Total revenue from the sale of a product divided by the quantity of the product sold.

total revenue
The total number of dollars received by a firm from the sale of a product.

marginal revenue
The change in total revenue that results from selling one more unit of a firm's product.

QUICK REVIEW

- In a purely competitive industry a large number of firms produce a standardized product and no significant barriers to entry exist.

- The demand of a competitive firm is perfectly elastic—horizontal on a graph—at the market price.

- Marginal revenue and average revenue for a competitive firm coincide with the firm's demand curve; total revenue rises by the product price for each additional unit sold.

8.3 Profit Maximization in the Short Run

Since the purely competitive firm is a price-taker, it can maximize its economic profit (or minimize its loss) only by adjusting its *output*. In the short run, the firm has a fixed plant. Thus, it can adjust its output only through changes in the amount of variable inputs (materials, labour) it uses. It adjusts its variable inputs to achieve the output level that maximizes its profit.

There are two ways to determine the level of output at which a competitive firm will realize maximum profit or the minimum amount of loss. One method is to compare total revenue and total cost; the other is to compare marginal revenue and marginal cost. Both approaches apply to all firms, whether they are pure competitors, pure monopolists, monopolistic competitors, or oligopolists.[1]

---

[1]To make sure you understand these two approaches, we will apply them both to output determination under pure competition, but since we want to emphasize the marginal approach, we will limit our graphical application of the total-revenue approach to a situation where the firm maximizes profits. We will then use the marginal approach to examine three cases: profit maximization, loss minimization, and shutdown.

Total-revenue – Total-cost Approach: Profit-maximization Case

With the price of its product given by the market, the competitive producer will ask: (1) Should we produce this product? (2) If so, in what amount? (3) What economic profit (or loss) will we realize?

Let's demonstrate how a firm in pure competition answers these questions, given certain cost data and a specific market price. Our cost data are already familiar to you because they are the fixed-cost, variable-cost, and total-cost data in Figure 8-1, repeated in columns 1 to 4 in the table of Figure 8-2. (Recall that these data reflect explicit and implicit costs, including a normal profit.) Assuming that the market price is $131, the total revenue for each output level is found by multiplying output (total product) by price. Total revenue data are in column 5. Then in column 6 we find the profit or loss at each output level by subtracting total cost, TC (column 4), from total revenue, TR (column 5).

Should the firm produce? Definitely. It can make a profit by doing so. How much should it produce? Nine units. Column 6 tells us that this is the output at which total economic profit is at a maximum. What economic profit (or loss) will the firm realize? A $299 economic profit—the difference between total revenue ($1179) and total cost ($880).

Figure 8-2(a) compares total revenue and total cost graphically for this profit-maximizing case. Observe again that the total revenue curve for a purely competitive firm is a straight line. Total cost increases with output in that more production requires more factors of production, but the rate of increase in total cost varies with the relative efficiency of the firm. Specifically, the cost data reflect Chapter 7's law of diminishing marginal returns. From zero to four units of output, total cost increases at a decreasing rate as the firm uses its fixed factors more efficiently. With additional output, total cost begins to rise by ever-increasing amounts because of the diminishing returns accompanying more intensive use of the plant.

Total revenue and total cost are equal where the two curves in Figure 8-2(a) intersect (at roughly two units of output). Total revenue covers all costs (including a normal profit, which is included in the cost curve) but there is no economic profit. For this reason economists call this output a **break-even point**: an output at which a firm makes a *normal profit* but not an economic profit. If we extended the data beyond 10 units of output, another break-even point would occur where total cost would catch up with total revenue somewhere between 13 and 14 units of output in Figure 8-2(a). Any output between the two break-even points identified in the figure will produce an economic profit. The firm achieves maximum profit, however, where the vertical distance between the total-revenue and total-cost curves is greatest. For our particular data, this is at nine units of output, where maximum profit is $299.

The profit-maximizing output is easier to see in Figure 8-2(b), where total economic profit is graphed for each level of output. Where the total-revenue and total-cost curves intersect in Figure 8-2(a), economic profit is zero, as shown by the total-profit line in Figure 8-2(b). Where the vertical distance between TR and TC is greatest in the upper graph, economic profit is at its peak ($299), as shown in the lower graph. This firm will choose to produce nine units, since that output maximizes its profit.

Marginal-revenue = Marginal-cost Approach

In the second approach, the firm compares the *marginal revenue* (MR) and the *marginal cost* (MC) of each successive unit of output. The firm will produce any unit of output whose marginal revenue exceeds its marginal cost because the firm would gain more in revenue from selling that unit than it would add to its costs by producing it. Conversely, if the marginal cost of a unit of output exceeds its marginal revenue, the firm will not produce that unit.

MR = MC RULE

In the short run, the firm will maximize profit or minimize loss by producing the output at which marginal revenue equals marginal cost. This profit-maximizing guide is known as the **MR = MC rule**.

break-even point
An output at which a firm makes a normal profit but not an economic profit.

Choosing a Little More or Less

MR = MC rule
A method of determining the total output at which economic profit is at a maximum (or losses at a minimum).

FIGURE 8-2

Total-revenue – Total-cost Approach to Profit Maximization for a Purely Competitive Firm

Panel (a): The firm's profit is maximized at that output (nine units) where total revenue, TR, exceeds total cost, TC, by the maximum amount. Panel (b): The vertical distance between TR and TC in panel (a) is plotted as a total-economic-profit curve. Maximum economic profit is $299 at nine units of output.

	PRICE: $131				
(1) Total product (output), Q	(2) Total fixed cost, TFC	(3) Total variable cost, TVC	(4) Total cost, TC	(5) Total revenue, TR	(6) Profit (+) or loss (−)
0	$100	$ 0	$ 100	$ 0	$−100
1	100	90	190	131	− 59
2	100	170	270	262	− 8
3	100	240	340	393	+ 53
4	100	300	400	524	+124
5	100	370	470	655	+185
6	100	450	550	786	+236
7	100	540	640	917	+277
8	100	650	750	1,048	+298
9	100	780	880	1,179	+299
10	100	930	1,030	1,310	+280

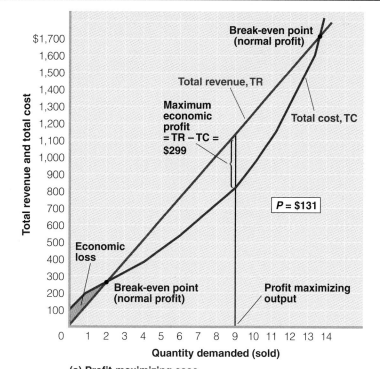

(a) Profit-maximizing case

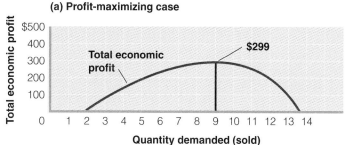

(b) Total economic profit

(For most sets of MR and MC data, MR and MC will be precisely equal at a fractional level of output. In such instances the firm should produce the last complete unit of output for which MR exceeds MC.) Note that we have arrived at exactly the same conclusions as we did in the TR – TC approach. The MR = MC rule and the TR – TC approach are two alternate ways of looking at the same thing.

THREE CHARACTERISTICS OF THE MR = MC RULE

Keep in mind these three features of the MR = MC rule:

1. The rule applies only if producing is preferable to shutting down. If marginal revenue does not equal or exceed average variable cost, the firm will prefer to shut down rather than produce the MR = MC output.

2. The rule is an accurate guide to profit maximization for all firms, whether they are purely competitive, monopolistic, monopolistically competitive, or oligopolistic.

3. The rule can be restated as P = MC when applied to a purely competitive firm. Because the demand schedule faced by a competitive seller is perfectly elastic at the going market price, product price and marginal revenue are equal. So under pure competition (and only under pure competition) we may substitute P for MR in the rule; *when producing is preferable to shutting down, the competitive firm should produce at that point where price equals marginal cost* (P = MC).

Now let's apply the MR = MC rule, first using the same price as in our total-revenue–total-cost approach to profit maximization. Then, by considering other prices, we will demonstrate two additional cases: loss minimization and shutdown. *It is crucial that you understand the MR = MC analysis that follows, since it reappears in Chapters 9 and 10.*

PROFIT-MAXIMIZING CASE

Five of the columns in the table of **Figure 8-3 (Key Graph)** reproduce the AFC, AVC, ATC, and MC data in Table 7-2. It is the marginal-cost data of column 6 that we will compare with price (equals marginal revenue) for each unit of output. Suppose first that the market price, and therefore marginal revenue, is $131, as shown in column 7.

What is the profit-maximizing output? Each of the first nine units adds to the firm's profit and will be produced. The tenth unit, however, will not be produced. It would add more to cost ($150) than to revenue ($131).

PROFIT CALCULATIONS

The economic profit realized by producing nine units can be calculated from the average-total-cost data. Multiplying price ($131) by output (9), we find that total revenue is $1179. Multiplying average total cost ($97.78) by output (9) gives us total cost of $880.[2] The difference of $299 (= $1179 – $880) is the economic profit. This firm will prefer to operate rather than shut down.

Another way to calculate profit is to determine the profit per unit by subtracting the average total cost ($97.78) from the product price ($131) and multiplying the difference (a per-unit profit of $33.22) by output (9). Take some time now to verify the numbers in column 8 in the table of Figure 8-3. You will find that any output other than those adhering to the MR = MC rule will mean either profits below $299 or losses.

GRAPHICAL PORTRAYAL

Figure 8-3 shows price (= MR) and marginal cost graphically. Price equals marginal cost at the profit-maximizing output of nine units. There the per-unit economic profit is P – A, where P is the

---

[2] Most of the unit-cost data are rounded figures. Therefore, economic profits calculated from them will typically vary by a few cents from the profits determined in the total-revenue–total-cost approach. Here we simply ignore the few-cents differentials to make our answers consistent with the results of the total-revenue–total-cost approach.

Key Graph

FIGURE 8-3 The Short-run Profit-maximizing Position of a Purely Competitive Firm

The MR = MC output enables the purely competitive firm to maximize profits or to minimize losses. In this case MR (= P in pure competition) and MC are equal at an output Q of nine units. There P exceeds the average total cost A = $97.78, so the firm realizes an economic profit of P − A per unit. The total economic profit is represented by the grey rectangle and is 9 × (P − A).

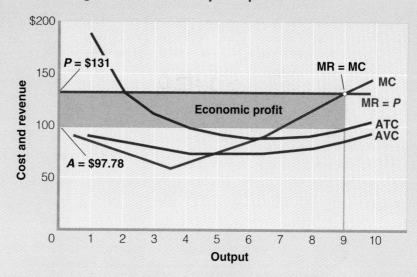

(1) Total product (output)	(2) Average fixed cost, AFC	(3) Average variable cost, AVC	(4) Average total cost, ATC	(5) Total cost, TC	(6) Marginal cost, MC	(7) Price = marginal revenue, MR	(8) Total economic profit (+) or loss (−)
0				$100			$−100
1	$100.00	$90.00	$190.00	190	$ 90	$131	− 59
2	50.00	85.00	135.00	270	80	131	− 8
3	33.33	80.00	113.33	340	70	131	+ 53
4	25.00	75.00	100.00	400	60	131	+124
5	20.00	74.00	94.00	470	70	131	+185
6	16.67	75.00	91.67	550	80	131	+236
7	14.29	77.14	91.43	640	90	131	+277
8	12.50	81.25	93.75	750	110	131	+298
9	11.11	86.67	97.78	880	130	131	+299
10	10.00	93.00	103.00	1,030	150	131	+280

Quick Quiz

1. **Curve MR is horizontal because**
   a. product price falls as output increases.
   b. the law of diminishing marginal utility is at work.
   c. the market demand for this product is perfectly elastic.
   d. the firm is a price-taker.

2. **At a price of $131 and 7 units of output**
   a. MR exceeds MC, and the firm should expand its output.

b. total revenue is less than total cost.

c. AVC exceeds ATC.

d. the firm would earn only a normal profit.

3. In maximizing profits at nine units of output, this firm is adhering to which of the following decision rules?

a. Produce where MR exceeds MC by the greatest amount.

b. Produce where P exceeds ATC by the greatest amount.

c. Produce where total revenue exceeds total cost by the greatest amount.

d. Produce where average fixed costs are zero.

4. Suppose price declined from $131 to $100. This firm's

a. marginal-cost curve would shift downward.

b. economic profit would fall to zero.

c. profit-maximizing output would decline.

d. total cost would fall by more than its total revenue.

ANSWERS: 1. d; 2. a; 3. c; 4. c

market price and A is the average total cost for an output of nine units. The total economic profit is $9 \times (P - A)$, shown by the grey rectangular area.

Note that the firm wants to maximize its total profit, not its per-unit profit. Per-unit profit is greatest at seven units of output, where price exceeds average total cost by $39.57 (= $131 – $91.43). But by producing only seven units, the firm would not produce two additional units of output that would clearly contribute to total profit.

LOSS-MINIMIZING CASE

Now let's assume that the market price is $81 rather than $131. Should the firm still produce? If so, how much? What will be the resulting profit or loss?

The first five columns in the table of Figure 8-4 on page 202 are the same as those in the table of Figure 8-3. Column 6 shows the new price (equal to MR), $81. Comparing columns 5 and 6, we find that the first unit of output adds $90 to total cost but only $81 to total revenue. One might conclude: "Don't produce—close down!" But that would be hasty. For units two through six, price exceeds marginal cost. Each of these five units adds more to revenue than to cost and, as shown in column 7, they decrease the total loss. Together they more than compensate for the loss taken on the first unit. Beyond six units, however, MC exceeds MR (= P). The firm should therefore produce six units.

LOSS DETERMINATION

Will production be profitable? No, because at six units of output the average total cost of $91.67 exceeds the price of $81 by $10.67 per unit. If we multiply that by the six units of output, we find the firm's total loss is $64.

Then why produce? Because this loss is less than the firm's $100 of fixed costs, which is the $100 loss the firm would incur in the short run by closing down. The firm receives enough revenue per unit ($81) to cover its average variable costs of $75 and also provide $6 per unit, or a total of $36, to apply against fixed costs. Therefore, the firm's loss is only $64 (= $100 – $36), not $100.

GRAPHICAL PORTRAYAL

This loss-minimizing case is also shown graphically in Figure 8-4. Wherever price P exceeds average variable cost, AVC, the firm can pay part, but not all, of its fixed costs by producing. The loss is minimized by producing the output at which MC = MR (here, six units). At that output, each unit

Consider This

Maximizing Profit

Have you ever driven by a poorly maintained business facility and wondered why the owner doesn't either fix up the property or go out of business? The somewhat surprising answer is that it may be unprofitable to improve the facility, yet profitable to continue to operate it as it deteriorates. Seeing why will aid your understanding of fixed cost, variable cost, profit-maximization, and shutdown points.

Consider the hypothetical story of the Highway View Inn, a one-story motel on Old Highway North, Any Town, Canada. The owner of Highway View built the motel on the basis of traffic patterns and competition that existed several decades ago. As more highways were built, Highway View found itself located on a relatively vacant stretch of road. Also, it faced greatly heightened competition from new "chain" motels located closer to the main highway that crossed the province.

In a typical early year, Highway View had annual total revenue of $300,000, annual fixed cost of $80,000, and annual variable cost of $130,000. Its profit was $90,000 (= $300,000 – $210,000).

But beginning a decade or so ago annual total revenue fell to $180,000, compared to fixed and variable costs of $80,000 and $110,000, respectively. In that year Highway View had a $10,000 (= $190,000 – $180,000) loss. Why did it stay open? The answer is that the motel's $180,000 of total revenue was sufficient to cover the $110,000 of variable cost and contribute $70,000 to the $80,000 payment of fixed cost. By staying open Highway View lost $10,000 instead of the $80,000 (equal to its fixed cost) it would have lost if it had shut down.

Highway View's total revenue of $180,000, however, did not cover its total cost of $190,000. Its owner therefore realized that the motel would have to be shut down in the long run. But rather than immediately close its doors, the owner decided to lower total cost by reducing maintenance. In effect, the owner decided to allow the motel property to deteriorate as a way to reduce total cost so as to match the reduced total revenue coming in.

But the deterioration of the motel structure will eventually result in lower occupancy rates and room rates, and therefore lower total revenue. The owner of Highway View knows that total revenue sooner or later will fall below total cost, even with an annual maintenance expense of zero. When that situation occurs, the owner is prepared to close its operations, tear down the motel, and sell its vacant property. But in the meantime, Highway View is open, deteriorating, and covering total cost, which includes a normal profit.

In general, it is a good business practice to maintain and improve one's property. But, as we have seen, there are interesting exceptions.

Question: Can government take action to persuade some motel owners that do not maintain their property to clean them up?

contributes $P - V$ to covering fixed cost, where V is the AVC at six units of output. The per-unit loss is $A - P = \$10.67$, and the total loss is $6 \times (A - P)$, or $64, as shown by the grey area.

SHUTDOWN CASE

Suppose now that the market price is only $71. Should the firm produce? No, because at every output the firm's average variable cost is greater than the price (compare columns 3 and 8 in the table of Figure 8-4). The smallest loss the firm can incur by producing is greater than the $100 fixed cost it will lose by shutting down (as shown by column 9). The best action is to shut down.

You can see this shutdown situation in Figure 8-5 on page 203. Price comes closest to covering average variable costs at the MR (= P) = MC output of five units. But even here, price or revenue per unit would fall short of average variable cost by $3 (= $74 – $71). So, it will make sense for the firm to shut down rather than produce at a $71 price—or at any price less than the minimum average variable cost of $74.

The shutdown case reminds us of the qualifier to our MR (= P) = MC rule. A competitive firm will maximize profit or minimize loss in the short run by producing that output at which MR (= P) = MC, *provided that market price exceeds minimum average variable cost.*

FIGURE 8-4   The Short-run Loss-minimizing Position of a Purely Competitive Firm

(1) Total product (output)	(2) Average fixed cost, AFC	(3) Average variable cost, AVC	(4) Average total cost, ATC	(5) Marginal cost, MC	(6) $81 price = marginal revenue, MR	(7) Profit (+) or loss (−), $81 price	(8) $71 price = marginal revenue, MR	(9) Profit (+) or loss (−), $71 price
0						$−100		$−100
1	$100.00	$90.00	$190.00	$ 90	$81	−109	$71	−119
2	50.00	85.00	135.00	80	81	−108	71	−128
3	33.33	80.00	113.33	70	81	− 97	71	−127
4	25.00	75.00	100.00	60	81	− 76	71	−116
5	20.00	74.00	94.00	70	81	− 65	71	−115
6	16.67	75.00	91.67	80	81	− 64	71	−124
7	14.29	77.14	91.43	90	81	− 73	71	−143
8	12.50	81.25	93.75	110	81	−102	71	−182
9	11.11	86.67	97.78	130	81	−151	71	−241
10	10.00	93.00	103.00	150	81	−220	71	−320

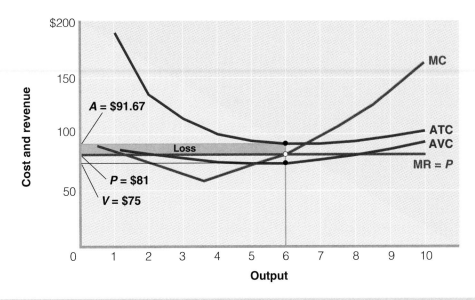

If price P exceeds the minimum AVC (here $74 at $Q = 5$) but is less than ATC, the MR = MC output (here six units) will permit the firm to minimize its losses. In this instance the loss is $A − P$ per unit, where A is the average total cost at six units of output. The total loss is shown by the grey area and is equal to $6 \times (A − P)$.

8.4   Marginal Cost and Short-run Supply

In the preceding section we simply selected three different prices and asked what quantity the profit-seeking competitive firm, faced with certain costs, would choose to offer in the market at each price. This set of product prices and corresponding quantities supplied constitutes part of the supply schedule for the competitive firm.

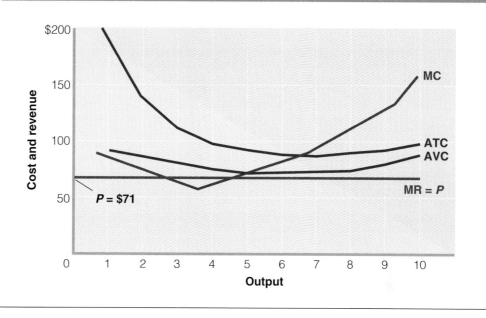

FIGURE 8-5 — The Short-run Shutdown Position of a Purely Competitive Firm

If price *P* falls below the minimum AVC (here $74 at *Q* = 5), the competitive firm will minimize its losses in the short run by shutting down. There is no level of output at which the firm can produce and realize a loss smaller than its total fixed cost.

TABLE 8-2 — The Supply Schedule of a Competitive Firm Confronted with the Cost Data in Figure 8-3

Price	Quantity supplied	Maximum profit (+) or minimum loss (–)
$151	10	$+480
131	9	+299
111	8	+138
91	7	– 3
81	6	– 64
71	0	–100
61	0	–100

Table 8-2 summarizes the supply schedule data for those three prices ($131, $81, and $71) and four others. This table confirms the direct relationship between product price and quantity supplied that we identified in Chapter 3. Note first that the firm will not produce at price $61 or $71, because both are less than the $74 minimum AVC. Then note that quantity supplied increases as price increases. Observe finally that economic profit is higher at higher prices.

Generalized Depiction

Figure 8-6 (Key Graph) generalizes the MR = MC rule and the relationship between short-run production costs and the firm's supply behaviour. The ATC, AVC, and MC curves are shown, along with several marginal-revenue lines drawn at possible market prices. Let's observe quantity supplied at each of these prices.

- Price P_1 is below the firm's minimum average variable cost, so at this price the firm won't operate at all. Quantity supplied will be zero, as it will be at all other prices below P_2.

- Price P_2 is just equal to the minimum average variable cost. The firm will supply Q_2 units of output (where $MR_2 = MC$) and just cover its total variable cost. Its loss will equal its total fixed cost. (Actually, the firm would be indifferent as to shutting down or supplying Q_2 units of output, but we assume it produces.)

- At price P_3 the firm will supply Q_3 units of output to minimize its short-run losses. At any other price between P_2 and P_4 the firm will minimize its losses by producing and supplying the quantity at which MR (= *P*) = MC.

Key Graph

FIGURE 8-6 The P = MC Rule and the Competitive Firm's Short-run Supply Curve

Application of the $P = MC$ rule, as modified by the shutdown case, reveals that the (solid) segment of the firm's MC curve that lies above AVC is the firm's short-run supply curve. More specifically, at price P_1, $P = MC$ at point a, but the firm will produce no output because P_1 is less than minimum AVC. At price P_2 the firm will operate at point b, where it produces Q_2 units and incurs a loss equal to its total fixed cost. At P_3 it operates at point c, where output is Q_3 and the loss is less than the total fixed cost. With the price of P_4, the firm operates at point d; in this case the firm earns a normal profit because at output Q_4 price equals ATC. At price P_5 the firm operates at point e and maximizes its economic profit by producing Q_5 units.

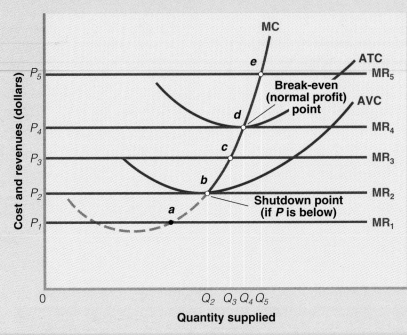

Quick Quiz

1. Which of the following might increase product price from P_3 to P_5?
   a. An improvement in production technology
   b. A decline in the price of a substitute good
   c. An increase in the price of a complementary good
   d. Rising incomes if the product is a normal good

2. An increase in price from P_3 to P_5 would
   a. shift this firm's MC curve to the right.
   b. mean that MR_5 exceeds MC at Q_3 units, inducing the firm to expand output to Q_5.
   c. decrease this firm's average variable costs.
   d. enable this firm to obtain a normal, but not an economic, profit.

3. At P_4
   a. this firm has no economic profit.
   b. this firm will earn only a normal profit and thus will shut down.
   c. MR_4 will be less than MC at the profit-maximizing output.
   d. the profit-maximizing output will be Q_5.

4. Suppose P_4 is $10, P_5 is $15, Q_4 is 8 units, and Q_5 is 10 units. This firm's
   a. supply curve is elastic over the Q_4–Q_5 range of output.
   b. supply curve is inelastic over the Q_4–Q_5 range of output.
   c. total revenue will decline if price rises from P_4 to P_5.
   d. marginal-cost curve will shift downward if price falls from P_5 to P_4.

ANSWERS: 1. d; 2. b; 3. a; 4. b

- The firm will just break even at price P_4, where it will supply Q_4 units of output (where $MR_4 = MC$), earning a normal profit but not an economic profit. Total revenue will just cover total cost, including a normal profit, because the revenue per unit ($MR_4 = P_4$) and the total cost per unit (ATC) are the same.

- At price P_5 the firm will earn an economic profit by producing and supplying Q_5 units of output. In fact, at any price above P_4 the firm will earn an economic profit by producing to the point where MR ($= P$) = MC.

Note that each of the MR ($= P$) = MC intersection points labelled *b*, *c*, *d*, and *e* in Figure 8-6 indicates a possible product price (on the vertical axis) and the corresponding quantity that the firm would supply at that price (on the horizontal axis). Thus, points such as these are on the upsloping supply curve of the competitive firm. Note, too, that quantity supplied would be zero at any price below the minimum average variable cost (AVC). We can conclude that the portion of the firm's marginal-cost curve lying above its average-variable-cost curve is its short-run supply curve. In Figure 8-6, the solid segment of the marginal-cost curve MC is this firm's **short-run supply curve**.

Diminishing Returns, Production Costs, and Product Supply

We have now identified the links between the law of diminishing returns (Chapter 7), production costs, and product supply in the short run. Because of the law of diminishing returns, marginal cost eventually rises as more units of output are produced. And because marginal cost rises with output, a purely competitive firm must get successively higher prices to motivate it to produce additional units of output.

Supply Curve Shifts

In Chapter 7 we saw that changes in such factors as the prices of variable inputs or in technology will shift the marginal-cost or short-run supply curve to a new location. All else being equal, a wage increase, for example, would shift the supply curve in Figure 8-6 upward and to the left, which means a decrease in supply. Similarly, technological progress that increases the productivity of labour would shift the marginal-cost or supply curve downward to the right, representing an increase in supply.

Firm and Industry: Equilibrium Price

From Chapter 3 we know that in a purely competitive market, equilibrium price is determined by total, or market, supply and total demand. To derive total supply, the supply curves of the individual competitive sellers must be added up. Columns 1 and 3 in Table 8-3 repeat the supply schedule for the individual competitive firm, as derived in Table 8-2. Let's assume there are 1000 competitive firms in this industry, all having the same total and unit costs as the single firm we discussed. This assumption allows us to calculate the market supply schedule (columns 2 and 3) by multiplying the quantity-supplied figures of the single firm (column 1) by 1000.

MARKET PRICE AND PROFITS

To determine the equilibrium price and output, these total-supply data must be compared with total-demand data. Let's assume that total demand is as shown in columns 3 and 4 in Table 8-3. By comparing the total quantity supplied and the total quantity demanded at the seven possible

short-run supply curve
A curve that shows the quantities of the product a firm in a purely competitive industry will offer to sell at various prices in the short run.

TABLE 8-3 — Firm and Market Supply and Market Demand

(1) Quantity supplied, single firm	(2) Total quantity supplied, 1000 firms	(3) Product price	(4) Total quantity demanded
10	10,000	$151	4,000
9	9,000	131	6,000
8	*8,000*	*111*	*8,000*
7	7,000	91	9,000
6	6,000	81	11,000
0	0	71	13,000
0	0	61	16,000

prices, we determine that the equilibrium price is $111 and the equilibrium quantity is 8000 units for the industry—eight units for each of the 1000 identical firms.

Will these conditions of market supply and demand make this a profitable industry? Multiplying product price ($111) by output (8 units), we find that the total revenue of each firm is $888. The total cost is $750, found by looking at column 4 in the table of Figure 8-2. The $138 difference is the economic profit of each firm. For the industry, total economic profit is $138,000. This, then, is a profitable industry.

Another way of calculating economic profit is to determine per-unit profit by subtracting average total cost ($93.75) from product price ($111) and multiplying the difference (per-unit profit of $17.25) by the firm's equilibrium level of output (8). Again we obtain an economic profit of $138 per firm and $138,000 for the industry.

GRAPHICAL PORTRAYAL

Figure 8-7 shows this analysis graphically. The individual supply curves of each of the 1000 identical firms—one of which is shown as s = MC in Figure 8-7(a)—are summed horizontally to get the total-supply curve $S = \sum MC$ of Figure 8-7(b). Together with total-demand curve D, it determines the equilibrium price $111 and equilibrium quantity (for the industry) 8000 units. This equilibrium price is given and unalterable to the individual firm; that is, each firm's demand curve is perfectly elastic at the equilibrium price, as indicated by d in Figure 8-7(a). Because the individual firm is a price-taker, the marginal-revenue curve coincides with the firm's demand curve d. This $111 price exceeds the average total cost at the firm's equilibrium MR = MC output of eight units, so the firm earns an economic profit represented by the grey area in Figure 8-7(a).

Assuming costs and market demand do not change, these diagrams reveal a genuine equilibrium in the short run. The market has no shortages or surpluses to cause price or total quantity to change. Nor can any one firm in the industry increase its profit by altering its output. Note, too, that higher unit and marginal costs on the one hand, or weaker market demand on the other, could change the situation so that Figure 8-7(a) resembles Figure 8-4 or Figure 8-5. In Figure 8-7(a) and (b), sketch how higher costs or decreased demand could produce short-run losses.

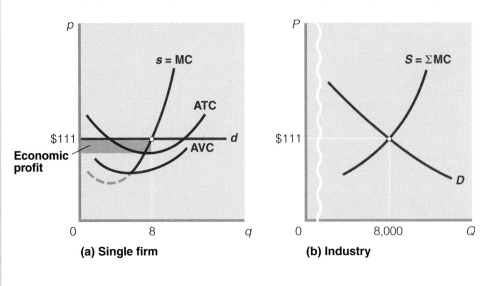

FIGURE 8-7

Short-run Competitive Equilibrium for a Firm (Panel A) and the Industry (Panel B)

The horizontal sum of the 1000 firms' individual supply curves (s) determines the industry supply curve (S). Given industry demand (D), the short-run equilibrium price and output for the industry are $111 and 8000 units. Taking the equilibrium price as given, the individual firm establishes its profit-maximizing output at eight units and, in this case, realizes the economic profit represented by the grey area.

(a) Single firm

(b) Industry

TABLE 8-4	Output Determination in Pure Competition in the Short Run

Question	Answer
Should this firm produce?	Yes, if price is equal to, or greater than, minimum average variable cost. This means that the firm is profitable or that its losses are less than its fixed cost.
What quantity should this firm produce?	Produce where MR (= *P*) = MC; there, profit is maximized (TR exceeds TC by a maximum amount) or loss is minimized.
Will production result in economic profit?	Yes, if price exceeds average total cost (TR will exceed TC). No, if average total cost exceeds price (TC will exceed TR).

FIRM VERSUS INDUSTRY

Figure 8-7 underscores a point made earlier: Product price is a given fact to the *individual* competitive firm, but the supply plans of all competitive producers *as a group* are a basic determinant of product price. If we recall the fallacy of composition, we find there is no inconsistency here. Although one firm, supplying a negligible fraction of total supply, cannot affect price, the industry supply curve does have an important bearing on price. *(Key Question 4)*

QUICK REVIEW

- Profit is maximized, or loss minimized, at the output at which marginal revenue (or price in pure competition) equals marginal cost.

- If the market price is below the minimum average variable cost, the firm will minimize its losses by shutting down.

- The segment of the firm's marginal-cost curve that lies above the average-variable-cost curve is its short-run supply curve.

- Table 8-4 summarizes the MR = MC approach to determining the competitive firm's profit-maximizing output. It also shows the equivalent analysis in terms of total revenue and total cost.

- Under pure competition, equilibrium price is a given to the individual firm and simultaneously is the result of the production (supply) decisions of all firms as a group.

8.5 Profit Maximization in the Long Run

In the short run a specific number of firms are in an industry, each with a fixed, unalterable plant. Firms may shut down in the sense that they can produce zero units of output in the short run, but they do not have enough time to liquidate their assets and go out of business. By contrast, in the long run firms already in an industry have sufficient time either to expand or to contract their plant capacities. More important, the number of firms in the industry may either increase or decrease as new firms enter or existing firms leave. We now examine how these long-run adjustments modify our conclusions concerning short-run output and price determination.

Assumptions

We make three simplifying assumptions, none of which affects our conclusions:

1. ***Entry and exit only***   The only long-run adjustment is the entry or exit of firms. Moreover, we ignore all short-run adjustments to concentrate on the effects of the long-run adjustments.

2. *Identical costs*   All firms in the industry have identical cost curves. This assumption allows us to discuss a representative firm, knowing that all other firms in the industry are similarly affected by any long-run adjustments that occur.

3. *Constant-cost industry*   The industry is a constant-cost industry, which means that the entry or exit of firms does not affect resource prices or, consequently, shift the average-total-cost or marginal curves of individual firms.

The Goal of Our Analysis

The basic conclusion we want to explain is this: After all long-run adjustments are completed, product price will be exactly equal to, and production will occur at, each firm's minimum average total cost.

This conclusion follows from two basic facts: (1) Firms seek profits and avoid losses, and (2) under pure competition, firms are free to enter and leave an industry. If market price in the short run exceeds average total costs, the resulting economic profits will attract new firms to the industry, but this industry expansion will increase supply until price is brought back down to equality with minimum average total cost in the long run. Conversely, if price in the short run is less than average total cost, resulting losses will cause firms to leave the industry in the long run. As they leave, total supply will decline, bringing the price back up to equality with minimum average total cost.

Long-run Equilibrium

Consider the average firm in a purely competitive industry that is initially in long-run equilibrium. This firm is represented in Figure 8-8(a), where MR = MC and price and minimum average total cost are equal at $50. Economic profit here is zero; the industry is in equilibrium and there is no tendency for firms to enter or to leave. The $50 market price is determined in Figure 8-8(b) by market demand D_1 and supply S_1. (S_1 is a short-run supply curve; we will develop the long-run industry supply curve in our discussion.)

As shown on the quantity axes of the two graphs, equilibrium output in the industry is 100,000, while equilibrium output for the single firm is 100. If all firms in the industry are identical, there must be 1000 firms (= 100,000/100).

| FIGURE 8-8 | Temporary Profits and the Re-establishment of Long-run Equilibrium in a Representative Firm (Panel A) and the Industry (Panel B) |

A favourable shift in demand (D_1 to D_2) will upset the original industry equilibrium and produce economic profits. But those profits will cause new firms to enter the industry, increasing supply (S_1 to S_2) and lowering product price until economic profits are once again zero.

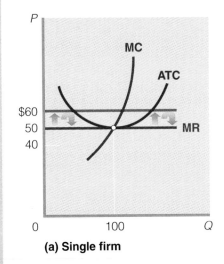

(a) Single firm

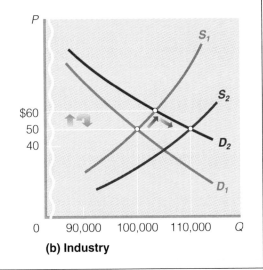

(b) Industry

ENTRY ELIMINATES ECONOMIC PROFITS

Let's upset the long-run equilibrium in Figure 8-8 and see what happens. Suppose a change in consumer tastes increases product demand from D_1 to D_2. Price will rise to $60, as determined at the intersection of D_2 and S_1, and the firm's marginal-revenue curve will shift upward to $60. This $60 price exceeds the firm's average total cost of $50 at output 100, creating an economic profit of $10 per unit. This economic profit will lure new firms into the industry. Some entrants will be newly created firms; others will shift from less prosperous industries.

As firms enter, the market supply of the product increases, pushing the product price below $60. Economic profits persist, and entry continues until short-run supply increases to S_2. Market price falls to $50, as does marginal revenue for the firm. Price and minimum average total cost are again equal at $50. The economic profits caused by the boost in demand have been eliminated, and, as a result, the previous incentive for more firms to enter the industry has disappeared. Long-run equilibrium has been restored.

Observe in Figure 8-8(a) and (b) that total quantity supplied is now 110,000 units and each firm is producing 100 units. Now 1100 firms rather than the original 1000 populate the industry. Economic profits have attracted 100 more firms.

EXIT ELIMINATES LOSSES

Now let's consider a shift in the opposite direction. We begin in Figure 8-9(b) with curves S_1 and D_1 setting the same initial long-run equilibrium situation as in our previous analysis, including the $50 price.

Suppose consumer demand declines from D_1 to D_3. This decline forces the market price and marginal revenue down to $40, making production unprofitable at the minimum ATC of $50. In time the resulting losses will induce firms to leave the industry. Their owners will seek a normal profit elsewhere rather than accept the below-normal profits (loss) now confronting them. Other firms will simply go out of business. As this exodus of firms proceeds, however, industry supply in the long run decreases, pushing the price up from $40 toward $50. Losses continue and more firms leave the industry until the supply curve shifts to S_3. Once this happens, price is again $50, just equal to the minimum average total cost. Losses have been eliminated and long-run equilibrium is restored.

FIGURE 8-9	Temporary Losses and the Re-establishment of Long-run Equilibrium in a Representative Firm (Panel A) and the Industry (Panel B)

An unfavourable shift in demand (D_1 to D_3) will upset the original industry equilibrium and produce losses, but those losses will cause firms to leave the industry, decreasing supply (S_1 to S_3) and increasing product price until all losses have disappeared.

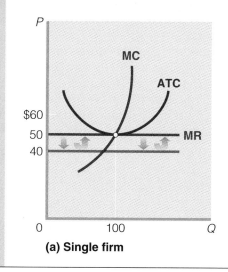

(a) Single firm

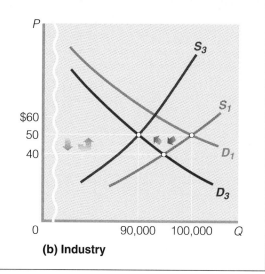

(b) Industry

In Figure 8-9(b), total quantity supplied is now 90,000 units and each firm is producing 100 units. Only 900 firms, not the original 1000, populate the industry. Losses have forced 100 firms out.

We have now reached an intermediate goal: Our analysis verifies that competition, reflected in the entry and exit of firms, eliminates economic profits or losses by adjusting price to equal minimum long-run average total cost. In addition, this competition forces firms to select output levels at which average total cost is minimized.

Long-run Supply for a Constant-cost Industry

long-run supply curve
A curve that shows the prices at which a purely competitive industry will make various quantities of the product available in the long run.

Although our analysis has dealt with the long run, we have noted that the market supply curves in Figures 8-8(b) and 8-9(b) are short-run curves. What then is the character of the **long-run supply curve** of a competitive industry? The analysis points us toward an answer. The crucial factor here is the effect, if any, that changes in the number of firms in the industry will have on costs of the individual firms in the industry. The long-run supply curve is the horizontal summation of long-run equilibrium points.

CONSTANT-COST INDUSTRY

constant-cost industry
An industry in which the entry of new firms has no effect on resource prices and thus no effect on production costs.

In our analysis of long-run competitive equilibrium we assumed that the industry under discussion was a **constant-cost industry**, which means that industry expansion or contraction will not affect resource prices or production costs. Graphically, it means that the entry or exit of firms does not shift the long-run ATC curves of individual firms. This is the case when the industry's demand for factors of production is small in relation to the total demand for those resources; the industry can expand or contract without significantly affecting factor prices and costs.

PERFECTLY ELASTIC LONG-RUN SUPPLY

<www.theshortrun.com/
classroom/glossary/macro/
marketequilibrium.html>
Market equilibrium

What does the long-run supply curve of a constant-cost industry look like? The answer is contained in our previous analysis. There we saw that the entry and exit of firms changes industry output but always brings the product price back to its original level, where it is just equal to the constant minimum ATC. Specifically, we discovered that the industry would supply 90,000, 100,000, or 110,000 units of output, all at a price of $50 per unit. In other words, the long-run supply of a constant-cost industry is perfectly elastic.

This is demonstrated graphically in Figure 8-10, which uses data from Figures 8-8 and 8-9. Suppose industry demand is originally D_1, industry output is Q_1 (100,000 units), and product price is P_1 ($50). This situation, from Figure 8-8, is one of long-run equilibrium. We saw that when demand increases to D_2, upsetting this equilibrium, the resulting economic profits attract new firms. Because this is a constant-cost industry, entry continues and industry output expands until the price is driven back down to the level of the unchanged minimum ATC, which is at price P_2 ($50) and output Q_2 (110,000).

From Figure 8-9, we saw that a decline in market demand from D_1 to D_3 causes an exit of firms and ultimately restores equilibrium at price P_3 ($50) and output Q_3 (90,000 units). The points Z_1, Z_2, and Z_3 in Figure 8-10 represent these three price–quantity combinations. A line or curve connecting all such points shows the various price–quantity combinations that firms would produce if they had enough time to make all desired adjustments to changes in demand. This line or curve is the industry's long-run supply curve. In a constant-cost industry this curve (straight line) is horizontal, as in Figure 8-10, thus representing perfectly elastic supply.

Long-run Supply for an Increasing-cost Industry

increasing-cost industry
An industry in which the entry of new firms raises the prices for resources and thus increases their production costs.

Constant-cost industries are a special case. Most industries are **increasing-cost industries**, in which firms' ATC curves shift upward as the industry expands and downward as the industry contracts. Usually, the entry of new firms will increase factor prices, particularly so in industries using specialized inputs whose supplies are not readily increased in response to an increase in input

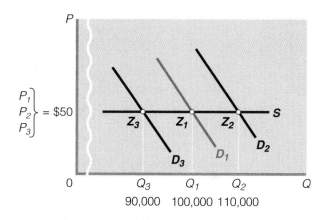

| FIGURE 8-10 | The Long-run Supply Curve for a Constant-cost Industry Is Horizontal |

Because the entry or exit of firms does not affect resource prices or, therefore, unit costs, an increase in demand (D_1 to D_2) causes an expansion in industry output (Q_1 to Q_2) but no alteration in price ($50). Similarly, a decrease in demand (D_1 to D_3) causes a contraction of output (Q_1 to Q_3) but no change in price. This means that the long-run industry supply curve (S) is horizontal through points Z_1, Z_2, and Z_3.

demand. Higher input prices result in higher long-run average total costs for all firms in the industry. These higher costs cause upward shifts in each firm's long-run ATC curve.

Thus, when an increase in product demand results in economic profits and attracts new firms to an increasing-cost industry, a two-way squeeze works to eliminate those profits. As before, the entry of new firms increases market supply and lowers the market price, but now the entire ATC curve shifts upward. The overall result is a higher-than-original equilibrium price. The industry produces a larger output at a higher product price because the industry expansion has increased factor prices and the minimum average total cost. We know that, in the long run, the product price must cover ATC.

Since greater output will be supplied at a higher price, the long-run industry supply curve is upsloping. Instead of supplying 90,000, 100,000, or 110,000 units at the same price of $50, an increasing-cost industry might supply 90,000 units at $45, 100,000 units at $50, and 110,000 units at $55. A higher price is required to induce more production, because costs per unit of output increase as production rises.

We show this in Figure 8-11. Original market demand is D_1 and industry price and output are P_1 ($50) and Q_1 (100,000 units), respectively, at equilibrium point Y_1. An increase in demand to D_2 upsets this equilibrium and leads to economic profits. New firms enter the industry, increasing both market supply and production costs of individual firms. A new price is established at point Y_2, where P_2 is $55 and Q_2 is 110,000 units.

Conversely, a decline in demand from D_1 to D_3 makes production unprofitable and causes firms to leave the industry. The resulting decline in factor prices reduces the minimum average total cost of production for firms that stay. A new equilibrium price is established at some level below the original price, say, at point Y_3, where P_3 is $45 and Q_3 is 90,000 units. Connecting these three equilibrium positions, we derive the upsloping long-run supply curve S in Figure 8-11.

Long-run Supply for a Decreasing-cost Industry

decreasing-cost industry
An industry in which the entry of firms lowers the prices of resources and thus decreases production costs.

In a **decreasing-cost industry**, a firm experiences lower costs as the industry expands. The personal computer industry is an example. As demand for personal computers increased, new manufacturers of computers entered the industry and greatly increased the input demand for the components used to build them (for example, memory chips, hard drives, monitors, and operating software). The expanded production of those components enabled the producers of those items to achieve

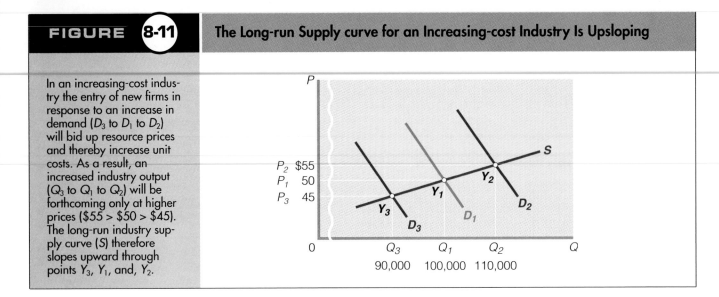

FIGURE 8-11   The Long-run Supply curve for an Increasing-cost Industry Is Upsloping

In an increasing-cost industry the entry of new firms in response to an increase in demand (D_3 to D_1 to D_2) will bid up resource prices and thereby increase unit costs. As a result, an increased industry output (Q_3 to Q_1 to Q_2) will be forthcoming only at higher prices ($\$55 > \$50 > \$45$). The long-run industry supply curve (S) therefore slopes upward through points Y_3, Y_1, and, Y_2.

substantial economies of scale. The decreased production costs of the components reduced their prices, which greatly lowered the computer manufacturers' average costs of production. The supply of personal computers increased by more than demand, and the price of personal computers declined.

We urge you to rework the analysis underlying Figure 8-11 to show that the long-run supply curve of a decreasing-cost industry is downsloping. *(Key Question 6)*

8.6   Pure Competition and Efficiency

Our final goal in this chapter is to investigate the efficiency of pure competition. As shown in **Figure 8-12 (Key Graph)**, in a pure competitive market structure price (and marginal revenue) will settle where it is equal to minimum average total cost: P (and MR) = minimum ATC. Since the marginal-cost curve intersects the average-total-cost curve at its minimum point, marginal cost and average total cost are equal: MC = minimum ATC. Thus, in long-run equilibrium a multiple equality exists: P (and MR) = MC = minimum ATC.

This triple equality tells us that although a competitive firm may realize economic profit or loss in the short run, it will earn only a normal profit by producing in accordance with the MR (= P) = MC rule in the long run. Also, this triple equality suggests certain conclusions of great social significance concerning the efficiency of a purely competitive economy.

Economists agree that, subject to qualifications discussed in later chapters, an idealized purely competitive economy leads to the most efficient use of society's scarce resources. A competitive market economy uses society's limited resources in a way that maximizes the satisfaction of consumers. As we demonstrated in Chapter 2, efficient use of limited resources requires both productive efficiency and allocative efficiency.

productive efficiency
The production of a good or service in the least costly way.

allocative efficiency
When resources are apportioned among firms and industries to obtain the mix of products and services most wanted by consumers.

Productive efficiency requires that goods and services be produced in the least costly way. **Allocative efficiency** requires that resources be apportioned among firms and industries so as to yield the mix of products and services most wanted by consumers. Allocative efficiency is achieved when it is impossible to change the composition of total output and achieve a net gain for society. Let's look at how productive and allocative efficiency are achieved under purely competitive conditions.

Key Graph

FIGURE 8-12 The Long-run Equilibrium Position of a Competitive Firm: P = MC = Minimum ATC

The equality of price and minimum average total cost indicates that the firm is using the most efficient technology, is charging the lowest price, *P*, and is producing the greatest output, *Q*, consistent with its costs. The equality of price and marginal cost indicates that resources are being allocated in accordance with consumer preferences.

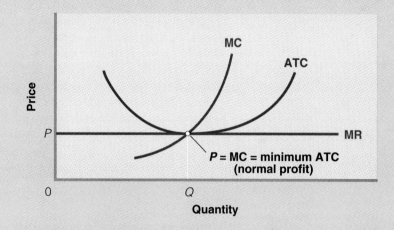

Quick Quiz

1. We know this firm is a price-taker because
   a. its MC curve slopes upward.
   b. its ATC curve is U-shaped.
   c. its MR curve is horizontal.
   d. MC and ATC are equal at the profit-maximizing output.

2. This firm's MC curve is rising because
   a. it is a price-taker.
   b. of the law of diminishing marginal utility.
   c. wage rates rise as output expands.
   d. of the law of diminishing marginal returns.

3. At this firm's profit-maximizing output
   a. total revenue equals total cost.
   b. it is earning an economic profit.
   c. allocative, but not necessarily productive, efficiency is achieved.
   d. productive, but not necessarily allocative, efficiency is achieved.

4. The equality of *P*, MC, and minimum ATC
   a. occurs only in constant-cost industries.
   b. encourages entry of new firms.
   c. means that the right goods are being produced in the right ways.
   d. results in a zero accounting profit.

ANSWERS 1. c; 2. d; 3. a; 4. c

Productive Efficiency: *P* = Minimum ATC

In the long run, pure competition forces firms to produce at the minimum average total cost of production and to charge a price that is just consistent with that cost, a highly favourable situation for the consumer. Unless firms use the best-available (least-cost) production methods and combinations of inputs, they will not survive. Stated differently, the minimum amount of resources will be used to produce any particular output. Let's suppose that output is cucumbers.

In the final equilibrium position shown in Figure 8-9(a), each firm in the cucumber industry is producing 100 units (say, pickup truckloads) of output by using $5000 (equal to average total cost of $50 $\times$ 100 units) worth of resources. If one firm produced that same output at a total cost of, say, $7000, its resources would be used inefficiently. Society would be faced with a net loss of $2000 worth of alternative products. In pure competition this firm's loss of $2000 would require it either to reduce its costs or go out of business.

Note, too, that consumers benefit from productive efficiency by paying the lowest product price with the prevailing technology and cost conditions.

Allocative Efficiency: *P* = MC

Productive efficiency alone does not ensure the efficient allocation of resources. Least-cost production must be used to provide society with the right goods—the goods that consumers want most. Before we can show that the competitive market system does just that, we must discuss the social meaning of product prices. There are two critical elements here.

1. The money price of any product is society's measure of the relative worth of an additional unit of that product—for example, cucumbers. So, the price of a unit of cucumbers is the marginal benefit derived from that unit of the product.

2. Similarly, recalling the idea of opportunity cost, we see that the marginal cost of an additional unit of a product measures the value of the other goods sacrificed to obtain it. In producing cucumbers, resources are drawn away from producing other goods. The marginal cost of producing a unit of cucumbers measures society's sacrifice of those other goods.

To understand why *P* = MC defines allocative efficiency, let's first look at situations where that is not the case.

UNDERPRODUCTION: *P* > MC

In pure competition, a firm will realize the maximum possible profit only by producing where price equals marginal cost (Figure 8-12). Producing fewer cucumbers such that MR (and thus *P*) exceeds MC yields less than maximum profit. It also entails, from society's viewpoint, an underallocation of resources to this product. The fact that price still exceeds marginal cost indicates that society values additional units of cucumbers more highly than the alternative products the resources could otherwise produce.

To illustrate, if the price or marginal benefit of a unit of cucumbers is $100 and its marginal cost is $50, producing an additional unit of cucumbers will increase total well-being by $50. Society will gain cucumbers valued at $100, while the alternative products sacrificed by allocating more resources to cucumbers would be valued at only $50. Whenever society can gain something valued at $100 by giving up something valued at $50, the initial allocation of resources must have been inefficient.

OVERPRODUCTION: *P* < MC

For similar reasons, the production of cucumbers should not go beyond the output at which price equals marginal cost. To produce where MC exceeds MR (and thus *P*) would yield less than the maximum profit for the producer and, from the viewpoint of society, would result in an overallocation of resources to cucumbers. Producing cucumbers at the level where marginal cost exceeds price (or marginal benefit) means that society is producing cucumbers by sacrificing alternative goods that it values more highly.

For example, if the price of a unit of cucumbers is $75 and its marginal cost is $100, then the production of one less unit of cucumbers would result in a net increase in society's total well-being of $25. Society would lose cucumbers valued at $75, but reallocating the freed resources to their best alternative uses would increase the output of some other good valued at $100. Thus, the original allocation of resources must have been inefficient.

EFFICIENT ALLOCATION

In pure competition, profit-motivated firms produce each good or service to the point where price (marginal benefit) and marginal cost are equal, resulting in an efficient allocation of society's resources. Each item is being produced to the point at which the value of the last unit is equal to the value of the alternative goods sacrificed by its production. To alter the production of cucumbers would reduce consumer satisfaction. *(Key Question 7)*

DYNAMIC ADJUSTMENTS

A further attribute of purely competitive markets is their ability to restore efficiency when disrupted by changes in the economy. A change in consumer tastes, resource supplies, or technology will automatically set in motion the appropriate realignments of resources. For example, suppose that cucumbers and pickles become dramatically more popular. First, the price of cucumbers will increase so that, at current output, the price of cucumbers will exceed its marginal cost. At this point efficiency will be lost, but the higher price will create economic profits in the cucumber industry and stimulate its expansion. The profitability of cucumbers will permit firms in the industry to bid factors of production away from now less pressing uses, say watermelons. Expansion of the industry will end only when the price of cucumbers and its marginal cost are equal—that is, when allocative efficiency has been restored.

Allocative Efficiency and Consumer and Producer Surplus

Recall that in Chapter 6 we introduced the concept of consumer surplus, the difference between what the consumer is willing to pay for a good and service, and what he or she actually pays. For example, you are very thirsty and thus willing to pay $3 for a can of orange juice. If the market price of a can of orange juice is $2, you are the beneficiary of $1 worth of consumer surplus.

The idea of producer surplus is somewhat similar to consumer surplus. **Producer surplus** is the difference producers receive for a product or service less the marginal cost of producing it. You will recall that the firm's supply curve is its marginal cost curve over and above its minimal AVC. As we did in Chapter 6 to introduce consumer surplus, we use a hypothetical market for jeans, but this time we focus on the supply side. Figure 8-13 depicts the supply curve for jeans with the same market price of $50 and quantity of Q^*. Analogous to consumers willing to pay different prices for jeans, producers are willing to supply jeans at different prices, depending on their costs.

At $30 suppliers are not willing to offer any jeans. But at any price above $30 and below $50 per pair of jeans, there is some producer surplus. For example, if Acme Corporation is willing to offer Q_1 of jeans at $40, but the market price is $50, the company would realize a producer surplus of $10 per pair of jeans. At a $50 market price producers collectively will realize a producer surplus represented by the blue triangle in Figure 8-13. The shaded area under the supply curve represents the marginal cost of producing jeans.

Efficiency Restated

Figure 8-14 brings together Figures 8-13 and 6-3. It depicts a market equilibrium in a purely competitive industry. What is apparent is that at the equilibrium price and quantity, the sum of consumer and producer surplus is maximized. Consumers are getting just the number of jeans they

producer surplus
The difference between what producers receive for a product or service and the marginal cost of producing it.

FIGURE 8-13   Producer Supply and Producer Surplus

At a price of $30 or less, no jeans are supplied. If Acme can supply jeans at $40 a pair but is able to sell them at $50, Acme realizes a $10 producer surplus on each pair. Collectively, producers realize a producer surplus represented by the blue triangle, while the grey area under the supply curve represents the total cost of producing jeans.

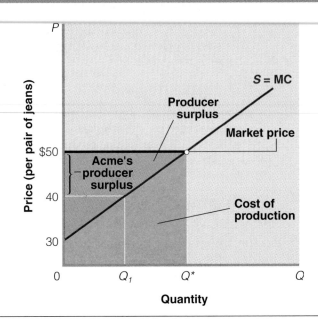

FIGURE 8-14   Allocative Efficiency and the Market for Jeans

Economic resources are used efficiently when the sum of consumer and producer surpluses are maximized. It is also the price and quantity at which MC = MB. Consumer surplus is depicted by the green area below the demand curve. Producer surplus is depicted by the blue area above the supply curve.

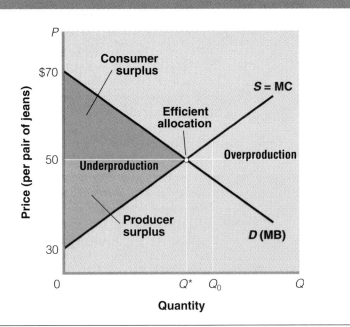

desire and value. Another way of looking at it is that at equilibrium price, the willingness to pay equals the opportunity cost of producing jeans. At less than Q^* fewer jeans and more of some other good, say cotton shirts, are produced that consumers value less than jeans. In a purely competitive industry, the price of jeans will rise, bringing about economic profit, which will induce more firms to produce jeans. The production of more jeans will reduce their price, until marginal cost equals marginal benefit again. The equilibrium quantity in Figure 8-14 reflects economic efficiency. In the terminology of Chapter 2, *productive efficiency* is achieved because competition forces producers to use the best techniques and combinations of factors in producing and selling jeans. Production costs of each level of output are minimized. *Allocative efficiency* is achieved because the correct quantity of output—Q^*—is produced relative to other goods and services. Points on the demand curve in Figure 8-14 measure the marginal benefit (MB) of jeans at each level of output. Points on the supply curve measure the marginal cost (MC) of jeans at each output level. The demand and supply curves intersect at the equilibrium output Q^*, indicating that MB = MC. (For the significance of the MB = MC equality for efficiency, review the discussion relating to Figure 2-2.)

Our analysis of consumer and producer surplus provides another way of thinking about efficiency. Each point on a demand curve identifies not only the marginal benefit of the corresponding unit of output but also the *maximum willingness to pay* for it. Willingness to pay derives from the benefit that a product provides. Similarly, each point on the supply curve identifies not only the marginal cost of a good but also the *minimum acceptable price* for the good. To stay profitable, sellers must receive minimum prices that "cover" their marginal costs.

In Figure 8-14 the maximum willingness to pay for each pair of jeans up to Q^* exceeds the corresponding minimum acceptable price. So each of these jeans adds a positive amount (maximum willingness to pay *minus* minimum acceptable price) to the *total* of consumer and producer surplus. Only at the equilibrium price Q^*, where maximum willingness to pay for the last unit equals minimum acceptable price for that unit, does society exhaust all the opportunities to add to combined consumer and producer surplus. So allocative efficiency occurs where "consumer surplus + producer surplus" is at its maximum size.

Other things equal, *competitive markets produce equilibrium prices and quantities that maximize the sum of consumer and producer surplus.* Allocative efficiency occurs at quantity levels where three conditions exist:

- MB = MC (Figure 2-2)

- Maximum willingness to pay = minimum acceptable price

- Combined consumer and producer surplus is at a maximum.

UNDERPRODUCTION AND OVERPRODUCTION

Note in Figure 8-14 that to the left of the equilibrium point, both consumer surplus and producer surplus are diminished. To the left of equilibrium there is underproduction of jeans. The welfare of both consumers and producers would increase if the production of jeans rose. To the left of equilibrium MB > MC, meaning that the cost of additional output is less than the additional benefit to society. Another way of expressing it is that all members of society would be better off, and no one worse off, if the output of jeans rose.

To the right of market equilibrium in Figure 8-14 there is a similar reduction of both consumer surplus and producer surplus. To the right of the equilibrium point, say at Q_0, there is overproduction of jeans. Both consumers and producers gain if production is reduced. To the right of equilibrium MC > MB, meaning that the cost of additional units of jeans is greater than the additional benefit to society. The two small triangles to the right of equilibrium in Figure 8-14 reflect the loss of consumer surplus and producer surplus, respectively.

THE INVISIBLE HAND REVISITED

Finally, the efficient allocation of resources in a purely competitive economy comes about because businesses and resource suppliers seek to further their self-interest. The invisible hand (Chapter 4) is at work in a competitive market system. The competitive system both maximizes profits for producers and maximizes consumer satisfaction. The invisible hand brings the private interests of producers in accord with society's interest in using scarce resources efficiently.

QUICK REVIEW

- In the long run, the entry of firms into an industry will compete away any economic profits, and the exit of firms will eliminate losses so that price and minimum average total cost are equal.

- The long-run supply curves of constant-cost, increasing-cost, and decreasing-cost industries are horizontal, upsloping, and downsloping, respectively.

- In purely competitive markets both productive efficiency (price equals minimum average total cost) and allocative efficiency (price equals marginal cost) are achieved in the long run.

- Producer surplus is the difference between the minimum price that a producer is willing to accept for a product and the higher price actually received.

- At the equilibrium price and quantity in competitive markets, marginal benefit equals marginal cost, maximum willingness to pay equals minimum acceptable price, and the total of consumer surplus and producer surplus is maximized. These individual conditions each define allocative efficiency.

THE LASTword | Efficiency and the Canadian Health Care System

The Canadian national health care system has been under strain in the last decade as patients have had to endure longer and longer line-ups for the medical services they need. Although the Canadian health care sector does not function in a competitive market structure, solutions have been put forward to improve the efficiency and delivery time of health-care services.

Productive efficiency implies getting the most output for the least cost. Another way of expressing productive efficiency is getting the most output from available resources. Although it is very difficult to accurately measure the efficiency of a country's national health care system, there are some measures that can be used as a rough proxy. One such proxy is the infant mortality rate per 1000 live births. According to this measure, some countries have much more efficient health care sectors than others. The Organization for Eco-

nomic Cooperation and Development (OECD) data shown here presents some interesting contrasts. The Czech Republic spends under $1000 per citizen and has 4.6 deaths per 1000 live births. (All spending is in U.S. dollars.) The United States spends over $4000 per citizen, but has a relatively high infant mortality rate of 7.2. This suggests the Czech health care system is more efficient than the American system. Indeed, the American system looks downright inefficient compared to many national health care systems, ranking a poor 24th even though its

per capita spending on health care is the highest in the world.

Canada's health care system does not fare much better when we use the infant mortality rate as a measure. It ranks only 17th in the world, though Canada has the world's 4th highest per capita expenditure on health care. Contrast this with Spain, which ranks 13th in the world in infant mortality despite being only the 22nd highest spender at about $1200 per person. Judging by the infant mortality rate, Iceland may have the most efficient health care system on the globe.

With an expenditure of $1750 per citizen, Iceland attains the lowest infant mortality rate in the world, with just 2.4 deaths per 1000 live births.

Of course, to measure the efficiency of a country's health care sector solely on the basis of the infant mortality rate is crude. We would also have to consider other measures, such as life expectancy of the average citizen in the country. Also missing from the expenditure data is the cost of inputs across countries. It may not be that the citizens of Iceland use less health care inputs than Canadians; they may simply pay lower relative incomes to physicians, nurses, and other health care workers. Moreover, the quality of the service also matters to consumers. A physician may be "very productive" because she sees ten patients in one hour, but these patients may feel dissatisfied if they feel rushed through their visit. On the other hand, if the physician sees only two patients per hour, the patients may be very satisfied with the quality of the care, but may have to book weeks in advance to secure an appointment. Finally, the data presented shed no light on the allocative efficiency question. We don't know which country or countries are allocating resources to reach the efficient level of output.

Proponents of Canada's national health care system suggest that recent dissatisfaction with its performance is attributable to the inadequacy of government resources apportioned to it. Meanwhile, critics emphasize that the efficiency of the Canadian health care system is just as important as the amount of money poured into it. They also point out that the lack of competition in the Canadian health care sector contributes to the growing line-ups patients have endured in the last few years. That's another way of saying that the productive efficiency of the Canadian health care system could be improved.

Infant Mortality in OECD Countries, 1999 (Deaths per 1,000 Live Births)

1. Iceland	2.4
2. Sweden	3.4
3. Japan	3.4
4. Finland	3.6
5. Norway	3.9
6. Denmark	4.2
7. France	4.3
8. Austria	4.4
9. Czech Republic	4.6
10. Germany	4.6
11. Switzerland	4.6
12. Luxembourg	4.7
13. Spain	4.9
14. Italy	5.1
15. Netherlands	5.2
16. Belgium	5.3
17. Canada[1]	5.5
18. Ireland	5.5
19. Portugal	5.5
20. Australia	5.7
21. United Kingdom	5.8
22. Greece	5.9
23. New Zealand[1]	6.8
24. United States[2]	7.2
25. Korea[3]	7.7
26. Slovak Republic	8.3
27. Hungary	8.5
28. Poland	8.9
29. Mexico	14.5
30. Turkey	37.5

Notes: 1. 1997; 2. 1998; 3. 1996.
Source: *Health at a Glance*, OECD, Paris, 2001.

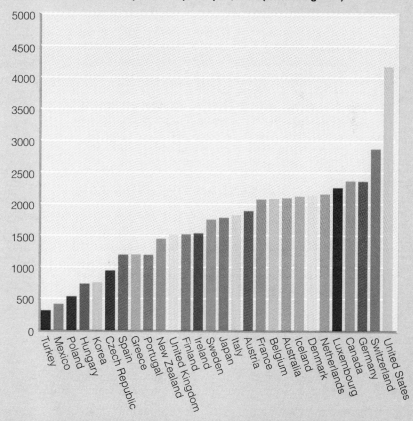

Health expenditure per capita, 1998 (US$ using PPP)

Source: *Health at a Glance*, OECD, Paris, 2001.

CHAPTER SUMMARY

8.1 FOUR MARKET STRUCTURES

- Industries can be grouped into four market structures: (a) pure competition, (b) pure monopoly, (c) monopolistic competition, and (d) oligopoly.

8.2 CHARACTERISTICS OF PURE COMPETITION AND THE FIRM'S DEMAND CURVE

- A purely competitive industry consists of a large number of independent firms producing a standardized product. Pure competition assumes that firms and factors of production are mobile among different industries.

- In a competitive industry, no single firm can influence market price, which means that the firm's demand curve is perfectly elastic and price equals marginal revenue.

8.3 PROFIT MAXIMIZATION IN THE SHORT RUN

- We can analyze short-run profit maximization by a competitive firm by comparing total revenue and total cost or by applying marginal analysis. A firm maximizes its short-run profit by producing the output at which total revenue exceeds total cost by the greatest amount.

- Provided price exceeds minimum average variable cost, a competitive firm maximizes profit or minimizes loss in the short run by producing the output at which price or marginal revenue equals marginal cost. If price is less than average variable cost, the firm minimizes its loss by shutting down. If price is greater than average variable cost but is less than average total cost, the firm minimizes its loss by producing the $P = MC$ output. If price also exceeds average total cost, the firm maximizes its economic profit at the $P = MC$ output.

8.4 MARGINAL COST AND THE SHORT-RUN SUPPLY

- Applying the MR ($= P$) $= MC$ rule at various possible market prices leads to the conclusion that the segment of the firm's short-run marginal-cost curve that lies above the firm's average-variable-cost curve is its short-run supply curve.

8.5 PROFIT MAXIMIZATION IN THE LONG RUN

- In the long run, the market price of a product will equal the minimum average total cost of production. At a higher price, economic profits would cause firms to enter the industry until those profits had been competed away. At a lower price, losses would force the exit of some firms from the industry until the product price rose to equal average total cost.

- The long-run supply curve is horizontal for a constant-cost industry, upsloping for an increasing-cost industry, and downsloping for a decreasing-cost industry.

8.6 PURE COMPETITION AND EFFICIENCY

- The long-run equality of price and minimum average total cost means that competitive firms will use the most efficient technology and charge the lowest price consistent with their production costs.

- The long-run equality of price and marginal cost implies that resources will be allocated in accordance with consumer tastes. The competitive price system will reallocate resources in response to a change in consumer tastes, in technology, or in factor supplies and will thereby maintain allocative efficiency over time.

- Graphically, the combined amount of producer and consumer surplus is represented by the triangle to the left of the intersection of the supply and demand curves that is below the demand curve and above the supply curve. At the equilibrium price and quantity in competitive markets, marginal benefit equals marginal cost, maximum willingness to pay equals minimum acceptable price, and the combined amount of consumer surplus and producer surplus is maximized.

- Output levels that are either less than or greater than the equilibrium output create efficiency losses—reductions in the combined amount of consumer surplus and producer surplus. Underproduction creates efficiency losses because output is not being produced for which maximum willingness to pay exceeds minimum acceptable price. Overproduction creates efficiency losses because output is being produced for which minimum acceptable price exceeds maximum willingness to pay.

TERMS AND CONCEPTS

STUDY QUESTIONS

1. Briefly state the basic characteristics of pure competition, pure monopoly, monopolistic competition, and oligopoly. Under which of these market classifications does each of the following most accurately fit? (a) a supermarket in your home town; (b) the steel industry; (c) a Satskatchewan wheat farm; (d) the chartered bank in which you or your family has an account; (e) the automobile industry. In each case justify your classification.

2. Strictly speaking, pure competition has never existed and probably never will. Then why study it?

3. **KEY QUESTION** Use the following demand schedule to determine total revenue and marginal revenue for each possible level of sales:

Product price	Quantity demanded	Total revenue	Marginal revenue
$2	0	$____	
2	1	____	$____
2	2	____	____
2	3	____	____
2	4	____	____
2	5	____	____

a. What can you conclude about the structure of the industry in which this firm is operating? Explain.

b. Graph the demand, total-revenue, and marginal-revenue curves for this firm.

c. Do the demand and marginal-revenue curves coincide? If so, why? If not, why not?

d. "Marginal revenue is the change in total revenue associated with additional units of output." Explain in words and graphically, using the data in the table.

4. **KEY QUESTION** Assume the following cost data are for a purely competitive producer:

Total product	Average fixed cost	Average variable cost	Average total cost	Marginal cost
0				
1	$60.00	$45.00	$105.00	$45
2	30.00	42.50	72.50	40
3	20.00	40.00	60.00	35
4	15.00	37.50	52.50	30
5	12.00	37.00	49.00	35
6	10.00	37.50	47.50	40
7	8.57	38.57	47.14	45
8	7.50	40.63	48.13	55
9	6.67	43.33	50.00	65
10	6.00	46.50	52.50	75

a. At a product price of $56, will this firm produce in the short run? Why or why not? If it does produce, what will be the profit-maximizing or loss-minimizing output? Explain. What economic profit or loss will the firm realize per unit of output?

b. Answer the questions in 4a assuming product price is $41.

c. Answer the questions in 4a assuming product price is $32.

d. In the table below, complete the short-run supply schedule for the firm (columns 1 and 2) and indicate the profit or loss incurred at each output (column 3).

(1) Price	(2) Quantity supplied, single firm	(3) Profit (+) or loss (−)	(4) Quantity supplied, 1500 firms
$26	____	$____	____
32	____	____	____
38	____	____	____
41	____	____	____
46	____	____	____
56	____	____	____
66	____	____	____

e. Explain: "That segment of a competitive firm's marginal-cost curve that lies above its average-variable-cost curve constitutes the short-run supply curve for the firm." Illustrate graphically.

f. Now assume that there are 1500 identical firms in this competitive industry; that is, that there are 1500 firms, each of which has the cost data shown in the table. Complete the industry supply schedule (column 4).

g. Suppose the market demand data for the product are as follows:

Price	Total quantity demanded
$26	17,000
32	15,000
38	13,500
41	12,000
46	10,500
56	9,500
66	8,000

What will be the equilibrium price? What will be the equilibrium output for the industry? for each firm? What will profit or loss be per unit? per firm? Will this industry expand or contract in the long run?

5. Why is the equality of marginal revenue and marginal cost essential for profit maximization in all market structures? Explain why price can be substituted for marginal revenue in the MR = MC rule when an industry is purely competitive.

6. **KEY QUESTION**   Using diagrams for both the industry and a representative firm, illustrate competitive long-run equilibrium. Assuming constant costs, employ these diagrams to show how (a) an increase and (b) a decrease in market demand will upset that long-run equilibrium. Trace graphically and describe in words the adjustment processes by which long-run equilibrium is restored. Now rework your analysis for increasing-cost and decreasing-cost industries and compare the three long-run supply curves.

7. **KEY QUESTION**   In long-run equilibrium, P = minimum ATC = MC. Of what significance for economic efficiency is the equality of P and minimum ATC? the equality of P and MC? Distinguish between productive efficiency and allocative efficiency in your answer.

8. Distinguish between the terms "maximum willingness to pay" and "minimum acceptable price." How do they relate, respectively, to consumer and producer surplus?

9. "Freely made exchanges in competitive markets benefit both buyers and sellers." Use the concepts of consumer surplus and producer surplus to verify this statement.

10. Draw a supply and demand graph and identify the areas of consumer surplus and producer surplus. Given the demand curve, what impact will an increase in supply have on the amount of consumer surplus shown in your diagram? Explain why.

11. Use the ideas of marginal benefit and marginal cost *and* the ideas of consumer surplus and producer surplus to explain why economists say competitive markets are efficient. Why are below- or above-equilibrium levels of output inefficient, according to these two sets of ideas?

12. **(The Last Word)** Besides the infant mortality rate, what other indicator can be used to measure productive efficiency of the Canadian health care system? Is there a trade-off between the quantity and quality of health care services?

INTERNET APPLICATION QUESTIONS

1. Suppose that you operate a purely competitive firm that buys and sells foreign currencies. Also suppose that yesterday, your business activity consisted of buying 100,000 Swiss francs at the market exchange rate and selling them for a 3 percent commission. Go to the McConnell-Brue-Barbiero Web site (Chapter 8) to get the most recent exchange rate. What was your total revenue in Canadian dollars yesterday? (Be sure to include your commission.) Why would your profit for the day be considerably less than this total revenue?

2. In a purely competitive market, individual firms produce homogeneous products and exert no significant control over product price. Go to the McConnell-Brue-Barbiero Web site (Chapter 8) to access the Alberta government site, which provides a brief overview of how a commodity exchange functions and has links to the main commodity exchanges in North America. Also, visit the Winnipeg Commodity Exchange and select "Daily Market Summary." Which of the main crops has had the largest price movement and why?

Pure Monopoly

We turn now from pure competition to pure monopoly, which is at the opposite end of the spectrum of market structures listed in Table 8-1. You deal with monopolies—sole sellers of products and services—more often than you might think. When you see the logo for Microsoft's Windows on your computer, you are dealing with a monopoly. When you purchase certain prescription drugs, you may be buying monopolized products. When you make a local telephone call, turn on your lights, or subscribe to cable TV, you may be patronizing a monopoly, depending on your location.

What precisely do we mean by *pure monopoly* and what conditions allow it to arise and survive? How does a pure monopolist determine its profit-maximizing price and output quantity? Does a pure monopolist achieve the efficiencies associated with pure competition? If not, what should the government do about it? A simplified model of pure monopoly will help us answer these questions.

9.1   Characteristics of Pure Monopoly

pure monopoly
An industry in which one firm is the sole producer or seller of a product or service for which there are no close substitutes.

Pure monopoly exists when a single firm is the sole producer of a product or service for which there are no close substitutes. Here are the main characteristics of pure monopoly.

- **Single seller**   A pure monopoly is an industry in which a single firm is the sole producer or seller of a specific good or the sole supplier of a service.

- **No close substitutes**   A pure monopoly's product is unique in that there are no close substitutes.

- **Price-maker**   The pure monopolist controls the total quantity supplied and thus has considerable control over price; it is a *price-maker*. The pure monopolist confronts the usual downward-sloping product demand curve. It can change its product price by changing the quantity of the product it supplies.

- **Blocked entry**   A pure monopolist has no competitors because certain barriers keep potential competitors from entering the industry. Those barriers may be economic, technological, legal, or of some other type, but entry is totally blocked in pure monopoly.

A pure monopoly exists when a single firm is the sole producer of a product or service for which there are no close substitutes.

Examples of Monopoly

Examples of *pure* monopoly are relatively rare in Canada, but there are many examples of less pure forms. In many cities, government-owned or government-regulated public utilities—natural gas and electric companies, the water company, the cable TV company, and the local telephone company—may be monopolies or virtually so. In some Canadian markets, competition has been introduced for some of these traditional monopolies. Many urban areas now have more than one gas supplier to choose from. Rapid technological change has dramatically altered the delivery of communications services, effectively eliminating what was a virtual monopoly by Bell Canada. In some urban markets, such as Toronto and Montreal, Sprint now competes with Bell Canada in the local telephone market. Wireless telephone services by newcomers Telus and Fido have further eroded Bell's monopoly position in local markets. Ontario and Alberta have moved towards deregulating their electricity markets, although the public furor that this has caused has delayed full deregulation.

Professional sports teams are, in a sense, monopolies because they are the sole suppliers of specific services in large geographic areas. With a few exceptions, a single major-league team in each sport serves each large Canadian city. If you want to see a live major-league baseball game in Toronto, you must patronize the Blue Jays. Other geographic monopolies exist. For example, a small town may be served by only one airline or railroad. In a small, isolated community, the local chartered bank, movie theatre, or bookstore may approximate a monopoly.

Of course, some competition almost always exists. Satellite television is a substitute for cable, and amateur softball is a substitute for professional baseball. The Linux operating system can substitute for Windows. But such substitutes are typically either more costly or in some way less appealing.

<money.york.pa.us/Articles/Microsoft.htm>
Predatory Pricing: Microsoft's Modus Operandi

Dual Objectives of the Study of Monopoly

We want to examine pure monopoly not only for its own sake but also because such a study will help you understand the more common market structures of monopolistic competition and oligopoly, to be discussed in Chapter 10. These two market structures combine, in differing degrees, characteristics of pure competition and pure monopoly.

Barriers to Entry

barriers to entry
Anything that artificially prevents the entry of firms into an industry.

The factors that prohibit firms from entering an industry are called **barriers to entry**. In pure monopoly, strong barriers to entry effectively block all potential competition. Somewhat weaker barriers may permit oligopoly, a market structure dominated by a few firms. Still weaker barriers may permit the entry of a fairly large number of competing firms, giving rise to monopolistic competition. The absence of any effective entry barriers permits the entry of a very large number of firms, which provides the basis of pure competition. So, the existence or absence of barriers to entry is pertinent not only to the extreme case of pure monopoly but also to other market structures.

ECONOMIES OF SCALE

Modern technology in some industries is such that economies of scale—declining average total cost with added firm size—are extensive. So, a firm's long-run average-cost schedule will decline over a wide range of output. Given market demand, only a few large firms or, in the extreme, only a single large firm, can achieve low average total costs.

Figure 9-1 indicates economies of scale over a wide range of outputs. If total consumer demand is within that output range, then only a single producer can satisfy demand at least cost. Note, for example, that a monopolist can produce 200 units at a per-unit cost of $10 and a total cost of $2000. If there are two firms in the industry and each produces 100 units, the unit cost is $15 and total cost rises to $3000 (= 200 units × $15). A still more competitive situation with four firms each producing 50 units would boost unit and total cost to $20 and $4000, respectively. Conclusion: When long-run ATC is declining, only a single producer, a monopolist, can produce any particular output at minimum total cost.

If a pure monopoly exists in such an industry, economies of scale will serve as an entry barrier and will protect the monopolist from competition. New firms that try to enter the industry as small-scale producers cannot realize the cost economies of the monopolist and therefore cannot obtain the normal profits necessary for survival or growth. A new firm might try to enter the industry as a large-scale producer so as to achieve the necessary economies of scale, but the massive plant facilities needed would require huge amounts of financing, which a new and untried enterprise would find difficult to secure. In most cases the financial obstacles and risks to starting big are prohibitive, which explains why efforts to enter such industries as automobiles, computer operating software, commercial aircraft, and basic steel are rarely successful.

In the extreme circumstance in which the market demand curve cuts the long-run ATC curve where average total costs are still declining, the single firm is called a *natural monopoly*. It might seem that a natural monopolist's lower unit cost would enable it to charge a lower price than if the

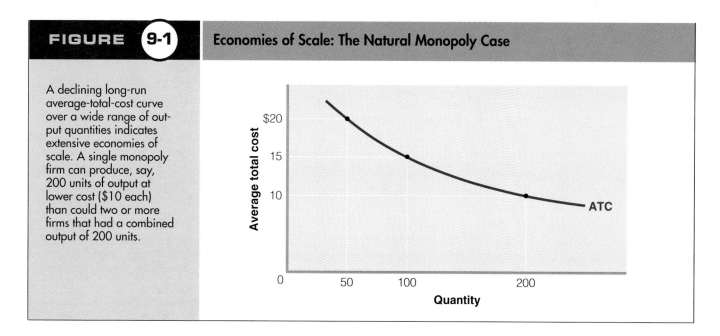

FIGURE 9-1

Economies of Scale: The Natural Monopoly Case

A declining long-run average-total-cost curve over a wide range of output quantities indicates extensive economies of scale. A single monopoly firm can produce, say, 200 units of output at lower cost ($10 each) than could two or more firms that had a combined output of 200 units.

industry were more competitive. But that won't necessarily happen. A pure monopolist may, instead, set its price far above ATC and obtain substantial economic profit. In that event, the cost advantage of a natural monopolist would accrue to the monopolist as profit and not as lower prices to consumers. That is why the government regulates some natural monopolies, specifying the price they may charge. We will say more about that later.

LEGAL BARRIERS TO ENTRY: PATENTS AND LICENCES

Government also creates legal barriers to entry by awarding patents and licences.

<www.aamc.org/newsroom/ reporter/feb2000/gene.htm> Does the gene patenting stampede threaten science?

Patents   A *patent* is the exclusive right of an inventor to use, or to allow another to use, her or his invention. Patent laws protect the inventor from rivals who would use the invention without having shared in the effort and expense of developing it. Patents thus provide the inventor with a monopoly position for the life of the patent. The world's nations have agreed on a uniform patent length of 17 years from the time of application. Patents have figured prominently in the growth of modern-day giants such as IBM, Microsoft, Kodak, Xerox, Bombardier, General Electric, and Nortel.

Research and development (R&D) is what leads to most patentable inventions and products. Firms that gain monopoly power through their own research or by purchasing the patents of others can use patents to strengthen their market position. The profit from one patent can finance the research required to develop new patentable products. In the pharmaceutical industry, patents on prescription drugs have produced large monopoly profits that have helped finance the discovery of new patentable medicines. So, monopoly power achieved through patents may well be self-sustaining, even though patents eventually expire and generic drugs then compete with the original brand.

Licences   Government may also limit entry into an industry or occupation through *licensing*. At the national level, the Canadian Radio-Television Telecommunications Commission (CRTC) licenses a limited number of radio and television stations in each geographic area. In many large cities one of a limited number of municipal licences is required to drive a taxicab. The consequent restriction of the supply of cabs creates economic profit for cab owners and drivers. New cabs cannot enter the industry to force prices and profit lower. In a few instances the government might license itself to provide some product and thereby create a public monopoly. For example, in some provinces, only province-owned retail outlets can sell liquor. Similarly, many provinces have licensed themselves to run lotteries.

OWNERSHIP OR CONTROL OF ESSENTIAL RESOURCES

A monopolist can use private property as an obstacle to potential rivals. For example, a firm that owns or controls a resource essential to the production process can prohibit the entry of rival firms. At one time the International Nickel Company of Canada (now called Inco) controlled 90 percent of the world's known nickel reserves. A municipal sand and gravel firm may own all the nearby deposits of sand and gravel. And it is very difficult for new sports leagues to be created because existing professional sports leagues have contracts with the best players and have long-term leases on the major stadiums and arenas.

PRICING AND OTHER STRATEGIC BARRIERS TO ENTRY

Even if a firm is not protected from entry by, say, extensive economies of scale or ownership of essential resources, entry may effectively be blocked by the way the monopolist responds to attempts by rivals to enter the industry. Confronted with a new entrant, the monopolist may create an entry barrier by slashing its price, stepping up its advertising, or taking other strategic action to make it difficult for the entrant to succeed. In 2000 an American federal court ruled that Microsoft had engaged in illegal actions to attempt to drive Netscape from the Internet browser market. Microsoft developed its own browser, Internet Explorer, and gave it away free. It also provided price discounts on its Windows operating system to computer manufacturers that featured Microsoft's Internet Explorer rather than Netscape's Navigator.

Monopoly Demand

Now that we have explained the sources of monopoly, we will build a model of pure monopoly so that we can analyze its price and output decisions. Let's start by making three assumptions:

1. Patents, economies of scale, or resource ownership secure our monopolist's status.

2. Government does not regulate the firm.

3. The firm is a single-price monopolist; it charges the same price for all units of output.

The crucial difference between a pure monopolist and seller in pure competition lies on the demand side of the market. The seller in a competitive market faces a perfectly elastic demand at the price determined by market supply and demand. It is a price-taker that can sell as much or as little as it wants at the going market price.

The demand curve for the monopolist is very different from that of a firm in pure competition. Because the pure monopolist *is* the industry, its demand curve is *the market demand curve,* which is downward-sloping. Columns 1 and 2 in Table 9-1 illustrate this; note that quantity demanded increases as price decreases.

In Chapter 8 we drew separate demand curves for the purely competitive industry and for a single firm in such an industry; only a single demand curve is needed in pure monopoly. The firm and the industry are one and the same. We have graphed part of the demand data in Table 9-1 as demand curve D in Figure 9-2. This is the monopolist's demand curve *and* the market demand curve. The downward-sloping demand curve has three implications that are essential to understanding the monopoly model.

| TABLE 9-1 | Revenue and Cost Data of a Pure Monopolist |

REVENUE DATA				COST DATA			
(1) Quantity of output (Q)	(2) Price (average revenue) (P)	(3) Total revenue (TR = P × Q)	(4) Marginal revenue MR = $\frac{\Delta TR}{\Delta Q}$	(5) Average total cost (ATC)	(6) Total cost Q × ATC (TC)	(7) Marginal cost (MC)	(8) Profit (+) or loss (−)
0	$172	$ 0			$ 100		$−100
1	162	162	$162	$190.00	190	$ 90	− 28
2	152	304	142	135.00	270	80	+ 34
3	142	426	122	113.33	340	70	+ 86
4	132	528	102	100.00	400	60	+128
5	*122*	*610*	*82*	*94.00*	*470*	*70*	*+140*
6	112	672	62	91.67	550	80	+122
7	102	714	42	91.43	640	90	+ 74
8	92	736	22	93.75	750	110	− 14
9	82	738	2	97.78	880	130	−142
10	72	720	−18	103.00	1030	150	−310

1. MARGINAL REVENUE IS LESS THAN PRICE

The monopolist's downward-sloping demand curve means that it can increase sales only by charging a lower price. Consequently marginal revenue is less than price (average revenue) for every level of output except the first. Why? The reason is that the lower price applies not only to the extra output sold but also to all prior units of output. Each additional unit of output sold increases total revenue by an amount equal to its own price less the sum of the price cuts that apply to all prior units of output.

Figure 9-2 confirms this point. We have highlighted two price–quantity combinations from the monopolist's demand curve. The monopolist can sell one more unit at $132 than it can at $142 and that way get an additional $132 of revenue. But to sell that fourth unit for $132, the monopolist must also sell the first three units at $132 rather than $142. This $10 reduction in revenue on three units results in a $30 revenue loss. The net difference in total revenue from selling a fourth unit is $102: the $132 gain minus the $30 loss. This net gain of $102—the marginal revenue of the fourth unit—is obviously less than the $132 price of the fourth unit.

Column 4 in Table 9-1 shows that marginal revenue is always less than the corresponding product price in column 2, except for the first unit of output. Because marginal revenue is the change in total revenue associated with each *additional* unit of output, the declining amounts of marginal revenue in column 4 mean that total revenue increases at a diminishing rate (as shown in column 3).

We show the relationship between the monopolist's marginal-revenue curve and total-revenue curve in Figure 9-3. For this figure, we extended the demand and revenue data of columns 1 through 4 in Table 9-1, assuming that successive $10 price cuts each increase sales by one unit. For example, the monopolist can sell 11 units at $62, 12 units at $52, and so on.

Note that the monopolist's MR curve lies below the demand curve, indicating that marginal revenue is less than price at every output quantity but the very first unit. Observe also the special relationship between total revenue and marginal revenue. Because marginal revenue is the change in total revenue, marginal revenue is positive while total revenue is increasing. When total revenue reaches its maximum, marginal revenue is zero. When total revenue is diminishing, marginal revenue is negative.

FIGURE 9-2	Price and Marginal Revenue in Pure Monopoly

A pure monopolist with a downsloping demand curve such as *D* must set a lower price to sell more output. Here, by charging $132 rather than $142, the monopolist sells an extra unit (the fourth unit) and gains $132 from that sale. But from this gain must be subtracted $30, which reflects the $10 less the monopolist charged for each of the first 3 units. Thus, the marginal revenue of the fourth unit is $102 (= $132 − $30), considerably less than its $132 price.

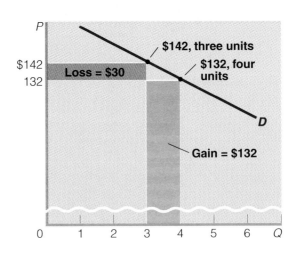

Demand, Marginal Revenue, and Total Revenue for an Imperfectly Competitive Firm

Panel (a): Because an imperfectly competitive firm must lower its price on all units sold in order to increase its sales, the marginal-revenue curve (MR) lies below its downsloping demand curve (D). The elastic and inelastic regions of demand are highlighted. Panel (b): Total revenue (TR) increases at a decreasing rate, reaches maximum, and then declines. Note that in the elastic region, TR is increasing and hence MR is positive. When TR reaches its maximum, MR is zero. In the inelastic region of demand, TR is declining, so MR is negative.

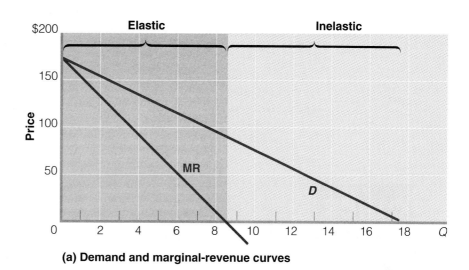

(a) Demand and marginal-revenue curves

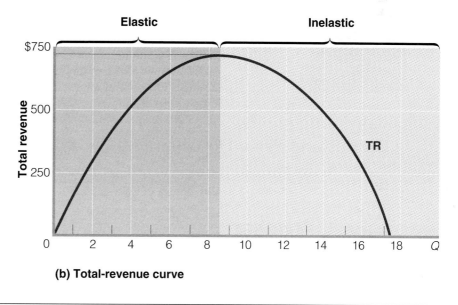

(b) Total-revenue curve

2. THE MONOPOLIST IS A PRICE-MAKER

Except in pure competition, firms face downward-sloping demand curves, whether they operate in pure monopoly, oligopoly, or monopolistic competition. So, firms in imperfectly competitive markets can to one degree or another influence total supply through their own output decisions. In changing market supply, they can also influence product price. Firms with downward-sloping demand curves are *price-makers*.

This fact is most evident in pure monopoly. In deciding what volume of output to produce, the monopolist is also indirectly determining the price it will charge. Through control of output, it can make the price. From columns 1 and 2 in Table 9-1 we find that the monopolist can charge a price of $72 if it produces 10 units, a price of $82 if it produces 9 units, and so forth.

3. THE MONOPOLIST SETS PRICES IN THE ELASTIC REGION OF DEMAND

The total-revenue test for price elasticity of demand is the basis for our third implication. Recall from Chapter 5 that the total-revenue test reveals that when demand is elastic, a decline in price will increase total revenue. Similarly, when demand is inelastic, a decline in price will *reduce* total revenue. Beginning at the top of demand curve D in Figure 9-3(a), observe that as the price declines from $172 to approximately $82, total revenue increases (and marginal revenue, therefore, is positive), which means that demand is elastic in this price range. For price declines below $82, total revenue decreases (marginal revenue is negative), which indicates that demand is inelastic there.

The implication is that a profit-maximizing monopolist will always want to avoid the inelastic segment of its demand curve in favour of some price–quantity combination in the elastic region. Here's why: to get into the inelastic region, the monopolist must lower price and increase output. In the inelastic region a lower price means less total revenue. And increased output always means increased total cost. Less total revenue and higher total cost yield lower profit. (*Key Question 4*)

> **QUICK REVIEW**
>
> • A pure monopolist is the sole supplier of a product or service for which there are no close substitutes.
>
> • A monopoly survives because of entry barriers such as economies of scale, patents and licences, the ownership of essential resources, and strategic actions to exclude rivals.
>
> • The monopolist's demand curve is downsloping, and its marginal-revenue curve lies below its demand curve.
>
> • The downsloping demand curve means that the monopolist is a price-maker.
>
> • The monopolist will operate in the elastic region of demand since it can increase total revenue and reduce total cost by reducing output.

9.2 Output and Price Determination in a Monopoly

At what specific price–quantity combination will a profit-maximizing monopolist choose to operate? To answer this question, we must add production costs to our analysis.

Cost Data

<hadm.sph.sc.edu/Courses/ Econ/Monopoly/Mon.html> Economics interactive tutorial: Monopoly price and output

On the cost side, we will assume that, although the firm is a monopolist in the product market, it hires factors of production in competitive markets and employs the same technology as Chapter 8's competitive firm. This assumption lets us use the cost data we developed in Chapter 7 and applied in Chapter 8, so we can compare the price–output decisions of a pure monopoly with those of a firm in pure competition. Columns 5 through 7 in Table 9-1 reproduce the relevant cost data from Table 7-2.

MR = MC Rule

A monopolist seeking to maximize total profit will employ the same rationale as a profit-seeking firm in a competitive industry. It will produce another unit of output as long as that unit adds more to total revenue than it adds to total cost. The firm will increase output up to the output at which marginal revenue equals marginal cost (MR = MC).

A comparison of columns 4 and 7 in Table 9-1 indicates that the profit-maximizing output is five units, because the fifth unit is the last unit of output whose marginal revenue exceeds its marginal cost. What price will the monopolist charge? The demand schedule shown as columns 1 and 2 in Table 9-1 indicates there is only one price at which five units can be sold: $122.

This analysis is shown in **Figure 9-4 (Key Graph)**, where we have graphed the demand, marginal-revenue, average-total-cost, and marginal-cost data of Table 9-1. The profit-maximizing output occurs at five units of output (Q_m) where the marginal-revenue (MR) and marginal-cost (MC) curves intersect (MR = MC).

To find the price the monopolist will charge, we extend a vertical line from Q_m up to the demand curve D. The price P_m at which Q_m units can be sold is $122, which is in this case the profit-maximizing price. The monopolist sets the quantity at Q_m to charge its profit-maximizing price of $122.

In columns 2 and 5 in Table 9-1 we see that, at five units of output, the product price ($122) exceeds the average total cost ($94). The monopolist thus earns an economic profit of $28 per unit and the total economic profit is then $140 (= 5 units × $28). In Figure 9-4, per-unit profit is $P_m - A$ where A is the average total cost of producing Q_m units. We find total economic profit by multiplying this per-unit profit by the profit-maximizing output Q_m.

Another way we can determine the profit-maximizing output is by comparing total revenue and total cost at each level of production and choosing the output with the greatest positive difference. Use columns 3 and 6 in Table 9-1 to verify our conclusion that five units is the profit-maximizing output. Graphing total revenue and total cost also shows the greatest difference (the maximum profit) at five units of output. Table 9-2 is a step-by-step summary of the process for determining the profit-maximizing output, the profit-maximizing price, and economic profit in pure monopoly. *(Key Question 5)*

No Monopoly Supply Curve

Recall that for firms in pure competition, MR equals P and the supply curve of a firm is determined by applying the MR (= P) = MC profit-maximizing rule. The supply curve for each firm is the portion of the firm's MC curve that lies above the average-variable-cost curve. At first glance we would suspect that the pure monopolist's marginal-cost curve would also be its supply curve, but that is *not* the case. *The pure monopolist has no supply curve.* Like the competitive firm, the monopolist equates marginal revenue and marginal cost to determine output, but for the monopolist marginal revenue is less than price. Because the monopolist does not equate marginal cost to price, it is possible for different demand conditions to bring about different prices for the same output. To convince yourself of this, refer to Figure 9-4 and pencil in a new, steeper marginal-revenue curve that intersects the marginal-cost curve at the same point as does the present marginal-revenue curve. Then draw in a new demand curve that roughly corresponds with your new marginal-revenue curve. With the new curves, the same MR = MC output of five units now corresponds with a higher profit-maximizing price. Conclusion: There is no supply curve for the pure monopolist.

TABLE 9-2	**Steps for Graphically Determining the Profit-maximizing Price and Economic Profit (If Any) in Pure Monopoly**

Step 1. Determine the profit-maximizing output by finding where MR = MC.

Step 2. Determine the profit-maximizing price by extending a vertical line upward from the output determined in step 1 to the pure monopolist's demand curve.

Step 3. Determine the pure monopolist's economic profit using one of two methods.

    Method 1. Find profit per unit by subtracting the average total cost of the profit-maximizing output from the profit-maximizing price. Then multiply the difference by the profit-maximizing output to determine economic profit (if any).

    Method 2. Find total cost by multiplying the average total cost of the profit-maximizing output by that output. Find total revenue by multiplying the profit-maximizing output by the profit-maximizing price. Then subtract total cost from total revenue to determine economic profit (if any).

Key Graph

FIGURE 9-4 The Profit-maximizing Position of a Pure Monopolist

The pure monopolist maximizes profit by producing the MR = MC output, here $Q_m = 5$ units. Then, as seen from the demand curve, it will charge price $P_m = \$122$. Average total cost will be $A = \$94$, meaning that per-unit profit is $P_m - A$ and total profit is $5 \times (P_m - A)$. Total economic profit is thus represented by the grey rectangle.

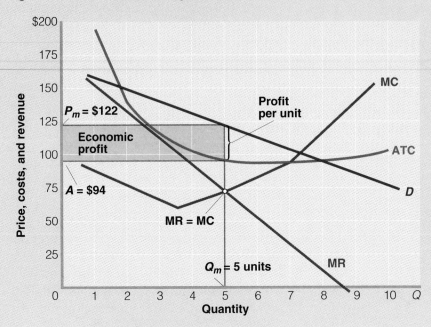

Quick Quiz

1. The MR curve lies below the demand curve in this figure because
  a. the demand curve is linear (a straight line).
  b. the demand curve is highly inelastic throughout its full length.
  c. the demand curve is highly elastic throughout its full length.
  d. the gain in revenue from an extra unit of output is less than the price charged for that unit of output.

2. The area labelled "Economic profit" can be found by multiplying the difference between *P* and ATC by quantity. It also can be found by
  a. dividing profit per unit by quantity.
  b. subtracting total cost from total revenue.
  c. multiplying the coefficient of demand elasticity by quantity.
  d. multiplying the difference between *P* and MC by quantity.

3. This pure monopolist
  a. charges the highest price it can get.
  b. earns only a normal profit in the long run.
  c. restricts output to create an insurmountable entry barrier.
  d. restricts output to increase its price and total economic profit.

4. At this monopolist's profit-maximizing output
  a. price equals marginal revenue.
  b. price equals marginal cost.
  c. price exceeds marginal cost.
  d. profit per unit is maximized.

ANSWERS: 1. d; 2. b; 3. d; 4. c

Misconceptions About Monopoly Pricing

Our analysis exposes two fallacies about a monopolist.

NOT THE HIGHEST PRICE

Because a monopolist can manipulate output and price, people often believe it will charge the highest price it can get. That is incorrect. Prices above P_m in Figure 9-4 yield less than maximum total profit. The monopolist seeks maximum total profit, not maximum price. Prices above P_m would reduce sales and total revenue by more than a decrease in total cost.

TOTAL, NOT UNIT, PROFIT

The monopolist seeks maximum *total* profit, not maximum *unit* profit. In Figure 9-4 a comparison of the vertical distance between average total cost and price at various possible outputs indicates that per-unit profit is greater at a point slightly to the left of the profit-maximizing output Q_m, where unit profit at four units of output is $32 (= $132 − $100) compared with $28 (= $122 − $94) at the profit-maximizing output of five units. Here the monopolist accepts a lower-than-maximum per-unit profit because additional sales more than compensate for the lower unit profit. A profit-maximizing monopolist prefers to sell five units at a profit of $28 per unit (for a total profit of $140) than four units at a profit of $32 per unit (for a total profit of only $128).

Possibility of Losses by Monopolist

The probability of economic profit is greater for a monopolist than for a firm in pure competition. In the long run only a normal profit is possible in a purely competitive industry, whereas barriers to entry mean that for the monopolist economic profits can persist.

But pure monopoly does not guarantee profit. The monopolist is not immune to changes in tastes that reduce the demand for its product. Nor is it immune to upward-shifting cost curves caused by escalating prices of factors of production. If the demand and cost situation faced by the monopolist is far less favourable than that in Figure 9-4, the monopolist will incur losses in the short run. Despite its dominance in the market, the monopoly enterprise in Figure 9-5 suffers a loss, as shown, because of weak demand and relatively high costs. Yet it will continue to operate because its total loss is less than its fixed cost. More precisely, at output Q_m the monopolist's price

---

FIGURE 9-5   **The Loss-minimizing Position of a Pure Monopolist**

If demand *D* is weak and costs are high, the pure monopolist may be unable to make a profit. Because P_m exceeds *V*, the average variable cost at the MR = MC output Q_m, the monopolist will minimize losses in the short run by producing at that output. The loss per unit is $A − P_m$, and the total loss is indicated by the pink rectangle.

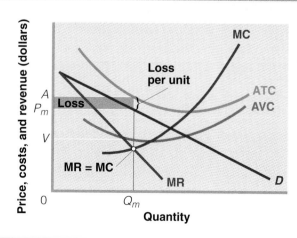

P_m exceeds its average variable cost V. Its loss per unit is $A - P_m$, and the total loss is shown by the pink rectangle.

The monopolist will not operate at a loss in the long run. The firm's owners will move their resources to other industries that offer better profit opportunities.

9.3   Economic Effects of Monopoly

Let's now evaluate pure monopoly from the standpoint of society as a whole. The standard reference for this evaluation is the long-run efficiency in a purely competitive market, identified by the triple equality $P = MC = $ minimum ATC.

Price, Output, and Efficiency

Figure 9-6 graphically contrasts the price, output, and efficiency outcomes of pure monopoly and a purely competitive *industry*. Recall that at the equilibrium price–output combination both productive efficiency and allocative efficiency are achieved. *Productive efficiency* is achieved because competitive pressures force firms to operate where average total cost is at a minimum, Q_c. Product price is at the lowest level consistent with minimum average total cost. Also, *allocative efficiency* is achieved because production occurs up to that output at which price (the measure of a product's value or marginal benefit to society) equals marginal cost (the worth of the alternative products forgone by society in producing any given commodity). In short: $P = MC = $ minimum ATC.

Now let's suppose that this industry becomes a pure monopoly [Figure 9-6(b)] because one firm buys out all its competitors. Also, assume that no changes in costs or market demand result from

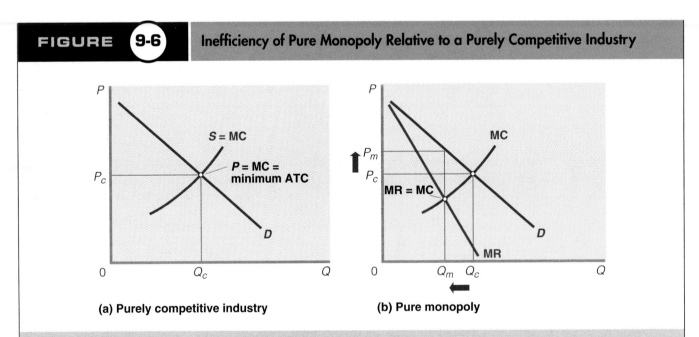

| FIGURE | 9-6 | Inefficiency of Pure Monopoly Relative to a Purely Competitive Industry |

(a) Purely competitive industry

(b) Pure monopoly

Panel (a): In a purely competitive industry, entry and exit of firms ensures that price (P_c) equals marginal cost (MC) and that the minimum average-total-cost output (Q_c) is produced. Both productive efficiency ($P = $ minimum ATC) and allocative efficiency ($P = $ MC) are obtained. Panel (b): In pure monopoly, the MR curve lies below the demand curve. The monopolist maximizes profit at output Q_m, where MR = MC, and charges price P_m. Thus, output is lower (Q_m rather than Q_c) and price is higher (P_m rather than P_c) than they would be in a purely competitive industry. Monopoly is inefficient, since output is less than that required for achieving minimum ATC (here at Q_c) and because the monopolist's price exceeds MC.

this dramatic change in the industry structure. What were formerly thousands of competing firms is now a single monopolist.

The competitive market supply curve S has become the marginal-cost curve (MC) of the monopolist. (Since the monopolist does not have a supply curve, as such, we have removed the S label.) The important change, however, is on the demand side. From the viewpoint of each of the individual competitive firms, demand was perfectly elastic, and marginal revenue was therefore equal to price. Each firm equated MR (= price) and MC in maximizing profits. But market demand and individual demand are the same to the monopolist. The firm *is* the industry, and thus the monopolist sees the downsloping demand curve D shown in Figure 9-6(b).

This means that marginal revenue is less than price, and that graphically the MR curve lies below demand curve D. In using the MR = MC rule, the monopolist selects output Q_m and price P_m. A comparison of both graphs in Figure 9-6 reveals that the monopolist finds it profitable to sell a smaller output at a higher price than would prevail in a competitive industry. Monopoly achieves neither productive nor allocative efficiency. The monopolist's output is less than Q_c, the output at which average total cost is lowest. Price is higher than the competitive price P_c, which in the long-run equilibrium of competitive firms equals minimum average total cost. Thus, the monopoly price *exceeds* minimum average total cost. Also, at the monopolist's Q_m output, product price is considerably higher than marginal cost, which means that society values additional units of the monopolist's output more highly than it values the alternative products the resources could otherwise produce. So the monopolist's profit-maximizing output results in an underallocation of resources, and thus it does not achieve allocative efficiency.

In monopoly, then, $P >$ MC and $P >$ minimum ATC.

Income Transfer

In general, monopoly transfers income from consumers to stockholders who own the monopoly. Since a monopoly charges a higher price than would a purely competitive firm with the same costs, it in effect levies a private tax on consumers and obtains substantial economic profits. Monopoly profit is not equally distributed, because higher income groups largely own corporate stock. The owners of a monopoly are enriched at the expense of the rest of consumers who overpay for the product. Because, on average, these owners have more income than the buyers, monopoly increases income inequality.

Cost Complications

Our evaluation of pure monopoly has led us to conclude that, given identical costs, a monopolist will charge a higher price, produce a smaller output, and allocate economic resources less efficiently than a purely competitive industry.

But costs may not be the same for a firm in a purely competitive industry and a monopolist. The unit cost incurred by a monopolist may be either larger or smaller than that incurred by a firm in a competitive industry. There are four reasons why costs may differ: (1) economies of scale, (2) a phenomenon called *X-inefficiency*, (3) the need for monopoly-preserving expenditures, and (4) the very long-run perspective, which allows for technological advance.

ECONOMIES OF SCALE ONCE AGAIN

Where there are extensive economies of scale, market demand may not be sufficient to support a large number of competing firms, each producing at minimum efficient scale. In such cases, an industry of one or two firms will have a lower average total cost than the same industry made up of numerous competitive firms. At the extreme, only a single firm—a natural monopoly—might be able to achieve the lowest long-run average total cost.

Some firms whose business is in new information technologies, for example, computer software, Internet service, and wireless communications, have displayed extensive economies of scale. As these firms have grown, their long-run average total costs have declined. Greater use of specialized inputs, the spreading of product development costs, and learning by doing all have produced economies of scale. Also, *simultaneous consumption* and *network effects* have reduced costs.

simultaneous consumption
A product's ability to satisfy a large number of consumers at the same time.

A product's ability to satisfy a large number of consumers at the same time is called **simultaneous consumption** (or *non-rivalrous consumption*). Dell Computers needs to produce a personal computer for each customer, but Microsoft needs to produce its Windows program only once. Then, at very low marginal cost, Microsoft delivers its program by disk to millions of consumers. The same is true for Internet service providers such as Rogers Communications and Bell Canada, music producers, and wireless communication firms such as Telus. Because marginal costs are so low, the average total cost of output declines as more customers are added.

network effects
Increases in the value of a product to each user as the total number of users rises.

Network effects are increases in the value of a product to each user, including existing users, as the total number of users rises. Computer software, cell phones, pagers, palm computers, and other products related to the Internet are good examples. When others have Internet service and devices to access it, you can conveniently send e-mail messages to them. When they have similar software, you can attach documents, spreadsheets, and photos to the e-mail message. The benefits of the product to each person are magnified the larger the number of people connected to the system.

Such network effects may drive a market toward monopoly, because consumers tend to choose standard products that everyone else is using. The focused demand for these products permits their producers to grow rapidly and thus achieve economies of scale. Smaller firms in the same sector get acquired or go out of business.

Economists generally agree that some new information firms have not yet exhausted their economies of scale, but it is questionable whether such firms are truly natural monopolies. Most firms eventually achieve their minimum efficient scale at less than the full size of the market, and, even if natural monopoly develops, it's unlikely that the monopolist will pass cost reductions along to consumers. So, with perhaps a handful of exceptions, economies of scale do not change the general conclusion that monopolies are less efficient than more competitive industries.

X-INEFFICIENCY

In constructing all the average-total-cost curves used in this book, we have assumed that the firm uses the most efficient technology. In other words, it uses the technology that permits it to achieve the lowest average total cost of whatever level of output it chooses to produce. **X-inefficiency** occurs when a firm's actual cost of producing any output is greater than the lowest possible cost of producing it. In Figure 9-7 X-inefficiency is represented by operation at points X and X′ above the lowest-cost ATC curve. At these points, per-unit costs are ATC_x (as opposed to ATC_1) for output Q_1 and $ATC_{x'}$ (as opposed to ATC_2) for output Q_2. Any point above the average-total-cost curve in Figure 9-7 is possible but reflects inefficiency or bad management by the firm.

X-inefficiency
Failure to produce any specific output at the lowest average (and total) cost possible.

Why does X-inefficiency occur if it reduces profits? The answer is that managers of a firm may have goals such as corporate growth, an easier work life, avoidance of business risk, or giving jobs to incompetent relatives that conflict with cost minimization. Or X-inefficiency may arise because a firm's workers are poorly motivated or ineffectively supervised.

<www.maths.tcd.ie/local/ JUNK/econrev/ser/html/ morton.html>
Monopoly and X-efficiency

For our purposes the relevant question is whether a monopolist suffers more X-inefficiency than competitive firms do. There is evidence that they do. Firms in competitive industries are continually under pressure from rivals, forcing them to be internally efficient to survive. But monopolists are sheltered from such competitive forces by entry barriers, making X-inefficiency more likely.

A reasonable estimate is that X-inefficiency may be 10 percent or more of costs for monopolists but only 5 percent for an average oligopolistic industry in which the four largest firms produce 60 percent of total output.[1] In the words of one authority: "The evidence is fragmentary, but it points in the same direction. X-inefficiency exists, and it is more apt to be reduced when competitive pressures are strong than when firms enjoy insulated market positions."[2]

---

[1]William G. Shepherd, *The Economics of Industrial Organization*, 4th ed. (Englewood Cliffs, NJ: Prentice-Hall, 1997), p. 107.

[2]F. M. Scherer and David Ross, *Industrial Market Structure and Economic Performance*, 3rd ed. (Chicago: Rand McNally College Publishing, 1990), p. 672.

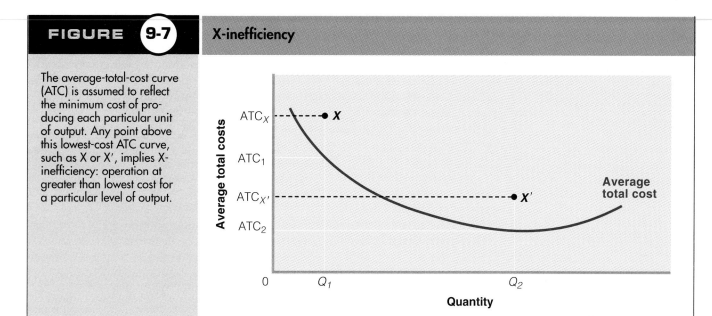

FIGURE 9-7

X-inefficiency

The average-total-cost curve (ATC) is assumed to reflect the minimum cost of producing each particular unit of output. Any point above this lowest-cost ATC curve, such as X or X′, implies X-inefficiency: operation at greater than lowest cost for a particular level of output.

rent-seeking behaviour
The actions by persons, firms, or unions to gain special benefits from government at taxpayers' or someone else's expense.

RENT-SEEKING EXPENDITURES

Rent-seeking behaviour is an attempt to transfer income or wealth to a particular firm or resource supplier at someone else's, or even society's, expense. We have seen that a monopolist can obtain an economic profit even in the long run. Therefore, it is no surprise that a firm may go to great expense to acquire or maintain a monopoly granted by government through legislation or an exclusive licence. Such rent-seeking expenditures add nothing to the firm's output, but they clearly increase its costs. Costs associated with rent-seeking behaviour imply that monopoly has even higher costs and less efficiency than suggested in Figure 9-6(b).

TECHNOLOGICAL ADVANCE

In the very long run, firms can reduce their costs through the discovery and implementation of new technology. If monopolists are more likely than competitive firms to develop more efficient production techniques over time, then the inefficiency of monopoly might be overstated. Since research and development (R&D) is the topic of Chapter 11, we will provide only a brief assessment here.

The general view of economists is that a pure monopolist will not be technologically progressive. Although its economic profit provides ample means to finance R&D, it has little incentive to implement new techniques (or products). Because of its sheltered market position, the pure monopolist can afford to be inefficient and lethargic; there simply is no penalty for being so.

One caveat: Research and technological advance may be one of the monopolist's barriers to entry. Thus, the monopolist may continue to seek technological advance to avoid falling prey to new rivals. In this case technological advance is essential to the maintenance of monopoly, but it is potential competition, not the monopoly market structure, that is driving the technological advance.

Assessment and Policy Options

Monopoly is a legitimate concern because the monopolist can charge higher-than-competitive prices that result in an underallocation of resources. Monopolists can stifle innovation, engage in rent-seeking behaviour, and foster X-inefficiency. Even when their costs are low because of economies of scale, monopolists are unlikely to charge a price that reflects those low costs. The cost savings may simply accrue to the monopoly as greater economic profit.

Fortunately, however, monopoly is not widespread in the Canadian economy. Barriers to entry are seldom completely successful. Although research and technological advance may strengthen the market position of a monopoly, technology may also undermine monopoly power. Over time, the creation of new technologies may work to destroy monopoly positions. For example, the development of courier delivery, fax machines, and e-mail has eroded the monopoly power of Canada Post Corporation. Cable television monopolies are now challenged by satellite TV and by new technologies that permit the transmission of audio and visual signals over the Internet.

Similarly, patents eventually expire and even before they do, the development of new and distinct products can undermine existing patent advantages. New sources of monopolized resources can be found, and competition from foreign firms may emerge. Finally, if a monopoly is sufficiently fearful of future competition from new products, it may keep its prices relatively low to discourage rivals from developing such products. If so, consumers may pay nearly competitive prices even though present competition is lacking.

So what should government do about monopoly when it arises in the real world? Government needs to look carefully at monopoly on a case-by-case basis. Three general policy options are available:

1. If the monopoly is achieved and sustained through anticompetitive actions, creates substantial economic inefficiency, and appears to be long lasting, the government can file charges against the monopoly under Canada'a anti-combines laws. If found guilty of monopoly abuse, the firm can either be prohibited from engaging in certain business activities or broken into two or more competing firms.

2. If the monopoly is a natural monopoly, it may be allowed to continue expanding. If no competition emerges from new products, government may then decide to regulate its prices and operations.

3. If the monopoly appears to be unsustainable over a long period, say, because of emerging new technology, government can simply choose to ignore it.

QUICK REVIEW

- The monopolist maximizes profit (or minimizes loss) at the output where MR = MC and charges the price that corresponds to that output on its demand curve.

- The monopolist has no supply curve, since any of several prices can be associated with a specific quantity of output supplied.

- Assuming identical costs, a monopolist will be less efficient than a purely competitive industry because the monopolist produces less output and charges a higher price.

- The inefficiencies of monopoly may be offset or lessened by economies of scale and, less likely, by technological progress, but may be intensified by the presence of X-inefficiency and rent-seeking expenditures.

9.4   Price Discrimination and Monopoly

So far, we have assumed that the monopolist charges a single price to all buyers. But under certain conditions the monopolist can increase its profit by charging different prices to different buyers. In so doing, the monopolist is engaging in **price discrimination**, the practice of selling a product or service at more than one price when the price differences are not justified by cost differences.

price discrimination
The selling of a product to different buyers at different prices when the price differences are not justified by differences in cost.

Conditions

A monopolist can engage in price discrimination if the following conditions are present:

- *Monopoly power*   The seller must be a monopolist with some ability to control output and price.
- *Market segregation*   The seller must be able to segregate buyers into distinct classes, each of which has a different willingness or ability to pay for the product. This separation of buyers is usually based on different elasticities of demand, as the examples that follow will make clear.
- *No resale*   The original purchaser cannot resell the product or service. If buyers in the low-price segment of the market could easily resell in the high-price segment, the monopolist's price-discrimination strategy would create competition in the high-price segment. This competition would reduce the price in the high-price segment and undermine the monopolist's price-discrimination policy. This suggests that service industries such as the transportation industry or legal and medical services, where resale is impossible, are candidates for price discrimination.

Examples of Price Discrimination

Price discrimination is widely practised in the Canadian economy. For example, Air Canada charges high fares to travelling executives, whose demand for travel is inelastic, and offers lower fares such as "family rates" and "advance purchase fares" to attract vacationers and others whose demands are more elastic.

Movie theatres and golf courses vary their charges on the basis of time (higher rates in the evening and on weekends when demand is strong) and age (ability to pay). Railways vary the rate charged per tonne-kilometre of freight according to the market value of the product being shipped. The shipper of 10 tonnes of television sets or costume jewellery is charged more than the shipper of 10 tonnes of gravel or coal.

The issuance of discount coupons, redeemable at purchase, is a form of price discrimination. It permits firms to give price discounts to their most price-sensitive customers who have elastic demand. Less price-sensitive consumers who have less elastic demand are not as likely to undertake the clipping and redeeming of coupons. The firm thus makes a larger profit than if it had used a single-price, no-coupon strategy.

Price discrimination can often occur in international trade. A Russian aluminum producer, for example, might sell aluminum for less in Canada than in Russia. In Canada, this seller faces an elastic demand because several substitute suppliers are available. But in Russia, where the manufacturer dominates the market and trade barriers impede imports, consumers have fewer choices and thus demand is less elastic. (See the Consider This box for another example of price discrimination.)

Consequences of Price Discrimination

As you will see shortly, a monopolist can increase its profit by practising price discrimination. At the same time, if the monopolist can achieve *perfect price discrimination* it will produce more output than at a single monopoly price. Perfect price discrimination occurs when the monopolist charges each customer the price that he or she would be willing to pay rather than forgo the product.

MORE PROFIT

Let's again consider our monopolist's downsloping demand curve in Figure 9-4, to see why price discrimination can increase profit. In that figure we saw that the profit-maximizing single price is $P_m = \$122$. However, the demand curve reveals that some buyers are willing to pay more than $122.

If the monopolist can identify those buyers, segregate them, and charge the maximum price each would be willing to pay, total revenue and economic profit would increase. Observe from columns 1 and 2 in Table 9-1 that buyers of the first four units of output would be willing to pay $162, $152, $142, and $132, respectively, for those units. If the seller could practise perfect price discrimination by charging the maximum price for each unit, total revenue would increase from $610 (= $122 × 5) to $710 (= $122 + $132 + $142 + $152 + $162) and profit would increase from $140 (= $610 − $470) to $240 (= $710 − $470).

MORE PRODUCTION

Other things being equal, the monopolist that can achieve perfect price discrimination will produce a larger output than the monopolist that does not. When the non-discriminating monopolist lowers its price to sell additional output, the lower price applies not only to the additional output but also to all the prior units of output. So the single-price monopolist's marginal revenue falls more rapidly than price. The decline of marginal revenue is a disincentive to increased production.

When a discriminating monopolist lowers its price, the reduced price applies only to the additional units sold and not to the prior units. Thus, marginal revenue equals price for each unit of output and the firm's marginal revenue curve and demand curve coincide. The disincentive to increased production is removed.

We can show the outcome through Table 9-1. Because marginal revenue and price are equal, the discriminating monopolist finds it profitable to produce seven units, not five units, of output. The additional revenue from the sixth and seventh units is $214 (= $112 + $102). Thus, total revenue for seven units is $924 (= $710 + $214). Since total cost for seven units is $640, profit is $284.

Ironically, although perfect price discrimination results in higher monopoly profit than that achieved by a non-discriminating monopolist, it also results in greater output and thus less allocative inefficiency. In our example, the output level of seven units matches the output that would have occurred in pure competition; that is, allocative efficiency ($P = MC$) is achieved.

GRAPHICAL PORTRAYAL

Figure 9-8 shows the effects of price discrimination graphically. Figure 9-8(a) reproduces Figure 9-4 in a generalized form to show the position of a non-discriminating monopolist as a benchmark. The non-discriminating monopolist produces output Q_1 (where MR = MC) and charges price P_1. Total revenue is area $0bce$ and economic profit is the grey area $abcd$.

Consider This

Price Discrimination

Take me out to the ball game....
Buy me some peanuts and Cracker Jack....

Professional baseball teams such as the Montreal Expos and the Toronto Blue Jays earn substantial revenues through ticket sales. To maximize profit they offer significantly lower ticket prices for youths (whose demand is elastic) than for adults (whose demand is inelastic). This discount may be as much as 50 percent.

If this type of price discrimination increases revenue and profit, why don't teams also price discriminate at the concession stands? Why don't they offer half-priced hot dogs, soft drinks, peanuts, and Cracker Jack to youths?

The answer involves the three requirements for successful price discrimination. All three requirements are met for game tickets: (1) The team has monopoly power; (2) it can segregate ticket buyers by age group, each group having a different elasticity of demand; and (3) youths cannot resell their discounted tickets to adults.

It's a different situation at the concession stands. Specifically, the third condition is *not* met. If the team had dual prices, it could not prevent the exchange or "resale" of the concession goods from youths to adults. Many adults would send youths to buy food and soft drinks for them: "Here's some money, Billy. Go buy *six* hot dogs." In this case, price discrimination would reduce, not increase, team profit. Thus, youths and adults are charged the same high prices at the concession stands. (These prices are high relative to those for the same goods at the local convenience store because the stadium sellers have a captive audience and thus considerable monopoly power.)

Question: Why does Air Canada charge those travellers who want to book a seat close to the departure date substantially more than what it charges people who are prepared to book at least a few weeks ahead of time?

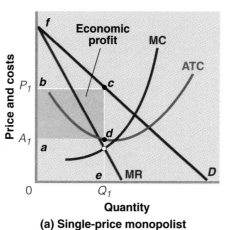
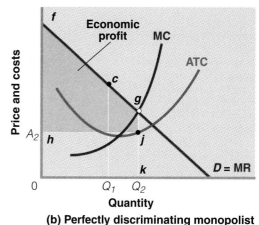

FIGURE 9-8   Single-price Versus Perfectly Discriminating Monopoly Pricing

Panel (a): The single-price monopolist produces output Q_1 at which MR = MC, charges price P_1 for all units, incurs an average total cost of A_1, and realizes an economic profit represented by area *abcd*. Panel (b): The perfectly discriminating monopolist has D = MR and, as a result, produces output Q_2 (where MR = MC). It then charges the maximum price for each unit of output, incurs average total cost A_2, and realizes an economic profit represented by area *hfgj*.

(a) Single-price monopolist

(b) Perfectly discriminating monopolist

The monopolist in Figure 9-8(b) engages in perfect price discrimination, charging each buyer the highest price he or she is willing to pay. Starting at the very first unit, each additional unit is sold for the price indicated by the corresponding point on the demand curve. This monopolist's demand and marginal-revenue curves coincide, because the monopolist does not cut price on preceding units to sell more output. Thus, the most profitable output is Q_2 (where MR = MC), which is greater than Q_1. Total revenue is area *0fgk* and total cost is area *0hjk*. The economic profit of *hfgj* for the discriminating monopolist is clearly larger than the profit of *abcd* for the single-price monopolist.

The impact of price discrimination on consumers is mixed. Those buying each unit up to Q_1 will pay more than the non-discriminatory price of P_1. But those additional consumers brought into the market by discrimination will pay less than P_1. Specifically, they will pay the various prices shown on segment *cg* of the D = MR curve.

Overall, perfect price discrimination results in greater profit, greater output, and higher prices for many consumers but lower prices for those purchasing the extra output. (***Key Question 6***)

9.5   Regulated Monopoly

The Role of Governments

Natural monopolies traditionally have been subject to *rate regulation* (price regulation), although the recent trend has been to deregulate those parts of the industries where competition seems possible. Government regulatory commissions still regulate the prices that natural gas distributors, regional telephone companies, and electricity suppliers can charge. But long-distance telephone, natural gas at the well-head, wireless communications, cable television, and long-distance electricity transmission have been, to one degree or another, deregulated over the past several decades, and competition among local telephone, electricity, and natural gas providers is now beginning.

Let's consider the regulation of a local natural monopoly, for example, a natural gas distributor. Figure 9-9 shows the demand and the long-run cost curves facing our firm. Because of extensive economies of scale, the demand curve cuts the natural monopolist's long-run average-total-cost curve at a point where that curve is still falling. It would be inefficient to have several firms in this industry because each firm's lowest average total cost would be substantially higher than that of a single firm. So, this circumstance requires a single seller.

We know by application of the MR = MC rule that Q_m and P_m are the profit-maximizing output and price that an unregulated monopolist would choose. Because price exceeds average total cost

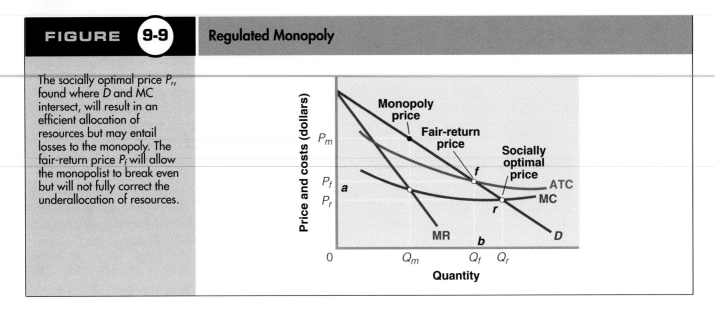

FIGURE 9-9 — Regulated Monopoly

The socially optimal price P_r, found where D and MC intersect, will result in an efficient allocation of resources but may entail losses to the monopoly. The fair-return price P_f will allow the monopolist to break even but will not fully correct the underallocation of resources.

at output Q_m, the monopolist enjoys a substantial economic profit. Furthermore, price exceeds marginal cost, indicating an underallocation of resources to this product or service. Can government regulation bring about better results from society's point of view?

Socially Optimal Price: *P* = MC

If the objective of a regulatory commission is to achieve allocative efficiency, it should establish a legal (ceiling) price for the monopolist equal to marginal cost. We see that P_r is the only price on the demand curve equal to marginal cost. The ceiling price effectively causes the monopolist's demand curve to become horizontal (indicating perfectly elastic demand) from zero out to point r, where the regulated price ceases to be effective. Also, out to point r we have $MR = P_r$.

Confronted with the ceiling price P_r, the monopolist will maximize profit or minimize loss by producing Q_r units of output, because at this output $MR (= P_r) = MC$. By making it illegal to charge more than P_r per unit, the regulatory agency has removed the monopolist's incentive to restrict output to Q_m to obtain a higher price and increase profit.

In short, the regulatory commission can simulate the allocative forces of pure competition by imposing the legal price P_r and letting the monopolist choose its profit-maximizing or loss-minimizing output. Production takes place where $P_r = MC$, and this equality indicates an efficient allocation of resources to this product or service. The price that achieves allocative efficiency is called the **socially optimal price**.

socially optimal price
The price of a product that results in the most efficient allocation of an economy's resources.

Fair-return Price: *P* = ATC

It is possible for the socially optimal price, P_r, that equals marginal cost to be so low that average total costs are not covered, as is the case in Figure 9-9. The result is a loss for the firm. The reason is that our firm is required to meet the heaviest peak demands (both daily and seasonally) for natural gas, and thus substantial excess production capacity when demand is relatively "normal." Its high level of investment in production facilities and economies of scale mean that its average total cost is likely to be greater than its marginal cost over a very wide range of outputs. In particular, as in Figure 9-9, average total cost is likely to be greater than the price P_r at the intersection of the demand curve and marginal-cost curve. Therefore, forcing the socially optimal price P_r on the regulated monopolist would result in short-run losses and long-run bankruptcy for the utility.

What to do? One option is to provide a public subsidy to cover the loss that marginal-cost pricing would entail. Another possibility is to condone price discrimination and hope that the additional revenue gained will permit the firm to cover costs.

In practice, regulatory commissions have pursued a third option: They modify the objective of allocative efficiency and $P = MC$ pricing. Most regulatory agencies in Canada establish a **fair-return price**.

Since total cost includes a normal or "fair" profit, we see in Figure 9-9 that a fair-return price is on the average-total-cost curve. Because the demand curve cuts average total cost only at point f, clearly P_f is the only price on the demand curve that permits a fair return. The corresponding output at regulated price P_f will be Q_f. Total revenue of $0afb$ will equal the utility's total cost of the same amount, and the firm will realize a normal profit.

fair-return price
The price of a product that enables its producer to obtain a normal profit and that is equal to the average cost of producing it.

Dilemma of Regulation

Comparing results of the socially optimal price ($P = MC$) and the fair-return price ($P = ATC$) suggests a policy dilemma, sometimes termed the *dilemma of regulation*. When its price is set to achieve the most efficient allocation of resources ($P = MC$), the regulated monopoly is likely to suffer losses. Survival of the firm would depend on permanent public subsidies from tax revenues. Conversely, although a fair-return price ($P = ATC$) allows the monopolist to cover costs, it only partially resolves the underallocation of resources that the unregulated monopoly price would foster. That is, the fair-return price would increase output only from Q_m to Q_f in Figure 9-9, while the socially optimal output is Q_r. Despite this dilemma, regulation can improve on the results of monopoly from the social point of view. Price regulation (even at the fair-return price) can simultaneously reduce price, increase output, and reduce the economic profits of monopolies. (*Key Question 11*)

9.6   Monopoly and Deadweight Loss

We can restate the efficiency of monopoly using *consumer surplus* and *producer surplus*. In Figure 9-10 we have once again put a purely competitive industry alongside a pure monopoly to compare them. We have indicated the extent of consumer and producer surplus in each of the market structures. You will recall from Chapter 8 that in a purely competitive market structure, equilibrium price P_c ($= MC = minimum ATC$) will create the maximum amount of consumer surplus and producer surplus, as indicated in Figure 9-10(a). We also noted that in pure competition marginal benefit equals marginal cost ($MB = MC$) at the equilibrium price and quantity, ensuring allocative efficiency.

In a pure monopoly, represented in Figure 9-10(b), the output is lower than in a pure competitive market structure, and the profit maximizing price P_m is above P_c, so consumers pay a price above the firm's (and the industry's) MC. At the lower output Q_m, the sum of consumer surplus and producer surplus has been reduced, compared to the pure competition scenario. The net loss of consumer surplus and producer surplus is referred to as **deadweight loss** of monopoly, and is indicated by the area covered by triangles B and C. At output Q_m, marginal benefit is greater than marginal cost ($MB > MC$), indicating that the monopolist is not producing as much output as consumers would like. Thus, allocative efficiency is not achieved.

deadweight loss
The loss of consumer surplus and producer surplus when output is either above or below its efficient level.

Figure 9-10(b) shows that there has been a redistribution of resources from the consumer to the monopolist. The higher price charged by the monopolist results in a gain represented the grey area A. Consumers lose the consumer surplus represented by triangle B, while the monopolist loses the producer surplus represented by the pink triangle C. But the monopolist will enjoy a net gain if its gain (area A) is larger than its loss of producer surplus (area C). The monopolist's gain is the difference between the monopoly price (P_m) and the equilibrium price in pure competition (P_c) multiplied by the quantity sold (Q_m).

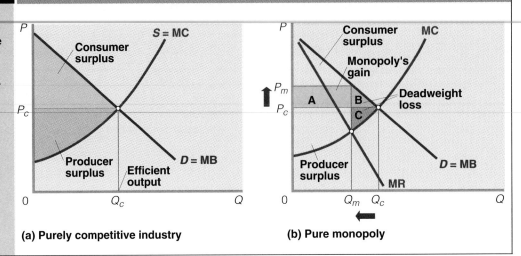

FIGURE 9-10

Monopoly and Deadweight Loss

Panel (a): In pure competition the long run equilibrium price (P_c) and quantity (Q_c) maximize the sum of consumer surplus and producer surplus. Panel (b): A pure monopolist restricts output to Q_m and increases price to P_m. Although the monopolist gains, a deadweight loss is created as a result of the lower consumer surplus brought about by the fall in output and rise in price.

(a) Purely competitive industry

(b) Pure monopoly

QUICK REVIEW

- Price discrimination occurs when a firm sells a product at different prices that are not based on cost differences.

- The conditions necessary for price discrimination are (1) monopoly power, (2) the ability to segregate buyers based on demand elasticities, and (3) the inability of buyers to resell the product.

- Compared with single pricing by a monopolist, perfect price discrimination results in greater profit and greater output. Many consumers pay higher prices, but other buyers pay prices below the single price.

- Monopoly price can be reduced and output increased through government regulation.

- The socially optimal price (P = MC) achieves allocative efficiency but may result in losses; the fair-return price (P = ATC) yields a normal profit but falls short of allocative efficiency.

- The inefficiency brought about by monopoly is referred to as deadweight loss.

THE LASTword

De Beers' Diamonds: Are Monopolies Forever?

De Beers was one of the world's strongest and most enduring monopolies. But in mid-2000 it announced that it could no longer control the supply of diamonds and thus would abandon its 66-year policy of monopolizing the diamond trade.

De Beers, a Swiss-based cartel controlled by a South African corporation, produces about 50 percent of the world's rough-cut diamonds and purchases for resale a sizable number of the rough-cut diamonds produced by other mines worldwide. As a result, De Beers markets 65 percent of the world's diamonds to a select group of diamond cutters and dealers—but that percentage has declined from 80 percent in the mid-1980s and continues to shrink. Therein lies De Beers' problem.

Classic Monopoly Behaviour
De Beers' past monopoly behaviour and results are a classic example of the unregulated monopoly model illustrated in Figure 9-4. No matter how many diamonds it mined or purchased, De Beers sold only that quantity of diamonds that would yield an appropriate (monopoly) price. That price was well above production costs, and De Beers and its partners earned monopoly profits.

When demand fell, De Beers reduced its sales to maintain price. The excess of production over sales was then reflected in growing diamond stockpiles held by De Beers. It also attempted to bolster demand through advertising ("Diamonds are forever"). When demand was strong, it increased sales by reducing its diamond inventories.

De Beers used several methods to control the production of many mines it did not own. First, it convinced a

number of independent producers that *single-channel* or monopoly marketing through De Beers would maximize their profit. Second, mines that circumvented De Beers often found their market suddenly flooded with similar diamonds from De Beers' vast stockpiles. The resulting price decline and loss of profit often would encourage the "rogue" mine into the De Beers fold. Finally, De Beers simply purchased and stockpiled diamonds produced by independent mines so their added supplies would not undercut the market.

The End of an Era? Several factors have come together to unravel the monopoly. New diamond discoveries resulted in a growing leakage of diamonds into world markets outside De Beers' control. For example, significant prospecting and trading in Angola occurred. Recent Canadian diamond discoveries, in the Northwest Territories, pose another threat. Although De Beers is a participant in Canada, a large uncontrolled supply of diamonds is expected to emerge. Similarly, although Russia is part of the De Beers' monopoly, that cash-

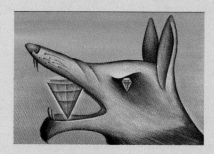

strapped country is allowed to sell part of its diamond stock directly into the world markets.

If that were not enough, Australian diamond producer Argyle opted to withdraw from the De Beers monopoly. Its annual production of mostly low-grade industrial diamonds accounts for about 6 percent of the global $8 billion diamond market. The international media has begun to focus heavily on the role that diamonds play in financing the bloody civil wars in Africa. Fearing a consumer boycott of diamonds, De Beers has pledged not to buy these conflict diamonds or do business with any firm that does. These diamonds, however, continue to find their way into the marketplace, eluding De Beers' control.

In mid-2000 De Beers abandoned its attempt to control the supply of diamonds. It announced that it planned to transform itself from a diamond cartel to a modern firm selling premium diamonds and other luxury goods under the De Beers label. It therefore would gradually reduce its $4 billion stockpile of diamonds and turn its efforts to increasing the overall demand for diamonds through advertising. De Beers proclaimed that it was changing its strategy to being "the diamond supplier of choice."

With its high market share and ability to control its own production levels, De Beers will still wield considerable influence over the price of rough-cut diamonds, but it turns out that the De Beers monopoly was not forever.

CHAPTER SUMMARY

9.1 CHARACTERISTICS OF PURE MONOPOLY

- A pure monopolist is the sole producer of a commodity for which there are no close substitutes.

- The existence of pure monopoly and other imperfectly competitive market structures is explained by barriers to entry, in the form of (a) economies of scale, (b) patent ownership and research, (c) ownership or control of essential factors of production, and (d) pricing and other strategic behaviour.

- The pure monopolist's market situation differs from that of a competitive firm in that the monopolist's demand curve is downsloping, causing the marginal-revenue curve to lie below the demand curve. Like the competitive seller, the pure monopolist will maximize profit by equating marginal revenue and marginal cost. Barriers to entry may permit a monopolist to acquire economic profit even in the long run. However, (a) the monopolist does not charge the highest price it can get; (b) the price that yields maximum total profit to the monopolist rarely coincides with the price that yields maximum unit profit; (c) high costs and a weak demand may prevent the monopolist from realizing any profit at all; and (d) the monopolist avoids the inelastic region of its demand curve.

9.2 OUTPUT AND PRICE DETERMINATION IN A MONOPOLY

- With the same costs, the pure monopolist will find it profitable to restrict output and charge a higher price than would sellers in a purely competitive industry. This restriction of output causes resources to be misallocated, as is shown by the fact that price exceeds marginal cost in monopolized markets.

9.3 ECONOMIC EFFECTS OF MONOPOLY

- In general, monopoly increases income inequality by transferring income from consumers to the owners of the monopoly.

- The costs monopolists and competitive producers face may not be the same. On the one hand, economies of scale may make lower unit costs available to monopolists but not to competitors, and pure monopoly may be more likely than pure competition to reduce costs via technological advance because of the monopolist's ability to realize economic profit, which can be used to finance research. On the other hand, X-inefficiency—the failure to produce with the least costly combination of inputs—is more common among monopolists than among competitive firms. Also, monopolists may make costly expenditures to maintain monopoly privileges that are conferred by government. Finally, the blocked entry of rival firms weakens the monopolist's incentive to be technologically progressive.

9.4 PRICE DISCRIMINATION AND MONOPOLY

- A monopolist can increase its profit by practising price discrimination, provided (a) it can segregate buyers on the basis of elasticities of demand and (b) its product or service cannot be readily transferred between the segregated markets. Other things being equal, the perfectly discriminating monopolist will produce a larger output than the non-discriminating monopolist.

9.5 REGULATED MONOPOLY

- Price regulation can be invoked to wholly or partially eliminate the tendency of monopolists to underallocate resources and to earn economic profits. The socially optimal price is determined where the demand and marginal-cost curves intersect; the fair-return price is determined where the demand and average-total-cost curves intersect.

9.6 MONOPOLY AND DEADWEIGHT LOSS

- The inefficiency of monopoly can be measured using the concepts of consumer surplus and producer surplus. The efficiency loss associated with pure monopoly is called deadweight loss.

TERMS AND CONCEPTS

pure monopoly, p. 224
barriers to entry, p. 224
simultaneous consumption, p. 236
network effects, p. 236

X-inefficiency, p. 236
rent-seeking behaviour, p. 237
price discrimination, p. 238
socially optimal price, p. 242

fair-return price, p. 243
deadweight loss, p. 243

STUDY QUESTIONS

1. "No firm is completely sheltered from rivals; all firms compete for consumer dollars. If that is so, then pure monopoly does not exist." Do you agree? Explain. How might you use Chapter 6's concept of cross elasticity of demand to judge whether monopoly exists?

2. Discuss the major barriers to entry into an industry. Explain how each barrier can foster either monopoly or oligopoly. Which barriers, if any, do you believe give rise to monopoly that is socially justifiable?

3. How does the demand curve faced by a purely monopolistic seller differ from that confronting a purely competitive firm? Why does it differ? Of what significance is the difference? Why is the pure monopolist's demand curve not perfectly inelastic?

4. **KEY QUESTION** Use the demand schedule that follows to calculate total revenue and marginal revenue at each quantity. Plot the demand, total-revenue, and marginal-revenue curves, and explain the relationships between them. Explain why the marginal revenue of the fourth unit of output is $3.50, even though its price is $5.00. Use Chapter 5's total-revenue test for price elasticity to designate the elastic and inelastic segments of your graphed demand curve. What generalization can you make about the relationship between marginal revenue and elasticity of demand? Suppose the marginal cost of successive units of output were zero. What output would the profit-seeking firm produce? Finally, use your analysis to explain why a monopolist would never produce in the inelastic region of demand.

Price (P)	Quantity demanded (Q)	Price (P)	Quantity demanded (Q)
$7.00	0	$4.50	5
6.50	1	4.00	6
6.00	2	3.50	7
5.50	3	3.00	8
5.00	4	2.50	9

5. **KEY QUESTION** Suppose a pure monopolist is faced with the demand schedule shown in the next column and the same cost data as the competitive producer discussed in question 4 at the end of Chapter 8. Calculate the missing total-revenue and marginal-revenue amounts, and determine the profit-maximizing price and profit-earning output for this monopolist. What is the monopolist's profit? Verify your answer graphically and by comparing total revenue and total cost.

Price	Quantity demanded	Total revenue	Marginal revenue
$115	0	$_____	
100	1	_____	$_____
83	2	_____	_____
71	3	_____	_____
63	4	_____	_____
55	5	_____	_____
48	6	_____	_____
42	7	_____	_____
37	8	_____	_____
33	9	_____	_____
29	10	_____	_____

6. **KEY QUESTION** If the firm described in question 5 could engage in perfect price discrimination, what would be the level of output? of profits? Draw a diagram showing the relevant demand, marginal-revenue, average-total-cost, and marginal-cost curves, and the equilibrium price and output for a non-discriminating monopolist. Use the same diagram to show the equilibrium position of a monopolist that is able to practise perfect price discrimination. Compare equilibrium outputs, total revenues, economic profits, and consumer prices in the two cases. Comment on the economic desirability of price discrimination.

7. Assume that a pure monopolist and a purely competitive firm have the same unit costs. Contrast the two with respect to (a) price, (b) output, (c) profits, (d) allocation of resources, and (e) impact on the distribution of income. Since both monopolists and competitive firms follow the MC = MR rule in maximizing profits, how do you account for the different results? Why might the costs of a purely competitive firm and a monopolist be different? What are the implications of such a cost difference?

8. Critically evaluate and explain:

   a. "Because they can control product price, monopolists are always assured of profitable production by simply charging the highest price consumers will pay."

   b. "The pure monopolist seeks the output that will yield the greatest per-unit profit."

   c. "An excess of price over marginal cost is the market's way of signalling the need for more production of a good."

   d. "The more profitable a firm, the greater its monopoly power."

   e. "The monopolist has a pricing policy; the competitive producer does not."

   f. "With respect to resource allocation, the interests of the seller and of society coincide in a purely competitive market but conflict in a monopolized market."

   g. "In a sense the monopolist makes a profit for not producing; the monopolist produces profit more than it does goods."

9. Assume a monopolistic publisher has agreed to pay an author 15 percent of the total revenue from the sales of a text. Will the author and the publisher want to charge the same price for the text? Explain.

10. Explain verbally and graphically how price (rate) regulation may improve the performance of monopolies. In your answer distinguish between (a) socially optimal (marginal-cost) pricing and (b) fair-return (average-total-cost) pricing. What is the "dilemma of regulation"?

www.mcgrawhill.ca/college/mcconnell

11. **KEY QUESTION** It has been proposed that natural monopolists should be allowed to determine their profit-maximizing outputs and prices and then government should tax their profits away and distribute them to consumers in proportion to their purchases from the monopoly. Is this proposal as socially desirable as requiring monopolists to equate price with marginal cost or average total cost?

12. U.S. pharmaceutical companies charge different prices for prescription drugs to buyers in different nations, including Canada, depending on elasticity of demand and government-imposed price ceilings. Explain why these companies oppose laws allowing the re-importation of drugs to the United States.

13. Use Figure 9-10 to explain why pure monopoly generates deadweight loss.

14. **(The Last Word)** How was De Beers able to control the world price of diamonds over the past several decades even though it produced only 50 percent of the diamonds? What factors ended its monopoly? What is De Beers' new strategy for earning economic profit, rather than just normal profit?

INTERNET APPLICATION QUESTIONS

1. In 2002 a U.S. Court of Appeals imposed remedies relating to a lower court's findings that Microsoft had a monopoly in personal computer (PC) operating systems and had maintained its monopoly through illegal actions. Go to the McConnell-Brue-Barbiero Web site (Chapter 9) to access the details of the case. On what basis did the court conclude that Microsoft was a monopoly (see Market Share)? What was Microsoft's market share of Intel-compatible PC operating systems? Of all operating systems, including Apple computers? What evidence did the court cite in claiming that Microsoft charged above-competitive prices (see Microsoft's Pricing Behaviour)?

10

Chapter

Monopolistic Competition and Oligopoly

Most market structures in the Canadian economy fall between the two extremes of pure competition and pure monopoly. In this chapter we develop models of *monopolistic competition* and *oligopoly* that more closely approximate real-world market structures.

Monopolistic competition exhibits a considerable amount of competition mixed with a small dose of monopoly power. For example, when you go out to eat, you have an amazing variety of choices. You can get a meal at a fast-food place such as McDonald's, Subway, or Taco Bell. You can go to a restaurant with a fuller menu and table service. For a special meal you can choose an Italian, a French, or a Japanese fine-food restaurant where your bill may be $40 or more per person. Each establishment serves food and beverages, but all have different menus and prices. Competition among them is based not only on price but also on product quality, location, and service.

Oligopoly, in contrast, displays a blend of greater monopoly power, less competition, and more strategic behaviour. There are only a few firms in an oligopolistic industry, and entry is difficult. For example, when you fly on a large commercial aircraft you are probably flying in a plane built by one of two world producers: Airbus or Boeing. In many manufacturing, mining, and wholesaling industries only a few firms dominate, not the thousands of producers present in pure competition, the many firms in monopolistic competition, or the single firm in monopoly.

10.1   Characteristics of Monopolistic Competition

monopolistic competition
A market structure in which many firms sell a differentiated product and entry into and exit from the market is relatively easy.

Let's begin by examining **monopolistic competition**, which is characterized by (1) a relatively large number of sellers, (2) differentiated products (often promoted by heavy advertising), and (3) easy entry to, and exit from, the industry. The first and third characteristics provide the competitive aspect of monopolistic competition; the second characteristic provides the monopolistic aspect. In general, however, monopolistically competitive industries are more competitive than they are monopolistic.

Relatively Large Number of Sellers

Monopolistic competition is characterized by a fairly large number of firms, say, 25, 35, 60, or 70, not by the hundreds or thousands of firms in pure competition. Consequently, monopolistic competition involves

<www.theshortrun.com/
classroom/glossary/micro/
monocomp.html>
Monopolistic competition

- **Small market shares**   Each firm has a comparatively small percentage of the total market and consequently has limited control over market price.

- **No collusion**   The presence of a relatively large number of firms makes collusion by a group of firms to restrict output and set prices unlikely.

- **Independent action**   With many firms in an industry, there is little interdependence among them; each firm can determine its own pricing policy without considering the possible reactions of rival firms. A single firm may realize a modest increase in sales by cutting its price, but the effect of that action on competitors' sales will be nearly imperceptible and will probably not trigger a response.

Differentiated Products

product differentiation
A form of non-price competition in which a firm tries to distinguish its product or service from all competing ones based on attributes such as design and quality.

In contrast to pure competition in which there is a standardized product, monopolistic competition is distinguished by **product differentiation**. Firms in monopolistic competition turn out variations of a particular product. They produce products with slightly different physical characteristics; offer varying degrees of customer service; provide varying amounts of location convenience; or proclaim special qualities, real or imagined, for their products.

Let's examine these aspects of product differentiation in more detail.

PRODUCT ATTRIBUTES

Product differentiation may take the form of physical or qualitative differences in the products themselves. Real differences in functional features, materials, design, and quality of work are vital aspects of product differentiation. Personal computers, for example, differ in terms of storage capacity, speed, graphic displays, and included software. There are dozens of competing principles of economics textbooks that differ in content, organization, presentation and readability, pedagogical aids, and graphics and design. Most cities have a variety of retail stores selling men's and women's clothing that differ greatly in styling, materials, and quality of work.

SERVICE

Service and the conditions surrounding the sale of a product are also forms of product differentiation. One grocery store may stress the helpfulness of its clerks who bag your groceries and carry them to your car. A warehouse supermarket may leave bagging and carrying to its customers but feature lower prices. Customers may prefer one-day over three-day dry cleaning of equal quality. The prestige appeal of a store, the courteousness and helpfulness of clerks, the firm's reputation for servicing or exchanging its products, and the credit it makes available are all service aspects of product differentiation.

LOCATION

Product differentiation may also be created through the use of brand names and trade marks, packaging, and celebrity connections.

Products may also be differentiated through the location and accessibility of the stores that sell them. Small convenience stores manage to compete with large supermarkets, even though these minimarts have a more limited range of products and charge higher prices. They compete mainly on the basis of location—being close to customers and situated on busy streets. A motel's proximity to a main highway gives it a locational advantage that may allow it to charge a higher room rate than nearby motels in less convenient locations.

BRAND NAMES AND PACKAGING

Product differentiation may also be created through the use of brand names and trademarks, packaging, and celebrity connections. Most aspirin tablets are very much alike, but many headache sufferers believe that one brand—for example, Bayer, Anacin, or Bufferin—is superior and worth a higher price than a generic substitute. A celebrity's name associated with jeans, perfume, or athletic equipment may enhance the appeal of those products for some buyers. Many customers prefer one style of ballpoint pen to another. Packaging that touts natural spring bottled water may attract additional customers versus other bottled waters.

SOME CONTROL OVER PRICE

Despite the relatively large number of firms, monopolistic competitors do have some control over their product prices because of product differentiation. If consumers prefer the products of specific sellers, then within limits they will pay more to satisfy their preferences. But control a firm in monopolistic competition has over price is quite limited, since there are numerous potential substitutes for its product.

Easy Entry and Exit

Entry into industries characterized by a monopolistic competition market structure is relatively easy compared to oligopoly or pure monopoly. Because firms are typically small, both absolutely and relatively, economies of scale are few and capital requirements are low. However, compared with pure competition, financial barriers may result from the need to develop and advertise a different product from one's rivals. Some firms may hold patents on their products or copyrights on their brand names, making it difficult and costly for other firms to imitate them.

Exit from industries in monopolistic competition is easier still. Nothing prevents an unprofitable firm from holding a going-out-of-business sale and shutting down.

Advertising

The expense and effort involved in product differentiation would be wasted if consumers were not made aware of product differences. Thus, firms in monopolistic competition advertise their prod-

252

non-price competition
A selling strategy in which one firm tries to distinguish its product or service from all competing ones based on attributes other than price.

ucts, often heavily. The goal of product differentiation and advertising—so-called **non-price competition**—is to make product differences a greater factor in consumer purchases than price. If successful, the firm's demand curve will shift to the right and will become less elastic.

Monopolistically Competitive Industries

Figure 10-1 lists several Canadian manufacturing industries that approximate monopolistic competition. In addition, many retail establishments in metropolitan areas fall into the category of monopolistic competition, including grocery stores, gasoline stations, barbershops, dry cleaners, clothing stores, and restaurants.

10.2   Price and Output in Monopolistic Competition

We now analyze the price and output decisions of a firm in monopolistic competition. Initially, we assume that each firm in the industry is producing a specific differentiated product and engaging in a particular amount of advertising. Later we'll see how changes in the product and in the amount of advertising modify our conclusions.

The Firm's Demand Curve

Our explanation is based on **Figure 10-2 (Key Graph)**. The basic feature of that diagram is the elasticity of demand, as shown by the individual firm's demand curve. The demand curve of each firm is highly, but not perfectly, elastic. It is precisely this feature that distinguishes monopolistic competition from pure monopoly and pure competition. The demand is more elastic than the demand

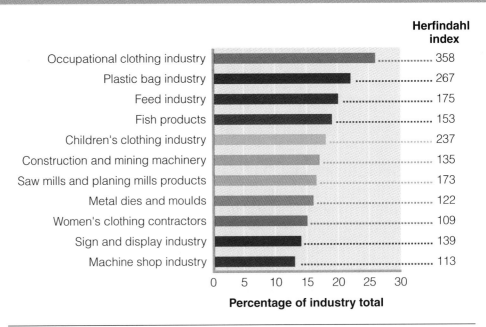

FIGURE 10-1

Percentage of Output Produced by the Four Largest Firms in Selected Low-concentration Sectors*

Several Canadian manufacturing industries approximate monopolistic competition, with a relatively large number of sellers, producing differentiated products. There is easy entry into the industry and firms often differentiate their products through advertising.

	Herfindahl index
Occupational clothing industry	358
Plastic bag industry	267
Feed industry	175
Fish products	153
Children's clothing industry	237
Construction and mining machinery	135
Saw mills and planing mills products	173
Metal dies and moulds	122
Women's clothing contractors	109
Sign and display industry	139
Machine shop industry	113

Percentage of industry total

Source: Statistics Canada, Industrial Organization and Concentration in Manufacturing, Mining and Logging Industries, Catalogue No. 31C0024.

*As measured by dollar value of shipments.

Key Graph

FIGURE 10-2 A Monopolistically Competitive Firm: Short Run and Long Run

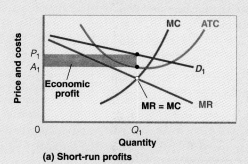

(a) Short-run profits

The firm in monopolistic competition maximizes profit or minimizes loss by producing the output at which MR = MC. The economic profit shown in panel (a) will induce new firms to enter, eventually eliminating economic profit. The loss shown in panel (b) will cause an exit of firms until normal profit is restored. After such entry and exit, the price will settle in panel (c) to where it just equals average total cost at the MR = MC output. At this price P_3 and output Q_3, the firm in monopolistic competition earns only a normal profit, and the industry is in long-run equilibrium.

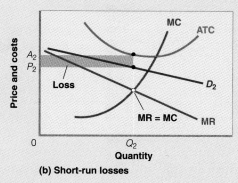

(b) Short-run losses

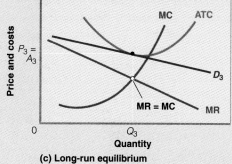

(c) Long-run equilibrium

Quick Quiz

1. Price exceeds MC in
   a. graph (a) only.
   b. graph (b) only.
   c. graphs (a) and (b) only.
   d. graphs (a), (b), and (c).

2. Price exceeds ATC in
   a. graph (a) only.
   b. graph (b) only.
   c. graphs (a) and (b) only.
   d. graphs (a), (b), and (c).

3. The firm represented by Figure 10-2(c) is
   a. making a normal profit.
   b. incurring a loss, once opportunity costs are considered.
   c. producing at the same level of output as a purely competitive firm.
   d. producing a standardized product.

4. Which of the following pairs are both competition-like elements in monopolistic competition?
   a. Price exceeds MR; standardized product.
   b. Entry is relatively easy; only a normal profit in the long run.
   c. Price equals MC at the profit-maximizing output; economic profits are likely in the long run.
   d. The firms' demand curve is downsloping; differentiated products.

ANSWERS: 1. d; 2. a; 3. a; 4. b

faced by a pure monopolist because the firm in monopolistic competition has many competitors producing close substitutes. The pure monopolist has no rivals at all. Yet, there are two reasons why the demand curve of a firm in monopolistic competition is not perfectly elastic, as is the case in pure competition. First, it has fewer rivals; second, its products are differentiated, so they are not perfect substitutes.

The price elasticity of demand faced by the firm in monopolistic competition depends on the number of rivals and the degree of product differentiation. The larger the number of rivals and the weaker the product differentiation, the greater the price elasticity of each firm's demand; that is, the closer monopolistic competition will be to pure competition.

The Short Run: Profit or Loss

The firm in monopolistic competition maximizes its profit or minimizes its loss in the short run just as firms in the other market structures we have discussed do: by producing the output at which marginal revenue equals marginal cost (MR = MC). In Figure 10-2(a) the firm produces output Q_1, where MR = MC. As shown by demand curve D_1, the firm then can charge price P_1. It realizes an economic profit, shown by the grey area $[= (P_1 - A_1) \times Q_1]$.

But with less favourable demand or costs, the firm may incur a loss in the short run. This possibility is shown in Figure 10-2(b), where the firm's best strategy is to minimize its loss. It does so by producing output Q_2 (where MR = MC) and, as determined by demand curve D_2, by charging price P_2. Because price P_2 is less than average total cost A_2, the firm incurs a per unit loss of $A_2 - P_2$ and a total loss represented as the pink area $[= (A_2 - P_2) \times Q_2]$.

The Long Run: Only a Normal Profit

In the long run, if there are economic profits, firms will enter an industry but exit an unprofitable one. So, a firm in monopolistic competition will earn only a normal profit in the long run. (Remember that the cost curves include both explicit and implicit costs, including a normal profit.)

PROFITS: FIRMS ENTER

In the case of short-run profit in Figure 10-2(a), economic profits attract new rivals because entry to the industry is relatively easy. As new firms enter, the demand curve faced by the typical firm shifts to the left (falls) because each firm has a smaller share of total demand. This decline in the firm's demand reduces its economic profit. When entry of new firms has reduced demand to the extent that the demand curve is tangent to the average-total-cost curve at the profit-maximizing output, the firm is just making a normal profit. This situation is shown in Figure 10-2(c), where demand is D_3 and the firm's long-run equilibrium output is Q_3. As Figure 10-2(c) indicates, any greater or lesser output will entail an average total cost that exceeds product price P_3, meaning a loss for the firm. At the tangency point between the demand curve and ATC, total revenue equals total costs. With the economic profit gone, no further incentive exists for additional firms to enter.

LOSSES: FIRMS LEAVE

When the industry suffers short-run losses, as in Figure 10-2(b), some firms will exit in the long run. Faced with fewer substitute products and with an expanded share of total demand, the surviving firms will see their demand curves shift to the right (rise), as to D_3. Their losses will disappear and give way to normal profits, shown in Figure 10-2(c). (For simplicity we have assumed constant costs; shifts in the cost curves as firms enter or leave would complicate our discussion slightly but would not alter our conclusions.)

COMPLICATIONS

The representative firm in the monopolistic competition model earns only a normal profit in the long run. That outcome may not always occur because of the following reasons:

- Some firms may achieve sufficient product differentiation that other firms cannot duplicate them, even over time. For example, one hotel in a major city may have the best location for business and tourist activities. Or a firm may have developed a well-known brand name that gives it a slight but very long-lasting advantage over imitators. Such firms may have sufficient monopoly power to realize modest economic profits even in the long run.

- Entry to some monopolistically competitive industries may not be easy. Because of product differentiation, greater financial barriers to entry are likely to exist than if the product were standardized. This suggests some monopoly power, with small economic profits continuing even in the long run.

 With all things considered, however, the normal profit outcome—the long-run equilibrium—shown in Figure 10-2(c) is a reasonable portrayal of reality.

Monopolistic Competition and Efficiency

We know from Chapter 8 that economic efficiency requires the triple equality $P = MC = $ minimum ATC. The equality of price and minimum average total cost yields *productive efficiency*. The good is being produced in the least costly way, and the price is just sufficient to cover average total cost, including a normal profit. The equality of price and marginal cost also yields *allocative efficiency*. The right amount of output is being produced, and thus the right amount of society's scarce resources is being devoted to this specific use.

How efficient is monopolistic competition, as measured against this triple equality?

NEITHER PRODUCTIVE NOR ALLOCATIVE EFFICIENCY

In monopolistic competition, neither productive nor allocative efficiency is achieved in long-run equilibrium. We show this in Figure 10-3, which includes an enlargement of part of Figure 10-2(c). First note that the profit-maximizing price P_3 slightly exceeds the lowest average total cost, A_4. Therefore, in producing the profit-maximizing output Q_3, the firm's average total cost is slightly higher than optimal from society's perspective—productive efficiency is not achieved. Also note that the profit-maximizing price P_3 exceeds marginal cost (here M_3), meaning that monopolistic competition causes an underallocation of resources. Society values each unit of output between Q_3 and Q_4 more highly than the goods it would have to forgo to produce those units. Thus, to a modest extent, monopolistic competition also fails the allocative-efficiency test. Consumers pay a higher-than-competitive price and obtain a less-than-optimal output. Indeed, firms in monopolistic competition must charge a higher-than-competitive price in the long run to achieve a normal profit.

EXCESS CAPACITY

excess capacity
Plant or equipment that is underused because the firm is producing less than the minimum-ATC output.

In monopolistic competition, the gap between the minimum-ATC output and the profit-maximizing output identifies **excess capacity**: plant or equipment that is underused because firms are producing less than the minimum-ATC output. We show this gap as the distance between Q_4 and Q_3 in Figure 10-3. If each firm could profitably produce at the minimum-ATC output, fewer firms could produce the same total output, and the product could be sold at a lower price. Industries that have a monopolistic-competition market structure are thus overcrowded with firms, each operating below its optimal capacity. This situation is typified by many kinds of retail establishments. For example, most cities have an abundance of small motels and restaurants that operate well below half capacity. *(Key Question 2)*

PRODUCT VARIETY

The situation portrayed in Figures 10-2(c) and 10-3 is not very satisfying to firms in monopolistic competition, since it allows only a normal profit. But the profit-realizing firm of Figure 10-2(a) need not stand by and watch new competitors eliminate its profit by imitating its product, match-

FIGURE 10-3 **The Inefficiency of Monopolistic Competition**

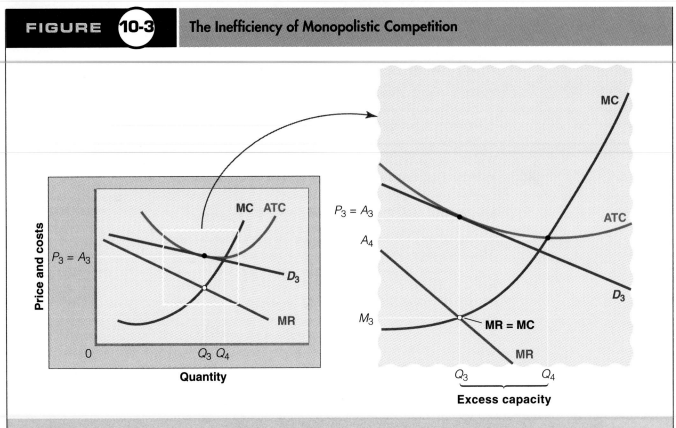

In long-run equilibrium a firm in monopolistic competition achieves neither productive nor allocative efficiency. Productive efficiency is not realized because production occurs where the average total cost A_3 exceeds the minimum average total cost A_4. Allocative efficiency is not realized because the product price P_3 exceeds the marginal cost M_3. The result is an underallocation of resources and excess productive capacity of $Q_4 - Q_3$.

ing its customer service, and copying its advertising. Each firm has a product that is distinguishable in some way from those of the other producers. So, the firm can attempt to stay ahead of competitors and sustain its profit through further product differentiation and more effective advertising. By developing or improving its product, it may be able to postpone, at least for a while, the outcome of Figure 10-2(c).

It is true that product differentiation and advertising will add to the firm's costs, but they can also increase the demand for its product. If demand increases by more than enough to compensate for the added costs, the firm will have improved its profit position. As Figure 10-3 suggests, the firm has little or no prospect of increasing profit by price-cutting. So why not engage in non-price competition?

Benefits of Product Variety   The product variety and product improvement that accompany the drive to maintain above-normal profit in monopolistic competition are a benefit for society—they may offset the cost of the inefficiency associated with monopolistic competition. Consumers have a wide diversity of tastes: Some like hip-hop bands, others like punk bands; some like contemporary furniture, others like traditional furniture. If a product is differentiated, then at any time the consumer will be offered a wide range of types, styles, brands, and quality gradations of that product. Compared with pure competition, this provides an advantage to the consumer. The range of choice is widened, and producers more fully meet the wide variation in consumer tastes.

In fact, product differentiation creates a tradeoff between consumer choice and productive efficiency. The stronger the product differentiation, the greater is the excess capacity and, hence, the greater is the productive inefficiency. But the greater the product differentiation, the more likely the firms will satisfy the great diversity of consumer tastes. The greater the excess capacity problem, the wider the range of consumer choice.

Further Complexity

Finally, the ability to engage in non-price competition makes the firm's situation in monopolistic competition more complex than Figure 10-3 indicates. That figure assumes a given (unchanging) product and a given level of advertising expenditures. But we know that, in practice, product attributes and advertising are not fixed. The firm in monopolistic competition juggles three factors—price, product, and advertising—in seeking maximum profit. It must determine what variety of product, selling at what price, and supplemented by what level of advertising will result in the greatest profit. This complex situation is not easily expressed in a simple economic model. At best, we can say that each possible combination of price, product, and advertising poses a different demand and cost (production cost plus advertising cost) situation for the firm, and that only one combination yields the maximum profit. In practice, this optimal combination cannot be readily forecast but must be found by trial and error.

QUICK R E V I E W	
• Monopolistic competition involves a relatively large number of firms operating in a non-collusive way and producing differentiated products, with easy industry entry and exit. • In the short run, a firm in monopolistic competition will maximize profit or minimize loss by producing that output at which marginal revenue equals marginal cost.	• In the long run, the easy entry and exit of firms in monopolistic competition means they earn only a normal profit. • The long-run equilibrium output for a firm in monopolistic competition is such that price exceeds the minimum average total cost (implying that consumers do not get the product at the lowest price attainable) and price exceeds marginal cost (indicating that resources are underallocated to the product).

10.3   The Characteristics of Oligopoly

oligopoly
A market structure dominated by a few large producers of homogeneous or differentiated products.

In terms of competitiveness, the spectrum of market structures reaches from pure competition to monopolistic competition, to oligopoly, to pure monopoly (review Table 8-1). We now direct our attention to **oligopoly**, a market structure dominated by a few large producers of a homogeneous or differentiated product. Because of their small number, oligopolists have considerable control over their prices, but each must consider the possible reaction of rivals to its own pricing, output, and advertising decisions.

<www.indiana.edu/~econed/pdffiles/fall99/meister.pdf>
Oligopoly: An in-class economic game

A Few Large Producers

The phrase "a few large producers" is necessarily vague because the market model of oligopoly covers much ground, ranging between pure monopoly on the one hand and monopolistic competition on the other. Oligopoly encompasses the Canadian steel industry, in which two firms dominate an entire national market, and the situation in which four or five much smaller auto parts stores enjoy roughly equal shares of the market in a medium-sized town. Generally, however, when you hear a term such as Big Three, Big Four, or Big Six, you can be sure it refers to an oligopolistic industry.

Homogeneous or Differentiated Products

homogeneous oligopoly
An oligopoly in which the firms produce a standardized product.

differentiated oligopoly
An oligopoly in which the firms produce a differentiated product.

An oligopoly may be either a **homogeneous oligopoly** or a **differentiated oligopoly**, depending on whether the firms in the oligopoly produce standardized or differentiated products. Many industrial products (steel, zinc, copper, aluminum, lead, cement, industrial alcohol) are virtually standardized products that are produced in oligopolies. Many consumer goods industries (automobiles, tires, household appliances, electronics equipment, breakfast cereals, cigarettes, and many sporting goods) are differentiated oligopolies. An example of a differentiated oligopoly in Canada is the media and telecommunications sector. It is dominated by CanWest Global Communications, which owns a daily newspaper in almost every big city in Canada and a variety of television stations; and BCE, which controls Bell Canada and owns satellite broadcaster Bell ExpressVu, television stations, and the *Globe and Mail*. These differentiated oligopolies typically engage in considerable non-price competition supported by heavy advertising.

Control over Price, but Mutual Interdependence

mutual interdependence
A situation in which a change in strategy (usually price) by one firm will affect the sales and profits of other firms.

Because firms are few in oligopolistic industries, each firm is a price-maker; like the monopolist, it can set its price and output levels to maximize its profit. But unlike the monopolist, which has no rivals, the oligopolist must consider how its rivals will react to any change in its price, output, product characteristics, or advertising. Oligopoly is thus characterized by **mutual interdependence**: a situation in which each firm's profit depends on its own price and sales strategies as well as those of its rivals. For example, in deciding whether to increase the price of its rolled steel, Dofasco will try to predict the response of the other major producer, Stelco (both firms are located in Hamilton, Ontario). In deciding on its advertising strategy, Burger King will take into consideration how McDonald's might react.

Entry Barriers

The same barriers to entry that create pure monopoly also contribute to the creation of oligopoly. Economies of scale are important entry barriers in a number of oligopolistic industries, such as the aircraft, rubber, and cement industries. In those industries, three or four firms might each have sufficient sales to achieve economies of scale, but new firms would have such a small market share that they could not do so. They would then be high-cost producers, and as such they could not survive. A closely related barrier is the large expenditure for capital—the cost of obtaining necessary plant and equipment—required for entering certain industries. The automobile, commercial aircraft, and petroleum-refining industries, for example, are all characterized by very high capital requirements. In Canada, the domestic automobile industry is dominated by Ford, General Motors, and Daimler-Chrysler, whose plants are concentrated in Ontario and Quebec; Quebec's Bombardier is one of the world's largest manufacturers of small short-haul passenger planes, such as the Dash 8; and Petro-Canada, which is 18 percent owned by the Canadian government, is Canada's largest oil refiner, as well as a major international player in the oil and gas sector.

The ownership and control of raw materials help explain why oligopoly exists in many mining industries, including gold, silver, and copper. In the electronics, chemicals, photographic equipment, office machine, and pharmaceutical industries, patents have served as entry barriers. Oligopolists can also preclude the entry of new competitors through preemptive and retaliatory pricing and advertising strategies.

Mergers

<distance-ed.bcc.ctc.edu/
econ100/ksttext/oligoply/
oligoply.htm>
The arthritic hand of oligopoly

Some oligopolies have emerged mainly through the growth of the dominant firms in a given industry (breakfast cereals, chewing gum, candy bars). But for other industries the route to oligopoly has been through mergers (examples: steel, in its early history; and, more recently, airlines, banking, and entertainment). The merging, or combining, of two or more competing firms may substantially increase their market share, which in turn may allow the new firm to achieve greater economies of scale.

Measures of Industry Concentration

Several measures exist to determine the degree to which oligopolistic industries are concentrated in their largest firms. The most-often-used measures are *concentration ratios* and the *Herfindahl index.*

CONCENTRATION RATIO

concentration ratio
The percentage of the total sales of an industry produced and sold by an industry's largest firms.

A **concentration ratio** reveals the percentage of total output produced and sold by an industry's largest firms. Figure 10-4 lists the four-firm concentration ratio—the percentage of total industry sales accounted for by the four largest firms—for a number of oligopolistic industries. For example, the four largest Canadian producers of tobacco products manufacture almost 100 percent of all cigarettes produced in Canada. (In fact, the domestic tobacco market is largely controlled by the *three* largest Canadian companies: Imperial Tobacco Ltd., owned by Imasco Ltd.; Rothmans, Benson & Hedges Inc.; and RJR-MacDonald Ltd.)

When the largest four firms in an industry control 40 percent or more of the market (as in Figure 10-4), that industry is considered oligopolistic. Using this benchmark, about one-half of all Canadian manufacturing industries are oligopolies.

Although concentration ratios provide useful insights into the competitiveness or monopoly power of various industries, they have three shortcomings.

Localized Markets Concentration ratios relate to the nation as a whole, whereas the markets for some products are highly localized because of high transportation costs. For example, the four-firm concentration ratio for concrete products is only 25 percent, suggesting a competitive industry in Canada. But the sheer bulk of this product limits the relevant market to a specific town or metropolitan area, and in such localized concrete markets we often find oligopolistic market structures.

interindustry competition
The competition between the products of one industry and the products of another industry.

Interindustry Competition We must be aware of **interindustry competition**—that is, competition between two products associated with different industries. The high concentration

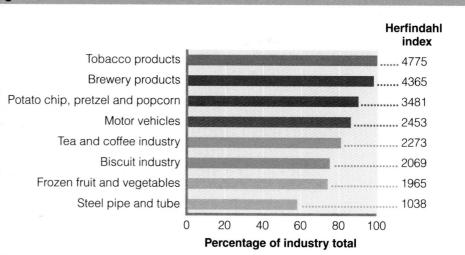

FIGURE 10-4

Percentage of Output Produced by the Four Largest Firms in Selected High-concentration Industries*

A concentration ratio reveals the percentage of total output produced and sold by an industry's four largest firms. The Herfindahl index is the sum of the squared percentage market share of all the firms in the industry. The higher the Herfindahl index, the greater the market power within an industry. The tobacco industry is the most concentrated sector in Canada.

Industry	Herfindahl index
Tobacco products	4775
Brewery products	4365
Potato chip, pretzel and popcorn	3481
Motor vehicles	2453
Tea and coffee industry	2273
Biscuit industry	2069
Frozen fruit and vegetables	1965
Steel pipe and tube	1038

Percentage of industry total

Source: Statistics Canada, Industrial Organization and Concentration in Manufacturing, Mining and Logging, Catalogue No. 31C0024.

*As measured by dollar value of shipments

ratio for the steel pipe and tube industry shown in Figure 10-4 understates the competition in that industry, because copper and plastic tubing compete with steel tubing in many applications.

World Trade   The data in Figure 10-4 are for Canadian production only, and may overstate concentration because they do not account for the **import competition** of foreign suppliers. The automobile industry is a good example. Although Figure 10-4 shows that three firms produce almost 90 percent of the domestic output of those goods, it ignores the fact that a large portion of the automobiles bought in Canada are imports. (Some foreign producers have actually set up production facilities in Canada. An example is Honda, in Alliston, Ontario.) Many of the world's largest corporations are foreign, and many of them do business in Canada, providing competition for domestic producers.

import competition
The competition domestic firms encounter from the products and services of foreign producers.

HERFINDAHL INDEX

The shortcomings of concentration ratios listed above actually apply to many measures of concentration, but one of those shortcomings can be eliminated: Suppose that in industry X one firm produces all the market output. A second industry, Y, has four firms, of which each has 25 percent of the market. The concentration ratio is 100 percent for both these industries. But industry X is a pure monopoly, while industry Y is an oligopoly that may be facing significant economic rivalry. Most economists would agree that monopoly power (or market power) is substantially greater in industry X than in industry Y, a fact disguised by their identical 100 percent concentration ratios.

The **Herfindahl index** addresses this problem. This index is the sum of the squared percentage market shares of all firms in the industry. In equation form:

Herfindahl index
The sum of the squared percentage market shares of all firms in the industry.

$$\text{Herfindahl index} = (\%S_1)^2 + (\%S_2)^2 + (\%S_3)^2 + \ldots + (\%S_n)^2$$

where $\%S_1$ is the percentage market share of firm 1, $\%S_2$ is the percentage market share of firm 2, and so on for each firm in the industry. By squaring the percentage market shares of all firms in the industry, the Herfindahl index gives much greater weight to larger, and thus more powerful, firms than to smaller ones. In the case of the single-firm industry X, the index would be at its maximum of 100^2 or 10,000, indicating an industry with complete monopoly power. For our supposed four-firm industry Y, the index would be $25^2 + 25^2 + 25^2 + 25^2$, or 2500, indicating much less market power. (For a purely competitive industry, the index would approach zero, since each firm's market share—$\%S$ in the equation—is extremely small.)

To generalize, the larger the Herfindahl index, the greater the market power within an industry. Note in Table 10-4 that the four-firm concentration ratios for the tobacco products industry and the brewery products industry are similar. But the Herfindahl index of 4775 for the tobacco products industry suggests greater market power than the 4365 index for the brewery products industry. Also, contrast the much larger Herfindahl indexes in Table 10-4 with those for the low-concentration industries in Table 10-1. *(Key Question 7)*

| 10.4 | Oligopoly Pricing Behaviour: A Game Theory Overview |

Oligopoly pricing behaviour has the characteristics of certain games of strategy, such as poker, chess, and bridge. The best way to play such a game depends on the way one's opponent plays. Players (and oligopolists) must plan their actions according to the actions and expected reactions of rivals. The study of how people behave in strategic situations is called *game theory*. We will use a simple **game theory model** to analyze the pricing behaviour of oligopolists. Game theory was first developed in the 1920s, and expanded rapidly during World War II in response to the military need of developing formal ways of thinking about strategy.

game theory model
A means of analyzing the pricing behaviour of oligopolists using the theory of strategy associated with games such as chess and bridge.

Basic Concepts

Any interaction in which individuals or firms must make choices and in which the final outcome depends on what each individual or firm chooses to do is termed a *game*. Games have four basic components: (1) the players, (2) the rules, (3) the possible strategies, and (4) the payoffs. Games may be *cooperative,* meaning players in the game make specific agreements that are binding on the parties, or *non-cooperative,* where agreements among the players are not possible.

Players   Each participant in a game is referred to as a player. The players in a game may be individuals, as in a chess game; a firm, usually in imperfectly competitive markets; or a country involved, for example, in a regional conflict. Game theory assumes players in a game can choose among a set of possible actions. The players (decision makers) are rational in that they pursue well-defined objectives. For individuals, the primary objective is utility maximization; for firms, it is profit maximization. Players are assumed to reason strategically, meaning they take into account other players' knowledge and expectations. Games can have any number of players, but for simplicity we will focus on two-player games. We assume that each player chooses a course of action that will yield the greatest benefit for himself or herself.

Rules   Games generally have clearly defined rules that players must follow in pursuing their strategies and goals. An example is the rules that chess players must follow as they choose their moves. The rules of a game may also be viewed as *constraints* that players face as they make choices.

Strategies   A possible course of action for a player in a game is called a strategy. There are usually a number of strategies from which a player can choose. In choosing a strategy, a player will have to consider the likely response from other players in the game. We will focus on possible strategies in cooperative (collusive) and noncooperative (non-collusive) games in a two-firm oligopoly.

Payoffs   Players in a game seek the best possible outcomes for themselves. The final returns to each player in a game are called *payoffs.* Payoffs may be large, small, or even negative. In some instances one player may gain exactly what the other player in the game loses. These are referred to as *zero-sum games.* Some games may offer positive payoffs to all players in the game. These are referred as *positive-sum games.*

EQUILIBRIUM

You will recall from Chapter 3 that competitive markets bring about equilibrium price and quantity for specific products or services. There is no unique equilibrium outcome in game theory. This is because outcomes depend not only on what one player may do, but also on how the other players in the game decide to react to any given initial move by the player making the first move. Still, we will see that there can be a **dominant strategy equilibrium**, in which there is a best strategy for all the players in a game, regardless of the strategies chosen by the other players. The dominant strategy equilibrium is a variant of the **Nash equilibrium**, named after John Nash, who won the Nobel Prize for Economic Science in 1994. A Nash equilibrium is an outcome in a non-cooperative game in which players choose their best strategy given the present strategies the others have chosen. Once a Nash equilibrium is reached, none of the players has an incentive to make a different decision.

Prisoner's Dilemma

To illustrate game theory in action, we'll look at the **prisoner's dilemma**, first introduced in the 1940s by Canadian economist A. W. Tucker, under whom John Nash studied. The prisoner's dilemma is a type of game between two prisoners that shows the difficulty of cooperating when the two cannot communicate with each other, even when it is in their best interests to do so. Let's take a look at an example.

Two individuals, Al and Bruno, are caught by police in the act of breaking into a warehouse containing valuable carpets. On the way to headquarters, the police investigators run a check on other crimes in the area and discover that two men closely matching Al's and Bruno's physical profiles stole $2 million dollars worth of diamonds just six months earlier, in a robbery for which the police have no leads or witnesses. (Al and Bruno had indeed carried out the diamond robbery.) In the hope of getting a confession, the police investigators decide to interrogate Al and Bruno in different rooms so they can't communicate with each other. The game has been set in motion.

dominant strategy equilibrium
An equilibrium in which there is a strategy for all players in a game, regardless of the strategies chosen by the other players.

Nash equilibrium
An outcome in a non-cooperative game in which players choose their best strategy given the present strategies the others have chosen.

prisoner's dilemma
A type of game where, whatever the other player does, each player is better off not co-operating.

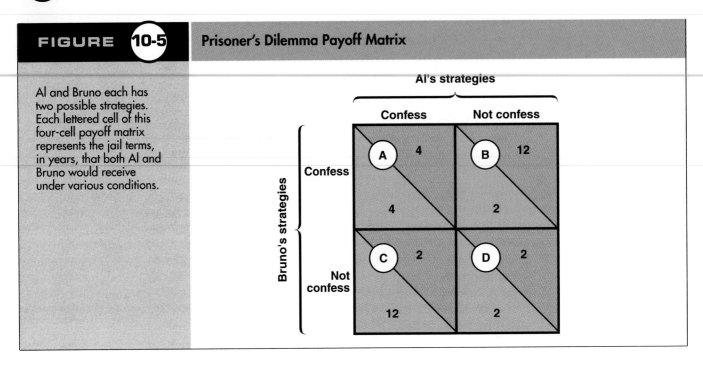

FIGURE 10-5 Prisoner's Dilemma Payoff Matrix

Al and Bruno each has two possible strategies. Each lettered cell of this four-cell payoff matrix represents the jail terms, in years, that both Al and Bruno would receive under various conditions.

The police investigators inform Al and Bruno that they are now suspects in the diamond robbery. Since they were caught red-handed trying to break into the carpet warehouse, Al and Bruno know they each will get the mandatory two-year jail sentence for that crime alone. If both confess to the diamond robbery each will get four years for both crimes. But if one confesses and the other does not, the one that confesses will still receive 2 years, while the one that does not confess will get 12 years.

What are the options for Al and Bruno given the "rules" for this game? Figure 10-5 sets out the *payoff matrix* for Al and Bruno. Four combinations are possible, and each of the four combinations is represented by a lettered cell. If both confess, they will get four years each (Cell A). If neither confesses to the diamond robbery, each will get only two years in jail (Cell D). If Bruno confesses, but Al does not, he gets 2 years and Al gets 12 (Cell B). Alternatively, if Al confesses, but Bruno does not, Al gets 2 years and Bruno goes to the slammer for 12 years (Cell C).

Recall that a player in a game will choose a strategy on the basis of what he or she expects the other players will do. If both Al and Bruno expect the other to deny they participated in the diamond robbery, then each will not confess. Both Al and Bruno know this, but each cannot be sure the other will deny participating in the diamond robbery. If they were allowed to communicate with each other they could cooperate (collude) to minimize their jail sentence. But they can't communicate, which means that they are in a non-cooperative game. The dilemma is that Al and Bruno should cooperate to minimize jail time, but if one confesses and the other does not, the one that does not confess will face a heavier penalty.

Given the uncertainty of what the other will do, confessing is the best strategy for both Al and Bruno in this game. The risk of a much higher jail term is too great for either Al or Bruno to consider denying involvement in the diamond robbery. By not confessing, the best that either Al or Bruno can hope for is a 2-year jail term, but the possibility exists for a 12-year term. If either Al or Bruno confesses, his worst-case scenario is a four-year jail sentence. You should be able to see that the *dominant strategy* for both Al and Bruno is to confess.

Strategies in a Two-firm Oligopoly

Let's now apply the game theory model to a two-firm oligopoly, also known as a *duopoly*. We assume a two-firm oligopoly producing athletic shoes. Each firm—let's call them RareAir and Uptown—

has a choice of two pricing strategies: price high or price low. The profit each firm earns will depend on the strategy it chooses and the strategy its rival chooses.

Four combinations of strategies are possible for the two firms, and a lettered cell in Figure 10-6 represents each combination. For example, cell C represents a low-price strategy for Uptown along with a high-price strategy for RareAir. Cell C shows that if Uptown adopts a low-price strategy and RareAir a high-price strategy, then Uptown will earn $15 million (green portion) and RareAir will earn $6 million (orange portion).

Mutual Interdependence Revisited

The data in Figure 10-6 are hypothetical, but their relationships are typical of real situations. Recall that oligopolistic firms can increase their profits, and influence their rivals' profits, by changing their pricing strategies. Each firm's profit depends on its own pricing strategy and that of its rivals. This mutual interdependence of oligopolists is the most obvious point demonstrated by Figure 10-6. If Uptown adopts a high-price strategy, its profit will be $12 million, provided that RareAir also employs a high-price strategy (cell A). But if RareAir uses a low-price strategy against Uptown's high-price strategy (cell B), RareAir will increase its market share and boost its profit from $12 million to $15 million. RareAir's higher profit will come at the expense of Uptown, whose profit will fall from $12 million to $6 million. Uptown's high-price strategy is a good strategy only if RareAir also employs a high-price strategy.

Collusive Tendencies

collusion
A situation in which firms act together and in agreement to fix prices, divide a market, or otherwise restrict competition.

Figure 10-6 also suggests that oligopolists often can benefit from **collusion**—that is, cooperation with rivals. To see the benefits of collusion, first suppose that both firms in Figure 10-6 are acting independently and following high-price strategies. Each realizes a $12 million profit (cell A).

Note that either RareAir or Uptown could increase its profit by switching to a low-price strategy (cell B or C). The low-price firm would increase its profit to $15 million, and the high-price firm's profit would fall to $6 million. The high-price firm would be better off if it, too, adopted a low-price policy. Doing so would increase its profit from $6 million to $8 million (cell D). The effect of all

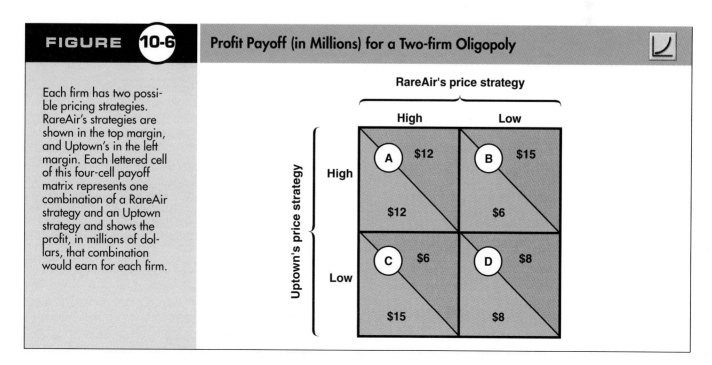

FIGURE 10-6

Profit Payoff (in Millions) for a Two-firm Oligopoly

Each firm has two possible pricing strategies. RareAir's strategies are shown in the top margin, and Uptown's in the left margin. Each lettered cell of this four-cell payoff matrix represents one combination of a RareAir strategy and an Uptown strategy and shows the profit, in millions of dollars, that combination would earn for each firm.

this independent strategy shifting would be to reduce both firms' profits from $12 million (cell A) to $8 million (cell D).

In real situations, too, independent action by oligopolists may lead to mutual competitive low-price strategies: Independent oligopolists compete with respect to price, which leads to lower prices and lower profits. This is clearly beneficial to consumers but not to the oligopolists' profits.

How could oligopolists avoid the low-profit outcome of cell D? The answer is that they could collude, rather than establish prices competitively or independently. In our example, the two firms could agree to establish and maintain a high-price policy. Each firm will increase its profit from $8 million (cell D) to $12 million (cell A).

Incentive to Cheat

The payoff matrix also explains why an oligopolist might be strongly tempted to cheat on a collusive agreement. Suppose Uptown and RareAir agree to maintain high-price policies, with each earning $12 million in profit (cell A). Both are tempted to cheat on this collusive pricing agreement, because either firm can increase its profit to $15 million by lowering its price. If Uptown cheats on the agreement by charging low prices, the payoff moves from cell A to cell C. Uptown's profit rises to $15 million, and RareAir's falls to $6 million. If RareAir cheats, the payoff moves from cell A to cell B, and RareAir gets the $15 million. *(Key Question 9)*

- An oligopoly is made up of relatively few firms producing either homogeneous or differentiated products; these firms are mutually interdependent.

- Barriers to entry such as scale economies, control of patents or strategic resources, or the ability to engage in retaliatory pricing characterize oligopolies. Oligopolies may result from internal growth of firms, mergers, or both.

- The four-firm concentration ratio shows the percentage of an industry's sales accounted for by its four largest firms; the Herfindahl index measures the degree of market power in an industry by summing the squares of the percentage market shares held by the individual firms in the industry.

- The prisoner's dilemma is a type of game that shows the difficulty of cooperating when the participants cannot communicate with each other.

- Game theory reveals that (1) oligopolies are mutually interdependent in their pricing policies, (2) collusion enhances oligopoly profits, and (3) there is a temptation for oligopolists to cheat on a collusive agreement.

10.5   Three Oligopoly Strategies

To gain further insight into oligopolistic pricing and output behaviour, we will examine three distinct pricing strategies: (1) the kinked-demand curve, (2) collusive pricing, and (3) price leadership. Why not a single model as in our discussions of the other market structures? There are two reasons:

1. **Diversity of oligopolies**   Oligopoly has a greater range and diversity of market situations than other market structures, including the *tight* oligopoly, in which two or three firms dominate an entire market, and the *loose* oligopoly, in which six or seven firms share, say, 70 or 80 percent of a market while a competitive fringe of firms shares the remainder. Oligopoly includes both differentiated and standardized products. It includes cases in which firms act in collusion and those in which they act independently. The diversity of oligopoly makes it impossible to explain all oligopolistic behaviours with a single market model.

2. **Complications of interdependence**   The mutual interdependence of oligopolistic firms is what complicates matters. Because firms cannot predict the reactions of their rivals with cer-

Consider This

Strategic Behaviour

The following story, offered with tongue in cheek, illustrates a localized market that exhibits some characteristics of oligopoly, including strategic behaviour.

Tracy Proudfoot's Native Canadian Arts and Crafts store is located in the centre of a small tourist town that borders on a national park. In the business's early days, Tracy had a mini-monopoly. Business was brisk and prices and profits were high.

But to Tracy's chagrin, two "copycat" shops opened up right next door, one on either side of her store. Worse yet, the competitors named their shops to take advantage of Tracy's advertising. One was "Native Arts and Crafts," the other "Indian Arts and Crafts." These new sellers drew business away from Tracy's store, forcing her to lower her prices. The three adjacent stores in the small, isolated town constituted a localized oligopoly for Native Canadian arts and crafts.

Tracy began to think strategically about ways to boost profit. She decided to distinguish her shop from those on either side by offering a greater mix of high-quality, expensive products and fewer inexpensive "souvenir" items. The tactic worked for a while, but the other stores eventually imitated her product mix.

Then, one of the competitors next door escalated the rivalry by hanging up a large sign proclaiming "We Sell for Less!" Shortly thereafter, the other shop put up a large sign stating, "We Won't Be Undersold!"

Not to be outdone, Tracy painted a colourful sign of her own and hung it above her door. It read, "Main Entrance."

Question: Will Tracy's last strategy succeed? What other strategy can Tracy pursue?

tainty, they cannot estimate their own demand and marginal-revenue data. Without such data, firms cannot determine their profit-maximizing price and output.

Despite these analytical difficulties, two interrelated characteristics of oligopolistic pricing have been observed. First, prices change less frequently under oligopoly than under pure competition, monopolistic competition, and, in some instances, pure monopoly. Second, when oligopolists do change prices, firms are likely to change their prices together, suggesting a tendency to act in concert, or collusively, in setting and changing prices (as we mentioned in the preceding section). The diversity of oligopolies and the presence of mutual interdependence are reflected in the models that follow.

Kinked-demand Theory: Non-collusive Oligopoly

Imagine an oligopolistic industry made up of three firms, Arch, King, and Dave's, each having about one-third of the total market for a differentiated product. Assume that the firms are independent, meaning that they do not engage in collusive (cooperative) price practices. Assume, too, that the going price for Arch's product is P_0 and its current sales are Q_0, as shown in **Figure 10-7(a)** (**Key Graph**).

Now the question is, "What does the firm's demand curve look like?" The location and shape of an oligopolist's demand curve depend on how the firm's rivals will react to a price change introduced by Arch. Two strategies are possible for Arch's rivals:

• **Match price changes** One possibility is that King and Dave's will exactly match any price change initiated by Arch. In this case, Arch's demand and marginal-revenue curves will look like the straight lines labelled D_1 and MR_1 in Figure 10-7(a). Why are they so steep? If Arch cuts its price, its sales will increase only modestly, because its two rivals will also cut their prices to prevent Arch from gaining an advantage over them. The small increase in sales that Arch (and its two rivals) will realize is at the expense of other industries; Arch will gain no sales from King and Dave. If Arch raises its price, its sales will fall only modestly, because King and Dave's will match its price increase. The industry will lose sales to other industries, but Arch will lose no customers to King and Dave's.

Key Graph

FIGURE 10-7 The Kinked-demand Curve

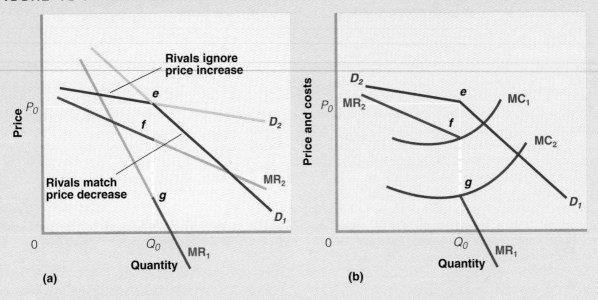

(a)

(b)

Panel (a): The slope of a non-collusive oligopolist's demand and marginal-revenue curves depends on whether the firm's rivals match (straight lines D_1 and MR_1) or ignore (straight lines D_2 and MR_2) any price changes that it may initiate from the current price P_0. Panel (b): In all likelihood an oligopolist's rivals will ignore a price increase but follow a price cut. This reaction causes the oligopolist's demand curve to be kinked (D_2eD_1) and the marginal-revenue curve to have a vertical break, or gap (fg). Because any shift in marginal costs between MC_1 and MC_2 will cut the vertical (dashed) segment of the marginal-revenue curve, no change in either price P_0 or output Q_0 will result from such a shift.

Quick Quiz

1. **Suppose Q_0 in this figure represents annual sales of five million units for this firm. The other two firms in this three-firm industry sell three million and two million units. The Herfindahl index for this industry is**
   a. 100 percent.   b. 400.   c. 10.   d. 3800.

2. **The D_2e segment of the demand curve D_2eD_1 in graph (b) implies that**
   a. this firm's total revenue will fall if it increases its price above P_0.
   b. other firms will match a price increase above P_0.
   c. the firm's relevant marginal-revenue curve will be MR_1 for price increases above P_0.
   d. the product in this industry is necessarily standardized.

3. **By matching a price cut, this firm's rivals can**
   a. increase their market shares.
   b. increase their marginal revenues.
   c. maintain their market shares.
   d. lower their total costs.

4. **A shift of the marginal-cost curve from MC_2 to MC_1 in graph (b) would**
   a. increase the going price above P_0.
   b. leave price at P_0 but reduce this firm's total profit.
   c. leave price at P_0 but reduce this firm's total revenue.
   d. make this firm's demand curve more elastic.

ANSWERS: 1. d; 2. a; 3. c; 4. b

- *Ignore price changes*   The other possibility is that King and Dave's will ignore any price change by Arch. In this case, the demand and marginal-revenue curves faced by Arch will resemble the straight lines D_2 and MR_2 in Figure 10-7(a). Demand in this case is considerably more elastic than under the previous assumption. The reasons are clear: If Arch lowers its price and its rivals do not, Arch will gain sales significantly at the expense of its two rivals, because it will be under-selling them. Conversely, if Arch raises its price and its rivals do not, Arch will lose many customers to King and Dave's, which will be underselling it.

A COMBINED STRATEGY

Now, which is the most likely assumption for Arch to make about how its rivals will react to any price change it might initiate? The answer is "it depends on the direction of price." Observation of oligopolistic industries suggests that a firm's rivals will match price declines below P_0 as they act to prevent the price-cutter from taking their customers. But the rivals will ignore price increases above P_0, because the rivals of the price-increasing firm stand to gain the business lost by the price-booster. In other words, the dark blue left-hand segment of the "rivals ignore" demand curve D_2 in Figure 10-7(a) is relevant for price increases, and the dark blue right-hand segment of the "rivals match" demand curve D_1 is relevant for price cuts. It is a reasonable assumption that the non-collusive oligopolist faces the **kinked-demand curve** D_2eD_1, as shown in Figure 10-7(b). Demand is highly elastic above the going price P_0 but much less elastic or even inelastic below that price.

Note also that if it is correct to suppose that rivals will follow a price cut but ignore an increase, the marginal-revenue curve of the oligopolist will also have an odd shape. It, too, will be made up of two segments: the dark purple left-hand part of marginal-revenue curve MR_2 in Figure 10-7(a) and the dark purple right-hand part of marginal-revenue curve MR_1. Because of the sharp difference in elasticity of demand above and below the going price, there is a gap, or what we can simply treat as a vertical segment, in the marginal-revenue curve. We show this gap as the dashed segment in the combined marginal-revenue curve MR_2fgMR_1 in Figure 10-7(b).

PRICE RIGIDITY

This analysis helps to explain why prices are generally stable in non-collusive oligopolistic industries; there are both demand and cost reasons.

On the demand side, the kinked-demand curve gives each oligopolist reason to believe that any change in price will be for the worse. If it raises its price, many of its customers will desert it. If it lowers its price, its sales will at best increase very modestly, since rivals will match the lower price. Even if a price cut increases the oligopolist's total revenue somewhat, its costs may increase by a greater amount. And if its demand is inelastic to the right of Q_0, then the firm's profit will fall. A price decrease in the inelastic region lowers the firm's total revenue, and the production of a larger output increases its total costs.

On the cost side, the broken marginal-revenue curve suggests that even if an oligopolist's costs change substantially, the firm may have no reason to change its price. In particular, all positions of the marginal-cost curve between MC_1 and MC_2 in Figure 10-7(b) will result in the firm's deciding on exactly the same price and output. For all those positions, MR equals MC at output Q_0; at that output, the firm will charge price P_0.

CRITICISMS OF THE MODEL

The kinked-demand analysis has two shortcomings. First, it does not explain how the going price gets to be at P_0 in Figure 10-7 in the first place. It only helps explain why oligopolists tend to stick with an existing price. The kinked-demand curve explains price rigidity but not price itself.

Second, oligopoly prices are not as rigid as the kinked-demand theory implies. During inflationary periods, many oligopolists have raised their prices often and substantially. And during downturns (recessions), some oligopolists have cut prices. In some instances these price reductions have set off a **price war**: successive and continuous rounds of price cuts by rivals as they attempt to maintain their market shares. *(Key Question 10)*

kinked-demand curve
The demand curve for a non-collusive oligopolist, that is based on the assumption that rivals will follow a price decrease and will not follow a price increase.

price war
Successive and continuous rounds of price cuts by rivals as they attempt to maintain their market shares.

Cartels and Other Collusion: Cooperative Strategies

Our game theory model demonstrates that one possible outcome of an oligopoly market structure is collusion. We can say that collusion occurs whenever firms in an industry reach an agreement to fix prices, divide up the market, or otherwise restrict competition among themselves. The danger of non-collusive, kinked-demand oligopolies is that a price war may break out, especially during a general business recession. Then each firm finds that, because of unsold goods and excess capacity, it can reduce per-unit costs by increasing market share. There is also the possibility that a new firm may surmount entry barriers and initiate aggressive price-cutting to gain a foothold in the market. In addition, the kinked-demand curve's tendency toward rigid prices may adversely affect profits if general inflationary pressures increase costs. But by controlling price through collusion, oligopolists may be able to reduce uncertainty, increase profits, and perhaps even prohibit the entry of new rivals.

PRICE AND OUTPUT

Assume once again that there are three oligopolistic firms (Gypsum, Sheetrock, and GSR) producing, in this instance, homogeneous products. All three firms have identical cost curves. Each firm's demand curve is indeterminate unless we know how its rivals will react to any price change. Therefore, we suppose each firm assumes that its two rivals will match either a price cut or a price increase. And, since they have identical cost data, and the same demand and thus marginal-revenue data, we can say that Figure 10-8 represents the position of each of our three oligopolistic firms.

What price and output combination should, say, Gypsum select? If Gypsum were a pure monopolist, the answer would be clear: Establish output at Q_0, where marginal revenue equals marginal cost, charge the corresponding price P_0, and enjoy the maximum profit attainable. However, firm Gypsum does have two rivals selling identical products, and if Gypsum's assumption that its rivals will match its price of P_0 proves to be incorrect, the consequences could be disastrous for Gypsum. Specifically, if Sheetrock and GSR actually charge prices below P_0 then Gypsum's demand curve D will shift sharply to the left as its potential customers turn to its rivals, which are now selling the same product at a lower price. Of course, Gypsum can retaliate by cutting its price too, but this will move all three firms down their demand curves, lowering their profits. It may even drive them to a point where average total cost exceeds price and losses are incurred.

FIGURE 10-8 | **Collusion and Joint-profit Maximization**

If oligopolistic firms face identical or highly similar demand and cost conditions, they may collude to limit their joint output and to set a single, common price. Thus each firm acts as if it were a pure monopolist, setting output at Q_0 and charging price P_0. This price and output combination maximizes each oligopolist's profit (grey area) and thus their combined or joint profit.

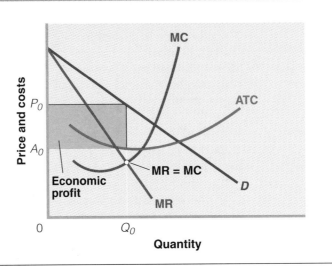

So the question becomes, will Sheetrock and GSR want to charge a price below P_0? Under our assumptions, and recognizing that Gypsum has little choice except to match any price they may set below P_0, the answer is, no. Faced with the same demand and cost circumstances, Sheetrock and GSR will find it in their interest to produce Q_0 and charge P_0. This is a curious situation; each firm finds it most profitable to charge the same price, P_0, but only if its rivals actually do so! How can the three firms ensure the price P_0 and quantity Q_0 solution in which each is keenly interested? How can they avoid the less profitable outcomes associated with either higher or lower prices?

The answer is evident: They could collude. They could get together, talk it over, and agree to charge the same price, P_0. In addition to reducing the possibility of price wars, this will give each firm the maximum profit. (But it will also subject them to anti-combines prosecution if they are caught!) For society, the result will be the same as would occur if the industry were a pure monopoly composed of three identical plants.

OVERT COLLUSION: THE OPEC CARTEL

cartel
A formal agreement among firms in an industry to set the price of a product and establish the outputs of the individual firms or to divide the market among them.

Collusion may assume a variety of forms. The most comprehensive form of collusion is the **cartel**, a group of producers that typically creates a formal written agreement specifying how much each member will produce and charge. Output must be controlled to maintain the agreed-on price. The collusion is overt, or open to view.

Undoubtedly the most significant international cartel is the Organization of Petroleum Exporting Countries (OPEC), comprising 11 oil-producing nations (see Global Perspective 10.1). OPEC produces 40 percent of the world's oil and supplies 60 percent of all oil traded internationally. In the late 1990s OPEC reacted vigorously to very low oil prices by greatly restricting supply. Some non-OPEC producers supported the cutback in production and within a 15-month period, the price of oil shot up from $11 a barrel to $34 a barrel. Gasoline prices in Canada rose by as much as 50 percent in some markets. Fearing a global political and economic backlash from the major industrial nations, OPEC upped the production quotas for its members in mid-2000. The increases in oil supply that resulted reduced oil prices somewhat. It is clear that the OPEC cartel has sufficient market power to hold the price of oil substantially above its marginal cost of production.

Global Perspective 10.1

The 11 OPEC nations, daily oil production, June 1, 2003

The OPEC nations produce about 40 percent of the world's oil and 60 percent of the oil sold in world markets.

OPEC Country	Barrels of Oil
Saudi Arabia	8,256,000
Iran	3,729,000
Venezuela	2,923,000
United Arab Emirates	2,217,000
Nigeria	2,092,000
Kuwait	2,038,000
Libya	1,360,000
Indonesia	1,317,000
Algeria	811,000
Qatar	658,000
Iraq	Not available

Source: OPEC Secretariat, <www.opec.org>.

In March 2003, the price of oil once again took a major jump, reaching almost $38 a barrel, as the U.S. attacked Iraq. But once the war ended in April, the price of oil quickly dropped again to below $30 a barrel.

COVERT COLLUSION: RELATIVELY RECENT EXAMPLES

Cartels are illegal in Canada, and hence any collusion that exists is covert, or secret. Yet there are examples, found in evidence from anti-combines (antimonopoly) cases. One example of covert collusion is the case of four cement firms in the Quebec City Region. In 1996, St. Lawrence Cement Inc., Lafarge Canada Inc., Cement Quebec Inc., and Beton Orleans Inc. were fined a total of $5.8 million for price fixing. The conspiracy was discovered by a Quebec City newspaper that reported that the cost of the city's new convention centre was higher than anticipated. The first three of these firms had previously been fined in 1983 for a similar violation of the *Competition Act*.

In many other instances collusion is even more subtle. **Tacit understandings** (historically called "gentlemen's agreements") are frequently made at cocktail parties, on golf courses, through phone calls, or at trade association meetings. In such agreements, competing firms reach a verbal understanding on product price, leaving market shares to be decided by non-price competition. Although these agreements, too, violate anti-combines laws—and can result in severe personal and corporate penalties—the elusive character of tacit understandings makes them difficult to detect.

tacit understanding
Any method by competing oligopolists to set prices and outputs that does not involve outright collusion.

OBSTACLES TO COLLUSION

Normally, cartels and similar collusive arrangements are difficult to establish and maintain. We look now at several reasons why this is so.

Demand and Cost Differences   When oligopolists face different costs and demand curves, it is difficult for them to agree on a price. Even with highly standardized products, firms usually have somewhat different market shares and operate with differing degrees of productive efficiency. Thus, it is unlikely that even homogeneous oligopolists would have the same demand and cost curves.

In either case, differences in costs and demand mean that the profit-maximizing price will differ among firms; no single price will be readily acceptable to all, as we assumed was true in Figure 10-8. So, price collusion depends on compromises and concessions that are not always easy to obtain, and hence they act as obstacles to collusion.

Number of Firms   Other things equal, the larger the number of firms, the more difficult it is to create a cartel or other form of price collusion. Agreement on price by three or four producers that control an entire market may be relatively easy to accomplish, but such agreement is more difficult to achieve where there are, say, 10 firms, each with roughly 10 percent of the market, or where the Big Three have 70 percent of the market while a competitive fringe of 8 or 10 smaller firms battles for the remainder.

Cheating   As the game theory model makes clear, there is a temptation for collusive oligopolists to engage in secret price cutting to increase sales and profit. The difficulty with such cheating is that buyers who are paying a high price for a product may become aware of the lower-priced sales and demand similar treatment. Or buyers receiving a price concession from one producer may use the concession as a wedge to get even larger price concessions from a rival producer. Buyers' attempts to play producers against one another may precipitate price wars among the producers. Although secret price concessions are potentially profitable, they threaten collusive oligopolies over time. Collusion is more likely to succeed when cheating is easy to detect and punish.

Recession   Long-lasting recession usually serves as an enemy of collusion, because slumping markets increase average total cost. In technical terms, as the oligopolists' demand and marginal-revenue curves shift to the left in Figure 10-8 in response to a recession, each firm moves leftward and upward to a higher operating point on its average-total-cost curve. Firms find they have substantial excess production capacity, sales are down, unit costs are up, and profits are being squeezed. Under such conditions, businesses may feel they can avoid serious profit reductions (or even losses) by cutting price and thus gaining sales at the expense of rivals.

Potential Entry   The greater prices and profits that result from collusion may attract new entrants, including foreign firms. Since that would increase market supply and reduce prices and profits, successful collusion requires that colluding oligopolists block the entry of new producers.

Legal Obstacles: Anti-Combines Law   Canadian anti-combines laws prohibit cartels and price-fixing collusion, so less obvious means of price control have evolved in Canada.

Price Leadership Model: Another Cooperative Strategy

price leadership
An implicit understanding that the dominant firm initiate price changes and all other firms follow.

Price leadership is a type of implicit understanding by which oligopolists can coordinate prices. A practice evolves whereby the "dominant firm" initiates price changes and all other firms more or less automatically follow the leader. Many industries, including cement, newsprint, glass containers, steel, beer, fertilizer, cigarettes, and tin, are practising, or have in the recent past practised, price leadership.

LEADERSHIP STRATEGY

An examination of price leadership in a variety of industries suggests that the price leader is likely to use the following strategies.

Infrequent Price Changes   Because price changes always carry the risk that rivals will not follow the lead, price adjustments are made only infrequently. Price is changed only when cost and demand conditions have been altered significantly.

Communications   The price leader often communicates impending price adjustments to the industry through speeches by major executives, trade publication interviews, or press releases. By publicizing the need to raise prices, the price leader seeks agreement among its competitors regarding the actual increase.

Limit Pricing   The price leader does not always choose the price that maximizes short-run profits for the industry because the industry may want to discourage new firms from entering. To discourage new competitors and to maintain the current oligopolistic structure of the industry, the price leader may keep price below the short-run profit-maximizing level. The strategy of establishing a price that blocks the entry of new firms is called *limit pricing*.

Breakdowns in Price Leadership: Price Wars   Price leadership in oligopoly occasionally breaks down, and sometimes results in a price war. An example of disruption of price leadership occurred in the breakfast cereal industry, in which Kellogg traditionally had been the price leader. General Mills countered Kellogg's leadership in 1995 by reducing the prices of its cereals by 11 percent. In 1996 Post responded with a 20 percent price cut, which Kellogg then followed. Not to be outdone, Post reduced its prices by another 11 percent.

Most price wars eventually run their course. When all firms recognize that low prices are severely reducing their profits, they again cede price leadership to one of the industry's leading firms. That firm then begins to raise prices, and the other firms willingly follow suit.

Oligopoly and Efficiency

Given the many possible outcomes in an oligopoly, it is impossible to say anything definitive about allocative and productive efficiency in this market structure. Certainly, if there are few firms in an oligopoly and they cooperate, society could end up in the situation depicted in Figure 10-8. That outcome would be identical to having a pure monopoly. We know that neither productive nor allocative efficiency is achieved in pure monopoly.

But such a negative outcome is increasingly unlikely for the three following reasons:

1. *Increased foreign competition*   In the past decade, foreign competition has increased rivalry in several oligopolistic industries—steel, automobiles, photographic film, electric shavers, outboard motors, and copy machines, for example.

2. *Limit pricing*   Recall that some oligopolists may intentionally keep prices below the short-run profit-maximizing level to bolster entry barriers. In essence, consumers and society may get

some of the benefits of competition—prices closer to marginal cost and minimum average total cost—even without the competition that free entry would provide.

3. ***Technological advance***   Over time, oligopolistic industries may foster more rapid product development and greater improvement of production techniques than would be possible if they were purely competitive. Oligopolists have large economic profits from which they can fund expensive research and development (R&D), and the existence of barriers to entry may give the oligopolist some assurance that it will reap the rewards of successful R&D. Thus, the short-run economic inefficiencies of oligopolists may be partly or wholly offset by the oligopolists' contributions to better products, lower prices, and lower costs over time. We will have more to say about these more dynamic aspects of rivalry in Chapter 11.

QUICK REVIEW

- In the kinked-demand theory of oligopoly, price is relatively inflexible because a firm contemplating a price change assumes that its rivals will follow a price cut and ignore a price increase.

- Cartels agree on production limits and set a common price to maximize the joint profit of their members as if each were a unit of a single pure monopoly.

- Collusion among oligopolists is difficult because of (1) demand and cost differences among sellers, (2) the complexity of output coordination among producers, (3) the potential for cheating, (4) a tendency for agreements to break down during recessions, (5) the potential entry of new firms, and (6) anti-combines laws.

- Price leadership involves an informal understanding among oligopolists to match any price change initiated by a designated firm (often the industry's dominant firm).

- Neither productive nor allocative efficiency is realized in oligopolistic markets, but oligopoly may be superior to the monopoly in promoting research and development and technological progress.

10.6   Oligopoly and Advertising

We have noted that oligopolists would rather not compete on the basis of price and may become involved in price collusion. Nonetheless, each firm's share of the total market is typically determined through product development and advertising, for two reasons:

1. Product improvements and successful advertising can produce more permanent gains in market share because they cannot be duplicated as quickly and completely as price reductions.

2. Oligopolists have sufficient financial resources to engage in product development and advertising.

Product development (or, more broadly, research and development) is the subject of the next chapter, so we will confine our present discussion to advertising. In recent years, Canadian advertising has exceeded $5 billion annually, and worldwide advertising, $420 billion. Advertising is prevalent in both monopolistic competition and oligopoly. Table 10-1 lists the five leading Canadian advertisers. Advertising may affect prices, competition, and efficiency both positively and negatively, depending on the circumstances. While our focus here is on advertising by oligopolists, the analysis is equally applicable to advertising by firms in monopolistic competition.

Positive Effects of Advertising

To make rational decisions, consumers need information about product characteristics and prices. Advertising may be a low-cost means of providing that information. Suppose you are in the market for a high-quality camera and such a product is advertised in newspapers or magazines. To make a rational choice, you may have to spend several days visiting stores to determine the prices and fea-

TABLE 10-1	The Largest Canadian Advertisers
Company	**Advertising spending (millions of dollars)**
General Motors	165.0
DaimlerChrysler	113.8
Ford Motor Co.	103.1
Bell Canada Enterprises	65.4
Government of Canada	45.2

Source: *Advertising Age*. Data are for 2000.

tures of various brands. This search has both direct costs (gasoline, parking fees) and indirect costs (the value of your time). Advertising reduces your search time and minimizes these costs.

By providing information about the various competing goods that are available, advertising diminishes monopoly power. In fact, advertising is frequently associated with the introduction of new products designed to compete with existing brands. Could Toyota and Honda have so strongly challenged North American auto producers without advertising? Could Federal Express have sliced market share away from UPS and Canada Post without advertising?

Viewed this way, advertising is an efficiency-enhancing activity. It is a relatively inexpensive means of providing useful information to consumers and thus lowering their search costs. By enhancing competition, advertising results in greater economic efficiency. By facilitating the introduction of new products, advertising speeds up technological progress. And by increasing output, advertising can reduce long-run average total cost by enabling firms to obtain economies of scale.

Potential Negative Effects of Advertising

Not all the effects of advertising are positive. Much advertising is designed simply to persuade consumers in favour of the advertiser's product. A television commercial that indicates that a popular personality drinks a particular brand of soft drink conveys little or no information to consumers about price or quality. Indeed, in some cases advertising may well persuade consumers to pay high prices for much-acclaimed but inferior products, forgoing better but unadvertised products selling at lower prices. For example, *Consumer Reports* recently found that heavily advertised premium motor oils and fancy additives provide no better engine performance and longevity than do cheaper brands.

Firms often establish substantial brand-name loyalty and thus achieve monopoly power via their advertising (see Global Perspective 10.2). As a consequence, they are able to increase their sales, expand their market share, and enjoy greater profits. Larger profit permits still more advertising and further enlargement of the firm's market share and profit. In time, consumers may lose the advan-

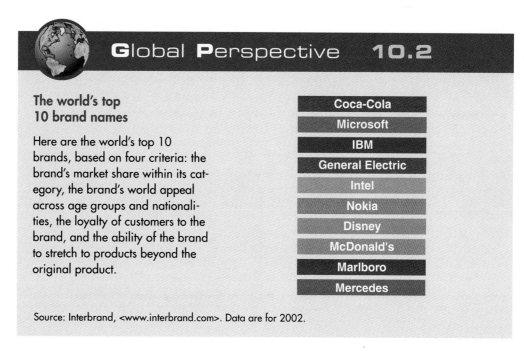

Global Perspective 10.2

The world's top 10 brand names

Here are the world's top 10 brands, based on four criteria: the brand's market share within its category, the brand's world appeal across age groups and nationalities, the loyalty of customers to the brand, and the ability of the brand to stretch to products beyond the original product.

- Coca-Cola
- Microsoft
- IBM
- General Electric
- Intel
- Nokia
- Disney
- McDonald's
- Marlboro
- Mercedes

Source: Interbrand, <www.interbrand.com>. Data are for 2002.

tages of competitive markets and face the disadvantages of monopolized markets. Moreover, new entrants to the industry need to incur large advertising costs in order to establish their products in the marketplace; thus, advertising costs may be a barrier to entry. *(Key Question 12)*

Advertising may also be self-cancelling. The advertising campaign of one fast-food hamburger chain may be offset by equally costly campaigns waged by rivals, so each firm's demand actually remains unchanged. Few, if any, extra burgers will be purchased, and each firm's market share will stay the same. But because of the advertising, the cost and hence the price of hamburgers will be higher.

When advertising either leads to increased monopoly power or is self-cancelling, economic inefficiency results.

THE LASTword | Oligopoly in the Beer Industry

The beer industry was once populated by dozens of firms and an even larger number of brands. It is now an oligopoly dominated by a handful of producers.

The brewing industry has undergone profound changes since World War II that have increased the degree of concentration in the industry. In 1945 more than 60 independent brewing companies existed in Canada. By 1967 there were 18, and by 1984 only 11. While the three largest brewers sold only 19 percent of the nation's beer in 1947, the Big Three brewers (Labatt, Molson, and Carling O'Keefe) sold 97 percent of the nation's domestically produced beer in 1989, the same year Molson and Carling O'Keefe merged. Currently, the Big Two—Labatt and Molson (each producing 45 percent)—brew most of the beer in Canada. The industry is clearly an oligopoly.

Changes on the demand side of the market have contributed to the shakeout of small brewers from the industry. First, consumer tastes have generally shifted from the stronger-flavoured beers of the small brewers to the light products of the larger brewers. Second, there has been a shift from the consumption of beer in taverns to consumption in the home.

The significance of this change is that taverns were usually supplied with kegs from local brewers to avoid the relatively high cost of shipping kegs. But the acceptance of aluminum cans for home consumption made it possible for large, distant brewers to compete with the local brewers, because the former could now ship their products by truck or rail without breakage.

Developments on the supply side of the market have been even more profound. Technological advances have increased the speed of the bottling and canning lines. Today, large brewers can fill and close 2000 cans per line per minute. Large plants are also able to reduce labour costs through automating brewing and warehousing. Furthermore, plant construction costs per barrel are about one-third

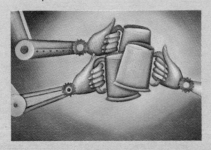

less for a 4.0 million hectolitres plant than for a 1.5-million-barrel plant. As a consequence of these and other factors, the minimum efficient scale in brewing is a plant size of about 4.0 million hectolitres, with multiple plants. Because the construction cost of a modern brewery that size is $450 million, economies of scale may now constitute a significant barrier to entry.

Blindfold taste tests confirm that most mass-produced Canadian beers taste alike, so brewers greatly emphasize advertising. Here, Labatt and Molson, who sell national brands, enjoy major cost advantages over producers that have regional brands (for example, Creemore Springs, Upper Canada, and Okanagan Spring). The reason is because national television advertising is less costly *per viewer* than local spot TV advertising.

Mergers in the brewing industry have been a fundamental cause of the rising concentration. Dominant firms have expanded by heavily advertising their main brands—such as Labatt Blue and Blue Light; and Molson

Canadian, Canadian Light, and Special Dry—sustaining significant product differentiation despite the declining number of major brewers.

Two factors dominate the Canadian beer industry: high transportation costs and provincial policies and practices. High transportation costs have translated into a regional structure of production compared with the brewing industry in the United States. As a consequence, a large number of breweries exist in Canada relative to the size of the domestic market. Especially outside the larger breweries in Ontario and Quebec, unit costs are markedly higher because of the inability to achieve economies of scale.

Even more important than transportation costs, provincial policies and practices in the past had a dominant impact on the Canadian brewing industry; until recently, brewers were not allowed to transport beer produced in one province to be sold in another. This restriction has now been relaxed, and brewers will centralize operations in the future to capture economies of scale.

Imported beers such as Beck's, Corona, Foster's, and Guinness constitute about 10 percent of the Canadian market, with individual brands seeming to wax and wane in popularity. Some local or regional microbreweries such as Upper Canada (purchased recently by Sleeman), which brew specialty beers and charge premium prices, have whittled into the sales of the major brewers. Labatt and Molson have taken notice, responding with specialty brands of their own (for example, John Labatt Classic, and Molson Signature Spring Bock and Rickards Red). Overall, however, it appears that imports such as Heineken and Budweiser may pose more of a threat to the majors than the microbreweries do.

Sources: Based on Kenneth G. Elzinga, "Beer," in Walter Adams and James Brock (eds.), *The Structure of American Industry*, 9th ed. (Englewood Cliffs, NJ: Prentice-Hall, 1995), pp. 119–151; Douglas F. Greer, "Beer: Causes of Structural Change," in Larry Duetsch (ed.), *Industry Studies*, 2nd ed. (New York: M. E. Sharpe, 1998), pp. 28–64; authors' updates; the Conference Board of Canada, *The Canadian Brewing Industry: Historical Evolution and Competitive Structure* (Toronto: International Studies and Development Group, 1989).

CHAPTER SUMMARY

10.1 CHARACTERISTICS OF MONOPOLISTIC COMPETITION

- The distinguishing features of monopolistic competition are (a) enough firms are in the industry to ensure that each firm has only limited control over price, mutual interdependence is absent, and collusion is nearly impossible; (b) products are characterized by real or perceived differences so that economic rivalry entails both price and non-price competition; and (c) entry to the industry is relatively easy. Many aspects of retailing, and some manufacturing industries in which economies of scale are few, approximate monopolistic competition.

10.2 PRICE AND OUTPUT IN MONOPOLISTIC COMPETITION

- Monopolistically competitive firms may earn economic profits or incur losses in the short run. The easy entry and exit of firms result in only normal profits in the long run.

- The long-run equilibrium position of the monopolistically competitive producer is less socially desirable than that of the pure competitor. Under monopolistic competition, price exceeds marginal cost, suggesting an underallocation of resources to the product, and price exceeds minimum average total cost, indicating that consumers do not get the product at the lowest price that cost conditions might allow.

- Non-price competition provides a means by which monopolistically competitive firms can offset the long-run tendency for economic profit to fall to zero. Through product differentiation, product development, and advertising, a firm may strive to increase the demand for its product more than enough to cover the added cost of such non-price competition. Consumers benefit from the wide diversity of product choice that monopolistic competition provides.

- In practice, the monopolistic competitor seeks the specific combination of price, product, and advertising that will maximize profit.

10.3 THE CHARACTERISTICS OF OLIGOPOLY

- Oligopolistic industries are characterized by the presence of few firms, each having a significant fraction of the market. Firms thus situated are mutually interdependent: the behaviour of any one firm directly affects, and is affected by, the actions of rivals. Products may be either virtually uniform or significantly differentiated. Various barriers to entry, including economies of scale, underlie and maintain oligopoly.

- Concentration ratios are a measure of oligopoly (monopoly) power. By giving more weight to larger firms, the Herfindahl index is designed to measure market dominance in an industry.

10.4 OLIGOPOLY PRICING BEHAVIOUR: A GAME THEORY OVERVIEW

- The prisoner's dilemma is a type of game that shows the difficulty of cooperating when the participants cannot communicate with one another.

- Game theory (a) shows the interdependence of oligopolists' pricing policies; (b) reveals the tendency of oligopolists to collude; and (c) explains the temptation of oligopolists to cheat on collusive arrangements.

10.5 THREE OLIGOPOLY STRATEGIES

- Non-collusive oligopolists may face a kinked-demand curve. This curve and the accompanying marginal-revenue curve help explain the price rigidity that often characterizes oligopolies; they do not, however, explain how the actual prices of products are first established.

- The uncertainties inherent in oligopoly promote collusion. Collusive oligopolists such as cartels maximize joint profits—that is, they behave like pure monopolists. Demand and cost differences, a large number of firms, cheating through secret price concessions, recessions, and the anti-combines laws are all obstacles to collusive oligopoly.

- Price leadership is an informal means of collusion whereby one firm, usually the largest or most efficient, initiates price changes and the other firms in the industry follow the leader.

- Market shares in oligopolistic industries are usually determined based on product development and advertising. Oligopolists emphasize non-price competition because (a) advertising and product variations are harder for rivals to match and (b) oligopolists frequently have ample resources to finance non-price competition.

- Neither productive nor allocative efficiency is realized in oligopolistic markets, but oligopoly may be superior to pure competition in promoting research and development and technological progress.

10.6 OLIGOPOLY AND ADVERTISING

- Advertising may affect prices, competition, and efficiency either positively or negatively. Positive: It can provide consumers with low-cost information about competing products, help introduce new competing products into concentrated industries, and generally reduce monopoly power and its attendant inefficiencies. Negative: It can promote monopoly power via persuasion and the creation of entry barriers. Moreover, when engaged in by rivals it can be self-cancelling by boosting costs and increasing economic inefficiency while accomplishing little else.

TERMS AND CONCEPTS

STUDY QUESTIONS

1. How does monopolistic competition differ from pure competition in its basic characteristics? from pure monopoly? Explain fully what product differentiation may involve. Explain how the entry of firms into its industry affects the demand curve facing a monopolistic competitor and how that, in turn, affects its economic profit.

2. **KEY QUESTION** Compare the elasticity of the monopolistic competitor's demand with that of a pure competitor and a pure monopolist. Assuming identical long-run costs, compare graphically the prices and outputs that would result in the long run under pure competition and under monopolistic competition. Contrast the two market structures in terms of productive and allocative efficiency. Explain: "Monopolistically competitive industries are characterized by too many firms, each of which produces too little."

3. "Monopolistic competition is monopolistic up to the point at which consumers become willing to buy close-substitute products and competitive beyond that point." Explain.

4. "Competition in quality and service may be just as effective as price competition in giving buyers more for their money." Do you agree? Why? Explain why

monopolistically competitive firms frequently prefer nonprice competition to price competition.

5. Critically evaluate and explain:

   a. "In monopolistically competitive industries, economic profits are competed away in the long run; hence, there is no valid reason to criticize the performance and efficiency of such industries."

   b. "In the long run, monopolistic competition leads to a monopolistic price but not to monopolistic profits."

6. Why do oligopolies exist? List five or six oligopolists whose products you own or regularly purchase. What distinguishes oligopoly from monopolistic competition?

7. **KEY QUESTION**   Answer the following questions, which relate to measures of concentration:

   a. What is the meaning of a four-firm concentration ratio of 60 percent? 90 percent? What are the shortcomings of concentration ratios as measures of monopoly power?

   b. Suppose that the five firms in industry A have annual sales of 30, 30, 20, 10, and 10 percent of total industry sales. For the five firms in industry B the figures are 60, 25, 5, 5, and 5 percent. Calculate the Herfindahl index for each industry and compare their likely competitiveness.

8. The following questions relate to the "prisoner's dilemma."

   a. Invent a prisoner's dilemma in which two students writing a multiple choice exam at opposite ends of a classroom are caught using hand signals to communicate. The professor in the room suspects they are cheating but has no definitive proof. Design a payoff matrix that gives each of the students an incentive to confess. Is there an equilibrium point in this game?

   b. Repeat the game assuming the two students are a brother and sister who care deeply about, and trust, each other.

9. **KEY QUESTION**   Explain the general meaning of the following payoff matrix for oligopolists C and D. All profit figures are in thousands.

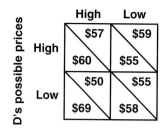

C's possible prices

		High	Low
D's possible prices	**High**	$57 / $60	$59 / $55
	Low	$50 / $69	$55 / $58

   a. Use the payoff matrix to explain the mutual interdependence that characterizes oligopolistic industries.

   b. Assuming no collusion between C and D, what is the likely pricing outcome?

   c. In view of your answer to 9b, explain why price collusion is mutually profitable. Why might a temptation to cheat on the collusive agreement exist?

10. **KEY QUESTION**   What assumptions about a rival's response to price changes underlie the kinked-demand curve for oligopolists? Why is there a gap in the oligopolist's marginal-revenue curve? How does the kinked-demand curve explain price rigidity in oligopoly? What are the shortcomings of the kinked-demand model?

11. Why might price collusion occur in oligopolistic industries? Assess the economic desirability of collusive pricing. What are the main obstacles to collusion? Speculate why price leadership is legal in Canada, whereas price fixing is not.

12. **KEY QUESTION**   Why is there so much advertising in monopolistic competition and oligopoly? How does such advertising help consumers and promote efficiency? Why might it be excessive at times?

13. **(Advanced analysis)** Construct a game theory matrix involving two firms and their decisions on high versus low advertising budgets and the effects of each decision on profits. Show a circumstance in which both firms select high advertising budgets even though both would be more profitable with low advertising budgets. Why won't they unilaterally cut their advertising budget?

14. **(The Last Word)** What firm(s) dominate the beer industry? What demand and supply factors have contributed to the small number of firms in this industry?

INTERNET APPLICATION QUESTIONS

1. Chapters.Indigo.ca is Canada's largest online bookseller, but it still has to compete with the very popular Amazon.com. Through the McConnell-Brue-Barbiero Web site (Chapter 10), search both sites for Viktor Frankl's *Man's Search for Meaning* (in paperback). Find the price and determine which company sells the book at a lower price (convert Amazon's price into Canadian dollars using the current exchange rate). Identify the non-price competition that might lead you to order from one company rather than the other.

Technology, R&D, and Efficiency

Just do it! In 1968 two entrepreneurs in Oregon developed a lightweight sport shoe and formed a new company called Nike, incorporating a "swoosh" logo (designed by a graduate student for $35). Today, Nike employs more than 20,000 workers and sells more than U.S.$9 billion worth of athletic shoes, hiking boots, and sports apparel annually.

"Intel inside." Intel? In 1967 neither this company nor its product existed. Today, it is the world's largest producer of microprocessors for personal computers, with 67,500 employees and more than U.S.$29 billion in annual sales.

Nortel Networks, headquartered in Brampton, Ontario, has become one of the largest manufacturers of wireless equipment in the world. Wireless networks allow transmission of electronic data to a variety of portable devices.

In 1996 Palm introduced its Palm Pilot, a palm-sized personal computer that now also has wireless Internet capabilities. A novel idea? Apparently, so: Microsoft, Handspring, OmniSky, and others have followed with similar products, and cellphone makers are incorporating Internet functionality into some of their new phones.

technological advance
New and better goods and services and new and better ways of producing or distributing them.

Each of these brief descriptions involves some elements of **technological advance**, broadly defined as new and better goods and services and new and better ways of producing or distributing them. In this chapter, we will look at some of the microeconomics of technological advance. Who motivates and implements technological advance? What determines a firm's optimal amount of research and development (R&D)? What are the extent and implications of the imitation problem that innovators face? Are certain market structures more conducive to technological advance than others? How does technological advance relate to efficiency? These are some of the questions we address in this chapter.

11.1 Technological Advance: Invention, Innovation, and Diffusion

very long run
A period in which technology can change and in which firms can develop and offer entirely new products.

For economists, technological advance occurs over a time period called the **very long run**, which can be as short as a few months or as long as many years. Recall that in our four market models (pure competition, monopolistic competition, oligopoly, and pure monopoly), the short run is a period in which technology, plant, and equipment are fixed; in the long run, technology is constant but firms can change their plant sizes and are free to enter or exit industries. In contrast, the very long run is a period in which technology can change and in which firms can develop and offer entirely new products.

In Chapter 2 we saw that technological advance shifts an economy's production possibilities curve outward, enabling the economy to obtain more goods and services. Technological advance is a three-step process of invention, innovation, and diffusion.

invention
The discovery of a product or process through the use of imagination, ingenious thinking, and experimentation and the first proof that it will work.

Invention

The basis of technological advance is **invention**: the discovery of a product or process through the use of imagination, ingenious thinking, and experimentation and the first proof that it will work. Invention is a process, and the result of the process is also called an invention. The prototypes (basic working models) of the telephone, the automobile, and the microchip are inventions. Invention usually is based on scientific knowledge and is the product of individuals, either working on their own or as members of corporate R&D staffs. Later on you will see how governments encourage invention by providing the inventor with a **patent**, an exclusive right to sell any new and useful process, machine, or product for a set time.

patent
An exclusive right to sell any new and useful process, machine, or product for a set time.

innovation
The first successful commercial introduction of a new product, the first use of a new method of production, or the creation of a new form of business organization.

Innovation

While invention is the "discovery and first proof of workability," **innovation** is the first successful commercial introduction of a new product, the first use of a new method, or the creation of a new form of business organization. Innovation is of two types: **product innovation**, which refers to new and improved products or services; and **process innovation**, which refers to new and improved methods of production or distribution.

product innovation
The development and sale of a new or improved product or service.

process innovation
The development and use of new or improved production or distribution methods.

Unlike inventions, innovations cannot be patented. Nevertheless, innovation is a major factor in competition, since it sometimes enables a firm to leapfrog competitors by rendering their products or processes obsolete. For example, personal computers coupled with software for word processing pushed some major typewriter manufacturers into obscurity. More recently, innovations in hardware retailing (large warehouse stores such as Home Depot) have threatened the existence of smaller, more traditional hardware stores.

Diffusion

diffusion
The widespread imitation of an innovation.

Diffusion is the spread of an innovation through imitation or copying. To take advantage of new profit opportunities or to slow the erosion of profit, both new and existing firms emulate the successful innovations of others. Years ago McDonald's successfully introduced the fast-food hamburger; Harvey's, Burger King, Swiss Chalet, and other firms soon copied that idea. Hertz greatly increased its auto rentals by offering customers unlimited mileage, and Avis, Budget, and others eventually followed. DaimlerChrysler profitably introduced a luxury version of its Jeep Grand Cherokee; other manufacturers, including Acura, Mercedes, and Lexus, countered with luxury sport-utility vehicles of their own.

R&D Expenditures

As related to *businesses*, the term "research and development" is used loosely to include direct efforts toward invention, innovation, and diffusion. However, *government* also engages in R&D. In 2001 *total* Canadian R&D expenditures (business *plus* government) were $14 billion. Relative to GDP, that amount was 1.5 percent, which is a reasonable measure of the emphasis the Canadian economy puts on technological advance. As shown in Global Perspective 11.1, this is a relatively low percentage of GDP compared to several other nations.

Modern View of Technological Advance

For decades most economists regarded technological advance as a random outside force to which the economy adjusted. Periodically fortuitous advances in scientific and technological knowledge occurred, paving the way for major new products (automobiles, airplanes) and new production processes (assembly lines). Firms and industries, each at its own pace, then incorporated the new technology into their products or processes to enhance or maintain their profit. Then after making the appropriate adjustments, they settled back into new long-run equilibrium positions.

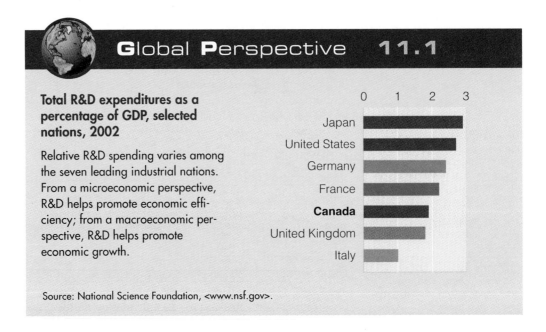

Global Perspective 11.1

Total R&D expenditures as a percentage of GDP, selected nations, 2002

Relative R&D spending varies among the seven leading industrial nations. From a microeconomic perspective, R&D helps promote economic efficiency; from a macroeconomic perspective, R&D helps promote economic growth.

Japan
United States
Germany
France
Canada
United Kingdom
Italy

Source: National Science Foundation, <www.nsf.gov>.

Most economists now have a different view. They see capitalism itself as the driving force of technological advance. In their view, invention, innovation, and diffusion occur in response to incentives within the economy, meaning that technological advance is *internal* to capitalism. Specifically, technological advance arises from intense rivalry among individuals and firms that motivates them to seek new profit opportunities or to expand existing opportunities. That rivalry occurs both among existing firms and between existing firms and new firms. In the modern view, entrepreneurs and other innovators are at the heart of technological advance.

<www.womenip.com>
Women inventors project

11.2   Role of Entrepreneurs and Other Innovators

The entrepreneur is an initiator, innovator, and risk bearer who combines resources in new and unique ways to produce new goods and services.

It will be helpful to distinguish between entrepreneurs and other innovators:

- **Entrepreneurs**   Recall that the entrepreneur is an initiator, innovator, and risk bearer—the catalyst who combines land, labour, and capital resources in new and unique ways to produce new goods and services. In the past a single individual, for example, Hart Massey in farm machinery, Henry Ford in automobiles, and Levi Strauss in blue jeans, carried out the entrepreneurial role. Such advances as air conditioning, the ballpoint pen, cellophane, the jet engine, insulin, xerography, and the helicopter all have an individualistic heritage. But in today's more technologically complex economy, entrepreneurship is just as likely to be carried out by entrepreneurial teams. Such teams may include only two or three people working as their own bosses on some new product or idea, or it may consist of larger groups of entrepreneurs who have pooled their financial resources.

- **Other innovators**   This designation includes other key people involved in the pursuit of innovation who do not bear personal financial risk. Among them are key executives, scientists, and other salaried employees engaged in commercial R&D activities.

Forming Start-ups

start-ups
Small new companies that focus on creating and introducing a new product or employing a new production or distribution technique.

Entrepreneurs often form small new companies called **start-ups** that focus on creating and introducing a new product or employing a new production or distribution technique. Two people, working out of their garages, formed such a start-up in the mid-1970s. Since neither of their employers—Hewlett-Packard and Atari, the developer of Pong (the first video game)—was interested in their prototype personal computer, they founded their own company: Apple Computers. Other examples of successful start-ups are Biovail, a biotechnology firm specializing in new medical treatments; Second Cup, a seller of gourmet coffee; and Corel, which develops innovative graphics and word-processing software.

Innovating Within Existing Firms

Innovators are also at work within existing corporations, large and small. Such innovators are salaried workers, though many firms have pay systems that provide them with substantial bonuses or shares of the profit. Examples of firms known for their skillful internal innovators are the 3M Corporation, the U.S. developer of Scotch tape, Post-it Notes, and Thinsulate insulation; and Canon, the Japanese developer of the laser engine for personal copiers and printers. R&D work in major corporations has produced significant technological improvements in such products as television sets, telephones, home appliances, automobiles, automobile tires, and sporting equipment.

Anticipating the Future

Some 50 years ago a writer for *Popular Mechanics* magazine boldly predicted, "Computers in the future may weigh no more than 1.5 tons." Today's notebook computers weigh less than 2 kilograms. It is difficult to anticipate the future, but that is what innovators try to do. Those with strong anticipatory ability and determination have a knack for introducing new and improved products or services at just the right time. Product innovation and development are creative endeavours, with such intangible rewards as personal satisfaction. Of course, the winners can reap huge monetary rewards in the form of economic profits, stock appreciation, or large bonuses. Extreme examples are Bill Gates and Paul Allen, who founded Microsoft in 1975 and had a net worth in 2002 of U.S.$43 billion and U.S.$21 billion, respectively, mainly in the form of Microsoft stock.

Past successes often give entrepreneurs and innovative firms access to resources for further innovations that anticipate consumer wants. Although they may not succeed a second time, the market tends to entrust the production of goods and services to businesses that have consistently succeeded in filling consumer wants. And the market does not care whether these winning entrepreneurs and innovative firms are Canadian, American, Brazilian, Japanese, German, or Swiss. Entrepreneurship and innovation are global in scope.

Exploiting University and Government Scientific Research

Only a small percentage of R&D spending goes to basic scientific research. The reason that percentage is so small is that scientific principles, as such, cannot be patented, nor do they usually have immediate commercial uses. Yet new scientific knowledge is highly important to technological advance. For that reason, entrepreneurs study the scientific output of university and government laboratories to identify discoveries with commercial applicability.

Government and university labs have been the scene of many technological breakthroughs. For example, insulin was first discovered at the University of Toronto with the help of government funding. Entire high-tech industries such as computers and biotechnology, for example, have their roots in major research universities and government laboratories, and nations with strong scientific communities tend to have the most technologically progressive firms and industries.

Also, firms increasingly help to fund university research that relates to their products. Business funding of R&D at universities has grown rapidly. Today, the separation between university scientists and innovators is narrowing; scientists and universities increasingly realize that their work may have commercial value and are teaming up with innovators to share in the potential profit.

QUICK REVIEW

- Broadly defined, technological advance means new or improved products and services and new or improved production and distribution processes.

- Invention is the *discovery* of a new product or method; innovation is the *successful commercial application* of some invention; and diffusion is the *widespread imitation* of the innovation.

- Many economists view technological advance as mainly a response to profit opportunities arising within a capitalist economy.

- Technological advance is fostered by entrepreneurs and other innovators and is supported by the scientific research of universities and government-sponsored laboratories.

11.3   A Firm's Optimal Amount of R&D

How does a firm decide on its optimal amount of research and development? That amount depends on the firm's perception of the marginal benefit and marginal cost of R&D activity. The decision rule here flows from the basic profit-maximizing rule: To earn the greatest profit, expand a particular activity until its marginal benefit (MB) equals its marginal cost (MC). A firm that sees the marginal benefit of a particular R&D activity, say, innovation, as exceeding the marginal cost should expand that activity. But the R&D spending decision is complex, since it involves a present sacrifice for a future expected gain. While the cost of R&D is immediate, the expected benefits occur at some future time and are highly uncertain, so estimating those benefits is often more art then science. Nevertheless, the MB = MC way of thinking remains relevant for analyzing R&D decisions.

Interest-rate Cost of Funds

Firms have several ways of obtaining the funds they need to finance R&D activities:

- **Bank loans**   Some firms are able to obtain a loan from a bank or other financial institution. The cost of using the funds is the interest paid to the lender. The marginal cost is the cost per extra dollar borrowed, which is simply the market interest rate for borrowed funds.

- **Bonds**   Established firms may be able to borrow funds for R&D by issuing bonds and selling them in the bond market. In this case, the cost is the interest paid to the lenders—the bondholders. Again, the marginal cost of using the funds is the interest rate.

- **Retained earnings**   A large, well-established firm may be able to draw on its own corporate savings to finance R&D. Typically, such a firm retains part of its profit rather than paying it all out as dividends to corporate owners. The marginal cost is the rate at which those funds could have earned interest as deposits in a financial institution.

- **Venture capital**   A smaller start-up firm might be able to attract venture capital to finance its R&D projects. **Venture capital** consists of that part of household saving used to finance high-risk business ventures in exchange for shares of the profit if the ventures succeed. The marginal cost of venture capital is the share of expected profit that the firm will have to pay to those who provided the money. This share can be stated as a percentage of the venture capital, so it is essentially an interest rate.

- **Personal savings**   Finally, individual entrepreneurs might draw on their own savings to finance the R&D for a new venture. The marginal cost of the financing is the forgone interest rate.

Thus, whatever the source of the R&D funds, we can state the marginal cost of these funds as an interest rate, *i*. For simplicity, let's assume that this interest rate is the same no matter how much financing is required. Further, we assume that a certain firm called MedTech must pay an interest rate of 8 percent, the least expensive funding available to it. Then a graph of the marginal cost of each funding amount for this firm is a horizontal line at the 8 percent interest rate, as shown in Figure 11-1. Such a graph is called an **interest-rate cost-of-funds curve**. This one tells us that MedTech can borrow $10, $10,000, $10,000,000 or more at the 8 percent interest rate. The table accompanying the graph contains the data used to construct the graph and tells us much the same thing.

With these data in hand, MedTech wants to determine how much R&D to finance in the coming year.

Expected Rate of Return

A firm's marginal benefit from R&D is its expected profit (or return) from the last (marginal) dollar spent on R&D. That is, the R&D is expected to result in a new product or production method that will increase revenue, reduce production costs, or both (in ways we will soon explain). This return is expected but not certain—there is risk in R&D decisions. Let's suppose that after considering such risks, MedTech anticipates that an R&D expenditure of $1 million will result in a new product that will yield a one-time added profit of $1.2 million a year later. The expected rate of return, *r*, on the $1 million R&D expenditure (after the $1 million has been repaid) is 20 percent (= $200,000/$1,000,000). This is the marginal benefit of the first $1 million of R&D. (Stretching the return over several years complicates the computation of *r*, but it does not alter the basic analysis.)

MedTech can use this same method to estimate the expected rates of return for R&D expenditures of $2 million, $3 million, $4 million, and so on. Suppose those marginal rates of return are the ones indicated in the table in Figure 11-2, where they are also graphed as the **expected-rate-of-return curve**. This curve shows the expected rate of return, which is the marginal benefit, of each

venture capital
Financial capital lent in return for a share in the business.

interest-rate cost-of-funds curve
A graph showing the interest rate a firm must pay to obtain funds to finance R&D.

<www.bothell. washington.edu/faculty/ danby/bls324/surplus.html>
Demand, supply, and surpluses

expected-rate-of-return curve
The increase in profit a firm anticipates it will obtain by investing in R&D.

FIGURE 11-1	The Interest-rate Cost-of-funds Schedule and Curve

R&D, millions	Interest-rate cost of funds, %
$10	8
20	8
30	8
40	8
50	8
60	8
70	8
80	8

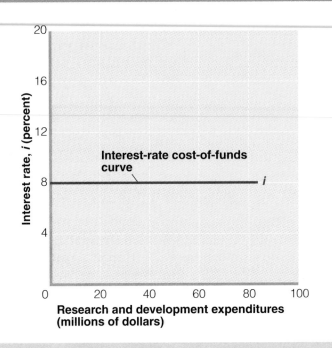

As it relates to R&D, a firm's interest-rate cost-of-funds schedule (the table) and curve (the graph) show the interest rate the firm must pay to obtain any particular amount of funds to finance R&D. Curve i indicates that the firm can finance as little or as much R&D as it wants at a constant 8 percent rate of interest.

dollar of expenditure on R&D. The curve slopes downward because of diminishing returns to R&D expenditures. A firm will direct its initial R&D expenditures to the highest expected-rate-of-return activities and then use additional funding for activities with successively lower expected rates of return.

Optimal R&D Expenditures

optimal amount of R&D
The amount of funding for which the expected rate of return and the interest cost of borrowing are equal.

Figure 11-3 on page 286 combines the interest-rate cost-of-funds curve (Figure 11-1) and the expected-rate-of-return curve (Figure 11-2). The curves intersect at MedTech's **optimal amount of R&D**, which is $60 million. Both the curve and the table tell us that at $60 million of R&D expenditures, the marginal benefit and marginal cost of the last dollar spent on R&D are equal. This firm should undertake all R&D expenditures up to $60 million, since those outlays yield a higher marginal benefit or expected rate of return, r, than the 8 percent marginal cost or interest-rate cost of borrowing, i. But MedTech should not undertake R&D expenditures beyond $60 million; for these outlays, r (marginal benefit) is less than i (marginal cost).

Our analysis reinforces two important points:

1. *Optimal versus affordable R&D*   From earlier discussions we know there can be too much, as well as too little, of a good thing. So it is with R&D and technological advance. Figure 11-3 shows that R&D expenditures make sense to a firm only as long as the expected return from the outlay equals or exceeds the cost of obtaining the funds needed to finance it. Many R&D expenditures may be affordable but not worthwhile, because their marginal benefit is likely to be less than their marginal cost.

FIGURE 11-2   **The Expected-rate-of-return Schedule and Curve**

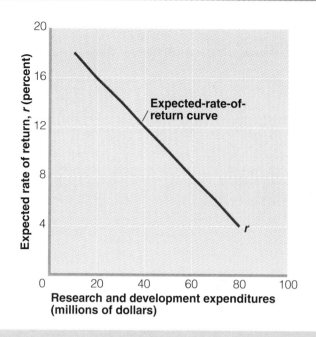

R&D, millions	Expected rate of return, %
$10	18
20	16
30	14
40	12
50	10
60	8
70	6
80	4

As they relate to R&D, a firm's expected-rate-of-return schedule (the table) and curve (the graph) show the firm's expected gain in profit, as a percentage of R&D spending, for each level of R&D spending. Curve r slopes downward because the firm assesses its potential R&D projects in descending order of expected rates of return.

2. ***Expected, not guaranteed, returns***   The outcomes from R&D are expected, not guaranteed. With 20/20 hindsight, a firm can always look back and decide whether a particular expenditure for R&D was worthwhile, but that assessment is irrelevant to the original decision. At the time of the decision, the expenditure was thought to be worthwhile, based on existing information and expectations. Invention and innovation carry with them a great deal of risk. For every successful outcome, there are scores of costly disappointments. ***(Key Questions 4 and 5)***

Increased Profit via Innovation

We have so far sidestepped the question of how technological change can increase a firm's profit. Although the answer may seem obvious—by increasing revenue or reducing production costs—insights can be gained by exploring these two potential outcomes in some detail.

INCREASED REVENUE VIA PRODUCT INNOVATION

Firms here and abroad have profitably introduced hundreds of new products in the past two or three decades. Examples include inline skates, microwave popcorn, cordless drills, digital cameras, camcorders, and projection TVs. Other new products are snowboards, cellular phones, telephone pagers, and automobile air bags.

How do such new products gain consumer acceptance? As you know from Chapter 6, to maximize their satisfaction, consumers purchase products that have the highest marginal utility per dollar. They determine which products to buy in view of their limited money income by comparing the ratios of MU/price for the various goods. They first select the unit of the good with the highest MU/price ratio, then the one with the next highest, and so on, until their income is used up.

FIGURE 11-3   A Firm's Optimal Level of R&D Expenditures

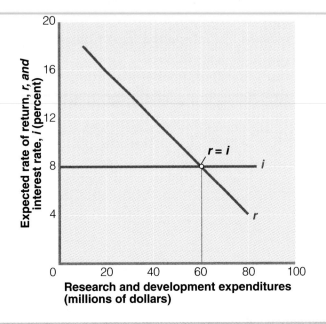

Expected rate of return, %	R&D, millions	Interest-rate cost of funds, %
18	$10	8
16	20	8
14	30	8
12	40	8
10	50	8
8	**60**	**8**
6	70	8
4	80	8

The firm's optimal level of R&D expenditures ($60 million) occurs where its expected rate of return equals the interest-rate cost of funds, as shown in both the table and the graph. At $60 million of R&D spending, the firm has taken advantage of all R&D opportunities for which the expected rate of return, *r*, exceeds or equals the 8 percent interest cost of borrowing, *i*.

The first five columns of Table 11-1 repeat some of the information in Table 6-1. Before the introduction of new product C, the consumer maximized total utility from $10 of income by buying two units of A at $1 per unit and four units of B at $2 per unit. The total $10 budget was thus used up, with $2 spent on A and $8 on B. As shown in columns 2(b) and 3(b), the marginal utility per dollar spent on the last unit of each product was 8 (= 8/$1 = 16/$2). The total utility, derived from columns 2(a) and 3(a), was 96 utils (= 10 + 8 from the first 2 units of A plus 24 + 20 + 18 + 16 from the first 4 units of B). (If you are uncertain about this outcome, please review the discussion of Table 6-1.)

Now suppose an innovative firm offers new product C (columns 4(a) and 4(b) in Table 11-1), priced at $4 per unit. Note that the first unit of C has a higher marginal utility per dollar (13) than any unit of A and B and that the second unit of C and the first unit of B have equal MU/price ratios of 12. To maximize satisfaction, the consumer now buys two units of C at $4 per unit, one unit of B at $2 per unit, and zero units of A. Our consumer has spent the entire $10 of income ($8 on C and $2 on B), and the MU/price ratios of the last units of B and C are equal at 12. But as determined via columns 3(a) and 4(a), the consumer's total utility is now 124 utils (= 24 from the first unit of B plus 52 + 48 from the first 2 units of C). Total utility has increased by 28 utils (= 124 utils – 96 utils) and that is why product C was purchased. *Consumers will buy a new product only if it increases their marginal utility, and thereby the total utility they obtain from their limited income.*

From the innovating firm's perspective, these dollar votes represent new-product demand that yields increased revenue. When per-unit revenue exceeds per-unit cost, the product innovation creates per-unit profit. Total profit rises by the per-unit profit multiplied by the number of units sold. As a percentage of the original R&D expenditure, the rise in total profit is the return on that R&D expenditure. It was the basis for the expected-rate-of-return curve *r* in Figure 11-2.

TABLE 11-1	Utility Maximization with the Introduction of a New Product (Income = $10)*					
(1) Unit of product	(2) Product A: price = $1		(3) Product B: price = $2		(4) New product C: price = $4	
	(a) Marginal utility, utils	(b) Marginal utility per dollar (MU/price)	(a) Marginal utility, utils	(b) Marginal utility per dollar (MU/price)	(a) Marginal utility, utils	(b) Marginal utility per dollar (MU/price)
First	10	10	24	*12*	52	13
Second	8	*8*	20	10	48	*12*
Third	7	7	18	9	44	11
Fourth	6	6	16	*8*	36	9
Fifth	5	5	12	6	32	8

*It is assumed in this table that the amount of marginal utility received from additional units of each of the three products is independent of the quantity purchased of the other products. For example, the marginal utility schedule for product C is independent of the amount of A and B purchased by the consumer.

Several other related points are worth noting:

- **Importance of price** Consumer acceptance of a new product depends on both its marginal utility and its price. (Confirm that the consumer represented in Table 11-1 would buy zero units of new product C if its price were $8 rather than $4.) To be successful, a new product must not only deliver utility to consumers but do so at an acceptable price.

- **Unsuccessful new products** For every successful new product, hundreds do not succeed; the expected return that motivates product innovation is not always realized. Examples of colossal product flops are Ford's Edsel automobile, 3-D movies, quadraphonic stereo, New Coke by Coca-Cola, Kodak disc cameras, and McDonald's McLean burger.

- **Product improvements** Most product innovation consists of incremental improvements to existing products rather than radical inventions, such as more fuel-efficient automobile engines, new varieties of pizza, lighter-weight shafts for golf clubs, more flavourful bubble-gum, rock shocks for mountain bikes, and clothing made of wrinkle-free fabrics. *(Key Question 6)*

REDUCED COST VIA PROCESS INNOVATION

The introduction of better methods of producing products is also a path toward lower costs and thus enhanced profit. Suppose a firm replaces old equipment with more productive equipment embodying technological advance. In either case, the innovation yields an upward shift in the firm's total-product curve from TP_1 to TP_2 in Figure 11-4(a). Now more units of output can be produced at each level of resource usage. Note from the figure, for example, that this firm can now produce 2500 units of output, rather than 2000 units, when using 1000 units of labour. So its average product has increased from 2 (= 2000 units of output ÷ 1000 units of labour) to 2.5 (= 2500 units of output ÷ 1000 units of labour).

The result is a downward shift in the firm's average-total-cost curve, from ATC_1 to ATC_2 in Figure 11-4(b). To understand why, let's assume this firm pays $1000 for the use of its capital and $9 for each unit of labour. Since it uses 1000 units of labour, its labour cost is $9000 (= $9 × 1000); its capital cost is $1000; and thus its total cost is $10,000. When its output increases from 2000 to 2500 units as a result of the process innovation, its total cost remains $10,000, and its average total cost declines from $5 (= $10,000/2000) to $4 (= $10,000/2500).

FIGURE 11-4 — Product Innovation, Total Product, and Average Total Cost

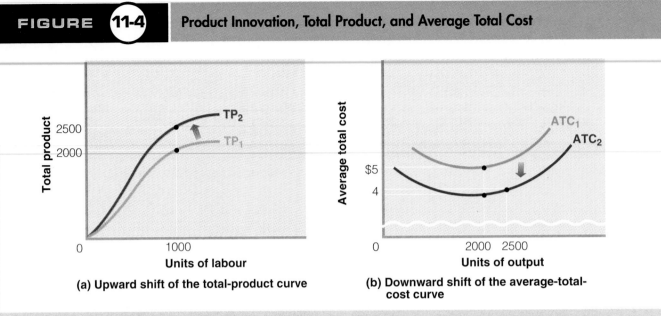

(a) Upward shift of the total-product curve

(b) Downward shift of the average-total-cost curve

Panel (a): Process innovation shifts a firm's total-product curve upward from TP_1 to TP_2, meaning that with a given amount of capital, the firm can produce more output at each level of labour input. As shown, with 1000 units of labour it can produce 2500 rather than 2000 units of output. Panel (b): The upward shift in the total-product curve results in a downward shift in the firm's average-total-cost curve, from ATC_1 to ATC_2. This shift means the firm can produce any particular unit of output at a lower average total cost than it could previously. For example, the original 2000 units can be produced at less than $4 per unit, versus $5 per unit originally. Or 2500 units can now be produced at $4 per unit.

This reduction in average total cost enhances the firm's profit. As a percentage of the R&D expenditure that fostered it, this extra profit is the expected return r, the basis for the rate-of-return curve in Figure 11-2.

Consider this example: Computer-based inventory control systems, such as those pioneered by Wal-Mart, enabled innovators to reduce the number of people keeping track of inventories and placing reorders of sold goods. They also enabled firms to keep goods arriving just in time, reducing the cost of storing inventories. The consequence? Significant increases in sales per worker, declines in average total cost, and increased profit. **(Key Question 8)**

Imitation and R&D Incentives

imitation problem
A firm's rivals may be able to imitate the new product or process, greatly reducing the originator's profit from its R&D effort.

Our analysis of product and process innovation explains how technological advance enhances a firm's profit, but it also hints at a potential **imitation problem**: a firm's rivals may be able to imitate the new product or process, greatly reducing the originator's profit from its R&D effort. As just one example, in the 1980s North American auto firms took apart Japanese Honda Accords, piece by piece, to discover the secrets of their high quality. This reverse engineering—which ironically was perfected earlier by the Japanese—helped the North American firms to incorporate innovative features into their own cars. This type of imitation is perfectly legitimate and fully anticipated; it is often the main path to widespread diffusion of an innovation.

fast-second strategy
The strategy of becoming the second firm to embrace an innovation, allowing the originator to incur the initial high costs of innovation.

In fact, a dominant firm that is making large profits from its existing products may let smaller firms in the industry incur the high costs of product innovation while it closely monitors their successes and failures. The dominant firm then moves quickly to imitate any successful new product; its goal is to become the second firm to embrace the innovation. In using this so-called **fast-second strategy**, the dominant firm counts on its own product-improvement abilities, marketing prowess, or economies of scale to help it succeed.

BENEFITS OF BEING FIRST

Imitation and the fast-second strategy raise an important question: What incentive is there for any firm to bear the expenses and risks of innovation if competitors can imitate their new or improved product? Why not let others bear the costs and risks of product development and then just imitate the successful innovations? Although we have seen that this may be a plausible strategy in some situations, there are several protections for, and potential advantages to, taking the lead (see the Consider This box).

Patents Some technological breakthroughs, specifically inventions, can be patented. Once patented, they cannot be legally imitated for almost two decades. The purpose of patents is, in fact, to reduce imitation and its negative effect on the incentive for engaging in R&D. For example, Polaroid's patent of its instant camera enabled it to earn high economic profits for many years.

Copyrights and Trademarks *Copyrights* protect publishers of books, computer software, movies, videos, and musical compositions from having their works copied. *Trademarks* give the original innovators of products the exclusive right to use a particular product name (WordPerfect, Barbie Doll, Wheaties). By reducing the problem of direct copying, these legal protections increase

Consider This

Innovation, Patents, and Profits

The board game Monopoly is an interesting example of a patented, trademarked product that is still earning a substantial profit after many decades.[1] The word "monopoly" goes back hundreds of years, but Monopoly (the game) is the registered trademark of Parker Brothers, now a unit of Hasbro.

The origin of modern Monopoly traces back to Elizabeth Magie, a Quaker from the U.S. state of Virginia. She invented a game in 1904 to advance the cause of Henry George, who advocated a single tax on land rent. Like Monopoly, Magie's game had 40 spaces, 4 railroads, 2 utilities, and 22 rental properties. The folk game was commonly played on the eastern seaboard, particularly within Quaker communities. The streets in the game were named after those between Inlet and Park Place, along the Boardwalk in Atlantic City.[2]

In the early 1930s, Charles Darrow of Germantown, Pennsylvania, copied and commercialized the game, selling it through Philadelphia department stores. Demand was so great that he could not keep up with the orders, so in 1934 he contacted Parker Brothers, a toy company, to see if they had any interest in it. Parker Brothers initially rejected the game, pointing out that it lasted too long, had rules that were too complicated, and contained 52 fundamental design errors. But Monopoly continued to sell briskly.

Legend has it that a friend telephoned Sally Barton, the daughter of the founder of Parker Brothers, to rave about a new game she had purchased. It was called Monopoly. Sally

relayed the information to her husband, Robert Barton, who was president of Parker Brothers. Barton purchased a copy of the game the next day and ended up playing Monopoly until 1:00 a.m. The next morning, he contacted Darrow and several days later Darrow agreed to sell the rights to his version of the game in return for royalties on each set sold.

Through copyright and trademark, Parker Brothers in effect gained a worldwide monopoly on Monopoly (although "The Original Monopoly Game" is an alternative[3]). Monopoly is available in 26 languages in 80 countries and is the best-selling copyrighted board game ever. More than 200 million sets have been sold, generating more than $3 billion of revenue for Parker Brothers.

---

[1] Maxine Brady, "The Monopoly Book: An Authorized History," Internet; "Hasbro/Parker Brothers, "Monopoly History," Internet; "History of Toys and Games," History Channel, Internet site.

[2] Ralph Anspach, the developer of the game Anti-Monopoly—and later, The Original Monopoly Game—uncovered this history of Monopoly (the game) in defending Anti-Monopoly in a court case relating to Parker Brother's trademark. See his *The Billion Dollar Monopoly Swindle* (San Francisco: Anspach Publication, 1998).

[3] Ibid.

Question: Pharmaceutical companies in Canada now have 20 years of protection for any new drug they develop before generic drug companies are allowed to produce the same drug. Is such a long period warranted?

the incentive for product innovation. They have been strengthened worldwide through recent international trade agreements.

Brand-name Recognition   Along with trademark protection, brand-name recognition may give the original innovator a major marketing advantage for years or even decades. Consumers often identify a new product with the firm that first introduced and popularized it in the mass market. Examples: Levi's blue jeans, Kleenex's soft tissues, Johnson and Johnson's Band-Aids, Sony's Walkman, and Kellogg's Corn Flakes.

Trade Secrets and Learning by Doing   Some innovations involve trade secrets, without which competitors cannot imitate the product or process. For example, Coca-Cola has successfully kept its formula for Coke a secret from potential rivals. In a related advantage, a firm's head-start with a new product often allows it to achieve substantial cost reductions through learning by doing. The innovator's lower cost may enable it to continue to profit even after imitators have entered the market.

Time Lags   Time lags between innovation and diffusion often enable innovating firms to realize a substantial economic profit. It takes time for an imitator to gain knowledge of the properties of a new innovation. Various entry barriers such as large financial requirements, economies of scale, and price-cutting may extend the time lag between innovation and imitation. It may take years or even decades before rival firms can successfully imitate a profitable new product and cut into the market share of the innovator.

Profitable Buyouts   A final advantage of being first arises from the possibility of a buyout (outright purchase) of the innovating firm by a larger firm. Here, the innovative entrepreneurs take their rewards immediately, as cash or as shares in the purchasing firm, rather than waiting for perhaps uncertain long-run profits from their own production and marketing efforts.

In short, despite the imitation problem, there are significant protections and advantages that enable most innovating firms to profit from their R&D efforts, as implied by the continuing high levels of R&D spending by firms year after year. As shown in Figure 11-5, business R&D spending in Canada not only remains substantial but has grown over the past quarter-century. The high levels of spending simply would not continue if imitation consistently and severely depressed rates of return on R&D expenditures.

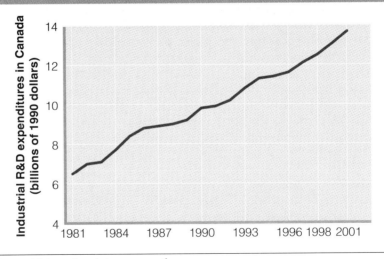

FIGURE 11-5   **The Growth of Business R&D Expenditures in Canada, 1981–2001**

Inflation-adjusted R&D expenditures by firms are substantial and growing, suggesting that R&D continues to be profitable for firms, even in the face of possible imitation.

Source: National Science Foundation. <www.nsf.gov>.

QUICK REVIEW

- A firm's optimal R&D expenditure is the amount at which the expected rate of return (marginal benefit) from the R&D expenditure just equals the interest-rate cost of borrowing (marginal cost) required to finance it.

- Product innovation can entice consumers to substitute a new product for existing products to increase their total utility, thereby increasing the innovating firm's revenue and profit.

- Process innovation can lower a firm's production costs and increase its profit by increasing total product and decreasing average total cost.

- A firm faces reduced profitability from R&D if competitors can successfully imitate its new product or process. Nevertheless, being first has significant potential protections and benefits, including patents, copyrights, and trademarks; brand-name recognition, trade secrets, and cost reductions from learning by doing; and major time lags between innovation and imitation.

11.4   Role of Market Structure

Is any particular market structure or firm size better suited to technological progress than others? Is a highly competitive industry comprising thousands of relatively small firms preferable to an industry comprising only two or three large firms?

Market Structure and Technological Advance

As a first step toward answering these questions, we survey the strengths and shortcomings of our four market models as related to technological advance.

PURE COMPETITION

Does a firm in pure competition have a strong incentive and strong ability to undertake R&D? On the positive side, strong competition provides a reason for these firms to innovate; competitive firms tend to be less complacent than monopolists. If a firm does not seize the initiative, one or more rivals may introduce a new product or cost-reducing production technique that could drive the firm from the market.

On the negative side, the expected rate of return on R&D may be low or even negative for a firm in pure competition. Because of easy entry, its profit rewards from innovation may quickly be competed away by existing or entering firms that also produce the new product or adopt the new technology. Observers have noted that the high rate of technological advance in the purely competitive agricultural industry, for example, has come not from the R&D of individual farmers but from government-sponsored research and from the development of fertilizers, hybrid seed, and farm implements by oligopolistic-firms.

MONOPOLISTIC COMPETITION

Firms in monopolistic competition also cannot afford to be complacent. But unlike firms in pure competition, which sell standardized products, firms in monopolistic competition have a strong profit incentive to engage in product development. This incentive to differentiate their products from those of competitors stems from the fact that sufficiently novel products may create monopoly power and thus economic profit. Examples abound of innovative firms (McDonald's, Rogers Video) that started out as monopolistic competitors in localized markets but soon gained considerable national market power, and higher economic profit.

For the typical firm, however, the shortcomings of monopolistic competition in relation to technological advance are the same as those of pure competition. Most firms in monopolistic competition remain small, which limits their ability to secure inexpensive financing for R&D. In addition, firms in monopolistic competition find it difficult to extract large profits from technological advances because entry to monopolistically competitive industries is relatively easy, leaving only normal profit in the long run. Firms in monopolistic competition, therefore, usually have relatively low expected rates of return on R&D expenditures.

OLIGOPOLY

Many of the characteristics of oligopoly are conducive to technological advance. First, the large size of oligopolists enables them to finance the often large R&D costs associated with major product or process innovation. Moreover, the existence of barriers to entry gives the oligopolist some assurance that it can maintain any economic profit it gains from innovation. Then, too, the large sales volume of the oligopolist enables it to spread the cost of specialized R&D equipment and teams of specialized researchers over a great many units of output. Finally, the broad scope of R&D activity within oligopolistic firms helps them offset the inevitable R&D misses with more than compensating R&D hits. Thus, oligopolists clearly have the means and incentive to innovate.

But R&D in oligopoly also has a negative side. In many instances, the oligopolist's incentive to innovate may be far less than we have implied above, because oligopoly tends to breed complacency. An oligopolist may reason that it makes little sense to introduce costly new technology and produce new products when it currently is earning a sizable economic profit without them. It is not difficult to cite oligopolistic industries in which the largest firms' interest in R&D has been quite modest— the steel, cigarette, and aluminum industries, for example.

PURE MONOPOLY

In general, the pure monopolist has little incentive to engage in R&D; it maintains its high profit through entry barriers that are complete. The only incentive for the pure monopolist to engage in R&D is defensive: to reduce the risk of some new product or production process destroying its monopoly. If such a product is out there to be discovered, the monopolist may have an incentive to find it. But, in general, pure monopoly is the market structure least conducive to innovation.

Inverted-U Theory

inverted-U theory of R&D
A theory that, other things equal, R&D expenditures as a percentage of sales rise with industry concentration, reach a peak at a four-firm concentration ratio of about 50 percent, and then fall as concentration further increases.

Analysis like this has led some experts on technological progress to postulate a so-called **inverted-U theory** of the relationship between market structure and technological advance. This theory is illustrated in Figure 11-6, which relates R&D spending as a percentage of a firm's sales (vertical axis) to the industry's four-firm concentration ratio (horizontal axis). The inverted-U shape of the curve suggests that R&D effort is at best weak in both very low concentration industries (pure competition) and very high concentration industries (pure monopoly). Starting from the lowest concentrations, R&D spending as a percentage of sales rises with concentration until a concentration ratio of 50 percent or so is reached, meaning that the four largest firms account for about one-half the total industry output. Beyond that, relative R&D spending decreases as concentration rises.

The logic of the inverted-U theory follows from our discussion. Firms in industries with very low concentration ratios are mainly competitive firms. They are small, which makes it difficult for them to finance R&D. Entry to these industries is easy, making it difficult to sustain economic profit from innovations that are not supported by patents. As a result, firms in these industries spend little on R&D relative to their sales. At the other end (far right) of the curve, where concentration is exceptionally high, monopoly profit is already high and innovation will not add much more profit. Finally, the lack of rivals makes the monopolist quite complacent about R&D.

The optimal industry structure for R&D is one in which expected returns on R&D spending are high and funds to finance it are readily available and inexpensive. From our discussion, those factors seem to occur in industries where a few firms are absolutely and relatively large but where the concentration ratio is not so high as to prohibit vigorous competition by smaller rivals. Rivalry among the larger oligopolistic firms and competition between the larger and smaller firms then

FIGURE 11-6 **The Inverted-U Theory of R&D Expenditures**

The inverted-U theory suggests that R&D expenditures as a percentage of sales rise with industry concentration until the four-firm concentration ratio reaches about 50 percent. Further increases in industry concentration are associated with lower R&D expenditures.

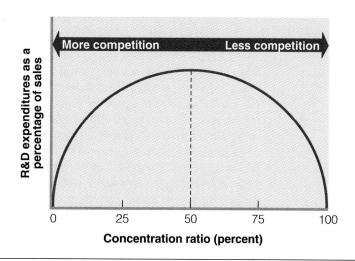

provide a strong incentive for R&D. The inverted-U theory, as represented by Figure 11-6, also points toward this loose oligopoly as the optimal structure for R&D spending.

Market Structure and Technological Advance: The Evidence

Dozens of industry studies have tried to pin down the relationship between market structure and technological advance. Because those studies dealt with different industries and time periods, and used different methodologies, they are not easy to compare and summarize. Nevertheless, they provide general support for the inverted-U theory.[1] Other things equal, the optimal market structure for technological advance seems to be an industry in which there is a mix of large oligopolistic firms (a 40 to 60 percent concentration ratio), with several highly innovative smaller firms.

Our "other things equal" qualification is quite important here. Whether a particular industry is highly technical may well be a more important determinant of R&D than its structure. While some concentrated industries (electronics, aircraft, and petroleum) devote large quantities of resources to R&D and are very innovative, others (cigarettes, aluminum, gypsum products) are not. The level of R&D spending within an industry seems to depend as much on its technical character and technological opportunities as on its market structure. There simply may be more opportunities to innovate in the computer and pharmaceutical industries, for example, than in the brick-making and coal-mining industries.

11.5 Technological Advance and Efficiency

Technological advance contributes significantly to economic efficiency. New and better processes and products enable society to produce more output, as well as a higher-valued mix of output.

Productive Efficiency

Technological advance improves *productive efficiency* by increasing the productivity of inputs, as indicated in Figure 11-4(a), and by reducing average total costs, as in Figure 11-4(b). In other words,

---

[1]Douglas F. Greer, *Industrial Organization and Public Policy,* 3rd ed. (New York: Macmillan, 1992), pp. 680–687.

it enables society to produce the same amount of a particular good or service while using fewer scarce resources, thereby freeing the unused resources to produce other goods and services. Process innovation enhances productive efficiency and is thus an important means of shifting an economy's production possibilities curve rightward.

Allocative Efficiency

Technological advance as embodied in *product* (or service) innovation enhances allocative efficiency by giving society a more preferred mix of goods and services. Recall from our earlier discussion that consumers buy a new product rather than an old product only when buying the new one increases the total utility obtained from their limited income. Obviously, then, the new product creates a higher level of total utility for society.

In terms of markets, the demand for the new product rises and the demand for the old product declines. The high economic profit created by the new product attracts resources away from less-valued uses and to the production of the new product. Such shifting of resources continues until the price of the new product equals its marginal cost.

There is a caveat here, however. Innovation (either product or process) can create monopoly power through patents or through the many advantages of being first. When new monopoly power results from an innovation, society may lose part of the improved efficiency it otherwise would have gained from that innovation. The reason is that the profit-maximizing monopolist restricts output to keep its product price above marginal cost. Microsoft used an early innovation in computer software (its DOS operating system) to achieve a commanding presence in some parts of the software industry. It built its monopoly power partly on a strategy of continual, identifiable product upgrades, from MS-DOS to Windows to Windows XP, with new versions in between. These product improvements are often announced well in advance, and the new versions contain more and more features of competing software. Moreover, Microsoft has extended some of its monopoly power to related software products (Word, PowerPoint). So although society has benefited greatly from the surge of product improvements flowing from Microsoft, another result has been rising entry barriers and monopoly in the software industry.

Innovation can reduce or even destroy monopoly power by providing competition where previously none existed. Economic efficiency is enhanced when that happens, because the new competition helps push prices down closer to marginal cost and minimum average total cost. Innovation that leads to greater competition within an industry reduces the inefficiency associated with reduced restriction of output and monopoly prices. In the Microsoft example, the new technology of the Internet has, at least temporarily, reduced Microsoft's dominance in some emerging areas of the software industry. Specifically, firms such as Sun Microsystems have pioneered new software relating to the Internet (Java programming language), leaving Microsoft working hard to catch up. So, it is difficult to judge whether Microsoft's monopoly power has hindered or aided innovation. Microsoft spends over $2 billion per year on research.

Health Care, Technological Advance, and Efficiency

Technological advance can help alleviate many of the problems presently facing the Canadian health care system. New pharmaceuticals and diagnostic equipment can help to reduce costs. For example, the new proton pump inhibitors (PPI), which reduce acid production in the stomach, have virtually eliminated the need for surgery in the case of ulcers. That is welcome news for many overcrowded hospital surgical departments that are often over budget.

Better diagnostic techniques, such as magnetic resonance imaging (MRI), can diagnose health problems more quickly, thus eliminating the need for additional testing. More accurate diagnoses can reduce the number of unnecessary medical interventions, such as exploratory surgery.

But while new and better pharmaceuticals and diagnostic equipment can help reduce waiting times for surgery—by eliminating either the need for some procedures or the need for other invasive exploratory diagnostic investigation—they are not cheap. Many new pharmaceuticals are prohibitively expensive for many patients, and an MRI machine costs millions of dollars. In late 2002, the Romanow Report, carried out by a former premier of Saskatchewan, recommended that provincial and federal governments inject more money into the national health care system to fund an insurance scheme that would cover the costs of pharmaceuticals for all Canadians. Presumably, the reasoning was that there are economies to be had from wider patient access to effective pharmaceuticals.

Still, we need studies that more accurately measure the costs and benefits associated with increased government spending on new pharmaceuticals and diagnostic equipment. In Canada, health care insurance effectively lowers the price of services for the consumer. Patients do not pay any out-of-pocket money for most essential health care services, meaning the price to the individual consumer is effectively zero. (However, recall that we should include the cost of travelling to the doctor's office and the required waiting time). Might a national insurance plan on pharmaceuticals lead to their overuse, driving costs ever higher? Might more sophisticated and expensive diagnostic equipment lead to ever-mounting demand for their use?

Critics of the present health care system in Canada answer in the affirmative. But proponents of our national health care system point out that Canadians use health care services as they need them, and that Canadians should not have to economize on potentially life-and-death procedures and pharmaceuticals.

Creative Destruction

creative destruction
The hypothesis that the creation of new products and production methods simultaneously destroys the market power of existing monopolies.

Innovation may even generate **creative destruction**, where the creation of new products and new production methods simultaneously destroys the monopoly market positions of firms committed to existing products and old ways of doing business. The term "creative destruction" was coined by the economist Joseph Schumpeter in the 1940s. Schumpeter's notion of creative destruction has become popular in our "information age" as technological advance has picked up speed. Many economists believe that innovation will become the main driver of wealth in the future, but it also means the near-certain failure of firms that do not innovate.

Many examples of creative destruction exist: In the 1800s wagons, ships, and barges were the only means of transporting freight until the railroads came along; the dominant market position of the railroads was, in turn, undermined by trucks, and, later, by airplanes. Movies brought new competition to live theatre, at one time the only show in town, but movies were later challenged by television. Vinyl long-playing (LP) records supplanted acetate 78-rpm phonograph records; cassettes then challenged LP records; and compact discs undermined cassettes. Now Internet music recording technology found on sites such as Kazaa threaten sales of traditional CDs. Aluminum cans and plastic bottles have displaced glass bottles in many uses. E-mail has challenged the postal service.

But some dominant firms may be able to use strategies such as selective price-cutting, buyouts, and massive advertising to block entry and competition from even the most innovative new firms and existing rivals. Moreover, rent-seeking dominant firms have been known to persuade government to give them tax breaks, subsidies, and tariff protection that strengthen their market power.

In short, while innovation in general enhances economic efficiency, in some cases it may lead to entrenched monopoly power. Further innovation may eventually destroy that monopoly power, but the process of creative destruction is neither automatic nor inevitable. However, rapid technological change, innovation, and efficiency clearly are not necessarily inconsistent with possession of monopoly power.

<www.asiaweek.com/asiaweek/magazine/2000/0324/cover1.html>
Creative Destruction City

<www.forbes.com/global/1998/1214/0119038a.html>
Creative Destruction 101

THE LASTword

On the Path to the Personal Computer and Internet

Technological advance is clearly evident in the development of the modern personal computer and the emergence of the Internet. Here is a brief history of those events.

1945 Grace Murray Hopper finds a dead moth between relay contacts in the experimental Mark II computer at Harvard University. Whenever the computer subsequently malfunctions, workers set out to "debug" the device.

1946 ENIAC is revealed. It is a precursor to the modern-day computer that relies on 18,000 vacuum tubes and fills 765 cubic metres of space.

1947 AT&T scientists invent the transfer resistance device, later known as the transistor. It replaces the less-reliable vacuum tubes in computers.

1961 Bob Noyce (who later founded Intel Corporation) and Jack Kilby invent the first integrated circuit, which miniaturizes electronic circuitry onto a single silicon chip.

1964 IBM introduces the System/360 computer. Configured as a system, it takes up nearly the same space as two tennis courts.

1965 Digital Equipment Corporation unveils its PDP-8, the first relatively small-sized computer (a minicomputer).

1969 A networking system called ARPANET is born; it is the beginning of the Internet.

1971 Intel introduces its 4004 processor (a microprocessor). The $200 chip is the size of a thumbnail and has as much computing capability as the 1946 ENIAC.

1975 Xerox markets Alto, the first personal computer (a microcomputer). Bill Gates and Paul Allen found Mi-

crosoft. MITS Corporation's Altair 8800 arrives on the scene. It contains Intel's 8080 microprocessor, which Intel developed a year earlier to control traffic lights.

1977 Apple II, Commodore's PET, and Tandy Radio Shack TRS-80 go on sale, setting the stage for the personal computer revolution.

1981 IBM enters the market with its personal computer powered by the Intel 8800 chip and operated by the Microsoft Disc Operating System (MS-DOS). Osborne Computer markets the Osborne 1, the first self-contained microcomputer, but within two years the firm declares bankruptcy. Logitech commercializes the X-Y Position Indicator for a Display System, invented earlier by Douglas Engelbart in a government-funded research lab. Someone dubs it a computer mouse because it appears to have a tail.

1982 Compaq Computer clones the IBM machines; others do the same. Eventually Compaq becomes the leading seller of personal computers.

1984 Apple introduces its Macintosh computer, with its user-friendly icons, attached mouse, and preloaded software. College student

Michael Dell founds Dell Computers, which builds personal computers and sells them through mail order. IBM, Sears Roebuck, and CBS team up to launch Prodigy Services, the first online computer business.

1985 Microsoft releases its Windows graphical user interface operating system that improves on MS-DOS. Ted Waitt starts a mail-order personal computer business (Gateway 2000) out of his South Dakota barn.

1990 Microsoft introduces Windows 3.0 which, like Macintosh, features windows, icons, and pull-down menus. Apple sues Microsoft for copyright infringement.

1991 The World Wide Web (an Internet system) is invented.

1993 Intel introduces its first Pentium chips, which greatly speed up computing. The courts reject Apple's claim that Microsoft violated its copyrights on its Macintosh operating system.

1994 Marc Andreessen starts up Netscape Communications and markets Netscape Navigator, which quickly becomes the leading software browser for the emerging Internet. David Filo and Jerry Yang develop Yahoo, a system for locating material stored on the Internet.

1995 Microsoft releases Windows 95 operating system, which becomes the dominant operating system of personal computers (90 percent market share). Microsoft is now well established as the world's leading software producer. Sun Microsystems introduces Java, an Internet programming language.

1996 Playing catch-up with Netscape, Microsoft develops Microsoft Internet Explorer and gives it away free.

1999 Netscape's market share plunges and it merges with America Online. More than 100 million personal computers are manufactured worldwide in this year alone.

2002 Sixty-eight percent of Canadian households have access to the Internet either at home or at work, and the Internet continues to spread worldwide (see table). Internet commerce in the Canada reaches $300 billion and an estimated 120,000 Canadian jobs are Internet-related.

TOP 10 INTERNET MARKETS BASED ON PENETRATION

Country	Have Internet access (millions)	Population (millions)	Penetration (%)
1 Canada	21.5	31.6	68.0
2 U.S.A.	174.0	278.1	62.6
3 South Korea	23.8	47.9	49.7
4 Australia	9.1	19.4	46.6
5 Taiwan	8.7	22.3	38.9
6 Japan	48.4	126.8	38.2
7 U.K.	20.6	59.6	34.5
8 Germany	26.0	83.0	31.3
9 Italy	16.7	57.7	28.9
10 France	12.4	60.0	20.6

Source: Canadian Media Directors' Council. <www.cmdc.ca/media_digest/001_51_55.htm>.

Source: Based partly on Diedtra Henderson, "Moore's Law Still Reigns," *Seattle Times*, Nov. 24, 1996. Augmented and updated.

CHAPTER SUMMARY

11.1 TECHNOLOGICAL ADVANCE: INVENTION, INNOVATION, AND DIFFUSION

- Technological advance is evidenced by new and improved goods and services and new and improved production or distribution processes. In economists' models, technological advance occurs only in the *very long run.*

- *Invention* is the discovery of a product or process through the use of imagination, ingenuity, and experimentation. *Innovation* is the first successful commercial introduction of a new product, the first use of a new method, or the creation of a new form of business enterprise. *Diffusion* is the spread of an earlier innovation among competing firms. Firms channel a majority of their R&D expenditures to innovation and imitation, rather than to basic scientific research and invention.

- Historically, most economists viewed technological advance as a random, external force to which the economy adjusted. Many contemporary economists see technological advance as occurring in response to profit incentives within the economy and thus as an integral part of capitalism.

11.2 ROLE OF ENTREPRENEURS AND OTHER INNOVATORS

- Entrepreneurs and other innovators try to anticipate the future. They play a central role in technological advance by initiating changes in products and processes. Entrepreneurs often form start-up firms that focus on creating and introducing new products. Sometimes, innovators work in the R&D labs of major corporations. Entrepreneurs and innovative firms often rely heavily on the basic research done by university and government scientists.

11.3 A FIRM'S OPTIMAL AMOUNT OF R&D

- A firm's optimal amount of R&D spending occurs where its expected return (marginal benefit) from R&D equals its interest-rate cost of funds (marginal cost) to finance R&D. Entrepreneurs and firms use several sources to finance R&D, including (a) bank loans, (b) bonds, (c) venture capital (funds lent in return for a share of the profits if the business succeeds), (d) undistributed corporate profits (retained earnings), and (e) personal savings.

- *Product innovation*, the introduction of new products, succeeds when it provides consumers with higher marginal utility per dollar spent than existing products do. The new product enables consumers to obtain greater total utility from a given income. From the firm's perspective, product innovation increases net revenue sufficiently to yield a positive rate of return on the R&D spending that produced the innovation.

- *Process innovation* can lower a firm's production costs by improving its internal production techniques. Such improvement increases the firm's total product, thereby lowering its average total cost and increasing its profit. The added profit provides a positive rate of return on the R&D spending that produced the process innovation.

- *Imitation* poses a potential problem for innovators, since it threatens their returns on R&D expenditures. Some dominant firms use a fast-second strategy, letting smaller firms initiate new products and then quickly imitating the successes. Nevertheless, significant protections and potential benefits go to firms that take the lead with R&D and innovation, including (a) patent protection, (b) copyrights and trademarks, (c) lasting brand-name recognition, (d) benefits from trade secrets and learning by doing, (e) high economic profits during the time lag between a product's introduction and its imitation, and (f) the possibility of lucrative buyout offers from larger firms.

11.4 ROLE OF MARKET STRUCTURE

- Each of the four basic market structures has potential strengths and weaknesses regarding the likelihood of

R&D and innovation. The *inverted-U theory* holds that a firm's R&D spending as a percentage of its sales rises with its industry four-firm concentration ratio, reaches a peak at a 50 percent concentration ratio, and then declines as concentration increases further. Empirical evidence is not clear-cut but lends general support to this theory. For any specific industry, however, the technological opportunities that are available may count more than market structure in determining R&D spending and innovation.

11.5 TECHNOLOGICAL ADVANCE AND EFFICIENCY

- In general, technological advance enhances both productive and allocative efficiency. But in some situations patents and the advantages of being first with an innovation can increase monopoly power. While in some cases creative destruction eventually destroys monopoly, most economists doubt that this process is either automatic or inevitable.

TERMS AND CONCEPTS

technological advance, p. 279
very long run, p. 279
invention, p. 279
patent, p. 279
innovation, p. 279
product innovation, p. 279

process innovation, p. 279
diffusion, p. 280
start-ups, p. 281
venture capital, p. 283
interest-rate cost-of-funds curve, p. 283

expected-rate-of-return curve, p. 283
optimal amount of R&D, p. 284
imitation problem, p. 288
fast-second strategy, p. 288
inverted-U theory of R&D, p. 292
creative destruction, p. 295

STUDY QUESTIONS

1. What is meant by technological advance, as broadly defined? How does technological advance enter into the definition of the very long run? Which of the following are examples of technological advance, and which are not: an improved production process; entry of a firm into a profitable purely competitive industry; the imitation of a new production process by another firm; an increase in a firm's advertising expenditures?

2. Listed below are several possible actions by firms. Write INV beside those that reflect invention, INN beside those that reflect innovation, and DIF beside those that reflect diffusion.

   a. An auto manufacturer adds heated seats as a standard feature in its luxury cars to keep pace with a rival firm whose luxury cars already have this feature.

   b. A television production company pioneers the first music video channel.

   c. A firm develops and patents a working model of a self-erasing whiteboard for classrooms.

   d. A light bulb firm is the first to produce and market lighting fixtures with halogen lamps.

   e. A rival toy maker introduces a new Jenny doll to compete with Mattel's Barbie doll.

3. Contrast the older and modern views of technological advance as they relate to the economy. What is the role of entrepreneurs and other innovators in technological advance? How does research by universities and government affect innovators and technological advance? Why do you think some university researchers are becoming more like entrepreneurs and less like pure scientists?

4. **KEY QUESTION**   Suppose a firm expects that a $20 million expenditure on R&D will result in a new product that will increase its revenue by a total of $30 million one year from now. The firm estimates that the production cost of the new product will be $29 million.

   a. What is the expected rate of return on this R&D expenditure?

b. Suppose the firm can get a bank loan at 6 percent interest to finance its $20 million R&D project. Will the firm undertake the project? Explain why or why not.

c. Now suppose the interest-rate cost of borrowing, in effect, falls to 4 percent because the firm decides to use its own retained earnings to finance the R&D. Will this lower interest rate change the firm's R&D decision? Explain.

5. **KEY QUESTION**   Answer the following questions on the basis of the information in this table:

Amount of R&D, millions	Expected rate of return on R&D, %
$10	16
$20	14
$30	12
$40	10
$50	8
$60	6

a. If the interest-rate cost of funds is 8 percent, what will be the optimal amount of R&D spending for this firm?

b. Explain why $20 million of R&D spending will not be optimal.

c. Why won't $60 million be optimal either?

6. **KEY QUESTION**   Refer to Table 11-1 and suppose the price of new product C is $2 instead of $4. How does this affect the optimal combination of products A, B, and C for the person represented by the data? Explain: "The success of a new product depends not only on its marginal utility but also on its price."

7. Learning how to use software takes time. So once customers have learned to use a particular software package, it is easier to sell them software upgrades than to convince them to switch to new software. What implications does this have for expected rates of return on R&D spending for software firms developing upgrades versus firms developing imitative products?

8. **KEY QUESTION**   Answer the following questions on the basis of this information for a single firm: total

cost of capital = $1000; price paid for labour = $12 per labour unit; price paid for raw materials = $4 per raw-material unit.

a. Suppose the firm can produce 5000 units of output by combining its fixed capital with 100 units of labour and 450 units of raw materials. What are the total cost and average total cost of producing the 5000 units of output?

b. Now assume the firm improves its production process so that it can produce 6000 units of output by combining its fixed capital with 100 units of labour and 450 units of raw materials. What are the total cost and average cost of producing the 6000 units of output?

c. Refer to your answers to 8a and 8b and explain how process innovation can improve economic efficiency.

9. Why might a firm making a large economic profit from its existing product employ a fast-second strategy in relationship to new or improved products? What risks does it run in pursuing this strategy? What incentive does a firm have to engage in R&D when rivals can imitate its new product?

10. Do you think the overall level of R&D would increase or decrease over the next 20 to 30 years if the lengths of new patents were extended from 17 years to, say, forever? What if the duration were reduced from 17 years to, say, 3 years?

11. Make a case that neither pure competition nor pure monopoly is conducive to a great deal of R&D spending and innovation. Why might oligopoly be more favourable to R&D spending and innovation than either pure competition or pure monopoly? What is the inverted-U theory and how does it relate to your answers to these questions?

12. Evaluate: "Society does not need laws outlawing monopolization and monopoly. Inevitably, monopoly causes its own self-destruction, since its high profit is the lure for other firms or entrepreneurs to develop substitute products."

13. **(The Last Word)** Identify a specific example of each of the following in The Last Word: (a) entrepreneurship, (b) invention, (c) innovation, and (d) diffusion.

INTERNET APPLICATION QUESTION

1. Visit NASA's Technology Transfer Office through the McConnell-Brue-Barbiero Web site (Chapter 11) to determine where significant commercial benefits have been realized from secondary use of NASA technology.

Are there any that have been inconsequential? How does the NASA Commercial Technology Network move technology from the lab to the marketplace?

12

Chapter

Competition Policy and Regulation

IN THIS CHAPTER YOU WILL LEARN:

12.1 What industrial concentration is and how governments combat it.

12.2 About industrial regulation and how government deals with it.

12.3 The definition of social regulations and what their goals are.

In the spirit of the TV show "Who Wants to Be a Millionaire?" try to answer these questions.

- Which one of the following companies was found guilty of violating Canadian anti-combines laws: (a) Kazaa, (b) Microsoft, (c) Toyo Tanso, (d) Colgate-Palmolive. Final answer?

- Firms subject to *industrial regulation* are often called (a) unnatural monopolies, (b) monopolistic competitors, (c) monopsonists, (d) public utilities. Final answer?

- The requirement that businesses make reasonable accommodations for disabled workers and customers is an example of (a) anti-combines policy; (b) an externality; (c) social regulation; (d) economies of scale. Final answer?

The answer, in order, are (c), (d), and (c).

In this chapter we look at three sets of government policies toward business: anti-combines policy, industrial regulation, and social regulation. Anti-combines policy consists of the laws and government actions designed to prevent monopoly and promote competition. Industrial regulation consists of government regulation of firms' prices (or rates) within selected industries. Social regulation is government regulation of the conditions under which goods are produced, the physical characteristics of goods, and the impact of the production and consumption of goods on society.

12.1   Industrial Concentration

In Chapter 9 we developed and applied a strict definition of monopoly. A *pure monopoly*, we said, is a one-firm industry—a situation whereby a unique product is being produced entirely by a single firm and entry to the industry is totally blocked.

In this chapter we will use the term *industrial concentration* to include pure monopoly and markets in which much potential monopoly power exists. Industrial concentration occurs whenever a single firm or a small number of firms control the major portion of the output of an industry. One, two, or three firms dominate the industry, potentially resulting in higher-than-competitive prices and profits. This definition, which is closer to how the general public understands the monopoly problem, includes many industries we have previously designated as oligopolies.

Industrial concentration in this chapter thus refers to industries in which firms are large in absolute terms and in relation to the total market. Examples are the telephone equipment industry, in which Nortel, large by any standard, dominates the market; the automobile industry, where General Motors of Canada, Ford of Canada, and DaimlerChrysler Canada are dominant; the petrochemical industry, dominated by Petro-Canada, Imperial Oil (Exxon), and Shell Canada; the aluminum industry, where industrial giant Alcan Aluminum reigns supreme; and the steel industry, where the two large producers, Dofasco, formerly Dominion Foundries & Steel, and Stelco, formerly Steel Company of Canada, command the lion's share of the market.

The Anti-combines Laws

The Role of Governments

anti-combines policy
The laws and government actions designed to prevent monopoly and promote competition.

The underlying purpose of **anti-combines policy** (antimonopoly policy) is to prevent industrial concentration or monopolization, to promote competition, and to achieve allocative efficiency. Although all economists would agree that these are praiseworthy goals, there is conflicting opinion about the effectiveness of Canadian anti-combines policy. As we will see, anti-combines policy over the years has been neither clear-cut nor consistent.

HISTORICAL BACKGROUND

With the advent of Confederation in 1867, local markets began to widen into national markets because of improved transportation facilities, mechanized production methods, and sophisticated corporate structures. In the 1880s and 1890s cartels emerged in several industries, including the cotton textile, salt, twine, flour, canning and packing, and tobacco industries.

Firms often used questionable tactics to monopolize these industries and then charged monopoly prices to customers and extracted price concessions from resource suppliers. Farmers and owners of small businesses were particularly vulnerable to the power of large corporate monopolies and were among the first to oppose them. Consumers and labour unions were not far behind in their opposition.

The main economic case against monopoly is familiar to you from Chapter 9. Monopolists produce less output and charge higher prices than if their industries were competitive. With pure competition, production occurs where $P = $ MC. This equality represents an efficient allocation of resources because P measures the marginal benefit to society of an extra unit of output, while marginal cost MC reflects the cost of an extra unit. When $P = $ MC, society cannot gain by producing one more or one less unit of the product. In contrast, a monopolist maximizes profit by equating marginal revenue (not price) with marginal cost. At this MR = MC point, price exceeds marginal cost, meaning that society would obtain more benefit than it would incur cost by producing extra units. There is an underallocation of resources to the monopolized product, and so the economic well-being of society is less than it would be with greater competition.

Government concluded in the late 19th century that market forces in monopolized industries did not provide sufficient control to protect consumers, achieve competition, and achieve allocative efficiency. So it instituted two alternative means of control as substitutes for, or supplements to, market forces.

- **Regulatory agencies**   In the few markets where the nature of the product or technology creates a *natural monopoly,* the government established public regulatory agencies to control such firms.

- **Anti-combines laws**   In most other markets, government control took the form of **anti-combines (antimonopoly) legislation** designed to inhibit or prevent the growth of monopoly.

anti-combines (anti-monopoly) legislation
Laws designed to prevent the growth of monopoly.

We will shortly review the anti-combines legislation that constitutes the basic law of the land with respect to corporate size and concentration. Before we do, let's examine merger types.

MERGER TYPES

There are three basic types of mergers, as represented in Figure 12-1. This figure shows two stages of production, one the input stage, the other the final-good stage of two distinct final-good industries: autos and blue jeans. Each rectangle (A, B, C … X, Y, Z) represents a particular firm.

horizontal merger
A merger between two competitors selling similar products in the same market.

A **horizontal merger** is a merger between two competitors selling similar products in the same market. In Figure 12-1 this type of merger is shown as a combination of glass producers T and U. Examples of horizontal mergers would be the buyout of Eatons by Sears, Air Canada's merger with Canadian Airlines, and Best Buy's merger with Future Shop.

vertical merger
The merger of firms engaged in different stages of production process of a final product.

A **vertical merger** is a merger between firms at different stages of the production process. In Figure 12-1 the merger between firm Z, a denim fabric producer, and firm F, a blue jeans producer, is a vertical merger. Vertical mergers involve firms having buyer–seller relationships. Examples of mergers of this type are PepsiCo's mergers with Pizza Hut, Taco Bell, and Kentucky Fried Chicken. PepsiCo supplies soft drinks to each of these fast-food outlets.

conglomerate merger
The merger of a firm in one industry with a firm in another industry or region.

A **conglomerate merger** is officially defined as any merger that is not horizontal or vertical; in general, it is the combination of firms in different industries or firms operating in different geo-

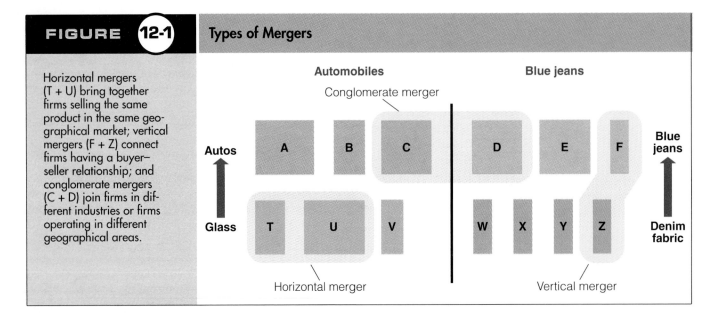

FIGURE 12-1   Types of Mergers

Horizontal mergers (T + U) bring together firms selling the same product in the same geographical market; vertical mergers (F + Z) connect firms having a buyer–seller relationship; and conglomerate mergers (C + D) join firms in different industries or firms operating in different geographical areas.

graphical areas. Conglomerate mergers can extend the line of products sold, or combine totally unrelated companies. In Figure 12-1, the merger between firm C, an auto manufacturer, and firm D, a blue jeans producer, is a conglomerate merger. A real-world example of a conglomerate is Power Corporation of Canada, headquartered in Montreal. Among its holdings are Great-West Life Co., Inc., a life insurance subsidiary, and Power Broadcast Inc., a subsidiary that owns newspapers and radio stations. In Europe, Power Corporation has investments in major communications, industrial, energy, utility, financial services, and food companies.

We now turn to look at the evolution of anti-combines legislation in Canada.

THE EVOLUTION OF ANTI-COMBINES LEGISLATION

The Act of 1889   Canadian anti-combines legislation began in 1889 with the passage of an Act that made it a *misdemeanour* to conspire to restrict either trade, output, or competition. Three years later, the Act of 1889 became a section of the Criminal Code and the offence became an indictable one. In the first ten years of the 20th century there were six prosecutions under the section, resulting in four convictions. Securing evidence to get a conviction under the Criminal Code was difficult, and further changes became necessary.

Combines Investigation Act
The Act, in 1910, that authorized a judge, on receiving an application by six people, to order an investigation into an alleged combine; became the Competition Act in 1986.

Combines Investigation Act, 1910   The result was the passing of the **Combines Investigation Act** in 1910, an Act whose name was changed in June 1986, when it became the Competition Act. The 1910 Act authorized a judge, on receiving an application by six persons, to order an investigation into an alleged combine.

The 1910 Act was unsuccessful for two reasons: (1) rarely could six private citizens be found willing to bear the publicity and expense of initiating an investigation; (2) each investigation started afresh; no person or body administered the Act continuously. Thus, there was only one investigation under the Act before World War I.

The next 50 years saw no fundamental change. Of note were the 1952 amendments to the Act, which split the duties of the combines commissioner and assigned them to two separate agencies—one for investigation and research, the other for appraisal and report. Thus were established a director of investigation and research and a Restrictive Trade Practices Commission, the latter being superseded in June 1986 by the Competition Tribunal (see below).

In 1960, the Combines Investigation Act was at last amended to include the provisions relating to combinations that had been laid down in the Criminal Code since 1892. As well, mergers and monopolies now were deemed unlawful only if a "detriment or against the interest of the public."

In 1967, the newly formed Department of Consumer and Corporate Affairs took over responsibility for combines, mergers, monopolies, and restraint of trade. Shortly thereafter, in 1969, the Economic Council of Canada reported that the provisions of the Combines Investigation Act making mergers and monopolies criminal offences were "all but inoperative" because a criminal offence had to be proved "beyond a shadow of a doubt"—a very difficult task. However, the Economic Council did *not* recommend barriers be placed in the way of a company achieving dominance through internal growth or superior efficiency. The Economic Council's whole approach then was based on the goal of economic efficiency. It was this same approach that led the Economic Council to recommend that competition policy be extended to services.

On January 1, 1976, new amendments to the Combines Investigation Act became effective, with the result that it became applicable to services as well.

Competition Act
The Act that replaced the Combines Investigation Act in 1986.

The Competition Act, 1986   Successive governments in Ottawa have attempted to bring about changes to Canada's law governing monopolies. Three attempts, Bills brought before Parliament in 1971, 1977, and 1977–79, met with opposition from business. Extensive consultations with the private sector and provincial governments preceded the introduction of yet another Bill in 1984. The 1984 election intervened and this Bill, too, was never enacted.

Finally, in June 1986, Parliament passed the Competition Tribunal Act and the **Competition Act**, the latter being the new name for the Combines Investigation Act. Some of the major changes are worth noting.

Uncompetitive market structures (monopoly and oligopoly) and uncompetitive structural change (merger) now come under the jurisdiction of the civil law, making it easier to prosecute those mergers and monopolies not in the public interest. Some behaviour, such as price fixing, is still handled by the regular courts, where the standard of evidence is "beyond a reasonable doubt" and the penalties are harsh. A **competition tribunal** adjudicates under a civil law framework that permits the issuing of remedial orders to restore and maintain competition in the market. The tribunal is made up of judges of the Federal Court and laypersons, with a judge as chairperson. The Restrictive Trade Practices Commission was abolished as a result.

competition tribunal
A government body that adjudicates under a civil law framework that permits the issuing of remedial orders to restore and maintain competition in the market.

The Competition Act does not directly attack monopoly; a firm can legally have 100 percent of the market. But it is the abuse of a monopoly position that is unlawful.

RECENT CASES

The Competition Act is designed to achieve economic efficiency and to be adaptable to changing market conditions and international trade. Only those mergers resulting in an unacceptable lessening of competition can be prohibited or modified by the competition tribunal. Mergers that result in efficiency gains through capturing economies of scale have generally been allowed. For example, in April 2003, the Competition Bureau reported it would not challenge the merger of certain assets of the coal businesses of Fording Inc., Teck Cominco Ltd., Luscar Ltd., and Consol Energy Inc., in the thermal coal, metallurgical coal, and coal terminal port businesses in Canada.

<canada.justice.gc.ca/en/ laws/C-36.4/index.html>
Competition Tribunal Act (R.S. 1985, c. 19 [2nd Supp.])

The Competition Bureau recommended allowing the merger of Air Canada and Canadian Airlines in 1999, provided the federal government opened up the Canadian market to foreign competition. Canadian Airlines was in financial difficulty and it was doubtful that it could survive on its own. Much can be said for the merger of Air Canada and Canadian Airlines on efficiency grounds, but concern is justified among the public about market concentration unless the federal government decides to pursue the so-called open skies policy.

The Competition Bureau recommended against chartered bank mergers in 1998, when the Royal Bank of Canada and the Bank of Montreal announced their intention to merge. Soon after, the Canadian Imperial Bank of Commerce and the Toronto Dominion Bank also decided to merge. The banks argued that they needed to merge to capture economies of scale and be able to compete internationally. The Competition Bureau was not convinced by the banks' argument, citing fears that competition would be greatly curtailed in smaller centres for both consumers and small and medium-sized firms. The Bureau noted that even if more foreign banks were allowed to compete in the Canadian market, the large established network of branches of the Canadian banks provided a large barrier to entry for any new competitor. The Royal Bank of Canada and the Bank of Montreal were, however, successful in merging their credit card operations.

<cb-bc.gc.ca>
Competition Bureau

In December 2002, the standing Senate Committee on Banking, Trade, and Commerce came out with an endorsement of mergers among Canada's chartered banks, with the proviso that the Competition Bureau ensure competition in the financial services sector to protect consumers. It remains to be seen whether the government will accept these recommendations and pass legislation to make it possible for the chartered banks to merge, if they so wish.

In April 2003 the Competition Bureau announced that Toyo Tanso USA Inc., whose world headquarters are in Japan, pleaded guilty to charges of attempting to maintain the price of isostatic graphite, which is used to make moulds and dies for various industries, including auto parts and semi-conductors. According to the Competition Bureau, Toyo Tanso met with independent distributors in Canada to attempt to raise prices of unmachined and semi-machined isostatic graphite. Toyo Tanso was fined $200,000 by the Federal Court of Canada under the price maintenance provision of the Competition Act. Two years earlier, the Competition Bureau's investigation in the same industry led to the conviction of the Carbone of America Industries Corp. after that company pleaded guilty to its role in an international price-fixing cartel for isostatic graphite.

ISSUES OF ENFORCEMENT: TRADEOFFS AMONG GOALS

Promoting competition is only one of society's goals and strict enforcement of the anti-combines laws may sometimes conflict with some other goal.

Occasionally, new technologies combine to create new products and services. A current example is the meshing of computer and communications technologies relating to the Internet. This interactive network has improved the communications capabilities of households, businesses, and governments across the globe. It also enables people to access unprecedented amounts of information and directly buy and sell goods and services. The emergence of this new technology has set off a spate of megamergers among entertainment companies, telecommunication companies, computer manufacturers, and software producers.

Should the government strictly enforce anti-combines laws to block some of those mergers, specifically ones that produce dominant firms and threaten to reduce competition? Or should the government temporarily suspend anti-combines rules to encourage the restructuring of industries and speed the expansion of this new technology? Hastening the advance of Internet-related technologies might also increase Canadian exports of electronic services.

Each of these enforcement tradeoffs, by itself, triggers controversy. Some argue that the gains from an anti-combines policy must be weighed against the effects of the policy on conflicting objectives. Others contend that selective enforcement of anti-combines laws dangerously interferes with the market process. Obviously, different policymakers and different administrations may view such considerations and tradeoffs differently. *(Key Questions 2 and 3)*

QUICK REVIEW

- Industrial concentration exists where a single firm or a small number of firms control the major portion of an industry's output.

- Three types of mergers can occur: horizontal, vertical, and conglomerate.

- The first Canadian anti-combines legislation was passed in 1889. Its purpose was to make it unlawful to restrict competition unduly.

- The original anti-combines legislation subsequently came under the Criminal Code, making successful prosecution difficult.

- The Competition Act, passed in 1986, removed anti-combines activity from the Criminal Code, making prosecution easier. This Act also stressed that even if some mergers lessen competition, they should be allowed if such mergers bring about significant efficiency gains.

12.2 Industrial Regulation

The Role of Governments

Anti-combines policy assumes that society will benefit if monopoly is prevented from evolving or if it is dissolved where it already exists. We now return to a special situation in which an economic reason exists for an industry to be a monopoly.

Natural Monopoly

natural monopoly
An industry in which economies of scale are so extensive that a single firm can supply the entire market at a lower unit cost than could a number of competing firms.

A **natural monopoly** exists when economies of scale are so extensive that a single firm can supply the entire market at a lower unit cost than could a number of competing firms. Clear-cut circumstances of natural monopoly are relatively rare, but such conditions exist for many *public utilities,* such as local electricity and water. As we discussed in Chapter 9, large-scale operations in some cases are necessary to obtain low unit costs and a low product price. Where natural monopoly exists, competition does not enhance efficiency. If the market were divided among many producers, economies of scale would not be achieved and unit costs and prices would increase.

TABLE 12-1	The Main Federal Regulatory Agencies

Atomic Energy Control Board

Canadian Dairy Commission

Canadian Grain Commission

Canadian Radio-Television and Telecommunications Commission

Canadian Wheat Board

National Energy Board

National Farm Products Marketing Council

National Harbours Board

National Transport Agency of Canada

public interest theory of regulation
The theory that industrial regulation is necessary to keep a natural monopoly from charging monopoly prices and thus harming consumers and society.

There are two possible alternatives for promoting better economic outcomes where natural monopoly exists. One is public ownership, and the other is public regulation.

Public ownership or some approximation of it has been established in a few instances, such as Canada Post, water supply systems, and garbage collection at the local level.

But *public regulation,* or what economists call industrial regulation, has been the preferred option in Canada. In this type of regulation, government commissions regulate the prices (usually called rates) charged by natural monopolists. Table 12-1 lists the major federal regulatory commissions.

The economic objective of industrial regulation is reflected in the **public interest theory of regulation**. According to that theory, industrial regulation is necessary to keep a natural monopoly from charging monopoly prices and thus harming consumers and society. The goal of such regulation is to garner for society at least part of the cost reductions associated with natural monopoly while avoiding the restrictions of output and high prices that come with unregulated monopoly. If competition is impractical, society should allow or even encourage a monopoly but regulate its prices. Regulation should then be structured so that ratepayers benefit from the economies of scale—the lower per-unit costs—that natural monopolists are able to achieve.

In practice, regulators seek to establish rates that will cover production costs and yield a fair return to the enterprise. The goal is to set price equal to average total cost, so that the regulated firm receives a normal profit, as described in the "Regulated Monopoly" section of Chapter 9. In particular, you should carefully review Figure 9-9.

Problems with Industrial Regulation

Considerable disagreement rages over the effectiveness of industrial regulation. Let's examine two criticisms.

COSTS AND INEFFICIENCY

An unregulated firm has a strong incentive to reduce its costs at each level of output, because that will increase its profit. The regulatory commission, however, confines the regulated firm to a normal profit or a fair return on the value of its assets. If a regulated firm lowers its operating costs, the rising profit eventually will lead the regulatory commission to require the firm to lower its rates and return its profits to normal. The regulated firm, therefore, has no incentive to reduce its operating costs.

Worse yet, higher costs do not result in lower profit. Because the regulatory commissions must allow the public utility a fair return, the regulated monopolist can simply pass through higher production costs to consumers by charging higher rates. A regulated firm may reason that it might as well have high salaries for its workers, luxurious working conditions for management, and the like, since the return is the same in percentage terms whether costs are minimized or not. So, although a natural monopoly reduces cost through economies of scale, industrial regulation fosters considerable X-inefficiency (Figure 9-7). Because of the absence of competition, the potential cost savings from natural monopoly may never actually materialize.

PERPETUATING MONOPOLY

A second general problem with industrial regulation is that it sometimes perpetuates monopoly long after the conditions of natural monopoly have evaporated.

Technological change often creates the potential for competition in at least some or all portions of the regulated industry, such as when trucks began competing with railroads; transmission of voice and data by microwave and satellites began competing with transmission over telephone wires; satellite television began competing with cable television, and cellphones began competing with regular phones. But, spurred by the firms they regulate and believing that the regulated firms are natural monopolies, commissions often protect the regulated firms from new competition by either blocking entry or extending regulation to competitors. The rationale usually is that the competitors simply want to skim the cream from selected highly profitable portions of the regulated industry but do no want to offer the universal service required of the regulated firm. By losing the highly profitable portion of their business, the regulated firms would have to increase rates for services that do not pay their own way to continue to receive a fair rate of return on their assets.

But where regulators block entry or extend regulation to competitive firms, industrial regulation may perpetuate a monopoly that is no longer a natural monopoly and that would otherwise erode. Ordinary monopoly, protected by government, may then supplant natural monopoly. If so, then the regulated prices may be higher than they would be with competition. The beneficiaries of outdated regulations are the regulated firms, their employees, and perhaps consumers of some services. The losers are all other consumers and the potential competitors who are barred from entering the industry. *(Key Question 8)*

Legal Cartel Theory

legal cartel theory of regulation
The hypothesis that some industries seek regulation or want to maintain regulation so that they may form a legal cartel.

The regulation of potentially competitive industries has produced the **legal cartel theory of regulation**. In place of socially minded officials forcing regulation on natural monopolies to protect consumers, holders of this view see practical politicians as supplying regulation to local, regional, and national firms that fear the impact of competition on their profits or even on their long-term survival. These firms desire regulation because it yields a legal monopoly that can guarantee a profit. Specifically, the regulatory commission performs such functions as blocking entry (for example, in local telephone service), or, where there are several firms, the commission divides up the market much like an illegal cartel (for example, before airline deregulation, the federal government assigned routes to specific airlines). The commission may also restrict potential competition by enlarging the "cartel."

Although private cartels are illegal, unstable, and often break down, the special attraction of a government-sponsored cartel under the guise of regulation is that it endures. The legal cartel theory of regulation suggests that regulation results from the rent-seeking activities of private firms and the desire of politicians to be responsive.

<csgb.ubc.ca/ccpp/>
Canadian competition policy

Occupational licensing is a labour-market application of the legal cartel theory. Certain occupational groups—dentists, barbers, hairstylists, dietitians, lawyers—demand stringent licensing on the grounds that it protects the public from charlatans and quacks, but skeptics say the real reason may be to limit entry into the occupational group so that practitioners can receive monopoly incomes. It is not surprising to these skeptics that a recent study found that, other things equal, dental fees were about 15 percent higher and dentist income 10 percent higher in areas with the most restrictive licensing laws. The quality of dentistry apparently was not affected.[1]

Deregulation

Beginning in the 1970s, the legal cartel theory, evidence of inefficiency in regulated industries, and the contention that the government was regulating potentially competitive industries all contributed to a wave of deregulation. Since then, Parliament and some provincial legislatures have

---

[1]Morris Kleiner and Robert Kudrie, "Does Regulation Affect Economic Outcomes? The Case of Dentistry," *Journal of Law and Economics*, October 2000, pp. 547–582.

passed legislation that has deregulated in varying degrees the airline, trucking, banking, railroad, natural gas, electricity, and television broadcasting industries. Deregulation has also occurred in the telecommunications industry. Bell Canada now competes with other carriers, such as Sprint, in the local and long-distance markets. Bell Canada also competes with cellular companies. Deregulation in the 1970s and 1980s was one of the most extensive experiments in economic policy to take place during the past 50 years.

CONTROVERSY

Deregulation was controversial, and the nature of the controversy was predictable. Proponents of deregulation, basing their arguments on erosion of natural monopoly and the legal cartel theory, contended that deregulation would lower prices, increase output, and eliminate bureaucratic inefficiencies.

Some critics of deregulation, embracing the view of continued natural monopoly and the public interest theory, argued that deregulation would result in destructive price wars and eventual re-monopolization of some of the deregulated industries by a single firm. They predicted higher prices, diminished output, and deteriorating service.

OUTCOMES OF DEREGULATION

Most economists believe that deregulation has benefited consumers and the economy. According to studies, deregulation of formerly regulated industries is now contributing hundreds of millions of dollars annually to society's well-being through lower prices, lower costs, and increased output.[2] Most of those gains are accruing in three industries: airlines, railroads, and trucking. Airfares (adjusted for inflation) have declined by about one-third, and airline safety has improved. Trucking and railroad freight rates (again, adjusted for inflation) have dropped by about one-half. Significant efficiency gains have occurred in long-distance telecommunications, and slight efficiency gains have been made in cable television, stock brokerage services, and the natural gas industry. Deregulation has unleashed a wave of technological advances that have resulted in such new and improved products and services as fax machines, cellular phones, fibre-optic cable, microwave systems in communications, and the Internet.

The success of past deregulation has led to further calls for deregulation. The latest industry to begin the deregulation process is electricity, led by Alberta and Ontario. Deregulation is now occurring at the wholesale level, where firms are free to build generating facilities and sell electricity at market prices.

QUICK REVIEW

- Natural monopoly occurs where economies of scale are so extensive that only a single firm can produce the product at minimum average total cost.

- The public interest theory of regulation says that government must regulate natural monopolies to prevent abuses arising from monopoly power. Regulated firms, however, have less incentive than competitive firms to reduce costs; that is, regulated firms tend to be X-inefficient.

- The legal cartel theory of regulation suggests that some firms seek government regulation to reduce price competition and ensure stable profits.

- Deregulation initiated by government in the past three decades has yielded large annual efficiency gains for society.

[2]Clifford Winston, "Economic Deregulation: Days of Reckoning for Microeconomists," *Journal of Economic Literature,* September 1993, p. 1284; and Robert Crandall and Jerry Ellig, *Economic Deregulation and Consumer Choice,* Center for Market Processes, Fairfax, Virginia, 1997.

12.3   Social Regulation

The Role of Governments

social regulation
Government regulation of the conditions under which goods are produced, the physical characteristics of goods, and the impact of the production on society.

The industrial regulation discussed in the preceding section has focused on the regulation of prices (or rates) in natural monopolies. But in the early 1960s, a new type of regulation began to emerge. **Social regulation** is concerned with the conditions under which goods and services are produced, the impact of production on society, and the physical qualities of the goods themselves.

Distinguishing Features

Social regulation differs from industrial regulation in several ways.

First, social regulation is often applied across the board to all industries and directly affects more producers than does industrial regulation. For instance, while the industrial regulation by the Air Transport Committee of the National Transport Agency of Canada controls only the air transport industry, the rules and regulations of the Canada Labour (Safety) Code and its provincial counterparts apply to every employer.

Second, social regulation intrudes into the day-to-day production process to a greater extent than industrial regulation. While industrial regulation focuses on rates, costs, and profits, social regulation often dictates the design of products, the conditions of employment, and the nature of the production process. As examples, rather than specify safety standards for vehicles, the Motor Vehicle Safety Act includes six standards limiting motor vehicle exhaust and noise emission.

Finally, social regulation has expanded rapidly during the same period in which industrial regulation has waned. Under this social regulation, firms must provide reasonable accommodations for qualified workers and job applicants with disabilities. Also, sellers must provide reasonable access for customers with disabilities. As much of our society had achieved a fairly affluent standard of living by the 1960s, attention shifted to improvement in the non-material quality of life. That focus called for safer products, less pollution, improved working conditions, and greater equality of economic opportunity.

The Optimal Level of Social Regulation

While economists agree on the need for social regulation, they disagree on whether the current level of such regulation is optimal. Recall that an activity should be expanded so long as its marginal benefit (MB) exceeds its marginal cost (MC). If the MB of social regulation exceeds its MC, then there is too little social regulation, but, if MC exceeds MB, there is too much social regulation. Unfortunately, the marginal costs and benefits of social regulation are not always easy to measure and therefore may be illusory. So, ideology about the proper size and role of government often drives the debate over social regulation as much as, or perhaps more than, economic cost–benefit analysis.

IN SUPPORT OF SOCIAL REGULATION

Defenders of social regulation say that it has achieved notable successes and, overall, has greatly enhanced society's well-being. They point out that the problems social regulation confronts are serious and substantial. Hundreds of workers die annually in job-related accidents and many thousands of workers suffer injuries that force them to miss a day or more of work. Air pollution continues to cloud major Canadian cities, imposing large costs in terms of reduced property values and increased health care expense. Numerous children and adults die each year because of poorly designed or manufactured products (for example, car tires) or tainted food (for example, *e-coli* in beef). Discrimination against some ethnic minorities, persons with disabilities, and older workers reduces their earnings and imposes heavy costs on society.

Proponents of social regulation acknowledge that social regulation is costly, but they correctly point out that a high price for something does not necessarily mean that it should not be purchased. They say that the appropriate economic test should not be whether the costs of social regulation are high or low but whether the benefits of social regulation exceed the costs. After decades of neglect, they further assert, society cannot expect to cleanse the environment, enhance the safety of the workplace, and promote economic opportunity for all without incurring substantial costs. So statements about the huge costs of social regulation are irrelevant, say defenders, since the benefits are even greater. The public often underestimates those benefits, since they are more difficult to measure than costs and often become apparent only after some time has passed (for example, the benefits of reducing global warming).

Proponents of social regulation point to its many specific benefits. It is estimated that highway fatalities would be 40 percent greater annually in the absence of auto safety features mandated through regulation. Compliance with child safety-seat and seat belt laws has significantly reduced the auto fatality rate for small children. The national air quality standards set by law have been reached in nearly all parts of the nation for sulphur dioxide, nitrogen dioxide, and lead. Recent studies clearly link cleaner air, other things equal, with increases in the values of homes. Employment equity regulations have increased the labour demand for ethnic minorities and females. The use of childproof lids has resulted in a 90 percent decline in child deaths caused by accidental swallowing of poisonous substances.

Some defenders of social regulation say many areas remain in which greater regulation would generate net benefits to society. For example, some call for greater regulation of the meat, poultry,

Consider This

Canada and the Kyoto Accord

In 1997, 38 industrialized countries agreed to cut emissions of greenhouse gases by 5.2 percent compared to their emissions in 1990. It is widely believed by scientists that greenhouse gases, primarily from the burning of fossil fuels, are significant contributors to global climate change. Developing nations were excluded from the Kyoto emission quotas on equity grounds. It was felt that such emission quotas would hinder economic growth in nations that needed growth to alleviate severe and widespread poverty.

At the end of 2002, the Canadian federal government ratified the Kyoto Accord on climate change, and committed Canada to reduce its greenhouse gas emissions by the required amount by the year 2012. In essence, the federal government passed social regulations that would reduce harmful pollutants to the environment. A federal government study revealed that the likely impact of the Kyoto Accord on the Canadian economy would be minimal. Moreover, the reduction of greenhouse gases had the approval of the majority of Canadians.

Not everyone in Canada agrees that reducing greenhouse gases will cost little, or that it is even necessary. Some scientists maintain the global climate change is a normal ecological occurrence, and is not created by the burning of fossil fuels. The business lobby is worried that the opting out of the Kyoto accord by the U.S., our largest trading partner, will put our exports at a competitive disadvantage in its market.

The premier of Alberta complained bitterly that the passage of the Kyoto Accord would mean his province's energy sector would bear a disproportionately large percentage of the implementation costs.

Given the many variables involved, it is difficult, if not impossible, to try to estimate the expected costs and benefits of the agreement for each of the provinces. For example, if there were rapid technological progress in the development of hydrogen fuel cells to power many of the machines and vehicles now using natural gas and oil, the expected costs of the Kyoto Accord would be negligible since consumers would shift to the new power source if the price were comparable.

The Kyoto Accord is a classic example of social regulations, with potential economic consequences. These regulations can be costly, but proponents of greenhouse gas reduction point out that continuing to pollute the earth's environment could be even more costly in the long run if extreme climate change makes the globe uninhabitable for human beings.

Question: What are some of the ways Canadians can be induced to reduce greenhouse gases to reach the goals set by the Kyoto Accord?

and seafood industries to improve food safety. Others say that more regulation is needed to ensure that violent movies, CDs, and video games are not marketed to children.

Advocates of social regulation claim that the benefits of such regulation are well worth the considerable costs. The costs are simply the price we must pay to create a hospitable, sustainable, and just society. *(Key Question 10)*

Criticisms of Social Regulation

Critics of social regulation contend that, in many instances, it has been expanded to the point where the marginal costs exceed the marginal benefits. In this view, society would achieve net benefits by cutting back on meddlesome social regulation. Critics say that many social regulation laws are poorly written, making regulatory objectives and standards difficult to understand. As a result, regulators pursue goals well beyond the original intent of the legislation. Businesses complain that regulators often press for additional increments of improvement, unmindful of costs.

Also, opponents of social regulation say that the regulatory agencies may attract overzealous workers who are hostile toward the market system and believe too fervently in regulation. For example, some Environment Canada staff allegedly see all pollution as bad and all polluters as "bad guys." They have been accused of avoiding the challenge of trying to identify the optimal amount of pollution based on a careful analysis of marginal costs and marginal benefits (see the Consider This box).

Two Reminders

The debate over the proper amount of social regulation will surely continue. We leave both proponents and opponents of social regulation with pertinent economic reminders.

THERE IS NO FREE LUNCH

On the one hand, fervent supporters of social regulation need to remember that there is no free lunch. Social regulation can produce higher prices, stifle innovation, and reduce competition.

Social regulation raises product prices in two ways. It does so directly because compliance costs normally get passed on to consumers, and it does so indirectly by reducing labour productivity. Resources invested in making workplaces accessible to workers with disabilities, for example, are not available for investment in new machinery designed to increase output per worker. Where the wage rate is fixed, a drop in labour productivity increases the marginal and average total costs of production. In effect, the supply curve for the product shifts leftward, causing the price of the product to rise.

Social regulation may have a negative impact on the rate of innovation. Technological advance may be stifled by, say, the fear that a new plant will not meet Environment Canada's guidelines or that a new medicine will require years of testing before being approved by the federal government.

Social regulation may weaken competition, since it usually places a relatively greater burden on small firms than on large ones. The costs of complying with social regulation are, in effect, fixed costs. Because smaller firms produce less output over which to distribute those costs, their compliance costs per unit of output put them at a competitive disadvantage with their larger rivals. Social regulation is more likely to force smaller firms out of business, thus contributing to the increased concentration of industry.

LESS GOVERNMENT IS NOT ALWAYS BETTER THAN MORE

On the other hand, fervent opponents of social regulation need to remember that less government is not always better than more government. Although the market system is a powerful engine for producing goods and services and generating income, it has its flaws. Through social regulation government can clearly increase economic efficiency and thus society's well-being. Ironically, by taking the rough edges off of capitalism, social regulation may be a strong pro-capitalist force. Properly conceived and executed, social regulation helps maintain political support for the market system. Such support could quickly wane if there were a steady stream of reports of unsafe workplaces, unsafe products, discriminatory hiring, choking pollution, ill-served medical patients, and the like. Social regulation helps the market system deliver not only goods and services but also a "good society."

QUICK REVIEW

- Social regulation is concerned with the conditions under which goods and services are produced, the effects of production on society, and the physical characteristics of the goods themselves.

- Defenders of social regulation point to the benefits arising from policies that keep dangerous products from the marketplace, reduce workplace injuries and deaths, contribute to clean air and water, and reduce employment discrimination.

- Critics of social regulation say uneconomical policy goals, inadequate information, unintended side effects, and overzealous personnel create excessive regulation, for which regulatory costs exceed regulatory benefits.

THE LASTword — The United States v. Microsoft

The recent Microsoft antitrust case in the U.S. is the most significant monopoly case since the break-up of AT&T in the early 1980s, and will have repercussions in Canada.

The Charges In May 1998 the U.S. Justice Department (under President Clinton), 19 individual states, and the District of Columbia (hereafter, "the government") filed antitrust charges against Microsoft under the Sherman Antitrust Act (a U.S. anti-combines law). The government charged that Microsoft had violated Section 2 of the Act through a series of unlawful actions designed to maintain its Windows monopoly. It also charged that some of that conduct violated Section 1 of the Act.

Microsoft denied the charges, arguing it had achieved its success through product innovation and lawful business practices. Microsoft contended that it should not be penalized for its superior foresight, business acumen, and technological prowess. It also pointed out that its monopoly was highly transitory because of rapid technological advances.

The District Court Findings In June 2000, the District Court ruled that the relevant market was software used to operate Intel-compatible personal computers (PCs). Microsoft's 95 percent share of that market clearly gave it monopoly power. The Court pointed out, however, that being a monopoly is not illegal. The violation of the Sherman Act occurred because Microsoft used anti-competitive means to maintain its monopoly power.

According to the Court, Microsoft feared that the success of Netscape's Navigator, which allowed people to browse the Internet, might allow Netscape to expand its software to include a competitive PC operating system—software that would threaten Microsoft's Windows monopoly. It also feared that the Internet applications of Sun's Java programming language might eventually threaten the Windows monopoly.

To counter these and similar threats, Microsoft illegally signed contracts with PC makers that required them to feature Internet Explorer on the PC desktop and penalized companies that promoted software products that competed with Microsoft products. Moreover, it gave friendly companies coding that linked Windows to software applications and withheld it from companies featuring Netscape. Finally, under license from Sun, Microsoft developed Windows-related Java software that made Sun's own software incompatible with Windows.

The District Court Remedy The District Court ordered Microsoft split into two competing companies, one initially selling the Windows operating system and the other initially selling Microsoft applications and services (such as Word, Hotmail, MSN, PowerPoint, and Internet Explorer).

Both companies would be free to develop new products that competed with each other, and both could derive those products from the intellectual property embodied in the common products existing at the time the company was split.

The Appeals Court's Ruling In late 2000 Microsoft appealed the District Court decision to a U.S. Court of Appeals. In 2001 the higher court affirmed that Microsoft illegally maintained its monopoly, but tossed out the District's Court decision to break up Microsoft. It agreed with Microsoft that it was denied due process during the penalty phase of the trial and concluded that the District Court judge had displayed an appearance of bias by holding extensive interviews with the press. The Appeals Court sent the remedial phase of the case to a new District Court judge to determine appropriate remedies. The Appeals Court also raised issues relating to the wisdom of a remedy that involved changing the structure of Microsoft.

The Final Settlement At the urging of the new District Court judge, the federal government (now under President Bush) and Microsoft negotiated a proposed settlement. With minor modification, the settlement became the final court order in 2002. The breakup was overturned and replaced with a remedy that places limits on the company's behaviour. It:

1. prevents Microsoft from retaliating against any firm that develops, sells, or uses software that competes with Microsoft Windows or Internet Explorer or that ships a personal computer that includes both Windows and a non-Microsoft operating system;

2. requires Microsoft to establish uniform royalty and licensing terms for computer manufacturers that want to include Windows on their PCs;

3. requires that manufacturers be allowed to remove Microsoft icons and replace them with other icons on the Windows desktop; and

4. calls for Microsoft to provide technical information to other companies so they can develop programs that work as well with Windows as Microsoft's own products do.

Source: United States v. Microsoft (District Court Conclusions of Law), April 2000; United States v. Microsoft (Court of Appeals), June 2001; U.S. v. Microsoft (Final Judgment), November 2002; and Reuters and Associate Press News Services.

CHAPTER SUMMARY

12.1 INDUSTRIAL CONCENTRATION

- Mergers can be of three types: horizontal, vertical, and conglomerate.

- The cornerstone of anti-combines policy consists of amendments to the Criminal Code in 1892 and the Combines Investigation Act of 1910. On the fifth attempt, the Competition Act was finally passed in mid-1986, supplanting the Combines Investigation Act.

12.2 INDUSTRIAL REGULATION

- The objective of industrial regulation is to protect the public from the market power of natural monopolies by regulating prices and quality of service.

- Critics of industrial regulation contend that it can lead to inefficiency and rising costs and that in many instances it constitutes a legal cartel for the regulated firms. Legislation passed in the late 1970s and the 1980s has brought about varying degrees of deregulation in the airline, trucking, banking, railroad, and television broadcasting industries. Studies indicate that deregulation is producing sizable annual gains to society through lower prices, lower costs, and increased output. The latest Canadian industries to begin the deregulation process are telecommunications, electricity, and natural gas.

12.3 SOCIAL REGULATION

- Social regulation is concerned with product safety, working conditions, and the effects of production on society. While industrial regulation is on the wane, social regulation continues to expand. The optimal amount of social regulation is where MB = MC.

- Those who support social regulation point to its numerous specific successes and assert that it has greatly enhanced society's well-being. Critics of social regulation contend that businesses are excessively regulated to the point where marginal costs exceed marginal benefits. They also say that social regulation often produces unintended and costly side effects.

TERMS AND CONCEPTS

STUDY QUESTIONS

1. Both anti-combines policy and industrial policy deal with monopoly. What distinguishes their approaches? How does government decide to use one form of remedy rather than the other?

2. **KEY QUESTION** Explain how strict enforcement of the anti-combines laws might conflict with (a) promoting exports to achieve a balance of trade, and (b) encouraging new technologies. Do you see any dangers in using selective anti-combines enforcement as part of a broader policy to increase exports?

3. **KEY QUESTION** How would you expect anti-combines authorities to react to (a) a proposed merger of Ford and General Motors; (b) evidence of secret meetings by contractors to rig bids for highway construction projects; (c) a proposed merger of a large shoe manufacturer and a chain of retail shoe stores; and (d) a proposed merger of a small life-insurance company and a regional candy manufacturer.

4. Suppose a proposed merger of firms would simultaneously lessen competition and reduce unit costs through economies of scale. Do you think such a merger should be allowed?

5. In the 1980s, PepsiCo Inc., which then had 28 percent of the soft-drink market, proposed to acquire the 7-Up Company. Shortly thereafter the Coca-Cola Company, with 39 percent of the market, indicated it wanted to acquire the Dr. Pepper Company. Seven-Up and Dr. Pepper each controlled about 7 percent of the market. In your judgment, was the government's decision to block these mergers appropriate?

6. "The anti-combines laws tend to penalize efficiently managed firms." Do you agree? Why or why not?

7. "The social desirability of any particular firm should be judged not on the basis of its market share but on the basis of its conduct and performance." Make a counterargument, referring to the monopoly model in your statement.

8. **KEY QUESTION** What types of industry, if any, should be subjected to industrial regulation? What specific problems does industrial regulation entail?

9. In view of the problems involved in regulating natural monopolies, compare socially optimal (marginal-cost) pricing and fair-return pricing by referring again to Figure 9-9. Assuming that a government subsidy might be used to cover any loss resulting from marginal-cost pricing, which pricing policy would you favour? Why? What problems might such a subsidy entail?

10. **KEY QUESTION** How does social regulation differ from industrial regulation? What types of benefits and costs are associated with social regulation?

11. Use economic analysis to explain why the optimal amount of product safety may be less than the amount that would totally eliminate risks of accidents and deaths. Use automobiles as an example.

12. **(The Last Word)** Under what law and on what basis did the U.S. federal government find Microsoft guilty of violating U.S. antitrust laws? What was the initial District Court's remedy? How did Microsoft fare with its appeal to the Court of Appeals? Was the final remedy in the case a structural or behavioural remedy?

INTERNET APPLICATION QUESTION

1. Connect to Canada's Competition Bureau's site through the McConnell-Brue-Barbiero Web site (Chapter 12). Review the current filings. What companies does the latest filing include? On what basis did the Competition Bureau make its decision on the Fording Coal Merger in April 2003?

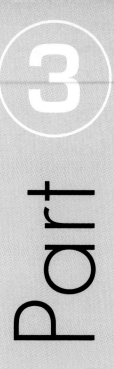

3

Part

Microeconomics of Factor Markets

13

Chapter

The Demand for Factors of Production

We now turn from the pricing and production of *goods and services* to the pricing and employment of *resources*, or *factors of production*. Although firms come in various sizes and operate under highly different market conditions, they each have a demand for factors of production. They obtain those resources from households—the owners of land, labour, capital, and entrepreneurial resources. So, referring to the circular flow model (Figure 2-6), we shift our attention from the bottom loop of the diagram (which shows that firms supply products and services that households want) to the top loop (which shows the demand for factors of production that households supply).

This chapter looks at the *demand* for factors of production. Although the discussion concentrates on labour, the principles we develop also apply to land, capital, and entrepreneurial ability. In Chapter 14 we will combine factor (labour) demand with labour *supply* to analyze wage rates. Then in Chapter 15 we will use factor demand and factor supply to examine the prices of, and returns to, other productive factors.

13.1   Factor Pricing and Demand

There are several good reasons to study how factor prices are determined:

- *Money-income determination*   Factor prices are a major determinant of household income. The expenditures that firms make in acquiring factors of production flow as wage, rent, interest, and profit incomes to households.

- *Resource allocation*   Just as product prices allocate finished goods and services to consumers, factor prices allocate inputs among industries and firms. In a dynamic economy, where technology and tastes often change, the efficient allocation of resources over time means a continuous shift of factors of production from one use to another. Changes in factor prices is a major determinant of those shifts.

- *Cost minimization*   To the firm, factor prices are costs, and to realize maximum profit, the firm must produce the profit-maximizing output with the most efficient (least costly) combination of resources. Factor prices determine the quantities of land, labour, capital and entrepreneurial ability that will be combined in producing each good or service.

<www.rci.rutgers.edu/~gag/
NOTES/micnotes11.html>
Marginal productivity theory of
distribution

- *Policy issues*   There are many policy issues surrounding the factor market. Examples: To what extent should government redistribute income through taxes and transfers? Should government do anything to discourage "excess" pay to corporate executives? Should it increase the legal minimum wage? Does it make sense to provide subsidies to farmers? Should it encourage or restrict labour unions? The facts and debates relating to these policy questions are based on resource pricing.

Marginal Productivity Theory of Factor Demand

To make things simple, we first assume that a firm hires a certain factor of production in a purely competitive factor market and sells its output in a purely competitive product market. The simplicity of this situation is twofold: In a competitive product market the firm is a price-taker and can dispose of as much output as it chooses at the market price. The firm sells such a negligible fraction of total output that it exerts no influence on product price. Similarly, in the competitive factor market, the firm is a wage-taker. It hires such a negligible fraction of the total supply of the factor that it cannot influence its price.

FACTOR DEMAND AS A DERIVED DEMAND

derived demand
The demand for a factor that
depends on the products it can
be used to produce.

The demand for factors is a **derived demand**: it is derived from the products or services that those factors of production help produce. Factors usually do not directly satisfy customer wants but do so indirectly through their use in producing goods and services. No one wants to consume a hectare of land, a John Deere tractor, or the labour services of a farmer, but households do want to consume the food products that these factors help produce. Similarly, the demand for cars generates a demand for assemblers, and the demands for such services as income-tax preparation, haircuts, and child care create derived demands for accountants, barbers, and child-care workers.

MARGINAL REVENUE PRODUCT (MRP)

The derived nature of factor demand means that the strength of the demand for any factor of production will depend on

- the productivity of the factor
- the price of the good it helps to produce

A factor that is highly productive in turning out a highly valued commodity will be in great demand, while a relatively unproductive factor that is capable of producing only a slightly valued commodity will be in little demand. There will be no demand at all for a factor of production that is phenomenally efficient in producing something that no one wants to buy.

marginal product (MP)
The extra output produced with one additional unit of a factor.

Productivity Table 13-1 shows the roles of productivity and product price in determining demand for factors of production. Here, we assume that a firm adds one variable factor, labour, to its fixed plant. Columns 1 and 2 give the number of units of the factor employed and the resulting total product (output). Column 3 shows the **marginal product** (MP), or additional output, from each additional factor unit. Columns 1 through 3 remind us that the law of diminishing returns applies here, causing the marginal product of labour to fall beyond some point. For simplicity, we assume that diminishing marginal returns begin after the first worker hired.

Product Price The derived demand for a factor depends also on the price of the commodity it produces. Column 4 in Table 13-1 adds this price information. Product price is constant, in this case at $2, because we are assuming a competitive product market. The firm is a price-taker and will sell units of output only at this market price.

marginal revenue product (MRP)
The change in total revenue from employing one additional unit of a factor.

Multiplying column 2 by column 4 gives us the total-revenue data of column 5. From these total-revenue data we can compute **marginal revenue product** (MRP), the change in total revenue resulting from the use of each additional unit of a factor (labour, in this case). In equation form,

$$\text{Marginal revenue product} = \frac{\text{change in total revenue}}{\text{one unit change in factor quantity}}$$

The MRPs are listed in column 6 in Table 13-1.

RULE FOR EMPLOYING FACTORS: MRP = MRC

The MRP schedule, shown as columns 1 and 6, is the firm's demand schedule for labour. To explain why, we must first discuss the rule that guides a profit-seeking firm in hiring any factor of produc-

The demand for factors is derived from the products or services that those factors help produce.

TABLE 13-1		The Demand for Labour: Pure Competition in the Sale of the Product			
(1) Units of a factor	(2) Total product (output)	(3) Marginal product, MP	(4) Product price	(5) Total revenue, or (2) × (4)	(6) Marginal revenue product, MRP
0	0		$2	$ 0	
		7			$14
1	7		2	14	
		6			12
2	13		2	26	
		5			10
3	18		2	36	
		4			8
4	22		2	44	
		3			6
5	25		2	50	
		2			4
6	27		2	54	
		1			2
7	28		2	56	

tion: *To maximize profit, a firm will hire additional units of a specific factor as long as each successive unit adds more to the firm's total revenue than it adds to total cost.*

We have seen that MRP measures how much each successive unit of a factor adds to total revenue. The amount that each additional unit of a factor adds to the firm's total (factor) cost is called its **marginal factor cost (MFC)**.

In equation form,

$$\text{Marginal factor cost} = \frac{\text{change in total (factor) cost}}{\text{one unit change in factor quantity}}$$

marginal factor cost (MFC)
The amount that each additional unit of a factor adds to the firm's total (factor) cost.

So we can restate our rule for hiring factors as follows: It will be profitable for a firm to hire additional units of a factor up to the point at which that factor 's MRP is equal to its MFC. If the number of workers a firm is currently hiring is such that the MRP of the last worker exceeds his or her MFC, the firm can increase profit by hiring more workers. But if the number being hired is such that the MFC of the last worker exceeds his or her MRP, the firm is hiring workers who are not paying their way, and it can increase its profit by laying off some workers. You may have recognized that this **MRP = MFC rule** is similar to the MR = MC profit-maximizing rule employed throughout our discussion of price and output determination. The rationale of the two rules is the same, but the point of reference is now *inputs* of a factor of production, not *outputs* of a product.

MRP = MFC rule
To maximize economic profit (or minimize losses) a firm should use the quantity of a factor at which its marginal revenue product is equal to its marginal factor cost.

MRP AS A FACTOR DEMAND SCHEDULE

In a purely competitive labour market, supply and demand establish the wage rate. Because each firm hires such a small fraction of market supply, it cannot influence the market wage rate; it is a wage-taker, not a wage-maker. This means that for each additional unit of labour hired, total factor cost increases by exactly the amount of the constant market wage rate. The MRC of labour exactly equals the market wage rate. Thus, factor "price" (the market wage rage) and factor "cost" (marginal factor cost) are equal for a firm that hires labour in a competitive labour market. Then the MRP = MFC rule tells us that, in pure competition, the firm will hire workers up to the point at which the market *wage rate* (its MFC) is equal to its MRP.

<cepa.newschool.edu/het/ essays/margrev/ distrib.htm#marginal>
Marginal productivity theory of distribution

In terms of the data in columns 1 and 6 in Table 13-1, if the market wage rate is, say, $13.95, the firm will hire only one worker, because the first worker adds $14 to total revenue and slightly less— $13.95—to total cost. In other words, because MRP exceeds MFC for the first worker, it is profitable to hire that worker. For each successive worker, however, MFC (= $13.95) exceeds MRP (= $12 or less), indicating that it will not be profitable to hire any of those workers. If the wage rate is $11.95, by the same reasoning we discover that it will pay the firm to hire both the first and second workers. Similarly, if the wage rate is $9.95, three will be hired. If $7.95, four. If $5.95, five. And so forth. Hence, *the MRP schedule constitutes the firm's demand for labour, because each point on this schedule (or curve) indicates the number of workers the firm would hire at each possible wage rate*. In Figure 13-1, we show the *D* = MRP curve based on the data in Table 13-1.

FACTOR DEMAND UNDER IMPERFECT PRODUCT MARKET COMPETITION

Our analysis of labour demand becomes more complex when the firm is selling its product in an imperfectly competitive market, one in which the firm is a price-maker. Pure monopoly, oligopoly, and monopolistic competition in the product market all mean that the firm's product demand curve is downsloping; the firm must set a lower price to increase its sales.

The productivity data in Table 13-1 are retained in columns 1 to 3 in Table 13-2. But here we show in column 4 that product price must be lowered to sell the marginal product of each successive worker. The MRP of the purely competitive seller of Table 13-1 falls for one reason: marginal product diminishes. The MRP of the imperfectly competitive seller of Table 13-2 falls for two reasons: marginal product diminishes *and* product price falls as output increases.

We emphasize that the lower price accompanying each increase in output (total product) applies not only to the marginal product of each successive worker but also *to all prior output.* Note that the second worker's marginal product is six units. These six units can be sold for $2.40 each, or, as

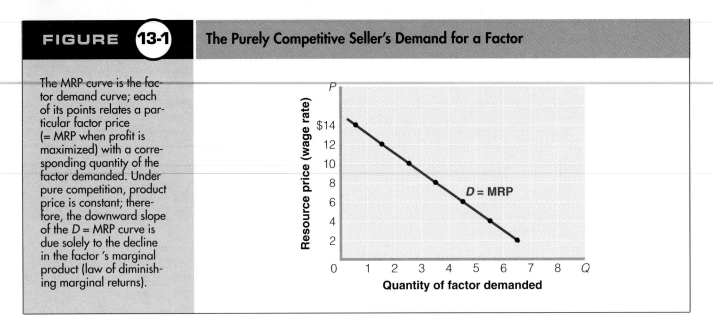

FIGURE 13-1 The Purely Competitive Seller's Demand for a Factor

The MRP curve is the factor demand curve; each of its points relates a particular factor price (= MRP when profit is maximized) with a corresponding quantity of the factor demanded. Under pure competition, product price is constant; therefore, the downward slope of the D = MRP curve is due solely to the decline in the factor's marginal product (law of diminishing marginal returns).

a group, for $14.40. But this is not the MRP of the second worker. To sell these six units, the firm must take a 20-cent price cut on the seven units produced by the first worker—units that otherwise could have been sold for $2.60 each. Thus, the MRP of the second worker is only $13.00 [= $14.40 − (7 × 20 cents)], as shown.

Similarly, the third worker adds five units to total product, and these units are worth $2.20 each, or $11.00 total. But to sell these five units the firm must take a 20-cent price cut on the 13 units produced by the first two workers. So the third worker's MRP is only $8.40 [= $11.00 − (13 × 20 cents)]. The other figures in column 6 are derived in the same way.

In Figure 13.2 we graph the MRP data from Table 13.2 and label it "D = MRP (imperfect competition)." The broken-line factor demand curve, in contrast, is that of the purely competitive seller represented in Figure 13.1. A comparison of the two curves demonstrates that, other things equal, the factor demand curve of an imperfectly competitive seller is less elastic than that of a purely

TABLE 13-2 The Demand for Labour: Imperfect Competition in the Sale of the Product

(1) Units of a factor	(2) Total product (output)	(3) Marginal product, MP	(4) Product price	(5) Total revenue, or (2) × (4)	(6) Marginal revenue product, MRP
0	0		$2.80	$ 0	
		7			$18.20
1	7		2.60	18.20	
		6			13.00
2	13		2.40	31.20	
		5			8.40
3	18		2.20	39.60	
		4			4.40
4	22		2.00	44.00	
		3			2.25
5	25		1.85	46.25	
		2			1.00
6	27		1.75	47.25	
		1			1.05
7	28		1.65	46.20	

competitive seller. Consider the effects of an identical percentage decline in the wage rate (factor price) from $11 to $6. Comparison of the two curves and a quick mental calculation reveals that the firm in imperfect competition does not expand the quantity of labour by as large a percentage as does the firm in pure competition.

The result is that the MRP curve—the factor demand curve—of the imperfectly competitive producer is less elastic than that of the purely competitive producer. At a wage rate or MRC of $11.95, both the purely competitive and the imperfectly competitive seller will hire two workers. But at $9.95 the competitive firm will hire three, and the imperfectly competitive firm only two. At $7.95 the purely competitive firm will employ four employees, and the imperfect competitor only three. You can see this difference in factor demand elasticity when we graph the MRP data in Table 13-2 and compare the graph with Figure 13-1, as we do in Figure 13-2.[1]

It is not surprising that the imperfectly competitive producer is less responsive to factor price cuts than the purely competitive producer. The imperfect competitor's relative reluctance to employ more factors of production, and produce more output, when factor prices fall reflects the imperfect competitor's tendency to restrict output in the product market. Other things equal, the imperfectly competitive seller produces less of a product than a purely competitive seller. In producing that smaller output, it demands fewer factors of production. *(Key Question 2)*

MARKET DEMAND FOR A FACTOR

We have now explained the individual firm's demand curve for a factor. Recall that the total, or market, demand curve for a *product* is found by summing horizontally the demand curves of all individual buyers in the market. The market demand curve for a particular *factor* is derived the same way—by summing the individual demand or MRP curves for all firms employing that factor (see the Consider This box for a story about the marginal revenue product of superstars.)

 FIGURE 13-2 **The Imperfectly Competitive Seller's Demand Curve for a Factor**

An imperfectly competitive seller's factor demand curve D (solid) slopes downward because both marginal product and product price fall as factor employment and output rise. This downward slope is greater than that for a purely competitive seller (dashed factor demand curve) because the pure competitor can sell the added output at a constant price.

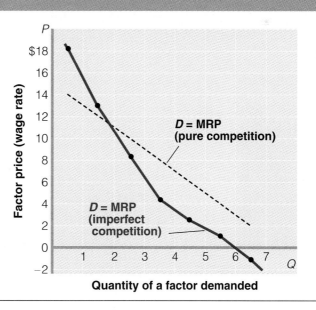

Quantity of a factor demanded

[1]Note that we plot the points in Figures 13-1 and 13-2 halfway between succeeding numbers of factor units, because MRP is associated with the addition of one more unit. Thus, in Figure 13-2, for example, we plot the MRP of the second unit ($13.00) not at 1 or 2, but rather at 1.5. This smoothing enables us to sketch a continuously downsloping curve rather than one that moves downward in discrete steps as each new unit of labour is hired.

www.mcgrawhill.ca/college/mcconnell

Consider This

Marginal Revenue Product

In what economist Robert Frank calls "winner-take-all markets," a few highly talented performers have huge earnings relative to the average performers in the market. Because consumers and firms seek out the best performers, small differences in talent or popularity get magnified into huge differences in pay. For example, gold-medal winners of major Olympic events receive lucrative endorsement and personal appearance contracts. Slightly less talented runners-up make little, if anything, from their participation. As a second example, professional sports teams pay a few marquee players between $5 million and $20 million a year, whereas their slightly less skilled teammates earn just one-tenth or one-twentieth as much.

In winner-take-all markets consumer spending gets channelled toward a few performers. The media then "hypes" these new stars, which further increases the public's awareness of their talents. More consumers then buy the stars' products. Although it is not easy to stay on top, several superstars emerge. Some become so well known that they can be identified by first name: Céline, Oprah, Martha, Tiger, Meg, Ken Jr., Jay, Ricky, Brad, Shania, etc.

The high earnings of superstars result from the high revenues they generate from their work. Consider the Canadian star Shania Twain. If she sold only a few thousand CDs and attracted only a few hundred fans to each concert, the revenue she would produce—her marginal revenue product—would be quite modest. So, too, would be her earnings.

But consumers have anointed Shania as queen of country/pop. For the moment, "*she*'s the one" and thus the demand for her CDs and concerts are extraordinarily high. She sells millions of CDs (41 million thus far), not thousands, and draws thousands to her concerts, not hundreds. Her extraordinarily high net earnings (an estimated $85 million in 2001) derive from her extraordinarily high marginal revenue product.

So it is for the other superstars in winner-take-all markets. Influenced by media hype but coerced by no one, consumers direct their spending toward a select few. The high marginal revenue product that results means strong demand for these stars' services. And because *top* talent (by definition) is very limited, superstars receive amazingly high earnings.

Question: The Montreal Canadiens pay their goaltender Jose Theodore $5.5 million per year and the Toronto Maple Leafs pay their goaltender Ed Belfour $6.5 million per year. Why do sports teams pay star players so much money?

QUICK REVIEW

- To maximize profit a firm will use a factor of production in an amount at which the factor's marginal revenue product equals its marginal factor cost (MRP = MFC).

- Application of the MRP = MFC rule to a firm's MRP curve demonstrates that the MRP curve is the firm's factor demand curve. In a purely competitive factor market, factor price (the wage rate) equals MFC.

- The factor demand curve of a firm in pure competition is downsloping solely because the marginal product of the factor diminishes; the factor demand curve of a firm in imperfect competition is downsloping because marginal product diminishes and product price falls as output is increased.

13.2   Determinants of Factor Demand

What will shift the factor demand curve? The fact that factor demand is derived from *product demand* and depends on *factor productivity* suggests two things that can shift factor demand. Also, our analysis of how changes in the prices of other products can shift a product's demand curve (Chapter 3) suggests another factor: changes in the prices of other *factors of production*.

<www.theshortrun.com/
classroom/glossary/micro/
resource.html>
Resource demand

Changes in Product Demand

Other things equal, *an increase in the demand for a product that uses a particular factor will increase the demand for that factor of production.*

Let's see how this works. The first thing to recall is that a change in the demand for a product will change its price. In Table 13-1, let's assume that an increase in product demand boosts the product price from $2 to $3. You should calculate the new factor demand schedule (columns 1 and 6), and plot it in Figure 13-1 to verify that the new factor demand curve lies to the right of the old demand curve. Similarly, a decline in the product demand (and price) will shift the factor demand curve to the left.

Changes in Productivity

Other things equal, *an increase in the productivity of a factor of production will increase the demand for that factor.* If we doubled the MP data of column 3 in Table 13-1, the MRP data of column 6 would also double, indicating an increase (rightward shift) in the factor demand curve.

The productivity of any resource can change for several reasons:

- *Quantities of other factors*   The marginal productivity of any factor will vary with the quantities of the other factors used with it. The greater the amount of capital land resources used with, say, labour, the greater will be labour's marginal productivity and, thus, labour demand.

- *Technological progress*   Technological improvements that increase the quality of other factors, such as capital, have the same effect. The better the *quality* of capital, the greater the productivity of labour used with it. Office workers employed with a specific amount of real capital in the form of desktop computers are more productive than office workers with the same amount of real capital embodied in typewriters and filing cabinets.

- *Quality of the variable factor*   Improvements in the quality of the variable factor, such as labour, will increase its marginal productivity and therefore its demand.

All these considerations help explain why the average level of (real) wages is higher in industrially advanced nations (for example, Canada, the U.S., Germany, Japan, and France) than in developing nations (for example, India, Ethiopia, Angola, and Cambodia). Workers in industrially advanced nations are generally healthier, better educated, and better trained than are workers in developing countries. Also, in most industries, workers in industrially advanced nations work with a larger and more efficient stock of capital goods and more abundant natural resources. This creates a strong demand for labour. On the supply side of the market, labour is *relatively* scarce compared with that in most developing nations. A strong demand and a relatively scarce supply of labour result in high wage rates in the industrially advanced nations.

Changes in the Prices of Other Factors

Just as changes in the prices of other products will change the demand for a specific product, changes in the prices of other factors of production will change the demand for a specific factor. Also recall that the effect of a change in the price of product X on the demand for product Y depends on whether X and Y are substitute goods or complementary goods *in consumption*. Similarly, the effect of a change in the price of factor A on the demand for factor B depends on their complementarity *in production*.

SUBSTITUTE RESOURCES

Suppose the technology in a certain production process is such that labour and capital can be substituted. A firm can produce a specific amount of output using a relatively small amount of labour and a relatively large amount of capital, or vice versa. Now assume that the price of machinery (capital) falls. The effect on the demand for labour will be the net result of two opposed effects: the substitution effect and the output effect.

- *Substitution effect*   The decline in the price of machinery prompts the firm to substitute machinery for labour. This substitution allows the firm to produce its output at a lower cost. So,

substitution effect
A firm will purchase more of an output whose relative price has declined and use less of an input whose relative price has increased.

at the fixed wage rate, smaller quantities of labour are now employed. This **substitution effect** decreases the demand for labour. More generally, the substitution effect indicates that a firm will purchase more of an input whose relative price has declined and, conversely, use less of an output whose relative price has increased.

- *Output effect*   Because the price of machinery has fallen, the costs of producing various outputs must also decline. With lower costs, the firm finds it profitable to produce and sell a greater output. The greater output increases the demand for all factors of production, including labour. So, this **output effect** increases the demand for labour. More generally, the output effect means that the firm will purchase more of one particular input when the price of the other input falls and less of that particular input when the price of the other input rises.

output effect
An increase in the price of one input will increase a firm's production costs and reduce its level of output, thus reducing the demand for other outputs (and vice versa).

- *Net effect*   The substitution and output effects are both present when the price of an input changes. The net change in factor demand depends on the relative sizes of the two effects. For example, if the substitution effect outweighs the output effect, a decrease in the price of capital decreases the demand for labour. If the output effect exceeds the substitution effect, a decrease in the price of capital increases the demand for labour.

COMPLEMENTARY FACTORS OF PRODUCTION

Recall from Chapter 3 that certain products, such as cameras and film or computers and software, are complementary goods; they go together and are jointly demanded. Factors of production can also be complementary; an increase in the quantity of one of them used in the production process requires an increase in the amount used of the other as well, and vice versa. Suppose a small design firm does computer-assisted design (CAD) with relatively expensive personal computers as its basic piece of capital equipment. Each computer requires a single design engineer to operate it.

Now assume that a technological advance in the production of these computers substantially reduces their price. No substitution effect can occur, because labour and capital must be used in *fixed proportions*, one person for one machine. Capital cannot be substituted for labour. But there is an output effect. Other things equal, the reduction in the price of capital goods means lower production costs. It will, therefore, be profitable to produce a larger output. In doing so, the firm will use both more capital and more labour. *When labour and capital are complementary, a decline in the price of capital increases the demand for labour through the output effect.*

We have cast our analysis of substitute factors and complementary factors mainly in terms of a decline in the price of capital. In Table 13-3 we summarize the effects of an *increase* in the price of capital on the demand for labour; study it carefully.

TABLE 13-3	**The Effect of an Increase in the Price of Capital on the Demand for Labour, D_L**		
(1) Relationship of inputs	**(2) Increase in the price of capital**		
	(a) Substitution effect	**(b) Output effect**	**(c) Combined effect**
Substitutes in production	Labour substituted for capital	Production costs up, output down, and less of both capital and labour used	D_L increases if the substitution effect exceeds the output effect; D_L decreases if the output effect exceeds the substitution effect
Complements in production	No substitution of labour for capital	Production costs up, output down, and less of both capital and labour used	D_L decreases

Now that we have discussed the full list of the determinants of labour demand, let's again review their effects. Stated in terms of the labour resource, the demand for labour will increase (the labour demand curve will shift rightward) when

- The demand for the product produced by that labour *increases*.
- The productivity (MP) of labour *increases*.
- The price of a substitute input *decreases*, provided the output effect exceeds the substitution effect.
- The price of a substitute input *increases*, provided the substitution effect exceeds the output effect.
- The price of a complementary input *decreases*.

Be sure that you can reverse these effects to explain a *decrease* in labour demand.

Table 13-4 provides several illustrations of the determinants of labour demand, listed by the categories of determinants we have discussed; give them a close look.

Occupational Employment Trends

Changes in labour demand have considerable significance, since they affect wage rates and employment in specific occupations. Increases in labour demand for certain occupational groups result in increases in their employment, and decreases in labour demand result in decreases in their employment. For illustration, let's look at occupations that are growing in demand. (Wage rates are the subject of the next chapter).

THE FASTEST GROWING OCCUPATIONS

The occupations that are growing quickly in the Canadian economy tend to be in the service sector. In general, the demand for service workers is rapidly outpacing the demand for manufacturing, construction, and mining workers. The top five fastest growing jobs are directly computer-related. The increase in the demand for computer engineers, computer support specialists, systems analysts, database managers, and desktop publishing specialists relates to the rapid rise in the demand for computers, computer services, and the Internet. It also relates to the rising productivity of these particular workers, given the vastly improved quality of the computer and communications equipment they work with. Price declines on such equipment have had a stronger output effect than substitution effect, increasing the demand for these types of labour.

Three of the other fastest growing occupations relate to health care: personal care and home health care aides, medical assistants, and physician assistants. The growing demands for these types of labour are derived from the growing demand for health services, caused by several factors. The aging of the Canadian population has brought with it more medical problems, and the rising standard of income has led to greater expenditures on health care.

<www.adin.org/lmi/fastest.htm>
Fastest growing and declining occupations, Ontario, 1995–2005

TABLE 13-4	Determinants of Labour Demand: Factors that Shift the Labour Demand Curve
Determinant	**Examples**
Changes in product demand	Gambling increases in popularity, increasing the demand for workers at casinos.
	Consumers decrease their demand for leather coats, decreasing the demand for tanners.
	The federal government reduces spending on the military, reducing the demand for military personnel.
Changes in productivity	An increase in the skill levels and output of glassblowers increases the demand for their services.
	Computer-assisted graphic design increases the productivity of, and demand for, graphic artists.
Changes in the price of another resource	An increase in the price of electricity increases the cost of producing aluminum and reduces the demand for aluminum workers.
	The price of security equipment used by businesses to protect against illegal entry falls, decreasing the demand for night guards.
	The price of telephone switching equipment decreases, greatly reducing the cost of telephone service, which in turn increases the demand for telemarketers.

13.3   Elasticity of Factor Demand

The employment changes we have just discussed result from shifts of factor demand curves. Such changes in demand must be distinguished from changes in the quantity demanded of a factor of production caused by a change in the price of the specific factor. Such a change is not caused by a shift of the demand curve but rather by a movement from one point to another on a fixed factor demand curve. For example, in Figure 13-1 we note that an increase in the wage rate from $5 to $7 will reduce the quantity of labour demanded from five to four units. This is a change in the *quantity of labour demanded* as distinct from a *change in demand*.

elasticity of factor demand
The percentage change in factor quantity divided by the percentage change in factor price.

The sensitivity of producers to changes in factor prices is measured by the **elasticity of factor demand**. In coefficient form,

$$E_{rd} = \frac{\text{percentage change in factor quantity}}{\text{percentage change in factor price}}$$

When E_{rd} is greater than one, factor demand is elastic; when E_{rd} is less than one, factor demand is inelastic; and when E_{rd} equals one, factor demand is unit-elastic. (Recall from Chapter 5 that demand elasticity has a negative sign, but we use the absolute value.) What determines the elasticity of factor demand? Several determinants are at work.

Ease of Factor Substitutability

The larger the number of satisfactory substitute factors available, the greater the elasticity of demand for a particular factor. If a furniture manufacturer finds that five or six different types of wood are equally satisfactory in making coffee tables, a rise in the price of any one type of wood may cause a sharp drop in the amount demanded as the producer substitutes one of the other woods. At the other extreme, no reasonable substitutes may exist; bauxite is absolutely essential in the production of aluminum ingots. Thus the demand for bauxite by aluminum producers is inelastic.

Time can play a role in the input substitution process. For example, a firm's truck drivers may obtain a substantial wage increase with little or no immediate decline in employment. But over time, as the firm's trucks wear out and are replaced, that wage increase may motivate the company to purchase larger trucks and in that way deliver the same total output with fewer drivers. Another example is the new commercial aircraft that require only two cockpit personnel rather than the former three, again indicating some substitutability between labour and capital if there is enough time.

Elasticity of Product Demand

The elasticity of demand for any factor depends on the elasticity of demand for the product it helps produce. *The greater the elasticity of product demand, the greater the elasticity of factor demand.* The derived nature of factor demand leads us to expect this relationship. A small rise in the price of a product with great elasticity of demand will sharply reduce output, bringing about relatively large declines in the amounts of various factors of production demanded; the demand for the factor is elastic.

Remember that the factor demand curve of Figure 13-1 is more elastic than the factor demand curve shown in Figure 13-2. The difference arises because in Figure 13-1, we assume a perfectly elastic product demand curve, while Figure 13-2 is based on a downsloping or less than perfectly elastic product demand curve.

Factor Cost as a Proportion of Total Cost

The larger the proportion of total production costs accounted for by a factor of production, the greater the elasticity of demand for that factor. For example, if labour cost is the only production cost, then a 20 percent increase in wage rates will shift all the firm's cost curves upward by the full 20 percent. If product demand is elastic, this substantial increase in wage costs will cause a relatively large decline in sales and a sharp decline in the amount of labour demanded. So labour demand is highly elastic. Conversely, if labour cost is a small percentage of the same firm's cost, labour demand would be relatively inelastic. *(Key Question 5)*

- A factor demand curve will shift because of changes in product demand, changes in the productivity of the factor, and changes in the prices of other inputs.

- If factors A and B are substitutable, a decline in the price of A will decrease the demand for B provided the substitution effect exceeds the output effect. If the output effect exceeds the substitution effect, the demand for B will increase.

- If factors C and D are complements, a decline in the price of C will increase the demand for D.

- Elasticity of factor demand measures the extent to which producers change the quantity of a factor they hire when its price changes.

- The elasticity of factor demand will be less the smaller the number of substitutes, the smaller the elasticity of product demand, and the smaller the proportion of total cost accounted for by the factor.

13.4 Optimal Combination of Factors

Choosing a Little More or Less

So far our main focus has been on one variable input, labour. But in the long run, firms can vary the amounts of all the factors of production they use. That's why we need to consider what combination of factors a firm will choose when *all* its inputs are variable. While our analysis is based on two factors, it can be extended to any number of inputs.

We will consider two interrelated questions:

1. What combination of factors will minimize costs at a specific level of output?

2. What combination of factors will maximize profit?

The Least-cost Rule

least-cost combination of factors
The quantity of each resource a firm must employ to produce a particular output at the lowest total cost.

A firm is producing a specific output with the **least-cost combination of factors** *when the last dollar spent on each factor yields the same marginal product.* In competitive factor markets marginal factor cost is the market factor price; the firm can hire as many or as few units of the factors as it wants at that price. Then, with just two factors, labour and capital, a competitive firm minimizes its total cost of a specific output when

$$\frac{\text{Marginal Product of Labour (MP}_L)}{\text{Price of Labour (P}_L)} = \frac{\text{Marginal Product of Capital (MP}_C)}{\text{Price of Capital (P}_C)} \qquad (1)$$

Throughout, we will refer to the marginal products of labour and capital as MP_L and MP_C, respectively, and symbolize the price of labour by P_L and the price of capital by P_C.

A concrete example shows why fulfilling the condition in equation (1) leads to least-cost production. Assume that the price of both capital and labour is $1 per unit, but that they are currently employed in such amounts that the marginal product of labour is 10 and the marginal product of capital is 5. Our equation immediately tells us that this is not the least costly combination of resources:

$$\frac{MP_L = 10}{P_L = \$1} > \frac{MP_C = 5}{P_C = \$1}$$

Suppose the firm spends $1 less on capital and shifts that dollar to labour. It loses five units of output produced by the last dollar's worth of capital, but it gains 10 units of output from the extra dollar's worth of labour. Net output increases by 5 (= 10 − 5) units for the same total cost. More such shifting of dollars from capital to labour will push the firm *down* along its MP curve for labour and *up* along its MP curve for capital, increasing output and moving the firm toward a position of equilibrium where equation (1) is fulfilled. At that equilibrium position, the MP per dollar for the last unit of both labour and capital might be, for example, seven. The firm will be producing a greater output for the same (original) cost.

Whenever the same total resource cost can result in a greater total output, the cost per unit—and therefore the total cost of any specific level of output—can be reduced. The cost of producing any specific output can be reduced as long as equation (1) does not hold. But when dollars have been shifted between capital and labour to the point where equation (1) holds, no additional changes in the use of capital and labour will reduce costs further. The firm is now producing that output using the least-cost combination of capital and labour.

All the long-run cost curves developed in Chapter 7 and used thereafter assume that the least-cost combination of inputs has been realized at each level of output. Any firm that combines factors of production in violation of the least-cost rule will have a higher-than-necessary average total cost at each level of output; that is, it will incur *X-inefficiency,* as shown in Figure 9-7.

The Profit-maximizing Rule

Minimizing cost is not sufficient for maximizing profit. A firm can produce any level of output in the least costly way by applying equation (1), but only one unique level of output can maximize profit. Our earlier analysis of product markets showed that this profit-maximizing output occurs where marginal revenue equals marginal cost (MR = MC). Near the beginning of this chapter, we determined that we could write this profit-maximizing condition as MRP = MFC as it relates to factor inputs.

In a purely competitive factor market, the marginal factor cost (MFC) is exactly equal to the factor price, *P*. Thus, for any competitive factor market, we have as our profit-maximizing equation

MRP (factor) = *P* (factor)

This condition must hold for every variable factor—and in the long run all factors are variable. In competitive markets, a firm will, therefore, achieve its **profit-maximizing combination of factors** when each factor is employed to the point at which its marginal revenue product equals its price. For two factors, labour and capital, we need both $P_L = \text{MRP}_L$ and $P_C = \text{MRP}_C$.

profit-maximizing combination of factors
The quantity of each factor a firm must employ to maximize its profits or minimize its losses.

We can combine these conditions by dividing both sides of each equation by their respective prices and equating the results, to get

$$\frac{\text{MRP}_L}{P_L} = \frac{\text{MRP}_C}{P_C} = 1 \qquad (2)$$

Note in equation (2) that it is not sufficient that the MRPs of the two resources be *proportionate* to their prices; the MRPs must be *equal* to their prices and the ratios, therefore, equal to one. For example, if $\text{MRP}_L = \$15$, $P_L = \$5$, $\text{MRP}_C = \$9$, and $P_C = \$3$, the firm is underemploying both capital and labour even though the ratios of MRP to resource price are identical for both factors. The firm can expand its profit by hiring additional amounts of both capital and labour until it moves down their downsloping MRP curves to the points at which $\text{MRP}_L = \$5$ and $\text{MRP}_C = \$3$. The ratios will then be 5/5 and 3/3 and equal to one.

The profit-maximizing position in equation (2) includes the cost-minimizing condition of equation (1). That is, if a firm is maximizing profit according to equation (2), then it must be using the least-cost combination of inputs to do so. However, the converse is not true: a firm operating at least cost according to equation (1) may not be operating at the output that maximizes its profit.

Numerical Illustration

A numerical illustration will help you understand the least-cost and profit-maximizing rules. In columns 2, 3, 2′, and 3′ in Table 13-5, we show the total products and marginal products for various amounts of labour and capital that are assumed to be the only inputs needed in producing some product, say, key chains. Both inputs are subject to diminishing returns.

We also assume that labour and capital are supplied in competitive factor markets at $8 and $12, respectively, and that key chains sell competitively at $2 per unit. For both labour and capital, we can determine the total revenue associated with each input level by multiplying total product by the $2 product price. These data are shown in columns 4 and 4′. They enable us to calculate the marginal revenue product of each successive input of labour and capital as shown in columns 5 and 5′, respectively.

PRODUCING AT LEAST COST

What is the least-cost combination of labour and capital to use in producing, say, 50 units of output? The answer, which we can obtain by trial and error, is three units of labour and two units of capital. Columns 2 and 2′ indicate that this combination of labour and capital does, indeed, result in the required 50 (= 28 + 22) units of output. Now, note from columns 3 and 3′ that hiring three units of labour gives us $MP_L/P_L = \frac{6}{8} = \frac{3}{4}$, and hiring two units of capital gives us $MP_C/P_C = \frac{9}{12} = \frac{3}{4}$. So, equation (1) is fulfilled. How can we verify that costs are actually minimized? First, we see that the total cost of employing three units of labour and two of capital is $48 [= (3 × $8) + (2 × $12)].

Other combinations of labour and capital will also yield 50 units of output but at a higher cost than $48. For example, five units of labour and one unit of capital will produce 50 (= 37 + 13) units, but total cost is higher at $52 [= (5 × $8) + (1 × $12)]. This result comes as no surprise, because five units of labour and one unit of capital violate the least-cost rule—$MP_L/P_L = \frac{4}{8}$, $MP_C/P_C = \frac{13}{12}$. Only the combination (three units of labour and two units of capital) that minimizes total cost will satisfy equation (1). All other combinations capable of producing 50 units of output violate the cost-minimizing rule, and, therefore, cost more than $48.

MAXIMIZING PROFIT

Will 50 units of output maximize the firm's profit? No, because the profit-maximizing terms of equation (2) are not satisfied when the firm employs three units of labour and two of capital. To

| TABLE 13-5 | Data for Finding the Least-cost and Profit-maximizing Combination of Labour and Capital* |

LABOUR (PRICE = $8)

(1) Quantity	(2) Total product (output)	(3) Marginal product	(4) Total revenue	(5) Marginal revenue product
0	0		$ 0	
		12		$24
1	12		24	
		10		20
2	22		44	
		6		12
3	28		56	
		5		10
4	33		66	
		4		*8*
5	37		74	
		3		6
6	40		80	
		2		4
7	42		84	

CAPITAL (PRICE = $12)

(1′) Quantity	(2′) Total product (output)	(3′) Marginal product	(4′) Total revenue	(5′) Marginal revenue product
0	0		$ 0	
		13		$26
1	13		26	
		9		18
2	22		44	
		6		*12*
3	28		56	
		4		8
4	32		64	
		3		6
5	35		70	
		2		4
6	37		74	
		1		2
7	38		76	

*To simplify, it is assumed in this table that the productivity of each resource is independent of the quantity of the other. For example, the total and marginal product of labour is assumed not to vary with the quantity of capital employed.

maximize profit, each input should be employed until its price equals its marginal revenue product. But for three units of labour, labour's MRP in column 5 is $12 while its price is only $8; the firm could increase its profit by hiring more labour. Similarly, for two units of capital, we see in column 5′ that capital's MRP is $18 and its price is only $12. This result indicates that more capital should also be employed. By producing only 50 units of output (even though they are produced at least cost), labour and capital are being used in less-than-profit-maximizing amounts. The firm needs to expand its employment of labour and capital, thereby increasing its output.

Table 13-5 shows that the MRPs of labour and capital are equal to their prices, so that equation (2) is fulfilled when the firm is employing five units of labour and three units of capital. This is the profit-maximizing combination of inputs.[2] The firm's total cost will be $76, made up of $40 (= 5 ×$8) of labour and $36 (= 3 × $12) of capital. Total revenue will be $130, found either by multiplying the total output of 65 (= 37 + 28) by the $2 product price or by summing the total revenues attributable to labour ($74) and to capital ($56). The difference between total revenue and total cost in this instance is $54 (= $130 − $76). Experiment with other combinations of labour and capital to demonstrate that they yield an economic profit of less than $54.

Note that the profit-maximizing combination of five units of labour and three units of capital is also a least-cost combination for this particular level of output. Using these factor amounts satisfies the least-cost requirement of equation (1) in that $MP_L/P_L = \frac{4}{8} = \frac{1}{2}$ and $MP_C/P_C = \frac{6}{12} = \frac{1}{2}$. (***Key Questions 6 and 7***)

Marginal Productivity Theory of Income Distribution

Our discussion of factor pricing is the cornerstone of the controversial view that fairness and economic justice are two of the outcomes of a competitive market economy. Table 13-5 tells us, in effect, that workers receive income payments (wages) equal to the marginal contributions they make to their employers' outputs and revenues. In other words, workers are paid according to the value of the labour services that they contribute to production. Similarly, owners of the other factors of production receive income based on the value of the factors they supply in the production process.

marginal productivity theory of income distribution
The contention that the distribution of income is fair when each unit of each factor receives a money payment equal to its marginal contribution to the firm's revenue (its marginal revenue product).

In this **marginal productivity theory of income distribution**, income is distributed according to the contribution to society's output. So, if you are willing to accept the ethical proposition "To each according to what he or she creates," income payments based on marginal revenue product seem to provide a fair and equitable distribution of society's income.

This idea sounds fair enough, but there are serious criticisms of this theory of income distribution:

- ***Inequality*** Critics argue that the distribution of income resulting from payment according to marginal productivity may be highly unequal because productive factors are very unequally distributed in the first place. Aside from their differences in mental and physical attributes, individuals encounter substantially different opportunities to enhance their productivity through education and training. Some people may not be able to participate in production at all because of mental or physical disabilities, and they would obtain no income under a system of distribution based solely on marginal productivity. Ownership of property resources is also highly unequal. Many landlords and capitalists obtain their property by inheritance rather than through their own productive effort. Hence, income from inherited property resources conflicts with the "To each according to what he or she creates" idea. This reasoning calls for government policies that modify the income distributions made strictly according to marginal productivity.

- ***Market Imperfections*** The marginal productivity theory rests on the assumptions of competitive markets. Yet labour markets, for example, are riddled with imperfections, as you will see in Chapter 14. Some employers exert pricing power in hiring workers. And some workers,

---

[2]Because we are dealing with discrete (non-fractional) units of the two outputs here, the use of four units of labour and two units of capital is equally profitable. The fifth unit of labour's MRP and its price (cost) are equal at $8, so that the fifth labour unit neither adds to nor subtracts from the firm's profit; similarly, the third unit of capital has no effect on profit.

through labour unions, professional associations, and occupational licensing laws, wield monopoly power in selling their services. Even the process of collective bargaining over wages suggests a power struggle over the division of income. In this struggle, market forces—and income shares based on marginal productivity—may get pushed into the background. In addition, discrimination in the labour market can distort earnings patterns. In short, because of real-world market imperfections, wage rates and other factor prices frequently are not based solely on contributions to output.

THE LASTword — Input Substitution: The Case of ABMs

Banks are using more automated banking machines (ABMs) and employing fewer human tellers.

As you have learned from this chapter, a firm achieves its least-cost combination of inputs when the last dollar it spends on each input makes the same contribution to total output. This raises an interesting real-world question: What happens when technological advance makes available a new, highly productive capital good for which MP/P is greater than it is for other inputs, say a particular type of labour? The answer is that the least-cost mix of factors abruptly changes and the firm responds accordingly. If the new capital is a substitute for labour (rather than a complement), the firm replaces the particular type of labour with the new capital. That is exactly what is happening in the banking industry, in which ABMs are replacing human bank tellers.

ABMs made their debut about 30 years age when Diebold, a U.S. firm, introduced the product. Today, Diebold and NCR (also a U.S. firm) dominate global sales, with the Japanese firm Fujitsu a distant third. The number of ABMs and their usage have exploded, and currently more than 35,000 ABMs are used in Canada. We rank number one in the world in ABM use, logging 48.3 transactions per Canadian in 2000, followed by the United States at 47.9

and Sweden at 36.1. There are now 800,000 ABMs worldwide.

ABMs are highly productive: A single machine can handle hundreds of transactions daily, thousands weekly, and millions over the course of several years. ABMs can not only handle cash withdrawals, but they can also accept deposits and facilitate switches of funds between various accounts. Although ABMs are expensive for banks to buy and install, they are available 24 hours a day, and their cost per transaction is one-fourth the cost for human tellers. They rarely get held up, and they do not quit their jobs (turnover among human tellers is nearly 50 percent per year). ABMs are highly convenient; unlike human tellers, they are located not only at banks but also at busy street corners, workplaces, colleges and universities, and shopping malls. The same bank card that enables you to withdraw cash from your local ABM also enables you to withdraw pounds from

an ABM in London, yen from an ABM in Tokyo, and even rubles from an ABM in Moscow. (All this, of course, assumes that you have money in your account.)

In the terminology of this chapter, the more productive, lower-priced ABMs have reduced the demand for a substitute in production—human tellers. Between 1990 and 2000, 6000 human teller positions were eliminated, and half the remaining teller positions may be gone by 2010. Where will the people holding these jobs go? Some will eventually move to other occupations. Others will be retrained and move to the chartered banks' extensive customer service departments to become investment advisors and wealth-management representatives. Although the lives of some individual tellers are disrupted, society clearly wins. Society gets cheaper, more convenient banking services and more of the other goods that these freed-up labour resources help to produce.

Source: Based partly on Ben Craig, "Where Have All the Tellers Gone?" *Economic Commentary* (Federal Reserve Bank of Cleveland), April. 15, 1997; and statistics compiled by the Canadian Bankers Association. These statistics can be found at www.cba.ca/

CHAPTER SUMMARY

13.1 FACTOR PRICING AND DEMAND

- Factor prices act as a determinant of money incomes, and they simultaneously ration factors of production to various industries and firms.

- The demand for any factor is derived from the product it helps produce. That means the demand for a factor will depend on its productivity and on the market value (price) of the good it is producing.

- Marginal revenue product is the extra revenue a firm obtains when it employs one more unit of a factor. The marginal-revenue-product curve for any factor is the demand curve for that factor, because the firm equates factor price and MRP in determining its profit-maximizing level of factor employment. Thus, each point on the MRP curve indicates how many factor units the firm will hire at a specific factor price.

- The firm's demand curve for a factor slopes downward, because the marginal product of additional units declines in accordance with the law of diminishing returns. When a firm is selling in an imperfectly competitive market, the factor demand curve falls for a second reason: Product price must be reduced for the firm to sell a larger output. We can derive the market demand curve for a factor by summing horizontally the demand curves of all the firms hiring that factor.

13.2 DETERMINANTS OF FACTOR DEMAND

- The demand curve for a factor will shift as the result of (a) a change in the demand for, and therefore the price of, the product the factor is producing; (b) changes in the productivity of the factor; and (c) changes in the prices of other factors.

- If factors A and B are substitutable for each other, a decline in the price of A will decrease the demand for B provided the substitution effect is greater than the output effect. But if the output effect exceeds the substitution effect, a decline in the price of A will increase the demand for B.

- If factors C and D are complementary or jointly demanded, there is only an output effect; a change in the price of C will change the demand for D in the opposite direction.

- The majority of the fastest growing occupations in Canada relate to computers or health care.

13.3 ELASTICITY OF FACTOR DEMAND

- The elasticity of demand for a factor measures the responsiveness of producers to a change in the factor's price. The coefficient of the elasticity of factor demand is

$$E_{rd} = \frac{\text{percentage change in factor quantity}}{\text{percentage change in factor price}}$$

When E_{rd} is greater than one, factor demand is elastic; when E_{rd} is less than one, factor demand is inelastic; and when E_{rd} equals one, factor demand is unit elastic.

- The elasticity of demand for a factor will be greater (a) the larger the number of good substitute factors available, (b) the greater the elasticity of demand for the product, and (c) the larger the proportion of total production costs attributable to the factor.

13.4 OPTIMAL COMBINATION OF FACTORS

- Any specific level of output will be produced with the least costly combination of variable factors when the marginal product per dollar's worth of each input is the same—that is, when

$$\frac{\text{MP of Labour}}{\text{Price of Labour}} = \frac{\text{MP of Capital}}{\text{Price of Capital}}$$

- A firm is employing the profit-maximizing combination of factors when each factor is used to the point where its marginal revenue product equals its price. In terms of labour and capital, that occurs when the MRP of labour equals the price of labour and the MRP of capital equals the price of capital—that is, when

$$\frac{\text{MRP of Labour}}{\text{Price of Labour}} = \frac{\text{MRP of Capital}}{\text{Price of Capital}} = 1$$

- The marginal productivity theory of income distribution holds that all factors are paid what they are economically worth: their marginal contribution to output. Critics assert that such an income distribution is too unequal and the real-world market imperfections result in pay above and below marginal contributions to output.

TERMS AND CONCEPTS

derived demand, p. 317
marginal product (MP), p. 318
marginal revenue product (MRP), p. 318
marginal factor cost (MFC), p. 319
MRP = MFC rule, p. 319

substitution effect, p. 324
output effect, p. 324
elasticity of factor demand, p. 326
least-cost combination of factors, p. 327

profit-maximizing combination of factors, p. 328
marginal productivity theory of income distribution, p. 330

STUDY QUESTIONS

1. What is the significance of factor pricing? Explain how the determinants of factor demand differ from those underlying product demand. Explain the meaning and significance of the fact that the demand for a factor is a derived demand. Why do factors demand curves slope downward?

2. **KEY QUESTION**   Complete the following labour demand table for a firm that is hiring labour competitively and selling its product in a competitive market.

   a. How many workers will the firm hire if the market wage rate is $27.95? $19.95? Explain why the firm will not hire a larger or smaller number of units of labour at each of these wage rates.

   b. Show in schedule form and graphically the labour demand curve of this firm.

   c. Now redetermine the firm's demand curve for labour, assuming that it is selling in an imperfectly competitive market and that, although it can sell 17 units at $2.20 per unit, it must lower product price by 5 cents to sell the marginal product of each successive labour unit. Compare this demand curve with that derived in question 2b. Which curve is more elastic? Explain.

Units of labour	Total product	Marginal product	Product price	Total revenue	Marginal revenue product
0	0		$2	$____	
		____			$____
1	17	____	2	____	
2	31	____	2	____	____
3	43	____	2	____	____
4	53	____	2	____	____
5	60	____	2	____	____
6	65	____	2	____	____

3. Suppose that marginal product tripled while product price fell by one-half in Table 13.1. What would be the new MRP values in Table 13.1? What would be the net impact on the location of the factor demand curve in Figure 13.1?

4. In 2002 Bombardier reduced employment by 3000 workers. What does this decision reveal about how it viewed its marginal revenue product (MRP) and marginal factor cost (MFC)? Why didn't Bombardier reduce employment by more than 3000 workers? By less than 3000 workers?

5. **KEY QUESTION**   What are the determinants of the elasticity of factor demand? What effect will each of the following have on the elasticity or the location of the demand for factor C, which is being used to produce commodity X? Where there is any uncertainty as to the outcome, specify the causes of that uncertainty.

   a. An increase in the demand for product X

   b. An increase in the price of substitute factor D

   c. An increase in the number of factors substitutable for C in producing X

   d. A technological improvement in the capital equipment with which factor C is combined

   e. A decline in the price of complementary factor E

   f. A decline in the elasticity of demand for product X due to a decline in the competitiveness of the product market

6. **KEY QUESTION**   Suppose the productivity of capital and labour are as shown in the accompanying table. The output of these factors sells in a purely competitive market for $1 per unit. Both capital and labour are hired under purely competitive conditions at $3 and $1, respectively.

Units of capital	MP of capital	Units of labour	MP of labour
0		0	
	24		11
1		1	
	21		9
2		2	
	18		8
3		3	
	15		7
4		4	
	9		6
5		5	
	6		4
6		6	
	3		1
7		7	
	1		½
8		8	

   a. What is the least-cost combination of labour and capital the firm should employ in producing 80 units of output? Explain.

   b. What is the profit-maximizing combination of labour and capital the firm should use? Explain. What is the resulting level of output? What is the economic profit? Is this the least costly way of producing the profit-maximizing output?

7. **KEY QUESTION**   In each of the following four cases, MRP_L and MRP_C refer to the marginal revenue products of labour and capital, respectively, and P_L and P_C refer to their prices. Indicate in each case whether the conditions are consistent with maximum profits for the firm. If not, state which factor(s) should be used in larger amounts and which factor(s) should be used in smaller amounts.

   a. $MRP_L = \$8$; $P_L = \$4$; $MRP_C = \$8$; $P_C = \$4$

   b. $MRP_L = \$10$; $P_L = \$12$; $MRP_C = \$14$; $P_C = \$9$

c. $MRP_L = \$6$; $P_L = \$6$; $MRP_C = \$12$; $P_C = \$12$

d. $MRP_L = \$22$; $P_L = \$26$; $MRP_C = \$16$; $P_C = \$19$

8. Florida citrus growers say that the recent crackdown on illegal immigration is increasing the market wage rates necessary to get their oranges picked. Some are turning to $100,000-to-$300,000 mechanical harvesters known as "trunk, shake, and catch" pickers, which vigourously shake oranges from the trees. If widely adopted, what will be the effect on the demand for human orange pickers? What does that imply about the relative strengths of the substitution and output effects?

9. **(The Last Word)** Explain the economics of the substitution of ABMs for human tellers. Some banks are beginning to assess transaction fees when customers use human tellers rather than ABMs. What are these banks trying to accomplish?

INTERNET APPLICATION QUESTIONS

1. Visit Human Resources Development Canada through the McConnell-Brue-Barbiero Web site (Chapter 13) to determine the specific employment outlooks for several occupations. For which jobs are prospects good now but only fair in 2007?

2. Increases in employment reflect increases in labour demand, accompanied by increases in labour supply. Go to the McConnell-Brue-Barbiero Web site (Chapter 13) and select International Labour Statistics (at the bottom). Find the percentage increases in employment for the United States, Japan, Germany, France, Great Britain, Italy, and Canada for the most recent 10-year period. Which three countries have had the fastest growth of labour demand, as measured by the employment outcome? which three the slowest?

14

Chapter

Wage Determination

Over 15 million of us go to work each day in Canada. We work at an amazing variety of jobs for thousands of different firms for considerable differences in pay. What determines our hourly wage or annual salary? Why is the salary for, say, a top major league baseball player $18 million a year, whereas the pay for a first-rate schoolteacher is $60,000? Why are starting salaries for university graduates who major in engineering and accounting so much higher than for graduates majoring in journalism and sociology?

Having explored the major factors that underlie labour demand, we now bring *labour supply* into our analysis to help answer these questions. Generally, labour supply and labour demand interact to determine the hourly wage rate or annual salary in each occupation. Collectively, those wages and salaries make up about 70 percent of the national income in Canada.

14.1   Labour, Wages, and Earnings

wage rate
A price paid per unit of labour services.

nominal wage
The amount of money received by a worker per unit of time (hour, day, etc.).

real wage
The amount of goods and services a worker can purchase with a nominal wage.

<www.internationalecon.com/ v1.0/ch40/40c200.html>
The real wage effects of free trade

Economists use the term "labour" broadly to apply to (1) blue-collar and white-collar workers of all varieties; (2) professionals such as lawyers, physicians, dentists, and teachers; and (3) owners of small businesses, including barbers, plumbers, and television repairers.

Wages are the price that employers pay for labour. Wages take the form not only of direct money payments such as hourly pay, annual salaries, bonuses, royalties, and commissions, but also fringe benefits, such as paid vacations and dental insurance. We will use the term "wages" to mean all such payments and benefits converted to an hourly basis. That will remind us that the **wage rate** is a price paid per unit of labour services, in this case, an hour of work. It will also let us distinguish between the wage rate and labour earnings, the latter being determined by multiplying the number of hours worked per week, per month, or per year by the hourly wage or wage rate.

We must also distinguish between nominal wages and real wages. A **nominal wage** is the amount of money received per hour, per day, and so on. A **real wage** is the quantity of goods and services a worker can obtain with nominal wages; real wages reveal the purchasing power of nominal wages.

Your real wage depends on your nominal wage and the prices of the goods and services you purchase. Suppose you receive an 8 percent increase in your nominal wage during a certain year, but in that same year the price level increases by 5 percent. Then your real wage has increased by 3 percent (= 8 percent *minus* 5 percent). Unless otherwise indicated, we will discuss only *real* wages.

14.2   Productivity and the General Level of Wages

Wages are the price that employers pay for labour.

Wages differ among nations, regions, occupations, and individuals. Wage rates are much higher in Canada than in China or India. Wages are slightly higher in central Canada and the west than in the east. Plumbers are paid less than NHL hockey players, and lawyer Adam may earn twice as much as lawyer Bharti for the same number of hours of work. Wage rates also differ by gender, race, and ethnic background.

The general level of wages includes a wide range of different wage rates. It includes the wages of bakers, barbers, brick masons, and brain surgeons. By averaging such wages, we can more easily compare wages among regions and among nations.

As Global Perspective 14.1 suggests, the general level of real wages in Canada, especially in the skilled trades, is relatively high—although not the highest in the world.

The explanation for the high real wages in Canada and other industrially advanced economies (referred to hereafter as advanced economies) is that the demand for labour in these nations is relatively large compared to the supply of labour.

The Role of Productivity

We know from the previous chapter that the demand for labour, or for any other factor, depends on its productivity. Generally, the greater the productivity of labour, the greater the demand for it. If the total supply of labour is fixed, then the stronger the demand for labour, and the higher the average level of real wages. The demand for labour in Canada and the other major advanced economies is large because labour in these countries is highly productive. There are several reasons for that high productivity:

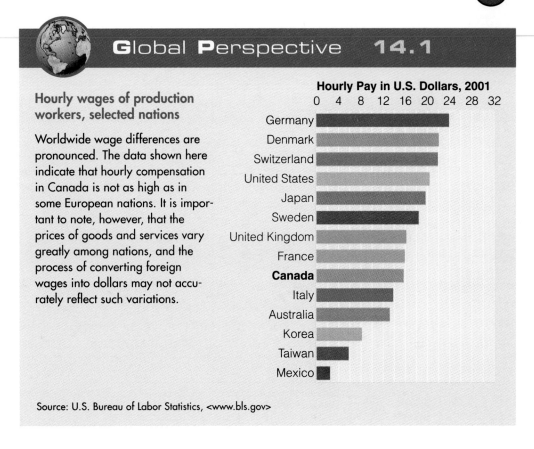

Global Perspective 14.1

Hourly wages of production workers, selected nations

Worldwide wage differences are pronounced. The data shown here indicate that hourly compensation in Canada is not as high as in some European nations. It is important to note, however, that the prices of goods and services vary greatly among nations, and the process of converting foreign wages into dollars may not accurately reflect such variations.

Hourly Pay in U.S. Dollars, 2001

0 4 8 12 16 20 24 28 32

Germany
Denmark
Switzerland
United States
Japan
Sweden
United Kingdom
France
Canada
Italy
Australia
Korea
Taiwan
Mexico

Source: U.S. Bureau of Labor Statistics, <www.bls.gov>

- **Plentiful capital** Workers in the advanced economies have access to large amounts of physical capital equipment (machinery and buildings). The total physical capital per worker in Canada is one of the highest in the world.

- **Access to abundant natural resources** In advanced economies, natural resources are abundant in relation to the size of the labour force. Some of those resources are available domestically and others are imported from abroad. Canada, for example, is richly endowed with arable land, mineral resources, and sources of energy for industry.

- **Advanced technology** The level of technological progress is generally high in advanced economies. Not only do workers in these economies have more capital equipment to work with but that equipment is also technologically superior to the equipment available to the vast majority of workers worldwide. Work methods in the advanced economies are also steadily being improved through scientific study and research.

- **Labour quality** The health, education, and training of workers in advanced economies are generally superior to those of workers in developing nations. Thus, even with the same quantity and quality of natural and capital resources, workers in advanced economies tend to be more productive than many of their counterparts in developing nations.

- **Intangible factors** Less tangible factors also underlie the high productivity in some of the advanced economies. In Canada, for example, such factors include (1) the efficiency and flexibility of management; (2) business, social, and political environments that emphasize production and productivity; (3) access to a large market, which enables firms to engage in mass production; and (4) increased specialization of production made possible by free trade agreements with other nations.

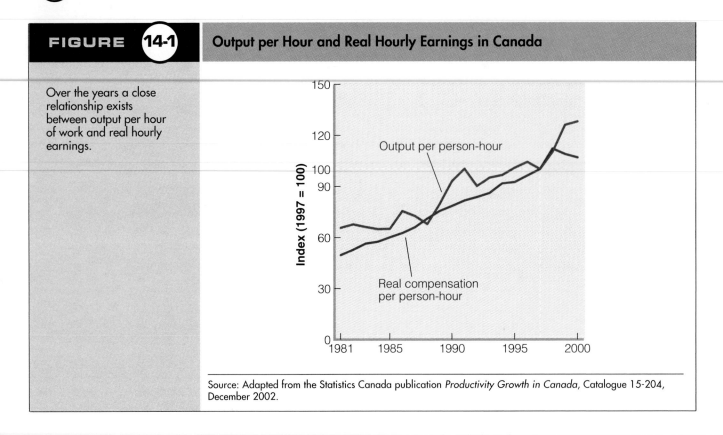

FIGURE 14-1   Output per Hour and Real Hourly Earnings in Canada

Over the years a close relationship exists between output per hour of work and real hourly earnings.

Source: Adapted from the Statistics Canada publication *Productivity Growth in Canada*, Catalogue 15-204, December 2002.

Real Wages and Productivity

Figure 14-1 shows the close long-run relationship between output per hour of work and real hourly earnings in Canada. Because real income and real output are two ways of viewing the same thing, real income (earnings) per worker can increase only at about the same rate as output per worker. When workers produce more real output per hour, more real income is available to distribute to them for each hour worked.

However, suppliers of land, capital, and entrepreneurial talent also share in the income from production. Real wages, therefore, do not always rise in lockstep with gains in productivity over short spans of time. But over long periods, productivity and real wages tend to rise together.

Growth of Real Wages

Basic supply and demand analysis helps explain the long-term trend of real-wage growth in Canada. The nation's labour force has grown significantly over the decades, but, as a result of the productivity-increasing factors we have mentioned, labour demand has increased more rapidly than labour supply. Figure 14-2 shows several such increases in labour supply and labour demand. The result has been a long-run increase in wage rates and employment.

14.3   Wages in a Purely Competitive Labour Market

Choosing a Little More or Less

We now turn from the average level of wages to specific wage rates. What determines the wage rate paid for some specific type of labour? Demand and supply analysis is again revealing. Let's begin

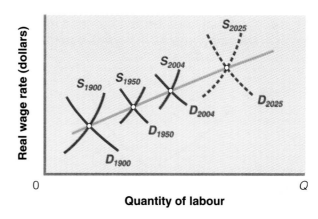

FIGURE 14-2

The Long-run Trend of Real Wages in Canada

The productivity of Canadian labour has increased substantially over the long run, causing the demand for labour, *D*, to shift rightward more rapidly than increases in the supply of labour, *S*. The result has been increases in real wages.

---

purely competitive labour market
A factor market in which a large number of firms demand a particular type of labour supplied by a large number of non-union workers.

by examining labour demand and labour supply in a **purely competitive labour market**. In this type of market

- Many firms compete with one another in hiring a specific type of labour.
- Many qualified workers with identical skills supply that type of labour.
- Individual firms and individual workers are wage-takers, since neither can exert any control over the market wage rate.

Market Demand for Labour

Suppose 200 firms demand a particular type of labour, say, carpenters. These firms need not be in the same industry. Thus, firms producing wood-framed furniture, wood windows and doors, houses and apartment buildings, and wood cabinets will demand carpenters. To find the total, or market, labour demand curve for a particular labour service, we sum horizontally the labour demand curves (the marginal revenue product curves) of the individual firms, as indicated in **Figure 14-3 (Key Graph)**. The horizontal summing of the 200 labour demand curves like *d* in Figure 14-3(b) yields the market labour demand curve *D* in Figure 14-3(a).

Market Supply of Labour

On the supply side of a purely competitive labour market, we assume that no union exists and that workers individually compete for available jobs. The supply curve for each type of labour slopes upward, indicating that employers must bid workers away from other industries, occupations, and localities. Within limits, workers have alternative job opportunities: for example, they may work in other industries in the same locality, or they may work in their present occupations in different cities or provinces, or they may work in other occupations.

Firms that want to hire these workers (here, carpenters) must pay higher wage rates to attract them away from the alternative job opportunities available to them. They must also pay higher wages to induce people who are not currently in the labour force—perhaps doing household activities or enjoying leisure—to seek employment. In short, assuming that wages are constant in other labour markets, higher wages in a particular labour market entice more workers to offer their labour services in that market—a fact confirmed by the upward-sloping market supply of labour curve *S* in Figure 14-3(a).

Key Graph

FIGURE 14-3 Labour Supply and Labour Demand in (Panel a) a Purely Competitive Labour Market and (Panel b) a Single Competitive Firm

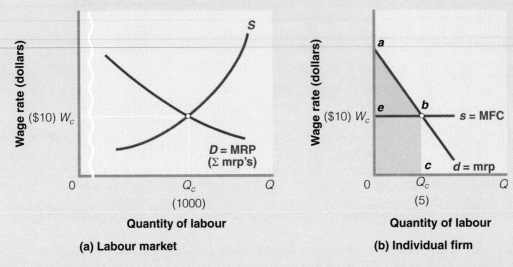

(a) Labour market

(b) Individual firm

In a purely competitive labour market (panel a), the equilibrium wage rate, W_c, and the number of workers, Q_c, are determined by labour supply S and labour demand D. Because this market wage rate is given to the individual firm (panel b) hiring in this market, its labour supply curve $s = MRC$ is perfectly elastic. Its labour demand curve is its MRP curve (here labelled mrp). The firm maximizes its profit by hiring workers up to where MRP = MFC. Area $0abc$ represents both the firm's total revenue and its total cost. The green area is its total wage cost; the lavender area is its non-labour costs, including a normal profit—that is, the firm's payments to the suppliers of land, capital, and entrepreneurship.

Quick Quiz

1. The supply of labour curve s slopes upward in graph (a) because
  a. the law of diminishing marginal utility applies.
  b. the law of diminishing returns applies.
  c. workers can afford to buy more leisure when their wage rates rise.
  d. higher wages are needed to attract workers away from other labour markets, household activities, and leisure.

2. This firm's labour demand curve d in graph (b) slopes downward because
  a. the law of diminishing marginal utility applies.
  b. the law of diminishing returns applies.
  c. the firm must lower its price to sell additional units of its product.
  d. the firm is a competitive employer, not a monopsonist.

3. In employing five workers, the firm represented in graph (b)
  a. has a total wage cost of $6000.
  b. is adhering to the general principle of undertaking all actions for which the marginal benefit exceeds the marginal cost.
  c. uses less labour than would be ideal from society's perspective.
  d. experiences increasing marginal returns.

4. A rightward shift of the labour supply curve in graph (a) would shift curve
  a. $d = mrp$ leftward in graph (b).
  b. $d = mrp$ rightward in graph (b).
  c. $s = MFC$ upward in graph (b).
  d. $s = MFC$ downward in graph (b).

ANSWERS: 1. d; 2. b; 3. b; 4. d

Labour Market Equilibrium

The intersection of the market labour demand curve and the market supply curve determines the equilibrium wage rate and level of employment in purely competitive labour markets. In Figure 14-3(a) the equilibrium wage rate is W_c ($10), and the number of workers hired is Q_c (1000). To the individual firm the market wage rate W_c is given. Each of the many firms employs such a small fraction of the total available supply of this type of labour that none of them can influence the wage rate. The supply of this labour is perfectly elastic to the individual firm, as shown by horizontal line *s* in Figure 14-3(b).

Each individual firm will find it profitable to hire this type of labour up to the point at which marginal revenue product is equal to marginal factor cost. This is merely an application of the MRP = MFC rule we developed in Chapter 13.

TABLE 14-1	The Supply of Labour: Pure Competition in the Hire of Labour		
(1) Units of labour	(2) Wage rate	(3) Total labour cost (wage bill)	(4) Marginal factor (labour) cost
0	$10	$ 0	
1	10	10	$10
2	10	20	10
3	10	30	10
4	10	40	10
5	10	50	10
6	10	60	10

As Table 14-1 indicates, when the price of a resource is given to the individual competitive firm, the marginal cost of that resource (MRC) is constant and is equal to the resource price. Here, MFC is constant and is equal to the wage rate. Each additional worker hired adds precisely his or her own wage rate ($10 in this case) to the firm's total resource cost. So the firm in a purely competitive labour market maximizes its profit by hiring workers to the point at which its wage rate equals MRP. In Figure 14-3(b) this firm will hire Q_c (five) workers, paying each of them the market wage rate, W_c ($10). So, too, will the other 199 firms (not shown) that are hiring workers in this labour market.

To determine a firm's total revenue from employing a particular number of labour units, we sum the MRPs of those units. For example, if a firm employs three labour units with marginal revenue products of $14, $13, and $12, respectively, then the firm's total revenue is $39 (= $14 + $13 + $12). In Figure 14-3(b), where we are not restricted to whole units of labour, total revenue is represented by area 0*abc* under the MRP curve to the left of Q_c. What area represents the firm's total cost, including a normal profit? For Q_c units, the same area—0*abc*. The green rectangle represents the firm's total wage cost (0Q_c × 0W_c). The lavender triangle (total revenue minus total wage cost) represents the firm's non-labour costs—its explicit and implicit payments to land, capital, and entrepreneurship. Thus, in this case, total cost (wages plus other income payments) equals total revenue. This firm and others like it are earning only a normal profit. Figure 14-3(b) represents a long-run equilibrium for a firm that is selling its product in a purely competitive product market and buying its labour in a purely competitive labour market. (*Key Questions 3 and 4*)

14.4 Monopsony Model

monopsony
A market structure in which there is only a single buyer.

In the purely competitive labour market described in the preceding section, each employer hires too small an amount of labour to influence the wage rate. The situation is quite different in **monopsony**, a market in which a single employer of labour has substantial buying (hiring) power. Labour market monopsony has the following characteristics:

- Only a single buyer of a particular type of labour exists.

- This type of labour is relatively immobile, either geographically or because workers would have to acquire new skills.

- The firm is a wage-maker, because the wage rate it must pay varies directly with the number of workers it employs.

As is true of monopoly power, there are various degrees of monopsony power. In *pure* monopsony such power is at its maximum, because only a single employer exists in the labour market. The best real-world examples are probably the labour markets in some towns that depend almost entirely on one major firm. For example, a copper-mining concern may be almost the only source of employment in a remote British Columbia town. A textile mill in Quebec's Eastern Townships, a Gatineau papermill, or a Newfoundland fish processor may provide most of the employment in its locale. Inco (the largest nickel producer in the world) is a dominant employer in the Sudbury, Ontario, area.

In other cases three or four firms may each hire a large portion of the supply of labour in a certain market and, therefore, have some monopsony power. If they tacitly or openly act in concert in hiring labour, they greatly enhance their monopsony power.

Upward-sloping Labour Supply to a Firm

When a firm hires most of the available supply of a particular type of labour, its decision to hire more or fewer workers affects the wage rate it pays to those workers.

When a firm hires most of the available supply of a particular type of labour, its decision to employ more or fewer workers affects the wage rate it pays to those workers. If a firm is large in relation to the size of the labour market, it will have to pay a higher wage rate to obtain more labour. Suppose only one employer of a particular type of labour exists in a certain geographic area. In that case, the labour supply curve for that firm and the total supply curve for the labour market are identical. This supply curve is upward sloping, indicating that the firm must pay a higher wage rate to attract more workers. The supply curve, S in Figure 14-4, is also the average-cost-of-labour curve for the firm; each point on it indicates the wage rate (cost) per worker that must be paid to attract the corresponding number of workers.

MRC Higher than the Wage Rate

When a monopsonist pays a higher wage to attract an additional worker, it must pay that higher wage to all the workers it is currently employing at a lower wage. If not, labour morale will deteriorate, and the employer will be plagued with labour unrest because of wage-rate differences for the same job. Paying a uniform wage to all workers means that the cost of an extra worker—the marginal factor (labour) cost (MFC)—is the sum of that worker's wage rate and the amount necessary to bring the wage rate of all current workers up to the new wage level.

FIGURE 14-4	**The Wage Rate and Level of Employment in a Monopsonistic Labour Market**

In a monopsonistic labour market, the employer's marginal factor (labour) cost curve (MFC) lies above the labour supply curve, S. Equating MFC with MRP at point b, the monopsonist hires Q_m workers (compared with Q_c under competition). As indicated by point c on S, it pays only wage rate W_m (compared with the competitive wage W_c).

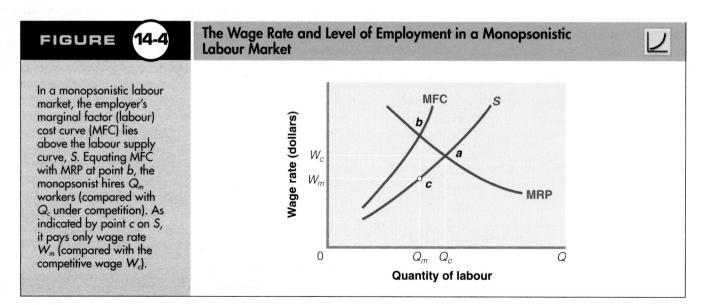

TABLE 14-2	The Supply of Labour: Monopsony in the Hire of Labour		
(1) Units of labour	(2) Wage rate	(3) Total labour cost (wage bill)	(4) Marginal factor (labour) cost
0	$ 5	$ 0	
1	6	6	$ 6
2	7	14	8
3	8	24	10
4	9	36	12
5	10	50	14
6	11	66	16

Table 14-2 illustrates this point. One worker can be hired at a wage rate of $6, but hiring a second worker forces the firm to pay a higher wage rate of $7. The marginal factor (labour) cost of the second worker is $8—the $7 paid to the second worker plus a $1 raise for the first worker. From another viewpoint, total labour cost is now $14 (= 2 × $7), up from $6. So the MRC of the second worker is $8 (= $14 – $6), not just the $7 wage rate paid to that worker. Similarly, the marginal labour cost of the third worker is $10—the $8 that must be paid to attract this worker from alternative employment, plus $1 raises, from $7 to $8, for the first two workers.

The important point is that to the monopsonist, marginal factor (labour) cost exceeds the wage rate. Graphically, the MFC curve lies above the average-cost-of-labour curve, or labour supply curve S, as is clearly shown in Figure 14-4.

Equilibrium Wage and Employment

How many units of labour will the monopsonist hire and what wage rate will it pay? To maximize profit, the monopsonist will employ the quantity of labour Q_m in Figure 14-4, because at that quantity MFC and MRP are equal (point b).[1] The monopsonist next determines how much it must pay to attract these Q_m workers. From the supply curve S, specifically point c, it sees that it must pay wage rate W_m. Clearly, it need not pay a wage equal to MRP; it can attract exactly the number of workers it wants (Q_m) with wage rate W_m. And that rate is what it will pay.

Contrast these results with those that would prevail in a competitive labour market. With competition in the hiring of labour, the level of employment would be greater (at Q_c) and the wage rate would be higher (at W_c). Other things equal, the monopsonist maximizes its profit by hiring a smaller number of workers and thereby paying a less-than-competitive wage rate. Society gets a smaller output, and workers get a wage rate that is less by bc than their marginal revenue product. Just as a monopolist finds it profitable to restrict product output to realize an above-competitive price for its goods, the monopsonist finds it profitable to restrict employment to depress wage rates and therefore costs—that is, to realize wage rates below those that would occur under competitive conditions.

Examples of Monopsony Power

Monopsonistic labour markets are not common in the Canadian economy, since more typically, many employers compete for workers, particularly for workers who are occupationally and geo-

---

[1]The fact that MFC exceeds factor price when factors are hired or purchased under imperfectly competitive (monopsonistic) conditions calls for adjustments in Chapter 13's least-cost and profit-maximizing rules for hiring factors. (See equations (1) and (2) in the "Optimal Combination of Factors" section of Chapter 13.) Specifically, we must substitute MFC for resource price in the denominators of our two equations. That is, with imperfect competition in the hiring of both labour and capital, equation (1) becomes

$$\frac{\text{MP}_L}{\text{MFC}_L} = \frac{\text{MP}_C}{\text{MFC}_C} \tag{1'}$$

and equation (2) is restated as

$$\frac{\text{MRP}_L}{\text{MFC}_L} = \frac{\text{MRP}_C}{\text{MFC}_C} \tag{2'}$$

In fact, equations (1) and (2) can be regarded as special cases of (1') and (2') in which firms happen to be hiring under purely competitive conditions and resource price is, therefore, equal to, and can be substituted for, marginal factor cost.

graphically mobile. Also, in a potential monopsony in a local labour market, unions spring up to counteract that power by forcing firms to negotiate wages. Nevertheless, there is evidence of monopsony power in such diverse labour markets as the markets for nurses, professional athletes, public-school teachers, newspaper employees, and some building trades workers.

In the case of nurses, the major employers in most locales are a relatively small number of hospitals. Further, the highly specialized skills of nurses are not readily transferable to other occupations. It has been found, in accordance with the monopsony model, that, other things equal, the smaller the number of hospitals in a town or city (that is, the greater the degree of monopsony), the lower the starting salaries of nurses.

Professional sports leagues also provide a good example of monopsony, particularly as it relates to the pay of first-year players. The National Hockey League, the National Basketball Association, and Major League Baseball assign first-year players to teams through player drafts. That device prohibits other teams from competing for the player's services, at least for several years, until the player becomes a free agent. In this way the league exercises monopsony power, which results in lower salaries than would occur under competitive conditions. *(Key Question 6)*

<www.bcnu.org/
backgrounder1.htm>
Nurses' opening demands in
new collective agreement

QUICK REVIEW

- Real wages have increased over time in Canada because labour demand has increased relative to labour supply.

- Over the long term, real wages per worker have increased at approximately the same rate as worker productivity.

- The competitive employer is a wage-taker and employs workers at the point where the wage rate (= MFC) equals MRP.

- The labour supply curve for a monopsonist is upward sloping, causing MFC to exceed the wage rate for each worker. Other things equal, the monopsonist, hiring where MFC = MRP, will employ fewer workers and pay a lower wage rate than would a purely competitive employer.

14.5   Unions and the Labour Market

We have assumed so far that workers compete with one another in selling their labour services. In some labour markets, however, workers sell their labour services collectively through unions. When a union is formed in an otherwise competitive labour market, it bargains with a relatively large number of employers. The union has many goals, the most important of which is to raise wage rates, and it can pursue that objective in several ways.

Demand-enhancement Model

From the union's viewpoint, the most desirable technique for raising wage rates is to increase the demand for labour. As Figure 14-5 shows, an increase in labour demand will create both higher wage rates and more jobs. How great those increases will be depends on the elasticity of labour supply. The less elastic the labour supply, the greater will be the wage increase; the more elastic the labour supply, the greater will be the employment increase.

To increase labour demand the union might try to influence one or more of the determinants of demand. For example, a union can attempt to increase the demand for the product or service its members are producing, enhance the productivity of labour, or alter the prices of other inputs.

INCREASE PRODUCT DEMAND

Unions can increase the demand for the products their members help produce—and thus raise the derived demand for labour services—through advertising and political lobbying.

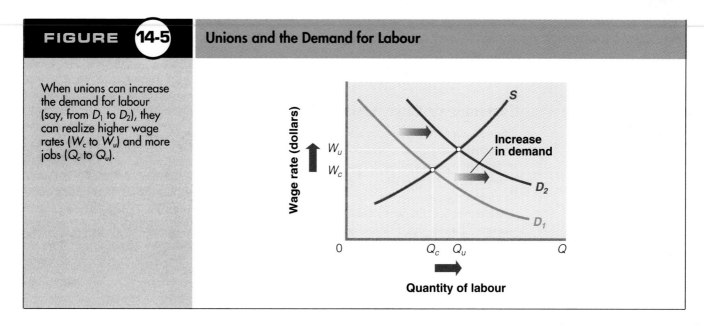

FIGURE 14-5

Unions and the Demand for Labour

When unions can increase the demand for labour (say, from D_1 to D_2), they can realize higher wage rates (W_c to W_u) and more jobs (Q_c to Q_u).

Occasionally, unions advertise union-produced goods or services. The long-running campaign urging consumers to "look for the union label" is an example. Less often, unions join with their employers to finance advertising campaigns designed to bolster product demand. Unions in Canada, such as the Canadian Auto Workers (CAW), have helped to finance "Buy Union" campaigns to convince consumers to purchase products made by their members.

On the political front, construction unions have lobbied for new highway, mass transit, and stadium projects. Teachers' unions and associations have pushed for increased public spending on education, and the steelworkers' union has at times supported employers in seeking protective tariffs designed to exclude competing foreign steel. The steelworkers recognize that an increase in the price of imported steel through tariffs or international agreements will increase the demand for domestically made steel, boosting the derived demand for Canadian steelworkers.

INCREASE PRODUCTIVITY

Many decisions affecting labour productivity—for example, decisions concerning the quantity and quality of real capital used by workers—are made unilaterally by management. There is a growing tendency, however, to set up joint labour–management committees designed to increase labour productivity.

RAISE THE PRICE OF OTHER INPUTS

Unions sometimes have tried to strengthen the demand for their labour by working to increase the price of substitute factors. For example, although union members are generally paid significantly more than the minimum wage, unions have strongly supported increases in the minimum wage. The purpose may be to raise the price of low-wage, non-union labour, which in some cases is substitutable for union labour. A higher minimum wage for non-union workers will discourage employers from substituting such workers for union workers and thereby increase the demand for union members.

Similarly, unions have sometimes sought to increase the demand for their labour by supporting public actions that reduce the price of a complementary factor of production. For example, unions in industries that use large amounts of imported factors of production might urge reductions in tariffs on those imports. Where labour and energy are complementary, a price decrease for the other factors will increase the demand for labour through Chapter 13's output effect.

Unions recognize that their ability to influence the demand for labour is very limited. Consequently they are more likely to try to prevent declines in labour demand than they are to promote increases. So, it is not surprising that union efforts to raise wage rates have concentrated on the supply side of the labour market.

Exclusive or Craft Union Model

One way in which unions can raise wage rates is to reduce the supply of labour, and over the years organized labour has favoured policies to do just that. The Canadian Labour Congress, an umbrella organization representing 2.5 million workers, has supported legislation that has (1) restricted immigration, (2) reduced child labour, (3) encouraged compulsory retirement, and (4) enforced a shorter workweek.

Moreover, certain types of workers have adopted techniques designed to restrict the number of workers who can join their union. This is especially true of *craft unions,* whose members possess a particular skill, such as carpenters or brick masons or plumbers. Craft unions have frequently forced employers to agree to hire only union members, thereby gaining virtually complete control of the labour supply. Then, by following restrictive membership policies—for example, long apprenticeships, very high initiation fees, and limits on the number of new members admitted—they artificially restrict labour supply. As indicated in Figure 14-6, such practices result in higher wage rates and constitute what is called **exclusive unionism**. By excluding workers from unions and therefore from the labour supply, craft unions succeed in elevating wage rates.

Occupational licensing is another means of restricting the supply of specific kinds of labour. Here a group of workers in a given occupation pressure provincial or municipal governments to pass a law that says that some occupational group (for example, barbers, or physicians, plumbers, cosmetologists, egg graders, pest controllers) can practise their trade only if they meet certain requirements. Those requirements might include level of education, amount of work experience, the passing of an examination, and personal characteristics ("the practitioner must be of good moral character"). Members of the licensed occupation typically dominate the licensing board that administers such laws. The result is self-regulation, which often leads to policies that serve only to restrict entry to the occupation and reduce the labour supply.

The purpose of licensing is supposedly to protect consumers from incompetent practitioners—surely a worthy goal. But such licensing also results in above-competitive wages and earnings for

exclusive unionism
The practice of a labour union of restricting the supply of skilled union labour to increase the wages received by union members.

occupational licensing
The laws of provincial or municipal governments that require a worker to satisfy certain specified requirements and obtain a licence from a licensing board before engaging in a particular occupation.

FIGURE 14-6   Exclusive or Craft Unionism

By reducing the supply of labour (say, from S_1 to S_2) through the use of restrictive membership policies, exclusive unions achieve higher wage rates (W_c to W_u). However, restriction of the labour supply also reduces the number of workers employed (Q_c to Q_u).

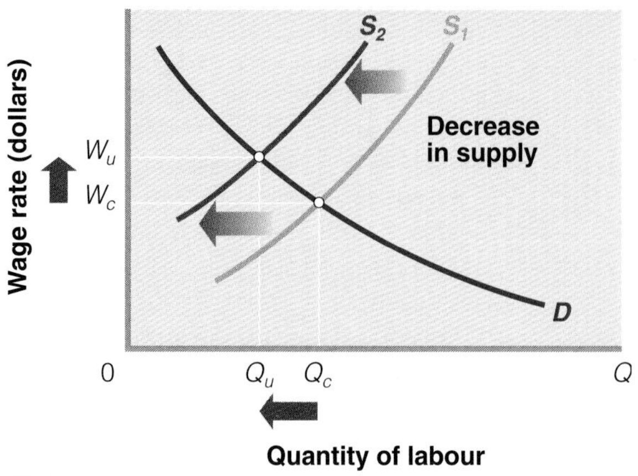

those in the licensed occupation (Figure 14-6). Moreover, licensing requirements often include a residency requirement, which inhibits the interprovincial movement of qualified workers. Some 300 occupations are now licensed in Canada.

Inclusive or Industrial Union Model

<www.amfanow.org/ craft.htm>
Craft union or industrial union?

inclusive unionism
The practice of a labour union of including as members all workers employed in an industry.

Instead of trying to limit their membership, however, most unions seek to organize all available workers. This is especially true of the *industrial unions,* such as the Canadian Auto Workers and the United Steelworkers. Such unions seek as members all available unskilled, semiskilled, and skilled workers in an industry. A union can afford to be exclusive when its members are skilled craft persons for whom there are few substitutes. But for a union composed of unskilled and semiskilled workers, a policy of limited membership would make available to the employers numerous non-union workers who can easily be substituted for the union workers.

An industrial union that includes virtually all available workers in its membership can put firms under great pressure to agree to its wage demands. Because of its legal right to strike, such a union can threaten to deprive firms of their entire labour supply, and an actual strike can do just that.

We illustrate such **inclusive unionism** in Figure 14-7. Initially, the competitive equilibrium wage rate is W_c and the level of employment is Q_c. Now suppose an industrial union is formed that demands a higher, above-equilibrium wage rate of, say, W_u. That wage rate W_u would create a perfectly elastic labour supply over the range *ae* in Figure 14-7. If firms wanted to hire any workers in this range, they would have to pay the union-imposed wage rate. If they decide against meeting this wage demand, the union will supply no labour at all, and the firms will be faced with a strike. If firms decide it is better to pay the higher wage rate than to suffer a strike, they will cut back on employment from Q_c to Q_u.

By agreeing to the union's W_u wage demand, individual employers become wage-takers. Because labour supply is perfectly elastic over range *ae*, the marginal resource (labour) cost is equal to the wage rate W_u over this range. The Q_u level of employment is the result of employers' equating this MFC (now equal to the wage rate) with MRP, according to our profit-maximizing rule.

Note from point *e* on labour supply curve *S* that Q_e workers desire employment at wage W_u. But as indicated by point *b* on labour demand curve *D*, only Q_u workers are employed. The result is a surplus of labour of $Q_e - Q_u$ (also shown by distance *eb*). In a purely competitive labour market

---

FIGURE **14-7**	**Inclusive or Industrial Unionism**

By organizing virtually all available workers to control the supply of labour, inclusive industrial unions may impose a wage rate, such as W_u, which is above the competitive wage rate W_c. The effect is to change the labour supply curve from *S* to *aeS*. At wage rate W_u, employers will cut employment from Q_c to Q_u.

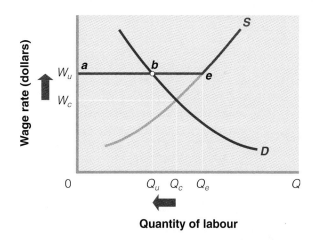

without the union, the effect of a surplus of unemployed workers would be lower wages. Specifically, the wage rate would fall to the equilibrium level, W_c, where the quantity of labour supplied equals the quantity of labour demanded (each Q_c).

Wage Increases and Unemployment

Have unions been successful in raising the wages of their members? Evidence suggests that union members on average achieve a 10 to 15 percent wage advantage over non-union workers.

As Figures 14-6 and 14-7 show, the effect of wage-raising actions by both exclusive and inclusive unionism is to reduce employment. That result acts as a restraining influence on union wage demands. A union cannot expect to maintain solidarity within its ranks if it demands a wage rate so high that joblessness will result for, say, 20 or 30 percent of its members.

The unemployment effect created by union-induced wage increases may be reduced in two ways:

1. *Growth*   The normal growth of the economy increases the demand for most kinds of labour over time. This continual rightward shift of the labour demand curves in Figures 14-6 and 14-7 might offset, or more than offset, the unemployment effects associated with the indicated wage increases. In that event, the increases in unemployment prompted by the unions would tend to *slow* the growth of job opportunities but would not reduce total employment by firms.

2. *Elasticity*   The size of the unemployment effect resulting from a union-induced wage increase depends on the elasticity of demand for labour. The more inelastic that demand, the smaller the amount of unemployment that accompanies a given wage-rate increase. And if unions have sufficient bargaining strength, they may be able to win provisions in their collective bargaining agreements that reduce the elasticity of demand for union labour by reducing the substitutability of other inputs for that labour. For example, a union may force employers to accept rules slowing the introduction of new machinery and equipment. Or the union may bargain successfully for severance pay or layoff pay, which increases the cost to the firm of substituting capital for labour when wage rates are increased.

Bilateral Monopoly Model

bilateral monopoly
A market in which there is a single seller (monopoly) and a single buyer (monopsony).

Suppose a strong industrial union is formed in a labour market that is monopsonistic rather than competitive, creating a combination of the monopsony model and the inclusive unionism model. The result is called **bilateral monopoly** because there is a single seller and a single buyer. The union is a monopolistic "seller" of labour that controls labour supply and can influence wage rates, but it faces a monopsonistic "buyer" of labour that can also affect wages by altering its employment. This is not an uncommon case, particularly in less-pure forms in which a single union confronts two, three, or four large employers, such as steel, automobiles, construction equipment, and professional sports.

INDETERMINATE OUTCOME OF BILATERAL MONOPOLY

This situation is shown in Figure 14-8, where we superimpose Figure 14-7 onto Figure 14-4. The monopsonistic employer will seek the below-competitive-equilibrium wage rate W_m, and the union will press for some above-competitive-equilibrium wage rate such as W_u. Which will be the outcome? We cannot say with certainty because the bilateral monopoly model does not explain what will happen at the collective bargaining table. We can expect the wage outcome to lie somewhere between W_m and W_u. Beyond that, about all we can say is that the party with the greater bargaining power and the more effective bargaining strategy will probably get a wage closer to the one it seeks.

DESIRABILITY OF BILATERAL MONOPOLY

The wage and employment outcomes in this situation might be more socially desirable than the term "bilateral monopoly" implies. The monopoly on one side of the market might in effect cancel out the monopoly on the other side, yielding competitive or near-competitive results. *(Key Question 7)*

FIGURE 14-8 **Bilateral Monopoly in the Labour Market**

A monopsonist seeks to hire Q_m workers (where MFC = MRP) and pay wage rate W_m corresponding to Q_m labour on labour supply curve S. The inclusive union it faces seeks the above-equilibrium wage rate W_u. The actual outcome cannot be predicted.

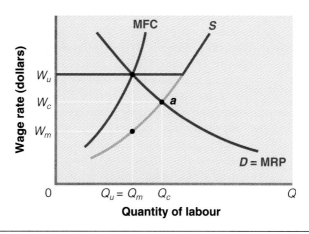

QUICK REVIEW

- In the demand-enhancement union model, a union increases the wage rate by increasing labour demand through actions that increase product demand, raise labour productivity, or alter the prices of related inputs.

- In the exclusive (craft) union model, a union increases wage rates by artificially restricting labour supply, through, say, long apprenticeships or occupational licensing.

- In the inclusive (industrial) union model, a union raises the wage rate by gaining control over a firm's labour supply and threatening to withhold labour via a strike unless a negotiated wage is obtained.

- Bilateral monopoly occurs in a labour market where a monopsonist bargains with an inclusive, or industrial, union. Wage and employment outcomes are determined by collective bargaining in this situation.

14.6 The Minimum-wage Controversy

minimum wage
The lowest wage employers may legally pay for an hour of work.

<info.load-otea.hrdc-drhc.gc.ca/federal_legislation/home.htm>
Canada's Labour Code

In Canada both the federal and provincial governments have enacted **minimum wage** legislation, but it is the provincial laws that cover most workers. The provincial minimum wage ranges from $5.80 per hour in Nova Scotia to $8.00 per hour in British Columbia. The purpose of the minimum wage is to provide a living wage for less-skilled workers to keep them and their families above the poverty line.

Case Against the Minimum Wage

Critics, reasoning in terms of Figure 14-7, contend that an above-equilibrium minimum wage (say, W_u) will push employers back up their labour demand curves, causing them to hire fewer workers. The higher labour costs may even force some firms out of business. Then, some of the poor, low-wage workers whom the minimum wage was designed to help will find themselves out of work. Critics point out that a worker who is *unemployed* at a minimum wage of $5.00 per hour is clearly worse off than if *employed* at a market wage rate of, say, $4.50 per hour.

A second criticism of the minimum wage is that it does not reduce poverty. Critics point out that much of the benefit of the minimum wage accrues to teenage workers, most of whom receive only minimum wages for just a few years.

Case for the Minimum Wage

Advocates of the minimum wage say that critics analyze its impact in an unrealistic context. Figure 14-7, advocates claim, assumes a competitive, static market. But in a more realistic, low-pay labour market where there is some monopsony power (Figure 14-8), the minimum wage can increase wage rates without causing unemployment. Indeed, a higher minimum wage may even produce more jobs by eliminating the motive that monopsonistic firms have for restricting employment. For example, a minimum wage floor of W_c in Figure 14-8 would change the firm's labour supply curve to $W_c aS$ and prompt the firm to increase its employment from Q_m workers to Q_c workers.

A minimum wage may increase labour productivity, shifting the labour demand curve to the right and offsetting any reduced employment that the minimum wage might cause. For example, the higher wage rate might prompt firms to find more productive tasks for low-paid workers, thereby raising their productivity. Alternatively, the minimum wage may reduce *labour turnover* (the rate at which workers voluntarily quit). With fewer low-productive trainees, the *average* productivity of the firm's workers would rise. In either case, the higher labour productivity would justify paying the higher minimum wage. So, the alleged negative employment effects of the minimum wage might not occur.

Evidence and Conclusions

Which view is correct? Unfortunately, there is no clear answer. All economists agree there is some minimum wage so high, say, $20 an hour, that it would severely reduce employment. But no current consensus exists on the employment effects of the present level of the minimum wage. Evidence in the 1980s suggested that minimum wage hikes reduced employment of minimum wage workers, particularly teenagers (16- to 19-year-olds). The consensus then was that a 10 percent increase in the minimum wage would reduce teenage employment by about 1 to 3 percent. But recent evidence suggests that the minimum wage hikes in the 1990s produced even smaller, and perhaps zero, employment declines among teenagers.[2]

The overall effect of the minimum wage is thus uncertain. On the one hand, the employment and unemployment effects of the minimum wage do not appear to be a great as many critics fear. On the other hand, because a large part of its effect is dissipated on non-poverty families, the minimum wage is not as strong an anti-poverty tool as many supporters contend.

It is clear, however, that the minimum wage has strong political support. Perhaps this stems from two realities: (1) more workers are helped by the minimum wage than are hurt and (2) the minimum wage gives society some assurance that employers are not taking undue advantage of vulnerable, low-skilled workers.

14.7   Wage Differentials

wage differentials
The difference between the wage received by one worker or group of workers and that received by another worker or group of workers.

Hourly wage rates and annual salaries differ greatly among occupations. In Table 14-3 we list average weekly wages for several industries to illustrate such occupational **wage differentials**. For example, observe that construction workers on average earn one-third more than those workers in the health and social service industry. Large wage differentials also exist within some of the occupations listed (not shown). For example, although average wages for retail salespersons are relatively low, some top salespersons selling on commission make several times the average wages for their occupation.

What explains wage differentials such as these? Once again, the forces of demand and supply are revealing. As we demonstrate in Figure 14-9 on page 352, wage differentials can arise on either the

---

[2]Alan Krueger, "Teaching the Minimum Wage in Econ 101 in Light of the New Economics of the Minimum Wage," *Journal of Economic Education,* Summer, 2001.

TABLE 14-3	Average Weekly Wages in Selected Industries, 2002
Industry	**Average weekly earnings (including overtime)**
All industries	**$ 681.09**
Mining, quarrying, and oil wells	1,167.98
Finance, insurance, and real estate	852.78
Logging and forestry	849.77
Manufacturing	830.15
Construction	804.22
Transportation, storage, communications, and other utilities	764.40
Educational and related services	725.27
Real estate services	609.79
Health and social services	605.12

Source: Adapted from the Statistics Canada Web site, www.statcan.ca/english/pgdb. Visit www.mcgrawhill.ca/college/mcconnell for data updates.

Σ-STAT

supply or demand side of labour markets. Figures 14-9(a) and (b) represent labour markets for two occupational groups that have identical *labour supply curves.* The labour market in panel (a) has a relatively high equilibrium wage (W_a) because labour demand is very strong. The labour market in panel (b) has an equilibrium wage that is relatively low (W_b) since labour demand is weak. Clearly, the wage differential between occupations (a) and (b) results solely from differences in the magnitude of labour demand.

Contrast that situation with Figure 14-9(c) and (d), where the *labour demand curves* are identical. In the labour market in panel (c), the equilibrium wage is relatively high (W_c) because labour supply is highly restricted. In the labour market in panel (d) labour supply is highly abundant, so the equilibrium wage (W_d) is relatively low. The wage differential between (c) and (d) results solely from the differences in the magnitude of the labour supply.

Although Figure 14-9 provides a good starting point for understanding wage differentials, we need to know *why* demand and supply conditions differ in various labour markets.

Marginal Revenue Productivity

The strength of labour demand—how far rightward the labour demand curve is located—differs greatly among occupations because of differences in how much various occupational groups contribute to their employers' revenue. This revenue contribution, in turn, depends on the workers' productivity and the strength of the demand for the products they are helping to produce. Where labour is highly productive and product demand is strong, labour demand also is strong and, other things equal, pay is high. Top professional athletes, for example, are highly productive at sports entertainment, for which millions of people are willing to pay billions of dollars over the course of a season. So the **marginal revenue productivity** of these top players is exceptionally high, as are their salaries, represented in Figure 14-9(a). In contrast, in most occupations workers generate much more modest revenue for their employers, so their pay is lower, as in Figure 14-9(b).

marginal revenue productivity
How much workers contribute to their employers' revenue.

Non-competing Groups

On the supply side of the labour market, workers are not homogeneous; they differ in their mental and physical capabilities and in their education and training. At any given time the labour force is made up of many **non-competing groups** of workers, each representing several occupations for which the members of a particular group qualify. In some groups qualified workers are relatively few, whereas in others they are highly abundant. Workers in one group do not qualify for the occupations of other groups.

non-competing groups
Collections of workers in the economy who do not compete with each other for employment because the skills and training of the workers in one group are substantially different from those in other groups.

ABILITY

Only a few workers have the ability or physical attributes to be brain surgeons, concert violinists, top fashion models, research scientists, or professional athletes. Because the supply of these particular types of labour is very small in relation to labour demand, their wages are high, as in Figure 14-9(c). The members of these and similar groups do not compete with one another or with other skilled or semiskilled workers. The violinist does not compete with the surgeon, nor does the surgeon compete with the violinist or the fashion model.

The concept of non-competing groups can be applied to various subgroups and even to specific individuals in a particular group. An especially skilled violinist can command a higher salary than colleagues who play the same instrument. A handful of top corporate executives earn 10 to 20 times

FIGURE 14-9   Labour Demand, Labour Supply, and Wage Differentials

The wage differential between labour markets (a) and (b) results solely from differences in labour demand. In labour markets (c) and (d), differences in labour supply cause the wage differential.

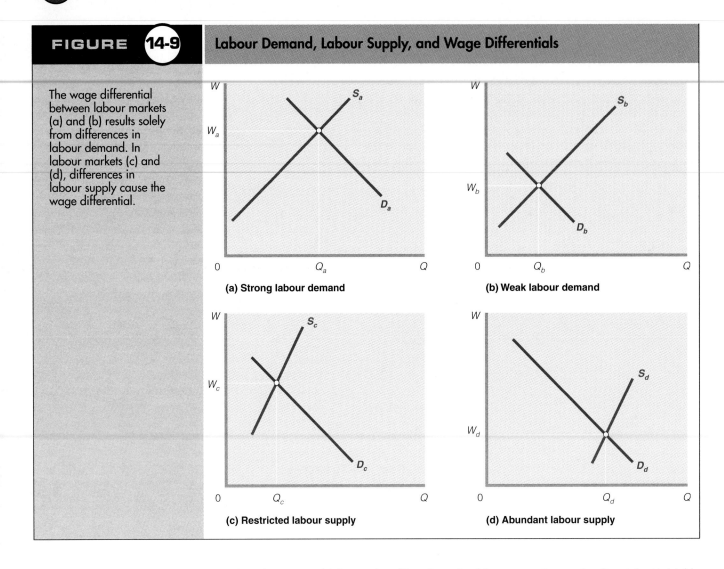

(a) Strong labour demand

(b) Weak labour demand

(c) Restricted labour supply

(d) Abundant labour supply

as much as the average chief executive officer. In each of these cases, the supply of top talent is highly limited, since less talented colleagues are only imperfect substitutes.

EDUCATION AND TRAINING

investment in human capital
Any expenditure to improve the education, skills, health, or mobility of workers, with an expectation of greater productivity and thus a positive return on the investment.

Another source of wage differentials has to do with differing amounts of investment in human capital. An **investment in human capital** is *an expenditure on education or training that improves the skills and, therefore, the productivity of workers.* Like expenditures on machinery and equipment, expenditures on education or training that increase a worker's productivity can be regarded as investments. In both cases, current costs are incurred with the intention that will lead to a greater *future* flow of earnings.

Although education yields higher incomes, it carries substantial costs. A college or university education involves not only direct costs (tuition, fees, books) but also indirect or opportunity costs (forgone earnings) as well. Does the higher pay received by better-educated workers compensate for these costs? The answer is yes. Rates of return are estimated to be 10 to 13 percent for investments in secondary education and 8 to 12 percent for investments in college and university education. One generally accepted estimate is that each year of schooling raises a worker's wage by about 8 percent. Also, the pay gap between college and university graduates and high-school graduates increased sharply between 1980 and 2001.

Compensating Differences

compensating differences
Differences in the wages received by workers in different jobs to compensate for non-monetary differences in the jobs.

If the workers in a particular non-competing group are equally capable of performing several different jobs, you might expect the wage rates to be identical for all these jobs. Not so. A group of high-school graduates may be equally capable of becoming sales clerks or construction workers, but these jobs pay different wages. In virtually all locales, construction labourers receive much higher wages than sales clerks. These wage differentials are called **compensating differences**, because they must be paid to compensate for non-monetary differences in various jobs.

The construction job involves dirty working conditions, the hazard of accidents, and irregular employment. The retail sales job means clean clothing, pleasant air-conditioned surroundings, and less fear of injury or layoff. Other things equal, it is easy to see why some workers would rather pick up a credit card than a shovel. So labour supply is less for construction firms, as in Figure 14-9(c), than for retail shops, as in Figure 14-9(d). Construction firms must pay higher wages than retailers to compensate for the unattractive aspects of construction jobs.

Compensating differences play an important role in allocating society's scarce labour resources. If very few workers want to be garbage collectors, then society must pay high wages to attract garbage collectors. If many more people want to be sales clerks than are needed, then society need not pay them as much as garbage collectors to get those services performed.

Compensating differences are more difficult to determine in Canada's publicly funded health care system. For example, many remote communities in Canada do not have enough physicians to serve the needs of the population. Many provincial governments offer bonuses to physicians who will move into remote communities. But it is not easy to determine an effective level for these government-determined bonuses, which are intended to compensate doctors for moving to what many of them believe to be less-desirable areas to live. Provincial bonuses to those physicians willing to relocate to remote areas have partially alleviated the chronic shortage of doctors in many parts of rural Canada.

Market Imperfections

Differences in marginal revenue productivity, amounts of human capital, and non-monetary aspects of jobs explain most of the wage differentials in the economy. But other persistent differentials result from various market imperfections that impede workers moving from lower-paying jobs to higher-paying jobs.

LACK OF JOB INFORMATION

Workers may simply be unaware of job opportunities and wage rates in other geographic areas and in other jobs for which they qualify. Consequently, the flow of qualified labour from lower-paying to higher-paying jobs may not be sufficient to equalize wages within occupations.

GEOGRAPHIC IMMOBILITY

Many workers are reluctant to move to new places, to leave friends, relatives, and associates, to force their children to change schools, to sell their houses, or to incur the costs and inconveniences of adjusting to a new job and a new community. As Adam Smith noted more than two centuries ago, "A [person] is of all sorts of luggage the most difficult to be transported." The reluctance of workers to move creates persistent geographic wage differentials within the same occupation. Some economists point out that Canada's employment insurance program contributes to labour immobility.

UNIONS AND GOVERNMENT RESTRAINTS

Wage differentials may be reinforced by artificial restrictions on mobility imposed by unions and government. We have noted that craft unions keep their wages high by restricting membership. Thus, the low-paid non-union carpenter of Edmonton, Alberta, may be willing to move to Vancouver in the pursuit of higher wages, but her chances of succeeding are slim. She may be unable to get a union card, and no card means no job. Similarly, an optometrist or lawyer qualified to practise in one province may not meet licensing requirements of other provinces, so his ability to move is limited. Other artificial barriers involve pension plans and seniority rights that might be jeopardized by moving from one job to another.

DISCRIMINATION

Despite legislation to the contrary, discrimination results in lower wages being paid to women and visible-minority workers than to white males doing virtually identical work. Also, women and minorities may be crowded into certain low-paying occupations, driving down wages there and raising them elsewhere. If discrimination keeps qualified women and minorities from taking the higher-paying jobs, then differences in pay will persist.

All four considerations—differences in marginal revenue productivity, non-competing groups, non-monetary differences, and market imperfections—come into play in explaining actual wage differentials. For example, the differential between the wages of a physician and those of a construction worker can be explained based on marginal revenue productivity and non-competing groups. Physicians generate considerable revenue because of their high productivity and the strong willingness of consumers (via provincial governments) to pay for health care. Physicians also fall into a non-competing group where, because of stringent training requirements, only a relatively few persons qualify. So the supply of labour is small in relation to demand.

14.8   Pay for Performance and the Principal–Agent Problem

The models of wage determination we have described in this chapter assume that worker pay is always a standard amount for each hour's work, for example, $15 per hour. But pay schemes are often more complex than that in both composition and purpose. For instance, many workers receive annual salaries rather than hourly pay. Many workers also receive fringe benefits: dental insurance, life insurance, paid vacations, paid sick-leave days, pension contributions, and so on. Finally, some pay plans are designed to elicit a desired level of performance from workers. This last aspect of pay plans requires further elaboration.

The Principal–Agent Problem Revisited

In Chapter 3 we first identified the *principal–agent problem* as it relates to possible differences in the interests of corporate stockholders (principals) and the executives (agents) they hire. This problem extends to all workers. Firms hire workers to help produce the goods and services the firms sell for a profit. Workers are the firms' agents; they are hired to advance the interest (profit) of the firms. The principals are the firms; they hire agents to advance their goals. Firms and workers have one interest in common: they both want the firm to survive and thrive. That will ensure profit for the firm and continued employment and wages for the workers.

But the interests of the firm and of the workers are not identical. A principal–agent problem arises when those interests diverge. Workers may seek to increase their utility by shirking on the job, that is, by providing less than the agreed-on effort or by taking unauthorized breaks. The night security guard in a warehouse may leave work early or spend time reading a novel rather than making the assigned rounds. A salaried manager may spend time away from the office visiting friends rather than attending to company business.

incentive pay plan
A compensation structure, such as piece rates, bonuses, stock options, commissions, and profit sharing, that ties worker pay directly to performance.

Firms (principals) have a profit incentive to reduce or eliminate shirking. One option is to monitor workers, but monitoring is difficult and costly. Hiring another worker to supervise or monitor the security guard might double the cost of maintaining a secure warehouse. Another way of resolving the principal–agent problem is through some sort of **incentive pay plan** that ties worker compensation more closely to output or performance. Such incentive pay schemes include piece rates, commissions and royalties, bonuses and profit sharing, and efficiency wages.

PIECE RATES

Piece rates are compensation paid according to the number of units of output a worker produces. If a principal pays fruit pickers by the bushel or typists by the page, it need not be concerned with shirking or with monitoring costs.

COMMISSIONS OR ROYALTIES

Unlike piece rates, commissions and royalties tie compensation to the value of sales. Employees who sell products or services—including real estate agents, insurance agents, stockbrokers, and retail salespersons—commonly receive *commissions* that are computed as a percentage of the monetary value of their sales. Recording artists and authors are paid *royalties,* computed as a certain percentage of sales revenues from their works. These types of compensation link the financial interests of the salespeople or artists and authors to the profit interest of the firms.

BONUSES, STOCK OPTIONS, AND PROFIT SHARING

Bonuses are payments in addition to one's annual salary that are based on some factor such as the performance of the individual worker, or of a group of workers, or of the firm itself. A professional baseball player may receive a bonus based on a high batting average, the number of home runs hit, or the number of runs batted in. A business manager may receive a bonus based on the profitability of her or his unit. *Stock options* allow workers to buy shares of their employer's stock at a fixed price. If the firm does well and its stock prices rise, the workers' stock holdings rise in value. Such options are part of the compensation packages of top corporate officials, as well as many workers in relatively new high-technology firms. *Profit-sharing plans* allocate a percentage of a firm's profit to its employees. Such plans have in recent years resulted in large annual payments to many Canadian workers.

EFFICIENCY WAGES

The rationale behind *efficiency wages* is that employers will get greater effort from their workers by paying them above-equilibrium wage rates. Glance back at Figure 14-3, which shows a competitive labour market in which the equilibrium wage rate is $10. What if an employer decides to pay an above-equilibrium wage of $12 per hour? Rather than putting the firm at a cost disadvantage compared with rival firms paying only $10, the higher wage might improve worker effort and productivity so that unit labour costs actually fall (see the Consider This box). For example, if each worker produces 10 units of output per hour at the $12 wage rate compared with only 6 units at the $10 wage rate, unit labour costs for the high-wage firm will be only $1.20 (= $12 ÷ 10) compared to $1.67 (= $10 ÷ 6) for firms paying the equilibrium wage.

An above-equilibrium wage may enhance worker efficiency in several ways. It enables the firm to attract higher-quality workers, it lifts worker morale, and it lowers turnover, resulting in a more experienced workforce, greater worker productivity, and lower recruitment and training costs. Because the opportunity cost of losing a higher-wage job is greater, workers are more likely to put forth their best efforts with less supervision and monitoring. In fact, efficiency wage payments have proven effective for many employers.

THE PRINCIPAL–AGENT PROBLEM AND HEALTH CARE SUPPLIERS

A difficult-to-solve principal–agent problem may arise in the doctor–patient relationship. Clearly, the physician has much more medical expertise than the patient, which gives rise to possible "demand creation" by the physician. If a doctor advises a patient to come back for a visit in two weeks, the patient is hardly in a position to disagree, given the physician's superior medical knowledge. Such a situation can result in unnecessary trips to doctors' offices, which in a health care sector dominated by private markets would lead to wasteful consumer expenditures. In a government-funded health care sector, such as Canada's, it also leads to wasteful *public* expenditures.

Consider This

Efficiency Wages

Ford Motor Company made headlines in 1914 by offering autoworkers $5 per day, up from $2.50 per day. The wage payment was newsworthy because the typical market wage in manufacturing at that time was just $2 to $3 per day.*

What was Ford's rationale for offering a higher-than-competitive wage? Statistics indicate that the firm was suffering from high rates of job quitting and absenteeism. It reasoned that a high wage rate would increase worker productivity by increasing morale and reducing employment turnover. Only workers who had worked at Ford for at least six months were eligible for the $5 per day wage. Nevertheless, 10,000 workers sought jobs with Ford in the period immediately following the announcement of the wage increase.

According to historians, the Ford strategy succeeded. The $5 wage raised the value of the job to Ford workers. That created worker incentives to keep working at Ford and to show up for work each day. It also encouraged labourers to work energetically so as not to be fired from a job that paid much more than alternative employment. The rates of job quitting and absenteeism both plummeted, and labour productivity at Ford rose by an estimated 51 percent that year.

The $5 wage was an *efficiency wage*—one that raised the marginal revenue product of Ford workers. Ford's pay plan addressed its principal–agent problem. The $2.50 wage hike "paid for itself" by more closely aligning the interests of Ford workers and owners.

---

*This application is from Campbell R. McConnell, Stanley L. Brue, and David A. Macpherson, *Contemporary Labor Economics*, 5th ed. (New York: McGraw-Hill, 1999), p. 233. It is based in part on Daniel M. G. Raff and Lawrence Summers, "Did Henry Ford Pay Efficiency Wages?" *Journal of Labor Economics*, pt. 2, October 1987, pp. S57–S86.

Question: If a company in a competitive sector pays a wage above the going equilibrium wage rate, or an efficiency wage, will it put that company at a competitive disadvantage?

In the Canadian health care system, in which patients do not pay out-of-pocket for a visit to the physician, the principal–agent problem between doctors and patients may be exacerbated. It probably contributes to the excess demand for physician services, which has resulted in longer waiting times to see a doctor. Unnecessary doctor visits have also contributed to rising health care expenditures for the federal and provincial governments.

Addendum: The Negative Side Effects of Pay for Performance

Although pay for performance may help to overcome the principal–agent problem and enhance worker productivity, such plans may have negative side effects and so require careful design. Here are a few examples:

- The rapid production pace that piece rates encourage may result in poor product quality and may compromise the safety of workers. Such outcomes can be costly to the firm over the long run.

- Commissions may cause some salespeople to engage in questionable or even fraudulent sales practices, such as making exaggerated claims about products or recommending unneeded repairs. Such practices may lead to private lawsuits or government legal action.

- Bonuses based on personal performance may disrupt the close cooperation needed for maximum team production. A professional hockey player who receives a bonus for goals scored may be reluctant to pass the puck to teammates.

- Since profit sharing is usually tied to the performance of the entire firm, less energetic workers can free-ride by obtaining their profit share based on the hard work of others.

- There may be a downside to the reduced turnover resulting from above-market wages: Firms that pay efficiency wages have fewer opportunities to hire new workers and suffer the loss of new blood that sometimes energizes the workplace.

QUICK REVIEW

- Proponents of the minimum wage argue that it is needed to assist the working poor and to counter monopsony where it might exist; critics say that it is poorly targeted to reduce poverty and that it reduces employment.

- Wage differentials are generally attributable to the forces of supply and demand, influenced by differences in workers' marginal revenue productivity, workers' education and skills, and non-monetary differences in jobs. Several labour market imperfections also play a role.

- As it applies to labour, the principal–agent problem is one of workers pursuing their own interests to the detriment of the employer's profit objective.

- Pay-for-performance plans (piece rates, commissions, royalties, bonuses, profit sharing, and efficiency wages) are designed to improve worker productivity by overcoming the principal–agent problem.

14.9   Immigration and Wages

Immigration has long been controversial in Canada, and views on the subject are often tied to discrimination and income inequality. Should more or fewer people be allowed to migrate to the Canada? Do immigrants lower the wages of Canadian workers? How should the problem of illegal entrants be handled?

Number of Immigrants

legal immigrants
People who lawfully enter a country and live there.

The annual flow of **legal immigrants** (who have permission to reside in Canada) was roughly 150,000 from the 1950s to the 1980s. In the 1990s, the number of immigrants averaged more than 200,000 per year. About one-third of recent annual population growth in Canada is the result of immigration. (Global Perspective 14.2 shows the countries of origin of Canada's legal immigrants in 2001.)

Such data are imperfect, however, because they do not include **illegal immigrants**, those who arrive without permission.

illegal immigrants
People who enter a country unlawfully and live there.

Economics of Immigration

Figure 14-10 provides some insight into the economic effects of immigration. In Figure 14-10(a), D_u is the demand for labour in Canada; in Figure 14-10(b), D_m is the demand for labour in Mexico. The demand for labour is greater in Canada, presumably because the nation has more capital and more advanced technologies that enhance the productivity of labour. (Recall from Chapter 13 that the labour demand curve is based on the marginal revenue productivity of labour.) Conversely, since machinery and equipment are presumably scarce in Mexico and technology less sophisticated, labour demand there is weak. We also assume that the before-migration labour forces of Canada and Mexico are c and C, respectively, and that both countries are at full employment.

WAGE RATES AND WORLD OUTPUT

If we further assume that migration (1) has no cost, (2) occurs solely in response to wage differentials, and (3) is unimpeded by law in either country, then workers will migrate from Mexico to Canada until wage rates in the two countries are equal at W_e. At that level, CF (equals cf) workers will have migrated from Mexico to Canada. Although the Canadian wage level will fall from W_u to W_e, domestic output (the sum of the marginal revenue products of the entire workforce) will increase from $0abc$ to $0adf$. In Mexico, the wage rate will rise from W_m to W_e, but domestic output will decline there from $0ABC$ to $0ADF$. Because the gain in domestic output $cbdf$ in Canada exceeds the output loss $FDBC$ in Mexico, the world's output has increased.

www.mcgrawhill.ca/college/mcconnell

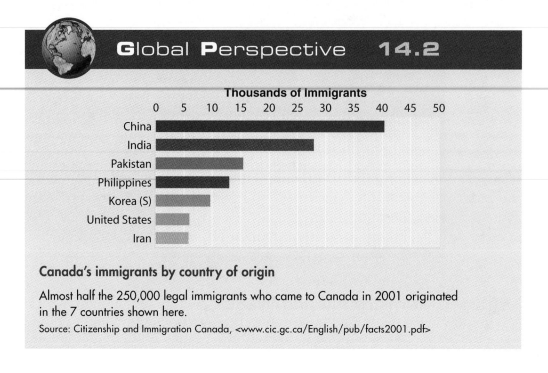

Global Perspective 14.2

Canada's immigrants by country of origin

Almost half the 250,000 legal immigrants who came to Canada in 2001 originated in the 7 countries shown here.

Source: Citizenship and Immigration Canada, <www.cic.gc.ca/English/pub/facts2001.pdf>

We can conclude that the elimination of barriers to the international flow of labour tends to increase worldwide economic efficiency. The world gains because the freedom to migrate enables people to move to countries where they can make larger contributions to world production. Migration involves an efficiency gain. It enables the world to produce a larger real output with a given amount of resources.

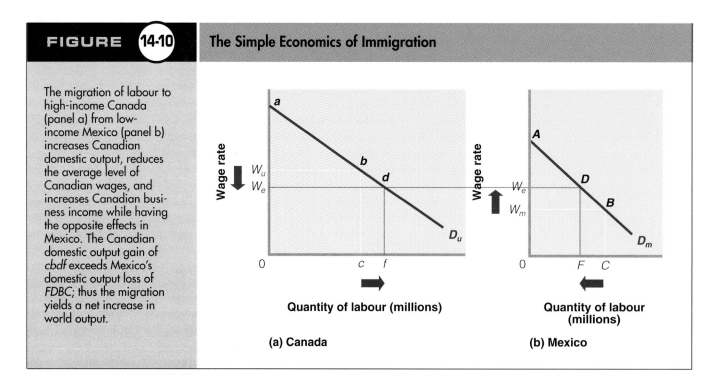

FIGURE 14-10

The Simple Economics of Immigration

The migration of labour to high-income Canada (panel a) from low-income Mexico (panel b) increases Canadian domestic output, reduces the average level of Canadian wages, and increases Canadian business income while having the opposite effects in Mexico. The Canadian domestic output gain of *cbdf* exceeds Mexico's domestic output loss of *FDBC*; thus the migration yields a net increase in world output.

(a) Canada

(b) Mexico

INCOME SHARES

Our model also suggests that the flow of immigrants will enhance business income in Canada and reduce it in Mexico. As just noted, before-immigration domestic output in Canada is represented by area $0abc$. The total wage bill is $0W_ubc$—the wage rate multiplied by the number of workers. The remaining triangular area W_uab represents business income before immigration. The same reasoning applies to Mexico, where W_mAB is before-immigration business income.

Unimpeded immigration increases business income from W_uab to W_ead in Canada and reduces it from W_mAB to W_eAD in Mexico. Canadian businesses benefit from immigration; Mexican businesses are hurt by emigration. This result is what we would expect intuitively; Canada is gaining "cheap" labour, and Mexico is losing "cheap" labour. This conclusion is consistent with the historical fact that Canadian employers have often actively recruited immigrants.

Complications and Modifications

Our model includes some simplifying assumptions and overlooks a relevant factor. We now relax some of the assumptions and introduce the omitted factor to see how our conclusions are affected.

COSTS OF MIGRATION

We assumed that international movement of workers is without personal cost, but obviously it is not. There are both the explicit, out-of-pocket costs of physically moving workers and their possessions and the implicit opportunity cost of lost income while the workers are moving and becoming established in the new country. Still more subtle costs are involved in adapting to a new culture, language, climate, and so forth. All such costs must be estimated by the potential immigrants and weighed against the expected benefits of higher wages in the new country. People who estimate that benefits exceed costs will migrate; people who see costs as exceeding benefits will stay put.

In terms of Figure 14-10, the existence of migration costs means that the flow of labour from Mexico to Canada will stop short of that needed to close the wage differential entirely. Wages will remain somewhat higher in Canada than in Mexico; the wage difference will not cause further migration and close up the wage gap because the marginal benefit of the higher wage does not cover the marginal cost of migration. Thus, the world production gain from migration will be reduced since wages will not equalize.

REMITTANCES AND BACKFLOWS

Most migration is permanent; workers who acquire skills in the receiving country tend not to return home. However, some migrants view their moves as temporary. They move to a more highly developed country, accumulate some wealth or education through hard work and frugality, and return home to establish their own enterprises. During their time in the new country, migrants frequently make sizable remittances to their families at home, which cause a redistribution of the net gain from migration between the countries involved. In Figure 14-10, remittances by Mexican workers in Canada to their relatives in Mexico would cause the gain in Canadian domestic output to be less than shown and the loss to Mexican domestic output also to be less than shown.

Actual backflows—the return of migrants to their home country—might also alter gains and losses through time. For example, if some Mexican workers who migrated to Canada acquired substantial labour market or managerial skills and then returned home, their enhanced human capital might make a substantial contribution to economic development in Mexico.

FULL EMPLOYMENT VERSUS UNEMPLOYMENT

Our model assumes full employment in the sending and receiving countries. Mexican workers presumably leave low-paying jobs to take (more or less immediately) higher-paying jobs in Canada. However, in many cases the factor that "pushes" immigrants from their homelands is not low wages but chronic unemployment and underemployment. Many developing countries are overpopulated and have surplus labour; workers are either unemployed or so grossly underemployed that their marginal revenue product is zero.

If we allow for this possibility, then Mexico actually gains, rather than loses, by having such workers emigrate. The unemployed workers are making no contribution to Mexico's domestic output and must be sustained by transfers from the rest of the labour force. The remaining Mexican labour force will be better off by the amount of the transfers after the unemployed workers have migrated to Canada. Conversely, if the Mexican immigrant workers are unable to find jobs in Canada and are sustained through transfers from employed Canadian workers, then the after-tax income of working Canadians will decline. *(Key Question 12)*

Immigration: Two Views

The traditional perception of immigration is that it consists of young, ambitious workers seeking opportunity in Canada. They are destined for success because of the courage and determination they exhibit in leaving their cultural roots to improve their lives. These energetic workers increase the supply of goods and services with their labour and simultaneously increase the demand for goods and services with their incomes and spending. In short, immigration is an engine of economic progress.

The counterview is that immigration is a socioeconomic drag on the receiving country. Immigrants compete with domestic workers for scarce jobs, pull down the average level of real wages, and burden the Canadian welfare system.

Both these views are far too simplistic. Immigration can either benefit or harm the receiving nation, depending on the number of immigrants; their education, skills, and work ethic; and the rate at which they can be absorbed into the economy without disruption. From a strictly economic perspective, nations seeking to maximize net benefits from immigration should expand immigration until its marginal benefits equal its marginal costs. The MB = MC conceptual framework explicitly recognizes that there can be too few immigrants, just as there can be too many. Moreover, the framework recognizes that from a strictly economic standpoint, not all immigrants are alike. The immigration of, say, a highly educated scientist has a different effect on the economy than does the immigration of a long-term welfare recipient.

QUICK REVIEW

- All else equal, immigration reduces wages, increases domestic output, and increases business income in the receiving nation; it has the opposite effects in the sending nation.

- Assessing the effects of immigration is complicated by such factors as unemployment, backflows and remittances, and fiscal impacts.

THE LASTword | Are Chief Executive Officers (CEOs) in Canada Overpaid?

The multimillion-dollar pay of major corporate CEOs has drawn considerable criticism.

Top executives of Canadian corporations typically receive total annual pay (salary, bonuses, and stock options) in the millions of dollars. As shown in the table below, each of the five highest-paid Canadian executives earned more than $15 million in 2002. The highest paid CEO earned over $50 million!

THE FIVE HIGHEST-PAID CANADIAN CEOS, 2002

Name	Company	Total Pay (in millions)
1. Frank Stronach	Magna International	$52.1
2. Robert Burton	Moore Corp.	20.9
3. Richard George	Suncor Energy	16.3
4. Conrad Black	Hollinger International	15.8
5. Pierre Lessard	Metro Inc.	15.3

Source: *Canadian Business*, May 12, 2003. This list is updated each year in the May issue of *Canadian Business*.

CEO pay in Canada is not only exceptionally high relative to the average pay of Canadian managers and workers, but is also the second highest CEO pay among industrialized countries. For example, in 2001 the CEO pay for firms with about $500 million in annual sales averaged $1,933,00 in the United States, $787,000 in Canada, $669,000 in the United Kingdom, $600,000 in Italy, $519,000 in France, $508,000 in Japan, and $455,000 in Germany.*

Is high CEO pay simply the outcome of labour supply and labour demand, as is the pay for star athletes and entertainers? Does it reflect marginal revenue productivity—that is, the contributions by CEOs to their company's output and revenue?

Observers who answer affirmatively point out that decisions made by the CEOs of large corporations affect the productivity of every employee in the organization. Good decisions enhance productivity throughout the organization and increase revenue; bad decisions reduce productivity and revenue. Only executives who have consistently made good business decisions attain the top positions in large corporations. Because the supply of these people is highly limited and their marginal revenue productivity is enormous, top CEOs command huge salaries and performance bonuses.

Also, some economists note that CEO pay in Canada may be like the prizes professional golfers and tennis players receive for winning tournaments. These valuable prizes are designed to promote the productivity of all those who aspire to achieve them. In corporations the top prizes go to the winners of the "contests" among managers to attain, at least eventually, the CEO positions. Thus high CEO pay does not derive solely from the CEO's direct productivity. Instead, it may exist because the high pay creates incentives that raise the productivity of scores of other corporate executives who seek to achieve the top position. In this view, high CEO pay is still based on high productivity.

Critics of existing CEO pay acknowledge that CEOs deserve substantially higher salaries than ordinary workers or typical managers, but they question pay packages that run into the millions of dollars. They reject the "tournament pay" idea on the grounds that corporations require cooperative team effort by managers and executives, not the type of high-stakes competition promoted by "winner-take-most" pay. They believe that corporations, although owned by their shareholders, are controlled by corporate boards and professional executives. Because many board members are present or past CEOs of other corporations, they often exaggerate CEO importance and, consequently, overpay their own CEOs. These overpayments are at the expense of the firm's stockholders.

In summary, defenders of CEO pay say that high pay is justified by the direct or indirect marginal revenue contribution of CEOs. Like it or not, CEO pay is market-determined pay. In contrast, critics say that multimillion-dollar CEO pay bears little relationship to marginal revenue productivity and is unfair to ordinary stockholders. It is clear from our discussion that these issues remain unsettled.

* Towers Perrin, New York, *Worldwide Total Remuneration, 2001–2002*. Amounts are in U.S. dollars.

CHAPTER SUMMARY

14.1 LABOUR, WAGES, AND EARNINGS

- The term "labour" encompasses all people who work for pay. The wage rate is the price paid per unit of time for labour. Labour earnings comprise total pay and are found by multiplying the number of hours worked by the hourly wage rate. The nominal wage rate is the amount of money received per unit of time; the real wage rate is the purchasing power of the nominal wage.

14.2 GENERAL LEVEL OF WAGES

- The long-run growth of real hourly earnings—the average real wage—roughly matches that of productivity, with both increasing over the long run.

- Global comparisons suggest that real wages in Canada are relatively high, but not the highest, internationally. High real wages in the advanced industrial countries stem largely from high labour productivity.

14.3 WAGES IN A PURELY COMPETITIVE LABOUR MARKET

- Specific wage rates depend on the structure of the particular labour market. In a competitive labour market, the equilibrium wage rate and level of employment are determined at the intersection of the labour supply curve and labour demand curve. For the individual firm, the market wage rate establishes a horizontal labour supply curve, meaning that the wage rate equals the firm's constant marginal resource cost. The firm hires workers to the point where its MRP equals this MFC.

14.4 MONOPSONY MODEL

- Under monopsony the marginal factor cost curve lies above the factor supply curve because the monopsonist must bid up the wage rate to hire extra workers and must pay that higher wage rate to all workers. The monopsonist hires fewer workers than are hired under competitive conditions, pays less-than-competitive wage rates (has lower labour costs), and thus obtains greater profit.

14.5 UNIONS AND THE LABOUR MARKET

- A union may raise competitive wage rates by (a) increasing the derived demand for labour, (b) restricting the supply of labour through exclusive unionism, or (c) directly enforcing an above-equilibrium wage rate through inclusive unionism.

- In many industries the labour market takes the form of bilateral monopoly, in which a strong union sells labour to a monopsonistic employer. The wage-rate outcome of this labour market model depends on union and employer bargaining power.

- On average, unionized workers realize wage rates 10 to 15 percent higher than comparable nonunion workers.

14.6 THE MINIMUM-WAGE CONTROVERSY

- Economists disagree about the desirability of the minimum wage as an antipoverty mechanism. While it causes unemployment for some low-income workers, it raises the incomes of those who retain their jobs.

14.7 WAGE DIFFERENTIALS

- Wage differentials are largely explainable in terms of (a) marginal revenue productivity of various groups of workers; (b) non-competing groups arising from differences in the capacities and education of different groups of workers; (c) compensating wage differences, that is, wage differences that must be paid to offset non-monetary differences in jobs; and (d) market imperfections in the form of lack of job information, geographical immobility, union and government restraints, and discrimination.

14.8 PAY FOR PERFORMANCE

- The principal–agent problem arises when workers provide less-than-expected effort. Firms may combat this by monitoring workers, by creating incentive pay schemes that link worker compensation to effort, or by paying efficiency wages.

14.9 IMMIGRATION AND WAGES

- Supply and demand analysis suggests that the movement of migrants from a poor country to a rich country (a) increases domestic output in the rich country, (b) reduces the average wage in the rich country, and (c) increases business income in the rich country. The opposite effects occur in the poor country, but the world as a whole realizes a larger total output.

- The outcomes of immigration predicted by simple supply and demand analysis become more complicated on consideration of (a) the costs of moving, (b) the possibility of remittances and backflows, (c) the level of unemployment in each country, and (d) the fiscal impact on the taxpayers of each country.

TERMS AND CONCEPTS

wage rate, p. 336
nominal wage, p. 336
real wage, p. 336
purely competitive labour market,
  p. 339
monopsony, p. 341
exclusive unionism, p. 346

occupational licensing, p. 346
inclusive unionism, p. 347
bilateral monopoly, p. 348
minimum wage, p. 349
wage differentials, p. 350
marginal revenue productivity, p. 351
non-competing groups, p. 351

investment in human capital, p. 352
compensating differences, p. 353
incentive pay plan, p. 354
legal immigrants, p. 357
illegal immigrants, p. 357

STUDY QUESTIONS

1. Explain why the general level of wages is high in Canada and other industrially advanced countries. What is the single most important factor underlying the long-run increase in average real-wage rates in Canada?

2. Why is a firm in a purely competitive labour market a *wage-taker*? What would happen if that firm decided to pay less than the going market wage rate?

3. **KEY QUESTION** Describe wage determination in a labour market in which workers are unorganized and many firms actively compete for the services of labour. Show this situation graphically, using W_1 to indicate the equilibrium wage rate and Q_1 to show the number of workers hired by the firms as a group. Show the labour supply curve of the individual firm and compare it with that of the total market. Why are there differences? In the diagram representing the firm, identify total revenue, total wage cost, and revenue available for the payment of non-labour resources.

4. **KEY QUESTION** Complete the following labour supply table for a firm hiring labour competitively:

Units of labour	Wage rate	Total labour cost (wage bill)	Marginal factor (labour) cost
0	$14	$_____	$_____
1	14	_____	_____
2	14	_____	_____
3	14	_____	_____
4	14	_____	_____
5	14	_____	_____
6	14	_____	

  a. Show graphically the labour supply and marginal factor (labour) cost curves for this firm. Explain the relationship of these curves to one another.

  b. Plot the labour demand data of question 2 in Chapter 13 on the graph used in *a* above. What are the equilibrium wage rate and level of employment? Explain.

5. Suppose the formerly competing firms in question 3 form an employers' association that hires labour as a monopsonist would. Describe verbally the effect on wage rates and employment. Adjust the graph you drew for question 3, showing the monopsonistic wage rate and employment level as W_2 and Q_2, respectively. Using this monopsony model, explain why hospital administrators sometimes complain about a shortage of nurses. How might such a shortage be corrected?

6. **KEY QUESTION** Assume a firm is a monopsonist that can hire its first worker for $6 but must increase the wage rate by $3 to attract each successive worker. Draw the firm's labour supply and marginal labour cost curves and explain their relationships to one another. On the same graph, plot the labour demand data of question 2 in Chapter 13. What are the equilibrium wage rate and level of employment? Why do these differ from your answer to question 4?

7. **KEY QUESTION** Assume a monopsonistic employer is paying a wage rate of W_m and hiring Q_m workers, as indicated in Figure 14-8. Now suppose an industrial union is formed that forces the employer to accept a wage rate of W_c. Explain verbally and graphically why in this instance the higher wage rate will be accompanied by an increase in the number of workers hired.

8. Have you ever worked for the minimum wage? If so, for how long? Would you favour increasing the minimum wage by a dollar? by two dollars? by five dollars? Explain your reasoning.

9. "Many of the lowest-paid people in society—for example, short-order cooks—also have relatively poor working conditions. Hence, the notion of compensating wage differentials is disproved." Do you agree? Explain.

10. What is meant by investment in human capital? Use this concept to explain (a) wage differentials, and (b) the long-run rise of real wage rates in Canada.

11. What is the principal–agent problem? Have you ever worked in a setting where this problem arose? If so, do

you think increased monitoring would have eliminated the problem? Why don't firms simply hire more supervisors to eliminate shirking?

12. **KEY QUESTION** Use graphical analysis to show the gains and losses resulting from the migration of workers from a low-income country to a high-income country. Explain how your conclusions are affected by (a) unemployment, (b) remittances to the home country, (c) backflows of migrants to their home country, and (d) the personal characteristics of the migrants. If the migrants are highly skilled workers, is there any justifica-

tion for the sending country to levy a "brain drain" tax on emigrants?

13. Evaluate: "If Canada deported, say, 100,000 illegal immigrants, the number of unemployed workers in Canada would decline by 100,000."

14. If a person favours the free movement of labour within Canada, is it then inconsistent to also favour restrictions on the international movement of labour? Why or why not?

15. **(The Last Word)** Do you think exceptionally high pay to CEOs is economically justified? Why or why not?

INTERNET APPLICATION QUESTION

1. Go to the McConnell-Brue-Barbiero Web site (Chapter 14) to access earnings of professional golfers. What are the annual earnings to date of the top 10 male golfers on the PGA tour? What are the earnings of the top 10

female golfers on the LPGA tour? What are the general differences in earnings between the male and female golfers? Can you explain them?

15 Chapter

Rent, Interest, and Profit

How do land prices (and land rents) get established and why do they differ? For example, a hectare of land in the middle of Toronto or Vancouver can sell for more than $50 million, while a hectare in Northern Manitoba may fetch no more than $500.

What determines interest rates and causes them to change? For instance, why were interest rates on a one-year Guaranteed Investment Certificate (GIC) 5.08 percent in Canada in March 2000, but only 3.10 percent in January 2003?

What are the sources of profits and losses? Why do profits change over time? For example, why did Molson, the brewer, turn a profit in 2001, whereas Rogers Communications incurred a loss in the same year?

In Chapter 14 we focused on wages and salaries, which account for about 75 percent of national income in Canada. In this chapter we examine the other factor payments—rent, interest, and profit—that make up the remaining 25 percent of national income. We begin by looking at rent.

15.1 Economic Rent

<www.theshortrun.com/classroom/glossary/micro/rent.html>
Economic rent

economic rent
The price paid for the use of land and other natural resources, the supply of which is fixed (perfectly inelastic).

To most people, "rent" means the money they must pay for the use of an apartment or a room. To the business executive, "rent" is a payment made for the use of a factory building, machine, or warehouse facility. Such definitions of rent can be confusing and ambiguous, however. Dormitory room rent, for example, may include other payments as well: interest on money the university borrowed to finance the dormitory, wages for maintenance services, utility payments, and so on.

Economists use rent in a much narrower sense. **Economic rent** is the price paid for the use of land and other natural resources that are completely fixed in total supply. As you will see, this fixed overall supply distinguishes rental payments from wage, interest, and profit payments.

Let's examine this idea and some of its implications through supply and demand analysis. We first assume that all land is of the same quality, meaning that each arable (tillable) hectare of land is as productive as every other hectare. We assume, too, that all land has a single use, for example, producing wheat. And we suppose that land is leased in a competitive market in which many producers are demanding land and many landowners are offering land in the market.

In Figure 15-1, curve S represents the supply of arable land available in the economy as a whole, and curve D_2 represents the demand of producers for use of that land. As with all economic resources, this demand is derived from the demand for the product being produced. The demand curve for land is downward sloping because of diminishing returns and because, for producers as a group, product price must be reduced to sell additional units of output.

Perfectly Inelastic Supply

The unique feature of our analysis is on the supply side. For all practical purposes the supply of land is perfectly inelastic (in both the short run and long run), as reflected in supply curve S. Land has

FIGURE 15-1	The Determination of Land Rent

Because the supply S of land (and other natural resources) is perfectly inelastic, demand is the sole active determinant of land rent. An increase in demand from D_2 to D_1 or a decrease in demand from D_2 to D_3 will cause a considerable change in rent: from R_2 to R_1 in the first instance and from R_2 to R_3 in the second. But the amount of land supplied will remain at L_0. If demand is very low (D_4) relative to supply, land will be a free good, commanding no rent.

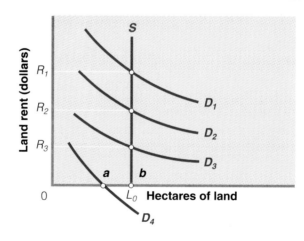

no production cost; it is a "free and non-reproducible gift of nature." The economy has only so much land, and that's that. Of course, within limits any parcel of land can be made more usable by clearing, drainage, and irrigation, but these are capital improvements and not changes in the amount of land itself.

Changes in Demand

Since the supply of land is fixed, demand is the only determinant of land rent; supply is passive. And what determines the demand for land? The factors we discussed in Chapter 13 do: the price of the product produced on the land, the productivity of land (which depends in part on the quantity and quality of the factors of production with which land is combined), and the prices of the other factors that are combined with land.

If the demand for land in Figure 15-1 increased from D_2 to D_1, land rent would rise from R_2 to R_1. If the demand for land declined from D_2 to D_3, land rent would fall from R_2 to R_3. In either case, the amount of land supplied would remain the same at quantity L_0. Changes in economic rent have no effect on the amount of land available since the supply of land cannot be augmented. If the demand for land were only D_4, land rent would be zero. Land would be a *free good*—a good for which demand is so low relative to supply that there is an excess supply of it even if the market price is zero. In Figure 15-1, we show this excess supply as distance $b - a$ at rent of zero. This essentially was the situation in the free-land era of Canadian history.

The ideas underlying Figure 15-1 help answer one of our chapter-opening questions. Land prices and rents are so high in central Toronto and Vancouver because the demand for that land is tremendous; it is capable of producing exceptionally high revenue from offices, hotel lodging, and entertainment. In contrast, the demand for isolated land in Northern Manitoba is highly limited because very little revenue can be generated from its use. (It is an entirely different matter, of course, if gold can be mined from the land!)

Land Rent: A Surplus Payment

The perfectly inelastic supply of land must be contrasted with the relatively elastic supply of capital, such as apartment buildings, machinery, and warehouses. In the long run, capital is *not* fixed in total supply. A higher price gives entrepreneurs the incentive to construct and offer larger quantities of property resources. Conversely, a decline in price induces suppliers to allow existing facilities to depreciate and not be replaced. The supply curves of these non-land factors of production are upward sloping, meaning that the prices paid to such factors have an **incentive function**. A high price provides an incentive to offer more of the factor, whereas a low price prompts factor suppliers to offer less.

Not so with land. Whether rent is $10,000, $500, $1, or $0 per hectare, the same amount of land is available to society for use in production, which is why economists consider rent a *surplus payment* not necessary to ensure that land is available to the economy as a whole.

incentive function of price
The inducement that an increase in the price of a commodity gives to sellers to make more of it available.

Productivity Differences and Rent Differences

So far we have assumed that all units of land are of the same grade. That is plainly not so. Different pieces of land vary greatly in productivity, depending on soil fertility and on such climatic factors as rainfall and temperature. Such factors explain, for example, why Southern Ontario soil is excellently suited to corn production, why the Prairies are less well suited, and why Yukon is nearly incapable of corn production. Such productivity differences are reflected in factor demand and prices. Competitive bidding by producers will establish a high rent for highly productive Southern Ontario land; less productive Prairie land will command a much lower rent; and Yukon land may command no rent at all.

Location itself may be just as important in explaining differences in land rent. Other things equal, renters will pay more for a unit of land that is strategically located with respect to materials, labour, and customers than they will for a unit of land whose location is remote from these things. For example, enormously high land prices are paid for major ski resorts in such places as Whistler, B.C., and for land in Alberta that has oil under it.

Figure 15-1, viewed from a slightly different perspective, reveals the rent differentials from quality differences in land. Assume, again, that only wheat can be produced on four grades of land, each of which is available in the fixed amount L_0. When combined with identical amounts of labour, capital, and entrepreneurial talent, the productivity or, more specifically, the marginal revenue product of each of the four grades of land is reflected in demand curves D_1, D_2, D_3, and D_4. Grade 1 land is the most productive, as shown by D_1, while grade 4 is the least productive, as shown by D_4. The resulting economic rents for grades 1, 2, and 3 land will be R_1, R_2, and R_3, respectively; the rent differential will mirror the differences in productivity of the three grades of land. Grade 4 land is so poor in quality that, given its supply S, farmers won't pay anything to use it. It will be a free good because it is not sufficiently scarce in relation to the demand for it to command a price or a rent.

Alternative Uses of Land

We have assumed that land has only one use. Actually, we know that land normally has alternative uses. A hectare of Ontario farmland may be useful not only for raising corn but also for raising oats, barley, and cattle; or it may be useful for building a house, or a highway, or as a factory site. In other words, any particular use of land involves an opportunity cost—the forgone production from the next best use of the resource. Where there are alternative uses, individual firms must pay rent to cover those opportunity costs to secure the use of land for their particular purpose. To the individual firm, rent is a cost of production, just as wages and interest are.

Recall that, as viewed by society, economic rent is not a cost. Society would have the same amount of land with or without the payment of economic rent. From society's perspective, economic rent is a surplus payment above that needed to gain the use of a resource. But individual firms do need to pay rent to attract land resources away from alternative uses. For firms, rental payments are a *cost.* **(Key Question 2)**

QUICK REVIEW

- Economic rent is the price paid for factors such as land whose supply is perfectly inelastic.

- Land rent is a surplus payment because land would be available to society even if this rent were not paid.

- Differential rents allocate land among alternative uses.

15.2   Interest: The Price of Money

Interest is the price paid for the use of money. It is the price that borrowers need to pay lenders for transferring purchasing power from the present to the future (see the Consider This box). It can be thought of as the amount of money that must be paid for the use of $1 for one year. Two points are important to this discussion.

1. ***Interest is stated as a percentage.***   Interest is paid in kind; that is, money (interest) is paid for the loan of money. For that reason, interest is stated as a percentage of the amount of money borrowed rather than as a dollar amount. By expressing interest as a percentage, we can immediately compare an interest payment of, say, $432 per year per $2880 with one of $1800 per year per $12,000. Both interest payments are 15 percent per year, which is not obvious from the actual dollar figures. This interest of 15 percent per year is referred to as a 15 percent interest rate.

2. ***Money is not a resource.***   Money is *not* a factor of production. Money is not productive; it cannot produce goods and services. However, businesses buy the use of money because it can be

Consider This

The Rate of "Interest"

Viewed from the supply side of the market for loanable funds, interest rates are the payments needed to entice individuals to sacrifice their present consumption, that is, to let someone else use their money for a period of time. The following story that was told by economist Irving Fisher (1867–1947) helps illustrate this "time-value of money."*

In the process of a massage, a masseur informed Fisher that he was a Socialist who believed that "interest is the basis of capitalism, and is robbery." Following the massage, Fisher asked, "How much do I owe you?"

The masseur replied, "Thirty dollars."

"Very well," said Fisher, "I will give you a note payable a hundred years hence. I suppose you have no objections to taking this note without any interest. At the end of that time, you, or perhaps your grandchildren, can redeem it."

"But I cannot afford to wait that long," said the masseur.

"I thought you said that interest was robbery. If interest is robbery, you ought to be willing to wait indefinitely for the money. If you are willing to wait ten years, how much would you require?"

"Well, I would have to get more than thirty dollars."

His point now made, Fisher replied, "That is interest."

---

* Irving Fisher, as quoted in Irving Norton Fisher, *My Father Irving Fisher* (New York: Comet, 1956), p. 77.

Question: Suppose you lend your close friend $100 for one year at zero interest rate and the inflation for the next year is projected at 10 percent. How much has this loan actually cost you?

used to acquire capital goods such as factories, machinery, warehouses, and so on. Such facilities clearly do contribute to production. Thus, in hiring the use of money capital, business executives are often indirectly buying the use of real capital goods.

Loanable Funds Theory of Interest

loanable funds theory of interest
The concept that the supply of and demand for loanable funds determine the equilibrium rate of interest.

In macroeconomics the interest rate is viewed through the lens of the economy's total supply of and demand for money. But since our present focus is on microeconomics, it will be useful to consider a more micro-based theory of interest here. Specifically, the **loanable funds theory of interest** explains the interest rate not in terms of the total supply of and demand for *money* but, rather, in terms of supply of and demand for *funds available for lending (and borrowing)*. As Figure 15-2 shows, the equilibrium interest rate (here, 8 percent) is the rate at which the quantities of loanable funds supplied and demanded are equal.

Let's first consider the loanable funds theory in simplified form. Specifically, assume households or consumers are the sole suppliers of loanable funds and businesses are the sole demanders. Also assume that lending occurs directly between households and businesses; there are no intermediate financial institutions.

SUPPLY OF LOANABLE FUNDS

The supply of loanable funds is represented by curve *S* in Figure 15-2. Its upward slope indicates that households will make available a larger quantity of funds at high interest rates than at low interest rates. Most people prefer to use their income to purchase pleasurable goods and services *today*, rather than to delay purchases to sometime in the *future*. For people to delay consumption and increase their saving, they must be compensated by an interest payment. The larger the amount of that payment, the greater the deferral of household consumption and thus the greater the amount of money made available for loans.

There is disagreement among economists as to how much the quantity of loanable funds made available by suppliers changes in response to changes in the interest rate. Most economists view sav-

FIGURE 15-2   The Market for Loanable Funds

The upsloping supply curve S for loanable funds reflects the idea that at higher interest rates, households will defer more of their present consumption (save more), making more funds available for lending. The downsloping demand curve D for loanable funds indicates that businesses will borrow more at lower interest rates than at higher interest rates. At the equilibrium interest rate (here, 8 percent), the quantities of loanable funds lent and borrowed are equal (here, F_0 each).

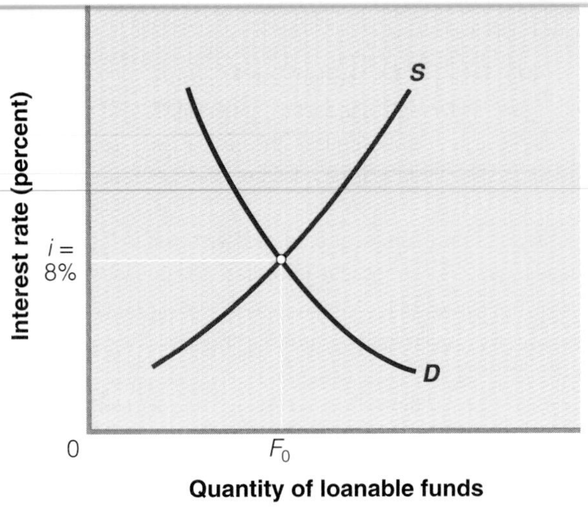

ing as being relatively insensitive to changes in the interest rate. The supply curve of loanable funds may, therefore, be more inelastic than S in Figure 15-2 implies.

DEMAND FOR LOANABLE FUNDS

Businesses borrow loanable funds primarily to add to their stocks of capital goods, such as new plants or warehouses, machinery, and equipment. Assume that a firm wants to buy a machine that will increase output and sales such that the firm's total revenue will rise by $110 for the year. Also assume that the machine costs $100 and has a useful life of just one year. Comparing the $10 earned with the $100 cost of the machine, we find that the expected rate of return on this investment is 10 percent (= $10/$100) for one year.

To determine whether the investment would be profitable and whether it should be made, the firm must compare the interest rate—the price of loanable funds—with the 10 percent expected rate of return. If funds can be borrowed at some rate less than the rate of return, say, at 8 percent, as in Figure 15-2, then the investment is profitable and should be made. But if funds can be borrowed only at an interest rate above the 10 percent rate of return, say, at 14 percent, the investment is unprofitable and should not be made.

Why is the demand for loanable funds downsloping, as in Figure 15-2? At higher interest rates fewer investment projects will be profitable and hence a smaller quantity of loanable funds will be demanded. At lower interest rates, more investment projects will be profitable and, therefore, more loanable funds will be demanded. Indeed, as we have just seen, it is profitable to purchase the $100 machine if funds can be borrowed at 8 percent but not if the firm must borrow at 14 percent.

Extending the Model

We now make this simple model more realistic in several ways.

FINANCIAL INSTITUTIONS

Households rarely lend their savings directly to businesses that are borrowing funds for investment. Instead, they place their savings in chartered banks (and other financial institutions). The banks pay

<www.mises.com/ humanaction/ chap19sec1.asp> The phenomenon of interest

interest to savers to attract loanable funds and in turn lend those funds to businesses. Businesses borrow the funds from the banks, paying them interest for the use of the money. Financial institutions profit by charging borrowers higher interest rates than the interest rates they pay savers. Both interest rates, however, are based on the supply of and demand for loanable funds.

CHANGES IN SUPPLY

Anything that causes households to be thriftier will prompt them to save more at each interest rate, shifting the supply curve rightward. For example, if interest earned on savings were to be suddenly exempted from taxation, we would expect the supply of loanable funds to increase and the equilibrium interest rate to decrease.

Conversely, a decline in thriftiness would shift the supply-of-loanable-funds curve leftward and increase the equilibrium interest rate. For example, if the government expanded social insurance to cover the costs of hospitalization, prescription drugs, and retirement living more fully, the incentive of households to save might diminish.

CHANGES IN DEMAND

On the demand side, anything that increases the rate of return on potential investments will increase the demand for loanable funds. Let's return to our earlier example, where a firm would receive additional revenue of $110 by purchasing a $100 machine and, therefore, would realize a 10 percent return on investment. What factors might increase or decrease the rate of return? Suppose a technological advance raised the productivity of the machine so that the firm's total revenue increased by $120 rather than $110. The rate of return would then be 20 percent, not 10 percent. Before the technological advance, the firm would have demanded zero loanable funds at, say, an interest rate of 14 percent, but now it will demand $100 of loanable funds at that interest rate, meaning that the demand curve for loanable funds has shifted to the right.

Similarly, an increase in consumer demand for the firm's product will increase the price of its product. So even though the productivity of the machine is unchanged, its potential revenue will rise from $110 to perhaps $120, increasing the firm's rate of return from 10 to 20 percent. Again, the firm will be willing to borrow more than previously at our presumed 8 or 14 percent interest rate, implying that the demand curve for loanable funds has shifted rightward. This shift in demand increases the equilibrium interest rate.

OTHER PARTICIPANTS

We must recognize there are other participants on both the demand and the supply sides of the loanable funds market. For example, while households are suppliers of loanable funds, many are also demanders of such funds. Households borrow to finance expensive purchases such as housing, automobiles, furniture, and household appliances. Governments also are on the demand side of the loanable funds market when they borrow to finance budgetary deficits. And businesses that have revenues in excess of their current expenditures may offer some of those revenues in the market for loanable funds. Thus, like households, businesses operate on both the supply and the demand sides of the market.

<www.bankofcanada.ca/en/>
Bank of Canada

Finally, in addition to gathering and making available the savings of households, banks and other financial institutions also increase funds through the lending process and decrease funds when loans are paid back and not lent out again. The Bank of Canada (the nation's central bank) controls the amount of this bank activity and thus influences interest rates.

This fact helps answer one of our chapter-opening questions: Why did the interest rate on a one-year Guaranteed Investment Certificate drop from 5.08 percent in March 2000 to 3.10 percent in January 2003? There are two reasons: (1) the demand for loanable funds decreased because businesses did not need to purchase more capital goods; and (2) the Bank of Canada took monetary actions that increased the supply of loanable funds. *(Key Question 5)*

TABLE 15-1	Selected Interest Rates, January 2003
Type of interest rate	**Annual percentage**
10-year Government of Canada bond	4.14
New Brunswick 2008 bond	4.55
B.C. 2008 bond	4.51
Bank of Montreal 2010 bond	5.03
5-year closed mortgage	6.70
91-day Treasury bill (Government of Canada)	2.65
Prime rate (rate charged by banks to their best corporate customers)	4.50
Visa interest rate	19.50

Range of Interest Rates

Although economists often speak in terms of a single interest rate, a number of interest rates exist. Table 15-1 lists several interest rates often referred to in the media. These rates range from 4.14 to 19.50 percent. Why are there differences?

- **Risk**   Loans to different borrowers for different purposes carry varying degrees of risk. The greater the chance that the borrower will not repay the loan, the higher the interest rate the lender will charge to compensate for that risk.

- **Maturity**   The time length of a loan or its *maturity* (when it needs to be paid back) also affects the interest rate. Other things equal, longer-term loans command higher interest rates than shorter-term loans. The long-term lender suffers the inconvenience and possible financial sacrifice of forgoing alternative uses for the money for a greater period.

- **Loan size**   If there are two loans of equal maturity and risk, the interest rate on the smaller of the two loans usually will be higher. The costs of issuing a large loan and a small loan are about the same in dollars, but the cost is greater *as a percentage* of the smaller loan.

- **Market imperfections**   Market imperfections also explain some interest rate differentials. The small-town bank that monopolizes local lending may charge high interest rates on consumer loans because households find it inconvenient and costly to shop around at banks in distant cities. The large corporation, however, can survey rival lenders to float a new bond issue and secure the lowest obtainable rate.

Pure Rate of Interest

pure rate of interest
An essentially risk-free, long-term interest rate not influenced by market imperfections.

Economists and financial specialists talk of "the" interest rate to simplify the cluster of rates (Table 15-1). When they do so, they usually have in mind the **pure rate of interest**. The pure rate is best approximated by the interest paid on long-term, virtually riskless securities such as 30-year long-term bonds of the Canadian government. This interest payment can be thought of as being made solely for the use of money over an extended time, because risk and administrative costs are negligible and the interest rate on these bonds is not distorted by market imperfections. In early 2003 the pure rate of interest in Canada was 5.42 percent.

Role of the Interest Rate

The interest rate is a critical price that affects the *level* and *composition* of investment goods production, as well as the *amount* of R&D spending.

INTEREST AND TOTAL OUTPUT

A lower equilibrium interest rate encourages businesses to borrow more for investment. As a result, total spending in the economy rises and, if the economy has unused resources, so does total output. Conversely, a higher equilibrium interest rate discourages business from borrowing for investment, reducing investment and total spending. Such a decrease in spending may be desirable if any economy is experiencing inflation.

Central banks often manipulate the interest rate to try to expand investment and output on the one hand, or to reduce investment and inflation on the other. Central banks affect the interest rate by changing the supply of money. Increases in the money supply increase the supply of loanable funds, causing the equilibrium interest rate to fall. This boosts investment spending and expands the economy. In contrast, decreases in the money supply decrease the supply of loanable funds, boosting the equilibrium interest rate. As a result, investment is constrained and so is the economy.

INTEREST AND THE ALLOCATION OF CAPITAL

Prices are rationing devices. The price of money—the interest rate—is certainly no exception. The interest rate rations the available supply of loanable funds to investment projects that have expected rates of return at or above the interest rate cost of the borrowed funds.

If, say, the computer industry expects to earn a return of 12 percent on the money it invests in physical capital and it can secure the required funds at an interest rate of 8 percent, it can borrow and expand its physical capital. If the expected rate of return on additional capital in the steel industry is only 6 percent, that industry will find it unprofitable to expand its capital stock at 8 percent interest. The interest rate allocates money, and ultimately physical capital, to those industries in which it will be most productive and, therefore, most profitable. Such an allocation of capital goods benefits society.

INTEREST AND THE LEVEL AND COMPOSITION OF R&D SPENDING

Recall from Chapter 11 that, like the investment decision, the decision on how much to spend on R&D depends on the cost of borrowing funds in relationship to the expected rate of return. Other things equal, the lower the interest rate, and thus the lower the cost of borrowing funds for R&D, the greater the amount of R&D spending that is profitable. The higher the interest rate, the less the amount of R&D spending.

Also, the interest rate allocates R&D funds to those firms and industries for which the expected rate of return on R&D is the greatest. Ace Microcircuits may have an expected rate of return of 16 percent on an R&D project, while Glow Paints has only a 2 percent expected rate of return on its R&D project. With the interest rate at 8 percent, loanable funds will flow to Ace, not to Glow. Society will benefit by having R&D spending allocated to projects that have sufficiently high expected rates of return to justify using scarce resources for R&D rather than for other purposes.

NOMINAL AND REAL INTEREST RATES

nominal interest rate
The interest rate expressed in terms of annual amounts currently charged for interest and not adjusted for inflation.

real interest rate
The interest rate expressed in dollars of constant value (adjusted for inflation); equal to the nominal interest rate less the expected rate of inflation.

This discussion of the role of the interest in investment decisions and in R&D decisions assumes that there is no inflation. If inflation exists, we must distinguish between nominal and real interest rates, just as we needed to distinguish between nominal and real wages in Chapter 14. The **nominal interest rate** is the rate of interest expressed in dollars of current value. The **real interest rate** is the rate of interest expressed in purchasing power—dollars of inflation-adjusted value. (For a comparison of nominal interest rates on bank loans in selected countries, see Global Perspective 15.1.)

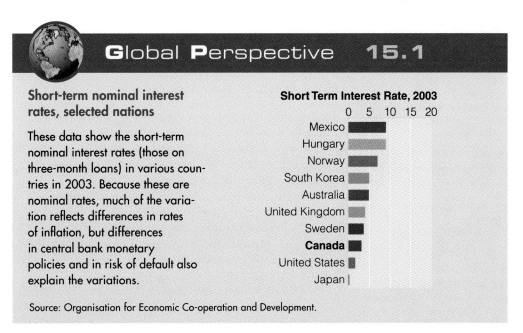

Global Perspective 15.1

Short-term nominal interest rates, selected nations

These data show the short-term nominal interest rates (those on three-month loans) in various countries in 2003. Because these are nominal rates, much of the variation reflects differences in rates of inflation, but differences in central bank monetary policies and in risk of default also explain the variations.

Short Term Interest Rate, 2003

	0	5	10	15	20
Mexico					
Hungary					
Norway					
South Korea					
Australia					
United Kingdom					
Sweden					
Canada					
United States					
Japan					

Source: Organisation for Economic Co-operation and Development.

For example, suppose the nominal interest rate and the rate of inflation are both 10 percent. If you borrow $100, you must pay back $110 a year from now. However, because of 10 percent inflation, each of these 110 dollars will be worth 10 percent less. Thus, the real value or purchasing power of your $110 at the end of the year is only $100. In inflation-adjusted dollars you are borrowing $100 and at year's end you are paying back $100. While the nominal interest rate is 10 percent, the real interest rate is zero. We determine this by subtracting the 10 percent inflation rate from the 10 percent nominal interest rate.

It is the real interest rate, not the nominal rate, that affects investment and R&D decisions. (**Key Question 7**)

QUICK REVIEW

- Interest is the price paid for the use of money.

- In the loanable funds model, the equilibrium interest rate is determined by the demand for and supply of loanable funds.

- The range of interest rates is influenced by risk, maturity, loan size, taxability, and market imperfections.

- The equilibrium interest rate affects the total level of investment and, therefore, the levels of total spending and total output; it also allocates money and real capital to specific industries and firms. Similarly, the interest rate affects the level and composition of R&D spending.

15.3   Economic Profit

explicit costs
The monetary payments a firm must make to an outsider to obtain a resource.

implicit costs
The monetary incomes a firm sacrifices when it uses a resource it owns rather than supplying the resource to the market.

economic (pure) profit
The total revenue of a firm less its economic costs (which includes both explicit costs and implicit costs); also called above normal profit.

<www.henrygeorge.org/cap.htm>
Capital, interest, and profit

normal profit
The payment made by a firm to obtain and retain entrepreneurial ability.

We have seen in previous chapters that economists define profit narrowly. To accountants, profit is what remains of a firm's total revenue after it has paid individuals and other firms for the materials, capital, and labour they have supplied to the firm. To the economist, this definition overstates profit. The reason is that the accountant's view of profit considers only **explicit costs**: payments made by the firm to outsiders. It ignores **implicit costs**: the monetary income the firm sacrifices when it uses resources that it owns, rather than supplying those resources to the market. The economist considers implicit costs to be opportunity costs and hence to be real costs that must be accounted for in determining profit. **Economic**, or **pure**, **profit** is what remains after all costs—both explicit and implicit costs, the latter including a normal profit—have been subtracted from a firm's total revenue. Economic profit may be either positive or negative (a loss).

Role of the Entrepreneur

The economist views profit as the return on a particular type of human resource: entrepreneurial ability. We know from earlier chapters that the entrepreneur (1) combines factors of production to produce a good or service, (2) makes basic, non-routine policy decisions for the firm, (3) introduces innovations in the form of new products or new production processes, and (4) bears the economic risks associated with all those functions.

Part of the entrepreneur's return is a **normal profit**, which is the minimum payment necessary to retain the entrepreneur in the current line of production. We saw in Chapter 7 that normal profit is a cost—the cost of using entrepreneurial ability for a particular purpose. We saw also that a firm's total revenue may exceed its total cost; the excess revenue above all costs is its economic profit. This *residual profit* also goes to the entrepreneur. The entrepreneur is the *residual claimant*: the factor that receives what is left after all costs are paid.

Why should there be residual profit? We next examine three possible reasons, two relating to the risks involved in business and one based on monopoly power.

Sources of Economic Profit

Let's first construct an artificial economic environment in which economic profit would be zero. Then, by noting how the real world differs from such an environment, we will see where economic profit arises.

We begin with a purely competitive, static economy. A **static economy** is one in which the basic forces such as factor supplies, technological knowledge, and consumer tastes are constant and unchanging. As a result, all cost and supply data, and all demand and revenue data, are constant.

Given the nature of these data, the economic future is perfectly certain. The outcome of any price or production policy can be accurately predicted. Furthermore, no product or production process is ever improved. Under pure competition any economic profit or loss that might have existed in an industry will disappear with the entry or exit of firms in the long run. All costs, explicit and implicit, are just covered in the long run, so no economic profit exists in our static economy.

The idea of zero economic profit in a static competitive economy suggests that profit is linked to the dynamic nature of real-world market economy and its accompanying uncertainty. Moreover, it indicates that economic profit may arise from a source other than the directing, innovating, and risk-bearing functions of the entrepreneur. That source is the presence of some amount of monopoly power.

static economy
An economy in which factor supplies, technological knowledge, and consumer tastes are constant and unchanging.

RISK AND PROFIT

In a real, dynamic economy the future is not predictable; there is uncertainty. This means that the entrepreneur must assume risks. Some or all economic profit may be a reward for assuming risks.

In linking economic profit with uncertainty and risk-bearing, we must distinguish between risks that are insurable and risks that are not. Some types of risk—fire, floods, theft, and accidents to employees—are measurable; that is, their frequency of occurrence can be estimated accurately. Firms can avoid losses due to **insurable risks** by paying an annual fee (an insurance premium) to an insurance company. The entrepreneur need not bear such risks.

However, the entrepreneur must bear the uninsurable risks of business, and those risks are a potential source of economic profit. **Uninsurable risks** are mainly the uncontrollable and unpredictable changes in the demand and supply conditions facing the firm (and hence its revenues and costs). Uninsurable risks stem from three general sources:

insurable risk
An event that would result in a loss but whose frequency of occurrence can be estimated with considerable accuracy.

uninsurable risk
An event that would result in a loss and whose occurrence is uncontrollable and unpredictable.

1. *Changes in the general economic environment*   A downturn in business (a recession), for example, can lead to greatly reduced demand, sales, and revenues, and thus to business losses. A prosperous firm may experience such losses through no fault of its own. A good example is Canada's largest telecommunications manufacturer, Nortel Networks. In the latter part of the 1990s the demand for fibre optics and wireless equipment was booming, and the company employed almost 100,000 people. By early 2003 it was experiencing losses and its workforce had shrunk to about 35,000 because of a drop in the demand for its output.

2. *Changes in the structure of the economy*   Consumer tastes, technology, factor availability, and prices change constantly in the real world, bringing changes in production costs and revenues. For example, an airline earning economic profit one year may find its profit plunging the next year as the result of a significant increase in the price of jet fuel. This is what happened to Air Canada in 2002: a combination of rising fuel prices and a slump in air travel reduced its profits. In 2003 Air Canada's revenues dropped precipitously due to the Iraq war and the outbreak in Ontario of Severe Acute Respiratory Syndrome (SARS), forcing Canada's largest airline into bankruptcy protection.

3. *Changes in government policy*   A newly instituted regulation, the removal of a tariff, or a change in a national policy may significantly alter the cost and revenue data of the affected industry and firms. An example is the electrical privatization fiasco in Ontario at the end of 2002. The provincial government first said it would privatize the electricity delivery market, and many firms sprung up to sign up customers. In the face of public controversy, the Ontario

government abruptly capped electricity rates, effectively ending competition. This sudden about-face by the provincial government put many of the new electricity supply firms in a difficult situation that may lead to the bankruptcy of some of them.

~~Regardless of how such revenue and cost changes come about, they are risks that the firm and~~ entrepreneur must take to stay in business. *Some or all the economic profit in a real, dynamic economy may be compensation for taking risks.*

INNOVATIONS AND PROFIT

One dynamic feature of a market economy, innovation, occurs at the initiative of the entrepreneur.

Such uncertainties are beyond the control of the individual firm or industry and thus are external to it. One dynamic feature of a market economy, however—innovation—occurs at the initiative of the entrepreneur. Business firms deliberately introduce new products and new methods of production to affect their costs and revenues favourably. The entrepreneur intentionally undertakes to upset existing cost and revenue data in a way that promises to be profitable.

Again, uncertainty enters the picture. Despite exhaustive market surveys, new products or modifications of existing products may be economic failures. Similarly, of the many new novels, textbooks, movies, and music CDs that appear every year, only a handful garner large profits. Nor is it certain whether new production machinery will actually yield projected cost economies. Thus, innovations undertaken by entrepreneurs entail uncertainty and the possibility of losses, not just the potential for increased profit. *Some of the economic profit in an innovative economy may be compensation for dealing with the uncertainty of innovation.*

MONOPOLY AND PROFIT

So far, we have linked economic profit with the uncertainties surrounding (1) the dynamic environment to which enterprises are exposed, and (2) the dynamic business processes they initiate themselves. *The existence of monopoly power is a final source of economic profit.* Because a monopolist can restrict output and deter entry, it may persistently enjoy above-competitive prices and economic profit if demand is strong relative to cost. *(Key Question 8)*

Functions of Profit

Economic profit is the main energizer of the market economy. It influences both the level of economic output and the allocation of resources among alternative uses.

PROFIT AND TOTAL OUTPUT

The expectation of economic profit motivates firms to innovate. Innovation stimulates new investment, increasing total output and employment.

PROFIT AND RESOURCE ALLOCATION

Profit also helps to allocate resources among alternative lines of production. Entrepreneurs seek profit and avoid losses. Economic profit in an industry is a signal that society wants that particular industry to expand. It attracts factors of production from industries that are not profitable. But the rewards of profit are more than an inducement for an industry to expand; they also attract the financing needed for expansion. In contrast, continuing losses penalize firms or industries that fail to adjust their productive efforts to match wants. Such losses signal society's desire for the afflicted industries to contract.

Profits and losses do not, however, result in an allocation of resources that is perfectly attuned to consumer preferences. The presence of monopoly, for example, impedes the movement of firms and resources from industry to industry in response to economic profit.

QUICK REVIEW

- Pure or economic profit is what remains after all explicit and implicit costs (including a normal profit) are subtracted from a firm's total revenue.

- Economic profit has three sources: the bearing of uninsurable risk, the uncer-

tainty of innovation, and monopoly power.

- Profit and profit expectations affect the levels of investment, total spending, and domestic output; profit and loss also allocate resources among alternative uses.

15.4 Income Shares

Our discussion in this and in the preceding chapter would not be complete without a brief re-examination of how Canadian national income is distributed among wages, rent, interest, and profit.

Let's look at Table 15-2. Although the income categories shown in the table do not neatly fit the economic definitions of wages, rent, interest, and profits, they do provide insight about income shares

TABLE 15-2	Relative Shares of Domestic Income, 1926–2002 (Selected Years or Period Averages of Shares for Individual Years)						
Year or period	Wages, salaries, and supplementary labour income	Corporation profits before taxes	Interest and miscellaneous investment income	Accrued net income of farmers from farm production	Net income of non-farm unincorporated business including rent	Inventory valuation adjustment	Net domestic income at basic prices
1926	55.3%	11.4%	3.2%	14.1%	14.9%	1.1%	100%
1929	60.0	12.9	3.7	8.0	15.7	−0.3	100
1937	62.6	15.6	3.1	6.9	13.9	−2.1	100
1941	61.9	18.1	2.8	7.0	12.6	−2.4	100
1945	63.4	13.1	2.7	9.2	12.0	−0.4	100
1951	60.7	17.9	2.5	10.5	12.0	−3.6	100
1957–60	67.0	13.7	3.9	3.6	12.0	−0.2	100
1961–65	67.7	14.2	4.3	3.6	10.6	−0.3	100
1966–70	70.9	13.5	4.7	2.7	8.8	−0.6	100
1971	73.0	12.2	5.5	2.0	8.2	−0.9	100
1973	70.6	16.0	5.7	3.0	7.2	−2.5	100
1975	71.2	14.8	7.1	2.9	6.0	−2.0	100
1979	69.3	16.4	10.7	1.7	5.4	−3.5	100
1982	72.7	9.2	12.2	1.2	5.8	−1.1	100
1990	72.6	8.7	11.1	0.6	7.0	−0.0	100
1994	73.5	10.0	10.1	0.4	6.9	−0.9	100
1999	75.2	10.5	5.0	0.2	6.2	2.9	100
2002	72.5	13.9	5.9	0.2	7.9	−0.2	100

Source: Adapted from Statistics Canada Web site, www.statcan.ca/english/pgdb/econ03.htm
Visit www.mcgrawhill.ca/college/mcconnell for data updates.

Σ-STAT

in Canada. Note the dominant role of labour resource and thus labour income in the Canadian economy. Even with labour income defined narrowly as "wages and salaries," labour receives about 73 percent of national income. But some economists contend that the income of proprietors is largely composed of implicit wages and salaries and should be added to the "wages and salaries" category to determine labour income. When we use this broad definition, labour's share rises to nearly 80 percent of national income, a percentage that has been remarkably stable in Canada since 1926. That leaves about 20 percent for capitalists in the form of rent, interest, and profit. Ironically, capitalist income is a relatively small share of the Canadian economy, which we call a capitalist system.

THE LASTword   Determining the Price of Credit

A variety of lending practices may cause the effective interest rate to be quite different from what it appears to be.

Borrowing and lending—receiving and granting credit—are a way of life. Individuals receive credit when they negotiate a mortgage loan and when they use their credit cards. Individuals make loans when they open a savings account in a chartered bank or buy a bond.

It is sometimes difficult to determine exactly how much interest we pay and receive when we borrow and lend. Let's suppose that you borrow $10,000, which you agree to repay with $1000 of interest at the end of one year. In this instance, the interest rate is 10 percent per year. To determine the interest rate i, we compare the interest paid with the amount borrowed:

$$i = \frac{\$1000}{\$10,000} = 10\%$$

But in some cases a lender—say, a bank—will discount the interest payment at the time the loan is made. Thus, instead of giving the borrower $10,000, the bank discounts the $1000 interest payment in advance, giving the borrower only $9000. This increases the interest rate:

$$i = \frac{\$1000}{\$9000} = 11\%$$

While the absolute amount of interest paid is the same, in this second case the borrower has only $9000 available for the year.

An even more subtle point is that, to simplify their calculations, some financial institutions assume a 360-day year (twelve 30-day months), which means the borrower has the use of the lender's funds for five days less than the normal year. This use of a short year also increases the actual interest rate paid by the borrower.

The interest rate paid may change dramatically if a loan is repaid in installments. Suppose a bank lends you $10,000 and charges interest in the amount of $1000 to be paid at the end of the year. But the loan contract requires that you repay the $10,000 loan in 12 equal monthly installments. In effect, then, the average amount of the loan outstanding during the year is only $5000. Therefore:

$$i = \frac{\$1000}{\$5000} = 20\%$$

Here interest is paid on the total amount of the loan ($10,000) rather than on the outstanding balance (which averages $5000 for the year), making for a much higher interest rate.

Another factor that influences the effective interest rate is whether interest is compounded. Suppose you deposit $10,000 in a savings account that pays a 10 percent interest rate compounded semiannually. In other words, interest is paid on your loan to the bank twice a year. At the end of the first six months, $500 of interest (10 percent of $10,000 for half a year) is added to your account. At the end of the year, interest is calculated on $10,500 so that the second interest payment is $525 (10 percent of $10,500 for half a year). Thus:

$$i = \frac{\$1025}{\$10,000} = 10.25\%$$

This means that a chartered bank advertising a 10 percent interest rate compounded semiannually is actually paying more interest to its customers than a competitor paying a simple (non-compounded) interest rate of 10.20 percent.

"Let the borrower (or depositor) beware" remains a fitting motto in the world of credit.

CHAPTER SUMMARY

15.1 ECONOMIC RENT

- Economic rent is the price paid for the use of land and other natural resources whose total supplies are fixed.

- Rent is a surplus payment that is socially unnecessary since land would be available to the economy even without rental payments.

- Differences in land rent result from differences in the fertility and climatic features of the land and difference in location.

- Although land rent is a surplus payment rather than a cost to the economy as a whole, to individual firms and industries rental payments are correctly regarded as costs. These payments must be made to gain the use of land, which has alternative uses.

15.2 INTEREST: THE PRICE OF MONEY

- Interest is the price paid for the use of money. In the loanable funds theory, the equilibrium interest rate is determined by the demand for and supply of loanable funds. Other things equal, an increase in the supply of loanable funds reduces the equilibrium interest rate, whereas a decrease in supply increases it; increases in the demand for loanable funds raise the equilibrium interest rate, whereas decreases in demand reduce it.

- Interest rates vary in size because loans differ as to risk, maturity, amount, and taxability; market imperfections cause additional variations. The pure rate of interest is the interest rate on long-term, virtually riskless, Government of Canada long-term bonds.

- The equilibrium interest rate influences the level of investment and helps ration financial and physical capital to specific firms and industries. Similarly, this rate influences the size and composition of R&D spending. The *real interest rate,* not the nominal rate, is critical to investment and R&D decisions.

15.3 ECONOMIC PROFIT

- Economic, or pure, profit is the difference between a firm's total revenue and the sum of its explicit and implicit costs, the latter including a normal profit. Profit accrues to entrepreneurs for assuming the uninsurable risks associated with organizing and directing economic resources and for innovating. Profit also results from monopoly power.

- Profit expectations influence innovation and investment activities and, therefore, the economy's levels of employment and economic growth. The basic function of profits and losses, however, is to allocate resources in accord with consumers' preferences.

15.4 INCOME SHARES

- The largest share of national income—about 70 percent—goes to labour, a share narrowly defined as "wages and salaries." When labour's share is more broadly defined to include "proprietors' income," it rises to about 80 percent of national income, leaving about 20 percent as capital's share.

TERMS AND CONCEPTS

economic rent, p. 366
incentive function of price, p. 367
loanable funds theory of interest,
  p. 369
pure rate of interest, p. 372

nominal interest rate, p. 373
real interest rate, p. 373
explicit costs, p. 374
implicit costs, p. 374
economic (pure) profit, p. 374

normal profit, p. 374
static economy, p. 375
insurable risks, p. 375
uninsurable risks, p. 375

STUDY QUESTIONS

1. How does the economist's use of the term "rent" differ from everyday usage? Explain: "Though rent need not be paid by society to make land available, rental payments are very useful in guiding land into the most productive uses."

2. **KEY QUESTION**   Explain why economic rent is a surplus payment when viewed by the economy as a whole but as a cost of production from the standpoint of individual firms and industries. Explain: "Rent performs no 'incentive function' in the economy."

3. In the 1980s land prices in Japan surged upward in a "speculative bubble." Land prices then fell for 11 straight years between 1990 and 2001. What can we safely assume happened to *land rent* in Japan over those 11 years? Use graphical analysis to illustrate your answer.

4. If money is not an economic resource, why is interest paid and received for its use? What considerations account for the fact that interest rates differ greatly on various types of loans? Use those considerations to

explain the relative sizes of the interest rates on the following:

a. A 10-year $1000 government bond

b. A $20 pawnshop loan

c. A 30-year mortgage loan on a $145,000 house

d. A 24-month $12,000 bank loan to finance the purchase of an automobile

e. A 60-day $100 loan from a personal finance company

5. **KEY QUESTION**   Why is the supply of loanable funds upsloping? Why is the demand for loanable funds downsloping? Explain the equilibrium interest rate. List some factors that might cause it to change.

6. What are the major economic functions of the interest rate? How might the fact that many businesses finance their investment activities internally affect the efficiency with which the interest rate performs its functions?

7. **KEY QUESTION**   Distinguish between nominal and real interest rates. Which is more relevant in making investment and R&D decisions? If the nominal interest rate is 12 percent and the inflation rate is 8 percent, what is the real rate of interest?

8. **KEY QUESTION**   How do the concepts of accounting profit and economic profit differ? Why is economic profit smaller than accounting profit? What are the three basic sources of economic profit? Classify each of the following according to those sources:

a. A firm's profit from developing and patenting a new medication that greatly reduces cholesterol and thus diminishes the likelihood of heart disease and stroke

b. A restaurant's profit that results from construction of a new highway past its door

c. The profit received by a firm due to an unanticipated change in consumer tastes

9. Why is the distinction between insurable and uninsurable risks significant for the theory of profit? Carefully evaluate: "All economic profit can be traced to either uncertainty or the desire to avoid it." What are the major functions of economic profit?

10. Explain the absence of economic profit in a purely competitive, static economy. Realizing that the major function of profit is to allocate resources according to consumer preferences, describe the allocation of resources in such an economy.

11. What is the rent, interest, and profit share of national income if proprietors' income is included within the labour (wage) share?

12. **(The Last Word)** Assume that you borrow $5000 and pay back the $5000 plus $250 in interest at the end of the year. Assuming no inflation, what is the real interest rate? What would the interest rate be if the $250 of interest had been discounted at the time the loan was made? What would the interest rate be if you were required to repay the loan in 12 equal monthly installments?

INTERNET APPLICATION QUESTION

1. The real interest rate is the nominal rate less the rate of inflation. Assume the Consumer Price Index (CPI) is a proxy for the inflation rate and one-year Treasury Bill rates represent the nominal interest rate. Find the current CPI at the McConnell-Brue-Barbiero Web site (Chapter 15), and then subtract it from the current one-year Treasury Bill rate. Repeat the process for the one-month Treasury Bills and the CPI rate of change for the past one month. Is there a difference between the 1-month and the 12-month real interest rates? If so, why is there a difference?

16

Chapter

Income Inequality, Poverty, and Discrimination

Evidence that suggests wide income disparity in Canada is easy to find. In 2002 the annual paycheque of Gerald Schwartz, the chief executive officer (CEO) of Onex Corporation totalled more than $49 million; the CEO of The Bank of Nova Scotia received more than $20 million; and the CEO of Alcan was paid more than $15 million. In contrast, the salary of the prime minister of Canada was $200,000 that year, and the typical schoolteacher earned $56,000. A full-time minimum-wage worker at a fast-food restaurant made about $12,000.

Average family income in Canada is among the highest in the world.

In 2000 about 4.4 million Canadians—or 14.7 percent of the population—lived in poverty. The richest one-fifth of the population received 40 percent of total income, while the poorest one-fifth received only 5 percent.

What are the sources of income inequality? Is income inequality rising or falling? Is Canada making progress against poverty? What are the major income maintenance programs in Canada? These are some of the questions that we will answer in the first part of this chapter. In the second part of the chapter we take a closer look at discrimination, which may be a contributing factor to the low income of some visible minorities, women, and other groups in Canadian society.

16.1   Facts about Income Inequality

Average family income in Canada is among the highest in the world; in 2000, it was $61,634 per family. But that average tells us nothing about income inequality. To learn about that, we must examine how income is distributed around the average.

Distribution of Personal Income by Income Category

income inequality
The unequal distribution of an economy's total income among households or families.

One way to measure **income inequality** is to look at the percentages of families in a series of income categories. Table 16-1 shows that 20 percent of all families had annual before-tax incomes of less than $20,000 in 2000, while 35.1 percent had annual incomes of $60,000 or more. The data in the table suggest considerable inequality of family income in Canada.

Distribution of Personal Income by Quintiles (Fifths)

Lorenz curve
A curve showing the distribution of income in an economy.

A second way to measure income inequality is to divide the total number of income receivers into five numerically equal groups, or *quintiles,* and examine the percentage of total personal (before-tax) income received by each quintile. We do this in Table 16-2.

TABLE 16-1	The Distribution of Total Income by Families, 2000
PANEL (A)	
Personal income category	**Percentage of all families in this category**
under $10,000	6.2
$10,001 to $19,999	13.8
$20,000 to $29,999	13.5
$30,000 to $49,999	22.3
$50,000 to $59,999	9.2
$60,000 and over	35.1
	100.0
PANEL (B)	
Average 2000 income for families	$61,634
Median 2000 income for families	$57,960
Number of families in Canada	8,427,000

Source: Statistics Canada, *Income Trends in Canada. 2000* (Ottawa, 2001).

The Lorenz Curve

We can display quintile distribution of personal income through a **Lorenz curve**. In Figure 16-1, we plot the cumulative percentage of families on the horizontal axis and the percentage of income they obtain on the vertical axis. The diagonal line 0*e* represents a *perfectly equal distribution of income* because each point along that line indicates that a particular percentage of families receive the same percentage of income. In other words, points representing 20 percent of all families receiving 20 percent of total income, 40 percent receiving 40 percent, 60 percent receiving 60 percent, and so on, all lie on the diagonal line.

By plotting the quintile data from Table 16-2, we obtain the Lorenz curve for 2000. Observe from point *a* that the bottom 20 percent of all families received 5.0 percent of the income; the bottom 40 percent received 16.1 percent (= 5.0 + 11.1), as shown by point *b*; and so forth. The blue area between the diagonal line and the Lorenz curve is determined by the extent that the Lorenz curve sags away from the diagonal and indicates the degree of income inequality. If the actual income distribution were perfectly equal, the Lorenz curve and the diagonal would coincide and the blue area would disappear.

At the opposite extreme is a situation of complete inequality, where all families but one have zero income. In that case the

TABLE 16-2	Percentage of Total Before-tax and After-tax Income Received by Each Quintile Group			
	BEFORE TAX			**AFTER TAX**
Quintile	1951	1965	2000	2000
Lowest 20%	4.4	4.4	4.1	5.0
Second 20%	11.2	11.8	9.8	11.1
Third 20%	18.3	18.2	16.0	16.8
Fourth 20%	23.3	24.5	24.5	24.3
Highest 20%	42.8	41.1	45.6	42.8
	100.0	100.0	100.0	100.0

Source: Statistics Canada, *Income Trends in Canada, 1980–2000.*

Lorenz curve would coincide with the horizontal axis from 0 to point f (at 0 percent of income) and then would move immediately up from f to point e along the vertical axis (indicating that a single family has 100 percent of the total income). The entire area below the diagonal line (area $0ef$) would indicate this extreme degree of inequality. To generalize, the farther the Lorenz curve sags away from the diagonal, the greater is the degree of income inequality.

The visual measurement of income inequality described by the Lorenz curve can easily be transformed into the **Gini ratio**—a numerical measure of the overall dispersion of income.

Gini ratio
A numerical measure of the overall dispersion of income.

$$\text{Gini ratio} = \frac{\text{area between Lorenz curve and diagonal}}{\text{total area below the diagonal}} = \frac{\text{A (light blue area)}}{\text{A + B (light blue + light green)}}$$

For the distribution of family after-tax market income shown in Figure 16.1, the Gini ratio is 0.424. As the area between the Lorenz curve and the diagonal gets larger, the Gini ratio rises to reflect greater inequality. (Test your understanding of this idea by confirming that the Gini coefficient for complete income equality is zero and for complete inequality is 1.)

Lorenz curves and Gini ratios can be used to contrast the income distributions of different subgroups, such as groups distinguished by age or marital status. For example, in 2000 the Gini ratio of lone-parent family income was 0.498; for elderly males, 0.685; and for non-elderly white females, 0.512. *(Key Question 2)*

FIGURE 16-1   **The Lorenz Curve**

The Lorenz curve is a graph of the percentage of total after-tax income obtained by cumulative percentages of families. The area between the diagonal (the line of perfect equality) and the Lorenz curve represents the degree of inequality in the Canadian distribution of total income. This inequality is measured numerically by the Gini ratio—area A (shown in light blue) divided by area A + B (the light blue area plus the light green area).

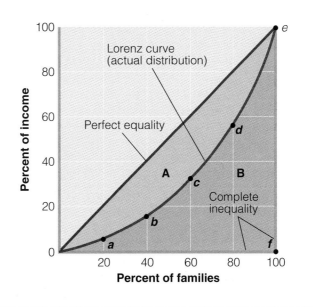

Income Mobility: The Time Dimension

The income data that we have been using so far have a major limitation: The income accounting period of one year is too short to be very meaningful. Because the Statistics Canada data portray the distribution of income in only a single year, they may conceal a more equal distribution over a few years, a decade, or even a lifetime. If Dushan earns $1000 in year one and $100,000 in year two, while Jamel earns $100,000 in year one and only $1000 in year two, do we have income inequality? The answer depends on the period of measurement. Annual data would reveal great income inequality, but there would be complete equality over the two-year period.

This point is important because evidence suggests considerable variation in the distribution of income over time. For most income receivers, income starts at a relatively low level, reaches a peak during middle age, and then declines. It follows that if all people received exactly the same stream of income over their lifetimes, considerable income inequality would still exist in any specific year because of age differences. In any single year, the young and the old would receive low incomes, while the middle-aged receive high incomes.

If we change from a snapshot view of income distribution in a single year to a view portraying incomes over much longer periods, we find considerable movement of income receivers among income classes. This movement correctly suggests that income is more equally distributed over a 5-year, 10-year, or 20-year period than in a single year. Such movement of individuals or families from one income quintile to another over time is called **income mobility**.

In short, there is significant individual and family income mobility over time; for many people, "low income" and "high income" are not permanent conditions. The longer the period considered, the more equal the distribution of income becomes.

income mobility
The movement of individuals and families from one income quintile to another over time.

Effect of Government Redistribution

The income data in Tables 16-1 and 16-2 include wages, salaries, dividends, and interest. They also include all cash transfer payments, such as employment insurance benefits and welfare assistance to needy families. The data are before tax and therefore do not take into account the effects of personal income and Canada Pension Plan contributions that are levied directly on income receivers. Nor do they include in-kind or **non-cash transfers**, which provide specific goods or services rather than cash. Non-cash transfers include such things as housing subsidies, dental care, and drug benefit plans. Such transfers are "incomelike," since they enable recipients to purchase goods and services.

non-cash transfer
Government transfer payments in the form of goods and services rather than money.

One economic function of government is to redistribute income, if society so desires. Table 16-2 reveals that government redistributes income from higher- to lower-income households through taxes and transfers. This point is made by the fact that the Canadian distribution of household income before taxes and transfers are taken into account is less equal than the distribution after taxes and transfers. Without government redistribution, the lowest 20 percent of households in 2000 would have received only 4.1 percent of total income. With redistribution, they received 5.0 percent, 22 percent more.

Which contributes more to redistribution, government taxes or government transfers? The answer is transfers. Roughly 80 percent of the reduction in income inequality is attributable to transfer payments, which account for more than 75 percent of the income of the lowest quintile. Together with growth of job opportunities, transfer payments have been the most important means of alleviating poverty in Canada.

<www.jewishworldreview.com/
cols/williams071699.asp>
The Vanishing Poor

16.2   Causes of Income Inequality

There are several causes of income inequality in Canada. In general, the market system is an impersonal mechanism that embodies no conscience concerning what is an equitable or just distribution of income. It permits a high degree of income inequality because it rewards individuals based on the contribution that their factors of production make to producing society's output.

The factors that contribute to income inequality follow.

Ability

People have different mental, physical, and aesthetic talents. Some have inherited the exceptional mental qualities that are essential to such high-paying occupations as medicine, corporate leadership, and law. Others are blessed with the physical capacity and coordination to become highly paid professional athletes. A few have the talent to become great artists or musicians, or have the beauty to become top fashion models. Others have very weak mental endowments and may work in low-paying occupations or may not be able to earn any income at all. The intelligence and skills of most people fall somewhere in-between.

Education and Training

Ability alone rarely produces high income; people must develop and refine their capabilities through education and training. Individuals differ significantly in the amount of education and training they obtain and thus in their capacity to earn income. Such differences may be a matter of choice: Chin enters the labour force after graduating from high school, while Rodriguez takes a job only after earning a college or university degree. Other differences may be involuntary: Chin and her parents may simply be unable to finance a postsecondary education.

People also receive varying degrees of on-the-job training, which contributes to income inequality. Some workers learn valuable new skills each year on the job and, therefore, experience significant income growth over time; others receive little or no on-the-job training and earn no more at age 50 than they did at age 30. Moreover, firms tend to select for advanced on-the-job training those workers who have the highest level of formal education. That added training magnifies the education-based income differences between less-educated and better-educated individuals.

Discrimination

Discrimination in education, hiring, training, and promotion undoubtedly contributes to income inequality in Canada, although the degree is uncertain. If discrimination restricts ethnic minorities or women to low-paying occupations, the supply of labour will be great relative to demand in those occupations. Wages and incomes will remain low. Conversely, discrimination reduces the competition that whites or men face in the occupations in which they are predominant. Thus, labour supply is artificially limited relative to demand in those occupations, with the result that wages and incomes are high. More will be said about discrimination later in this chapter.

Preferences and Risks

Incomes also differ because of differences in preferences for market work relative to leisure, market work relative to work in the household, and types of market work. People who choose to stay home with children, work part time, or retire early usually have less income than people who make other choices. For example, those who are willing to take arduous, unpleasant jobs, such as underground mining or heavy construction, to work long hours with great intensity, or to moonlight will tend to earn more.

Individuals also differ in their willingness to assume risk. We refer here not only to the race car driver or the professional boxer but also to the entrepreneur. Although many entrepreneurs fail, many of those who develop successful new products or services realize very substantial incomes. That contributes to income inequality.

Unequal Distribution of Wealth

Income is a *flow*; it represents a stream of wage and salary earnings, along with rent, interest, and profits, as depicted in Chapter 2's circular flow diagram. In contrast, wealth is a *stock*, reflecting at a particular moment the financial and real assets an individual has accumulated over time. A retired person may have very little income and yet own a home, mutual fund shares, and a pension plan that add up to considerable wealth. A new university graduate may be earning a substantial income as an accountant, middle manager, or engineer but have yet to accumulate significant wealth.

The ownership of wealth in Canada is more unequal than the distribution of income. This inequality of wealth leads to inequality in rent, interest, and dividends, which in turn contributes to income inequality. Those who own more machinery, real estate, farmland, stocks and bonds, and savings accounts obviously receive greater income from that ownership than people with less or no such wealth.

Market Power

The ability to "rig the market" on your own behalf also contributes to income inequality. For example, in *factor* markets certain unions and professional groups have adopted policies that limit the supply of their services, thereby boosting the incomes of those on the inside. Also, legislation that requires occupational licensing for, say, doctors, dentists, and lawyers can bestow market power that favours the licensed groups. In *product* markets, rigging the market means gaining or enhancing monopoly power, which results in greater profit and thus greater income to the firms' owners.

Luck, Connections, and Misfortune

Other forces also play a role in producing income inequality. Luck and being in the right place at the right time have helped individuals to stumble into fortunes. Discovering oil on a ranch, owning land along a proposed highway interchange, and hiring the right press agent have accounted for some high incomes. Personal contacts and political connections are other potential routes to attaining high income.

In contrast, economic misfortunes such as prolonged illness, serious accident, death of the family breadwinner, or unemployment may plunge a family into the low range of income. The burden of such misfortune is borne very unevenly by the population and thus contributes to income inequality. *(Key Question 4)*

Trends in Income Inequality

Over a period of years economic growth has raised incomes in Canada: In *absolute* dollar amounts, the entire distribution of income has been moving upward. But incomes may move up in *absolute* terms while leaving the *relative* distribution of income less equal, or unchanged. Table 16-2 shows the relative distribution of personal income over time. Recall that personal income is before tax and includes cash transfers but not non-cash transfers. As you can see, the distribution of income in Canada has remained remarkably constant over the past 50 years.

Global Perspective 16.1 compares inequality in Canada (here by individuals, not by families) with that in several other nations. Income inequality tends to be highest in developing nations.

CAUSES OF GROWING INEQUALITY

Economists suggest several major explanations for the rise in income inequality over the past three decades.

Greater Demand for Highly Skilled Workers   Perhaps the most significant contributor to the growing income inequality has been an increasing demand by many firms for workers who are highly skilled and well educated. Several industries requiring highly skilled workers have either recently emerged or expanded greatly, such as the computer software, business consulting, biotechnology, health care, and Internet industries. Because highly skilled workers remain relatively scarce, their wages have been bid up. Consequently, the wage differences between them and less-skilled workers have increased.

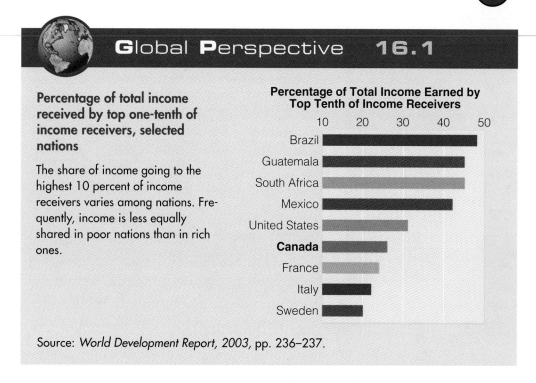

Global Perspective   16.1

Percentage of total income received by top one-tenth of income receivers, selected nations

The share of income going to the highest 10 percent of income receivers varies among nations. Frequently, income is less equally shared in poor nations than in rich ones.

Percentage of Total Income Earned by Top Tenth of Income Receivers

Brazil
Guatemala
South Africa
Mexico
United States
Canada
France
Italy
Sweden

Source: *World Development Report, 2003,* pp. 236–237.

The rising demand for skill has also evidenced itself in rapidly rising pay for CEOs (chief executive officers), sizable increases in income from stock options, substantial increases in incomes of professional athletes and entertainers, and huge fortunes for successful entrepreneurs. This growth of "superstar" pay has also contributed to rising income inequality.

Demographic Changes   The entrance of large numbers of less-experienced and less-skilled baby boomers into the labour force during the 1970s and 1980s may have contributed to greater income inequality in those two decades. Because younger workers tend to earn less income than older workers, their growing numbers contributed to income inequality. There has also been a growing tendency for men and women with high earnings potential to marry each other, thus increasing family income among the highest-income quintiles. Finally, the number of families headed by single or divorced women has increased greatly. That trend has increased income inequality because such families lack a second major wage earner, and also because the poverty rate for female-headed households is very high.

International Trade, Immigration, and Decline in Unionism   Other factors are likely at work. Stronger international competition from imports has reduced the demand for and employment of less-skilled (but highly paid) workers in such industries as the automobile and steel industries. The decline in such jobs has reduced the average wage for less-skilled workers. It also has swelled the ranks of workers in already low-paying industries, placing further downward pressure on wages there. Similarly, the transfer of jobs to lower-wage workers in developing countries exerts downward wage pressure on less-skilled workers in Canada. Finally, the decline in unionism in Canada undoubtedly contributes to wage inequality, since unions tend to equalize pay within firms and industries.

Two cautions are in order: First, when we note growing income inequality, we are not saying that the rich are getting richer and the poor are getting poorer in terms of absolute income. Both the rich and the poor are experiencing rises in real income. Rather, what has happened is that, while incomes have risen in all quintiles, income growth was fastest in the top quintile. Second, increased income inequality is not solely a Canadian phenomenon. The recent move toward greater inequality has also occurred in several other industrially advanced nations.

QUICK REVIEW

- Data reveal considerable income inequality in Canada; in 2000 the richest fifth of all families received 42.8 percent of after-tax income, and the poorest fifth received 5.0 percent.

- The Lorenz curve depicts income inequality graphically by comparing percentages of total families and percentages of total income. The Gini ratio is a measure of the overall dispersion of income and is found by dividing the area between the diagonal and the Lorenz curve by the total area below the diagonal.

- The distribution of income is less unequal over longer periods.

- Government taxes and transfers significantly reduce income inequality by redistributing income from higher-income groups to lower-income groups; the bulk of this redistribution results from transfer payments.

- Differences in ability, education and training, tastes for market work versus non-market activities, property ownership, and market power—along with discrimination and luck—help explain income inequality.

16.3   Equality versus Efficiency

The main policy issue concerning income inequality is how much is necessary and justified. While no general agreement exists on the justifiable amount, we can gain insight by exploring the cases for and against greater inequality.

The Case for Equality: Maximizing Total Utility

The basic argument for an equal distribution of income is that income equality maximizes the total consumer satisfaction (utility) from any particular level of output and income. The rationale for this argument is shown in Figure 16-2, in which we assume that the money incomes of two individuals, Anderson and Brooks, are subject to diminishing marginal utility. In any period, income receivers spend the first dollars received on the products they value most—products whose marginal utility is high. As their most pressing wants become satisfied, consumers then spend additional dollars of income on less important, lower-marginal-utility goods. The identical diminishing-marginal-utility-from-income curves (MU_A and MU_B in the figure) reflect the assumption that Anderson and Brooks have the same capacity to derive utility from income.

Now suppose $10,000 worth of income (output) is to be distributed between Anderson and Brooks. According to proponents of income equality, the optimal distribution is an equal distribution, which causes the marginal utility of the last dollar spent to be the same for both persons. We can prove this by demonstrating that if the income distribution is initially unequal, then distributing income more equally can increase the combined utility of the two individuals.

Suppose that the $10,000 of income initially is distributed unequally, with Anderson getting $2500 and Brooks $7500. The marginal utility, a, from the last dollar received by Anderson is high, and the marginal utility, b, from Brooks's last dollar of income is low. If a single dollar of income is shifted from Brooks to Anderson—that is, toward greater equality—then Anderson's utility increases by a and Brooks's utility decreases by b. The combined utility then increases by a minus b (Anderson's large gain minus Brooks's small loss). The transfer of another dollar from Brooks to Anderson again increases their combined utility, this time by a slightly smaller amount. Continued transfer of dollars from Brooks to Anderson increases their combined utility until the income is evenly distributed and both receive $5000. At that time their marginal utilities from the last dollar of income are equal (at a' and b'), and any further income redistribution beyond the $2500 already transferred would begin to create inequality and decrease their combined utility.

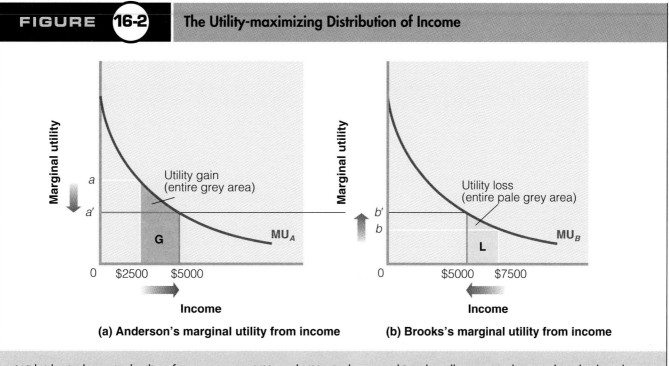

FIGURE 16-2 The Utility-maximizing Distribution of Income

(a) Anderson's marginal utility from income

(b) Brooks's marginal utility from income

With identical marginal-utility-of-income curves MU_A and MU_B, Anderson and Brooks will maximize their combined utility when any amount of income (say, $10,000) is equally distributed. If income is unequally distributed (say, $2500 to Anderson and $7500 to Brooks), the marginal utility derived from the last dollar will be greater for Anderson than for Brooks, and a redistribution toward equality will result in a net increase in total utility. The utility gained by equalizing income at $5000 each, shown by the full area G below curve MU_A in panel (a), exceeds the utility lost, indicated by the full area L below curve MU_B in panel (b).

The area under the MU curve, and to the left of the individual's particular level of income, represents the total utility of that income. Therefore, as a result of the transfer of the $2500, Anderson has gained utility represented by the full area G below the curve MU_A, and Brooks has lost utility represented by the full area L below the curve MU_B. Area G is obviously greater than area L, so income equality yields greater combined total utility than income inequality does.

The Case for Inequality: Incentives and Efficiency

Although the logic of the argument for equality is sound, critics attack its fundamental assumption that there is some fixed amount of output produced and therefore income to be distributed. Critics of income equality argue *that the way in which income is distributed is an important determinant of the amount of output or income that is produced and is available for distribution.*

Suppose once again in Figure 16-2 that Anderson earns $2500 and Brooks earns $7500. In moving toward equality, society (the government) must tax away some of Brooks's income and transfer it to Anderson. This tax-and-transfer process diminishes the income rewards of high-income Brooks and raises the income rewards of low-income Anderson; in so doing, it reduces the incentives of both to earn high incomes. Why should high-income Brooks work hard, save, invest, or undertake entrepreneurial risks when the rewards from such activities will be reduced by taxation? Why should low-income Anderson be motivated to increase his income through market activities when the government stands ready to transfer income to him? Taxes are a reduction in the rewards from increased productive effort; redistribution through transfers is a reward for diminished effort.

In the extreme, imagine a situation in which the government levies a 100 percent tax on income and distributes the tax revenue equally to its citizenry. Why would anyone work hard? Why would anyone work at all? Why would anyone assume business risk? Or why would anyone save (forgo current consumption) in order to invest? The economic incentives to get ahead would be removed, greatly reducing society's total production and income. In other words, the way the income pie is distributed affects the size of that pie. The basic argument for income inequality is that inequality is essential to maintain incentives to produce output and income—that is, to get the pie baked year after year.

The Equality–Efficiency Tradeoff

equality–efficiency tradeoff
The decrease in economic efficiency that may accompany a decrease in income inequality.

The essence of this income equality–inequality debate is that there is a fundamental tradeoff between equality and efficiency. In this **equality–efficiency tradeoff**, greater income equality (achieved through redistribution of income) comes at the opportunity cost of reduced production and income. And greater production and income (through reduced redistribution) comes at the expense of less equality of income. The tradeoff obligates society to choose how much redistribution it wants, in view of the costs. If society decides it wants to redistribute income, it needs to determine methods that minimize the adverse effects on economic efficiency.

16.4   The Nature of Poverty

We next turn from the larger issue of income distribution to the more specific issue of very low income, or poverty. A society with a high degree of income inequality can have either a high, moderate, or low amount of poverty. We need to learn about the extent of poverty in Canada, the characteristics of the poor, and the programs designed to reduce poverty.

Definition of Poverty

absolute poverty
A situation in which the basic material needs of an individual or a family (food, clothing, shelter) are not met.

relative poverty
A situation in which an individual's or a family's income is low relative to others in society.

Poverty does not lend itself to precise definition, but it helps to distinguish between absolute and relative poverty. **Absolute poverty** occurs when the basic material needs—food, clothing, and shelter—of an individual or a family are not met. **Relative poverty** refers to an individual's or a family's low income relative to others in society. While a family's basic material needs may be met, it would still be considered poor if its income relative to others is much lower.

While it is possible to eradicate absolute poverty, relative poverty will probably always be around, at least in a market economy, where some individuals are able to earn much more than others.

A family's needs have many determinants: its size, its health, the ages of its members, and so forth. Its means include currently earned income, transfer payments, past savings, property owned, and so on. Statistics Canada uses a (revised 1992) low income cut-off (LICO) that depends on the percentage that a family spends on necessities compared to an average family. Statistics Canada uses the 1992 Family Expenditure Survey, which found that, on average, families spend 44 percent of their after-tax income on these necessities. Canadian families that spend 20 percent more than this figure (that is, about 53 percent or more) on food, shelter, and clothing compared to an average family are considered to be below the cut-off. In total, 10.9 percent of Canadians were considered to be living in poverty in 2000.

Who Are the Poor?

Unfortunately for purposes of public policy, the poor are heterogeneous: they can be found in all geographic regions; they are whites, non-whites, and Native peoples; they include large numbers of both rural and urban people; they are both old and young.

Yet, despite this pervasiveness, poverty is far from randomly distributed, as Table 16-3 demonstrates. An aging widow with four years of schooling living in an Atlantic town and prevented from

TABLE 16-3	Incidence of Low Income by Selected Characteristics, 2000		
		ESTIMATED PERCENTAGE BELOW LOW INCOME CUT-OFF*	
		All persons	**Unattached Individuals**
All persons and unattached individuals		10.9	28.6
By region:	Nova Scotia	10.4	28.8
	Quebec	13.6	34.8
By age of household head:	Under 18	12.5	—
	18–64	11.0	—
	65 and over	9.5	—
By sex of household head—female		33.9	37.0
—male†		20.1	30.2

Source: Statistics Canada, *Income in Canada, 2001*, Catalogue No. 75-202, June 2003.

*Families that spent 20 percent more on food, shelter, and clothing than the average family were considered to be in straitened circumstances and, therefore, below the 1992 LICO. According to this criterion, it is estimated that 3.3 million people were below the LICO in 2000, which represents 10.9 percent of the covered population (of whom 868,000 were children).

†Divorced, separated, or widowed.

seeking paid work by her four under-16 children still at home—well, she is likely to be poor. When her children have left home and she is over 70, her fortunes look no brighter.

The high poverty rate for children is especially disturbing because poverty tends to breed poverty. There were almost 900,000 poor children in Canada in 2000. Poor children are at greater risk for a range of long-term problems, including poor health and inadequate education, crime, drugs, and teenage pregnancy. Many of today's impoverished children will reach adulthood unhealthy, illiterate, and unable to earn above-poverty incomes.

From our discussion of income mobility, we know that there is considerable movement out of poverty. Only slightly more than half of those who are in poverty one year will remain below the poverty line the next year. However, poverty is much more persistent for some groups, in particular families headed by women, those with little education and few labour market skills, and those who are dysfunctional because of drugs, alcoholism, or mental illness.

The Invisible Poor

The facts and figures on the extent and character of poverty may be difficult to accept. After all, ours is an affluent society. How do we reconcile the depressing statistics on poverty with everyday observations of abundance? The answer lies mainly in the fact that much Canadian poverty is hidden; it is largely invisible.

There are three reasons for this invisibility. First, a sizable proportion of the people in the poverty pool change from year to year. Research has shown that as many as one-half of those in poverty are poor for only one or two years before successfully climbing out of poverty. Many of these people are not visible as being permanently downtrodden and needy. Second, the "permanently poor" are increasingly isolated geographically. Poverty persists in depressed areas of large cities and is not readily visible from the expressway or commuter train. Similarly, rural poverty and the chronically depressed areas of eastern Quebec and the Atlantic provinces are also off the beaten path. Third, and perhaps most important, the poor are politically invisible. They often do not have interest groups fighting the various levels of governments for their rights.

<www.statcan.ca/Daily/English/000306/d000306a.htm>
Poverty and the elderly

Canada Pension Plan (CPP)
A national retirement plan funded by obligatory employer and employee contributions.

Old Age Security (OAS)
A pension paid on application at age 65 to everyone resident in Canada for at least 10 years immediately before turning 65.

TABLE 16-4	Estimated Federal Government Transfer Payments, 2002–2003	
Program	**Estimated expenditures*, millions of dollars**	
Major transfers to other levels of government		
Fiscal Equalization	10,545	
Canada Health and Social Transfers	18,600	
Territorial governments	1,598	
Alternative payments for standing programs	(2,522)	
Other	(526)	
Subtotal	27,695	
Major transfers to persons		
Elderly Benefits	26,350	
Employment Insurance	15,900	
Subtotal	42,250	
Other transfer payments and subsidies	20,255	
Total transfer payments	**90,200**	

Source: Treasury Board of Canada Secretariat *2002–2003 Estimates, Part I: The Government Expenditure Plan*, <www.tbs-sct.gc.ca/est-pre/20022003/ page.asp?page=001_e_3.htm>. Reproduced with the permission of the Minister of Public Works and Government Services Canada, 2003.

*Fiscal year ending March 31, 2003
Visit www.mcgrawhill.ca/college/mcconnell for data updates.

Guaranteed Income Supplement (GIS)
Money paid on application, subject to a means test, to those receiving an OAS pension who have an income below a certain level.

Employment Insurance (EI)
A program that insures workers against the hazards of losing their jobs.

The Income Maintenance System

The existence of a wide variety of income-maintenance programs is evidence that alleviation of poverty has been accepted as a legitimate goal of public policy. In recent years, income-maintenance programs have involved substantial monetary outlays and large numbers of beneficiaries. About one-half of the federal government's 2002–03 expenditures were transfer payments. The government estimated these $90 billion of expenditures would be disbursed as shown in Table 16-4. It should be noted, however, that the bulk of these transfers go to the non-poor, and only a few of these programs are specifically targeted at the poor.

In addition to all these programs, there is the **Canada Pension Plan (CPP)**—funded by obligatory employee and employer contributions.[1] It increases each year by the percentage increase in the cost of living in the previous year.

The **Old Age Security (OAS)** pension is paid on application at age 65 to everyone resident in Canada for at least 10 years immediately before turning 65. The **Guaranteed Income Supplement (GIS)** is paid on application, subject to a means test, to those receiving the OAS pension who have an income below a certain level. Considerably more than half of Canadians over 65 draw the GIS. Both the OAS pension and the GIS are increased every three months by the percentage increase in the cost of living in the previous three months.

Employment insurance (EI) was started in 1940 to insure workers against the hazards of losing their jobs. Certainly it has lessened the misery of the very large number of the involuntarily unemployed during recessionary periods. In the early 1970s, employment insurance benefits were greatly increased so a positive incentive was created for marginal workers to enter the labour force not to work, but to qualify for benefits. In 1977, benefits were decreased slightly while qualifying for them was made more difficult. By the 1990s the federal government tightened the rules to qualify for EI, as it coped with mounting deficits. By early 2002 the number of persons receiving EI had fallen significantly, partly as a result of a healthy economy.

QUICK REVIEW

- The fundamental argument for income equality is that it maximizes total utility by equalizing the marginal utility of the last dollar of income received by all people.

- The basic argument for income inequality is that it is necessary as an economic incentive for production.

- By government standards, more than three million Canadians, or 10.9 percent of the population, live in poverty.

- The Canadian income maintenance system includes both employment insurance programs and pension programs.

---

[1]The Quebec Pension Plan, for residents of that province, is similar.

16.5　Welfare Policy: Goals and Conflicts

An ideal public assistance (welfare) program should simultaneously achieve three goals. First, the plan should be effective in getting individuals and families out of poverty. Second, it should provide adequate incentives for able-bodied, non-retired people to work. Third, the plan's cost should be reasonable. Unfortunately, these three goals conflict, causing tradeoffs and necessitating compromises. To understand this, consider the three hypothetical welfare plans shown in Table 16-5.

Common Features

We first examine the two common elements in each of the three plans (and in real-world public assistance plans). First, there is a *minimum annual income* that government will provide if the family has no earned income. Second, each plan has a *benefit-reduction rate,* which is the rate at which benefits are reduced or lost as a result of earned income.

Consider plan 1. The minimum annual income provided by government is $8000, and the benefit-reduction rate is 50 percent. If a family earns no income, it will receive cash transfer payments totalling $8000. If it earns $4000, it will lose $2000 ($4000 of earnings times the 50 percent benefit-reduction rate) of transfer payments; its total income will then be $10,000 (= $4000 of earnings *plus* $6000 of transfer payments). If $8000 is earned, transfer payments will fall to $4000, and so on. Note that at an income of $16,000, transfer payments are zero. The level of earned income at which the transfer payments disappear is called the *break-even income.*

We might criticize plan 1 on the grounds that a 50 percent benefit-reduction rate is too high and therefore does not provide sufficient incentives to work. As earned income increases, the loss of transfer payments constitutes a tax on earnings. Some people may choose not to work when they lose 50 cents of each extra dollar earned. Thus in plan 2 the $8000 minimum income is retained, but the benefit-reduction rate is reduced to 25 percent. But note that the break-even level of income increases to $32,000, so many more families would now qualify for transfer payments. Furthermore, a family with any earned income under $32,000 will receive a larger total transfer payment. For both reasons, a reduction of the benefit-reduction rate to enhance work incentives will raise the cost of the income-maintenance plan.

After examining plans 1 and 2, we might argue that the $8000 minimum annual income is too low—it does not get families out of poverty. Plan 3 raises the minimum income to $12,000 and retains the 50 percent benefit-reduction rate of plan 1. While plan 3 does a better job of raising the

TABLE 16-5	Tradeoffs Among Goals: Three Public Assistance Plans							
PLAN 1 ($8000 MINIMUM INCOME AND 50% BENEFIT-REDUCTION RATE)			**PLAN 2 ($8000 MINIMUM INCOME AND 25% BENEFIT-REDUCTION RATE)**			**PLAN 3 ($12,000 MINIMUM INCOME AND 50% BENEFIT-REDUCTION RATE)**		
Earned income	**Transfer payment**	**Total income**	**Earned income**	**Transfer payment**	**Total income**	**Earned income**	**Transfer payment**	**Total income**
$ 0	$8,000	$ 8,000	$ 0	$8,000	$ 8,000	$ 0	$12,000	$12,000
4,000	6,000	10,000	8,000	6,000	14,000	8,000	8,000	16,000
8,000	4,000	12,000	16,000	4,000	20,000	16,000	4,000	20,000
12,000	2,000	14,000	24,000	2,000	26,000	24,000*	0	24,000
16,000*	0	16,000	32,000*	0	32,000			

*Indicates break-even income. Determined by dividing the minimum income by the benefit-reduction rate.

incomes of the poor, it too yields a higher break-even income than plan 1 and therefore will be more costly. Also, if the $12,000 income guarantee of plan 3 were coupled with plan 2's 25 percent benefit-reduction rate to strengthen work incentives, the break-even income level would shoot up to $48,000 and add even more to the costs of the public assistance program.

Conflicts among Goals

<www.un.org/esa/socdev/
poverty/poverty.htm>
UN declares 1997–2006 the
Decade for the Eradication of
Poverty

Clearly, the goals of eliminating poverty, maintaining work incentives, and holding down program costs are in conflict.

Plan 1, with a low minimum income and a high benefit-reduction rate, keeps costs down. But the low minimum income means that this plan is not very effective in eliminating poverty, and the high benefit-reduction rate weakens work incentives.

In comparison, plan 2 has a lower benefit-reduction rate and therefore stronger work incentives. But it is more costly because it sets a higher break-even income and therefore pays benefits to more families.

Compared with plan 1, plan 3 has a higher minimum income and is more effective in eliminating poverty. While work incentives are the same as those in plan 1, the higher guaranteed income in plan 3 makes the plan more costly. *(Key Question 9)*

16.6   Labour Market Discrimination

<is.dal.ca/~eequity/INFO/
question.htm>
Frequently asked employment
equity questions

We have already pointed out that one of the potential causes of income inequality is labour market discrimination. Let's take a more in-depth look at this phenomenon. Broadly defined, labour market discrimination occurs when equivalent labour resources are paid or treated differently even though their productive contributions are equal. These differences result from a combination of non-discriminatory and discriminatory factors. For example, studies indicate that about one-half the differences in earnings between men and women and between whites and visible minorities can be explained by such non-discriminatory factors as differences in education, age, training, industry and occupation, union membership, location, work experience, continuity of work, and health. (Of course, some of these factors may be influenced by discrimination.) The other half is an unexplained difference, the bulk of which economists attribute to discrimination.

In labour market discrimination, certain groups of people are often accorded inferior treatment with respect to hiring, occupational access, education and training, promotion, wage rates, or working conditions even though they have the same abilities, education and training, and experience as the more preferred groups. People who practise discrimination are said to exhibit a prejudice or bias against the targets of their discrimination.

Types of Discrimination

Labour market discrimination can take several forms:

wage discrimination
The payment of a lower wage to members of a less-preferred group than to members of a more-preferred group for the same work.

- **Wage discrimination** occurs when women or members of minorities are paid less than white males for doing the same work. This kind of discrimination is declining because of its explicitness and the fact that it clearly violates federal and provincial labour law. But wage discrimination can be subtle and difficult to detect. For example, women and minorities sometimes find that their job classifications carry lower pay than job classifications held by white males, even though they are performing essentially the same tasks.

employment discrimination
Inferior treatment in hiring, promotion, and work assignment for a particular group of employees.

- **Employment discrimination** takes place when women or visible-minority workers receive inferior treatment in hiring, promotions, assignments, temporary layoffs, and permanent discharges (see the Consider This box). This type of discrimination also encompasses sexual and racial harassment—demeaning treatment in the workplace by coworkers or administrators.

occupational discrimination
Arbitrary restriction of particular groups from more desirable, higher-paying occupations.

• **Occupational discrimination** occurs when women or visible-minority workers are arbitrarily restricted or prohibited from entering the more desirable, higher-paying occupations. Businesswomen have found it difficult to break through the "glass ceiling" that prevents them from moving up to executive ranks. Visible minorities in executive and sales positions are relatively rare. In addition, skilled and unionized work such as electrical work, bricklaying, and plumbing do not have high visible minority representation.

Consider This

Gender Discrimination

There have long been allegations of discrimination against women in the hiring process in some occupations, but such discrimination is usually difficult to demonstrate. Economists Claudia Goldin and Cecilia Rouse spotted a unique opportunity for testing such discrimination as it relates to major symphony orchestras. In the past, orchestras relied on their musical directors to extend invitations to candidates, audition them, and handpick new members. Concerned with the potential for hiring bias, in the 1970s and 1980s orchestras altered the process in two ways. First, orchestra members were included as judges, and, second, orchestras began open competitions using blind auditions with a physical screen (usually a room divider) to conceal the identity of the candidates. (These blind auditions, however, did not extend to the final competition in most orchestras.) Did the change in procedures increase the probability of women being hired?

To answer this question, Goldin and Rouse studied the orchestral management files of auditions for eight major orchestras. These records contained the names of all candidates and identified those who had advanced to the next round, including the ultimate winners of the competition. The researchers then looked for women in the sample who had competed in auditions both before and after the introduction of the blind screening.

A strong suspicion existed of bias against women in hiring musicians for the nation's finest orchestras. These positions are highly desirable, not only because they are prestigious but also because they offer high pay (often more than $75,000 annually). In 1970 only 5 percent of the members of the top five orchestras were women, and many music directors publicly suggested that women players, in general, have less musical talent.

The change to screens provided direct evidence of past discrimination. The screens increased by 50 percent the probability that a woman would be advanced from the preliminary rounds. The screens also greatly increased the likelihood that a woman would be selected in the final round. Without the screens about 10 percent of all hires were women, but with the screens about 35 percent were women. Today, about 25 percent of the membership of top symphony orchestras are women. The screens explain from 25 to 45 percent of the increases in the proportion of women in the orchestras studied.

Was the past discrimination in hiring an example of statistical discrimination based on, say, a presumption of greater turnover by women or more leaves for medical (including maternity) or other reasons? To answer that question, Goldin and Rouse examined information on turnover and leaves of orchestra members between 1960 and 1996. They found that neither differed by gender, so leaves and turnover should not have influenced hiring decisions.

Instead, the discrimination in hiring seemed to reflect a taste for discrimination by musical directors. Male musical directors apparently had a positive discrimination coefficient d. At the fixed (union-determined) wage, they simply preferred male musicians, at women's expense.

Source: Claudia Goldin and Cecilia Rouse, "Orchestrating Impartiality: The Impact of 'Blind' Auditions on Female Musicians," *American Economic Review*, September 2000, pp. 715–741.

Question: What two types of discrimination are represented by the discrimination evidenced here?

396

**human capital
discrimination**
Arbitrary restriction of particular groups from productivity-enhancing investments in education and training.

• **Human capital discrimination** occurs when women or members of minorities do not have the same access to productivity-enhancing investments in education and training as white males. For example, the lower average educational attainment of visible minorities has reduced their opportunities in the labour market.

Costs of Discrimination

Discrimination imposes costs on those who are discriminated against. Where it exists, discrimination actually diminishes the economy's output and income; like any other artificial barrier to free competition, it decreases economic efficiency and reduces production. By arbitrarily blocking certain qualified groups of people from high-productivity (and thus high-wage) jobs, discrimination prevents them from making their maximum contribution to society's output, income, and well-being.

The effects of discrimination can be depicted as a point inside the economy's production possibilities curve, such as point D in Figure 16-3. At such a point, the economy obtains some combination of capital and consumption goods—here, $K_d + C_d$—that is less desirable than combinations represented by points such as X, Y, or Z on the curve. By preventing the economy from achieving productive efficiency, discrimination reduces the nation's real output and income. Very rough estimates suggest that the Canadian economy would gain $35 billion per year by eliminating racial and ethnic discrimination and some $20 billion per year by ending gender discrimination.

Economic Analysis of Discrimination

Prejudice reflects complex, multifaceted, and deeply ingrained beliefs and attitudes. Thus, economic analysis can contribute some insight into discrimination but no detailed explanations. With this caution in mind, let's look more deeply into the economics of discrimination.

FIGURE 16-3   **Discrimination and Production Possibilities**

Discrimination represents a failure to achieve productive efficiency. The cost of discrimination to society is the sacrificed output associated with a point such as D inside the nation's production possibilities curve, compared with points such as X, Y, and Z on the curve.

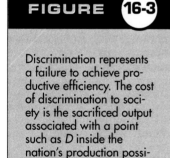

TASTE-FOR-DISCRIMINATION MODEL

taste-for-discrimination model
A theory of discrimination that views it as a preference for which an employer is willing to pay.

The **taste-for-discrimination** model examines prejudice by using the emotion-free language of demand theory. It views discrimination as resulting from a preference or taste for which the discriminator is willing to pay. The model assumes that, for whatever reason, prejudiced people experience a subjective or psychic cost—a disutility—whenever they must interact with those they are biased against. Consequently, they are willing to pay a certain price to avoid interactions with the non-preferred group. The size of this price depends directly on the degree of prejudice.

The taste-for-discrimination model is general since it can be applied to race, gender, age, and religion, but our discussion focuses on employer discrimination, in which employers discriminate against non-preferred workers. For concreteness, we will look at a white employer discriminating against visible-minority workers.

discrimination coefficient
A measure of the cost or disutility of prejudice.

Discrimination Coefficient

A prejudiced white employer behaves as if employing visible-minority workers would add a cost. The amount of this cost—this disutility—is reflected in a **discrimination coefficient**, d, measured in monetary units. Because the employer is not prejudiced against whites, the cost of employing a white worker is the white wage rate, W_w. However, the employer's perceived cost of employing a visible-minority worker is the visible-minority worker's wage rate, W_b, plus the cost d involved in the employer's prejudice, or $W_b + d$.

The prejudiced white employer will have no preference between visible-minority and white workers when the total cost per worker is the same, that is, when $W_w = W_b + d$. Suppose the market wage rate for whites is $10 and the monetary value of the disutility the employer attaches to hiring visible minorities is $2 (that is, $d = \$2$). This employer will be indifferent between hiring visible minorities and whites only when the visible-minority wage rate is $8, since at this wage the perceived cost of hiring either a white or a visible-minority worker is $10: $10 white wage = $8 visible-minority wage + $2 discrimination coefficient.

It follows that our prejudiced white employer will hire visible minorities only if their wage rate is sufficiently below that of whites. By "sufficiently" we mean at least the amount of the discrimination coefficient.

The greater a white employer's taste for discrimination, as reflected in the value of d, the larger the difference between white wages and the lower wages at which visible minorities will be hired. A colour-blind employer whose d is $0 will hire equally productive visible minorities and whites impartially if their wages are the same. A blatantly prejudiced white employer whose d is infinity would refuse to hire visible minorities even if the visible minority wage were zero.

Most prejudiced white employers will not refuse to hire visible minorities under all conditions. They will, in fact, *prefer* to hire visible minorities if the actual white–visible minority wage difference in the market exceeds the value of d. In our example, if whites can be hired at $10 and equally productive visible minorities at only $7.50, the biased white employer will hire visible minorities. That employer is willing to pay a wage difference of up to $2 per hour for whites to satisfy his or her bias, but no more. At the $2.50 actual difference, the employer will hire visible minorities.

Conversely, if whites can be hired at $10 and visible minorities at $8.50, whites will be hired. Again, the biased employer is willing to pay a wage difference of up to $2 for whites; a $1.50 actual difference means that hiring whites is a "bargain" for this employer.

Prejudice and the Market Visible Minority–White Wage Ratio

For a particular supply of visible-minority workers, the actual visible minority–white wage ratio—the ratio determined in the labour market—will depend on the collective prejudice of white employers. To see why, consider Figure 16-4, which shows a labour market for *visible-minority* workers. Initially, suppose the relevant labour demand curve is D_1, so the equilibrium visible-minority wage is $8 and the equilibrium level of visible-minority employment is 6 million. If we assume that the *white* wage (not shown) is $10, then the initial visible minority–white wage ratio is .80 (= $8/$10).

Now assume that prejudice against visible-minority workers increases—that is, the collective d of white employers rises. An increase in d means an increase in the perceived cost of visible-minority

FIGURE 16-4 The Visible-minority Wage and Employment Level in the Taste-for-discrimination Model

An increase in prejudice by white employers as reflected in higher discrimination coefficients would decrease the demand for visible-minority workers, here from D_1 to D_2, and reduce the visible-minority wage rate and level of visible-minority employment. This drop in the visible-minority wage rate would lower the visible minority–white wage ratio (not shown). In contrast, if prejudice were reduced such that the discrimination coefficients of employers declined, the demand for visible-minority labour would increase, as from D_1 to D_3, boosting the visible-minority wage rate and level of employment. The higher visible-minority wage rate would increase the visible minority–white wage ratio.

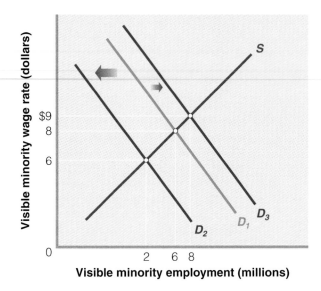

labour at each visible-minority wage rate, and that reduces the demand for visible-minority labour, say, from D_1 to D_2. The visible-minority wage rate falls from $8 to $6 in the market, and the level of visible-minority employment declines from six million to two million. The increase in white employer prejudice reduces the visible-minority wage rate and thus the actual visible minority–white wage ratio. If the white wage rate remains at $10, the new visible minority–white ratio is .6 (= $6/$10).

Conversely, suppose social attitudes change such that white employers become less biased and their discrimination coefficient as a group declines. This change decreases the perceived cost of visible-minority labour at each visible-minority wage rate, so the demand for visible-minority labour increases, as from D_1 to D_3. In this case, the visible-minority wage rate rises to $9, and employment of visible-minority workers increases to eight million. The decrease in white employer prejudice increases the visible-minority wage rate and thus the actual visible minority–white wage ratio. If the white wage remains at $10, the new visible minority–white wage ratio is .9 (= $9/$10).

Competition and Discrimination The taste-for-discrimination model suggests that competition will reduce discrimination in the very long run, as follows: The actual visible minority–white wage difference for equally productive workers—say, $2—allows non-discriminators to hire visible minorities for less than whites. Firms that hire visible-minority workers will, therefore, have lower actual wage costs per unit of output and lower average total costs than will the firms that discriminate. These lower costs will allow non-discriminators to underprice discriminating competitors, eventually driving them out of the market.

Critics of this implication of the taste-for-discrimination model note that progress in eliminating racial discrimination has been modest. Discrimination based on race has persisted in Canada and other market economies decade after decade. To explain why, economists have proposed other models. *(Key Question 10)*

STATISTICAL DISCRIMINATION

statistical discrimination
Judging individuals on the average characteristic of the group to which they belong rather than on their own personal characteristics.

A second theory of discrimination centres on the concept of **statistical discrimination**, in which people are judged based on the average characteristics of the group to which they belong, rather than on their own personal characteristics or productivity. The uniqueness of this theory is its suggestion that discriminatory outcomes are possible even where no prejudice exists.

Basic Idea   Suppose you are given a complex, but solvable, mathematical problem and told you will get $1 million in cash if you can identify a student on campus who is capable of solving it. The catch is that you have only 15 minutes, are restricted to the campus area, and must approach students one at a time. Who among the thousands of students—all strangers—would you approach first? Obviously, you would prefer to choose a mathematics, physics, or engineering major. Would you choose a man or a woman? A white person or a member of a visible minority? If gender or race plays any role in your choice, you are engaging in statistical discrimination.

Labour Market Example   How does statistical discrimination show itself in labour markets? Employers with job openings want to hire the most productive workers available. They have their personnel department collect information concerning each job applicant, including age, education, and work experience. They may supplement that information with preemployment tests, which they believe are helpful indicators of potential job performance. But it is very expensive to collect detailed information about job applicants, and it is difficult to predict job performance based on limited data. Consequently, some employers looking for inexpensive information may consider the *average* characteristics of women and minorities in determining whom to hire. They are practising statistical discrimination when they do so. They are using gender, race, or ethnic background as a crude indicator of production-related attributes.

Note what happens when such a crude indicator is used. Average characteristics for a *group* are being applied to *individual* members of that group. The employer may falsely assume, for example, that *each and every* female worker has the same employment tendencies as the *average* woman. Such stereotyping means that numerous women who are career-oriented, who plan to work after having children, or who don't plan to have children, and who are flexible as to geographical transfers will be discriminated against.

Profitable, Undesirable, but Not Malicious   The firm that practises statistical discrimination is not being malicious in its hiring behaviour (although it may be violating antidiscrimination laws). The decisions it makes will be rational and profitable, because *on average* its hiring decisions are likely to be correct. Nevertheless, many people suffer because of statistical discrimination, since it blocks the economic betterment of capable people. Since it is profitable, statistical discrimination tends to persist.

OCCUPATIONAL SEGREGATION: THE CROWDING MODEL

occupational segregation
The crowding of women or minorities into less desirable, lower-paying occupations.

The practice of **occupational segregation**—the crowding of women, visible minorities, and certain ethnic groups into less desirable, lower-paying occupations—is still apparent in the Canadian economy. Statistics indicate that women are disproportionately concentrated in a limited number of occupations such as teaching, nursing, and secretarial and clerical jobs. Visible minorities are crowded into low-paying jobs such as those of laundry workers, cleaners and household aides, hospital orderlies, agricultural workers, and other manual labourers.

Let's look at a model of occupational segregation, using women and men as an example.

The Model   The character and income consequences of occupational discrimination are revealed through a labour supply and demand model. We make the following assumptions:

- The labour force is equally divided between male and female workers. Let's say there are six million male and six million female workers.

- The economy comprises three occupations, X, Y, and Z, with identical labour demand curves, as shown in Figure 16-5.

- Men and women have the same labour force characteristics; each of the three occupations could be filled equally well by men or by women.

Effects of Crowding   Suppose that, as a consequence of discrimination, the six million women are excluded from occupations X and Y and crowded into occupation Z, where they earn wage W. The men distribute themselves equally among occupations X and Y, meaning that three million male workers are in each occupation and have a common wage of M. (If we assume that there are no barriers to mobility between X and Y, any initially different distribution of males between X and Y would result in a wage differential between the two occupations. That differential would prompt labour shifts from the low-wage to the high-wage occupation until an equal distribution occurred.)

Because women are crowded into occupation Z, labour supply (not shown) is larger and their wage rate W is much lower than M. Because of the discrimination, this is an equilibrium situation that will persist as long as the crowding occurs. The occupational barrier means women cannot move into occupations X and Y in pursuit of a higher wage.

The result is a loss of output for society. To see why, recall again that labour demand reflects labour's marginal revenue product, which is labour's contribution to domestic output. Thus, the grey areas for occupations X and Y in Figure 16-5 show the decrease in domestic output—the market value of the marginal output—caused by subtracting one million women from each of these occupations. Similarly, the orange area for occupation Z shows the increase in domestic output caused by moving two million women into occupation Z. Although society would gain the added output represented by the orange area in occupation Z, it would lose the output represented by the sum of the two grey areas in occupations X and Y. That output loss exceeds the output gain, producing a net output loss for society.

Eliminating Occupational Segregation   Now assume that through legislation or sweeping changes in social attitudes, discrimination disappears. Women, attracted by higher wage

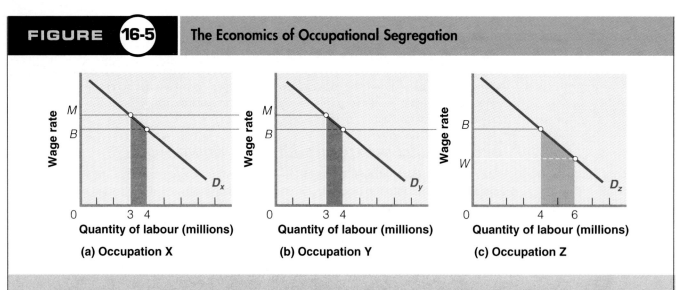

FIGURE 16-5   **The Economics of Occupational Segregation**

(a) Occupation X

(b) Occupation Y

(c) Occupation Z

By crowding women into one occupation, men enjoy high wage rates of M in occupations X and Y, while women receive low wages of W in occupation Z. The elimination of discrimination will equalize wage rates at B and result in a net increase in the nation's output.

rates, shift from occupation Z to X and Y; one million women move into X and another one million move into Y. Now there are four million workers in Z and occupational segregation is eliminated. At that point there are four million workers in each occupation, and wage rates in all three occupations are equal, here at *B*. That wage equality eliminates the incentive for further reallocations of labour.

The new, non-discriminatory equilibrium clearly benefits women, who now receive higher wages; it hurts men, who now receive lower wages. But women were initially harmed and men benefited through discrimination; removing discrimination corrects that situation.

Society also gains. The elimination of occupational segregation reverses the net output loss just discussed. Adding one million women to each of occupations X and Y in Figure 16-5 increases domestic output by the sum of the two grey areas. The decrease in domestic output caused by losing two million women from occupation Z is shown by the orange area. The sum of the two increases in domestic output in X and Y exceeds the decrease in domestic output in Z. With the end of the discrimination, two million women workers have moved from occupation Z, where their contribution to domestic output (their MRP) is low, to higher paying occupations X and Y, where their contribution to domestic output is high. Thus society gains a more efficient allocation of resources from the removal of occupational discrimination. (In terms of Figure 16-3, society moves from a point inside its production possibilities curve to a point closer to, or on, the curve.) *(Key Question 12)*

QUICK REVIEW

- Discrimination reduces domestic output and occurs when workers who have the same abilities, education, training, and experience as other workers receive inferior treatment with respect to hiring, occupational access, promotion, or wages.

- Non-discriminatory factors explain about one-half of the gender and racial earnings gap; most of the remaining gap is thought to reflect discrimination.

- The taste-for-discrimination model sees discrimination as representing a preference or taste for which the discriminator is willing to pay.

- The theory of statistical discrimination says that employers often wrongly judge individuals based on average group characteristics rather than on personal characteristics, thus harming those discriminated against.

- The crowding model of discrimination suggests that when women and minorities are systematically excluded from high-paying occupations and crowded into low-paying ones, their wages and society's domestic output are reduced.

THE LASTword   Poverty in the Voices of Poor People

While statistics tell us much about poverty and inequality, the statements below attest to the human suffering caused by insufficient material means in many nations.

Poor people in 60 countries were asked to analyze and share their ideas of well-being (a good experience of life) and "ill-being" (a bad experience of life).

Well-being was variously described as happiness, harmony, peace, freedom from anxiety, and peace of mind. In Russia people say, "Well-being is a life free from daily worries about lack of money." In Bangladesh, "to have a life free from anxiety." In Brazil, "not having to go through so many rough spots."

People describe ill-being as lack of material things, as bad experiences, and as bad feelings about oneself. A group of young men in Jamaica ranks lack of self-confidence as the second biggest impact of poverty: "Poverty means we don't believe in [ourselves], we hardly travel out of the community—so frustrated, just locked up in a house all day."

Universal Problems Although the nature of ill-being and poverty varies among locations and people—something that policy responses must take into account—there is a striking commonality across countries. Not sur-

prisingly, material well-being turns out to be very important. Lack of food, shelter, and clothing is mentioned everywhere as critical. In Kenya a man says: "Don't ask me what poverty is because you have met it outside my house. Look at the house and count the number of holes. Look at my utensils and the clothes I am wearing. Look at everything and write what you see. What you see is poverty."

Alongside the material, physical well-being features prominently in the characterizations of poverty. And the two meld together when lack of food leads to ill health—or when ill health leads to an inability to earn income. People speak about the importance of looking well fed. In Ethiopia poor people say, "We are skinny," "We are deprived and pale," and speak of life that "makes you older than your age."

More Than Material Goods Security of income is also closely tied to health. But insecurity extends beyond ill health. Crime and violence are often mentioned by poor people. In Ethiopia women say, "We live hour to hour," worrying about whether it will rain. An Argentine says, "You have

work, and you are fine. If not, you starve. That's how it is." Two social aspects of ill-being and poverty also emerged. For many poor people, well-being means the freedom of choice and action and the power to control one's life. A young woman in Jamaica says that poverty is "like living in jail, living in bondage, waiting to be free."

Linked to these feelings are definitions of well-being as social well-being and comments on the stigma of poverty. As an old woman in Bulgaria says, "to be well means to see your grandchildren happy and well dressed and to know that your children have settled down; to be able to give them food and money whenever they come to see you, and not to ask them for help and money." A Somali proverb captures the other side: "Prolonged sickness and persistent poverty cause people to hate you."

Source: *World Development Report 2000–2001,* "Introduction," (Oxford University Press, New York, 2000), <www.worldbank.org/poverty/wdrpoverty/report/ch1.pdf>.

CHAPTER SUMMARY

16.1 FACTS ABOUT INCOME INEQUALITY

- The distribution of income in Canada reflects considerable inequality. After taxes, the top 20 percent of families earn 42.8 percent of total income, while the bottom 20 percent earn only 5.0 percent.

- The Lorenz curve shows the percentage of total income received by each percentage of families. The extent of

the gap between the Lorenz curve and a line of total equality illustrates the degree of income inequality.

- Recognizing that the positions of individual families in the distribution of income change over time and incorporating the effects of non-cash transfers and taxes would reveal less income inequality than do standard census data. Government transfers (cash and non-cash) greatly lessen the degree of income inequality; taxes also reduce inequality but not nearly as much as transfers.

16.2 CAUSES OF INCOME INEQUALITY

- Causes of income inequality include differences in abilities, education and training, and job tastes, along with discrimination, inequality in the distribution of wealth, and an unequal distribution of market power.

16.3 EQUALITY VERSUS EFFICIENCY

- The basic argument for income equality is that it maximizes consumer satisfaction (total utility) from a particular level of total income. The main argument for income inequality is that it provides the incentives to work, invest, and assume risk; it is necessary for the production of output that, in turn, creates income that is then available for distribution.

16.4 THE NATURE OF POVERTY

- Absolute poverty occurs when the basic material needs are not met. Relative poverty refers to an individual's or a family's low income relative to the rest of society. Absolute poverty can be eradicated, but relative poverty is much more difficult to resolve.

- Current statistics suggest that about 10.9 percent of the country lives in poverty. Poverty is concentrated among the poorly educated, the aged, and families headed by women.

- Our present income maintenance system is made up of social insurance programs (Canada Pension Plan and Employment Insurance benefits), universal programs (Old Age Security Pension), and public assistance or welfare programs.

16.5 WELFARE POLICY: GOALS AND CONFLICTS

- Public assistance programs (welfare) are difficult to design because their goals of reducing poverty, main-

taining work incentives, and holding down program costs often conflict.

16.6 LABOUR MARKET DISCRIMINATION

- Discrimination relating to the labour market occurs when women or minorities having the same abilities, education, training, and experience as men or white workers receive inferior treatment with respect to hiring, occupational choice, education and training, promotion, and wage rates. Forms of discrimination include wage discrimination, employment discrimination, occupational discrimination, and human capital discrimination. Discrimination redistributes national income and, by creating inefficiencies, diminishes its size.

- In the taste-for-discrimination model, some white employers have a preference for discrimination, measured by a discrimination coefficient d. Prejudiced white employers will hire visible-minority workers only if their wages are at least d dollars below those of whites. The model indicates that declines in the discrimination coefficients of white employers will increase the demand for visible-minority workers, raising the visible-minority wage rate and the ratio of visible-minority wages to white wages. It also suggests that competition may eliminate discrimination in the long run.

- Statistical discrimination occurs when employers base employment decisions about *individuals* on the average characteristics of *groups* of workers. That practice can lead to discrimination against individuals even in the absence of prejudice.

- The crowding model of occupational segregation indicates how white males gain higher earnings at the expense of women and minorities who are confined to a limited number of occupations. The model shows that discrimination also causes a net loss of a nation's output.

TERMS AND CONCEPTS

STUDY QUESTIONS

1. Using quintiles, briefly summarize the degree of income inequality in Canada.

2. **KEY QESTION**   Assume Syed, Beth, Sabine, David, and Mikkel receive incomes of $500, $250, $125, $75, and $50 respectively. Construct and interpret a Lorenz curve for this five-person economy. What percentage of total income is received by the richest quintile and by the poorest quintile?

3. Why is the lifetime distribution of income more equal than the distribution in any specific year?

4. **KEY QUESTION** Briefly discuss the major causes of income inequality. With respect to income inequality, is there any difference between inheriting property and inheriting a high IQ? Explain.

5. Use the leaky-bucket analogy to discuss the equality–efficiency tradeoff.

6. Should a nation's income be distributed to its members according to their contributions to the production of that total income or according to the members' needs? Should society attempt to equalize income or economic opportunities? Are the issues of equity and equality in the distribution of income synonymous? To what degree, if any, is income inequality equitable?

7. Analyze in detail: "There need be no tradeoff between equality and efficiency. An efficient economy that yields an income distribution many regard as unfair may cause those with meagre income rewards to become discouraged and stop trying. Hence, efficiency is undermined. A fairer distribution of rewards may generate a higher average productive effort on the part of the population, thereby enhancing efficiency. If people think they are playing a fair economic game and this belief causes them to try harder, an economy with an equitable income distribution may be efficient as well."

8. Comment on or explain:

   a. "To endow everyone with equal income will certainly make for very unequal enjoyment and satisfaction."

   b. "Equality is a superior good: the richer we become, the more of it we can afford."

   c. "The mob goes in search of bread, and the means it employs is generally to wreck the bakeries."

   d. "Some freedoms may be more important in the long run than freedom from want on the part of every individual."

   e. "Capitalism and democracy are really a most improbable mixture. Maybe that is why they need each other—to put some rationality into equality and some humanity into efficiency."

   f. "The incentives created by the attempt to bring about a more equal distribution of income are in conflict with the incentives needed to generate increased income."

9. **KEY QUESTION** The following table contains three hypothetical public assistance plans.

   a. Determine the minimum income, the benefit-reduction rate, and the break-even income for each plan.

   b. Which plan is the most costly? the least costly? Which plan is the most effective in reducing poverty? the least effective? Which plan embodies the strongest disincentive to work? the weakest disincentive to work?

   c. Use your answers in part (b) to explain the following statement: "The dilemma of public assistance is that you cannot bring families up to the poverty level and simultaneously preserve work incentives and minimize program costs."

| Plan One | | | Plan Two | | | Plan Three | | |
Earned income	Transfer payment	Total income	Earned income	Transfer payment	Total income	Earned income	Transfer payment	Total income
$ 0	$4,000	$4,000	$ 0	$4,000	$ 4,000	$ 0	$8,000	$ 8,000
2,000	3,000	5,000	4,000	3,000	7,000	4,000	6,000	10,000
4,000	2,000	6,000	8,000	2,000	10,000	8,000	4,000	12,000
6,000	1,000	7,000	12,000	1,000	13,000	12,000	2,000	14,000

10. **KEY QUESTION** The labour demand and supply data in the table below relate to a single occupation. Use them to answer the questions that follow. Base your answers on the taste-for-discrimination model.

Quantity of labour demanded, thousands	Visible minority wage rate	Quantity of visible minority labour supplied (thousands)
24	$16	52
30	14	44
35	12	35
42	10	28
48	8	20

a. Plot the labour demand and supply curves for visible minority workers in this occupation.

b. What are the equilibrium visible minority wage rate and quantity of visible minority employment?

c. Suppose the white wage rate in this occupation is $16. What is the visible minority–white wage ratio?

d. Suppose a particular employer has a discrimination coefficient d of $5 per hour. Will that employer hire visible-minority or white workers at the visible minority–white wage ratio indicated in part (c)? Explain.

e. Suppose employers as a group become less prejudiced against visible minorities and demand 14 more units of visible-minority labour at each visible-minority wage rate in the table. What are the new equilibrium visible-minority wage rate and level of visible-minority employment? Does the visible minority–white wage ratio rise or fall? Explain.

f. Suppose visible minorities as a group increase their labour services in that occupation, collectively offering 14 more units of labour at each visible-minority wage rate. Disregarding the changes indicated in part (e), what are the new equilibrium visible-minority wage rate and level of visible-minority employment? Does the visible minority–white wage ratio rise, or does it fall?

11. Males under the age of 25 must pay far higher auto insurance premiums than females in this age group. How does this fact relate to statistical discrimination? Statistical discrimination implies that discrimination can persist indefinitely, while the taste-for-discrimination model suggests that competition might reduce discrimination in the long run. Explain the difference.

12. **KEY QUESTION**   Use a demand and supply model to explain the effect of occupational segregation or crowding on the relative wage rates and earnings of men and women. Who gains and who loses from the elimination of occupational segregation? Is there a net gain or a net loss to society? Explain.

13. "Current employment equity programs are based on the belief that to overcome discrimination, we must practise discrimination. That perverse logic has created a system that undermines the fundamental values it was intended to protect." Do you agree? Why or why not?

14. Suppose Ann and Becky are applicants to your university and that they have identical admission qualifications. Ann, who is a member of a visible minority, grew up in a public housing development; Becky, who is white, grew up in a wealthy suburb. You can admit only one of the two. Which would you admit and why? Now suppose that Ann is white and Becky is a member of a visible minority, all else being equal. Does that change your selection? Why or why not?

15. **(The Last Word)** How do poor people describe "well-being" and "ill-being"?

INTERNET APPLICATION QUESTION

1. Statistics Canada compiles information about low income in Canada. Access its site through the McConnell-Brue-Barbiero Web site (Chapter 16) and answer the following questions:

Σ-STAT

a. Is the percentage of the population living below Statistics Canada's low income cut-off higher or lower than in the previous year reported? Compared to a decade earlier?

b. Is the poverty rate (in percent) higher or lower than the previous year for the general population and children under 18 and the elderly?

4

Part

Microeconomics of Government and Public Policy

17

Government and Market Failure

The economic activities of government affect your well-being every day. If you drive to work or to school, you are using publicly provided highways and streets. If you attend a college or university, taxpayers subsidize your education. When you receive a cheque from your job, you see deductions for income taxes and social insurance taxes. Government antipollution laws affect the air you breathe. Laws requiring seat belts and motorcycle helmets and the sprinkler system in university dormitories are all government mandates.

In this chapter we examine *market failure*—instances in which private markets do not bring about the allocation of resources that best satisfies society's wants. Where private markets fail, there may be an economic role for government. We will examine that role as it relates to three types of market failure: public goods, externalities, and information asymmetries. Our discussion of externalities in turn facilitates a discussion of pollution and pollution policies.

In Chapter 18 our discussion of the microeconomics of government continues with an analysis of potential government inefficiencies—called *government failure*—and the economics of taxation.

17.1   Public Goods

One person's consumption of a public good does not preclude consumption of the same good by others.

Recall from Chapter 4 that a private good is characterized by *rivalry* and *excludability*. "Rivalry" means that when one person buys and consumes a product, it is not available for purchase and consumption by another person. "Excludability" means that sellers can keep people who do not pay for the product from obtaining its benefits. Because of these characteristics, the demand for a private good gets expressed in the market, and profit-seeking suppliers satisfy that demand. In contrast, the characteristics of a public good have the opposite characteristics: *non-rivalry* and *non-excludability*. Once a producer has provided a public good, everyone can obtain the benefit. One person's consumption of the good does not preclude consumption of the same good by others. And, once a producer has provided a public good, it cannot bar non-payers from receiving the benefit. Because of free riders, the demand for a public good does not get expressed in the market and therefore the good does not get produced. Only government will provide it. Two simple examples will help clarify these ideas.

The market demand for a private good is the horizontal summation of the demand curves representing all individual buyers (review Figure 3-2). Suppose just two people in society enjoy hot dogs, which cost $.80 each to produce. If Adams wants to buy three hot dogs at $1 each and Benson wants to buy two hot dogs at that same price, the market demand curve will reflect that five hot dogs are demanded at a $1 price. A seller charging $1 for each hot dog can gain $5 of revenue and earn $1 of profit ($5 of total revenue minus $4 of cost).

The situation is different with public goods. Suppose an enterprising sculptor creates a piece of art costing $600 and places it in the town square. Also suppose that Adams gets $300 of enjoyment from the art and Benson gets $400. Sensing this enjoyment and hoping to make a profit, the sculptor approaches Adams for a donation equal to his satisfaction. Adams falsely says that he doesn't much like the piece. The sculptor then tries Benson, hoping to get $400 or so. Benson professes not to like the piece either. Adams and Benson have become *free riders*. Although feeling a bit guilty, both reason that it makes no sense to pay for something when you can receive the benefits without paying for them. The artist is a quick learner; he vows never to try anything like that again.

Conclusion: Because of non-rivalry and non-excludability, private firms cannot profitably produce a public good. If society wants the good, it must direct government to provide it. Government can finance the provision of the good through taxation.

Demand for Public Goods

<members.aol.com/trajcom/private/commons.htm>
The commons

If consumers need not reveal their true demand for a public good in the marketplace, then how can the optimal amount of that good be determined? The answer is that the government has to try to estimate the demand for a public good through surveys or public votes. Suppose Adams and Benson are the only two people in the society, and their marginal willingness to pay for a public good, this time national defence, is as shown in columns 1, 2, and 3 in Table 17-1.

Notice that the schedules in Table 17-1 are demand schedules. Rather than depicting demand in the usual way—the quantity of a product someone is willing to buy at each possible price—these schedules show the price someone is willing to pay for the marginal unit of each possible quantity. That is, Adams is willing to pay $4 for the first unit of the public good, $3 for the second, $2 for the third, and so on.

410

TABLE 17-1	Demand for a Public Good, Two Individuals		
(1) Quantity of public good	(2) Adams's willingness to pay (price)	(3) Benson's willingness to pay (price)	(4) Collective willingness to pay (price)
1	$4 +	$5 =	$9
2	3 +	4 =	7
3	2 +	3 =	5
4	1 +	2 =	3
5	0 +	1 =	1

Suppose the government produces one unit of this public good. Because of the non-excludability characteristic of a public good, Adams's consumption of the good does not preclude Benson from also consuming it, and vice versa. So both consume the good, and neither volunteers to pay for it. But from Table 17-1 we can find the amount these two people would be willing to pay, together. Columns 1 and 2 show that Adams would be willing to pay $4 for the first unit of the public good; columns 1 and 3 show that Benson would be willing to pay $5 for it. So the two people are jointly willing to pay $9 (= $4 + $5) for this unit.

For the second unit of the public good, the collective price they are willing to pay is $7 (= $3 from Adams plus $4 from Benson); for the third unit they will pay $5 (= $2 plus $3); and so on. By finding the collective willingness to pay for each additional unit (column 4), we can construct a collective demand schedule (a willingness-to-pay schedule) for the public good. Here, we are not adding the quantities demanded at each possible price as when we determine the market demand for a private good. Instead, we are adding *the prices that people are willing to pay for the last unit of the public good at each possible quantity demanded.*

Figure 17-1 shows the same adding procedure graphically, using the data from Table 17-1. Note that we sum Adams's and Benson's willingness-to-pay curves *vertically* to derive the collective willingness-to-pay curve (demand curve). For example, the height of the collective demand curve D_c at two units of output is $7, the sum of the amounts that Adams and Benson are each willing to pay for the second unit (= $3 + $4). Likewise, the height of the collective demand curve at four units of the public good is $3 (= $1 + $2).

What does it mean in Figure 17-1(a) that, for example, Adams is willing to pay $3 for the second unit of the public good? It means that Adams expects to receive $3 of extra benefit or utility from that unit. And we know from the law of diminishing marginal utility that successive units of any good yield less and less added benefit. This is also true for public goods, explaining the downward slope of the willingness-to-pay curves of both Adams and Benson, and of the collective demand curve. These curves, in essence, are marginal-benefit curves. *(Key Question 1)*

Supply of Public Goods

The supply curve for any good, private or public, is its marginal-cost curve. Marginal cost rises as more of a good is produced. In the short run, government has fixed factors (public capital) with which to produce public goods such as national defence. As it adds more units of a variable factor (labour) to these fixed factors, total product eventually rises at a diminishing rate. That means that marginal product falls and marginal cost rises, explaining why curve S in Figure 17-1(c) slopes upward.

Optimal Quantity of a Public Good

We can now determine the optimal quantity of the public good. The collective demand curve D_c in Figure 17-1(c) measures society's marginal benefit of each unit of this particular good. The supply curve S in that figure measures society's marginal cost of each unit. The optimal quantity of this public good occurs where marginal benefit equals marginal cost, or where the two curves intersect. In Figure 17-1(c) that point is three units of the public good, where the collective willingness to pay for the last (third) unit—the marginal benefit—just matches that unit's marginal cost ($5 = $5). As we saw in Chapter 2, equating marginal benefit and marginal cost efficiently allocates society's scarce resources. *(Key Question 2)*

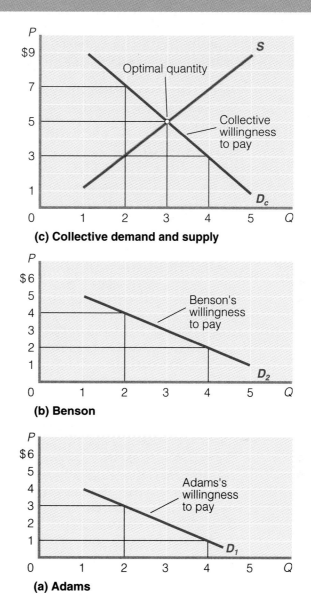

FIGURE **17-1**

The Optimal Amount of a Public Good

The collective demand curve for a public good, as shown by D_c in panel (c), is found by summing vertically the individual willingness-to-pay curves D_1 in panel (a) and D_2 in panel (b) of Adams and Benson, the only two people in the economy. The supply curve of the public good represented in panel (c) slopes upward and to the right, reflecting rising marginal costs. The optimal amount of the public good is three units, determined by the intersection of D_c and S. At that output, marginal benefit (reflected in the collective demand curve D_c) equals marginal cost (reflected in the supply curve S).

Cost–Benefit Analysis

cost–benefit analysis
Comparing the marginal costs of a government project with the marginal benefits to decide whether to employ more or less resources in that project.

The above example suggests a practical means, called **cost–benefit analysis**, for deciding whether to provide a particular public good and how much of it to provide. Like our example, cost–benefit analysis (or marginal benefit–marginal cost analysis) involves a comparison of marginal costs and marginal benefits.

CONCEPT

Suppose the federal government is contemplating a highway construction plan. Because the economy's resources are limited, any decision to use more resources in the public sector will mean fewer resources for the private sector. There will be both a cost and a benefit. The cost is the loss of satisfaction resulting from the accompanying decline in the production of private goods; the benefit is the extra satisfaction resulting from the output of more public goods. Should the needed resources be shifted from the private to the public sector? The answer is yes if the benefit from the extra public goods exceeds the cost that results from having fewer private goods. The answer is no if the cost of the forgone private goods is greater than the benefit associated with the extra public goods.

Cost–benefit analysis, however, can indicate more than whether a public program is worth doing. It can also help the government decide on the extent to which a project should be pursued. Economic questions can rarely be answered simply by yes or no but, rather, are matters of how much or how little.

ILLUSTRATION

Although a few private toll roads exist, highways clearly have public-good characteristics because the benefits are widely diffused and the exclusion principle is not easily applied. Should the federal government expand the national highway system? If so, what is the proper size or scope for the overall project?

Table 17-2 lists a series of increasingly costly highway projects: widening existing two-lane highways; building new two-lane highways; building new four-lane highways; building new six-lane highways. The extent to which government should undertake highway construction depends on the costs and benefits. The costs are largely the costs of constructing and maintaining the highways; the benefit is an improved flow of people and goods throughout the nation.

The table shows that total benefit (column 4) exceeds total cost (column 2) for plans A, B, and C, indicating that some highway construction is economically justifiable. We see this directly in column 6, where total costs (column 2) are subtracted from total annual benefits (column 4). Net benefits are positive for plans A, B, and C. Plan D is not justifiable because net benefits are negative.

But the question of optimal size or scope for this project remains. Comparing the additional, or marginal, cost and the additional, or marginal, benefit relating to each plan determines the answer. In this case plan C (building new four-lane highways) is the best plan. For plans A and B, the marginal benefits exceed the marginal costs. Plan D's marginal cost ($10 billion) exceeds the marginal benefit ($3 billion) and therefore cannot be justified; it overallocates resources to the project. Plan C is closest to the optimum because its marginal benefit ($10 billion) still exceeds marginal cost ($8 billion) but approaches the MB = MC (or MC = MB) ideal.

MC = MB rule
For a government project, marginal benefit should equal marginal cost to produce maximum benefit to society.

This **marginal cost = marginal benefit rule** actually tells us which plan provides society with the maximum net benefit. You can confirm directly in column 6 that the maximum net benefit (of $5 billion) is associated with plan C.

Cost–benefit analysis shatters the myth that "economy in government" and "reduced government spending" are synonymous. "Economy" is concerned with using scarce resources efficiently.

TABLE 17-2	Cost-benefit Analysis for a National Highway Construction Project, Billions of Dollars				
(1) Plan	(2) Total cost of project	(3) Marginal cost	(4) Total benefit	(5) Marginal benefit	(6) Net benefit or (4) – (2)
No new construction	$ 0		$ 0		$0
A: Widen existing highways	4	$ 4	5	$ 5	1
B: Two-lane highways	10	6	13	8	3
C: Four-lane highways	18	8	23	10	5
D: Six-lane highways	28	10	26	3	–2

If the cost of a proposed government program exceeds its benefits, then the proposed public program should not be undertaken, but if the benefits exceed the cost, then it would be uneconomical or "wasteful" not to spend on that government program. Economy in government does not mean minimization of public spending; it means allocating resources between the private and public sectors to achieve maximum net benefit. *(Key Question 3)*

QUICK REVIEW

- The demand (marginal-benefit) curve for a public good is found by vertically adding the prices all the members of society are willing to pay for the last unit of output at various output levels.

- The socially optimal amount of a public good is the amount at which the marginal

cost and marginal benefit of the good are equal.

- Cost–benefit analysis is the method of evaluating alternative projects by comparing the marginal cost and marginal benefits and applying the MC = MB rule.

17.2   Externalities Revisited

externalities
Benefits or costs from production or consumption accruing without compensation to non-buyers and non-sellers of the product.

Government not only produces public goods but also corrects for kinds of market failure called **externalities** or spillovers. Recall from Chapter 4 that a spillover is a cost or a benefit accruing to an individual or group—a third party—that is *external* to a market transaction. An example of a spillover cost or a negative externality is the cost of breathing polluted air; an example of a spillover benefit or a positive externality is the benefit of having everyone else inoculated against some communicable disease. When there are spillover costs, there is an overproduction of the product and an overallocation of resources to this product. Conversely, underproduction and underallocation of resources result when spillover benefits are present. We can demonstrate both graphically.

Spillover Costs

Figure 17-2(a) illustrates how spillover costs affect the allocation of resources. When producers shift some of their costs onto the community as spillover costs, producers' marginal costs are lower than otherwise. So their supply curves do not include or capture all the costs associated with the production of their goods. A polluting producer's supply curve such as S in Figure 17-2(a), therefore, understates the total cost of production. The firm's supply curve lies to the right of the full-cost supply curve S_t that would include the spillover cost. Through polluting and thus transferring cost to others in society, the firm enjoys lower production costs and has the supply curve S.

The outcome is shown in Figure 17-2(a), where equilibrium output Q_e is larger than the optimal output Q_o. This means that resources are overallocated to the production of this commodity; too many units of it are produced.

Spillover Benefits

Figure 17-2(b) shows the impact of spillover benefits on resource allocation. When spillover benefits occur, the market demand curve D lies to the left of the full-benefits demand curve. That is, D does not include the spillover benefits of the product, whereas D_t does. Consider inoculations against a communicable disease. Watson and Weinberg benefit when they get vaccinated but so do their associates Singh and Anderson who are less likely to contract the disease from them. The market demand curve reflects only the direct, private benefits to Watson and Weinberg; it does not reflect the spillover benefits—the positive externalities—to Singh and Anderson, which are included in D_t.

An example of a negative externality is the cost of breathing polluted air.

FIGURE 17-2   Spillover Costs and Spillover Benefits

Panel (a): With spillover costs borne by society, the producers' supply curve S is to the right of (below) the full-cost curve S_t. Consequently, the equilibrium output Q_e is greater than the optimal output Q_o. Panel (b): When spillover benefits accrue to society, the market demand curve D is to the left of (below) the full-benefit demand curve D_t. As a result, the equilibrium output Q_e is less than the optimal output Q_o.

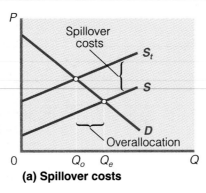

(a) Spillover costs

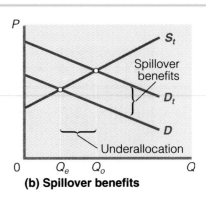

(b) Spillover benefits

The outcome is that the equilibrium output Q_e is less than the optimal output Q_o. The market fails to produce enough vaccinations and resources are underallocated to this product.

Economists have explored several approaches to the problems of spillover costs and benefits. Let's first look at situations where government intervention is not needed and then at some possible government solutions.

The Effectiveness of Markets

Coase theorem
The idea first stated by economist Ronald Coase that spillover problems may be resolved through private negotiations of the affected parties.

Individual Bargaining: Coase Theorem

In the **Coase theorem**, conceived by economist Ronald Coase at the University of Chicago, government is not needed to remedy spillover costs or benefits where (1) property ownership is clearly defined, (2) the number of people involved is small, and (3) bargaining costs are negligible. Under these circumstances the government should confine its role to encouraging bargaining between affected individuals or groups. Because the economic self-interests of the parties are at stake, bargaining will enable them to find a mutually acceptable solution to the externality problem, no matter who has the property rights.

EXAMPLE OF THE COASE THEOREM

Suppose the owner of a large parcel of forest land is considering a plan to clear-cut (totally level) hundreds of hectares of mature fir trees. The complication is that the forest surrounds a lake with a popular resort on its shore. The resort is on land it owns. The unspoiled beauty of the general area attracts vacationers from all over the nation to the resort, and the resort owner is against the clear-cutting. Should provincial or municipal government intervene to allow or prevent the tree cutting?

According to the Coase theorem, the forest owner and the resort owner can resolve this situation without government intervention. As long as one of the parties to the dispute has property rights to what is at issue, an incentive will exist for both parties to negotiate a solution acceptable to each. In our example, the owner of the timberland holds the property rights to the land to be logged and thus has the right to clear-cut it. The owner of the resort, therefore, has an economic incentive to negotiate with the forest owner to reduce the logging impact. Excessive logging of the forest surrounding the resort will reduce tourism and revenues to the resort owner.

What is the economic incentive to the forest owner to negotiate with the resort owner? The answer draws directly on the idea of opportunity cost. One cost incurred in logging the forest is the

<www.best.com/~ddfr/ Academic/Coase_World.html> Coase and the Nobel Prize

forgone payment that the forest owner could obtain from the resort owner for agreeing not to clear-cut the fir trees. The resort owner might be willing to make a lump-sum or annual payment to the owner of the forest to avoid or minimize the spillover cost. Or perhaps the resort owner might be willing to buy the forested land to prevent the logging. As viewed by the forest owner, a payment for not clear-cutting or a purchase price above the market value of the land is an opportunity cost of logging the land.

It is likely that both parties would regard a negotiated agreement as better than clear-cutting the firs.

LIMITATIONS

Unfortunately, many externalities involve large numbers of affected parties, high bargaining costs, and community property such as air and water. In such situations private bargaining often does not work. As an example, the global warming problem affects billions of people in many nations. The vast number of affected parties could not individually negotiate an agreement to remedy this problem. Instead, they must rely on their governments to represent the billions of affected parties and find an acceptable solution.

Nevertheless, the Coase theorem reminds us that in many situations, bargaining between private parties can remedy spillover costs and spillover benefits.

Liability Rules and Lawsuits

Although private negotiation may not be a realistic solution to many externality problems, clearly established property rights may help in another way. The government has erected a framework of laws that define private property and protect it from damage done by other parties. Those laws, and the damage recovery system to which they give rise, permit parties suffering spillover costs to sue for compensation.

Suppose the Ajax Degreaser Company regularly dumps leaky barrels containing solvents into a nearby canyon owned by Bar Q Ranch. Bar Q eventually discovers this dumpsite and, after tracing the drums to Ajax, immediately contacts its lawyer. Soon after, Bar Q sues Ajax. Not only will Ajax have to pay for the cleanup, but it may also have to pay Bar Q additional damages for ruining its property.

Clearly defined property rights and government liability laws thus help remedy some externality problems. They do so directly by forcing the perpetrator of the harmful externality to pay damages to those injured. They do so indirectly by discouraging firms and individuals from generating spillover costs for fear of being sued. It is not surprising, then, that many spillovers do not involve private property but rather property held in common by society. It is the public bodies of water, the public lands, and the public air, where ownership is less clear, that often bear the brunt of spillovers.

A caveat is in order here: like private negotiations, private lawsuits to resolve externalities have their own limitations. Large legal fees and major time delays in the court system are commonplace. Also, the uncertainty associated with the court outcome reduces the effectiveness of this approach. Will the court accept your claim that your emphysema has resulted from the smoke emitted by the factory next door, or will it conclude that your ailment is unrelated to the plant's pollution? Can you prove that a specific firm in the area is the source of the contamination of your well? What happens to Bar Q's suit if Ajax Degreaser goes out of business during the litigation?

Government Intervention

Government intervention may be needed to achieve economic efficiency when externalities affect large numbers of people or when community interests are at stake. Government can use direct controls and taxes to counter spillover costs; government may provide subsidies or public goods to deal with spillover benefits.

DIRECT CONTROLS

The direct way to reduce spillover costs from a certain activity is to pass legislation limiting that activity. Such direct controls force the offending firms to incur the actual costs of the offending activity. To date, this approach has dominated public policy in Canada. Historically, direct controls in the form of uniform emissions standards—limits on allowable pollution—have dominated Canadian air pollution policy. Clean air legislation forces factories, cars, and businesses to install "maximum achievable control technology" to reduce emissions. Clean-water legislation limits the amount of heavy metals, detergents, and other pollutants firms can discharge into rivers and bays. Toxic-waste laws dictate special procedures and dump sites for disposing of contaminated soil and solvents. Violating these laws means fines and, in some cases, imprisonment.

Direct controls raise the marginal cost of production because the firms must operate and maintain pollution-control equipment. The supply curve S in Figure 17-3(b), which does not reflect the spillover costs, shifts leftward (upward) to the full-cost supply curve, S_t. Product price increases, equilibrium output falls from Q_e to Q_o, and the initial overallocation of resources shown in Figure 17-3(a) is corrected.

SPECIFIC TAXES

A second policy approach to spillover costs is for government to levy taxes or charges specifically on the related good. For example, the government has placed a manufacturing tax on CFCs, which deplete the stratospheric ozone layer protecting the earth from excessive solar ultraviolet radiation. Facing such a tax, manufacturers must decide whether to pay the tax or expend additional funds to purchase or develop substitute products. In either case, the tax raises the marginal cost of producing CFCs, shifting the private supply curve for this product leftward.

In Figure 17-3(b), a tax equal to T per unit increases the firm's marginal cost, shifting the supply curve from S to S_t. The equilibrium price rises and the equilibrium output declines from Q_e to the economically efficient level Q_o. The tax thus eliminates the initial overallocation of resources.

SUBSIDIES AND GOVERNMENT PROVISION

Where spillover benefits are large and diffuse, as in our earlier example of inoculations, government has three options for correcting the underallocation of resources:

FIGURE 17-3	**Correcting for Spillover Costs (Negative Externalities)**

Panel (a): Spillover costs result in an overallocation of resources. Panel (b): Government can correct this overallocation in two ways: (1) the use of direct controls, which would shift the supply curve from S to S_t and reduce output from Q_e to Q_o, or (2) the imposition of a specific tax T, which would also shift the supply curve from S to S_t, eliminating the overallocation of resources.

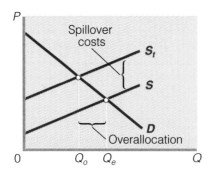

(a) Spillover costs

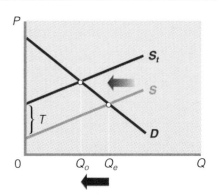

(b) Correcting the overallocation of resources via direct controls or via a tax

1. ***Subsidies to buyers***   Figure 17-4(a) shows the supply–demand situation for spillover benefits. Government could correct the underallocation of resources, for example, to inoculations, by subsidizing consumers of the product. It could give each new mother in Canada a discount coupon to be used to obtain a series of inoculations for her child. The coupon would reduce the price to the mother by, say, 50 percent. As shown in Figure 17-4(b), this program would shift the demand curve for inoculations from too-low D to the appropriate D_t. The number of inoculations would rise from Q_e to the optimal Q_o, eliminating the underallocation of resources shown in Figure 17-4(a).

2. ***Subsidies to producers***   A subsidy to producers is a specific tax in reverse. Taxes impose an extra cost on producers, while subsidies reduce producers' costs. As shown in Figure 17-4(c), a subsidy of U per inoculation to physicians and medical clinics would reduce their marginal costs and shift their supply curve rightward from S_t to S'_t. The output of inoculations would increase from Q_e to the optimal level Q_o, correcting the underallocation of resources shown in Figure 17-4(a).

3. ***Government provision***   Finally, where spillover benefits are large, the government may decide to provide the product as a public good. The Canadian government largely eradicated the crippling disease polio by administering free vaccines to all children. India ended smallpox by paying people in rural areas to come to public clinics to have their children vaccinated. *(**Key Question 4**)*

tragedy of the commons
Air, water, and public land rights are held in common by society and freely available, so no incentive exists to maintain or use them carefully; the result is overuse, degradation, and pollution.

A Market-based Approach to Spillover Costs

One novel approach to spillover costs involves the creation of a market for externality rights. But before describing that approach, we first need to understand the **tragedy of the commons**.

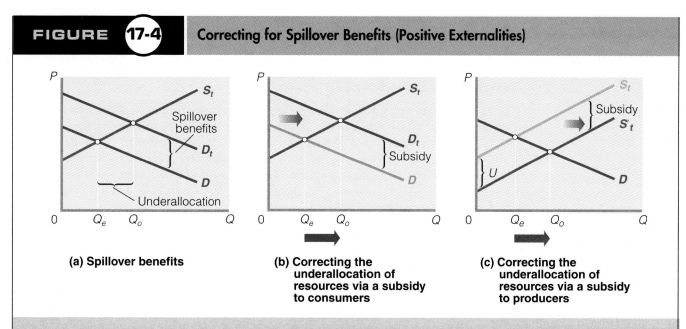

FIGURE 17-4   Correcting for Spillover Benefits (Positive Externalities)

(a) Spillover benefits

(b) Correcting the underallocation of resources via a subsidy to consumers

(c) Correcting the underallocation of resources via a subsidy to producers

Panel (a): Spillover benefits result in an underallocation of resources. Panel (b): This underallocation can be corrected by a subsidy to consumers, which shifts market demand from D to D_t and increases output from Q_e to Q_o. Panel (c): Alternatively, the underallocation can be eliminated by providing producers with a subsidy of U, which shifts their supply curve from S_t to S'_t, increasing output from Q_e to Q_o.

418

THE TRAGEDY OF THE COMMONS

<www.ecoplan.org/
com_index.htm>
The commons sustainability
agenda

The air, rivers, lakes, oceans, and public lands, such as parks and streets, are prone to being polluted because the rights to use those resources are held in common by society. No private individual or institution has an incentive to maintain the purity or quality of such resources.

We maintain the property we own—we paint and repair our homes periodically, for example—in part because we will recoup the value of these improvements at the time of sale. But as long as rights to air, water, and certain land resources are commonly held and are freely available, no incentive exists to maintain them or use them carefully. As a result, these natural resources are overused or polluted.

For example, a common pasture in which anyone can graze cattle will quickly be overgrazed, because each rancher has an incentive to graze as many cattle as possible. Similarly, manufacturers will choose to dump waste chemicals into rivers and lakes rather than pay for proper disposal. Firms will discharge smoke into the air if they can, rather than purchase expensive abatement facilities. Even federal, provincial, and municipal governments sometimes discharge inadequately treated waste into rivers, lakes, or oceans to avoid the expense of constructing expensive treatment facilities. Many individuals avoid the costs of proper refuse pickup and disposal by burning their garbage or dumping it on public lands.

**market for externality
rights**
A market in which firms can buy
rights to discharge pollutants.

The problem is mainly one of incentives. There is no incentive to incur internal costs associated with reducing or eliminating pollution when those costs can be transferred externally to society. Each person and company reasons their individual contribution to pollution is so small that it has little or no overall consequence. But their actions, multiplied by hundreds, thousands, or millions, overwhelm the absorptive capacity of the common resources. Society ends up with a degradation or pollution problem.

A MARKET FOR EXTERNALITY RIGHTS

A novel policy approach to spillover costs—one that is market oriented—is the idea that the government can create a **market for externality rights**. We confine our discussion to pollution, although this same approach can be used with other externalities.

OPERATION OF THE MARKET

In this market approach, a pollution-control agency determines the amount of pollutants that firms can discharge into the water or air of a specific region annually while maintaining the water or air quality at some acceptable level. Suppose the agency decides that 500 tonnes of pollutants can be discharged into Metropolitan Lake and "recycled" by nature each year. Then 500 pollution rights, each entitling the owner to dump one tonne of pollutants into the lake in one year, are made available for sale to producers each year. The supply of these pollution rights is fixed and, therefore, perfectly inelastic, as shown in Figure 17-5.

The demand for pollution rights, represented by D_{2004} in the figure, is the same downsloping form as the demand for any other input. At higher prices there is less pollution, as polluters either stop polluting or pollute less by acquiring pollution-abatement equipment. An equilibrium market price for pollution rights, here $100, will be determined at which the environment-preserving quantity of pollution rights is rationed to polluters. Figure 17-5 shows that if the use of the lake as a dumpsite for pollutants were free, 750 tonnes of pollutants would be discharged into the lake; it would be overconsumed, or polluted, in the amount of 250 tonnes.

Over time, as human and business populations expand, demand will increase, as from D_{2004} to D_{2014}. Without a market for pollution rights, pollution in 2014 would be 1000 tonnes, 500 tonnes beyond what can be assimilated by nature. With the market for pollution rights, the price would rise from $100 to $200, and the amount of pollutants would remain at 500 tonnes—the amount that the lake can recycle.

FIGURE **17-5**	A Market for Pollution Rights

The supply of pollution rights, S, is set by the government, which determines that a specific body of water can safely recycle 500 tonnes of waste. In 2004, the demand for pollution rights is D_{2004} and the one-tonne price is $100. The quantity of pollution is 500 tonnes, not the 750 tonnes it would have been without the pollution rights. Over time, the demand for pollution rights increases to D_{2014} and the one-tonne price rises to $200. But the amount of pollution stays at 500 tonnes, rather than rising to 1000 tonnes.

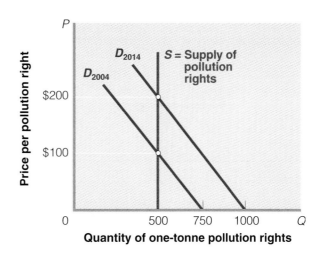

ADVANTAGES

This scheme has several advantages over direct controls, the most important of which is that it reduces society's costs by allowing pollution rights to be bought and sold. Suppose it costs Acme Pulp Mill $20 a year to reduce a specific noxious discharge by one tonne while it costs Zemo Chemicals $8000 a year to accomplish the same one-tonne reduction. Also assume that Zemo wants to expand production, but doing so will increase its pollution discharge by one tonne.

Without a market for pollution rights, Zemo would have to use $8000 of society's scarce resources to keep the one-tonne pollution discharge from occurring. But with a market for pollution rights, Zemo has a better option: it buys one tonne of pollution rights for the $100 price shown in Figure 17-5. Acme is willing to sell Zemo one tonne of pollution rights for $100 because that amount is more than Acme's $20 cost of reducing its pollution by one tonne. Zemo increases its discharge by one tonne; Acme reduces its discharge by one tonne. Zemo benefits (by $8000 − $100), Acme benefits (by $100 − $20), and society benefits (by $8000 − $20). Rather than using $8000 of its scarce resources to hold the discharge at the specified level, society uses only $20 of those resources.

Market-based plans have other advantages. Potential polluters have a monetary incentive not to pollute because they must pay for the rights to discharge effluent. Conservation groups can fight pollution by buying up and withholding pollution rights, thereby reducing pollution below governmentally determined standards. As the demand for pollution rights increases over time, the growing revenue from the sale of a fixed quantity of pollution rights could be devoted to environmental improvement. At the same time, the rising price of pollution rights stimulates the search for improved pollution-control techniques.

Table 17-3 reviews the major methods for correcting externalities.

Society's Optimal Amount of Externality Reduction

Negative externalities such as pollution reduce the utility of those affected. These spillovers are not economic goods but economic "bads." If something is bad, shouldn't society eliminate it? Why should society allow firms or municipalities to discharge *any* impure waste into public waterways or to emit *any* pollution into the air?

TABLE 17-3	Methods for Dealing with Externalities	
Problem	**Resource allocation outcome**	**Ways to correct externalities**
Spillover costs (negative externalities)	Overallocation of resources	1. Individual bargaining 2. Liability rules and lawsuits 3. Tax on producers 4. Direct controls 5. Market for externality rights
Spillover benefits (positive externalities)	Underallocation of resources	1. Individual bargaining 2. Subsidy to consumers 3. Subsidy to producers 4. Government provision

Reducing a negative externality has a price. Society must decide how much of a reduction it wants to buy. Eliminating pollution entirely might not be desirable, even if it were technologically feasible. Because of the law of diminishing returns, cleaning up the last 10 percent of pollutants from an industrial smokestack is normally far more costly than cleaning up the prior 10 percent.

The marginal cost (MC) to the firm and hence to society—the opportunity cost of the extra resources used—rises as pollution is reduced further. At some point MC may rise so high that it exceeds society's marginal benefit (MB) of further pollution abatement (reduction). Additional actions to reduce pollution will therefore lower society's well-being; total cost will rise more than total benefit.

MC, MB, AND EQUILIBRIUM QUANTITY

Figure 17-6 shows both the rising marginal-cost curve, MC, for pollution reduction and the downsloping marginal-benefit curve, MB, for this outcome. MB slopes downward because of the law of diminishing marginal utility: the more pollution reduction society accomplishes, the lower the utility (and benefit) of the next unit of pollution reduction.

optimal reduction of an externality
The point at which society's marginal cost and marginal benefit of reducing that externality are equal.

The **optimal reduction of an externality** occurs when society's marginal cost and marginal benefit of reducing that externality are equal (MC = MB). In Figure 17-6 this optimal amount of pollution abatement is Q_1 units. When MB exceeds MC, additional abatement moves society toward economic efficiency; the added benefit of cleaner air or water exceeds the benefit of any alternative use of the required resources. When MC exceeds MB, additional abatement reduces economic efficiency; there would be greater benefits from using resources in some other way than to further reduce pollution.

In reality, it is difficult to measure the marginal costs and benefits of pollution control. Nevertheless, Figure 17-6 demonstrates that some pollution may be economically efficient not because pollution is desirable but because beyond some level of control, further abatement may reduce our net well-being.

SHIFTS IN LOCATIONS OF CURVES

The locations of the marginal-cost and marginal-benefit curves in Figure 17-6 are not fixed. They can shift over time. For example, if the technology of pollution-control equipment were to improve noticeably, we would expect the cost of pollution abatement to fall, society's MC curve to shift rightward, and the optimal level of abatement to rise. Or suppose that society were to decide that it wanted cleaner air and water because of new information about the adverse health effects of pollution. The MB curve in Figure 17-6 would shift rightward, and the optimal level of pollution control would increase beyond Q_1. Test your understanding of these statements by drawing the new MC and MB curves in Figure 17-6. (*Key Question 7*)

FIGURE **17-6**

Money Facilitates Trade when Wants Do Not Coincide

The optimal amount of externality reduction—in this case, pollution abatement—occurs at Q_1, where society's marginal cost MC and marginal benefit MB of reducing the spillover are equal.

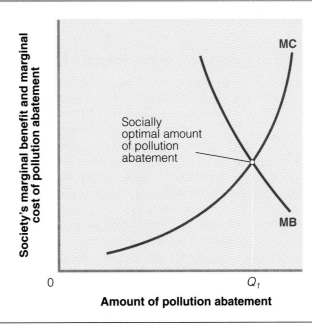

QUICK REVIEW

- Policies for coping with the overallocation of resources caused by spillover costs are (1) private bargaining, (2) liability rules and lawsuits, (3) direct controls, (4) specific taxes, and (5) markets for externality rights.

- Policies for correcting the underallocation of resources associated with spillover ben-

efits are (1) private bargaining, (2) subsidies to producers, (3) subsidies to consumers, and (4) government provision.

- The optimal amount of negative-externality reduction occurs where society's marginal cost and marginal benefit of reducing the externality are equal.

17.3   The Economics of Solid-waste Disposal and Recycling

Recycling

Production and consumption of goods and services result in millions of tonnes of solid waste (garbage) annually in Canada. The major means of disposing of solid waste are garbage dumps and incinerators, but these methods often produce spillover costs to nearby communities. Landfills in southern Ontario in particular are either completely full or rapidly filling up. Garbage from there is now being transported hundreds of kilometres to dumps in other municipal jurisdictions, as well as to the neighbouring state of Michigan.

On the receiving end, people in rural areas near newly expanding dumps are understandably upset about the increased truck traffic on their highways and the growing mounds of smelly garbage in municipal dumps. Moreover, some landfills are producing serious water-supply pollution.

The high opportunity cost of urban and suburban land and the negative externalities created by dumps make landfills increasingly expensive. An alternative policy is to incinerate garbage in plants that produce electricity. But people object to having garbage incinerators, with their accompanying truck traffic and air pollution, close to their homes.

Is there a better solution to the growing problem of solid waste? Increasing attention has been given to recycling: the reuse of old materials to make new products. Should government encourage more recycling? If so, how, and to what extent?

MARKET FOR RECYCLABLE INPUTS

Figure 17-7(a), which shows the demand and supply curves for some recyclable product, such as glass, suggests the incentives for recycling.

The demand for recyclable glass comes from manufacturers that use recycled glass as a resource in producing new glass. This demand curve slopes downward, telling us that manufacturers will increase their purchases of recyclable glass as its price falls.

The location of the demand curve in Figure 17-7(a) depends partly on the demand for the products for which the recycled glass is used. The greater the demand for those products, the greater the demand for the recyclable input. The location of the curve also depends on the technology and thus the cost of using original raw materials rather than recycled glass in the production process. The more costly it is to use original materials relative to recycled glass, the farther to the right will be the demand curve for recyclable glass.

The supply curve for recyclable glass slopes upward, because higher prices increase the incentive for households to recycle. The location of the supply curve depends on such factors as the attitudes of households toward recycling and the cost to them of alternative disposal.

The equilibrium price P_1 and quantity Q_1 in Figure 17-7(a) are determined at the intersection of the supply and demand curves. At price P_1 the market clears; there is neither a shortage nor a surplus of recyclable glass.

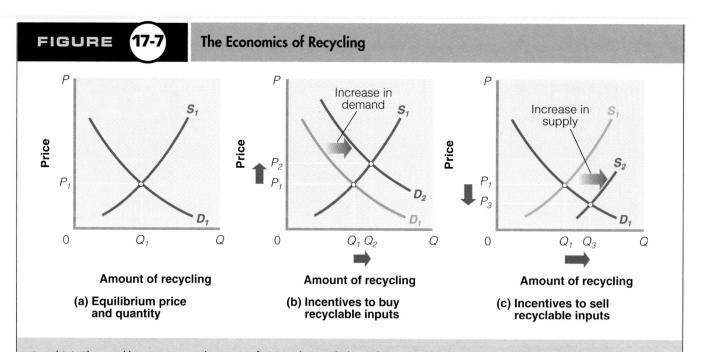

FIGURE 17-7 The Economics of Recycling

(a) Equilibrium price and quantity

(b) Incentives to buy recyclable inputs

(c) Incentives to sell recyclable inputs

Panel (a): The equilibrium price and amount of materials recycled are determined by supply S_1 and demand D_1. Panel (b): Policies that increase the incentives for producers to buy recyclable inputs shift the demand curve rightward, say, to D_2, and raise both the equilibrium price and the amount of recycling. Panel (c): Policies that encourage households to recycle shift the supply curve rightward, say, to S_2, and expand the equilibrium amount of recycling. These policies, however, also reduce the equilibrium price of the recycled inputs.

POLICY

Suppose the government wants to encourage recycling as an alternative to land dumps or incineration. It could do that in one of two ways.

Demand Incentives   The government could increase recycling by increasing the demand for recycled inputs. If the demand curve in Figure 17-7(b) shifts from D_1 rightward to D_2, the equilibrium price and quantity of recycled glass will increase to P_2 and Q_2; more recycling will occur. A policy that will increase demand is to tax the inputs that are substitutable for recycled glass in the production process. Such a tax would encourage firms to use more of the untaxed recycled glass and less of the taxed inputs.

Environmental awareness by the public can also contribute to rightward shifts of the demand curve for recycled resources. Many large firms that produce waste-intensive goods have concluded that it is in their interest to support recycling, for fear of a consumer backlash against their products. Procter & Gamble (disposable diapers) and McDonald's (packaging of fast food) have undertaken multimillion-dollar campaigns to use recycled plastic and paper.

Supply Incentives   As shown in Figure 17-7(c), government can also increase recycling by shifting the supply curve rightward, as from S_1 to S_2. The equilibrium price would fall from P_1 to P_3, but the equilibrium quantity—in this case recyclable glass—would rise from Q_1 to Q_3. That is, more recycling would occur. Many municipal governments have implemented specific policies to encourage recycling by providing curbside pickup of recyclable goods such as glass, aluminum cans, and newspapers at a lower monthly fee than for the pickup of other garbage, or free of charge.

In a few cases, supply incentives for recyclables have been so effective that the price of a recycled item has fallen to zero. You can envision this outcome by shifting the supply curve in Figure 17-7(c) farther rightward. Some cities are now paying users of recyclable inputs such as mixed paper to truck them away from the recycling centre, which means that these items have a negative price. If the cost of paying firms to take away recyclable products is lower than the cost of alternative methods, even such paid-for recycling will promote economic efficiency.

Global Warming

Canada has made progress in cleaning its air. But significant air pollution problems remain. Millions of Canadians live in areas, such as southern Ontario, that have unhealthy levels of harmful air pollutants. Moreover, Canada and the other nations of the world face the risks of *global warming*. The balance of scientific evidence suggests that carbon dioxide and other gas emissions from factories, power plants, and automobiles are accumulating in the atmosphere and creating a greenhouse effect. As a result, many scientists predict that average temperatures will rise by 1 to 3 degrees Celsius by 2100. In turn, almost all regions of the world will experience noticeable climatic changes. Ocean levels will gradually rise by several inches, and rainfall patterns will change. Snow accumulations will decline in some regions and rise in others. Violent storms such as tornadoes, typhoons, and hurricanes could increase in frequency and severity. But the economic effects of global warming will not be uniform; cool and temperate regions and nations may economically benefit, and hot and dry regions and nations may be harmed. Global Perspective 17.1 lists carbon dioxide emissions on a per capita basis for selected nations.

The world's nations have responded to the global warming problem by promising to limit the growth of carbon dioxide and other greenhouse emissions. Specifically, the industrially advanced nations agreed in the 1997 Kyoto Protocol to cut their greenhouse gas emissions 6 to 8 percent below 1990 levels by 2012. Canada committed to a 6 percent reduction below 1990 levels by 2012. The Canadian government ratified the Kyoto Protocol in 2002. Many contentious issues remain to be resolved through further meetings and negotiations. For example, to what extent should developing nations such as China and India, currently exempt from the limits, participate in reducing emissions? Should all industrial countries be forced to make, say, at least half their agreed reduction at home, rather than buying tradable emissions credits from other nations and making no reductions at home? Such credits were established as part of the Kyoto Protocol.

<www.crt.umontreal.ca/
~amit/papers/cjm.pdf>
The Kyoto Protocol

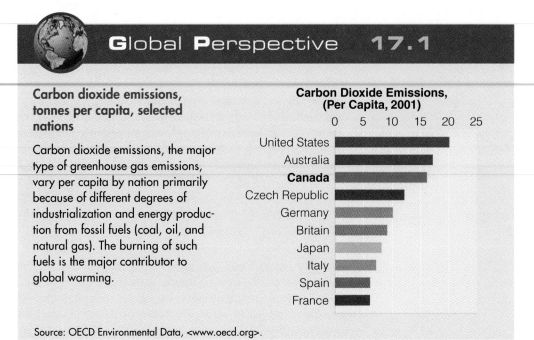

Global Perspective 17.1

Carbon dioxide emissions, tonnes per capita, selected nations

Carbon dioxide emissions, the major type of greenhouse gas emissions, vary per capita by nation primarily because of different degrees of industrialization and energy production from fossil fuels (coal, oil, and natural gas). The burning of such fuels is the major contributor to global warming.

Carbon Dioxide Emissions, (Per Capita, 2001)

United States	~20
Australia	~18
Canada	~17
Czech Republic	~12
Germany	~10
Britain	~9
Japan	~9
Italy	~8
Spain	~7
France	~6

Source: OECD Environmental Data, <www.oecd.org>.

Economists stress that global warming policies that reduce greenhouse gas emissions and thus slow or eliminate global warming create costs as well as benefits. It is imperative to consider the marginal costs and marginal benefits carefully when making policy decisions. Greenhouse gas limits should not be so stringent that they end up costing society more than the value of the benefits they produce. But limits should not be so lenient that society forgoes substantial potential benefits that it would have otherwise achieved.

Economists also stress that the market mechanism will make appropriate adjustments based on new climatic realities. Air conditioner sales will rise; snow shovel sales will fall. Some agricultural lands will be deserted; others further north will be cultivated. The maple syrup industry in Canada may benefit if production in New England falls as a result of global warming. Nevertheless, the *transition costs*—the costs associated with making economic adjustments—of global warming will undoubtedly be very high if no actions are taken to reduce greenhouse gases. The reduction or elimination of these transition costs is part of the benefit of slowing or eliminating the greenhouse effect. Such benefits must be fully considered in the cost–benefit analysis.

Complicating the cost–benefit analysis for both the private and public sectors is the unwillingness of the U.S. to sign the Kyoto Protocol. Given that the U.S. is Canada's largest export market, Canadian firms and the government have to consider what the private costs will be of reducing greehouse gases when competing with American firms that do not have to meet the same emission standards.

QUICK REVIEW

- Society's pollution problem has worsened because of increasing population, rising per capita consumption, certain changes in technology, and the so-called tragedy of the commons.

- The government can encourage recycling through demand and supply incentives; its task is to determine the optimal amount of recycling.

- Under the terms of the 1997 Kyoto Protocol, the industrial nations agreed to cut emissions of greenhouse gases by 6 to 8 percent below the 1990 levels by 2012.

17.4   Information Failures

asymmetric information
A situation in which one party to a market transaction has much more information about a product or service than the other does.

Thus far, we have looked at two types of market failure: public goods and externalities. There is another market failure that results when either buyers or sellers have incomplete or inaccurate information, and their cost of obtaining better information is prohibitive. Technically stated, this market failure is the result of **asymmetric information**—unequal information available to buyers and sellers about price, quality, or some other aspect of the good or service.

Sufficient market information is normally available to ensure that goods and services are produced and purchased efficiently. But in some cases, inadequate information makes it difficult to distinguish trustworthy from untrustworthy sellers or buyers (see the Consider This box). In these markets, society's scarce resources may not be used efficiently, implying that the government should intervene by increasing the information available to the market participants. Under rare circumstances the government may itself supply a good for which information problems have prohibited efficient production.

Inadequate Information About Sellers

Inadequate information about sellers and their products can cause market failure in the form of underallocation of resources. Examining the markets for gasoline and for the services of surgeons will show us how this comes about.

EXAMPLE: THE GASOLINE MARKET

Assume an absurd situation: Suppose no system of weights and measures was established by law, no government inspection of gasoline pumps took place, and no law against false advertising existed. Each gas station can define a litre of gas as it pleases. A station can advertise that its gas is

Consider This

Asymmetric Information

A new car loses substantial market value when it is purchased, even though the same new car can sit on the dealer's lot for weeks, or even months, and retain its market value.

One explanation of this paradox is that many people obtain considerable utility from owning new things and are willing to pay premiums to get them. But there is a second, complementary explanation that relates to *asymmetric information.*

Used-car owners (potential sellers) have much better information about the mechanical condition of their cars than do potential buyers. Owners of defective cars—so-called "lemons"—have an incentive to sell them to unsuspecting buyers, whereas owners of perfectly operating cars have an incentive to retain their cars. Although both good and bad used cars are offered for sale, the *average* quality of the used cars offered on the market is poorer than the same makes and models that are *not* for sale. The typical

consumer finds it difficult to identify the poorer quality used cars simply by looking at them or taking them for a test drive. Thus the demand for used cars, and used-car prices in general, are lowered because of the risk of getting a poor-quality car.

So we have a solution to the paradox. When purchased, the market values of new cars drop quickly to the average market value established in the used-car market. This is true even though new cars may be in perfect operating condition. Their market value is depressed relative to cars still on the lot because (1) many people are willing to pay premiums for brand new cars and (2) buyers of used cars assume the risk of "buying someone else's problem."

Question: When you buy a textbook, why doesn't its resale value plummet instantly as happens with automobiles?

426

87 octane when in fact it is only 75. It can rig its pumps to indicate that it is providing more gas than the amount being delivered.

Obviously, the consumers' cost of obtaining reliable information under such chaotic conditions is exceptionally high, if not prohibitive. Customers or their representatives would have to buy samples of gas from various gas stations, have them tested for octane level, and test the accuracy of calibrations at the pump. These activities would have to be repeated regularly, because a station owner could alter the product quality and the accuracy of the pump at will.

Because of the high costs of obtaining information about the seller, many customers would opt out of this chaotic market. One tankful of a 50 percent solution of gasoline and water would be enough to discourage most motorists from further driving. More realistically, the conditions in this market would encourage consumers to vote for political candidates who promised to provide a governmental solution. Oil companies and honest gasoline stations would not object to government intervention because accurate information, by enabling this market to work, would expand their total sales and profit.

The government has in fact intervened in the market for gasoline and other markets with similar potential information difficulties. It established a system of weights and measures, employs inspectors to check the accuracy of gasoline pumps, and passed laws against fraudulent claims and misleading advertising. These government activities have produced clear net benefits for society.

EXAMPLE: LICENSING OF SURGEONS

Suppose now that anyone could hang out a shingle and claim to be a surgeon, much as anyone can become a house painter. The market would eventually sort out the true surgeons from those who were learning by doing or were fly-by-night operators who moved into and out of an area. As people died from unsuccessful surgery, lawsuits for malpractice eventually would eliminate the medical impostors. People needing surgery for themselves or their loved ones could obtain information from newspaper reports or from people who had undergone similar operations.

But this process of obtaining information for those needing surgery would take considerable time and would impose unacceptably high human and economic costs. There is a fundamental difference between getting an amateurish paint job on one's house and being on the receiving end of heart surgery by a bogus physician. The marginal cost of obtaining information about surgeons would be excessively high. The risk of proceeding without good information would result in much less surgery than desirable—an underallocation of resources to surgery.

The government has remedied this market failure through a system of qualifying tests and licensing. The licensing provides consumers with inexpensive information about a service they buy infrequently. The government has taken a similar role in several other areas of the economy. For example, it approves new medicines, regulates the securities industry, and requires warnings on containers of potentially hazardous substances. It also requires warning labels on cigarette packages and disseminates information about communicable diseases. And it issues warnings about unsafe toys and inspects restaurants for health-related violations.

Inadequate Information About Buyers

Just as inadequate information involving sellers can keep markets from achieving economic efficiency, so can inadequate information relating to buyers. The buyers may be consumers who buy products or firms that buy resources.

moral hazard problem
The possibility that individuals will change their behaviour as the result of a contract or agreement.

MORAL HAZARD PROBLEM

Private markets may underallocate resources to a particular good or service for which there is a severe **moral hazard problem**. The moral hazard problem is the tendency of one party to a contract to alter her or his behaviour after the contract is signed in ways that could be costly to the other party.

Suppose a firm offers an insurance policy that pays a set amount of money per month to couples that divorce. The attractiveness of such insurance is that it would pool the economic risk of divorce among thousands of people and, in particular, would protect spouses and children from the economic hardship that divorce often brings. Unfortunately, the moral hazard problem reduces the likelihood that insurance companies can profitably provide this type of insurance.

After taking out such insurance, married couples would have less incentive to get along and to iron out marital difficulties. Some couples might be motivated to obtain a divorce, collect the insurance, and then continue to live together. Such insurance could even promote more divorces, the very outcome it is intended to protect against. The moral hazard problem would force the insurer to charge such high premiums for this insurance that few policies would be bought. If the insurer could identify in advance those people most prone to alter their behaviour, the firm could exclude them from buying it. But the firm's marginal cost of getting such information is too high compared with the marginal benefit. Thus, this market would fail.

Although divorce insurance is not available in the marketplace, society recognizes the benefits of insuring against the hardships of divorce. It has corrected for this underallocation of hardship insurance through child-support laws that dictate payments to the spouse who retains the children, when the economic circumstances warrant such payments. Alimony laws also play a role.

The moral hazard problem is also illustrated in the following statements:

- Drivers may be less cautious because they have car insurance.

- Medical malpractice insurance may increase the amount of malpractice.

- Guaranteed contracts for professional athletes may reduce the quality of their performance.

- Employment compensation insurance may lead some workers to shirk.

- Government insurance on bank deposits may encourage banks to make risky loans.

The Moral Hazard Problem and Canada's Health Care System The moral hazard problem can help us understand some issues in the current debate on Canada's publicly funded health care system. Critics of the health care system point out that with zero deductibility for most essential health care services, there is "excess demand" for these services, which has created longer and longer waiting periods. Part of this "excess demand" may be due to the moral hazard problem: some individuals may lead unhealthy lifestyles because they know they will get the medical services they need if they get sick.

Advocates of Canada's publicly funded health care system believe this argument is ludicrous. No one willingly gets sick because he or she is fully insured. Being sick is hardly a pleasant state for any individual. Moreover, many diseases are not connected to lifestyles, but may be hereditary or caused by environmental factors over which individuals have no control.

ADVERSE SELECTION PROBLEM

adverse selection problem
A problem arising when information known to one party to a contract is not known to the other party, causing the latter to incur major costs.

Another information problem resulting from inadequate information involving buyers is the **adverse selection problem**. This problem arises when information known by the first party to a contract is not known by the second and, as a result, the second party incurs major costs. Unlike the moral hazard problem, which arises after a person signs a contract, the adverse selection problem arises at the time a person signs a contract.

In insurance, the adverse selection problem is that people who are most likely to need insurance payouts are those who buy insurance. For example, those in poorest health are more likely to buy the most generous health insurance policies. Or, at the extreme, a person planning to hire an arsonist to torch his failing business has an incentive to buy fire insurance.

The adverse selection problem thus tends to eliminate the pooling of low and high risks, which is the basis of profitable insurance. Insurance rates then must be so high that few people would want to (or be able to) buy such insurance.

Where private firms underprovide insurance because of information problems, the government often establishes some type of social insurance. It can require everyone in a particular group to take the insurance and thereby can overcome the adverse selection problem. For example, in Canada every citizen is covered by publicly funded health care insurance. The national health care program requires universal participation: People who are most likely to need the health care benefits are automatically participants in the program. So, too, are those not likely to need the benefits. No adverse selection problem exists.

Advocates of our publicly funded health care system point out that we need such a system because private markets would make it impossible for many Canadians who are seriously ill, or are at high risk of serious diseases, to get adequate health insurance. Private insurers would be unwilling to take on clients at high risk for developing serious diseases because of the very high costs that would entail for the insurer. Thus advocates of our present health care system claim that private markets would underallocate resources to health care. Such underallocation of resources in private markets is a powerful argument for a fully publicly funded health care system.

WORKPLACE SAFETY

The labour market also provides an example of how inadequate information about buyers (employers) can produce market failures.

For several reasons employers have an economic incentive to provide safe workplaces. A safe workplace reduces the amount of disruption of the production process created by job accidents, and lowers the costs of recruiting, screening, training, and retaining new workers. It also reduces a firm's worker compensation insurance premiums (legally required insurance against job injuries).

But a safe workplace is expensive: safe equipment, protective gear, and a slower work pace all entail costs. The firm will decide how much safety to provide by comparing the marginal cost and marginal benefit of providing a safer workplace. Will this amount of job safety achieve economic efficiency, as well as maximize the firm's profit?

The answer is yes if the labour and product markets are competitive and if workers are fully aware of the job risks at various places of employment. With full information, workers will avoid employers having unsafe workplaces. The supply of labour to these establishments will be greatly restricted, forcing them to raise their wages to attract a workforce. The higher wages will then give these employers an incentive to provide increased workplace safety; safer workplaces will reduce wage expenses. Only firms that find it very costly to provide safer workplaces will choose to pay high compensating wage differentials rather than reduce workplace hazards.

A serious problem arises when workers do not know that particular occupations or workplaces are unsafe. Because information about the buyer—that is, about the employer and the workplace—is inadequate, the firm may not need to pay a wage premium to attract its workforce. Its incentive to remove safety hazards, therefore, will be diminished. In brief, the labour market will fail because of asymmetric information—in this case, sellers (workers) having less information than buyers (employers).

The government has several options for remedying this information problem:

- It can directly provide information to workers about the injury experience of various employers, much as it publishes the on-time performance of airlines.

- It can require that firms provide information to workers about known workplace hazards.

- It can establish standards of workplace safety and enforce them through inspections and penalties.

Although provincial governments have mainly employed the standards-and-enforcement approach to improve workplace safety, some critics contend that an information strategy might be less costly and more effective. *(Key Question 12)*

Qualification

There are many ways to overcome information difficulties without government intervention. For example, many firms offer product warranties to overcome the lack of information about themselves and their products. Franchising also helps overcome this problem. When you visit a McDonald's or a Holiday Inn, you know precisely what you are going to get, unlike when you stop at Bob's Hamburger Shop or the Bates Motel.

Also, some private firms and organizations specialize in providing information to buyers and sellers. *Consumer Reports* provides product information; labour unions collect and disseminate information about job safety; and credit bureaus provide information to insurance companies. Brokers, bonding agencies, and intermediaries also provide information to clients.

Economists agree, however, that the private sector cannot remedy all information problems. In some situations, government intervention is desirable to promote an efficient allocation of society's scarce resources.

QUICK REVIEW

- Asymmetric information is a source of potential market failure, causing society's scarce resources to be allocated inefficiently.

- Inadequate information about sellers and their products may lead to an underallocation of resources to those products.

- The moral hazard problem is the tendency of one party to a contract to alter its behaviour in ways that are costly to the other party; for example, a person who buys insurance may willingly incur added risk.

- The adverse selection problem arises when one party to a contract has less information than the other party and incurs a cost because of that asymmetrical information. For example, an insurance company offering "no-medical-exam-required" life insurance policies may attract customers who have life-threatening diseases.

THE LASTword — Lojack: A Case of Positive Externalities

Economists Ian Ayres and Steven Levitt find that an auto antitheft device called Lojack produces large spillover benefits.

Private expenditures to reduce crime are estimated to be $30 billion annually and are growing at a faster rate than spending on public crime prevention. Unfortunately, some forms of private crime prevention simply redistribute crime rather than reduce it. For example, car alarm systems that have red blinking warning lights may simply divert professional auto thieves to vehicles that do not have such lights and alarms. The owner of a car with such an alarm system benefits through the reduced likelihood of theft but imposes a cost on other car owners who do not have such alarms. Their cars are more likely to be targeted by thieves because other cars have visible security systems.

Some private crime prevention measures, however, actually reduce crime, rather than simply redistributing it. One such measure is installation of a Lojack (or some similar) car retrieval system. Lojack is a tiny radio transmitter that is hidden in one of many possible places within the car. When an owner reports a stolen car, the police can remotely activate the transmitter. They can then determine its precise location and track its subsequent movements.

The owner of the car benefits because the 95 percent retrieval rate on cars with the Lojack system is higher than the 60 percent retrieval rate for cars without the system. But, according to a study by Ayres and Levitt, the benefit to the car owner is only 10 percent of the total benefit. Ninety percent of the total benefit is external; it is a spillover benefit to other car owners in the community.

There are two sources of this positive externality. First, the presence of the Lojack device sometimes enables police to intercept the car while the thief is still driving it. For example, in California the arrest rate for cars with Lojack was three times greater than for cars without it. The arrest puts the car thief out of commission for a time and thus reduces subsequent car thefts in the community. Second, and far more important, the device enables police to trace cars to "chop-shops," where crooks disassemble cars for resale of the parts. When police raid the chop-shop, they put the entire theft ring out of business. In Los Angeles alone, Lojack has eliminated 45 chop-shops in just a few years. The purging of the chop-shop and theft ring reduces auto theft in the community. So, auto owners who do not have Lojack devices in their cars benefit from car owners who do. Ayres and Levitt estimate the *marginal social benefit* of Lojack—the marginal benefit to the Lojack car owner *plus* the spillover benefit to other car owners—is 15 times greater than the marginal cost of the device.

We saw in Figure 17-4(a) that the existence of positive externalities causes an insufficient quantity of a product and thus an underallocation of scarce resources to its production. The two general ways to correct the outcome are to subsidize the consumer, as shown in Figure 17-4(b) or to subsidize the producer, as shown in Figure 17-4(c). Currently, there is only one form of government intervention in place: provincial-mandated insurance discounts for people who install auto retrieval systems such as Lojack. Those discounts on insurance premiums, in effect, subsidize the consumer by lowering the price of the system to consumers: the lower price raises the number of systems installed. But based on their research, Ayres and Levitt contend that the current levels of insurance discounts are far too small to correct the underallocation that results from the positive externalities created by Lojack.

Source: Based on Ian Ayres and Steven D. Levitt, "Measuring Positive Externalities from Unobservable Victim Precaution: An Empirical Analysis of Lojack," *Quarterly Journal of Economics*, February 1998, pp. 43–77. The authors point out that Lojack did not fund their work in any way, nor do they have any financial stake in Lojack.

CHAPTER SUMMARY

17.1 PUBLIC GOODS

- Graphically, the collective demand curve for a particular public good can be found by summing vertically the individual demand curves for that good. The demand curve resulting from this process indicates the collective willingness to pay for the last unit of any given amount of the public good.

- The optimal quantity of a public good occurs where the combined willingness to pay for the last unit—the marginal benefit of the good—equals the good's marginal cost.

- Cost–benefit analysis can provide guidance as to the economic desirability and most efficient scope of public goods output.

17.2 EXTERNALITIES REVISITED

- Spillovers, or externalities, cause the equilibrium output of certain goods to vary from the optimal output. Spillover costs (negative externalities) result in an over-allocation of resources that can be corrected by legislation or specific taxes. Spillover benefits (positive externalities) are accompanied by an underallocation of resources that can be corrected by subsidies to consumers, subsidies to producers, or government provision.

- According to the Coase theorem, private bargaining is capable of solving potential externality problems where (a) the property rights are clearly defined, (b) the number of people involved is small, and (c) bargaining costs are negligible.

- Clearly established property rights and liability rules permit some spillover costs to be prevented or remedied through private lawsuits. Lawsuits, however, can be costly, time-consuming, and uncertain as to their results.

- Direct controls and specific taxes can improve resource allocation in situations where negative externalities affect many people and community resources. Both direct controls (e.g., smokestack emission standards) and specific taxes (e.g., taxes on firms producing toxic chemicals) increase production costs and hence product price. As product price rises, the externality is reduced, because less of the output is bought and sold.

- Markets for pollution rights, where firms can buy and sell the right to discharge a fixed amount of pollution, put a price on pollution and encourage firms to reduce or eliminate it.

- The socially optimal amount of externality abatement occurs where society's marginal cost and marginal benefit of reducing the externality are equal. This optimal amount of pollution abatement is likely to be less than a 100 percent reduction. Changes in technology or changes in society's attitudes toward pollution can affect the optimal amount of pollution abatement.

17.3 THE ECONOMICS OF SOLID-WASTE DISPOSAL AND RECYCLING

- Recycling is a recent response to the growing garbage disposal problem. The equilibrium price and quantity of recyclable inputs depend on their demand and supply. The government can encourage recycling through either demand or supply incentives.

- A growing body of scientific evidence suggests that accumulation of carbon dioxide and other greenhouse gases in the earth's atmosphere is contributing to a global warming problem. In the Kyoto Protocol of 1997, the world's industrial nations agreed to reduce their emissions of greenhouse gases to 6 to 8 percent below 1990 levels by 2012. Canada ratified the agreement in late 2002. The United States refused to sign the Kyoto agreement, which could have potential negative short-term consequences for Canada's exporters to the U.S. market.

17.4 INFORMATION FAILURES

- Asymmetric information between sellers and buyers can cause markets to fail. The moral hazard problem occurs when people alter their behaviour after they sign a contract, imposing costs on the other party. The adverse selection problem occurs when one party to a contract takes advantage of the other party's inadequate information, resulting in an unanticipated loss to the latter party.

TERMS AND CONCEPTS

cost–benefit analysis, p. 411
marginal cost = marginal benefit (MC = MB) rule, p. 412
externalities, p. 413
Coase theorem, p. 414

tragedy of the commons, p. 417
market for externality rights, p. 418
optimal reduction of an externality, p. 420
asymmetric information, p. 425

moral hazard problem, p. 426
adverse selection problem, p. 427

STUDY QUESTIONS

1. **KEY QUESTION** Based on the following three individual demand schedules for a particular good, and assuming these three people are the only ones in the society, determine (a) the market demand schedule on the assumption that the good is a private good, and (b) the collective demand schedule on the assumption that the good is a public good. Explain the differences, if any, in your schedules.

Individual 1		Individual 2		Individual 3	
P	Q_d	P	Q_d	P	Q_d
$8	0	$8	1	$8	0
7	0	7	2	7	0
6	0	6	3	6	1
5	1	5	4	5	2
4	2	4	5	4	3
3	3	3	6	3	4
2	4	2	7	2	5
1	5	1	8	1	6

2. **KEY QUESTION**   Use your demand schedule for a public good, determined in question 1, and the following supply schedule to ascertain the optimal quantity of this public good. Why is this the optimal quantity?

P	Q_s
$19	10
16	8
13	6
10	4
7	2
4	1

3. **KEY QUESTION**   The following table shows the total costs and total benefits in billions for four different antipollution programs of increasing scope. Which program should be undertaken? Why?

Program	Total cost	Total benefit
A	$ 3	$ 7
B	7	12
C	12	16
D	18	19

4. **KEY QUESTION**   Why are spillover costs and spillover benefits also called negative and positive externalities? Show graphically how a tax can correct for a spillover cost and how a subsidy to producers can correct for a spillover benefit. How does a subsidy to consumers differ from a subsidy to producers in correcting for a spillover benefit?

5. An apple grower's orchard provides nectar to a neighbour's bees, while the beekeeper's bees help the apple grower by pollinating the apple blossoms. Use Figure 17-2(b) to explain why this situation might lead to an underallocation of resources to apple growing and to beekeeping. How might this underallocation get resolved via the means suggested by the Coase theorem?

6. Explain: "Without a market for pollution rights, dumping pollutants into the air or water is costless; in the presence of the right to buy and sell pollution rights, dumping pollution creates an opportunity cost for the polluter." What is the significance of this opportunity cost to the search for better technology to reduce pollution?

7. **KEY QUESTION**   Explain the following statement using the MB curve in Figure 17-6 to illustrate: "The optimal amount of pollution abatement for some substances, say, water from storm drains, is very low; the optimal amount of abatement for other substances, say, cyanide poison, is close to 100 percent."

8. What is the global-warming problem? How is it being addressed? Using an example other than those given in the text, explain how global warming might hurt one particular region or country but help another.

9. Explain how marketable emission credits add to overall economic efficiency, compared to across-the-board limitations on maximum discharges of air pollutants by firms.

10. Explain why there may be insufficient recycling of products when the externalities associated with landfills and garbage incinerators are not considered. What demand and supply incentives might the government provide to promote more recycling? Explain how there could be too much recycling in some situations.

11. Why is it in the interest of new homebuyers and builders of new homes to have government building codes and building inspectors?

12. **KEY QUESTION**   Place an M beside those items in the following list that describe a moral hazard problem and an A beside those that describe an adverse selection problem.

   a. A person with a terminal illness buys several life insurance policies through the mail.

   b. A person drives carelessly because he or she has automobile insurance.

   c. A person who intends to torch his warehouse takes out a large fire insurance policy.

   d. A professional athlete who has a guaranteed contract fails to stay in shape during the off-season.

   e. A woman who anticipates having a large family takes a job with a firm that offers exceptional child-care benefits.

13. Explain how Canada's publicly funded health care system resolves the adverse selection problem.

14. **(The Last Word)** Explain how a global positioning antitheft device installed by one car owner can produce a positive spillover to thousands of others in a city.

INTERNET APPLICATION QUESTION

1. Government can use direct controls in the form of legislation to reduce negative externalities such as water pollution. Go to the McConnell-Brue-Barbiero Web site (Chapter 17) to access the Environment Canada Web site. Environment Canada is responsible for getting environmental results on clean water. What success has Environment Canada had? What is it doing now?

18

Chapter

Public Choice Theory and the Economics of Taxation

IN THIS CHAPTER YOU WILL LEARN:

18.1 How public preferences are revealed through majority voting.

18.2 What government failure is and why it occurs.

18.3 Different ways of apportioning the tax burden.

18.4 About the efficiency cost of taxes.

In Chapter 17 we saw that private markets can occasionally produce *market failures,* which impede economic efficiency and justify government intervention in the economy. But the government's response to market failures is not without its own problems and pitfalls. Perhaps that is why government policies and decisions are the focus of hundreds of radio talk shows, television debates, and newspaper articles each day.

In this chapter, we explore a number of *government failures* that impede economic efficiency in the public sector. Our spotlight is first on selected aspects of **public choice theory**—the economic analysis of government decision making—and then on the economics of taxation.

18.1 Revealing Preferences Through Majority Voting

Which public goods should government produce and in what amounts? How should the tax burden of financing government be apportioned?

Decisions like these are made collectively in Canada through a democratic process that relies heavily on majority voting. Candidates for office offer alternative policy packages, and citizens elect the people they think will make the best decisions on their collective behalf. Voters retire officials who do not adequately represent their collective wishes. Citizens also periodically have opportunities at the provincial and municipal levels to vote directly on public expenditures or new legislation.

Although the democratic process does a reasonably good job of revealing society's preferences, it is imperfect. **Public choice theory** demonstrates that majority voting can produce inefficiencies and inconsistencies.

public choice theory
The economic analysis of collective and government decision making.

Inefficient Voting Outcomes

Society's well-being is enhanced when government provides a public good whose total benefit exceeds its total cost. Unfortunately, majority voting does not always produce that outcome. Voters may defeat a proposal to provide a public good even though it may yield total benefits that exceed its total cost. Conversely, majority voting may result in the provision of a public good that costs more than the benefits it yields.

ILLUSTRATION: INEFFICIENT "NO" VOTE

Assume that the government can provide a public good, say, national defence, at a total expense of $900. Assume that there are only three individuals—Adams, Benson, and Conrad—in the society and that they will share the $900 tax expense equally, each being taxed $300 if the proposed public good is provided. And assume, as Figure 18-1(a) illustrates, that Adams would receive $700 worth of benefits from having this public good; Benson, $250; and Conrad, $200.

What will be the result if a majority vote determines whether this public good is provided? Although people do not always vote strictly according to their own economic interest, it is likely that Benson and Conrad will vote no because they will incur tax costs of $300 each while gaining benefits of only $250 and $200, respectively. Adams will vote yes. So the majority vote will defeat the proposal even though the total benefit of $1150 (= $700 for Adams + $250 for Benson + $200 for Conrad) exceeds the total cost of $900.

ILLUSTRATION: INEFFICIENT "YES" VOTE

Now consider a situation in which the majority favours a public good even though its total cost *exceeds* its total benefit. Figure 18-1(b) shows the details. Again, Adams, Benson, and Conrad will equally share the $900 cost of the public good; they will each be taxed $300. But since Adams's benefit now is only $100 from the public good, she will vote against it. Meanwhile, Benson and Conrad will benefit by $350 each. They will vote for the public good because that benefit ($350) exceeds their tax payments ($300). The majority vote will provide a public good costing $900 that produces total benefits of only $800 (= $100 for Adams + $350 for Benson + $350 for Conrad). Society's resources will be inefficiently allocated to this public good, and there will be too much of it.

CONCLUSION

An inefficient outcome may occur as either an overproduction or an underproduction of a specific public good and, therefore, as an overallocation or underallocation of resources for that particular use. In our examples, each person has only a single vote, no matter how much he or she might gain

FIGURE 18-1

Inefficient Voting Outcomes

Majority voting can produce inefficient decisions. Panel (a): Majority voting leads to rejection of a public good that has greater total benefit than total cost. Panel (b): Majority voting results in acceptance of a public good that has a higher total cost than total benefit.

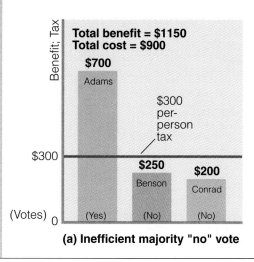

(a) Inefficient majority "no" vote

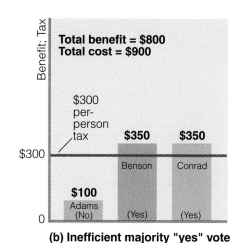

(b) Inefficient majority "yes" vote

or lose from a public good. In the first example (inefficient no vote), Adams would be willing to purchase a vote from either Benson or Conrad if buying votes were legal. That way Adams could be assured of obtaining the national defence she so highly values. But since buying votes is illegal, many people with strong preferences for certain public goods may have to go without them.

When individual consumers have a strong preference for a specific *private good,* they usually can find that good in the marketplace even though it may be unpopular with the majority of consumers. But a person cannot easily buy a *public good* such as national defence once the majority has decided against it.

Conversely, a consumer in the marketplace can decide not to buy a particular product, even a popular one. But although you may not want national defence, you must "buy" it through your tax payments when it is favoured by the majority.

Because majority voting fails to incorporate the strength of the preferences of the individual voter, it may produce economically inefficient outcomes.

Interest Groups and Logrolling

There are avenues for resolving the inefficiencies associated with majority voting. Two examples follow.

INTEREST GROUPS

Those who have a strong preference for a public good may band together into an interest group and use advertisements, mailings, and direct persuasion to convince others of the merits of that public good. Adams might try to persuade Benson and Conrad that it is in their best interest to vote for national defence—that national defence is much more valuable to them than their $250 and $200 valuations. Such appeals are common in democratic politics. Sometimes they are successful; sometimes they are not.

POLITICAL LOGROLLING

Logrolling—the trading of votes to secure favourable outcomes—can also turn an inefficient outcome into an efficient one. In our first example [Figure 18-1(a)], perhaps Benson has a strong preference for a different public good, for example, a new road, which Adams and Conrad do not think

logrolling
The trading of votes by legislators to secure favourable outcomes on decisions concerning the provision of public goods and quasipublic goods.

is worth the tax expense. That would provide an opportunity for Adams and Benson to trade votes to ensure provision of both national defence and the new road. That is, Adams and Benson would each vote yes on both measures. Adams would get the national defence and Benson would get the road. Without the logrolling, both public goods would have been rejected. Logrolling will add to society's well-being if, as was true for national defence, the road creates a greater overall benefit than cost.

Logrolling need not increase economic efficiency. Even if national defence and the road each cost more than the total benefit they produced, both might still be provided because of the vote trading.

Paradox of Voting

paradox of voting
A situation in which paired-choice voting by majority rule fails to provide a consistent ranking of society's preferences for public goods or services.

<www.magnolia.net/~leonf/sd/vp-brf.html>
The voter's paradox

Another difficulty with majority voting is the **paradox of voting**, a situation in which society may not be able to rank its preferences consistently through paired-choice majority voting.

PREFERENCES

Consider Table 18-1, in which we again assume a community of three voters: Adams, Benson, and Conrad. Suppose the community has three alternative public goods from which to choose: national defence, a road, and a severe-weather warning system. We expect that each member of the community prefers the three alternatives in a certain order. For example, one person might prefer national defence to a road, and a road to a severe-weather warning system. We can attempt to determine the preferences of the community through paired-choice majority voting. Specifically, a vote can be held between any two of the public goods, and the winner of that vote can then be matched against the third public good in another vote.

The three goods and the assumed individual preferences of the three voters are listed in the top part of Table 18-1. The data indicate that Adams prefers national defence to the road and the road to the severe-weather warning system. This implies also that Adams prefers national defence to the severe-weather warning system. Benson values the road more than the severe-weather warning system and the warning system more than national defence. Conrad's order of preference is severe-weather warning system, national defence, and road.

VOTING OUTCOMES

The lower part of Table 18-1 shows the outcomes of three hypothetical decisions of the majority vote. In the first, national defence wins against the road because a majority of voters (Adams and Conrad) prefer national defence to the road. In the second election to see whether this community wants a road or a severe-weather warning system, a majority of voters (Adams and Benson) prefer the road.

We have determined that the majority of people in this community prefer national defence to a road and prefer a road to a severe-weather warning system. It seems logical to conclude that the community prefers national defence to a weather warning system, but the community does not!

To demonstrate this conclusion, we hold a direct election between national defence and the warning system. Row (3) shows that a majority of voters (Benson and Conrad) prefer the severe-weather warning system to national defence. As listed in Table 18-1, then, the three paired-choice majority votes imply that this community is irrational: it seems to prefer national defence to a road and a road to a warning system, but would rather have a severe-weather warning system than national defence.

TABLE 18-1 Paradox of Voting

Preferences

Public Good	Adams	Benson	Conrad
National defence	1st choice	3rd choice	2nd choice
Road	2nd choice	1st choice	3rd choice
Severe-weather warning system	3rd choice	2nd choice	1st choice

Election	Voting outcomes: winner
1. National defence vs. road	National defence (preferred by Adams and Conrad)
2. Road vs. warning system	Road (preferred by Adams and Benson)
3. National defence vs. warning system	Warning system (preferred by Benson and Conrad)

The problem is not irrational community preferences but rather a flawed procedure for determining those preferences. We see that the outcome from paired-choice majority voting may depend on the order in which the votes are taken up. Under some circumstances majority voting fails to make consistent choices that reflect the community's underlying preferences. As a consequence, government may find it difficult to provide the "correct" public goods by acting in accordance with majority voting. One important note: this critique is not meant to suggest that there is some better procedure. Majority voting is much more likely to reflect community preferences than decisions made by, say, a dictator or a group of self-appointed leaders. *(Key Question 2)*

Median-voter Model

median-voter model
The theory that under majority rule the median (middle) voter will be in the dominant position to determine the outcome of an election.

One final aspect of majority voting reveals insights into real-world phenomena. The **median-voter model** suggests that, under majority rule and consistent voting preferences, the median voter will in a sense determine the outcomes of elections. The median voter is the person holding the middle position on an issue: half the other voters have stronger preferences for a public good, amount of taxation, or degree of government regulation, and half have weaker or negative preferences. The extreme voters on each side of an issue prefer the median choice rather than the other extreme position, so the median voter's choice predominates.

EXAMPLE

Suppose a society composed of Adams, Benson, and Conrad has reached agreement that as a society it needs a severe-weather warning system. Each independently is to submit a total dollar amount he or she thinks should be spent on the warning system, assuming each will be taxed one-third of that amount. An election will determine the size of the system. Because each person can be expected to vote for his or her own proposal, no majority will occur if all the proposals are placed on the ballot at the same time. Thus, the group decides on a paired-choice vote: they will first vote between two of the proposals and then match the winner of that vote against the remaining proposal.

The three proposals are as follows: Adams desires a $400 system; Benson wants an $800 system; Conrad opts for a $300 system. Which proposal will win? The median-voter model suggests it will be the $400 proposal submitted by the median voter, Adams. Half the other voters favour a more costly system; half favour a less costly system. To understand why the $400 system will be the outcome, let's conduct the two elections.

First, suppose that the $400 proposal is matched against the $800 proposal. Adams naturally votes for her $400 proposal, and Benson votes for his own $800 proposal. Conrad, who proposed the $300 expenditure for the warning system, votes for the $400 proposal because it is closer to his own. So Adams's $400 proposal is selected by a 2-to-1 majority vote.

Next, we match the $400 proposal against the $300 proposal. Again the $400 proposal wins. It gets a vote from Adams and one from Benson, who proposed the $800 expenditure and for that reason prefers a $400 expenditure to a $300 one. Adams, the median voter in this case, is in a sense the person who has decided the level of expenditure on a severe-weather warning system for this society.

REAL-WORLD APPLICABILITY

Although our illustration is a simple one, it explains a great deal. We do note a tendency for public choices to match most closely the median view. Political candidates, for example, take one set of positions to win the nomination of their political parties; in so doing, they tend to appeal to the median voter within their party to get the nomination. They then shift their views more closely to the political centre when they square off against opponents from the opposite political party. In effect, they redirect their appeal toward the median voter within the total population. They also try to label their opponents as being too liberal, or too conservative, and out of touch with mainstream Canada. They then conduct polls and adjust their positions on issues accordingly.

IMPLICATIONS

The median-voter model has two important implications:

1. Many people will be dissatisfied by the extent of government involvement in the economy. The size of government will largely be determined by the median preference, leaving many people desiring a much larger, or a much smaller, public sector. In the marketplace you can buy zero zucchinis, two zucchinis, or 200 zucchinis, depending on how much you enjoy them. In the public sector you get the public health funding the median voter prefers.

2. Some people may "vote with their feet" by moving into political jurisdictions where the median voter's preferences are closer to their own. They may move from one province to another where the level of government services, and therefore taxes, is lower. Or they may move into an area known for its excellent, but expensive, school system.

For these reasons, and because our personal preferences for government activity are not static, the median preference shifts over time. Moreover, information about people's preferences is imperfect, leaving much room for politicians to misjudge the true median position. When they misjudge, they may have a difficult time getting re-elected. *(Key Question 3)*

18.2   Government Failure

We have seen that government has a legitimate function in dealing with instances of market failure. But as implied in our discussion of voting problems, government does not always perform its economic functions effectively and efficiently. Public choice theory reveals that inherent shortcomings within the public sector can produce inefficient outcomes. Such shortcomings result in **government failure**—inefficiency because of certain characteristics of the public sector. Let's consider some of these characteristics and outcomes.

government failure
Inefficiencies in resource allocation caused by problems in the operation of the public sector (government).

Special Interests and Rent Seeking

Casual reflection suggests there may be a significant gap between "sound economics" and "sound politics." Sound economics calls for the public sector to pursue various programs as long as marginal benefits exceed marginal costs. Good politics, however, suggests that politicians support programs and policies that will maximize their chance of getting elected and staying in office. The result may be that the government will promote the goals of groups of voters that have special interests to the detriment of the larger public. In the process, economic inefficiency may result.

SPECIAL-INTEREST EFFECT

special-interest effect
Any result of government promotion of the interests (goals) of a small group at the expense of a much larger group.

Efficient public decision making is often impaired by the **special-interest effect**. This is any outcome of the political process whereby a small number of people obtain a government program or policy that gives them large gains at the expense of a much greater number of persons who individually suffer small losses.

The small group of potential beneficiaries is well informed and highly vocal on the issue in question, and they press politicians for approval. The large numbers facing very small individual losses, however, are generally uninformed on the issue. Politicians feel they will lose the campaign contributions and votes of the small special-interest group that backs the issue if they legislate against it but will not lose the support of the large group of uninformed voters, who are likely to evaluate the politicians on other issues of greater importance to them.

The special-interest effect is also evident in so-called *pork-barrel politics,* a means of securing a government project that yields benefits mainly to a single political district and its political representative. In this case, the special-interest group comprises municipal constituents, while the larger group consists of relatively uninformed taxpayers scattered across a much larger geographic area. Politicians clearly have a strong incentive to secure public goods ("pork") for their municipal constituents.

Finally, a politician's inclination to support the smaller group of special beneficiaries is enhanced because special-interest groups are often quite willing to help finance the campaigns of right-minded politicians and politicians who bring home the pork. The result is that politicians may support special-interest programs and projects that cannot be justified on economic grounds.

RENT-SEEKING BEHAVIOUR

rent seeking
The actions by persons, firms, or unions to gain special benefits from government at the taxpayers' or someone else's expense.

The appeal to government for special benefits at taxpayers' or someone else's expense is called **rent seeking**. To economists, rent is a payment beyond what is necessary to keep a resource supplied in its current use. Corporations, trade associations, labour unions, and professional organizations employ vast resources to secure favourable government policies that result in rent—higher profit or income than would occur under competitive market conditions. The government is able to dispense such rent directly or indirectly through laws, rules, hiring, and purchases. Elected officials are willing to provide such rent because they want to be responsive to key constituents, who in turn help them remain in office.

Here are some examples of "rent-providing" legislation or policies: tariffs on foreign products that limit competition and raise prices to consumers; tax breaks that benefit specific corporations; government construction projects that create union jobs but cost more than the benefits they yield; occupational licensing that goes beyond what is needed to protect consumers; and large subsidies to farmers by taxpayers. None of these is justified by economic efficiency (see the Consider This box).

 ## Consider This

Rent Seeking

The French economist Frédéric Bastiat (1801–50) is remembered for his wit and his capacity to point out absurdities in the arguments of his opponents. In the following passage, he satirizes appeals to government for special benefits at someone else's expense, or what today we call "rent seeking." His message is timeless: When rent-seekers succeed, it is often at the expense of the general interest.

> When, unfortunately, one has regard to the interest of the producer, and not to that of the consumer, it is impossible to avoid running counter to the general interest, because the demand of the producer, as such, is only for efforts, wants, and obstacles.
>
> I find a remarkable illustration of this in a Bordeaux newspaper. M. Simiot proposes this question: Should the proposed railway from Paris to Madrid offer a solution of continuity at Bordeaux?
>
> [Mr. Simiot argues that] the railway from Paris to Bayonne should have a break at Bordeaux, for if goods and passengers are forced to stop at that town, profits will accrue to bargemen, pedlars, *commissionaires*, hotel-keepers, etc.
>
> Here we have clearly the interest of labour put before the interest of consumers.
>
> But if Bordeaux has a right to profit by a gap in the line of railway, and if such profit is consistent with the public interest, then Angoulême, Poitiers, Tours, Orleans, nay, more, all the intermediate places, Ruffec, Châtellerault, etc., should also demand gaps, as being for the general interest, and, of course, for the interest of national industry; for the more these breaks in the line are multiplied, the greater will be the increase of consignments, commissions, transhipments, etc., along the whole extent of the railway. In this way, we shall succeed in having a line of railway composed of successive gaps, and which may be denominated a *Negative Railway*.
>
> The *principle of restriction* is the very same as the *principle of gaps*; the sacrifice of the consumer's interest to that of the producer, in other words, the sacrifice of the ends to the means.*

---

*Frédéric Bastiat, *Economic Sophisms* (Edinburgh: Oliver & Boyd, Ltd., 1873), pp. 80–81, abridged.

Question: If self interest is one of the main driving forces of the market economy, why does Bastiat, a proponent of the market system, take objection to the expressions of self interest by the various groups in the construction of the French railway ?

Clear Benefits, Hidden Costs

Some critics say that vote-seeking politicians will not weigh objectively all the costs and benefits of various programs in deciding which to support and which to reject. Because political officeholders must seek voter support every few years, they favour programs that have immediate and clear-cut benefits and vague or deferred costs.

Such biases may lead politicians to reject economically justifiable programs and to accept programs that are economically irrational. For example, a proposal to construct or expand mass-transit systems in large metropolitan areas may be economically rational on the basis of benefit–cost analysis, but if (1) the program is to be financed by immediate increases in highly visible income or sales taxes and (2) benefits will occur only years from now when the project is completed, then the vote-seeking politician may oppose the program.

Another example of possible political bias is the distribution of health care expenditures by both the federal and provincial governments in Canada. Certain government health care expenditures on a relatively small number of Canadians may lead to much media attention, but may not be the most efficient expenditures of health care resources from society's standpoint. But it is this kind of positive and visible "front page coverage" that politicians desire in their attempts to get re-elected.

Limited and Bundled Choice

Public choice theorists point out that the political process forces citizens and their elected representatives to be less selective in choosing public goods and services than they are in choosing private goods and services.

In the marketplace, the citizen as a consumer can exactly satisfy personal preferences by buying certain goods and not buying others. However, in the public sector the citizen as a voter is confronted with, say, only two or three candidates for an office, each representing a different bundle of programs (public goods and services). None of these bundles of public goods is likely to fit exactly the preferences of any particular voter, yet the voter must choose one of them. The candidate who comes closest to voter Smith's preference may endorse national health insurance, increases in Old Age Security benefits, subsidies to tobacco farmers, and tariffs on imported goods. Smith is likely to vote for that candidate even though Smith strongly opposes tobacco subsidies.

Parliament is confronted with a similar limited-choice, bundled-goods problem. Appropriations legislation combines hundreds, even thousands, of spending items into a single bill. Many of these spending items may be completely unrelated to the main purpose of the legislation, yet members of Parliament must vote the entire package—yea or nay. Unlike consumers in the marketplace, they cannot be selective. *(Key Question 4)*

Bureaucracy and Inefficiency

Some economists contend that public agencies are generally less efficient than private businesses. The reason is that the market system creates incentives and pressures for internal efficiency that are absent from the public sector. The market system imposes a very obvious test of performance on private firms: the test of profit and loss. An efficient firm is profitable and therefore successful; it survives, prospers, and grows. An inefficient firm is unprofitable and unsuccessful; it declines and in time goes bankrupt and ceases to exist. But no similar, clear-cut test exists with which to assess the efficiency or inefficiency of public agencies.

Furthermore, economists assert that government employees, together with the special-interest groups they serve, often gain sufficient political clout to block attempts to pare down or eliminate their agencies. Politicians who attempt to reduce the size of huge federal bureaucracies such as those relating to agriculture, education, and health and welfare incur sizable political risk because bureaucrats and special-interest groups will team up to defeat them.

Finally, critics point out that there is a tendency for government bureaucrats to justify their continued employment by looking for and eventually finding new "problems" to solve. It is not surprising that social problems, as defined by government, tend to persist or even expand.

Imperfect Institutions

Such criticisms of public sector inefficiency shatter the concept of a benevolent government that responds with precision and efficiency to the wants of its citizens. The market system of the private sector is far from perfectly efficient, and government's economic function is mainly to correct that system's shortcomings. But the public sector too is subject to deficiencies in fulfilling its economic function.

Because the market system and public agencies are both imperfect, it is sometimes difficult to determine whether a particular activity can be performed with greater success in the private sector or the public sector. It is easy to reach agreement on opposite extremes: national defence must lie with the public sector, while computer production can best be accomplished by the private sector. But what about health insurance? parks and recreation areas? fire protection? garbage collection? housing? education? It is hard to say absolutely that it should be assigned to either the public sector or the private sector. After all, the goods and services just mentioned are provided in part by *both* private enterprises and public agencies.

QUICK REVIEW

- Majority voting can produce voting outcomes that are inefficient; projects having greater total benefits than total costs may be defeated and projects having greater total costs than total benefits may be approved.

- The paradox of voting occurs when voting by majority rule does not provide a consistent ranking of society's preferences for public goods and services.

- The median-voter model suggests that under majority rule and consistent voting preferences, the voter who has the middle preference will determine the outcome of an election.

- Public sector failure occurs as a result of rent-seeking, pressure by special-interest groups, shortsighted political behaviour, limited and bundled choices, and bureaucratic inefficiency.

18.3 Apportioning the Tax Burden

The Role of Governments

We now turn from the difficulties of making collective decisions about public goods to the difficulties of deciding how those goods should be financed.

It is difficult to measure precisely how the benefits of public goods are apportioned among individuals and institutions. We cannot accurately determine how much citizen Raheed Singh benefits from military installations, a network of highways, a public school system, the national weather bureau, and municipal police and fire protection.

The situation is different when it comes to paying for those benefits. Studies reveal with reasonable clarity how the overall tax burden is apportioned. (By "tax burden" we mean the total cost of taxes imposed on society.) The overall level of taxes is important, but the average citizen is much more concerned with his or her part of the overall tax burden.

Benefits Received versus Ability to Pay

There are two basic philosophies on how the economy's tax burden should be apportioned.

BENEFITS-RECEIVED PRINCIPLE

benefits-received principle
The idea that those who receive the benefits of goods and services provided by government should pay the taxes required to finance them.

The **benefits-received principle** of taxation asserts that households and businesses should purchase the goods and services of government in the same way they buy other commodities. Those who benefit most from government-supplied goods or services should pay the taxes necessary to finance them. A few public goods are now financed on this basis. For example, money collected as gasoline taxes is typically used to finance some highway construction and repairs. Thus people who benefit from good roads pay the cost of those roads. Difficulties immediately arise, however, when we consider widespread application of the benefits-received principle.

- How will the government determine the benefits that individual households and businesses receive from national defence, education, the court system, and police and fire protection? Recall that public goods provide widespread spillover benefits and that the exclusion principle does not apply. Even in the seemingly straightforward case of highway financing, it is difficult to measure benefits. Owners of cars benefit in different degrees from good roads, but others also benefit. For example, businesses benefit because good roads bring them customers.

- The benefits-received principle cannot logically be applied to income redistribution programs. It would be absurd and self-defeating to ask poor families to pay the taxes needed to finance their welfare payments. It would be ridiculous to think of taxing only unemployed workers to finance the unemployment compensation payments they receive.

ABILITY-TO-PAY PRINCIPLE

ability-to-pay principle
The idea that those who have greater income (or wealth) should pay a greater proportion of it as taxes than those who have less income (or wealth).

The **ability-to-pay principle** of taxation asserts that the tax burden should be apportioned according to taxpayers' income and wealth. In Canada this means that individuals and businesses with larger incomes should pay more taxes in both absolute and relative terms than those with smaller incomes.

What is the rationale of ability-to-pay taxation? Proponents argue that each additional dollar of income received by a household yields a smaller amount of satisfaction or marginal utility when it is spent. Because consumers act rationally, the first dollars of income received in any period will be spent on high-urgency goods that yield the greatest marginal utility. Successive dollars of income will go for less urgently needed goods and finally for trivial goods and services. This process means that a dollar taken through taxes from a poor person who has few dollars represents a greater utility sacrifice than a dollar taken through taxes from a rich person who has many dollars. To balance the sacrifices that taxes impose on income receivers, taxes should be apportioned according to the amount of income a taxpayer receives.

This argument is appealing, but application problems arise here, too. Although we might agree that the household earning $100,000 per year has a greater ability to pay taxes than a household receiving $10,000, we don't know exactly how much more ability to pay the first family has. Should the wealthier family pay the same *percentage* of its larger income, and hence a larger absolute amount, as taxes? Or should it be made to pay a larger *fraction* of its income as taxes? How much larger should that fraction be?

There is no scientific way of measuring someone's ability to pay taxes—and that's the main problem.

BENEFITS RECEIVED VERSUS ABILITY TO PAY AND HEALTH CARE

In the ongoing debate about Canada's publicly funded national health care system, one of the options is to pursue a taxation policy based on the benefits-received principle. Canadians who use the health care system more frequently would be expected to pay more taxes than Canadians who use it rarely. Those in favour of funding the health care system along these lines do so at least partly because they believe this will reduce inefficient usage of health care services. Critics of this scheme point out that it violates the universality principle: very sick people who cannot afford to pay higher taxes would not be able to access essential health care services. The benefits-received principle of taxation in the case of health care amounts to user fees for medical services. There appears to be a consensus among Canadians that the universality principle in health care should not be violated.

Progressive, Proportional, and Regressive Taxes

Any discussion of taxation leads ultimately to the question of tax rates. Note that an *average tax rate* is the total tax paid divided by some base against which the tax is compared.

DEFINITIONS

Taxes are classified as progressive, proportional, or regressive, depending on the relationship between average tax rates and taxpayer incomes. We focus on incomes because all taxes, whether on income or on a product or a building or a parcel of land, are ultimately paid out of someone's income.

progressive tax
A tax whose average tax rate increases as the taxpayer's income increases.

regressive tax
A tax whose average tax rate decreases as the taxpayer's income increases.

proportional tax
A tax whose average tax rate remains constant as the taxpayer's income increases or decreases.

- A tax is **progressive** if its average rate increases as income increases. Such a tax claims not only a larger absolute (dollar) amount but also a larger percentage of income as income increases.

- A tax is **regressive** if its average rate declines as income increases. Such a tax takes a smaller proportion of income as income increases. A regressive tax may or may not take a larger absolute amount of income as income increases. (You may want to derive an example to confirm this conclusion.)

- A tax is **proportional** if its average rate *remains the same* regardless of the size of income.

We can illustrate these ideas with the personal income tax. Suppose tax rates are such that a household pays 10 percent of its income in taxes regardless of the size of its income. This is a *proportional* income tax. Now suppose the rate structure is such that a household with an annual taxable income of less than $10,000 pays 5 percent in income taxes; a household with an income of $10,000 to $20,000 pays 10 percent; one with a $20,000 to $30,000 income pays 15 percent; and so forth. This is a *progressive* income tax.

Finally, suppose the rate declines as taxable income rises: you pay 15 percent if you earn less than $10,000; 10 percent if you earn $10,000 to $20,000; 5 percent if you earn $20,000 to $30,000; and so forth. This is a regressive income tax.

In general, progressive taxes are those that fall relatively more heavily on those with high incomes; regressive taxes are those that fall relatively more heavily on the poor. *(Key Question 7)*

APPLICATIONS

Let's examine the progressivity, or regressivity, of several taxes. In Table 18-2 you will find the yields of the main taxes in Canada and what these yields are as a percentage of gross domestic product.

Personal Income Tax The federal personal income tax is progressive, with marginal tax rates (those assessed on additional income) ranging from 17 to 29 percent. In 2002 the federal income tax was 17 percent on the first $30,004; 26 percent for income between $30,005 and $60,008; and 29 percent for income above $60,009. Rules that allow individuals to deduct from income contributions to their registered retirement saving plan (RRSP) tend to make the tax less progressive than these marginal rates suggest. Nevertheless, average tax rates rise with income. Table 18-2 shows that the personal income tax is the largest source of government revenue.

TABLE 18-2 Tax Revenue Sources of Canadian Governments, 2001–02		
	Billions of dollars	**Percent of GDP**
Personal income taxes	142.0	13.0
Corporation income taxes	39.0	3.6
Sales taxes	89.0	8.1
Property and related taxes	34.0	3.1
Other taxes	128.9	11.8
Total tax revenues	432.9	39.6

Source: Adapted from the Statistics Canada website, www.statcan.ca/english/pgdb/govt01a.htm. Visit www.mcgrawhill.ca/college/mcconnell for data updates.

Σ-STAT

Sales Taxes At first thought, a general sales tax with, for example, a 5 percent rate would seem to be proportional, but in fact it is regressive with respect to income. A larger portion of a low-income person's income is taxed than is the case for a high-income person; the rich pay no tax on the part of income that is saved, whereas the poor are unable to save. For example, "Low-income" Goldstein has an income of $15,000 and spends it all. "High-income" Jones has an income of $300,000 but spends only $200,000 and saves the rest. Assuming a 5 percent sales tax applies to all expenditures of each individual, we find that Goldstein pays $750 (5 percent of $15,000) in sales taxes and Jones pays $10,000 (5 percent of $200,000). But Goldstein pays $750/$15,000 or 5 percent of income as sales taxes, while Jones pays $10,000/$300,000 or 3.3 percent of income as sales tax. The general sales tax, therefore, is regressive.

<sbinfocanada.about.com/
library/weekly/
aa032101a.htm>
Provincial tax comparison for
small businesses

Corporate Income Tax   The federal corporate income tax is essentially a proportional tax with a flat 28 percent tax rate in 2002. But this assumes that corporation owners (shareholders) bear the tax. Some tax experts argue that at least part of the tax is passed through to consumers in the form of higher product prices. To the extent that this occurs, the tax is like a sales tax and is thus regressive.

Property Taxes   Most economists conclude that property taxes on buildings are regressive for the same reasons as are sales taxes. First, property owners add the tax to the rents that tenants are charged. Second, property taxes, as a percentage of income, are higher for low-income families than for high-income families because the poor must spend a larger proportion of their incomes for housing. The regressivity of property taxes may be increased by differences in property-tax rates from municipality to municipality.

18.4   Tax Incidence and Efficiency Loss

tax incidence
The person or group who ends up paying a tax.

Determining whether a particular tax is progressive, proportional, or regressive is complicated, because those on whom taxes are levied do not always pay the taxes. We therefore need to try to locate the final resting place of a tax, or the **tax incidence**. The tools of elasticity of supply and demand will help. Let's focus on a hypothetical tax levied on wine producers. Do the producers really pay this tax, or do they shift it to wine consumers?

Elasticity and Tax Incidence

In Figure 18-2, S and D represent the before-tax market for a certain domestic wine; the no-tax equilibrium price and quantity are $8 per bottle and 15 million bottles. If government levies a tax of $2 per bottle directly on the winery for every bottle sold, who will actually pay it?

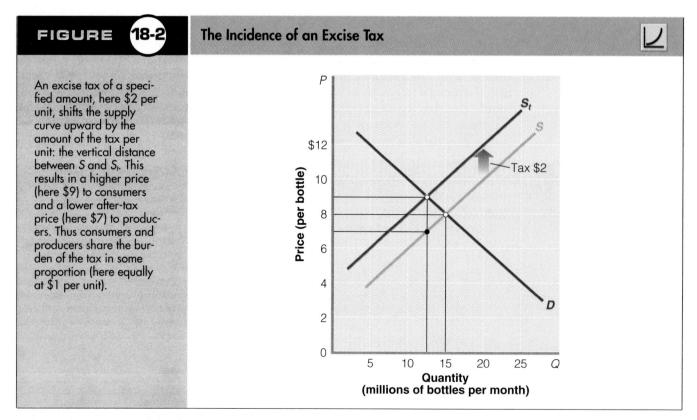

| FIGURE 18-2 | The Incidence of an Excise Tax |

An excise tax of a specified amount, here $2 per unit, shifts the supply curve upward by the amount of the tax per unit: the vertical distance between S and S_t. This results in a higher price (here $9) to consumers and a lower after-tax price (here $7) to producers. Thus consumers and producers share the burden of the tax in some proportion (here equally at $1 per unit).

DIVISION OF BURDEN

Since the government imposes the tax on the sellers (suppliers), we can view the tax as an addition to the marginal cost of the product. Now sellers must get $2 more for each bottle to receive the same per-unit profit they were getting before the tax. While sellers are willing to offer, for example, five million bottles of untaxed wine at $4 per bottle, they must now receive $6 per bottle (= $4 plus the $2 tax) to offer the same five million bottles. The tax shifts the supply curve upward (leftward) as shown in Figure 18-2, where S_t is the after-tax supply curve.

The after-tax equilibrium price is $9 per bottle, whereas the before-tax equilibrium price was $8. So, in this case, consumers pay half the $2 tax as a higher price; producers pay the other half in the form of a lower after-tax per-unit revenue. That is, after remitting the $2 tax per unit to government, producers receive $7, or $1 less than the $8 before-tax price. In this instance, consumers and producers share the burden of the tax equally: producers shift half the tax to consumers in the form of a higher price and bear the other half themselves.

Note also that the equilibrium quantity declines because of the tax levy and the higher price that it imposes on consumers. In Figure 18-2 that decline in quantity is from 15 million bottles to 12.5 million bottles per month.

ELASTICITIES

If the elasticities of demand and supply were different from those shown in Figure 18-2, the incidence of tax would also be different. Two generalizations are relevant.

First, *with a specific supply, the more inelastic the demand for the product, the larger is the portion of the tax shifted to consumers.* To verify this, sketch graphically the cases in which demand is perfectly elastic and perfectly inelastic. In the first case, the incidence of the tax is entirely on sellers; in the second, the tax is shifted entirely to consumers.

Figure 18-3 contrasts the more usual cases where demand is either relatively elastic or relatively inelastic in the relevant price range. With elastic demand in panel (a), a small portion of the tax $(P_e - P_1)$ is shifted to consumers, and most of the tax $(P_1 - P_a)$ is borne by the producers. With inelastic demand in panel (b), most of the tax $(P_i - P_1)$ is shifted to consumers, and only a small amount $(P_1 - P_b)$ is paid by producers. In both graphs the per-unit tax is represented by the vertical distance between S_t and S.

Note also that the decline in equilibrium quantity $(Q_1 - Q_2)$ is smaller when demand is more inelastic. This is the basis of our previous applications of the elasticity concept: Revenue-seeking

---

FIGURE 18-3   **Demand Elasticity and the Incidence of an Excise Tax**

Panel (a): If demand is elastic in the relevant price range, price rises modestly (P_1 to P_e) when an excise tax is levied. Hence, the producer bears most of the tax burden. Panel (b): If demand is inelastic, the price to the buyer increases substantially (P_1 to P_i) and most of the tax is shifted to consumers.

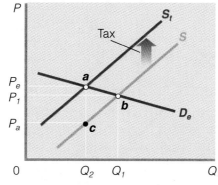

(a) Tax incidence and elastic demand

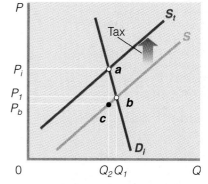

(b) Tax incidence and inelastic demand

legislatures place heavy sales taxes on liquor, cigarettes, automobile tires, telephone service, and other products whose demand is inelastic. Since demand for these products is relatively inelastic, the tax does not reduce sales by much, so the tax revenue stays high.

Second, *with a specific demand, the more inelastic the supply, the larger is the portion of the tax borne by producers.* When supply is elastic [Figure 18-4(a)], the producers shift most of the tax $(P_e - P_1)$ to consumers and bear only a small portion $(P_1 - P_a)$ themselves. But where supply is inelastic [Figure 18-4(b)], the reverse is true: the major portion of the tax $(P_1 - P_b)$ falls on sellers, and a relatively small amount $(P_i - P_1)$ is shifted to buyers. The equilibrium quantity also declines less with an inelastic supply than it does with an elastic supply.

Gold is an example of a product with an inelastic supply and one where the burden of a tax (such as an extraction tax) would mainly fall on producers. Conversely, because the supply of baseballs is relatively elastic, producers would pass on to consumers much of an excise tax on baseballs.

Efficiency Loss of a Tax

We just observed that producers and consumers typically each bear part of a tax levied on producers. Let's now look more closely at the overall economic effect of a sales tax. Consider Figure 18-5, which is identical to Figure 18-2 but contains the additional detail we need for our discussion.

TAX REVENUES

In our example, a $2 tax on wine increases its market price from $8 to $9 per bottle and reduces the equilibrium quantity from 15 million bottles to 12.5 million. Government tax revenue is $25 million (= $2 × 12.5 million bottles), an amount shown as the rectangle *efac* in Figure 18-5. The elasticities of supply and demand in this case are such that consumers and producers each pay half this total amount, or $12.5 million apiece (= $1 × 12.5 million bottles). The government uses this $25 million of tax revenue to provide public goods and services. So this transfer of dollars from consumers and producers to government involves no loss of well-being to society.

EFFICIENCY LOSS

The $2 tax on wine does more than require consumers and producers to pay $25 million in taxes; it also reduces the equilibrium amount of wine produced and consumed by 2.5 million bottles. The

---

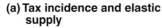

| FIGURE | 18-4 | Supply Elasticity and the Incidence of an Excise Tax |

Panel (a): With elastic supply, an excise tax results in a large price increase (P_1 to P_e), and the tax is, therefore, paid mainly by consumers. Panel (b): If supply is inelastic, the price rise is small (P_1 to P_i), and sellers bear most of the tax.

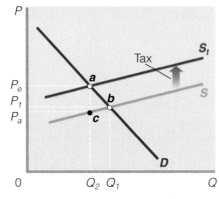

(a) Tax incidence and elastic supply

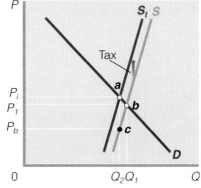

(b) Tax incidence and inelastic supply

FIGURE 18-5   Efficiency Loss of a Tax

The levy of a $2 tax per bottle of wine increases the price per bottle from $8 to $9 and reduces the equilibrium quantity from 15 million to 12.5 million. Tax revenue to the government is $25 million (area *efac*). The efficiency loss of the tax arises from the 2.5 million decline in output; the amount of that loss is shown as triangle *abc*.

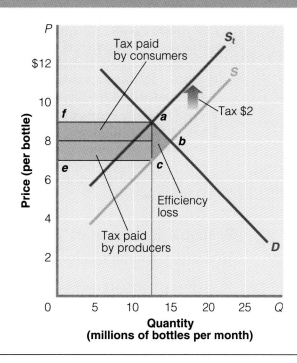

fact that consumers and producers demanded and supplied 2.5 million more bottles of wine before the tax means that those 2.5 million bottles provided benefits in excess of their production costs. This is clear from the following analysis.

Segment *ab* of demand curve *D* in Figure 18-5 indicates the willingness to pay—the marginal benefit—associated with each of the 2.5 million bottles consumed before (but not after) the tax. Segment *cb* of supply curve *S* reflects the marginal cost of each bottle of wine. For all but the very last one of these 2.5 million bottles, the marginal benefit (shown by a point on *ab*) exceeds the marginal cost (shown by a point on *cb*). Not producing all 2.5 million bottles of wine reduces well-being by an amount represented by the triangle *abc*. The area of this triangle identifies the **efficiency loss of the tax** (also called the *deadweight loss of the tax*). This loss is society's sacrifice of net benefit, because the tax reduces production and consumption of the product below their levels of economic efficiency at which marginal benefit and marginal cost are equal.

efficiency loss of a tax
The loss of net benefits to society because a tax reduces the production and consumption of a taxed good below the level of allocative efficiency.

ROLE OF ELASTICITIES

Most taxes create some degree of efficiency loss, but just how much depends on the supply and demand elasticities. Glancing back at Figure 18-3, we see that the efficiency loss area *abc* is greater in panel (a), where demand is relatively elastic, than in panel (b), where demand is relatively inelastic. Similarly, area *abc* is greater in panel (a) of Figure 18-4 than in panel (b), indicating a larger efficiency loss where supply is more elastic. Other things equal, *the greater the elasticities of supply and demand, the greater the efficiency loss of a particular tax.*

Two taxes yielding equal revenues do not necessarily impose equal costs on society. The government must keep this fact in mind when designing a tax system to finance beneficial public goods and services. In general, government should minimize the efficiency loss of the tax system in raising any specific dollar amount of tax revenue.

QUALIFICATIONS

But there may be other tax goals as important as, or even more important than, minimizing efficiency losses from taxes. Here are two examples:

1. *Redistributive goals*   Government may want to impose progressive taxes as a way to redistribute income. A 10 percent sales tax placed on selected luxuries would be an example. Because the demand for luxuries is elastic, substantial efficiency losses from this tax are to be expected. However, if government concluded that the benefits from the redistribution effects of the tax would exceed the efficiency losses, then it would levy the luxury tax.

2. *Reducing negative externalities*   The government may have intended the $1 tax on wine in Figure 18-5 to reduce the consumption of wine by 2.5 million bottles. It may have concluded that such consumption of alcoholic beverages produces certain negative externalities. Therefore, it might have intentionally levied this tax to shift the market supply curve such that the price of wine increased and the amount of resources allocated to wine declined, as in Figure 18-3(b). *(Key Question 9)*

Probable Incidence of Taxes in Canada

Let's look now at the probable incidence of each of the major sources of tax revenue in Canada.

PERSONAL INCOME TAX

The incidence of the personal income tax is generally on the individual because there is little chance for shifting it. But there might be exceptions. Individuals and groups who can control the price of their labour services may be able to shift a part of the tax. Dentists, lawyers, and other professional people who can readily increase their fees may do so because of the tax. Unions might regard personal income taxes as part of the cost of living and, as a result, strengthen their bargaining resolve for higher wages when personal income tax rates rise. If they are successful, they may shift part of the tax from workers to employers, who, by increasing prices, shift the wage increase to the public. Generally, however, the individual on whom the tax is initially levied bears the burden of the personal income tax.

CORPORATE INCOME TAX

The incidence of the corporate income tax is much less certain. The traditional view is that a firm currently charging the profit-maximizing price and producing the profit-maximizing output will have no reason to change price or output when a tax on corporate income (profit) is imposed. The price and output combination yielding the greatest profit before the tax will still yield the greatest profit after a fixed percentage of the firm's profit is taken away via an income tax. In this view, the company's stockholders (owners) must bear the burden of the tax through lower dividends or a smaller amount of retained earnings.

However, where a small number of firms control a market, producers may be able to shift part of their corporate income tax to consumers through higher prices and to resource suppliers through lower prices and wages. That is, some firms may be able to use their monopoly power as product sellers and monopsony power as resource buyers to reduce the actual amount of the tax paid by their corporate stockholders.

There is no consensus among experts on the overall incidence of the corporate income tax. Stockholders, customers, and resource suppliers may share the tax burden in some unknown proportion.

SALES AND EXCISE TAXES

A *sales tax* is a general excise tax levied on a wide range of consumer goods and services, whereas a *specific excise tax* is one levied only on a particular product. Sales taxes are usually transparent to the buyer, whereas excise taxes are often hidden in the price of the product. An example of a general sales tax is the federal Goods and Services Tax (GST), which is levied on most goods and services sold across Canada. Sellers often shift both kinds of taxes partly or largely to consumers through higher product prices. There may be some difference in the extent to which sales taxes and excise taxes are shifted, however. Because a sales tax covers a much wider range of products than an excise tax does, consumers have little chance to resist the price boosts that sales taxes entail. They cannot reallocate their expenditures to untaxed, lower-priced products. Therefore, sales taxes tend to be shifted in their entirety from producers to consumers.

Excise taxes, however, fall on a select list of goods. Therefore, the possibility of consumers turning to substitute goods and services is greater. An excise tax on theatre tickets that does not apply to other types of entertainment might be difficult to pass on to consumers via price increases. Why? The answer is provided in Figure 18-3(a), where demand is elastic. A price boost to cover the excise tax on theatre tickets might cause consumers to substitute alternative types of entertainment. The higher price would reduce sales so much that a seller would be better off to bear all, or a large portion of, the excise tax. (See Global Perspective 18.1 for a comparison of taxes on goods and services in various countries.)

With other products, modest price increases to cover taxes may have smaller effects on sales. The excise taxes on gasoline, cigarettes, and alcoholic beverages provide examples—for these products few good substitutes exist to which consumers can turn as prices rise. For these goods, the seller is better able to shift nearly all the excise tax to consumers; prices of cigarettes have gone up in lockstep with the recent, substantial increases in excise taxes on cigarettes.

<www.taxpayer.com/
opinioneditorials/
nationalpost/jan5-1999.htm>
Gasoline and taxes

PROPERTY TAXES

Many property taxes are borne by the property owner because there is no other party to whom they can be shifted. This is typically true for taxes on land, personal property, and owner-occupied residences. Even when land is sold, the property tax is not likely to be shifted. The buyer understands that future taxes will have to be paid on it, and this expected taxation will be reflected in the price the buyer is willing to offer for the land.

Many property taxes are borne by the property owner because there is no other party to whom they can be shifted.

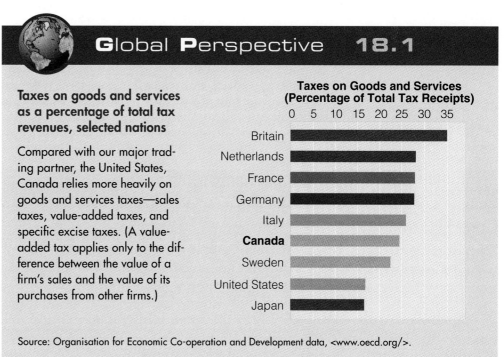

Global Perspective 18.1

Taxes on goods and services as a percentage of total tax revenues, selected nations

Compared with our major trading partner, the United States, Canada relies more heavily on goods and services taxes—sales taxes, value-added taxes, and specific excise taxes. (A value-added tax applies only to the difference between the value of a firm's sales and the value of its purchases from other firms.)

**Taxes on Goods and Services
(Percentage of Total Tax Receipts)**

0   5   10   15   20   25   30   35

Britain
Netherlands
France
Germany
Italy
Canada
Sweden
United States
Japan

Source: Organisation for Economic Co-operation and Development data, <www.oecd.org/>.

Taxes on rented and business property are a different story. Taxes on rented property can be shifted wholly or in part from the owner to the tenant through higher rent. Business property taxes are treated as a business cost and are taken into account in establishing product price; hence, such taxes are ordinarily shifted to the firm's customers.

Table 18-3 summarizes this discussion of the shifting and incidence of taxes.

Recent Canadian Tax Reform

Goods and Services Tax (GST)
Federal tax that replaced the federal sales tax in Canada; it is 7 percent on a broad base of goods and services.

<www.ctf.ca>
Canadian Tax Foundation

The Canadian tax system has undergone three major changes within the past two decades: (1) the 1987 Tax Reform, (2) the **Goods and Services Tax (GST)**, and (3) reforms since 2000. Keep in mind that we refer to the federal government only; each province also levies taxes, some in conjunction with the federal government.

THE 1987 TAX REFORM

Spurred on by the tax reform in the United States that significantly lowered marginal tax rates, the Canadian government simplified the personal income tax from 11 categories to only 3. The result was a lower marginal tax rate, which, combined with provincial levies, had been as high as 64 percent. The tax reforms also eliminated tax deductions in favour of tax credits. The top federal marginal tax rate has come down to 29 percent.

After these reforms, the federal surtax was increased and a claw-back provision was introduced that in effect took back part of the social insurance benefits, primarily employment insurance and family allowance, paid to higher-income Canadians. Both of these provisions made the income tax system more progressive.

THE GST

value-added tax (VAT)
A tax imposed on the difference between the value of the products sold by a firm and the value of the goods purchased from other firms to produce the product.

The controversy surrounding the introduction of the GST was unprecedented. Much of the dispute arose because of misunderstandings and a concerted and highly publicized effort by the official opposition in Parliament, the Liberal Party, to defeat the legislation.

The GST is similar to a **value-added tax (VAT)**. It is much like a sales tax, except that it applies only to the difference between the value of a firm's sales and the value of its purchases from other firms. Firms are allowed a tax credit equal to the taxes paid on their inputs. Most European nations currrently use VATs as a source of revenue (see Global Perspective 18.1).

The GST replaced the federal sales tax, which was levied primarily on manufactured goods and was as high as 13 percent on some products. The GST at present stands at 7 percent and is levied on a much broader base that includes both goods and services. The only exemptions are agricultural and fish products, prescription drugs, and medical devices.

An important feature of the GST is that exports are exempt since producers can claim a credit equal to the taxes paid on the inputs used to produce the product. Moreover, imported goods are subject to the GST, so they do not have an advantage compared to domestically produced goods.

TABLE 18-3	The Probable Incidence of Taxes
Type of tax	**Probable incidence**
Personal income tax	The household or individual on which it is levied.
Corporate income tax	Some economists conclude the firm on which it is levied bears the tax; others conclude the tax is shifted, wholly or in part, to consumers and resource suppliers.
Sales tax	Consumers who buy the taxed products.
Specific excise taxes	Consumers, producers, or both, depending on elasticities of demand and supply.
Property taxes	Owners in the case of land and owner-occupied residences; tenants in the case of rented property; consumers in the case of business property.

REFORMS SINCE 2000

In the federal government budget of February 2000, major changes to the tax system were announced. The most important features are

- Full indexation of the personal income tax system to protect taxpayers against automatic tax increases caused by inflation.
- The reduction of the middle income tax rate to 23 from 26 percent over five years.
- The reduction of the corporate income tax rate to 21 percent from 28 percent on small business income.
- The reduction of the capital gains tax.
- The elimination of the 5 percent deficit reduction surtax on middle-income taxpayers.

The federal government claims that over five years, the year 2000 tax reforms will save Canadians some $58 billion in taxes. These tax reforms were at least partly due to the elimination of the budget deficit in 1998 and the projection of increasing surplus in the first decade of the new millennium. But as in the case of the 1987 reforms, some economists believe that the lower tax rates in the United States also played a role. An ongoing debate is whether a brain drain to our neighbour to the south is primarily due to its lower tax rates. It is difficult to assess whether the assertion has any truth to it because of the difficulty of determining whether those that did leave did so because of the differential tax burden.

In February 2003 the federal government brought down the latest budget before this book went to press. The main change to taxes was the federal government's commitment to eliminate the federal capital tax by 2008.

THE LASTword   Public Choice Theory

The founder of public choice theory is James M. Buchanan (b. 1919). He received the Nobel Prize in Economics in 1986 for his groundbreaking contributions to public choice theory.

Buchanan belongs to a group known as welfare economists. Welfare economists are concerned with maximizing social well-being, and focus on such things as redistribution policies and voting (decision) rules. Buchanan focused on the latter. As part of the creation of public choice theory (also known as the economics of politics), he also developed *constitutional economics* (the economics of rules).

Buchanan was not alone in his work on public choice theory. He co-authored the groundbreaking book *The Calculus of Consent: Logical Foundations of Constitutional Democracy* with Gordon Tullock (b. 1922) at the University of Virginia. Together they advanced public choice theory by incorporating rent-seeking behavior, interest groups, and voting rules.

Swedish economist Knut Wicksell (1851–1926), though recognized primarily for his work in monetary economics, influenced Buchanan's ideas through his 1896 dissertation on taxes. Wicksell argued that only a unanimous collective choice can guarantee that a public policy action will result in a just and efficient outcome. This is today referred to as a *unanimity rule*. According to Wicksell, if a policy action "holds out any prospect at all of creating utility exceeding costs, it will always be theoretically possible, and approximately so in practice, to find a distribution of costs such that all parties regard the expenditure as beneficial and may therefore approve it unanimously."*

The philosophy underlying Buchanan's public choice theory is that only individuals know what provides them utility or creates disutility. While individuals vary in such things as ability, information, and tastes, they all pursue their own self-interest. Classical economists such as Adam Smith argued that the pursuit of economic self-interest would create a harmony of interests in the market place. Buchanan extended the principle to political self-interest and to identifying mechanisms by which a harmony of political interests (primarily in terms of economic policy actions) could be achieved.

---

*Knut Wicksell, "A New Principle of Just Taxation," translated by James M. Buchanan, in *Classics in the Theory of Public Finance*, eds. Richard A. Musgrave and A.T. Peacock (London: Macmillan, 1958), pp. 89–90.

CHAPTER SUMMARY

18.1 REVEALING PREFERENCES THROUGH MAJORITY VOTING

- Public choice theory examines the economics of collective and government decision making, politics, and elections.

- Majority voting creates a possibility of (a) an underallocation or an overallocation of resources to a particular public good and (b) inconsistent voting outcomes. The median-voter model predicts that, under majority rule, the person holding the middle position on an issue will determine the outcome of an election involving that issue.

18.2 GOVERNMENT FAILURES

- Public choice theorists cite reasons why government might be inefficient in providing public goods and services: (a) There are strong reasons for politicians to support special-interest legislation; (b) Politicians may be biased in favour of programs with immediate and clear-cut benefits and difficult-to-identify costs and against programs with immediate and easily identified costs and vague or deferred benefits; (c) Citizens as voters and governmental representatives face limited and bundled choices as to public goods and services, whereas consumers in the private sector can be highly selective in their choices; (d) Government bureaucracies have less incentive to operate efficiently than do private businesses.

18.3 APPORTIONING THE TAX BURDEN

- The benefits-received principle of taxation states that those who receive the benefits of goods and services provided by government should pay the taxes required to finance them. The ability-to-pay principle states that those who have greater income should be taxed more,

absolutely and relatively, than those who have less income.

- The federal personal income tax is progressive. The flat rate corporate income tax is regressive. General sales, excise, and property taxes are regressive.

18.4 TAX INCIDENCE AND EFFICIENCY LOSS

- Excise taxes affect supply and, therefore, equilibrium price and quantity. The more inelastic the demand for a product, the greater is the portion of an excise tax that is shifted to consumers. The greater the inelasticity of supply, the larger the portion of the tax that is borne by the seller.

- Taxation involves the loss of some output whose marginal benefit exceeds its marginal cost. The more elastic the supply and demand curves, the greater the efficiency loss resulting from a particular tax.

- Sales taxes normally are shifted to consumers; personal income taxes are not shifted. Specific excise taxes may or may not be shifted to consumers, depending on the elasticities of demand and supply. Disagreement exists as to whether corporate income taxes are shifted. Property taxes on owner-occupied property are borne by the owner; those on rental property are borne by tenants.

- The 1987 federal tax reform simplified income taxes and lowered the marginal tax rate. The 2000 federal tax reform lowered the personal income tax rate for middle-income Canadians.

- The GST is similar to a value-added tax. It is an improvement over the federal sales tax it replaced because it introduces fewer distortions, exports are exempt, and imports compete on equal footing with domestic goods.

TERMS AND CONCEPTS

public choice theory, p. 434
logrolling, p. 435
paradox of voting, p. 436
median-voter model, p. 437
government failure, p. 438
special-interest effect, p. 438

rent seeking, p. 439
benefits-received principle, p. 441
ability-to-pay principle, p. 442
progressive tax, p. 443
regressive tax, p. 443
proportional tax, p. 443

tax incidence, p. 444
efficiency loss of a tax, p. 447
Goods and Services Tax (GST),
   p. 450
value-added tax (VAT), p. 450

STUDY QUESTIONS

1. Explain how affirmative and negative majority votes can sometimes lead to inefficient allocations of resources to public goods. Is this problem likely to be greater under a benefits-received or under an ability-to-

pay tax system? Use the information in Figure 18-1(a) and (b) to show how society might be better off if Adams were allowed to buy votes.

2. **KEY QUESTION** Explain the paradox of voting through reference to the accompanying table, which shows the ranking of three public goods by voters Larry, Curley, and Moe:

Rankings

Public good	Larry	Curley	Moe
Courthouse	2nd choice	1st choice	3rd choice
School	3rd choice	2nd choice	1st choice
Park	1st choice	3rd choice	2nd choice

3. **KEY QUESTION** Suppose there are only five people in a society and each favours one of the five highway construction options in Table 17-2 (include no highway construction as one of the options). Explain which of these highway options will be selected using a majority paired-choice vote. Will this option be the optimal size of the project from an economic perspective?

4. **KEY QUESTION** How does the problem of limited and bundled choice in the public sector relate to economic efficiency? Why are public bureaucracies alleged to be less efficient than private enterprises?

5. Explain: "Politicians would make more rational economic decisions if they weren't running for re-election every few years."

6. Distinguish between the benefits-received and the ability-to-pay principles of taxation. Which philosophy is more evident in our present tax structure? Justify your answer. To which principle of taxation do you subscribe? Why?

7. **KEY QUESTION** Suppose a tax is such that an individual with an income of $10,000 pays $2000 of tax, a person with an income of $20,000 pays $3000 of tax, a person with an income of $30,000 pays $4000 of tax, and so forth. What is each person's average tax rate? Is this tax regressive, proportional, or progressive?

8. What is meant by a progressive tax? A regressive tax? A proportional tax? Comment on the progressivity or regressivity of each of the following taxes, indicating your assumption concerning tax incidence: (a) the federal personal income tax, (b) a 7 percent general sales tax, (c) a federal excise tax on automobile tires, (d) a municipal property tax on real estate, (e) the federal corporate income tax.

9. **KEY QUESTION** What is the incidence of an excise tax when demand is highly inelastic? elastic? What effect does the elasticity of supply have on the incidence of an excise tax? What is the efficiency loss of a tax, and how does it relate to elasticity of demand and supply?

10. **Advanced analysis** Suppose the equation for the demand curve for some product X is $P = 8 - .6Q$ and the supply curve is $P = 2 + .4Q$. What are the equilibrium price and quantity? Now suppose an excise tax is imposed on X such that the new supply equation is $P = 4 + .4Q$. How much tax revenue will this excise tax yield the government? Graph the curves and label the area of the graph that represents the tax collection "TC" and the area that represents the efficiency loss of the tax "EL." Briefly explain why area EL is the efficiency loss of the tax but TC is not.

11. **(The Last Word)** According to public choice theory there is no such thing as a "public interest." Explain why.

INTERNET APPLICATION QUESTION

1. Some economists contend that public agencies are generally less efficient than private businesses. Federal Express competes directly with Canada Post for delivery of express mail and packages. Assume you need to send an express letter and a package from your address to either Halifax or Vancouver. Access the Web sites of federal Express and Canada Post through the McConnell-Brue-Barbiero Web site (Chapter 18). Based on their interactive rate and options calculators, which service is more competitive as to price and delivery? Does a lower rate with greater delivery options mean greater efficiency? Why or why not?

Credits

Text Credits

Chapter 2

p. 38 From Organisation for Economic Co-operation and Development (OECD).

Chapter 4

p. 79 From The Heritage Foundation and *The Wall Street Journal*; p. 90 From Organisation for Economic Co-operation and Development (OECD); p. 93 From Kerney, A.T., *Foreign Policy*, www.foreignpolicy.com.

Chapter 6

p. 140 From World Bank, www.worldbank.com.

Chapter 7

p. 178 From U.S. Bureau of Labor Statistics, www.bls.gov.

Chapter 8

p. 218 From Organisation for Economic Co-operation and Development (OECD), *Health at a Glance*, Paris, 2001.

Chapter 10

p. 252 Adapted from the Statistics Canada publication, "Industrial Organization and Concentration in Manufacturing Industries," Catalogue No. 31C0024, April 2002; p. 259 Adapted from the Statistics Canada publication, "Industrial Organization and Concentration in Manufacturing Industries," Catalogue No. 31C0024, April 2002; p. 269 From OPEC Secretariat, www.opec.org; p. 273 From Interbrand, www.interbrand.com.

Chapter 11

p. 280 From National Science Foundation, www.nsf.gov; p. 297 Data from Canadian Media Directors' Council, www.cmdc.ca/media_digest/001_51_55.htm.

Chapter 14

p. 337 From U.S. Bureau of Labor Statistics, www.bls.gov; p. 338 Adapted from the Statistics Canada publication, "Productivity Growth in Canada", Catalogue No. 15-204, December 2002; p. 351 Adapted from the Statistics Canada web site, www.statcan.ca/english/pgdb/econ03.htm; p. 358 From Citizenship and Immigration Canada, www.cic.gc.ca; p. 361 From *Canadian Business*, May 12, 2003. This list is updated each year in the May issue of *Canadian Business*.

Chapter 15

p. 373 From Organisation for Economic Co-operation and Development (OECD); p. 377 Adapted from the Statistics Canada web site, www.statcan.ca/english/pgdb/econ03.htm.

Chapter 16

p. 382 Adapted from the Statistics Canada publication, "Income Trends in Canada," Catalogue No. 13F0022, 180-2000, Ottawa, 2001; p. 383 From the Statistics Canada publication, "Income Trends in Canada, 1980–2000"; p. 387 From *World Development Report*, 2003, pp. 236–237; p. 391 Adapted from the Statistics Canada publication, "Income in Canada, 2001," Catalogue No. 75-202, June 2003; p. 392 Adapted from the 2002–2003 Estimates Part 1 – The Government Expenditure Plan, www.tbs-sct.gc.ca/est-pre/20022003/page.asp?page=001_e_3.htm, Treasury Board of Canada Secretariat, 2002. Reproduced with the permission of the Minister of Public Works and Government Services, 2003.

Chapter 17

p. 424 From Organisation for Economic Co-operation and Development (OECD), Environmental Data.

Chapter 18

p. 443 Adapted from the Statistics Canada web site, www.statcan.ca/english/pgdb/govt01a.htm; p. 449 From Organisation for Economic Co-operation and Development (OECD).

Photographs

Chapter 1

p. 3, PhotoDisc

Chapter 2

p. 35, PhotoDisc

Chapter 3

p. 49, PhotoDisc; p. 65, PhotoDisc; p. 67, PhotoDisc

Chapter 4

p. 88, Canapress; p. 92, PhotoDisc

Chapter 5

p. 112, PhotoDisc; p. 124, Corel; p. 128, PhotoDisc

Chapter 6

p. 137, PhotoDisc; p. 147, PhotoDisc

Chapter 7

p. 165, PhotoDisc; p. 184, PhotoDisc

Chapter 8

p. 192, PhotoDisc; p. 194, PhotoDisc

Chapter 9

p. 224, PhotoDisc

Chapter 10

p. 251, PhotoDisc

Chapter 11

p. 281, PhotoDisc

Chapter 13

p. 318, PhotoDisc

Chapter 14

p. 336, PhotoDisc; p. 342, PhotoDisc

Chapter 15

p. 376, PhotoDisc

Chapter 16

p. 382, PhotoDisc

Chapter 17

p. 409, Canapress; p. 413, PhotoDisc

Chapter 18

p. 449, Corel

Glossary

A

Ability-to-pay principle   The idea that those who have greater income (or wealth) should pay a greater proportion of it as taxes than those who have less income (or wealth).

Absolute advantage When a given amount of resources can produce more of a commodity in one country than in another.

Absolute poverty A situation in which the basic material needs of an individual or a family (food, clothing, shelter) are not met.

Adverse selection problem A problem arising when information known to one party to a contract is not known to the other party, causing the latter to incur major costs.

Aggregate A collection of specific economic units treated as if they were one unit.

Agribusiness Large corporate firms in farming.

Allocative efficiency The apportionment of resources among firms and industries to obtain the production of the products most wanted by society (consumers); the output of each product at which its marginal cost and price or marginal benefit are equal.

Anti-combines (antimonopoly) legislation Laws designed to prevent the growth of monopoly.

Anti-combines policy The laws and government actions designed to prevent monopoly and promote competition.

Appreciation (of the dollar) An increase in the value of the dollar relative to the currency of another nation so that a dollar buys a larger amount of the foreign currency and thus of foreign goods.

Asymmetric information A situation in which one party to a market transaction has much more information about a product or service than the other does; the result may be an underallocation or overallocation of resources.

Average fixed cost (AFC) A firm's total fixed cost divided by output (the quantity of product produced).

Average product (AP) The total output produced per unit of a resource employed (total product divided by the quantity of that employed resource).

Average revenue Total revenue from the sale of a product divided by the quantity of the product sold.

Average total cost (ATC) A firm's total cost divided by output (the quantity of product produced); equal to average fixed cost plus average variable cost.

Average variable cost (AVC) A firm's total variable cost divided by output (the quantity of product produced).

B

Barriers to entry Anything that artificially prevents the entry of firms into an industry.

Barter The exchange of one good or service for another good or service.

Benefits-received principle The idea that those who receive the benefits of goods and services provided by government should pay the taxes required to finance them.

Bilateral monopoly A market in which there is a single seller (monopoly) and a single buyer (monopsony).

Bonds Financial devices through which a borrower (a firm or government) is obligated to pay the principle and interest on a loan at a specific date in the future.

Break-even point An output at which a firm makes a normal profit but not an economic profit.

Budget constraint The limit that the size of a consumer's income (and the prices that must be paid for goods and services) imposes on the ability of that consumer to obtain goods and services.

Budget line A line that shows the different combinations of two products a consumer can purchase with a specific money income, given the products' prices.

C

Canada Pension Plan (CPP) A national retirement plan funded by obligatory employer and employee contributions.

Capital Human-made resources (buildings, machinery, and equipment) used to produce goods and services; goods that do not directly satisfy human wants; also called capital goods.

Cartel A formal agreement among firms in an industry to set the price of a product and establish the outputs of the individual firms or to divide the market among them.

Change in demand A change in the quantity demanded of a good or service at every price; a shift of the demand curve to the left or right.

Change in quantity demanded A movement from one point to another on a fixed demand curve caused by a change in price of the product under consideration.

Change in quantity supplied A movement from one point to another on a fixed supply curve caused by a change in the price of a product under consideration.

Change in supply A change in the quantity supplied of a good or service at every price; a shift of the supply curve to the left or right.

Circular flow model The flow of resources from households to firms and of products from firms to households. These flows are accompanied by reverse flows of money from firms to households and from households to firms.

Coase theorem The idea first stated by economist Ronald Coase that spillover problems may be resolved through private negotiations of the affected parties.

Collusion A situation in which firms act together and in agreement to fix prices, divide a market, or otherwise restrict competition.

Combines Investigation Act The Act, in 1910, that authorized a judge, on receiving an application by six people, to order an investigation into an alleged combine; became the Competition Act in 1986.

Command system An economic system in which property resources are owned by the government and the economic decisions are made by a central government body.

Comparative advantage A lower relative or comparative cost than another producer.

Compensating differences Differences in the wages received by workers in different jobs to compensate for nonmonetary differences in the jobs.

Competition Act The Act that replaced the Combines Investigation Act in 1986.

Competition Tribunal A government body that adjudicates under a civil law framework that will permit the issuing of remedial orders to restore and maintain competition in the market.

Competition The presence in a market of a large number of independent buyers and sellers competing with one another and the freedom of buyers and sellers to enter and leave the market.

Complementary goods Products and services that are used together; when the price of one falls the demand for the other increases (and conversely).

Concentration ratio The percentage of the total sales of an industry produced and sold by an industry's largest firms.

Conglomerate merger The merger of a firm in one industry with a firm in another industry or region.

Constant returns to scale The range of output between the output at which economies of scale end and diseconomies of scale begin.

Constant-cost industry An industry in which the entry of new firms has no effect on resource prices and thus no effect on production costs.

Consumer goods Products and services that satisfy human wants directly.

Consumer sovereignty Determination by consumers of the types and quantities of goods and services that will be produced with the scarce resources of the economy; consumer direction of production through their dollar votes.

Corporation A legal entity chartered by the federal government that operates as a distinct and separate body from the individuals who own it.

Cost–benefit analysis Comparing the marginal costs of a government project or program with the marginal benefits to decide whether to employ resources in that project or program and to what extent.

Creative destruction The hypothesis that the creation of new products and production methods simultaneously destroys the market power of existing monopolies.

Crop restriction In return for guaranteed prices for their crops, farmers

agree to limit the number of hectares they plant in that crop.

Cross elasticity of demand The ratio of the percentage change in quantity demanded of one good to the percentage change in the price of some other good; a positive coefficient indicates the two products are substitute goods; a negative coefficient indicates they are complementary goods.

D

Deadweight loss The loss of consumer surplus and producer surplus when output is either below or above its efficient level.

Decreasing-cost industry An industry in which the entry of firms lowers the prices of resources and thus decreases production costs.

Deficiency payments Subsidies that make up the difference between market prices and government-supported prices; a method of price support.

Demand curve A curve that illustrates demand.

Dependent variable A variable that changes as a consequence of a change in some other (independent) variable; the "effect" or outcome.

Depreciation (of the dollar) A decrease in the value of the dollar relative to another currency so that a dollar buys a smaller amount of the foreign currency and therefore of foreign goods.

Derived demand The demand for a resource that depends on the products it can be used to produce.

Determinants of demand Factors other than its price that determine the quantities demanded of a good or service.

Determinants of supply Factors other than its price that determine the quantities supplied of a good or service.

Differentiated oligopoly An oligopoly in which the firms produce a differentiated product.

Diffusion The widespread imitation of an innovation.

Direct relationship The relationship between two variables that change in the same direction, for example, product price and quantity supplied.

Discrimination coefficient A measure of the cost or disutility of prejudice; the monetary amount an employer is willing to pay to hire a preferred worker rather than a nonpreferred worker.

Diseconomies of scale Increase in the average total cost of producing a product as the firm expands the size of its plant (its output) in the long run.

Division of labour Dividing the work required to produce a product into a number of different tasks that are performed by different workers; specialization of workers.

Dollar votes The "votes" that consumers and entrepreneurs cast for the production of consumer and capital goods, respectively, when they purchase them in product and resource markets.

Dominant strategy equilibrium An equilibrium in which there is a strategy for all players in a game, regardless of the strategies chosen by the other players.

Double taxation The taxation of both corporate net income (profits) and the dividends paid from this net income when they become the personal income of households.

E

Economic (opportunity) cost A payment that must be made to obtain and retain the services of a resource; the income a firm must provide to a resource supplier to attract the resource away from an alternative use; equal to the quantity of other products that cannot be produced when resources are instead used to make a particular product.

Economic (pure) profit The total revenue of a firm less its economic costs (which includes both explicit costs and implicit costs); also called above normal profit.

Economic growth (1) An outward shift in the production possibilities curve that results from an increase in resource supplies or quality or an improvement in technology; (2) an increase either in real output (gross domestic product) or in real output per capita.

Economic perspective A viewpoint that envisions individuals and institutions making rational decisions by comparing the marginal benefits and marginal costs associated with their actions.

Economic problems Choices are necessary because society's material wants for goods and services are unlimited but the resources available to satisfy these wants are limited (scarce).

Economic profit The total revenue of a firm less its economic costs (which includes both explicit costs and implicit costs); also called "pure profit" and "above normal profit."

Economic rent The price paid for the use of land and other natural resources, the supply of which is fixed (perfectly inelastic).

Economic resources The land, labour, capital, and entrepreneurial ability that are used in the production of goods and services; productive agents; factors of production.

Economic system A particular set of institutional arrangements and a coordinating mechanism for solving the economizing problem; a method of organizing an economy; of which the market economy, command economy, and traditional economy are three general types.

Economics The social science dealing with the use of scarce resources to obtain the maximum satisfaction of society's virtually unlimited economic wants.

Economies of scale Reductions in the average total cost of producing a product as the firm expands the size of plant (its output) in the long run; the economies of mass production.

Efficiency loss of a tax The loss of net benefits to society because a tax reduces the production and consumption of a taxed good below the level of allocative efficiency.

Elastic demand Product or resource demand whose price elasticity is greater than one; means the resulting change in quantity demanded is greater than the percentage change in price.

Elasticity of resource demand The percentage change in resource quantity divided by the percentage change in resource price; if the result is greater than one, resource demand is elastic; if the result is less than one, resource demand is inelastic; and when the result equals one, resource demand is unit-elastic.

Employment discrimination Inferior treatment in hiring, promotion, and work assignment for a particular group of employees.

Employment equity Policies and programs that establish targets of increased employment and promotion for women and minorities.

Employment insurance (EI) A program that insures workers against the hazards of losing their jobs.

Entrepreneurial ability The human resources that combine the other resources to produce a product, make non-routine decisions, innovate, and bear risks.

Equality–efficiency tradeoff The decrease in economic efficiency that may accompany a decrease in income inequality; the presumption that some income inequality is required to achieve economic efficiency.

Equilibrium position The combination of products that yields the greatest satisfaction or utility; the combination will lie on the highest attainable indifference curve.

Equilibrium price The price in a competitive market at which the quantity demanded and the quantity supplied are equal, where there is neither a shortage nor a surplus, and where there is no tendency for price to rise or fall.

Equilibrium quantity The quantity demanded and supplied at the equilibrium price in a competitive market.

Euro The common currency unit used by 12 European nations in the Euro zone, which includes all nations of the European Union except Great Britain, Denmark, and Sweden.

European Union (EU) An association of 15 European nations that has eliminated tariffs and import quotas among them, established common tariffs for goods imported from outside the member nations, allowed the free movement of labour and capital among them, and created other common economic policies; includes Austria, Belgium, Denmark, Finland, France, Germany, Great Britain, Greece, Ireland, Italy, Luxembourg, the Netherlands, Portugal, Spain, and Sweden.

Excess capacity Plant or equipment that is underused because the firm is producing less than the minimum-ATC output.

Exchange rate The rate of exchange of one nation's currency for another nation's currency.

Exclusive unionism The practice of a labour union of restricting the supply of skilled union labour to increase the wages received by union members; the policies typically employed by a craft union.

Expected-rate-of-return curve The increase in profit a firm anticipates it will obtain by investing in R&D.

Explicit costs The monetary payments a firm must make to an outsider to obtain a resource.

Export subsidies Government payments to domestic producers to enable them to reduce the price of a good or service to foreign buyers.

Externalities A benefit or cost from production or consumption accruing without compensation to nonbuyers and nonsellers of the product.

F

Factor market A market in which households sell and firms buy resources or the services of resources.

Factors of production Economic resources: land, capital, labour, and entrepreneurial ability.

Fair-return price The price of a product that enables its producer to obtain a normal profit and that is equal to the average cost of producing it.

Fallacy of composition Incorrectly reasoning that what is true for the individual (or part) is necessarily true for the group (or whole).

Fast-second strategy The strategy of becoming the second firm to embrace an innovation, allowing the originator to incur the initial high costs of innovation.

Firm An organization that employs resources to produce a good or service for profit and that owns and operates one or more plants.

Fixed costs Any cost that in total does not change when the firm changes its output; the cost of fixed resources.

Foreign exchange market A market in which the money (currency) of one nation can be used to purchase (can be exchanged for) the money of another nation.

Freedom of choice The freedom of owners of property resources to employ or dispose of them as they see fit, of workers to enter any line of work for which they are qualified, and of consumers to spend their incomes in a manner that they think is appropriate.

Freedom of enterprise The freedom of firms to obtain economic resources, to use these resources to produce products of the firm's own choosing, and to sell their products in markets of their choice.

Free-rider problem The inability of potential providers of an economically desirable but indivisible good or service to obtain payment from those who benefit, because the exclusion principle is not applicable.

Full employment (1) Use of all available resources to produce want-satisfying goods and services. (2) The situation when the unemployment rate is equal to the full-employment unemployment rate and there is frictional and structural but no cyclical unemployment (and the real output of the economy equals its potential real output).

Full production Employment of available resources so that the maximum amount of (or total value of) goods and services is produced; occurs when both productive efficiency and allocative efficiency are realized.

G

Game theory model A means of analyzing the pricing behaviour of oligopolists using the theory of strategy associated with games such as chess and bridge.

General Agreement on Tariffs and Trade (GATT) The international agreement reached in 1947 in which 23 nations agreed to give equal and nondiscriminatory treatment to the other nations, to reduce tariff rates by multinational negotiations, and to eliminate import quotas. Now includes most nations and has become the World Trade Organization.

Generalizations Statements of the nature of the relation between two or more sets of facts.

Gini ratio A numerical measure of the overall dispersion of income.

Goods and Services Tax (GST) Federal tax that replaced the federal sales tax in Canada; it is 7 percent on a broad base of goods and services (the only exemptions are agricultural and fish products, prescription drugs, and medical devices); businesses remit the difference between the value of their sales and the value of its purchases from other firms.

Government failure Inefficiencies in resource allocation caused by problems in the operation of the public sector (government); occurs because of rent-seeking pressure by special-interest groups, short-sighted political behaviour, limited and bundled choices, and bureaucratic inefficiencies.

Guaranteed Income Supplement (GIS) Money paid on application, subject to a means test, to those receiving an OAS pension who have an income below a certain level.

Guiding function of prices The ability of price changes to bring about changes in the quantities of products and resources demanded and supplied.

H

Herfindahl index The sum of the squared percentage market share of all firms in the industry.

Homogeneous oligopoly An oligopoly in which the firms produce a standardized product.

Horizontal axis The "left–right" or "west–east" axis on a graph or grid.

Horizontal merger A merger between two competitors selling similar products in the same market.

Household An economic unit (of one or more persons) that provides the economy with resources and uses the income received to purchase goods and services that satisfy material wants.

Human capital discrimination Arbitrary restriction of particular groups from productivity-enhancing investments in education and training.

I

Illegal immigrants People who enter a country unlawfully and live there.

Imitation problem A firm's rivals may be able to imitate the new product or process, greatly reducing the originator's profit from its R&D effort.

Imperfect competition The market models pure monopoly, monopolistic competition, and oligopoly considered as a group.

Implicit costs The monetary income a firm sacrifices when it uses a resource it owns rather than supplying the resource in the market; equal to what the resource could have earned in the best-paying alternative employment; includes a normal profit.

Import competition The competition domestic firms encounter from the products and services of foreign producers.

Import quota A limit imposed by a nation on the quantity (or total value) of a good that may be imported during some period.

Incentive function of price The inducement that an increase in the price of a commodity gives to sellers to make more of it available (and conversely for a decrease in price), and the inducement that an increase in price offers to buyers to purchase smaller quantities (and conversely for a decrease in price).

Incentive pay plan A compensation structure that ties worker pay directly to performance such as piece rates, bonuses, stock options, commissions, and profit sharing.

Inclusive unionism The practice of a labour union of including as members all workers employed in an industry.

Income effect A change in the quantity demanded of a product that results from the change in real income (purchasing power) produced by a change in the product's price.

Income elasticity of demand The ratio of the percentage change in the quantity demanded of a good to a percentage change in consumer income; measures the responsiveness of consumer purchases to income changes.

Income inequality The unequal distribution of an economy's total income among households or families.

Income mobility The movement of individuals and families from one income quintile to another over time.

Increasing-cost industry An industry in which the entry of new firms raises the prices for resources and thus increases their production costs.

Independent variable The variable causing a change in some other (dependent) variable.

Indifference curves Curves showing the different combinations of two products that yield the same satisfaction or utility to a consumer.

Indifference map A series of indifference curves, each of which represents a different level of utility and together show the preferences of a consumer.

Industry A group of firms that produce the same or similar products.

Inelastic demand Product or resource demand for which the price elasticity coefficient is less than one; means the resulting percentage change in quantity demanded is less than the percentage change in price.

Inferior good A good or service whose consumption declines as income rises (and conversely), price remaining constant.

Innovation The first successful commercial introduction of a new product, the first use of a new method of production, or the creation of a new form of business organization.

Insurable risk An event that would result in a loss but whose frequency of occurrence can be estimated with considerable accuracy; insurance companies are willing to sell insurance against such losses.

Interest-rate cost-of-funds curve A graph showing the interest rate a firm must pay to obtain funds to finance R&D.

Interindustry competition The competition between the products of one industry and the products of another industry.

Invention The discovery of a product or process using imagination, ingenious thinking, and experimentation and the first proof that it will work.

Inverse relationship The relationship between two variables that change in opposite directions, for example, product price and quantity demanded.

Inverted-U theory A theory saying that, other things being equal, R&D expenditures as a percentage of sales rise with industry concentration, reach a peak at a four-firm concentration ratio of about 50 percent, and then fall as concentration further increases.

Investment in human capital Any expenditure undertaken to improve the education, skills, health, or mobility of workers, with an expectation of greater productivity and thus a positive return on the investment.

Investment Spending for the production and accumulation of capital and additions to inventories.

Invisible hand The tendency of firms and resource suppliers seeking to further their own self-interests in competitive markets to also promote the interest of society as a whole.

K

Kinked-demand curve The demand curve for a noncollusive oligopolist that is based on the assumption that rivals will follow a price decrease and will not follow a price increase.

L

Labour The physical and mental talents and efforts of people that are used to produce goods and services.

Land Natural resources ("free gifts of nature") used to produce goods and services.

Law of demand The principle that, other things equal, an increase in a product's price will reduce the quantity of it demanded; and conversely for a decrease in price.

Law of diminishing marginal utility As a consumer increases the consumption of a good or service, the marginal utility obtained from each additional unit of the good or service decreases.

Law of diminishing returns As successive increments of a variable resource are added to a fixed resource, the marginal product of the variable resource will eventually decrease.

Law of increasing opportunity costs As the production of a good increases, the opportunity cost of producing an additional unit rises.

Law of supply The principle that, other things equal, an increase in the price of a product will increase the quantity of it supplied; and conversely for a price decrease.

Least-cost combination of resources The quantity of each resource a firm must employ to produce a particular output at the lowest total cost.

Legal cartel theory of regulation The hypothesis that some industries seek regulation or want to maintain regulation so that they may form a legal cartel.

Legal immigrants People who lawfully enter a country and live there.

Limited liability Restriction of the maximum loss to a predetermined amount for the owners (stockholders) of a corporation, the maximum loss is the amount they paid for their shares of stock.

Loanable funds theory of interest The concept that the supply of and demand for loanable funds determine the equilibrium rate of interest.

Logrolling The trading of votes by legislators to secure favourable outcomes on decisions concerning the provision of public goods and quasipublic goods.

Long run A period of time long enough to enable producers of a product to change the quantities of all the resources they employ; period in which all resources and costs are variable and no resources or costs are fixed.

Long-run farm problem The tendency for agriculture to be a declining industry as technological progress increases supply relative to an inelastic and slowly increasing demand.

Long-run supply curve A curve that shows the prices at which a purely competitive industry will make various quantities of the product available in the long run.

Lorenz curve A curve showing the distribution of income in an economy; the cumulated percentage of families (income receivers) is measured along the horizontal axis and cumulated percentage of income is measured along the vertical axis.

M

Macroeconomics The part of economics concerned with the economy as a whole; with such major aggregates as the household, business, and governmental sectors; and with measures of the total economy.

Marginal analysis The comparison or marginal ("extra" or "additional") benefits and marginal costs, usually for decision making.

Marginal cost (MC) The extra (additional) cost of producing one more unit of output; equal to the change in total cost divided by the change in output (and in the short run to the change in total variable cost divided by the change in output).

Marginal product (MP) The extra output produced with one additional unit of a resource.

Marginal productivity theory of income distribution The contention that the distribution of income is fair when each unit of each resource receives a money payment equal to its marginal contribution to the firm's revenue (its marginal revenue product).

Marginal rate of substitution The rate at which a consumer is prepared to substitute one good for another (from a given combination of goods) and remain equally satisfied (have the same total utility); equal to the slope of a consumer's indifference curve at each point on the curve.

Marginal resource cost (MRC) The amount that each additional unit of resource adds to the firm's total (resource) cost.

Marginal revenue product (MRP) The change in total revenue from employing one additional unit of a resource.

Marginal revenue productivity How much workers contribute to their employers' revenue; usually reflected in their pay level.

Marginal revenue The change in total revenue that results from selling one more unit of a firm's product.

Marginal utility The extra utility a consumer obtains from the consumption of one additional unit of a good or service; equal to the change in total utility divided by the change in the quantity consumed.

Market failure The inability of markets to bring about the allocation of resources that best satisfies the wants of society.

Market for externality rights A market in which firms can buy rights to discharge pollutants; the price of such rights is determined by the demand for the right and a perfectly inelastic supply of such rights (the latter is determined by the quantity of discharges that the environment can assimilate).

Market period A period in which producers of a product are unable to change the quantity produced in response to a change in its price; in which there is a perfectly inelastic supply.

Market system All the product and resource markets of a market economy and the relationships among them; a method that allows the prices determined in these markets to allocate the economy's scarce resources and to communicate and coordinate the decisions made by consumers, firms, and resource suppliers.

Market Any institution or mechanism that brings together buyers (demanders) and sellers (suppliers) of a particular good or service.

MC = MB rule For a government project, marginal benefit should equal marginal cost to produce maximum benefit to society.

Median-voter model The theory that under majority rule the median (middle) voter will be in the dominant position to determine the outcome of an election.

Medium of exchange Items sellers generally accept and buyers generally use to pay for a good or service; money; a convenient means of exchanging goods and services without engaging in barter.

Microeconomics The part of economics concerned with such individual units as industries, firms, and households; and with individual markets, particular prices, and specific goods and services.

Minimum efficient scale (MES) The lowest level of output at which a firm can minimize long-run average costs.

Minimum wage The lowest wage employers may legally pay for an hour of work.

Money Any item that is generally acceptable to sellers in exchange for goods and services.

Monopolistic competition A market structure in which many firms sell a differentiated product and entry into and exit from the market is relatively easy.

Monopsony A market structure in which there is only a single buyer of a good, service, or resource.

Moral hazard problem The possibility that individuals or institutions will change their behaviour as the result of a contract or agreement.

Most-favoured-nation (MFN) clause An agreement by Canada to allow some other nation's exports into Canada at the lowest tariff level levied by Canada, then or later.

MR = MC rule A method of determining the total output at which economic profit is at a maximum (or losses at a minimum).

MRP = MRC rule To maximize economic profit (or minimize losses) a firm should use the quantity of a resource at which its marginal revenue product is equal to its marginal resource cost.

Multinational corporation A firm that owns production facilities in other countries and produces and sells its product abroad.

Mutual interdependence A situation in which a change in strategy (usually price) by one firm will affect the sales and profits of other firms.

N

Nash equilibrium An outcome in a non-cooperative game in which players choose their best strategy given the present strategies the others have chosen.

Natural monopoly An industry in which economies of scale are so great that a single firm can produce the product at a lower average total cost than if more than one firm produced the product.

Network effects Increases in the value of a product to each user, including existing ones, as the total number of users rises.

Nominal interest rate The interest rate expressed in terms of annual amounts currently charged for interest and not adjusted for inflation.

Nominal wage The amount of money received by a worker per unit of time (hour, day, etc.).

Non-cash transfer Government transfer payments in the form of goods and services rather than money; for example, food stamps, housing assistance, and job training; also called in-kind transfers.

Non-competing groups Collections of workers in the economy who do not compete with each other for employment because the skill and training of the workers in one group are substantially different from those in other groups.

Non-price competition A selling strategy in which one firm tries to distinguish its product or service from all competing ones based on attributes other than price and then advertising the distinguished product to consumers.

Non-tariff barriers All barriers other than protective tariffs that nations erect to impede international trade, including import quotas, licensing requirements, unreasonable product-quality standards, unnecessary red tape in customs procedures, and so on.

Normal good A good or service whose consumption increases when income increases and falls when income decreases, price remaining constant.

Normal profit The payment made by a firm to obtain and retain entrepreneurial ability; the minimum income entrepreneurial ability must receive to induce it to perform entrepreneurial functions for a firm.

Normative economics The part of economics involving value judgments about what the economy should be like; concerned with which economic goals and policies should be implemented.

North American Free Trade Agreement (NAFTA) A 1993 agreement establishing, over a 15-year period, a free trade zone composed of Canada, Mexico, and the United States.

O

Occupational discrimination Arbitrary restriction of particular groups from more desirable, higher-paying occupations.

Occupational licensing The laws of provincial or municipal governments that require a worker to satisfy certain specified requirements and obtain a licence from a licensing board before engaging in a particular occupation.

Occupational segregation Crowding women or minorities into less desirable, lower-paying occupations.

Old Age Security (OAS) A pension paid on application at age 65 to everyone resident in Canada for at least 10 years immediately before turning 65.

Oligopoly A market structure in which a few large firms produce homogeneous or differentiated products.

Opportunity cost The amount of other products that must be forgone or sacrificed to produce a unit of a product.

Optimal amount of R&D The amount of funding for which the expected rate of return and the interest cost of borrowing are equal.

Optimal reduction of an externality The point at which society's marginal cost and marginal benefit of reducing that externality are equal.

Other-things-equal assumption The assumption that factors other than those being considered are held constant.

Output effect An increase in the price of one input will increase a firm's production costs and reduce its level of output, thus reducing the demand for other inputs (and vice versa).

P

Paradox of voting A situation in which paired-choice voting by majority rule fails to provide a consistent ranking of society's preferences for public goods or services.

Partnership An unincorporated firm owned and operated by two or more people.

Patent An exclusive right to sell any new and useful process, machine, or product for a set time.

Perfectly elastic demand Product or resource demand in which quantity demanded can be of any amount at a particular product price; graphs as a horizontal demand curve.

Perfectly elastic supply Product or resource supply in which quantity supplied can be of any amount at a particular product or resource price; graphs as a horizontal supply curve.

Perfectly inelastic demand Product or resource demand in which price can be of any amount at a particular quantity of the product or resource demanded; quantity demanded does not respond to a change in price; graphs as a vertical demand curve.

Perfectly inelastic supply Product or resource supply in which price can be of any amount at a particular quantity of the product or resource demanded; quantity supplied does not respond to a change in price; graphs as a vertical supply curve.

Plant A physical establishment that performs one or more functions in the production, fabrication, and distribution of goods and services.

Policy economics The formulation of courses of action to bring about desired economic outcomes or to prevent undesired occurrences.

Positive economics The analysis of facts or data to establish scientific generalizations about economic behaviour.

Post hoc, ergo propter hoc fallacy Incorrectly reasoning that when one event precedes another the first event must have caused the second event.

Price ceiling A legally established maximum price for a good or service.

Price discrimination The selling of a product to different buyers at different prices when the price differences are not justified by differences in cost.

Price elasticity of demand The ratio of the percentage change in quantity demanded of a product or resource to the percentage change in its price; a measure of the responsiveness of buyers to a change in the price of a product or resource.

Price elasticity of supply The ratio of the percentage change in quantity supplied of a product or resource to the percentage change in its price; the responsiveness of producers to a change in the price of a product or resource.

Price floors Legally determined prices above the equilibrium price.

Price leadership An implicit understanding oligopolists use to coordinate prices without engaging in outright collusion by having the dominant firm initiate price changes and all other firms follow.

Price war Successive and continuous rounds of price cuts by rivals as they attempt to maintain their market shares.

Price-taker A firm in a purely competitive market that cannot change market price but only adjust to it.

Principal–agent problem A conflict of interest that occurs when agents (workers or managers) pursue their own objectives to the detriment of the principal's (stockholders) goals.

Principles Statements about economic behaviour that enable prediction of the probable effect of certain actions.

Prisoner's dilemma A type of game where, whatever the other player does, each player is better off not cooperating.

Private property The right of private persons and firms to obtain, own, control, employ, dispose of, and bequeath land, capital, and other property.

Process innovation The development and use of new or improved production or distribution methods.

Product differentiation A strategy in which one firm's product is distinguished from competing products by means of its design, related services, quality, location, or other attributes (except price).

Product innovation The development and sale of a new or improved product or service.

Product market A market in which products are sold by firms and bought by households.

Production possibilities curve A curve that shows the different combinations of two goods or services that can be produced in a full-employment, full-production economy where the available supplies of resources and technology are fixed.

Production possibilities table A table showing the different combinations of two products that can be used produced with a specific set of resources in a full-employment, full-production economy.

Productive efficiency The production of a good in the least costly way; occurs when production takes place at the output at which average total cost is a minimum and at which marginal product per dollar's worth of input is the same for all inputs.

Profit-maximizing combination of resources The quantity of each resource a firm must employ to maximize its profits or minimize its losses.

Progressive tax A tax whose average tax rate increases as the taxpayer's income increases and decreases as the taxpayer's income decreases.

Proportional tax A tax whose average tax rate remains constant as the taxpayer's income increases or decreases.

Protective tariff A tariff designed to shield domestic producers of a good or service from the competition of foreign producers.

Public choice theory The economic analysis of collective and government decision making, politics, and the democratic process.

Public good A good or service that is indivisible and to which the exclusion principle does not apply; a good or service with these characteristics provided by government.

Public interest theory of regulation The theory that industrial regulation is necessary to keep a natural monopoly from charging monopoly prices and thus harming consumers and society.

Pure competition A market structure in which a very large number of firms produce a standardized product.

Pure monopoly A market structure in which one firm is the sole seller of a product or service.

Pure rate of interest An essentially risk-free, long-term interest rate not influenced by market imperfections.

Purely competitive labour market A resource market in which a large number of (noncolluding) firms demand a particular type of labour supplied by a large number of nonunion workers.

Q

Quasi-public good A good or service to which the exclusion principle could apply, but that has such a large spillover benefit that government sponsors its production to prevent an underallocation of resources.

Quota A restriction on the amount of a product that a farm is allowed to produce in a given period.

R

Rational behaviour Human behaviour based on comparison of marginal costs and marginal benefits; behaviour designed to maximize total utility.

Rationing function of prices The ability of market forces in a competitive market to equalize quantity demanded and quantity supplied and to eliminate shortages and surpluses via changes in prices.

Real interest rate The interest rate expressed in dollars of constant value (adjusted for inflation); equal to the nominal interest rate less the expected rate of inflation.

Real wage The amount of goods and services a worker can purchase with a nominal wage; the purchasing power of the nominal wage.

Regressive tax A tax whose average tax rate decreases as the taxpayer's income increases and decreases as the taxpayer's income decreases.

Relative poverty A situation in which an individual's or a family's income is low relative to others in society.

Rent-seeking behaviour The actions by persons, firms, or unions to gain special benefits from government at taxpayers' or someone else's expense.

Reverse discrimination The view that the preferential treatment associated with employment equity constitutes discrimination against other groups.

Roundabout production The construction and use of capital to aid in the production of consumer goods.

S

Scientific method The systematic pursuit of knowledge through the formulation of a problem, collection of data, and the formulation and testing of hypotheses.

Self-interest That which each firm, property owner, worker, and consumer believes is best for itself and seeks to obtain.

Short run A period of time in which producers are able to change the quantities of some but not all of the resources they employ; a period in which some resources (usually plant) are fixed and some are variable.

Shortage The amount by which the quantity demanded of a product

exceeds the quantity supplied at a particular (below-equilibrium) price.

Short-run farm problem The sharp year-to-year changes in the prices of agricultural products and in the incomes of farmers.

Short-run supply curve A curve that shows the quantities of the product a firm in a purely competitive industry will offer to sell at various prices in the short run.

Simultaneous consumption A product's ability to satisfy a large number of consumers at the same time.

Slope of a line The ratio of the vertical change (the rise or fall) to the horizontal change (the run) between any two points on a line. The slope of an upward sloping line is positive, reflecting a direct relationship between two variables; the slope of a downward sloping line is negative, reflecting an inverse relationship between two variables.

Social regulation Government regulation of the conditions under which goods are produced, the physical characteristics of goods, and the impact of the production on society.

Socially optimal price The price of a product that results in the most efficient allocation of an economy's resources.

Sole proprietorship An unincorporated firm owned and operated by one person.

Special-interest effect Any result of government promotion of the interests (goals) of a small group at the expense of a much larger group.

Specialization The use of the resources of an individual, a firm, a region, or a nation to produce one or a few goods and services.

Spillover benefit A benefit obtained without compensation by third parties from the production or consumption of sellers or buyers. Example: A beekeeper benefits when a neighbouring farmer plants clover.

Spillover costs A cost imposed without compensation on third parties by the production or consumption of sellers or buyers. Example: A manufacturer dumps toxic chemicals into a river, killing the fish sought by sport fishers.

Start-ups Small new companies that focus on creating and introducing a new product or employing a new production or distribution technique.

Static economy An economy in which resource supplies, technological knowledge, and consumer tastes are constant and unchanging.

Statistical discrimination Judging individuals on the average characteristic of the group to which they belong rather than on their own personal characteristics.

Stocks (corporate) Ownership shares in a corporation.

Substitute goods Products or services that can be used in place of each other. When the price of one falls the demand for the other falls, and conversely with an increase of price.

Substitution effect (1) A change in the quantity demanded of a consumer good that results from a change in its relative expensiveness produced by a change in the product's price. (2) The effect of a change in the price of a resource on the quantity of the resource employed by a firm, assuming no change in its output.

Supply curve A curve that illustrates supply.

Support prices Government-supported minimum prices for agricultural products.

Surplus The amount by which the quantity supplied of a product exceeds the quantity demanded at a specific (above-equilibrium) price.

T

Tacit understandings Any method by competing oligopolists to set prices and outputs that does not involve outright collusion.

Taste-for-discrimination model A theory of discrimination that views it as a preference for which an employer is willing to pay.

Tax incidence The person or group who ends up paying a tax.

Technological advance New and better goods and services and new and better ways of producing or distributing them.

Terms of trade The rate at which units of one product can be exchanged for units of another product; the price of a good or service; the amount of one good or service that must be given up to obtain one unit of another good or service.

Theoretical economics The process of deriving and applying economic theories and principles.

Total cost The sum of fixed cost and variable cost.

Total product (TP) The total output of a particular good or service produced by a firm (or a group of firms or the entire economy).

Total revenue The total number of dollars received by a firm (or firms) from the sale of a product; equal to the total expenditures for the product produced by the firm (or firms); equal to the quantity sold (demanded) multiplied by the price at which it is sold.

Total utility The total amount of satisfaction derived from the consumption of a single product or a combination of products.

Total-revenue test A test to determine elasticity of demand between any two prices: Demand is elastic if total revenue moves in the opposite direction as price; it is inelastic when it moves in the same direction as price; and it is of unitary elasticity when it does not change when price changes.

Trade bloc A group of nations that lower or abolish trade barriers among members. Examples include the European Union and the nations of the North American Free Trade Agreement.

Tradeoffs The sacrifice of some or all of one economic goal, good, or service to achieve some other goal, good, or service.

Tragedy of the commons Air, water, and public land rights are held in common by society and freely available, so no incentive exists to maintain or use them carefully; the result is overuse, degradation, and pollution.

U

Uninsurable risk An event that would result in a loss and whose occurrence is uncontrollable and unpredictable; insurance companies are not willing to sell insurance against such a loss.

Unit elasticity Demand or supply for which the elasticity coefficient is equal to one; means that the percentage change in the quantity demanded or supplied is equal to the percentage change in price.

Utility The want-satisfying power of a good or service; the satisfaction or pleasure a consumer obtains from the consumption of a good or service (or from the consumption of a collection of goods and services).

Utility-maximizing rule To obtain the greatest utility the consumer should allocate money income so that the last dollar spent on each good or service yields the same marginal utility.

V

Value-added tax (VAT) A tax imposed on the difference between the value of the products sold by a firm and the value of the goods purchased from other firms to produce the product; used in several European countries.

Variable costs Costs that in total increase when the firm increases its output and decrease when it reduces its output.

Venture capital Financial capital lent in return for a share in the business.

Vertical axis The "up–down" or "north–south" axis on a graph or grid.

Vertical intercept The point at which a line meets the vertical axis of a graph.

Vertical merger The merger of firms engaged in different stages of the production process of a final product.

Very long run A period in which technology can change and in which firms can develop and offer entirely new products.

W

Wage differentials The difference between the wage received by one worker or group of workers and that received by another worker or group of workers.

Wage discrimination The payment of a lower wage to members of a less-preferred group than to members of a more-preferred group for the same work.

Wage rate A price paid per unit of labour services.

World Trade Organization (WTO) An organization established in 1994, replacing GATT, to oversee the provisions of the Uruguay Round and resolve any disputes stemming from it.

X

X-inefficiency Failure to produce any specific output at the lowest average (and total) cost possible.

Index